PYTHON
PROGRAMMING
Using Problem Solving Approach,
Second Edition

Reema Thareja

Assistant Professor, Department of Computer Science,
Shyama Prasad Mukherji College for Women,
University of Delhi

OXFORD
UNIVERSITY PRESS

OXFORD
UNIVERSITY PRESS

Oxford University Press is a department of the University of Oxford.
It furthers the University's objective of excellence in research, scholarship,
and education by publishing worldwide. Oxford is a registered trade mark of
Oxford University Press in the UK and in certain other countries.

Published in India by
Oxford University Press
22 Workspace, 2nd Floor, 1/22 Asaf Ali Road, New Delhi 110002

ISBN-13 (Print): 978-93-5497-376-5
ISBN-10 (Print): 93-5497-376-0

eISBN-13 (eBook): 978-93-5497-552-3
eISBN-10 (eBook): 93-5497-552-6

Typeset in Times New Roman and Gill Sans Std
by B2K-BYTES 2 KNOWLEDGE, Tamil Nadu
Printed in India by Gopsons Papers Pvt. Ltd., Noida
Cover image: © cash1994/Shutterstock

For product information and current price, please visit www.india.oup.com

I dedicate this book to my family and my uncle, Mr B.L. Theraja,
who is a well-known author

Preface

Python is an open-source, excellent, easy, high-level, interpreted, interactive, object-oriented and a reliable language that uses English like words. It is also a versatile language that supports development of a wide range of applications ranging from simple text processing to WWW browsers to games. Moreover, Programmers can embed Python within their C, C++, COM, ActiveX, CORBA, and Java programs to give 'scripting' capabilities for users.

Python has a huge user base that is constantly growing. The strength of Python can be understood from the fact that this programming language is the most preferred language of companies like Nokia, Google, YouTube and even NASA for its easy syntax. The support for multiple programming paradigms, including object-oriented programming, functional Python programming, and parallel programming models makes it an ideal choice for the programmers.

However, no student can learn to program just by reading a book; rather it is a skill that must be developed by practice. So, after learning the rudiments of program writing, students should find a number of examples and exercises that would help them to learn to design efficient programs. The book presents various programming examples that have already been implemented and tested using the latest version of Python.

About the Book

This book is aimed at serving as a textbook for undergraduate and postgraduate courses of computer applications. The objective of this book is to introduce the concepts of Python programming language to young learners and apply them for solving real world problems. The book will also be useful for computer professionals working in the area of Python programming as a reference and resource.

Every chapter in this book contains multiple programming examples to impart practically sound knowledge of the concept. To further enhance the understanding of the subject, there are numerous objective types, subjective type and programming exercises at the end of each chapter.

The overall objective of this book is to give the reader a sound understanding of the fundamentals of Python language and prepare them for taking up challenging tasks in the area. Efforts have been made to acquaint the reader with the techniques and applications in the area. The salient features of the book include:

- Easy to understand
- Explanation of the concept using diagrams
- Solved examples within the chapters
- Glossary of important terms at the end of each chapter
- Comprehensive exercises at the end of each chapter
- Lots of programs that have been executed
- Appendices to give additional information
- Interesting videos by author to augment learning
- Case studies which include programs that apply concepts learnt in chapters

Organization of the Book

The book is organized into 12 chapters.

Chapter 1 provides an introduction to the basics of designing efficient programs and discusses the concept of algorithms, flowcharts and pseudocodes. It then talks about programming languages and their evolution through generations.

Chapter 2 describes different programming paradigms, concepts of OOP along with merits and demerits of object-oriented programming languages. The chapter also gives a comparative study of some OOP languages and highlights the applications of OOP.

Chapter 3 discusses basic features of Python and its building blocks (like keywords, identifiers, constants variables, operators, expressions, statements and naming conventions supported by the language.

New in 2e- Internal working of Python

Chapter 4 deals with special types of statements like decision control, iterative, break, continue, pass and the else statement.

Chapter 5 provides a detailed explanation of defining and calling functions. It also talks about vital concepts like variable length arguments, recursive functions, modules and packages.

New in 2e: Higher Orders Functions, Function Composition, Tail Recursion

Chapter 6 unleashes the concept of strings. The chapter lays special focus on the operators used with strings, slicing operation, built-in string methods and functions, comparing and iterating through strings and the string module.

New in 2e: String Formatting Operator using Verbose in Regular Expression

Chapter 7 discusses how data can be stored in files. The chapter deals with opening, processing (reading, writing, appending) and closing of files though a Python program. These files are handled in text mode as well as binary mode for better clarity of the concepts. The chapter also explains the concept of file, directory and the OS module.

New in 2e: Get File Permissions, Set File Permissions (Chmod), Change Ownership (Chown), Get File Timestamp, Set File Timestamp, Get File Extension, Seek A Position In A File, Symlink, Starting A File With Default Application, Opening Files using Command Line Arguments, More Programming Examples.

Chapter 8 details the different data structures that are extensively used in Python. It discusses creating, accessing, cloning, updating of lists. It also talks about list methods and functions, functional programming, creating, accessing, updating tuples. It also provides the concepts to work with sets, dictionaries, nested lists, nested tuples, nested sets, nested dictionaries, list comprehensions and dictionary comprehensions.

New to 2e: List Aliasing, List Cloning, Set Comprehension, Nested Set Comprehensions, Additional Programming Examples.

Chapter 9 introduces the concept of classes, objects, public, private, class and instance variables. It also talks about special methods, built- in attributes, built-in methods, garbage collection, class method and static method.

Chapter 10 introduces inheritance in its various forms. It gives a detail explanation on method overriding, containership, abstract class, interface and metaclass.

Chapter 11 is all about overloading arithmetic and logical operators. It also discusses reverse adding, overriding __getitem__, __setitem__, in, __call__ and other miscellaneous functions.

Chapter 12 gives the concepts of exception handling that can be used to make your programs robust. For this, the chapter demonstrates the concepts of try, except, finally blocks, raising and re-raising exceptions, built-in and user defined exceptions, assertions and handling invoked functions.

New to Second Edition: ***Difference between Syntax and Logical Error, More Programming Examples***

The book also provides appendices and annexures along with author videos for specific important topics for a more robust understanding of the subject. List of appendices, annexures, and videos is given below.

These can be assessed through the AREAL icon placed on page xvii of this book.

Appendix A: Types of Operating Systems
Appendix B: Python IDEs

Appendix C: Multi-threading
Appendix D: Turtle Graphics
Appendix E: Searching and Sorting Operations on List
Appendix F: Web Programming
Appendix H: Network Programming *(new)*
Appendix I: GUI Programming with `tkinter` Package
Appendix J: Working with Images *(new)*
Appendix K: Data Science with Numpy and Pandas *(new)*
Appendix L: Interfacing Python with Mysql *(new)*
Appendix M: Python for NoSQL *(new)*
Appendix N: Plotting with Matplotlib and seaborn *(new)*
Appendix O: Event Driven Programming
Appendix P: Drawing Flowcharts with RAPTOR *(new)*
Appendix Q: Scratch Programming *(new)*

Annexure 1: Installing Python
Annexure 2: Testing and debugging of Python programs
Annexure 3: Comparison between Python 2.X and Python 3.X
Annexure 5: Plotting graphs
Annexure 5: Functions as Objects (Please include as annexure)
Annexure 6: Iterator, Getters, Setters, @property and @deleter
Annexure 7: Object Relational Mapper (ORM) *(new)*
Annexure 8: Lists as Arrays *(new)*
Annexure 9: Iterator and Generator
Annexure 10: Beautiful Idiomatic Approach to Solve Programming Problems *(new)*

Interesting videos by authors have also been provided to augment learning for some of the chapters. These can be accessed through Areal icon.

Chapter 4: Decision_Control_Statements
Chapter 5: Functions and Modules
Chapter 6: Strings
Chapter 7: File Handling
Chapter 8: Lists
Chapter 8: List Comprehensions
Chapter 8: Tuple
Chapter 8: Sets
Chapter 8: Dictionaries
Numpy/Appendix

Acknowledgements

The writing of this textbook was a mammoth task for which a lot of help was required from many people. Fortunately, I have had the fine support of my family, friends and fellow members of the teaching staff at the Shyama Prasad Mukherji College.

My special thanks would always go to my father Late Sh. Janak Raj Thareja, my mother Smt. Usha Thareja, my brother Pallav and sisters Kimi and Rashi who were a source of abiding inspiration and divine blessings for me. I am especially thankful to my son Goransh who has been very patient and cooperative in letting me realize my dreams. My sincere thanks go to my uncle Mr. B.L. Theraja for his inspiration and guidance in writing this book.

Finally, I would like to acknowledge the technical assistance provided to me by Mr. Mitul Kapoor. I would like to thank for sparing out his precious time to help me to design, and test the programs.

Last but not the least, my acknowledgements will always be incomplete if I do not thank Oxford University Press, India who have supported my creative writing activities over the past few years.

Reema Thareja

Brief Contents

Detailed Contents

OXFORD AREAL

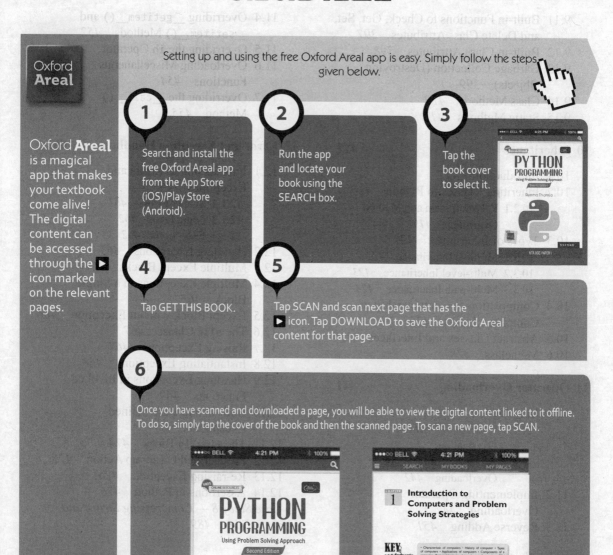

Oxford **Areal** is a magical app that makes your textbook come alive! The digital content can be accessed through the ▶ icon marked on the relevant pages.

Setting up and using the free Oxford Areal app is easy. Simply follow the steps given below.

1 Search and install the free Oxford Areal app from the App Store (iOS)/Play Store (Android).

2 Run the app and locate your book using the SEARCH box.

3 Tap the book cover to select it.

4 Tap GET THIS BOOK.

5 Tap SCAN and scan next page that has the ▶ icon. Tap DOWNLOAD to save the Oxford Areal content for that page.

6 Once you have scanned and downloaded a page, you will be able to view the digital content linked to it offline. To do so, simply tap the cover of the book and then the scanned page. To scan a new page, tap SCAN.

Use Oxford Areal to view Videos of chapters.

Appendices & Annexure

Videos

Introduction to Computers and Problem Solving Strategies

KEY
••• Concepts

• Characteristic of computers • History of computer • Types of computers • Applications of computers • Components of a computer • Basic architecture and organization of computer • CPU • Input and Output devices • Computer memory • Generations of programming languages • Computer hardware and software • Translators, linkers, loaders, assemblers • Stored program concept • System software • Application software • Software development process languages • Pseudocodes • Flowcharts • Algorithms • Types of errors • Testing and debugging

1.1 INTRODUCTION

We all have seen computers in our homes, schools, or colleges. In fact, in today's scenario we find computers in most aspects of daily life, and for some it is hard to even imagine a world without them. A computer is basically a machine that takes instructions and performs computations based on those instructions.

Nowadays computers come in different sizes. Their size may vary from very small to very large. In the past, computers were extremely large in size and required an entire room for installation. These computers consumed enormous amounts of power and were too expensive to be used for commercial applications. Therefore, they were used only for limited tasks, such as computing trajectories for astronomical or military applications.

However, with technological advancements, the size of computers became smaller and their energy requirements lowered immensely. This opened the way for adoption of computers for commercial purposes.

These days, computers have become so prevalent in the market that all interactive devices such as cellular phones, global positioning system (GPS) units, portable organizers, automated teller machines (ATMs), and gas pumps work with computers.

1.2 WHAT IS A COMPUTER?

A computer is an electronic machine that takes instructions and performs computations based on those instructions. Before going into details, let us learn some key terms that are frequently used in computers.

Data Data is a collection of raw facts or figures.

Information Information comprises processed data to provide answers to *'who'*, *'what'*, *'where'*, and *'when'* type of questions.

Knowledge Knowledge is the application of data and information to answer *'how'* part of the question (refer Figure 1.1).

Instructions Commands given to the computer that tells what it has to do are instructions.

Programs A set of instructions in computer language is called a program.

Software A set of programs is called software.

Hardware A computer and all its physical parts are known as hardware.

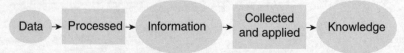

Data → Processed → Information → Collected and applied → Knowledge

Figure 1.1   Data, information, and knowledge

1.3 HISTORY OF COMPUTERS

History of computers can be understood by looking into five generations. With each new generation of computers, there had been advancement in computer technology. The circuitry became smaller with enhanced speed, less consumption of power, and efficient memory.

Therefore, each generation of computer is characterized by a major technological development that has drastically changed the way in which computers operate.

First Generation (1942–1955)

Hardware Technology First generation computers were manufactured using thousands of vacuum tubes. Vacuum tube (as shown in Figure 1.2) is a device made of fragile glass.

Software Technology Programming was done in machine language or assembly language.

Used for Scientific applications

Examples ENIAC, EDVAC, EDSAC, UNIVAC I, IBM 701

Highlights

- They were the fastest calculating device of those times.
- Computers were too bulky and required a complete room for storage.
- Highly unreliable as vacuum tubes emitted a large amount of heat and burnt frequently.
- Required air-conditioned room for installation.
- Costly.
- Difficult to use.
- Required constant maintenance because vacuum tubes used filaments that had limited lifetime. Therefore, these computers were prone to frequent hardware failures.

Figure 1.2   Vacuum tube
Source: Vladyslav Danilin/Shutterstock

Second Generation (1955–1964)

Hardware Technology Second generation computers were manufactured using transistors (as shown in Figure 1.3). Transistors were reliable, powerful, cheaper, smaller, and cooler than vacuum tubes.

Software Technology Programming was done in high-level programming language.

Used for Scientific and commercial applications

Examples Honeywell 400, IBM 7030, CDC 1604,

UNIVAC LARC

Highlights
- Faster, smaller, cheaper, reliable, and easier to use than the first generation computers.
- Consumed 1/10th the power consumed by first generation computers.
- Bulky in size and required a complete room for its installation.
- Dissipated less heat than first generation computers but still required air-conditioned room.
- Costly.
- Difficult to use.

Figure 1.3 Transistors
Source: yurazaga/Shutterstock

> **Note** Initially, ICs contained 10–20 components. This technology was called Small Scale Integration (SSI). Later it was enhanced to contain about 100 components. This was called MSI (Medium Scale Integration).

Third Generation (1964–1975)

Hardware Technology Third generation computers were manufactured using integrated chips (ICs) as shown in Figure 1.4. ICs consist of several components such as transistors, capacitors, and resistors on a single chip to avoid wired interconnection between components. These computers used SSI and MSI technology. Minicomputers came into existence.

Software Technology Programming was done in high-level programming language such as FORTRAN, COBOL, Pascal, and BASIC.

Figure 1.4 Integrated chip
Source: cooldesign/FreeDigitalPhotos.net

Used for Scientific, commercial, and interactive online applications.

Examples IBM 360/370, PDP-8, PADP-11, CDC6600

Highlights
- Faster, smaller, cheaper, reliable, and easier to use than the second generation computers.
- They consumed less power than second generation computers.
- Bulky in size and required a complete room for its installation.
- Dissipated less heat than second generation computers but still required air-conditioned room.
- Costly.
- Easier to use and upgrade.

Fourth Generation (1975–1989)

Hardware Technology Fourth generation computers were manufactured using ICs with LSI (Large Scale Integrated) and later with VLSI (Very Large Scale Integrated) technology as shown in Figure 1.5. Microcomputers came

Figure 1.5 VLSI

into existence, and use of personal computers became widespread during this period. High speed computer networks in the form of LANs, WANs, and MANs started growing. Besides mainframes, supercomputers were also used.

> **Note** LSI contained 30,000 components on a single chip and VLSI technology had about 1 million electronic components on a single chip.

Software Technology Programming was done in high-level programming language such as C++ and Java. Graphical user interface (GUI) based operating system (like Windows) was introduced. It had icons and menus among other features to allow computers to be used as a general purpose machine by all users.

Used for Scientific, commercial, interactive online, and network applications.

Examples IBM PC, Apple II, TRS-80, VAX 9000, CRAY-1, CRAY-2, CRAY-X/MP

Highlights Faster, smaller, cheaper, powerful, reliable, and easier to use than the previous generation computers.

Fifth Generation (1989–Present)

Hardware Technology Fifth generation computers were manufactured using ICs with ULSI (Ultra Large Scale Integrated) technology as shown in Figure 1.6. Use of Internet became widespread. Very powerful mainframes, desktops, portable laptops, and smartphones are being used commonly. Super computers use parallel processing techniques.

> **Note** ULSI contained about 10 million electronic components on a single chip.

Software Technology Programming was done in high-level programming language such as Java, Python, and C#.

Used for Scientific, commercial, interactive online, multimedia (graphics, audio, video), and network applications.

Examples IBM notebooks, Pentium PCs, SUM workstations, IBM SP/2, Param supercomputer.

Highlights

- Faster, smaller, cheaper, powerful, reliable, and easier to use than the previous generation computers.
- Speed of microprocessors and the size of memory are growing rapidly.
- High-end features available on mainframe computers in the fourth generation are now available on the microprocessors.

Figure 1.6 ULSI

- Consume less power than computers of prior generations.
- Air-conditioned rooms required for mainframes and supercomputers but not for microprocessors.

1.4 CHARACTERISTICS OF COMPUTERS

The important characteristics of a computer (as shown in Figure 1.7) are as follows.

Speed Computers can perform millions of operations in a single second. This means that a computer can process the data in blink of an eye which otherwise may take multiple days to complete. The speed of the computer is usually given in *nano second* and *pico second,* where

$$1 \text{ nano second} = 1 \times 10^{-9} \text{ second and } 1 \text{ pico second} = 1 \times 10^{-12} \text{ second}$$

Accuracy Computers are a reliable electronic device. It never makes mistakes. It always gives accurate results provided that correct data and set of instructions are input to it. So in the advent of an error, only the user who has fed the incorrect data/program is responsible. If the input data is wrong, then the output will also be erroneous. In computer terminology, it is known as garbage-in garbage-out (GIGO).

Automatic Besides being very fast and accurate, computers are automatic devices that can perform without any user intervention. The user just needs to assign the task to the computer after which the computer automatically controls different devices attached to it and executes the program instructions one by one.

Diligence Computers can never get tired as humans do. It can continually work for hours without creating any error. If a large number of executions have to be made then each and every execution will require the same amount of time and accuracy.

Versatile Versatile means flexible. Today, computers are being used in our daily lives in different fields. For

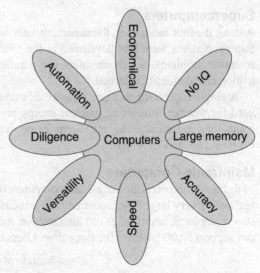

Figure 1.7   Characteristics of a computer

example, they are used as personal computers (PCs) for home use, for business-oriented tasks, weather forecasting, space explorations, teaching, railways, banking, medicine, etc. On the PC that you use at home, you may play a game, compose and send e-mails, listen to music, etc. Therefore, computers are versatile devices as they can perform multiple tasks of different nature at the same time.

Memory Similar to humans, computers also have memory. Human beings cannot store everything in their memory and need secondary media, such as a notebook to record certain important things. Similarly, computers have internal memory (storage space) as well as external or secondary memory. While the internal memory of computers is very expensive and limited in size, the secondary storage is cheaper and bigger in size.

The computer stores a large amount of data and programs in the secondary storage space. The stored data and programs can be used whenever required. Secondary memory devices include CD, DVD, hard disk, pen drives, etc.

> **Note**   When data and programs have to be used they are copied from the secondary memory into the internal memory (often known as RAM).

No IQ Although the trend today is to make computers intelligent by inducing artificial intelligence (AI) in them, they do not have any decision-making abilities of their own, that is, their IQ level is zero. They need guidance to perform various tasks.

Economical Today, computers are considered as short-term investment for achieving long-term gain. Using computers also reduces manpower requirements and leads to an elegant and efficient way for doing tasks. Hence, computers save time, energy, and money. When compared to other systems, computers can do more work in lesser time. For example, using the conventional postal system to send an important document takes at least 2–3 days, whereas the same information when sent using the Internet (e-mail) will be delivered instantaneously.

1.5 CLASSIFICATION OF COMPUTERS

Computers can be broadly classified into four categories based on their speed, amount of data that they can process, and price (refer to Figure 1.8). These categories are as follows:

- Supercomputers
- Mainframe computers
- Minicomputers
- Microcomputers

Supercomputers

Among the four categories, the supercomputer is the fastest, most powerful, and most expensive computer. Supercomputers were first developed in the 1980s to process large amounts of data and to solve complex scientific problems. Supercomputers use parallel processing technology and can perform more than one trillion calculations in a second.

A single supercomputer can support thousands of users at the same time. Such computers are mainly used for weather forecasting, nuclear energy research, aircraft design, automotive design, online banking, controlling industrial units, etc. Some examples of supercomputers are CRAY-1, CRAY-2, Control Data CYBER 205, and ETA A-10.

Mainframe Computers

Mainframe computers are large-scale computers (but smaller than supercomputers). These are very expensive and need a very large clean room with air conditioning, thereby making them very costly to deploy. As with supercomputers, mainframes can also support multiple processors. For example, the IBM S/390 mainframe can support 50,000 users at the same time. Users can access mainframes by either using terminals or via PCs.

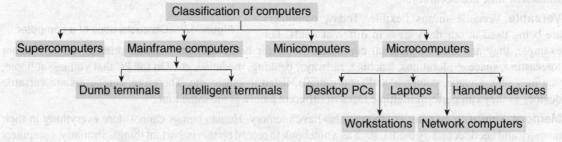

Figure 1.8 Classification of computers

Mainframe computers are typically used as servers on the World Wide Web. They are also used in organizations such as banks, airline companies, and universities, where a large number of users frequently access the data stored in their databases. IBM is the major manufacturer of mainframe computers. Some examples of mainframe computers include IBM S/390, Control Data CYBER 176, and Amdahl 580.

Minicomputers

As the name suggests, minicomputers are smaller, cheaper, and slower than mainframes. They are called minicomputers because they were the smallest computer of their times. Also known as *midrange computers,* the capabilities of minicomputers fall between mainframe and personal computers.

Minicomputers are widely used in business, education, hospitals, government organizations, etc. While some minicomputers can be used only by a single user, others are specifically designed to handle multiple users simultaneously. Usually, single-user minicomputers are used for performing complex design tasks.

As with mainframes, minicomputers can also be used as servers in a networked environment, and hundreds of PCs can be connected to it.

The first minicomputer was introduced by Digital Equipment Corporation (DEC) in the mid-1960s. Other manufacturers of minicomputers include IBM Corporation (AS/400 computers), Data General Corporation, and Prime Computer.

Microcomputers

Microcomputers, commonly known as PCs, are very small and cheap. The first microcomputer was designed by IBM in 1981 and was named IBM-PC. Later on, many computer hardware companies copied this design and termed their microcomputers *PC-compatible,* which refers to any PC that is based on the original IBM PC design.

Another type of popular PC is designed by Apple. PCs designed by IBM and other PC-compatible computers have a different architecture from that of Apple computers. Moreover, PCs and PC-compatible computers commonly use the Windows operating system, while Apple computers use the Macintosh operating system (MacOS). PCs can be classified into the following categories:

Desktop PCs A desktop PC is the most popular model of PCs. The system unit of the desktop PC can be placed flat on a desk or table. It is widely used in homes and offices.

Laptops Laptops (Figure 1.9) are small microcomputers that can easily fit inside a briefcase. They are very handy and can easily be carried from one place to another. They may also be placed on the user's lap (thus the name). Hence, laptops are very useful, especially when going on long journeys. Laptops operate on a battery and do not always have to be plugged in like desktop computers.

The memory and storage capacity of a laptop is almost equivalent to that of a desktop computer. As with desktop computers, laptops also have hard disk drives, USB drives, etc. For input, laptops have a built-in keyboard and a trackball/touchpad, which is used as a pointing device (as a mouse is used for a desktop PC).

Today, laptops have the same features and processing speed as the most powerful PCs. However, a drawback is that laptops are generally more

Figure 1.9 Laptop
Source: You can more/Shutterstock

expensive than desktop computers. These computers are very popular among business travellers.

Workstations Workstations are single-user computers that have the same features as PCs, but their processing speed matches that of a minicomputer or mainframe computer. Workstation computers have advanced processors, and more RAM and storage capacity than PCs. Therefore, they are more expensive and powerful than a normal desktop computer.

Although workstation computers are widely used as powerful single-user computers by scientists, engineers, architects, and graphic designers, they can also be used as servers in a networked environment.

Network Computers Network computers have less processing power, memory, and storage than a desktop computer. These are specially designed to be used as terminals in a networked environment. For example, some network computers are specifically designed to access data stored on a network (including the Internet and intranet).

Some network computers do not have any storage space and merely rely on the network's server for data storage and processing tasks. The concept of network computers had become popular in the mid-1990s when several variations of computers such as Windows terminals, NetPCs, and diskless workstations were widely used.

Network computers that are specifically designed to access only the Internet or intranet are often known as Internet PCs or Internet boxes. Some network computers used in homes do not even have a monitor. Such computers may be connected to a television, which serves as the output device. The most common example of a home-based network computer is Web TV, which enables the user to connect a television to the Internet. The other reason for the popularity of network computers is that they are cheaper to purchase and maintain than PCs.

Handheld Computers The mid-1990s witnessed a range of small personal computing devices that are commonly known as handheld computers, or mobile computers. These computers are called handheld computers because they can fit in one hand, while users can use the other hand to operate them. Handheld computers are very small in size, and hence they have small-sized screens and keyboards. These computers are preferred by business travellers and mobile employees whose jobs require them to move from place to place.

Some examples of handheld computers are as follows:

- Smartphones
- Tablet PCs
- Phablets

Smartphones These days, cellular phones are web-enabled telephones that have features of both analog and digital devices. Such phones are also known as smartphones because, in addition to basic phone capabilities, they also facilitate the users to access the Internet and send e-mails and faxes.

Tablet PCs A tablet PC (refer Figure 1.10) is a computing device that is smaller than a laptop, but bigger than a smartphone. Features such as user-friendly interface, portability, and touch screen have made them very popular in the last few years. These days, a wide range of high-performance tablets are available in the market. While all of them look similar from outside, they may differ in features such as operating system, speed of data connectivity, camera specifications, size of the screen, processing power, battery life, and storage capability.

Some operating systems that are used in tablets are Android Jellybean (an open-source operating system built by Google), Windows 8, and iOS (developed by Apple).

Figure 1.10 Tablet
Source: bloomua/Shutterstock/OUP Picture Bank

While users can easily type directly on the surface of a tablet, some users prefer a wireless or bluetooth-connected keyboard. These days, tablets also offer an optional docking station with keyboards that transforms the tablet into a full-featured netbook.

Uses The following are the uses of tablet PCs:

- Viewing presentations
- Video conferencing
- Reading e-books, e-newspaper
- Watching movies
- Playing games
- Sharing pictures, video, songs, documents, etc.
- Browsing the Internet
- Keeping in touch with friends and family on popular social networks, sending emails
- Business people use them to perform tasks such as editing documents, exchanging documents, taking notes, and giving presentations
- Tablets are best used in crowded places such as airports and coffee shops, where size and portability become more important.

Note Tablets may replace laptops if users don't have to perform heavy processing tasks and do not require a CD or DVD player.

Phablet (Phone + Tablet) Phablet is a class of mobile device that combines the functions of a smartphone and tablet. Usually, mobile devices with screen size 4–5 inch are termed as smartphones and those with size ranging from 7–10 inch are known as tablets. A phablet fills the void between the two types of devices. Therefore, phablet is a half-smartphone and half-tablet mobile device (refer Figure 1.11). A phablet can be easily held and used in one hand. These days, phablets support 3G as well as 4G networks for cellular calls and are Wi-Fi-enabled.

Smartphones   Phablets   Tablets
5-inch and less Between 5-7 inches 7 inches and above

Figure 1.11 Comparison between Smartphone, Phablet, and Tablet

The trend of phablet started with Samsung's Galaxy Note in 2011 and its popularity grew dramatically in 2012 due to the falling costs and increasing power efficiency of smartphone display. Following the competition, other smartphone manufacturers, including Lenovo, LG, HTC, Huawei, Micromax, and Sony came up with their models of phablets.

Raspberry Pi

Raspberry Pi is a credit card sized computer which was originally designed for education. It is a low-cost device that has been specifically created to improve programming skills and hardware understanding at the pre-university level. Raspberry Pi was originally intended to be a microcomputer to teach children coding. But later on its scope was expanded and it has now become a very popular device.

Although the Raspberry Pi is slower than a modern laptop or desktop, it is a complete Linux computer that provides all the expected abilities at a low-power consumption level. Raspberry Pi is being widely used around the world either as a desktop computer or as a device to build smart devices. For example, some common use of Raspberry Pi include:

- Teach coding
- Used as a desktop
- Create a retro gaming console
- Make a world clock or an FM radio with the Pi Zero
- Make a media center with Rasplex or an always-on downloading machine
- Build a motion capture security camera

1.6 BASIC APPLICATIONS OF COMPUTERS

When the first computers were developed, they were used only in the fields of mathematics and science. In fact, the first effective utilization of computers was for decoding messages in military applications. Later on, computers were used in real-time control systems, such as for landing on the moon. However, with the advancement of technology, the cost of a computer and its maintenance declined. This opened the way for computers extensively being used in business and commercial sector for information processing. Today, computers are widely used in different fields as discussed below.

Communication Internet which connects computers all over the world. Internet gives you access to enormous amount of information, much more than you could have in a library. Then using electronic mail you can communicate in seconds with a person who is thousands of miles away. The chat software enables you to chat with another person in real-time (irrespective of the physical location of that person). Then, video conferencing tools are becoming popular for conducting meetings with people who are unable to be present at a particular place.

Desktop Publishing Desktop publishing software enables you to create page layouts for entire books.

Government Computers are used to keep records on legislative actions, Internal Revenue Service records, etc.

Traffic Control It is used by governments for city planning and traffic control.

Legal System Computers are being used by lawyers to shorten the time required to conduct legal precedent and case research. Lawyers use computers to look through millions of individual cases and find whether similar or parallel cases were approved, denied, criticized, or overruled. This enables the lawyers to formulate strategies based on past case decisions. Moreover, computers are also used to keep track of appointments and prepare legal documents and briefs in time for filling cases.

Retail Business Computers are used in retail shops to enter the order, calculate the cost, and print a receipt. They are also used to keep an inventory of the products available and a complete description about them.

Sports In sports, computers are used to compile statistics, identify weak players and strong players by analyzing statistics, sell tickets, create training programs and diets for athletes, and suggest game plan strategies based on the competitor's past performance. Computers are also used to generate most of the graphic art displays flashed on scoreboards.

Computers are used in the control room to display action replays and insert commercial breaks on schedule. Moreover, sports shoes manufacturing companies, like NIKE, use computers for designing footwears. They calculate stress points and then create the style and shape that offer maximum support for the foot.

Music Computers are used to generate a variety of sounds. Moreover, the background music in movies, television shows, and commercials are all generated electronically using computers.

Movies Computers are used to create sets, special effects, animations, cartoons, imaginary characters, videos, and commercials.

Travel and Tourism Computers are used to prepare ticket, monitor the train's or airplane's route, or guide the plane to a safe landing. They are also used to know about hotels in an area, reserve room, or rent a car.

Business and Industry In business and industry, computers are used mainly for entering and analysing data, pay roll processing, personnel record keeping, inventory management, etc.

Hospitals Hospitals use computers to record every information about a patient from the time of his admission till his exit. For example the date, time, reason of admit, the doctor being consulted, all prescribed medications, doctor visits, other hospital services, bill, etc. are all stored in computers. Moreover, computer-controlled devices are widely used to monitor pulse rate, blood pressure, and other vital signs of the patient and in an emergency situation an alarm is used to notify the nurses and other attendants.

Moreover, computers are used as an aid to physically handicapped people. For example, computers are used to develop more effective artificial limbs for amputees.

Simulation Computers enable the engineers to design aircraft models and simulate the effects that winds and other environmental forces might have on those designs. Even the astronauts at NASA are trained using computer-simulated problems that could be encountered during launch, in space, or upon return to Earth.

Geology Civil engineers use computers to evaluate the effects of an earthquake on the structure of buildings based on age, proximity to the fault, soil type, size, shape, and construction material.

Astronomy Spacecrafts are usually monitored using computers which not only keep a continuous record of the voyage and the records of the speed, direction, fuel, temperature, and such performance but also suggests a corrective action if the vehicle makes any mistake. The remote stations on the earth compares all these quantities with the desired values and in case these values need to be modified to enhance the performance of the space craft, signals are immediately sent which set in motion the mechanics to rectify the situation. With the help of computers, these are done within a fraction of seconds.

Weather Forecasting When computers are fed with mathematical equations along with data about air pressure, temperature, humidity, and other values, the solution of these equations gives an accurate prediction of weather in a particular area. For example, a Crax XMP Supercomputer installed at Mausam Bhavan in New Delhi is used to predict weather and climatic changes in the Indian subcontinent.

Education A computer is a powerful teaching aid and acts as another teacher in the classroom. Teachers use computers to develop instructional material. They may use pictures, graphs, and graphical presentations to easily illustrate an otherwise difficult concept. Moreover, teachers at all levels can use computers to administer assignments and keep track of grades of the students. Besides teachers, students also prefer to learn from an E-learning software rather than learning from a book. Students can also give online exams and get instant results.

Online Banking The world today is moving towards a cashless society, where you need not have money in your pocket to purchase anything. You can just have your credit card or debit card with you.

The ATM machines (Automated Teller Machine) provides a 24 × 7 service and allows you to draw cash, check the balance in your account, and order a product.

Industry and Engineering Computers are found in all kinds of industries like thermal power plant, oil refineries, chemical industries, etc. for process control, computer aided designing, and computer aided manufacturing.

Computerized process control (with or without human intervention) is used to enhance efficiency in applications such as production of various chemical products, oil refining, paper manufacture, rolling and cutting steel to customer requirements, etc.

In Computer Aided Design (CAD) the computers are used for automating the design and drafting process. It helps an engineer to design a part, analyse its characteristics, and then subject it to simulated stresses. In case a part fails the stress test, its specifications can be modified on the computer and retested. The final design specifications are released for production only when the engineer is satisfied that the part meets strength and other quality considerations.

Computer-aided manufacturing (CAM) phase comes up where CAD leaves off. In this phase, the metal or other materials are manufactured while complying with their specification. For this computer-controlled manufacturing tools are used to produce high-quality products.

Robots Robots are computer-controlled machines mainly used in manufacturing process in extreme conditions where humans cannot work. For example, in high temperature, high pressure conditions, or in processes that demand very high level of accuracy.

Decision Support Systems Computers help managers to analyse their organization's data to understand the present scenario of their business, view the trends in the market, and predict the future of their products. Managers also use decision support systems to analyse market research data, to size up the competition, and to plan effective strategies for penetrating their markets.

Expert System Expert systems are used to automate the decision-making process in a specific area like analysing the credit histories for loan approval and diagnosing a patient's condition for prescribing an appropriate treatment. Expert systems analyse the available data in depth to recommend a course of action. A medical expert system can provide the most likely diagnosis of a patient's condition.

Others Adding more to it, in today's scenario computers are used to find jobs on the Internet, find a suitable match for a boy or girl, read news and articles online, find one's batchmates, send and receive greetings pertaining to different occasions, etc.

1.7 STORED PROGRAM CONCEPT

All digital computers are based on the principle of stored program concept, which was introduced by Sir John von Neumann in the late 1940s. The following are the key characteristic features of this concept:

- Before any data is processed, instructions are read into memory.
- Instructions are stored in the computer's memory for execution.
- Instructions are stored in binary form (using binary numbers—only 0s and 1s).
- Processing starts with the first instruction in the program, which is copied into a control unit circuit. The control unit executes the instructions.
- Instructions written by the users are performed sequentially until there is a break in the current flow.
- Input/output and processing operations are performed simultaneously. While data is being read/written, the central processing unit (CPU) executes another program in the memory that is ready for execution.

Note A stored program architecture is a fundamental computer architecture wherein the computer executes the instructions that are stored in its memory.

A stored program architecture is a fundamental computer architecture wherein the computer executes the instructions that are stored in its memory. John W. Mauchly, an American physicist, and J. Presper Eckert, an American engineer, further contributed to the stored program concept to make digital computers much more flexible and powerful. As a result, engineers in England built the first stored-program computer, Manchester Mark I, in the year 1949. They were shortly followed by the Americans who designed EDVAC in the very same year.

Today, a CPU chip can handle billions of instructions per second. It executes instructions provided both the data and instructions are valid. In case either one of them or both are not valid, the computer stops the processing of instructions.

1.7.1 Types of Stored Program Computers

A computer with a Von Neumann architecture stores data and instructions in the same memory (refer Figure 1.12(a)). There is a serial machine in which data and instructions are selected one at a time. Data and instructions are transferred to and from memory through a shared data bus. Since there is a single bus to carry data and instructions, process execution becomes slower.

Later Harvard University proposed a stored program concept in which there was a separate memory to store data and instructions (refer Figure 1.12(b)). Instructions are selected serially from the instruction memory and executed in the processor. When an instruction needs data, it is selected from the data memory. Since there are separate memories, execution becomes faster.

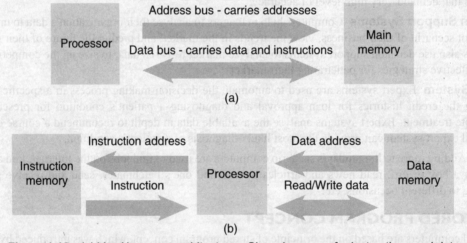

Figure 1.12   (a) Von Neumann architecture—Shared memory for instructions and data
(b) Harvard architecture—Separate memories for instructions and data

1.8 COMPONENTS AND FUNCTIONS OF A COMPUTER SYSTEM

A computer is an electronic device which basically performs five major operations, which are as follows:

1. accepting data or instructions (input)
2. storing data
3. processing data
4. displaying results (output) and
5. controlling and coordinating all operations inside a computer

In this section, we will discuss all these functions and see how one component of a computer interacts with another unit to perform these operations using the block diagram of a computer as shown in Figure 1.13.

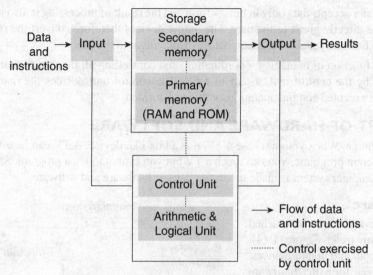

Figure 1.13 Block diagram of a computer

Input This is the process of entering data and instructions (also known as programs) into the computer system. The data and instructions can be entered into the computer system by using different input devices such as keyboard, mouse, scanner, trackball, etc.

| Note | Computers understand binary language which consists of only two symbols (0s and 1s). Therefore, it is the responsibility of the input devices to convert the input data into binary codes. |

Storage Storage is the process of saving data and instructions permanently in the computer so that it can be used for processing. The computer storage space stores not only the data and programs but also the intermediate results and the final results of processing. A computer has two types of storage areas:

Primary Storage Primary storage also known as the main memory is that storage area which is directly accessible by the CPU at a very fast speed. It is used to store the data and program, the intermediate results of processing, and the recently generated results. The primary storage is very expensive and therefore limited in capacity. Another drawback of main memory is that it is volatile in nature, that is, as soon as the computer is switched off, the information stored in it gets erased. Hence, it cannot be used as a permanent storage of useful data and programs for future use. For example, RAM (Random Access Memory).

Secondary Storage Also known as the secondary memory or auxiliary memory is just the opposite of primary memory. It basically overcomes all the drawbacks of the primary storage. It is cheaper, non-volatile, and used to permanently store data and programs of those jobs which are not being currently executed by the CPU. Secondary memory supplements the limited storage capacity of the primary memory. For example, using a magnetic disk you can store your data in C drive, D drive, etc. for future use.

Processing The process of performing operations on the data as per the instructions specified by the user (program) is called processing. Data processing is an activity that involves handling or manipulating data in some way to assign meaning to it. The main aim of processing is to transform data into information. Data and instructions are taken from the primary memory and are transferred to the Arithmetic and Logical Unit (ALU), a part of CPU, which performs all sorts of calculations. When the processing completes, the final result is transferred to the main memory.

Output Output is the reverse of input. It is the process of giving the result of data processing to the outside world (external to the computer system). The results are given through output devices like monitor, printer, etc.

Now that the computer accepts data only in binary form and the result of processing is also in the binary form, the result cannot be directly given to the user. The output devices therefore convert the results available in binary codes into a human-readable language before displaying it to the user.

Controlling The function of managing, coordinating, and controlling all the components of the computer system is handled by the control unit, a part of CPU. The control unit decides the manner in which the instructions will be executed and the operations will be performed.

1.9 CONCEPT OF HARDWARE AND SOFTWARE

You have a TV at home. When you purchase a TV, it is a box like device. A TV can be used only when it is able to display different programs. You can touch a TV but you cannot touch a program. Same is the concept in a computer. A computer system is made up of two parts— hardware and software.

1.9.1 Hardware

All the physical parts that can be touched are called hardware (refer Figure 1.14). For example, all input and output devices, and memory devices form the hardware part of the computer.

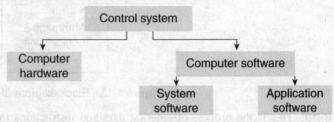

Figure 1.14   Parts of a computer system

If we think of computer as a living being, then the hardware would be the body that does things like seeing with eyes, lifting objects, and filling the lungs with air; the software would be the intelligence that helps in interpreting the images that come through the eyes, instructing the arms how to lift objects, and forcing the body to fill the lungs with air.

Since the computer hardware is a part of a machine, it can only understand two basic concepts: 'on' and 'off'. The 'on' and 'off' concept is called *binary*. Computer software was developed to tell the computer hardware what to do.

1.9.2 Software

The computer hardware cannot think and make decisions on its own. So, it cannot be used to analyse a given set of data and find a solution on its own. The hardware needs a software (a set of programs) to instruct what has to be done. A program is a set of instructions that is arranged in a sequence to guide a computer to find a solution for the given problem. The process of writing a program is called *programming*.

Let us now discuss the CPU and the other hardware components of a computer system in the following sections.

1.10 CENTRAL PROCESSING UNIT (CPU): BASIC ARCHITECTURE

Central Processing Unit can be called the brain of the computer system because the entire processing of data and execution of instructions is done here. It is made up of one or more than one microprocessors which consist of two main parts—Arithmetic and Logical Unit (ALU) and Control Unit (CU). It also contains registers and a Bus Interface Unit (BIU) of shown in Figure 1.15.

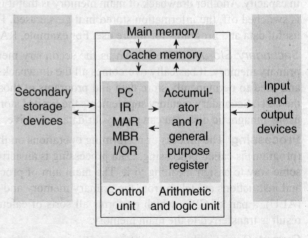

Figure 1.15   Basic computer organization

Arithmetic and Logical Unit

The ALU performs all kinds of calculations, such as arithmetic (add, subtract, multiply, divide, etc.), comparison (less than, greater than, or equal to), and other operations. The intermediate results of processing may be stored in the main memory, as they might be required again. When the processing completes, the final result is then transferred to the main memory. Hence, the data may move from main memory to the ALU multiple times before the processing is over.

Control Unit

The main function of the CU is to direct and coordinate the computer operations. It interprets the instructions (program) and initiates action to execute them. The CU controls the flow of data through the computer system and directs the ALU, input/output (I/O) devices, and other units. It is, therefore, called the central nervous system of the computer system. In addition, the CU is responsible for fetching, decoding, executing instructions, and storing results.

Registers

A processor register is a computer memory that provides quick access to the data currently being used for processing. The ALU stores all temporary results and the final result in the processor registers. As mentioned earlier, registers are at the top of memory hierarchy and are always preferred to speed up program execution.

Registers are also used to store the instructions of the program currently being executed. There are different types of registers, each with a specific storage function.

Accumulator and general-purpose registers These are frequently used to store the data brought from the main memory and the intermediate results during program execution. The number of general-purpose registers present varies from processor to processor. When program execution is complete, the result of processing is transferred from the accumulator to the memory through the memory buffer register (MBR).

Special-purpose registers These include the following:
- The memory address register (MAR) stores the address of the data or instruction to be fetched from the main memory. The value stored in the MAR is copied from the program counter.
- The MBR stores the data or instruction fetched from the main memory (Figure 1.16). If an instruction is fetched from the memory, then the contents of the MBR are copied into the instruction register (IR). If a data is fetched

| Processor | ⇄ | Memory buffer register | ⇄ | Memory |

Figure 1.16 Data to and from memory comes from and to processor through the MBR

from the memory, the contents are either transferred to the accumulator or to the I/O register. The MBR is also used while writing contents in the main memory. In this case, the processor first transfers the contents to the MBR, which then writes them into the memory.
- The IR stores the instructions currently being executed. In general, an instruction consists of two parts—operation and address of the data on which the operation has to be performed. When the IR is loaded with an instruction, the address of the data is transferred to the MAR and the operation part is given to the CU, which interprets it and executes it.
- The I/O register is used to transfer data or instructions to or from an I/O device. An input device transfers data to the I/O register for processing. Correspondingly, any data to be sent to the output device is written in this register.
- The program counter stores the address of the next instruction to be executed.

The size of a register is usually specified by the number of bits it can store. For example, a register can be of 8 bits, 16 bits, 32 bits, or 64 bits. Higher the register size, more the data that can be stored in it.

Instruction cycle To execute an instruction, a processor normally follows a set of basic operations that are together known as an instruction cycle (Figure 1.17). The operations performed in an instruction cycle involve the following:

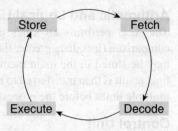

Fetch Retrieving an instruction or a data from memory.

Decode Interpreting the instruction.

Execute Running the corresponding commands to process the data.

Store Writing the results of processing into memory.

Figure 1.17 Instruction cycle

This instruction cycle is repeated continuously until the power is turned off.

Bus Interface Unit

The BIU provides functions for transferring data between the execution unit of the CPU and other components of the computer system that lie outside the CPU. Every computer system has three different types of busses to carry information from one part to the other. These are the data bus, control bus, and address bus (Figure 1.18).

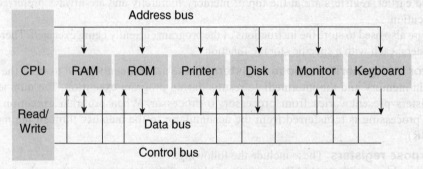

Figure 1.18 Buses with a computer system

The BIU puts the contents of the program counter on the address bus. Note that the content of the program counter is the address of the next instruction to be executed. Once the memory receives an address from the BIU, it places the contents at that address on the data bus, which is then transferred to the IR of the processor through the MBR. At this time, the contents of the program counter are modified (e.g., incremented by 1) so that it now stores the address of the next instruction.

1.11 INPUT AND OUTPUT DEVICES

An input device is used to feed data and instructions into the computer. In the absence of an *input device,* a computer would have only been a display device. Correspondingly, any device that outputs/gives information from a computer is called an *output device.* Refer to Figure 1.19 which shows some basic I/O devices that are generally connected with our computer system.

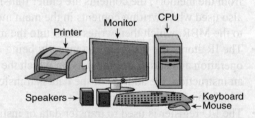

Figure 1.19 Basic I/O device computer system

Input Devices

Some of the input devices that are widely used by computer users to feed data or instruction to the computer are keyboard, mouse, trackball, joystick, stylus, touch screen, barcode reader, optical character recognition (OCR) device, optical mark recognition (OMR), MICR, web and digital cameras, etc.

Output Devices

We can classify the output devices in two categories as shown in Figure 1.20.

Soft copy output devices are those output devices which produce an electronic version of an output. For example, a file which is stored on hard disk, CD, pen drive, etc. and is displayed on the computer screen (monitor). Features of a soft copy output include:

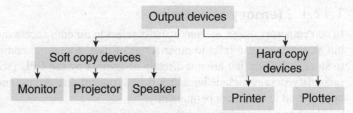

Figure 1.20   Classification of output devices

- The output can be viewed only when the computer is switched On.
- The user can easily edit the soft copy output.
- Soft copy cannot be used by people who do not have a computer.
- Searching data in a soft copy is easy and fast.
- Electronic distribution of a soft copy is cheaper. It can be done easily and quickly.

Hard copy output devices are those output devices which produce a physical form of output. For example, the content of a file printed on a paper (using printer and plotters) is a form of hard copy output. Features of a hard copy output include:

- Computer is not needed to see the output.
- Editing the hard copy is difficult.
- Hard copy output can be easily distributed to people who do not have a computer.
- Searching data in a hard copy is a tiring and difficult job.
- Distribution of a hard copy is not only costly but also slower.

1.12 COMPUTER MEMORY

Computer memory is an internal storage area in the computer used to store data and programs either temporarily or permanently. No processing is done in the computer memory. A computer memory can be broadly divided into two groups: primary (main) memory and secondary memory. While the main memory holds instructions and data when a program is executing, the secondary memory holds data and programs not currently in use and provides long-term storage. Refer to Table 1.1 to understand the key differences between primary and secondary memory.

Table 1.1   Differences between primary and secondary memory

Primary memory	Secondary memory
• It is more expensive.	• It is cheaper.
• It is faster and more efficient than secondary memory.	• It is slower and less efficient than secondary memory.
• Directly accessed by the CPU.	• Cannot be accessed directly by the CPU.
• It is volatile in nature.	• It is non-volatile in nature.
• Storage capacity is limited.	• It has large storage capacity.
• It has no moving parts.	• It has moving parts.
• The memory is power dependent.	• The memory is power independent.
• The memory is integrated circuit based.	• The memory is magnetic or optical based.
• It consumes less power.	• It consumes more power.
• It stores data temporarily.	• It stores data permanently.

1.12.1 Memory Hierarchy

In contemporary usage, *memory* usually refers to random access memory, typically DRAM (Dynamic RAM) but *memory* can also refer to other forms of data storage. In computer terminology, the term *storage* refers to storage devices that are not directly accessible by the CPU (secondary or tertiary storage). Examples of secondary storage include hard disk drives, optical disc drives, and other devices that are slower than RAM but are used to store data permanently.

These days, computers use different types of memory which can be organized in a hierarchy around the CPU, as a trade-off between performance and cost. The memory at a higher level in the storage hierarchy has less capacity to store data, is more expensive, and is fastest to access as shown in Figure 1.21.

CPU Registers

CPU registers are located inside the processor and are therefore directly accessed by the CPU. Registers are the fastest of all forms of computer data storage.

Cache Memory

Cache memory is an intermediate form of storage between registers and the primary memory. It is used to store instructions and data that are repeatedly required to execute programs thereby improving the overall system speed and increase the performance of the computer. Keeping frequently accessed data and instructions in the cache avoids accessing the slower primary memory.

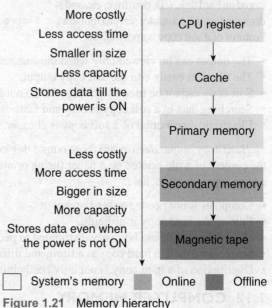

Figure 1.21   Memory hierarchy

Working of the Cache Memory When a program is being executed and the CPU wants to read data or instructions, then the following steps will be performed:

CPU first checks whether the data or instruction is available in cache memory. If it is not present, the CPU reads the data or instructions from the main memory into the processor registers. The CPU also copies it into the cache memory. When the same piece of data/instruction is needed, the CPU reads it from the cache memory instead of the main memory.

1.12.2 Primary Memory

Primary memory (or main memory or internal memory) can be directly accessed by the CPU. The CPU continuously reads instructions stored in the primary memory and executes them. Any data that has to be operated by the CPU is also stored there. There are two types of primary memory: RAM and ROM, which are discussed as follows.

Random Access Memory (RAM)

RAM is a volatile (stores data only when the power is On) storage area within the computer typically used to store data temporarily so that it can be accessed by the CPU. The information stored in RAM is loaded from the computer's hard disk, and includes data related to the operating system and applications that are currently being executed by the processor.

RAM is considered as *random access* because any memory cell can be directly accessed if its address is known. When the RAM gets full, the computer system operates at a slow speed. When multiple applications are being executed simultaneously and the RAM gets fully occupied by the application's data, it is searched to identify memory portions that have not been utilized. The contents of those locations are then copied onto the hard drive. This action frees up RAM space and enables the system to load other pieces of required data.

These days, the applications' and operating system's demand for system RAM has drastically increased. For example, in the year 2000, a personal computer (PC) had only 128 MB of RAM, but today PCs have 1–2 GB of RAM installed, and may include graphics cards with their own additional 512 MB or more of RAM. As discussed earlier, there are two types of RAM—static RAM (SRAM) and dynamic RAM (DRAM).

Static RAM This is a type of RAM that holds data without an external refresh as long as it is powered. This is in striking contrast with the DRAM which must be refreshed multiple times in a second to hold its data contents. SRAM is made of D flip-flops in which the memory cells flip-flop between 0 and 1 without the use of capacitors. Therefore, there is no need for an external refresh process to be carried out.

The limitation of SRAM is that it occupies more space and is more expensive than DRAM. While each transistor on a DRAM chip can store one bit of information, the SRAM chip, on the other hand, requires four to six transistors to store a bit. This means that a DRAM chip can hold at least four times as much data as an SRAM chip of the same size, thereby making SRAM much more expensive.

However, SRAM is faster, more reliable than DRAM, and is often used as cache memory. SRAM chips are also used in cars, household appliances, and handheld electronic devices.

Dynamic RAM This is the most common type of memory used in personal computers, workstations, and servers today. A DRAM chip contains millions of tiny memory cells. Each cell is made up of a transistor and a capacitor, and can contain 1 bit of information—0 or 1. To store a bit of information in a DRAM chip, a tiny amount of power is put into the cell to charge the capacitor. Hence, while reading a bit, the transistor checks for a charge in the capacitor. If a charge is present, then the reading is 1; if not, the reading is 0.

However, the problem with DRAM is that the capacitor leaks energy very quickly and can hold the charge for only a fraction of a second. Therefore, a refresh process is required to maintain the charge in the capacitor so that it can retain the information. This refreshing process is carried out multiple times in a second and requires that all cells be accessed, even if the information is not needed.

However, the advantage of DRAM over SRAM is that it is cheap, can hold more data per chip, and generates less heat than SRAM. DRAM is widely used to build the main memory. The following are the different types of DRAM:

Synchronous DRAM (SDRAM) SDRAM synchronizes itself with the clock speed of the microprocessor to enable faster access to memory.

Enhanced SDRAM (ESDRAM) This version of SDRAM, though not widely used, includes a small SRAM cache to reduce delays in data access and speed up operations.

Double data rate SDRAM (DDR) DDR allows data transfers on both the rising and falling edges of the clock cycle, which doubles the data throughput. DDR SDRAM chips are available in capacities of 128 MB to 1 GB. Although DDR memory is very common, the technology is becoming outdated and is being replaced by DDR2.

DDR2 chips are the next generation of DDR SDRAM memory. It can hold 256 MB to 2 GB of memory and can operate at higher bus speeds. Although DDR2 has twice the latency (data access delays) of DDR, it delivers data at twice the speed, thereby performing at the same level.

Rambus DRAM (RDRAM) It is a proprietary, protocol-based, high-speed memory technology developed by Rambus Inc. RDRAM can operate at extremely high frequencies as compared to other types of DRAMs.

Synchronous link dynamic RAM (SLDRAM) This version of SDRAM, not used widely, was basically designed as a royalty-free, open-industry standard design alternative to RDRAM.

Read Only Memory (ROM)

ROM refers to computer memory chips containing permanent data. Unlike RAM, ROM is non-volatile, that is, the data is retained in it even when the computer is turned Off. Refer Table 1.2 to understand the key differences between RAM and ROM.

Table 1.2   Differences between RAM and ROM

RAM	ROM
• Data can be read as well as written.	• Data can only be read.
• Data is stored temporarily.	• Data is stored permanently.
• Data is stored while the computer is being used by users to hold their data.	• Data is stored during the time of fabrication.
• It is required while the computer is being used by users to run their applications.	• It is required for starting the computer, and storing important programs.

Most computers contain a small amount of ROM that stores critical programs which are used to start the computer when it is turned On. Originally, ROM was actually read only. So, in order to update the programs stored in ROM, the ROM chip had to be removed and physically replaced by the ROM chip that has a new version of the program. However, today ROM chips are not literally *read only,* as updates to the ROM chip are possible. The process of updating a ROM chip is a bit slower as memory must be erased in large portions before it can be re-written.

Rewritable ROM chips include PROMs, EPROMs, and EEPROMs.

* *Programmable read-only memory (PROM)* also called one-time programmable ROM can be written to or programmed using a special device called a PROM programmer. The working of a PROM is similar to that of a CD-ROM recorder which enables the users to write programs just once but the recorded data can be read multiple times. Programming a PROM is also called *burning.*
* *Erasable programmable read-only memory (EPROM)* is a type of ROM that can be erased and re-programmed. The EPROM can be erased by exposing the chip to strong ultraviolet light typically for 10 minutes or longer and then rewritten with a process that again needs higher than usual voltage applied.
* *Electrically erasable programmable read-only memory (EEPROM)* allows its entire or selected contents to be electrically erased, then rewritten electrically. The process of writing an EEPROM is also known as flashing.

1.12.3 Secondary Storage Devices

Secondary storage (also known as external memory or auxiliary storage) differs from main memory in that it is not directly accessible by the CPU. The secondary storage devices hold data even when the computer is switched off. An example of such a device is the hard disk.

The computer usually uses its input/output channels to access data from the secondary storage devices to transfer the data to an intermediate area in the main memory. Secondary storage devices are non-volatile in nature, cheaper than the primary memory, and thus can be used to store huge amounts of data. While the CPU can read the data stored in the main memory in nanoseconds, the data from the secondary storage devices can be accessed in milliseconds.

The secondary storage devices are basically formatted according to a file system that organizes the data into files and directories. The file system also provides additional information to describe the owner of a certain file, the access time, the access permissions, and other information.

Some of the secondary storage devices are magnetic tape, hard disks, compact disks, USB flash drive, memory card, and blue-ray disc.

1.13 CLASSIFICATION OF COMPUTER SOFTWARE

Computer software is written by programmers using a programming language. The programmer writes a set of instructions (program) using a specific programming language. Such programs are known as the *source code.* Another computer program called a *compiler* is then used on the source code, to transform the instructions into a language that the computer can understand. The result is an executable computer program, which is another name for software.

Examples of computer software include the following:

- *Driver software,* which allows a computer to interact with hardware devices such as printers, scanners, and video cards.
- *Educational software,* which includes programs and games that help in teaching and providing drills to help memorize facts. Educational software can be used in diverse areas, from teaching computer-related activities like typing to subjects like chemistry.
- *Media players* and *media development software,* which are specifically designed to play and/or edit digital media files such as music and videos.
- *Productivity software,* which is an older term used to denote any program that allows the user to be more productive in a business sense. Examples of such software include word processors, database management utilities, and presentation software.
- *Operating systems software,* which helps in coordinating system resources and allows execution of other programs. Some examples of operating systems are Windows, Mac OS X, and Linux.
- *Computer games,* which are widely used as a form of entertainment software that has many genres. Computer software can be broadly classified into two groups, namely application software and system software.
- *Application software* is designed for users to solve a particular problem. It is generally what we think of when we refer to a computer program. Examples of application software include spreadsheets, database systems, desktop publishing software, program development software, games, and web browsers. Simply put, application software represents programs that allow users to do something besides merely run the hardware.
- On the contrary, *system software,* provides a general programming environment in which programmers can create specific applications to suit their needs. This environment provides new functions that are not available at the hardware level and performs tasks related to executing the application program. System software represents programs that allow the hardware to run properly. It acts as an interface between the hardware of the computer and the application software that users need to run on the computer. Figure 1.22 illustrates the relationship between application software and system software.

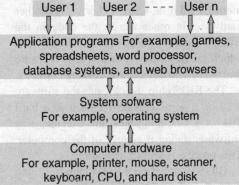

Figure 1.22 Relationship among hardware, system software, and application software

Table 1.3 lists the differences between system and application software.

Table 1.3 Differences between system and application software

System software	Application software
• It is a collection of programs that enable users to interact with hardware components efficiently.	• It is a collection of programs written for a specific application, such as a library system, inventory control system, and so on.
• It controls and manages the hardware.	• It uses the services provided by the system software to interact with hardware components.
• The programmer must understand the architecture of the machine and hardware details to write system software.	• In most cases, the programmer ignores the architecture of the machine and hardware details to write application software.

(Contd)

Table 1.3   (*Contd*)

System software	Application software
• It interacts with the hardware directly.	• It interacts with the hardware indirectly through calls provided by system software.
• Writing system software is a complicated task.	• Writing application programs is relatively easy.
• Examples include compilers and operating systems.	• Examples include Microsoft Word and Microsoft Paint.

1.13.1 System Software

System software is computer software designed to operate computer hardware and to provide and maintain a platform for running application software. Some of the most widely used system software are discussed in this section.

Computer BIOS and Device Drivers

Basic Input/Output System (BIOS) and device drivers provide basic functionality to operate and control the hardware connected to or built into the computer.

BIOS is built into the computer and is the first code run by the computer when it is switched on. The key role of BIOS is to load and start the operating system (OS).

When the computer starts, the first function that BIOS performs is to initialize and identify system devices such as the video display card, keyboard, mouse, hard disk, CD/DVD drive, and other hardware. In other words, the code in the BIOS chip runs a series of tests called POST, which stands for power on self test, to ensure that the system devices are working correctly.

The BIOS chip then locates the software held on a peripheral device such as a hard disk or a CD, and loads and executes that software, giving it control of the computer. This process is known as *booting*.

BIOS is stored on a ROM chip built into the system. It also has a user interface similar to a menu, which can be accessed by pressing a certain key on the keyboard when the PC starts. A BIOS screen is shown in Figure 1.23.

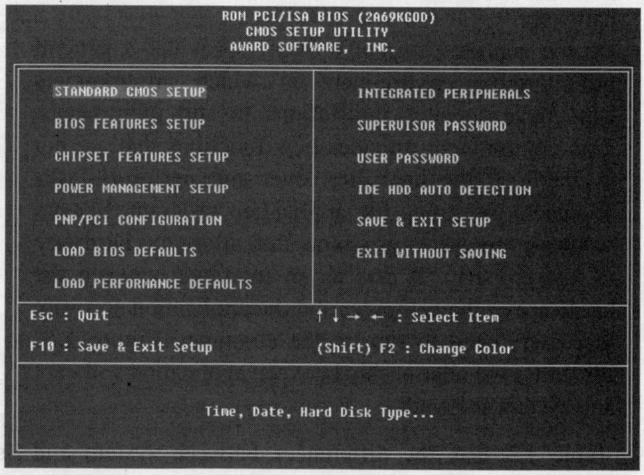

```
ROM PCI/ISA BIOS (2A69KG0D)
CMOS SETUP UTILITY
AWARD SOFTWARE, INC.

STANDARD CMOS SETUP            INTEGRATED PERIPHERALS
BIOS FEATURES SETUP            SUPERVISOR PASSWORD
CHIPSET FEATURES SETUP         USER PASSWORD
POWER MANAGEMENT SETUP         IDE HDD AUTO DETECTION
PNP/PCI CONFIGURATION          SAVE & EXIT SETUP
LOAD BIOS DEFAULTS             EXIT WITHOUT SAVING
LOAD PERFORMANCE DEFAULTS

Esc : Quit                     ↑ ↓ → ← : Select Item
F10 : Save & Exit Setup        (Shift) F2 : Change Color

        Time, Date, Hard Disk Type...
```

Figure 1.23   The BIOS menu

The BIOS menu enables the user to configure hardware, set the system clock, enable or disable system components, and, most importantly, select the devices which are eligible to be a potential boot device and set various password prompts.

In summary, BIOS performs the following functions:

- Initializes system hardware
- Initializes system registers
- Initializes power management system
- Tests RAM
- Tests all the serial and parallel ports
- Initializes CD/DVD disk drive and hard disk controllers
- Displays system summary information

Operating System

An operating system is a group of computer programs that controls the computer's resources such as CPU, memory, I/O devices, etc. and provides the users with an interface that makes it easier to use. The primary goal of an operating system is to make the computer system (or any other device in which it is installed, such as a cell phone) convenient and efficient to use. It provides users an environment in which a user can execute programs conveniently and efficiently. It is the most important software in a computer system. To understand its utility, let us first understand the basic functions that an operating system performs (shown in Figure 1.24).

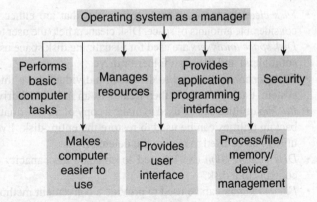

Figure 1.24 Operating system as a computer system manager

- *Manages the computer's resources*: The OS controls and efficiently utilizes hardware components such as CPU, memory, and I/O devices.
- *Provides a user interface*: The OS enables users to easily interact with the computer hardware. For example, the Windows operating system displays icons, using which the users can interact with the system.
- *Process management*: The OS enables a user to execute more than one job at the same time to enhance productivity. Multiple processes being executed at the same time calls for efficient utilization of the system's resources by the operating system.
- *Memory management*: Finding vacant spaces in the primary memory, loading the appropriate data and programs in the located space, executing them, and removing them from the memory is all done by the operating system.
- *File management*: The OS allows users to create, copy, delete, and rename files.
- *Security management*: The OS protects stored information from malicious users. It ensures that the data and files stored cannot be accessed by unauthorized users.
- *Device Management*: The operating system manages and controls all I/O devices such as disks, tapes, terminal, printer, and keyboard to ensure correct data transmission to and from devices. It also provides an intuitive interface so that the users can easily work with them.
- *Booting Services*: Booting means loading an operating system into the computer's main memory. After the operating system is loaded, it becomes ready for users to run their applications. During the boot process, the computer performs a self-diagnostic test, also known as a POST (Power On Self Test) to ensure that all components are operational. It also loads necessary drivers and programs that help the computer and devices communicate with each other.

For further reading on Operating Systems, refer to Annexure 1.

Utility Software

Utility software is used to analyse, configure, optimize, and maintain the computer system. Utility programs may be requested by application programs during their execution for multiple purposes. Some examples of utility programs include the following:

- *Disk defragmenters* can be used to detect computer files whose contents are broken across several locations on the hard disk, and the fragments can be moved to one location in order to increase efficiency.
- *Disk checkers* can be used to scan the contents of a hard disk to find files or areas that are either corrupt in some way, or were not correctly saved, and eliminate/repair them in order to make the hard drive operate more efficiently.

- *Disk cleaners* can be used to locate files that are either not required for computer operation, or take up considerable amounts of space. Disk cleaners help the user to decide what to delete when their hard disk is full.
- *Disk space analysers* are used for visualizing disk space usage by obtaining the size of all folders (including subfolders) and files in a folder or drive.
- *Disk partitions* are used to divide an individual drive into multiple logical drives, each with its own file system. Each partition is then treated as an individual drive.
- *Backup* utilities can be used to make a copy of all information stored on a disk. In case a disk failure occurs, backup utilities can be used to restore the entire disk. Even if a file gets deleted accidentally, the backup utility can be used to restore the deleted file.
- *Disk compression* can be used to enhance the capacity of the disk by compressing/uncompressing the contents of a disk.
- *File managers* can be used to provide a convenient method of performing routine data management tasks, such as deleting, renaming, cataloguing, moving, copying, merging, generating, and modifying data sets.
- *System profilers* can be used to provide detailed information about the software installed and hardware attached to the computer.
- *Anti-virus* utilities are used to scan the computer for viruses.
- *Data compression* utilities are used to compress files to a smaller size.
- *Cryptographic* utilities are used to encrypt and decrypt files.
- *Launcher applications* are used as a convenient access point for application software.
- *Registry cleaners* are used to clean and optimize the Windows registry by deleting old registry keys that are no longer in use.
- *Network* utilities are used to analyse the computer's network connectivity, configure network settings, and check data transfer or log events.
- *Command line interface (CLI)* and *graphical user interface (GUI)* are used to interface the operating system with other software.

Translators

In this section we shall discuss the functions of translators which are computer programs used to translate a code written in one programming language to a code in another language that the computer understands.

Compiler

A compiler is a special type of program that transforms the source code written in a programming language (the *source language)* into machine language, which uses only two digits—0 and 1 (the *target language)*. The resultant code in 0s and 1s is known as the object *code.* The object code is used to create an executable program.

Therefore, a compiler (Figure 1.25) is used to translate the source code from a high-level programming language to a lower-level language (e.g., assembly language or machine code). There is a one-to-one correspondence between the high-level language code and machine language code generated by the compiler.

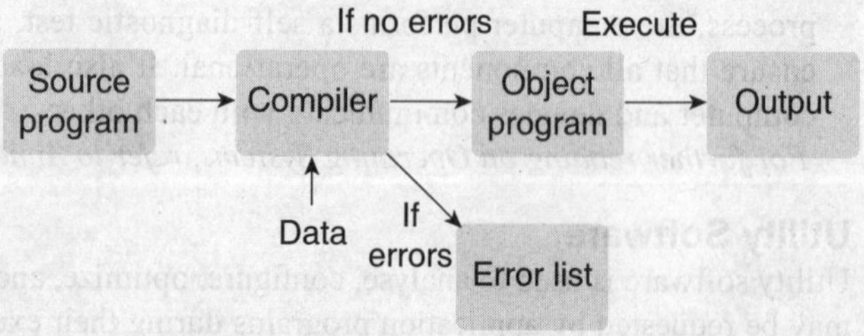

Figure 1.25 Compiler

If the source code contains errors, then the compiler will not be able to do its intended task. Errors that limit the compiler in understanding a program are called *syntax errors*. Examples of syntax errors are spelling mistakes, typing mistakes, illegal characters, and use of undefined variables. The other type of error is the logical error, which occurs when the program does not function accurately. Logical errors are much harder to locate and correct than syntax errors. Whenever errors are detected in the source code, the compiler generates a list of error messages indicating the type of error and the line in which the error has occurred. The programmer makes use of this error list to correct the source code.

How Compilers Work?

Compilers, like other programs, reside on the secondary storage. To translate a source code into its equivalent machine language code, the computer first loads the compiler and the source program from the secondary memory into the main memory. It then executes the compiler along with the source program as its input. The output of this execution is the object file, which is also stored in the secondary storage. Whenever the program is to be executed, the computer loads the object file into the memory and executes it. Thus, it is not necessary to compile the program every time it needs to be executed. Compilation will be needed again only if the source code is modified.

The work of a compiler is only to translate the human-readable source code into a computer-executable machine code. It can locate syntax errors in the program (if any) but cannot fix it. Unless the syntactical error is rectified, the source code cannot be converted into the object code.

Each high-level language has a separate compiler. A compiler can translate a program in one particular high-level language into machine language. For a program written in some other programming language, a compiler for that specific language is needed. For example, to compile a C program you may need gcc compiler, for C++ code you may use g++ compiler, and for Java program you need a javac compiler.

Interpreter

Similar to the compiler, the *interpreter* also executes instructions written in a high-level language. Basically, a program written in a high-level language can be executed in any of the two ways—by compiling the program or by passing the program through an interpreter.

The compiler translates instructions written in a high-level programming language directly into machine language; the interpreter, on the other hand, translates the instructions into an intermediate form, which it then executes. The interpreter takes one statement of high-level code, translates it into the machine level code, executes it, and then takes the next statement and repeats the process until the entire program is translated.

> **Note** An interpreter not only translates the code into machine language but also executes it.

Figure 1.26 shows an interpreter that takes a source program as its input and gives the output. This is in contrast with the compiler, which produces an object file as the output of the compilation process. Usually, a compiled program executes faster than an interpreted program. Moreover, since there is no object file saved for future use, users will have to reinterpret the entire program each time they want to execute the code. Examples of some interpreted languages include Ruby, Python, and PHP.

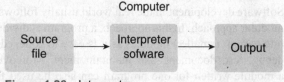

Figure 1.26 Interpreter

Overall, compilers and interpreters both achieve similar purposes, but they are inherently different as to how they achieve that purpose. The differences between compilers and interpreters are given in Table 1.4.

Table 1.4 Differences between compilers and interpreters

Compiler	Interpreter
• It translates the entire program in one go.	• It interprets and executes one statement at a time.
• It generates error(s) after at a time. translating the entire program.	• It stops translation after getting the first error.
• Execution of code is faster.	• Execution of code is slower as every time reinterpretation of statements has to be done.

(Contd)

Table 1.4 (*Contd*)

Compiler	Interpreter
• An object file is generated.	• No object file is code. generated.
• Code need not be recompiled every time it is executed.	• Code has to be reinterpreted every time it is executed.
• It merely translates the code.	• It translates as well as executes the code.
• It requires less memory space (to save the object file).	• It requires more memory space (no object file).

Assembler Since computers can execute only codes written in machine language, a special program, called the assembler, is required to convert the code written in assembly language into an equivalent code in machine language, which contains only 0s and 1s. The working of an assembler is shown in Figure 1.27; it can be seen that the assembler takes an assembly language program as input and gives a code in machine language (also called object program) as output. There is a one-to-one correspondence between the assembly language code and the machine language code. However, if there is an error, the assembler gives a list of errors. The object file is created only when the assembly language code is free from errors. The object file can be executed as and when required. For example, MASM, TASM, NASM, YASM, VASM, etc.

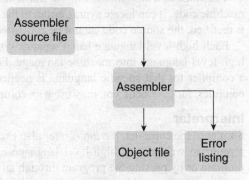

Figure 1.27 Assembler

> **Note** An assembler only translates an assembly program into machine language, the result of which is an object file that can be executed. However, the assembler itself does not execute the object file.

Linker

Software development in the real world usually follows a modular approach. In this approach, a program is divided into various (smaller) modules as it is easy to code, edit, debug, test, document, and maintain them. Moreover, a module written for one program can also be used for another program. When a module is compiled, an object file of that module is generated.

Once the modules are coded and tested, the object files of all the modules are combined together to form the final executable file. Therefore, a linker, also called a *link editor* or *binder*, is a program that combines the object modules to form an executable program (see Figure 1.28). Usually, the compiler automatically invokes the linker as the last step in compiling a program.

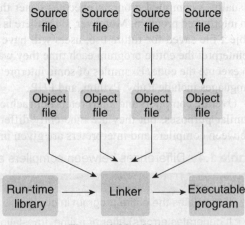

Figure 1.28 Linker

Loader

A *loader* is a special type of program that is part of an operating system and which copies programs from a storage device to the main memory, where they can be executed. Most loaders are transparent to the users.

Debugger

Debugging is a necessary step in software development process. Since it is very common for real world applications to have thousands of lines of code, the possibility of having errors in them cannot be ruled out. Therefore, identifying bugs (errors) and removing them as early as possible is very important.

Debugging tools, commonly known as *debuggers*, are used to identify coding errors at different stages of software (or program) development. These days, many programming language packages have a facility for checking the code for errors while it is being written.

A debugger is a program that runs other programs allowing users to exercise some degree of control over their programs so that they can examine them when things go wrong. A debugger helps the programmer to discover the following things:

- Which statement or expression was being executed when the error occurred?
- If an error occurred during the execution of a function, what parameters were passed to it while it was called?
- What is the value of variables at different lines in the program?
- What is the result of evaluating an expression?
- What is the sequence of statements actually executed in a program?

When a program crashes, debuggers show the position of the error in the program. Many debuggers allow programmers to run programs in a step-by-step mode. They also allow them to stop on specific points at which they can examine the value of certain variables.

1.13.2 Application Software

Application software is a type of computer software that employs the capabilities of a computer directly to perform a user-defined task. This is in contrast with system software, which is involved in integrating a computer's capabilities, but does not directly apply them in the performance of tasks that benefit the user.

To understand application software better, consider an analogy where hardware would depict the relationship of an electric light bulb (an application) to an electric power generation plant (a system).

The power plant merely generates electricity, which is not by itself of any real use until harnessed through an application such as the electric light, which performs a service that actually benefits the user.

Typical examples of software applications are word processors, spreadsheets, media players, education software, CAD, CAM, data communication software, statistical and operational research software, etc. Multiple applications bundled together as a package are sometimes referred to as an *application suite*.

Examples of Application Software These days, we have a number of application software packages available in the market for a wide range of applications. The range of these applications vary from simple applications such as word processing, and inventory management to complex and scientific applications such as weather forecasting, oil and natural gas exploration. In this section we will discuss some popular application software.

Word Processing Software (MS Word) A word processor is a software package that enables its users to create, edit, print, and save documents for future retrieval and reference as shown in Figure 1.29. The key advantage of using a word processor is that it allows the users to make changes to a document without retyping the entire document.

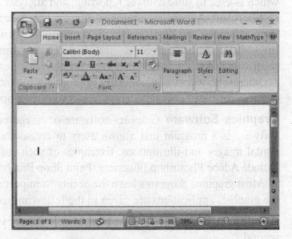

Figure 1.29 MS Word

Microsoft Word is the world's leading word processing application. Users can create a variety of documents such as letters, memos, resumes, forms, or any other document that can be typed and printed.

Spreadsheet Program (Microsoft Excel) A spreadsheet software is the one in which data is stored into spreadsheet rows and columns, or 'cells' which can be formatted in various fonts or colours. Microsoft Excel is an example of a spreadsheet software (as shown in Figure 1.30) that is basically used to store, organize, and manipulate data. The stored data can also be converted into graphs for analysis.

Microsoft Excel includes a number of simple as well as complex formulas and functions to calculate variables in the data. Excel is therefore widely used in finance to automatically calculate variables such as profit, loss, or expenditure.

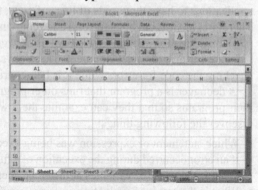

Figure 1.30   MS Excel

Presentation Software (Microsoft PowerPoint) Microsoft PowerPoint (as shown in Figure 1.31) is used to create multimedia presentations and slide shows. When designing presentations on Microsoft PowerPoint, users can add effects on slide transitions, add sound clips, images, animations, or video clips to make the presentation even more interesting for the target audience.

In addition to slide shows, PowerPoint also offers printing options to facilitate the users to provide handouts and outlines for the audience as well as note pages for the speaker to refer to during the presentation.

All in all, PowerPoint is a one-stop-shop for creating beautiful presentations for business and classrooms. It is also an effective tool for training purposes.

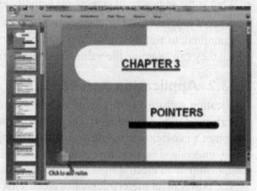

Figure 1.31   MS PowerPoint

Database Software (Microsoft Access) Microsoft Access (as shown in Figure 1.32) is a database application which is used to store data for reporting, and analysis.

Microsoft Access is equipped with query interface, forms to input and display data, and reports for printing. In addition to this, Access has features to automate repetitive tasks.

Microsoft Access is particularly appropriate for meeting end-user database needs and for rapid application development.

Graphics Software Graphics software or image editing software is a program that allows users to create and edit digital images and illustrations. Examples of such software include Adobe Photoshop Illustrator, Paint Shop Pro, MS Paint, etc.

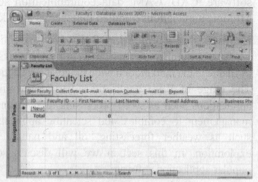

Figure 1.32   MS Access

Most graphics programs have the ability to import and export one or more graphics file formats. Some of the graphics applications are given in the following section:

Animation Software It simulates a movement by displaying a sequence of images in a fraction of a second.

CAD Software It is used by architects and engineers to create architectural drawings, product designs, landscaping plans, and engineering drawings. CAD software enables the designers to work much faster. The drawings that were created in several days can now be drawn in a few hours.

Desktop Publishing Software It facilitates users with a full set of word-processing features along with a fine control over placement of text and graphics. Using such an application, the users can easily create newsletters, advertisements, books, and other types of documents.

Multimedia Software *Multimedia* is a comprehensive term which means different types of media. It includes a combination of text, audio, still images, animation, video, and interactivity content forms.

Multimedia is used for creating exciting advertisements to grab and keep attention of the target audience. It is also used in business to design training programs. In the entertainment industry, multimedia is used to create special effects in movies and animations. It is also used in computer games and some video games that are a popular pastime.

Edutainment which combines education with multimedia entertainment is now emerging as a trend in school as well as higher education. This has made learning theories much simpler than ever before. Moreover, visually impaired or people with other kinds of disabilities can pursue their careers by using training programs specially designed for them.

Multimedia is used by engineers and researchers for modeling and simulation. For example, a scientist can look at a molecular model of a particular substance and manipulate it to arrive at a new substance. Even in medicines, doctors are now trained by looking at a virtual surgery.

Ability Media allows those with disabilities to gain qualifications in the multimedia field so they can pursue careers that give them access to a wide array of powerful communication forms.

1.14 REPRESENTATION OF DATA: BITS AND BYTES

We have seen that computers store and process data to retrieve information. Here,

- *data* refers to anything that has some interest to the user, and
- *information* is the result of data processing

The term *data representation* refers to the technique used to represent data internally stored in the computer.

These days, computers store massive amounts of a variety of data such as numbers, text, images, audio, and video (as shown in Figure 1.33). Though all these types of data belong to a different class but internally they all are stored in the same simple format of 1s and 0s.

Computers are electronic machines which operate using binary logic.

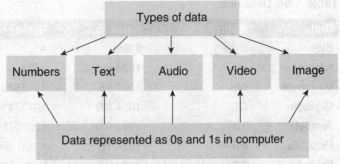

Figure 1.33   Different types of data

These devices use two different values to represent the two voltage levels (0 V for logic 0 and +5 V for logic 1). The two values 0 and 1, therefore, correspond to the two digits used by the binary number system.

The binary number system works like the decimal number system with the following exceptions:

- While the decimal number system uses a base 10, the binary number system on the other hand uses base 2.
- The decimal number system uses digits from 0 to 9 but the binary number system uses only two digits 0 and 1. Any other digit is considered to be invalid in this number system.

Some important terms in binary number system include (as shown in Table 1.5):

Table 1.5 Important terms in binary number system

Term	Size (bits)	Example
Bit	1	0
Nibble	4	1010
Byte	8	0101 1100
Word	16	0101 1100 0101 1100

Bit Bit is a short form of binary digit. It is the smallest possible unit of data. In computerized data, a bit can either be 0 or 1.

Nibble Nibble is a group of four binary digits.

Byte Byte is a group of eight bits. A nibble is a half byte. Bits 0 through 3 are called the low order nibble, and bits 4 through 7 form the high order nibble as shown in Figure 1.34.

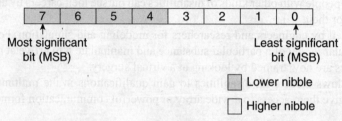

Figure 1.34 Lower and upper nibble

While a single bit can store two different values 2^0 (0 or 1), a byte comprised of 8 bits can store 2^8 or 256 different values.

If a code has 128 different values, then it needs at least 7 bits to represent its values because $2^7 = 128$. Besides bytes, data is also specified using the units shown in Table 1.6.

Table 1.6 Data units

Unit	Abbreviation	Equal to	Bytes	Power of 2
Byte	Byte	8 Bits	1	2^0 bytes
Kilobyte	KB	1024 Bytes	1024	2^{10} bytes
Megabyte	MB	1024 KB	1048576	2^{20} bytes
Gigabyte	GB	1024 MB	1073741824	2^{30} bytes
Terabyte	TB	1024 GB	1099511627776	2^{40} bytes
Petabyte	PB	1024 TB	1 000 000 000 000 000	2^{50} bytes
Exabyte	EB	1024 PB	1 000 000 000 000 000 000	2^{60} bytes

Word A group of two bytes is called a word. Bits 0 through 7 form the low order byte and bits 8 through 15 form the high order byte (refer Figure 1.35). However, computers today have redefined word as a group of 4 bytes (32 bits). With 16 bits, the computer can represent 216 (65536) different values.

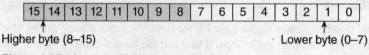

Figure 1.35 Lower and upper byte

Binary Representation with 2 Digits

We have seen that the number of values that can be encoded in binary depends on the number of binary digits. For example, if we have a single digit, we can represent only $2^1 = 2$ values 0 or 1. If we have two digits, we can represent $2^2 = 4$ values—00, 01, 10, and 11. Look at Tables 1.7 and 1.8, which summarize this concept.

Table 1.7 Data values using 2 bits

Number of digits—2	
Data values that can be represented = 2^2 = 4	
0	000
1	001
2	010
3	011
4	100
5	101
6	110
7	111

Table 1.8 Data values using 3 bits

Number of digits—3	
Data values that can be represented = 2^3 = 8	
0	000
1	001
2	010
3	011
4	100
5	101
6	110
7	111

1.15 PROBLEM SOLVING STRATEGIES

As discussed earlier, computer is a very powerful and versatile machine. Despite the fact that it has no intelligence of its own, it can perform a wide range of tasks. Basically, a computer can do any task given to it provided that the programmer has already fed correct instructions to direct what, how, and when the steps have to be done to solve the particular problem at hand.

A wrong or ambiguous instruction may prove to be disastrous. So it lays a big responsibility on the programmer to clearly understand the problem and instruct a computer correctly and precisely. For this, he should work to develop a step by step solution to the problem. These steps can be given as,

- Clearly define the problem in very simple and precise language.
- Analyze the problem to find out different ways to solve the problem. Evaluate all the options and decide the best possible solution.
- Once the best possible solution is decided, clearly define the steps in which the solution can be obtained. That is, define the selected solution in a detailed step by step manner.
- Write the steps in a particular programming language so that it can be executed by the computer.

The design and development of correct, efficient, and maintainable programs depend on the approach adopted by the programmer to perform various activities that need to be performed during the development process. The entire program or software (collection of programs) development process is divided into a number of phases, where each phase performs a well-defined task. Moreover, the output of one phase provides the input for its subsequent phase.

The phases in the software development life cycle (SDLC) process is shown in Figure 1.36.

The phases in the SDLC process can be summarized as follows:

Requirements analysis In this phase, the user's expectations are gathered to know why the program/software has to be built. Then, all the gathered requirements are analysed to arrive at the scope or the objective of the overall software product. The last activity in this phase includes documenting every identified requirement of the users in order to avoid any doubts or uncertainty regarding the functionality of the programs.

The functionality, capability, performance, and availability of hardware and software components are all analysed in this phase.

Design The requirements documented in the previous phase acts as an input to the design phase. In the design phase, a plan of actions is made before the actual development process can start. This plan will be followed throughout the development process. Moreover, in the design phase, the core structure of the software/program is broken down into modules. The solution of the program is then specified for each module in the form of algorithms or flowcharts. The design phase, therefore, specifies how the program/software will be built.

Implementation In this phase, the designed algorithms are converted into program code using any of the high-level languages. The particular choice of language will depend on the type of program, such as whether it is a system or an application program. While C is preferred for writing system programs, Visual Basic might be preferred for writing an application program. The program codes are tested by the programmer to ensure their correctness.

This phase is also called construction or code generation phase as the code of the software is generated in this phase. While constructing the code, the development team checks whether the software is compatible with the available hardware and other software components that were mentioned in the Requirements Specification Document created in the first phase.

Testing In this phase, all the modules are tested together to ensure that the overall system works well as a whole product. Although individual pieces of codes are already tested by the programmers in the implementation phase, there is always a chance for bugs to creep into the program when the individual modules are integrated to form the overall program structure. In this phase, the software is tested using a large number of varied inputs, also known as test data, to ensure that the software is working as expected by the user's requirements that were identified in the requirements analysis phase.

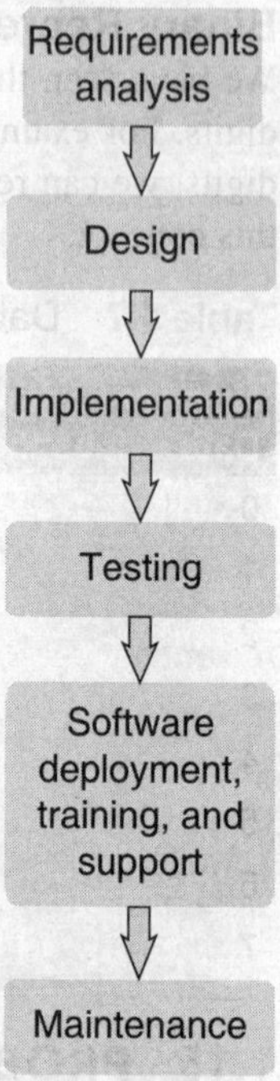

Figure 1.36 Phases in software development life cycle

Software deployment, training, and support After the code is tested and the software or the program has been approved by the users, it is installed or deployed in the production environment. This is a crucial phase that is often ignored by most developers. Program designers and developers spend a lot of time to create software but if nobody in an organization knows how to use it or fix up certain problems, then no one would like to use it. Moreover, people are often resistant to change and avoid venturing into an unfamiliar area, so as a part of the deployment phase, it has become very crucial to have training classes for the users of the software.

Maintenance Maintenance and enhancements are ongoing activities that are done to cope with newly discovered problems or new requirements. Such activities may take a long time to complete as the requirement may call for the addition of new code that does not fit the original design or an extra piece of code, required to fix an unforeseen problem. As a general rule, if the cost of the maintenance phase exceeds 25% of the prior phase's cost, then it clearly indicates that the overall quality of at least one prior phase is poor. In such cases, it is better to re-build the software (or some modules) before the maintenance cost shoots out of control.

1.15.1 Fundamentals of Computing – Identification of Computational Problems

Computational thinking is the process of breaking down a problem into a number of simple steps. It is a step that comes before programming. We all know that computer is a machine with no IQ. To make a computer solve any program, it requires instructions. Computers work on GIGO concept, that is, Garbage-In-Garbage-Out principle. GIGO means that if we give incorrect data or instructions, then it will give wrong results. So, we must take utmost care to ensure that the data and instructions given as input to the computer are not only technically correct but also simple enough to understand.

Moreover, computers perform several *computations to process the* information. As we know, **information** is derived by processing **data**. This data includes the raw *facts* or observations and **computation** is the manipulation of *data* using a systematic **procedure**. To write this systematic procedure, we need to develop scientific thinking. This approach to thinking is known as **computational thinking**.

Computational thinking is not a formal methodology for reasoning but is useful in all fields and disciplines. Such a thinking specifies a way of reasoning or thinking logically and methodically to solve any problem in any area.

To solve problems using computational thinking, we need to follow the steps given below:

Problem Specification First, analyse the problem, describe it and then specify the criteria for the solution. For this, the best approach is to break a complex problem down into a number of smaller and manageable sub-problems. This is known as **problem decomposition**.

Software Engineering *Techniques like* Problem Requirements' Document, Problem Specifications' Document, UML diagrams, etc. are extensively used in this phase.

Algorithmic Expression In this phase, an algorithm (a precise sequence of steps) that can be performed to solve the problem using appropriate data structures is penned down. This step is, therefore, known as **algorithmic thinking**.

In this phase, data representation is done through some symbolic system and the algorithm is developed using techniques like modularity, flow control (sequential/ selection/iteration), recursion, encapsulation, and parallel computing. For this, Flowcharts, Pseudocodes, Data Flow Diagrams, State Diagrams, Class-responsibility-collaboration (CRC) cards for Class Diagrams, Use Cases for Sequence Diagrams, etc. are prepared to give a detailed view of the proposed solution.

The first step in Algorithmic expression is **pattern recognition**. Once a complex problem is decomposed into smaller problems, the next step is to look at the similarities they share. For this, patterns in shared characteristics are identified to deduce similarities in small decomposed problems. This helps to solve complex problems more efficiently.

The second step is **Abstraction**, which involves ignoring unessential details and *prioritizing* relevant information about the system under examination.

The next step is **Generalization**. In this step, characteristics that are common across disparate models are identified to adapt a solution from one domain to an unrelated domain.

Solution Implementation and Evaluation: In this step, the final solution is implemented and systematically evaluated to determine its *correctness* and *efficiency*. In this step, the programmer also checks for generalized solutions via automation or extension to other solutions.

In simpler words,
> **Data + How to Think about that Data = Computational Thinking**
> This means that computational thinking is all about representing data and manipulating it to obtain a computational solution to a computable problem.

1.16 PROGRAM DESIGN TOOLS: ALGORITHMS, FLOWCHARTS, PSEUDOCODES

This section will deal with different tools, which are used to design solution(s) of a given problem at hand.

1.16.1 Algorithms

The typical meaning of an algorithm is a formally defined procedure for performing some calculation. If a procedure is formally defined, then it must be implemented using some formal language, and such languages are known as *programming languages.* The algorithm gives the logic of the program, that is, a step-by-step description of how to arrive at a solution.

In general terms, an algorithm provides a blueprint to writing a program to solve a particular problem. It is considered to be an effective procedure for solving a problem in a finite number of steps. That is, a well-defined algorithm always provides an answer, and is guaranteed to terminate.

Algorithms are mainly used to achieve *software reuse.* Once we have an idea or a blueprint of a solution, we can implement it in any language, such as C, C++, Java, and so on. In order to qualify as an algorithm, a sequence of instructions must possess the following characteristics:

- Be precise
- Be unambiguous
- Not even a single instruction must be repeated infinitely.
- After the algorithm gets terminated, the desired result must be obtained.

Different Approaches to Designing an Algorithm

Algorithms are used to manipulate the data for a given problem. For a complex problem, its algorithm is often divided into smaller units called modules. This process of dividing an algorithm into modules is called *modularization.* The key advantages of modularization are as follows:

- It makes the complex algorithm simpler to design and implement.
- Each module can be designed independently. While designing one module, the details of other modules can be ignored, thereby enhancing clarity in design which in turn simplifies implementation, debugging, testing, documenting, and maintenance of the overall algorithm.

There are two main approaches to design an algorithm—top-down approach and bottom-up approach, as shown in Figure 1.37.

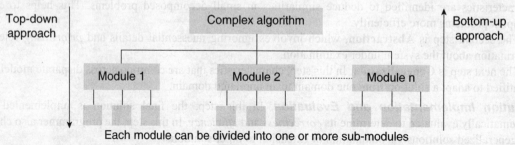

Figure 1.37   Different approaches of designing an algorithm

Top-down approach A top-down design approach starts by dividing the complex algorithm into one or more modules. These modules can further be decomposed into one or more sub-modules, and this process of decomposition is iterated until the desired level of module complexity is achieved. Top-down design method is a form of stepwise refinement where we begin with the topmost module and incrementally add modules that it calls.

Therefore, in a top-down approach, we start from an abstract design and then at each step, this design is refined into more concrete levels until a level is reached that requires no further refinement.

Bottom-up approach A bottom-up approach is just the reverse of top-down approach. In the bottom-up design, we start with designing the most basic or concrete modules and then proceed towards designing higher level modules. The higher level modules are implemented by using the operations performed by lower level modules. Thus, in this approach sub-modules are grouped together to form a higher level module. All the higher level modules are clubbed together to form even higher level modules. This process is repeated until the design of the complete algorithm is obtained.

Top-down vs bottom-up approach Whether the top-down strategy should be followed or a bottom-up is a question that can be answered depending on the application at hand. While top-down approach follows a stepwise refinement by decomposing the algorithm into manageable modules, the bottom-up approach on the other hand defines a module and then groups together several modules to form a new higher level module.

Top-down approach is highly appreciated for ease in documenting the modules, generation of test cases, implementation of code, and debugging. However, it is also criticized because the sub-modules are analysed in isolation without concentrating on their communication with other modules or on reusability of components and little attention is paid to data, thereby ignoring the concept of information hiding.

The bottom-up approach allows information hiding as it first identifies what has to be encapsulated within a module and then provides an abstract interface to define the module's boundaries as seen from the clients. But all this is difficult to be done in a strict bottom-up strategy. Some top-down activities need to be performed for this.

All in all, design of complex algorithms must not be constrained to proceed according to a fixed pattern but should be a blend of top-down and bottom-up approaches.

Control Structures Used In Algorithms

An algorithm has a finite number of steps and some steps may involve decision making and repetition. Broadly speaking, an algorithm may employ three control structures, namely, sequence, decision, and repetition.

Sequence Sequence means that each step of the algorithm is executed in the specified order. An algorithm to add two numbers is given in Figure 1.38. This algorithm performs the steps in a purely sequential order.

```
Step 1 : Input first number as A
Step 2 : Input second number as B
Step 3 : Set Sum = A + B
Step 4 : Print Sum
Step 5 : End
```

Figure 1.38 Algorithm to add two numbers

Decision Decision statements are used when the outcome of the process depends on some condition. For example, if x = y, then print "EQUAL". Hence, the general form of the if construct can be given as follows:

```
IF condition then process
```

A condition in this context is any statement that may evaluate either to a true value or a false value. In the preceding example, the variable *x* can either be equal or not equal to *y*. However, it cannot be both true and false. If the condition is true then the process is executed.

A decision statement can also be stated in the following manner:

```
IF condition
then process!
ELSE process2
```

This form is commonly known as the if-else construct. Here, if the condition is true then process1 is executed, else process2 is executed. An algorithm to check the equality of two numbers is shown in Figure 1.39.

```
Step 1 : Input first number as A
Step 2 : Input second number as B
Step 3 : IF A = B
              Print "Equal"
         ELSE
              Print "Not equal"
         [END of IF]
Step 4 : End
```

Figure 1.39 Algorithm to test the equality of two numbers

Repetition Repetition, which involves executing one or more steps for a number of times, can be implemented using constructs such as the while, do-while, and for loops. These loops execute one or more steps until some condition is true. Figure 1.40 shows an algorithm that prints the first 10 natural numbers.

```
Step 1 : [initialize] Set I = 1, N = 10
Step 2 : Repeat Steps 3 and 4 while I <= N
Step 3 : Print I
Step 4 : SET I = I + 1
         [END OF LOOP]
Step 5 : End
```

Figure 1.40 Algorithm to print the first 10 natural numbers

Example 1.1   Write an algorithm for interchanging/swapping two values.

Solution

```
Step 1: Input first number as A
Step 2: Input second number as B
Step 3: Set temp = A
Step 4: Set A = B
Step 5: Set B = temp
Step 6: Print A, B
Step 7: End
```

Example 1.2   Write an algorithm to find the larger of two numbers.

Solution

```
Step 1: Input first number as A
Step 2: Input second number as B
Step 3: IF A > B
    Print A
  ELSE IF A < B
  Print B
  ELSE
Print "The numbers are equal"
    [END OF IF]
Step 4: End
```

Example 1.3   Write an algorithm to find whether a number is even or odd.

Solution

```
Step 1: Input number as A
Step 2: IF A % 2 = 0
    Print "Even"
    ELSE
    Print "Odd"
  [END OF IF]
Step 3: End
```

Example 1.4   Write an algorithm to print the grade obtained by a student using the following rules:

Marks	Grade
Above 75	O
60-75	A
50-60	B
40-50	C
Less than 40	D

Solution

```
Step 1: Enter the marks obtained as M
Step 2: IF M > 75
      Print "O"
Step 3: IF M >= 60 and M < 75
      Print "A"
 Step 4: IF M >= 50 and M < 60
      Print "B"
Step 5: IF M >= 40 and M < 50
      Print "C"
    ELSE
      Print "D"
  [END OF IF]
Step 6: End
```

Example 1.5 Write an algorithm to find the sum of first N natural numbers.

Solution

```
Step 1: Input N
Step 2: Set I = 1, sum = 0
Step 3: Repeat Steps 4 and 5 while I <= N
Step 4: Set sum = sum + I
Step 5: Set I = I + 1
    [END OF LOOP]
Step 6: Print sum
Step 7: End
```

Recursion Recursion is a technique of solving a problem by breaking it down into smaller and smaller sub-problems until you get to a small enough problem that it can be easily solved. Usually, recursion involves a function calling itself until a specified condition is met.

Example 1.6 Write a recursive algorithm to find the factorial of a number.

Solution

```
Step 1: Start
Step 2: Input number as n
Step 3: Call factorial(n)
Step 4: Stop

factorial(n)
Step 1: Set f = 1
Step 2: If n==1 then return 1
Step 2: Else
    Set f=n*factorial(n-1)
Step 3: Print f
```

If you don't have any idea of functions, then do not worry. We will revisit recursion in Chapter 5 and discuss it in detail.

1.16.2 Flowcharts

A flowchart is a graphical or symbolic representation of a process. It is basically used to design and document virtually complex processes to help the viewers to visualize the logic of the process, so that they can gain a better understanding of the process and find flaws, bottlenecks, and other less obvious features within it.

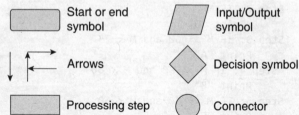

Figure 1.41 Symbols of flowchart

When designing a flowchart, each step in the process is depicted by a different symbol and is associated with a short description. The symbols in the flowchart (refer Figure 1.41) are linked together with arrows to show the flow of logic in the process.

The symbols used in a flowchart include the following:

- *Start and end symbols* are also known as the terminal symbols and are represented as circles, ovals, or rounded rectangles. Terminal symbols are always the first and the last symbols in a flowchart.
- *Arrows* depict the flow of control of the program. They illustrate the exact sequence in which the instructions are executed.
- *Generic processing step,* also called as an activity, is represented using a rectangle. Activities include instructions such as add a to b or save the result. Therefore, a processing symbol represents arithmetic and data movement instructions. When more than one process has to be executed simultaneously, they can be placed in the same processing box. However, their execution will be carried out in the order of their appearance.
- *Input/Output symbols* are represented using a parallelogram and are used to get inputs from the users or display the results to them.
- A *conditional or decision symbol* is represented using a diamond. It is basically used to depict a Yes/No question or a True/False test. The two symbols coming out of it, one from the bottom point and the other from the right point, corresponds to Yes or True, and No or False, respectively. The arrows should always be labelled. A decision symbol in a flowchart can have more than two arrows, which indicates that a complex decision is being taken.
- *Labelled connectors* are represented by an identifying label inside a circle and are used in complex or multi-sheet diagrams to substitute for arrows. For each label, the 'outflow' connector must have one or more 'inflow' connectors. A pair of identically labelled connectors is used to indicate a continued flow when the use of lines becomes confusing.

Significance of Flowcharts

A flowchart is a diagrammatic representation that illustrates the sequence of steps that must be performed to solve a problem. It is usually drawn in the early stages of formulating computer solutions. It facilitates communication between programmers and users. Once a flowchart is drawn, programmers can make users understand the solution easily and clearly.

Flowcharts are very important in the programming of a problem as they help the programmers to understand the logic of complicated and lengthy problems. Once a flowchart is drawn, it becomes easy for the programmers to write the program in any high-level language. Hence, the flowchart has become a necessity for better documentation of complex programs.

A flowchart follows the top-down approach in solving problems.

Example 1.7 Draw a flowchart to calculate the sum of the first 10 natural numbers.

Solution

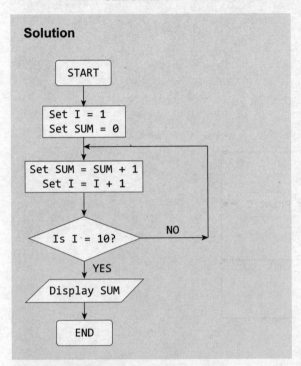

Example 1.8 Draw a flowchart to add two numbers.

Solution

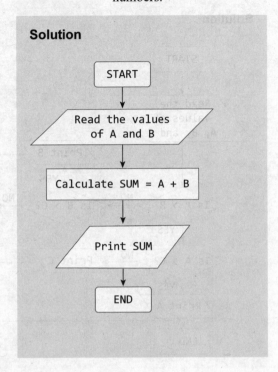

Example 1.9 Draw a flowchart to calculate the salary of a daily wager.

Solution

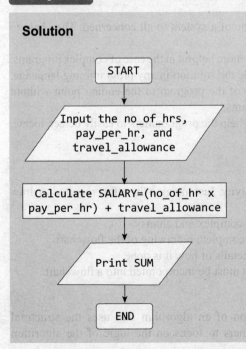

Example 1.10 Draw a flowchart to determine the largest of three numbers.

Solution

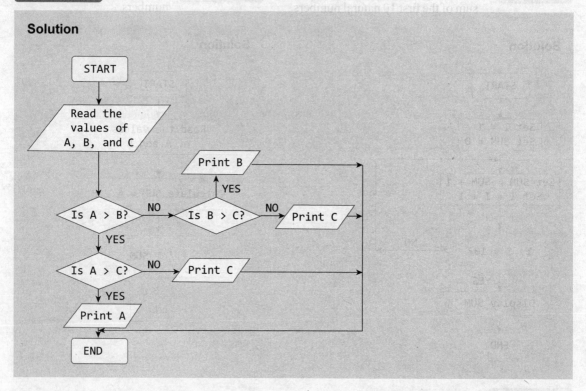

Advantages

- They are very good communication tools to explain the logic of a system to all concerned. They help to analyse the problem in a more effective manner.
- They are also used for program documentation. They are even more helpful in the case of complex programs.
- They act as a guide or blueprint for the programmers to code the solution in any programming language. They direct the programmers to go from the starting point of the program to the ending point without missing any step in between. This results in error-free programs.
- They can be used to debug programs that have error(s). They help the programmers to easily detect, locate, and remove mistakes in the program in a systematic manner.

Limitations

- Drawing flowcharts is a laborious and a time-consuming activity. Just imagine the effort required to draw a flowchart of a program having 50,000 statements in it!
- Many a times, the flowchart of a complex program becomes complex and clumsy.
- At times, a little bit of alteration in the solution may require complete redrawing of the flowchart.
- The essentials of what is done may get lost in the technical details of how it is done.
- There are no well-defined standards that limit the details that must be incorporated into a flowchart.

1.16.3 Pseudocodes

Pseudocode is a compact and informal high-level description of an algorithm that uses the structural conventions of a programming language. It facilitates designers to focus on the logic of the algorithm without getting bogged down by the details of language syntax. An ideal pseudocode must be complete, describing the entire logic of the algorithm, so that it can be translated straightaway into a programming language.

It is basically meant for human reading rather than machine reading, so it omits the details that are not essential for humans. Such details include variable declarations, system-specific code, and subroutines.

Pseudocodes are an outline of a program that can easily be converted into programming statements. They consist of short English phrases that explain specific tasks within a program's algorithm. They should not include keywords in any specific computer language.

The sole purpose of pseudocodes is to enhance human understandability of the solution. They are commonly used in textbooks and scientific publications for documenting algorithms, and for sketching out the program structure before the actual coding is done. This helps even non-programmers to understand the logic of the designed solution. There are no standards defined for writing a pseudocode, because a pseudocode is not an executable program. Flowcharts can be considered as graphical alternatives to pseudocodes, but require more space on paper.

Example 1.11   Write a pseudocode for calculating the price of a product after adding the sales tax to its original price.

Solution

1. Read the price of the product
2. Read the sales tax rate
3. Calculate sales tax = price of the item x* sales tax rate
4. Calculate total price = price of the product + sales tax
5. Print total price
6. End
Variables: price of the item, sales tax rate, sales tax, total price

Example 1.12   Write a pseudocode to calculate the weekly wages of an employee. The pay depends on wages per hour and the number of hours worked. Moreover, if the employee has worked for more than 30 hours, then he or she gets twice the wages per hour, for every extra hour that he or she has worked.

Solution

1. Read hours worked
2. Read wages per hour
3. Set overtime charges to 0
4. Set overtime hrs to 0
5. IF hours worked > 30 then
   a. Calculate overtime hrs = hours worked - 30
   b. Calculate overtime charges = overtime hrs x (2 x wages per hour)
   c. Set hours worked = hours worked - overtime hrs
   ENDIF
6. Calculate salary = (hours worked x wages per hour) + overtime charges
7. Display salary
8. End
Variables: hours worked, wages per hour, overtime charges, overtime hrs, salary

Example 1.13   Write a pseudocode to read the marks of 10 students. If marks is greater than 50, the student passes, else the student fails. Count the number of students passing and failing.

Solution

```
1. Set pass to 0
2. Set fail to 0
3. Set no of students to 1
4. WHILE no of students < 10
   a. input the marks
   b. IF marks >= 50 then
   Set pass = pass + 1
   ELSE
   Set fail = fail + 1
   ENDIF ENDWHILE
5. Display pass
6. Display fail
7. End
Variables: pass,fail, no of students, marks
```

1.17 TYPES OF ERRORS

While writing programs, very often we get errors in our programs. These errors if not removed will either give erroneous output or will not let the compiler to compile the program. These errors are broadly classified under four groups as shown in Figure 1.42.

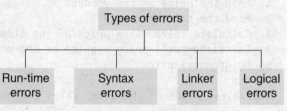

Figure 1.42 Types of errors

Run-time Errors As the name suggests, run-time errors occur when the program is being run executed. Such errors occur when the program performs some illegal operations like

- dividing a number by zero
- opening a file that already exists
- lack of free memory space
- finding square or logarithm of negative numbers

Run-time errors may terminate program execution, so the code must be written in such a way that it handles all sorts of unexpected errors rather terminating it unexpectedly.

Syntax Errors Syntax errors (also known as compile-time errors) are generated when rules of a programming language are violated. Python interprets (executes) each instruction in the program line by line. The moment the interpreter encounters a syntactic error, it stops further execution of the program.

Semantic or Logical Errors Semantic errors are those errors which may comply with rules of the programming language but gives an unexpected and undesirable output which is obviously not correct. For example, if you write a program to add two numbers but instead of writing '+' symbol, you put the '-' symbol. Then Python will subtract the numbers and returns the result. But, actually the output is different from what you expected.

Logical errors are errors in the program code. Such errors are not detected by the compiler, and programmers must check their code line by line or use a debugger to locate and rectify the errors. Logical errors occur due to incorrect statements.

Linker Errors These errors occur when the linker is not able to find the function definition for a given prototype.

1.18 TESTING AND DEBUGGING APPROACHES

Testing is an activity that is performed to verify correct behaviour of a program. It is specifically carried out with an intent to find errors. Ideally, testing should be conducted at all stages of program development. However, in the implementation stage, the following three types of tests can be conducted:

Unit Tests Unit testing is applied only on a single unit or module to ensure whether it exhibits the expected behaviour.

Integration Tests These tests are a logical extension of unit tests. In this test, two units that have already been tested are combined into a component and the interface between them is tested. The guiding principle is to test combinations of pieces and then gradually expanding the component to include other modules as well. This process is repeated until all the modules are tested together. The main focus of integration testing is to identify errors that occur when the units are combined.

System Tests System testing checks the entire system. For example, if our program code consists of three modules, then each of the module is tested individually using unit tests and then system test is applied to test this entire system as one system.

Debugging, on the other hand, is an activity that includes execution testing and code correction. The main aim of debugging is locating errors in the program code. Once the errors are located, they are then isolated and fixed to produce an error-free code. Different approaches applied for debugging a code includes:

Brute-Force Method In this technique, a printout of CPU registers and relevant memory locations is taken, studied, and documented. It is the least efficient way of debugging a program and is generally done when all the other methods fail.

Backtracking Method It is a popular technique that is widely used to debug small applications. It works by locating the first symptom of error and then tracing backward across the entire source code until the real cause of error is detected. However, the main drawback of this approach is that with increase in number of source code lines, the possible backward paths become too large to manage.

Cause Elimination In this approach, a list of all possible causes of an error is developed. Then relevant tests are carried out to eliminate each of them. If some tests indicate that a particular cause may be responsible for an error then the data is refined to isolate the error.

For further details on testing and debugging techniques in Python, refer to Annexure 4.

Example 1.14 Let us take a problem statement, do requirement analysis, design and implement the solution in Python, and then test the program.

Problem Statement To develop an automatic system that accepts marks of a student and generates his/her grade.

Requirements Analysis Ask the users to enlist the rules for assigning grades. These rules are:

Marks	Grade
Above 75	O
60–75	A
50–60	B
40–50	C
Less than 40	D

Design In this phase, write an algorithm that gives a solution to the problem.

```
Step 1: Enter the marks obtained as M
Step 2: If M > 75 then print "O"
Step 3: If M >= 60 and M < 75 then print "A"
Step 4: If M >= 50 and M < 60 then print "B"
Step 5: If M >= 40 and M < 50 then print "C"
    else
    print "D"
Step 6: End
```

Implementation Write the Python program to implement the proposed algorithm.

```python
marks = int(input("Enter the marks : "))
grade = ''
if marks > 75:
    grade = 'O'
elif marks > 60 and marks <=75:
    grade = 'A'
elif marks > 50 and marks <=60:
    grade = 'B'
elif marks > 40 and marks <=50:
    grade = 'C'
else:
    grade = 'D'
print("GRADE = ", grade)
```

Test The above program is then tested with different test data to ensure that the program gives correct output for all relevant and possible inputs. The test cases are shown in the table given below.

Test Case ID	Input	Expected Output	Actual Output
1	-12	Not Possible	Not Possible
2	112	Not Possible	Not Possible

Test Case ID	Input	Expected Output	Actual Output
3	32	D	D
4	46	C	C
5	54	B	B
6	68	A	A
7	91	O	O
8	40	C	C
9	50	B	B
10	60	A	A
11	75	O	O
12	100	O	O
13	0	D	D

Note in the above table, we have identified test cases for the following,

1. "Not Possible" Combinations
2. A middle value from each range
3. Boundary values for each range

Summary

- A computer is an electronic machine that accepts data and instructions and performs computations on the data based on those instructions.
- Modern day computers are based on the principle of the stored program concept, which was introduced by Sir John von Neumann in the late 1940s.
- The speed of the computer is usually given in nanoseconds and picoseconds.
- The term computer generation refers to the different advancements of new computer technology.
- A computer has two parts—hardware, which does all the physical work computers are known for, and software, which tells the hardware what to do and how to do it.
- The CPU is a combination of the ALU and the CU. The CPU is known as the brain of the computer system.
- The CU is the central nervous system of the entire computer system. It manages and controls all the components of the computer system.
- An input device is used to feed data and instructions into the computer.
- Output devices are electromechanical devices that accept digital data from the computer and convert them into human understandable language.
- Computer memory is an internal storage area in the computer that is used to store data and programs either temporarily or permanently. It also stores the intermediate results and the final results of processing.
- While the main memory holds instructions and data when a program is being executed, the auxiliary or the secondary memory holds data and programs not currently in use and provides long-term storage.
- The primary memory is volatile, so the data can be retained in it only when the power is on. Moreover, it is very expensive and therefore limited in capacity.
- On the contrary, the secondary memory stores data or instructions permanently, even when the power is turned off. It is cheap and can store large volumes of data, which is highly portable.
- Processor registers are located inside the processor and are therefore directly accessed by the CPU. Each register stores a word of data (which is either 32 or 64 bits).

- Cache memory is an intermediate form of storage between the ultra-fast registers and the RAM.
- Computer software is written by computer programmers using a programming language.
- Application software is designed to solve a particular problem for users.
- System software represents programs that allow the hardware to run properly. System software acts as an interface between the hardware of the computer and the application software that users need to run on the computer.
- Compilers and interpreters are special types of programs that convert source code written in a programming language (source language) into machine language comprising of just two digits—1s and 0s (target language).
- The number of unique digits used to form numbers within a number system is called radix of that system. Decimal number system has a radix of 10, binary has a radix of 2, octal has a radix of 8, and hexadecimal has a radix of 16.
- The entire program or software (collection of programs) development process is divided into a number of phases, where each phase performs a well-defined task.
- During requirements analysis, users' expectations are gathered to know why the program/software has to be built.
- In the design phase, a plan of action is made.
- In the implementation phase, the designed algorithms are converted into program code using any of the high-level languages
- In the testing phase, all the modules are tested together to ensure that the overall system works well as a whole product.
- After the code is tested and the software or the program has been approved by the users, it is then installed or deployed in the production environment.
- Maintenance and enhancements are on-going activities that are done to cope with newly discovered problems or new requirements.

Glossary

Algorithm A formally defined procedure for performing some calculation and provides a blueprint to write a program that solves a particular problem.

Assembler System software that converts the code written in assembly language into machine language.

Basic input output system (BIOS) Program that tells the computer what to do when it starts up, e.g., running hardware diagnostics and loading the operating system into RAM.

Bit It is short form of binary digit. It is the smallest possible unit of data, which can either be 0 or 1.

Byte A group of eight bits.

Command line interface Command line interface (CLI) is a type of interface in which users interact with a program.

Compile-time errors These are errors that occur at the time of compilation of the program.

Compiler/Interpreter System software that translates the source code from a high-level programming language to a lower-level language.

Computer A machine that takes instructions and performs computations based on those instructions.

Data A collection of raw facts or figures.

Debugging An activity that includes execution testing and code correction. The main aim of debugging is to locate errors in the program code.

DRAM A type of RAM that must be refreshed multiple times in a second to retain its data contents.

Erasable programmable read-only memory A type of ROM that can be erased and re-programmed. The EPROM can be erased by exposing the chip to strong ultraviolet light.

Flash memory A type of EEPROM in which the contents can be erased under software control. It is the most flexible type of ROM.

Flowchart A graphical or symbolic representation of a process.

Graphical user interface Graphical user interface (GUI) is a type of user interface that enables users to interact with programs in more ways than typing. A GUI offers graphical icons and visual indicators to display the information and actions available to a user.

Hard copy output devices Output devices that produce a physical form of output.

Information Processed data that provide answers to 'who', 'what', 'where', and 'when' types of questions.

Input The process of entering data and instructions into the computer system.

Instructions Commands given to the computer that tell what it has to do.

Knowledge The application of data and information to answer the 'how' part of the question.

Linker System software that combines object modules to form an executable program.

Loader System software that copies programs from a storage device to the main memory, where they can be executed.

Memory An internal storage area in the computer used to store data and programs either temporarily or permanently.

Modularization The process of dividing an algorithm into smaller units or modules.

Output The process of giving the result of data processing to the outside world.

Processing The process of performing operations on the data as per the instructions specified by the user.

Program A set of instructions that are arranged in a sequence to guide a computer to find a solution for the given problem.

Programmable read-only memory A type of ROM that can be programmed using high voltages.

Pseudocode A compact and informal high-level description of an algorithm that uses the structural conventions of a programming language.

Run-time errors These are errors that occur when the program is being executed.

Soft copy output devices Output devices that produce an electronic version of an output.

Software A set of programs.

SRAM A type of RAM that holds data without an external refresh as long as it is powered.

Storage The process of saving data and instructions permanently in the computer so that it can be used for processing.

Testing An activity performed to verify the correct behaviour of a program. It is specifically carried out with the intent to find errors.

Translator A computer program, which translates a code written in one programming language to a code in another language that the computer understands.

Word A group of two bytes.

Exercises

Fill in the Blanks

1. A program is the _____.
2. Computers operate on _____ based on _____.
3. The speed of computers is expressed in _____ or _____.
4. Raw facts or figures are called _____.
5. _____ and _____ are examples of first-generation computing devices.
6. Second-generation computers were first developed for the _____ industry.
7. _____ packages allow easy manipulation and analysis of data organized in rows and columns.
8. CRAY-1, CRAY-2, Control Data CYBER 205, and ETA A-10 are _____.

9. _____ concept was introduced by Sir John von Neumann in the late 1940s.
10. Android Jellybean, Windows, and iOS are all examples of popular operating systems used in _____ and _____.
11. _____ unit directs and coordinates the computer operations.
12. Intermediate results during program execution are stored in _____.
13. _____ stores the address of the data or instruction to be fetched from memory.
14. An instruction consists of _____ and _____.
15. The instruction cycle is repeated continuously until _____.
16. Buses in a computer system can carry _____ and _____.
17. In an instruction, _____ specifies the computation to be performed.
18. Giga is _____ and tera is _____.
19. _____ instructs the hardware what to do and how to do it.
20. The hardware needs a _____ to instruct what has to be done.
21. _____ is used to feed data and instructions into the computer.
22. The _____ memory holds data and programs that are currently being executed by the CPU.
23. _____ memory is volatile.
24. _____ memory stores data or instructions permanently.
25. _____ are the fastest of all forms of computer data storage.
26. Static RAM is made of _____.
27. _____ is a one-time programmable ROM.
28. The process of writing data to an optical disk is called _____.

29. The process of writing a program is called _____.
30. _____ is used to write computer software.
31. _____ transforms source code into binary language.
32. _____ helps in coordinating system resources and allows other programs to execute.
33. _____ provides a platform for running application software.
34. _____ is a software package that enables its users to create, edit, print, and save documents for future retrieval and reference.
35. Information from a database is extracted in the form of a _____.
36. Adobe Photoshop is an example of _____ software.
37. _____ and _____ statements are used to change the sequence of execution of instructions.
38. _____ is a formally defined procedure for performing some calculation.
39. _____ statements are used when the outcome of the process depends on some condition.
40. Repetition can be implemented using constructs such as _____, _____, and _____.
41. A complex algorithm is often divided into smaller units called _____.
42. _____ design approach starts by dividing the complex algorithm into one or more modules.
43. The _____ symbol is always the first and the last symbol in a flowchart.
44. _____ is a form of structured English that describes algorithms.
45. _____ is used to express algorithms and as a mode of human communication.
46. In the _____ phase, a plan of action is made.
47. In the _____ phase, designed algorithms are converted into program code.
48. User's expectations are gathered in the _____ phase.

State True or False

1. Computers work on the GIGO concept.
2. 1 nanosecond $= 1 \times 10 - 12$ seconds.
3. Floppy disks and hard disks are examples of primary memory.
4. First-generation computers used a very large number of transistors.
5. First-generation computers could be programmed only in binary language.
6. Fifth-generation computers are based on AI.
7. Network computers have more processing power, memory, and storage than a desktop computer.
8. RAM stores the data and parts of program, the intermediate results of processing, and the recently generated results of jobs that are currently being worked on by the computer.
9. Computer hardware does all the physical work computers are known for.
10. The computer hardware cannot think and make decisions on its own.
11. The term software refers to a set of instructions arranged in a sequence to guide a computer to find a solution for the given problem.
12. BIOS defines the firmware interface.
13. Primary memory is faster than secondary memory.
14. The ALU initiates action to execute the instructions.
15. The program counter stores the address of the next instruction to be executed.

16. A byte is a group of eight bits.
17. A computer can perform thousands of instructions in one second.
18. First generation of computers were used for commercial applications.
19. Computer and all its physical parts are known as software.
20. 1942–1955 marks the second generation of computers.
21. Machine/assembly language was used in first generation of computers.
22. SSI and MSI technology was used in fourth generation of computers.
23. Computer is a reliable machine.
24. When data and programs have to be used, they are copied from the primary memory into the secondary memory accuracy.
25. CPU can directly access primary memory.
26. Primary memory can be used for storing data permanently.
27. ALU manages and controls all the components of the computer system.
28. Critical programs which are used to start the computer when it is turned on are stored in RAM.
29. Hard disk drive is an example of ROM.
30. Application software provides a general programming environment in which programmers can create specific applications to suit their needs.
31. Compiler and operating system is an example of application software.
32. MS Word and Paint are examples of application software.

33. Compiler translates one statement of high-level language program into machine language and executes it.
34. An interpreted program gets executed faster than a compiled program.
35. Microsoft Excel is a word-processing software.
36. An algorithm solves a problem in a finite number of steps.
37. Flowcharts are drawn in the early stages of formulating computer solutions.
38. The main focus of pseudocodes is on the details of the language syntax.
39. In the deployment phase, all the modules are tested together to ensure that the overall system works well as a whole product.
40. Maintenance is an ongoing activity.
41. Algorithms are implemented using a programming language.
42. Logical errors are detected by the compiler.
43. Repetition means that each step of the algorithm is executed in a specified order.
44. Terminal symbol depicts the flow of control of the program.
45. Labelled connectors are square in shape.
46. It takes less time to write a structured program than other programs.
47. Logic errors are much harder to locate and correct than syntax errors.
48. An interpreter translates the code and also executes it.

Multiple Choice Questions

1. A computer works on _____ given to it.
   (a) Computations   (b) Instructions
   (c) Data   (d) b and c
2. Computer is a _____ machine.
   (a) Electrical   (b) Mechanical
   (c) Electronic   (d) Physical
3. _____ comprises processed data.
   (a) Data   (b) Information
   (c) Knowledge   (d) Instructions
4. Commands given to the computer that tells what it has to do are _____ .
   (a) Data   (b) Information
   (c) Knowledge   (d) Instructions
5. Which generation of computers were used in the period 1955–1964?
   (a) First   (b) Second
   (c) Third   (d) Fourth

6. Which of the following were used for manufacturing first generation computers?
   (a) Vacuum tubes   (b) Transistors
   (c) Integrated chips (d) ULSI
7. Select the computer(s) in the first generation of computers.
   (a) ENIAC   (b) EDVAC
   (c) EDSAC   (d) All of these
8. Which technology was used to manufacture second generation computers?
   (a) Vacuum tubes   (b) Transistors
   (c) ICs   (d) None of these
9. Select the computer(s) in the second generation of computers.
   (a) UNIVAC LARC   (b) EDVAC
   (c) EDSAC   (d) All of these
10. Which generation of computers were manufactured using ICs with LSI and later with VLSI technology?

(a) First   (b) Second

(c) Third   (d) Fourth

11. In which computer generation did microcomputers come into existence?

    (a) First   (b) Second

    (c) Third   (d) Fourth

12. Currently on which generation of computers are we working?

    (a) First   (b) Fifth

    (c) Third   (d) Fourth

13. Name an Indian supercomputer.

    (a) UNIVAC LARC   (b) EDVAC

    (c) EDSAC   (d) CRAY XMP

14. The process of entering data and instructions into the computer system is called _____.

    (a) Input   (b) Output

    (c) Processing   (d) Result

15. Computer understands only _____ language.

    (a) Assembly   (b) Binary

    (c) High level   (d) SQL

16. In which part of the CPU are all computations performed?

    (a) CU   (b) MU

    (c) ALU   (d) Registers

17. _____ is the main input device.

    (a) Mouse   (b) Joystick

    (c) Keyboard   (d) Touch screen

18. Which output device is used in home theatre systems?

    (a) Printer   (b) Plotter

    (c) Projector   (d) Speakers

19. Which memory holds data and programs not currently in use and provides long-term storage?

    (a) RAM   (b) ROM

    (c) Primary memory   (d) Secondary memory

20. Which storage device will you use to back up large amount of data?

    (a) Magnetic hard disk   (b) ROM

    (c) RAM   (d) Magnetic tape

21. Which of the following enables the users to interact with hardware components efficiently?

    (a) Application software

    (b) Communication software

    (c) Presentation software

    (d) System software

22. Which of the following copies programs from a storage device to the main memory?

    (a) Compiler   (b) Interpreter

    (c) Assembler   (d) Loader

23. Code written in which language can be directly executed by the computer?

    (a) Compiled   (b) Assembly

    (c) Binary   (d) Interpreter

24. _____ is a mnemonic that specifies the operation that has to be performed.

    (a) Operand   (b) Opcode

    (c) Label   (d) Comment

25. A group of 4 binary digits is called a _____.

    (a) Bit   (b) Nibble

    (c) Byte   (d) Word

26. A group of 8 binary digits is called a _____.

    (a) Bit   (b) Nibble

    (c) Byte   (d) Word

27. The brain of the computer is the

    (a) Control unit   (b) ALU

    (c) CPU   (d) All of these

28. The memory used by the CPU to store instructions and data that are repeatedly required to execute programs to improve overall system performance is

    (a) primary memory   (b) auxiliary memory

    (c) cache memory   (d) flash memory

29. Magnetic tapes, floppy disks, optical disks, flash memory, and hard disks are examples of

    (a) Primary memory   (b) Auxiliary memory

    (c) Cache memory   (d) Flash memory

30. The memory used in MP3 players, PDAs, laptops, and digital audio players is

    (a) Primary memory   (b) Optical memory

    (c) Cache memory   (d) Flash memory

31. The component of the processor that controls the flow of data through the computer system is

    (a) BIU   (b) Execution unit

    (c) CU   (d) ALU

32. Which keys are used by applications and operating systems to perform specific commands?

    (a) Typing keys   (b) Arrow keys

    (c) Control keys   (d) Function keys

33. BIOS is stored in

    (a) RAM   (b) ROM

    (c) Hard disk   (d) None of these

34. Which of the following languages is a symbolic language?

    (a) Machine language   (b) C

    (c) Assembly language   (d) All of these

35. Choose the odd one out from the following:

    (a) Compiler   (b) Interpreter

    (c) Assembler   (d) Linker

36. Windows Vista, Linux, and UNIX are examples of

    (a) Operating systems   (b) Computer hardware

    (c) Firmware   (d) Device drivers

37. Which among the following is an excellent analytical tool?
    (a) Microsoft Word (b) Microsoft Excel
    (c) Microsoft Access (d) Microsoft PowerPoint
38. Which interface makes use of the graphical components to allow users to easily interact with the computer system?
    (a) CPU (b) CLI
    (c) GUI (d) CUI
39. The register or location in main memory from where the data to be processed is located is specified by
    (a) Label (b) Opcode
    (c) Operand(s) (d) None of these
40. The code in 0s and 1s is
    (a) Source code (b) Object code
    (c) Executable code (d) None of these
41. The system software that creates the final executable file is
    (a) Assembler (b) Compiler
    (c) Loader (d) Linker
42. Which among the following is an on-going activity in software development?
    (a) Requirements analysis (b) Implementation
    (c) User training (d) Maintenance
43. The functionality, capability, performance, availability of hardware and software components are all analyzed in which phase?
    (a) Requirements analysis (b) Design
    (c) Implementation (d) Testing
44. In which phase are algorithms, flowcharts, and pseudocodes prepared?
    (a) Requirements analysis (b) Design
    (c) Implementation (d) Testing
45. Algorithms should be
    (a) precise (b) unambiguous
    (c) clear (d) all of these
46. To check whether a given number is even or odd, you will use which type of control structure?
    (a) Sequence (b) Decision
    (c) Repetition (d) All of these
47. Which one of the following is a graphical or symbolic representation of a process?
    (a) Algorithm (b) Flowchart
    (c) Pseudocode (d) Program
48. In a flowchart, which symbol is represented using a rectangle?
    (a) Terminal (b) Decision
    (c) Activity (d) Input/Output
49. Which of the following details are omitted in pseudocodes?
    (a) Variable declaration
    (b) System specific code
    (c) Subroutines
    (d) All of these
50. Trying to open a file that already exists, will result in which type of error?
    (a) Run time (b) Compile time
    (c) Linker error (d) Logical error
51. Which of the following errors is generated when rules of a programming language are violated?
    (a) Syntax error (b) Semantic error
    (c) Linker error (d) Logical error

Review Questions

1. Define a computer.
2. Differentiate between data and information.
3. Differentiate between primary memory and secondary memory.
4. Write a short note on the characteristics of a computer.
5. Computers work on the garbage-in and garbage-out concept. Comment.
6. Explain the evolution of computers. Further, state how computers in one generation are better than their predecessors.
7. Broadly classify computers based on their speed, the amount of data that they can hold, and price.
8. Discuss the variants of microcomputers that are widely used today.
9. Explain the areas in which computers are being applied to carry out routine and highly specialized tasks.
10. What are input devices and output devices?
11. Differentiate between a soft copy and a hard copy output.
12. What do you understand by computer memory?
13. Differentiate between primary memory and secondary memory.
14. Give the characteristics of the memory hierarchy chart.
15. Differentiate between static RAM and dynamic RAM.
16. Give the organization of computer memory. How does the CPU access a memory cell?
17. Briefly discuss the importance of cache memory.
18. What do you understand by re-programmable ROM chips?
19. Draw and explain the basic architecture of a processor.
20. 'CPU is the brain of the computer.' Justify.

21. Broadly classify the computer system into two parts. In addition, make a comparison between a human body and the computer system, thereby explaining which part performs what function.
22. Differentiate between computer hardware and software.
23. What is booting?
24. Explain the role of the operating system.
25. Why are compilers and interpreters used? Is there any difference between a compiler and an interpreter?
26. What is application software? Give examples.
27. Differentiate between syntax errors and logical errors.
28. How is application software different from system software?
29. Define an algorithm. How is it useful in the context of software development?
30. Explain and compare the approaches for designing an algorithm.
31. What is modularization?
32. Explain sequence, repetition, and decision statements. Also give the keywords used in each type of statement.
33. With the help of an example, explain the use of a flowchart.
34. How is a flowchart different from an algorithm? Do we need to have both of them for program development?
35. What do you understand by the term pseudocode?
36. Differentiate between algorithm and pseudocodes.
37. Write a short note on assembly language.
38. What is an assembler?
39. Differentiate between an assembler and an interpreter.

40. Briefly explain the phases in software development project.
41. Write an algorithm and draw a flowchart that calculates salary of an employee. Prompt the user to enter the Basic Salary, HRA, TA, and DA. Add these components to calculate the Gross Salary. Also deduct 10% salary from the Gross Salary to be paid as tax.
42. Draw a flowchart and write an algorithm and a psuedocode for the following problem statements
    a. Cook maggi
    b. Cross road
    c. Calculate bill of items purchased
    d. To find out whether a number is positive or negative
    e. Print "Hello" five times on the screen
    f. Find area of a rectangle
    g. Convert meters into centimeters
    h. Find the sum of first 10 numbers

Answers

Fill in the Blanks

1. set of instructions that is arranged in a sequence to guide a computer to find a solution for the given problem.
2. Data, instructions
3. Nano second, pico second
4. Data
5. ENIAC, EDVAC
6. Scientific and commercial applications
7. Spreadsheet
8. Super computers
9. Stored program
10. Smart phones, tablets
11. Control
12. Accumulator
13. MAR
14. Opcode, operand
15. The computer is halted or switched off
16. Data, address
17. Opcode
18. 2^{30} bytes, 2^{40} bytes
19. Software
20. Software
21. Input device
22. Primary
23. Primary
24. Secondary
25. CPU Registers
26. D flip flops
27. PROM
28. Burning
29. Programming
30. Programming language
31. Translator
32. Operating system
33. System software
34. Report
35. Word processing
36. Graphics
37. Decision, repetition
38. Algorithm
39. Decision
40. while, do-while, and for loops
41. functions or modules
42. top-down
43. Terminal symbols
44. Psuedocode
45. Flowcharts
46. Design
47. Implementation
48. Requirements analysis

State True or False

1. True   2. False   3. False   4. False   5. True   6. True   7. False   8. True   9. True   10. True
11. True   12. True   13. True   14. False   15. False   16. True   17. False   18. False   19. False   20. False
21. False   22. False   23. True   24. False   25. True   26. False   27. False   28. False   29. False   30. False
31. False   32. True   33. False   34. False   35. False   36. True   37. True   38. True   39. False   40. True
41. False   42. False   43. False   44. False   45. False   46. True   47. True   48. True

Multiple Choice Questions

1. (d)   2. (c)   3. (b)   4. (d)   5. (b)   6. (a)   7. (d)   8. (b)   9. (a)   10. (d)   11. (d)   12. (b)
13. (d)   14. (a)   15. (b)   16. (c)   17. (c)   18. (d)   19. (d)   20. (d)   21. (d)   22. (d)   23. (c)   24. (b)
25. (b)   26. (c)   27. (c)   28. (c)   29. (b)   30. (d)   31. (a)   32. (d)   33. (c)   34. (c)   35. (d)   36. (a)
37. (b)   38. (c)   39. (a)   40. (b)   41. (d)   42. (d)   43. (a)   44. (b)   45. (d)   46. (b)   47. (b)   48. (c)
49. (d)   50. (a)   51. (a)

Introduction to Object Oriented Programming (OOP)

2.1 COMPUTER PROGRAMMING AND PROGRAMMING LANGUAGES

A *program* is a collection of instructions that tells the computer how to solve a particular problem. We have already written algorithms and pseudocdes and drawn flowcharts that gives a blueprint of the solution (or the program to be written). Computer programming goes a step further in problem solving process. *Programming* is the process of taking an algorithm and writing it in a particular programming language, so that it can be executed by a computer. Programmers can use any of the programming languages that exist to write a program.

A *programming language* is a language specifically designed to express computations that can be performed by a computer. Programming languages are used to create programs that control the behaviour of a system, to express algorithms, or as a mode of human communication.

Usually, programming languages have a vocabulary of syntax and semantics for instructing a computer to perform specific tasks. The term *programming language* refers to high-level languages such as BASIC (Beginners' All-purpose Symbolic Instruction Code), C, C++, COBOL (Common Business Oriented Language), FORTRAN (Formula Translator), Python, Ada, and Pascal, to name a few. Each of these languages has a unique set of keywords (words that it understands) and a special syntax for organizing program instructions.

Though high-level programming languages are easy for humans to read and understand, the computer can understand only machine language, which consists of only numbers. Each type of central processing unit (CPU) has its own unique machine language.

In between machine languages and high-level languages, there is another type of language known as assembly language. Assembly languages are similar to machine languages, but they are much easier to program because they allow a programmer to substitute names for numbers.

However, irrespective of the language that a programmer uses, a program written using any programming language has to be converted into machine language so that the computer can understand it. There are two ways to do this: *compile* the program or *interpret* the program.

When planning a software solution, the software development team often faces a common question— which programming language to use? Many programming languages are available today and each one has its own strengths and weaknesses. Python can be used to write an efficient code, whereas a code in BASIC is easy to write and understand; some languages are compiled, whereas others are interpreted; some languages are well known to the programmers, whereas others are completely new. Selecting the perfect language for a particular application at hand is a daunting task.

The selection of language for writing a program depends on the following factors:

- The type of computer hardware and software on which the program is to be executed.
- The type of program.
- The expertise and availability of the programmers.
- Features to write the application.
- It should have built-in features that support the development of software that are reliable and less prone to crash.
- Lower development and maintenance costs.
- Stability and capability to support even more than the expected simultaneous users.
- Elasticity of a language that implies the ease with which new features (or functions) can be added to the existing program.
- Portability.
- Better speed of development that includes the time it takes to write a code, time taken to find a solution to the problem at hand, time taken to find the bugs, availability of development tools, experience and skill of the programmers, and testing regime.

For example, FORTRAN is a particularly good language for processing numerical data, but it does not lend itself very well to organizing large programs. Pascal can be used for writing well-structured and readable programs, but it is not as flexible as the C programming language. C++ goes one step ahead of C by incorporating powerful object oriented features, but it is complex and difficult to learn. Python, however is a good mix of the best features of all these languages.

2.2 GENERATIONS OF PROGRAMMING LANGUAGES

We now know that programming languages are the primary tools for creating software. As of now, hundreds of programming languages exist in the market, some more used than others and each claiming to be the best. However, in the 1940s when computers were being developed, there was just one language—machine language.

The concept of generations of programming languages (also known as levels) is closely connected to the advances in technology. The five generations of programming languages include machine language, assembly language, high-level language (also known as the third generation language or 3GL), very high-level language (also known as the fourth generation language or 4GL), and fifth generation language that includes artificial intelligence.

2.2.1 First Generation: Machine Language

Machine language was used to program the first stored-program computer systems. This is the lowest level of programming language and is the only language that a computer understands. All the commands and data values are expressed using 0s and 1s, corresponding to the *off* and *on* electrical states in a computer.

In the 1950s, each computer had its own native language, and programmers had primitive systems for combining numbers to represent instructions such as *add* and *subtract*. Although there were similarities between each of the machine languages, a computer could not understand programs written in another machine language (refer to Figure 2.1).

In machine language, all instructions, memory locations, numbers, and characters are represented in strings of 0s and 1s. Although machine language programs are typically displayed with the *binary* numbers represented in *octal* (base 8) or *hexadecimal* (base 16) number systems, these programs are not easy for humans to read, write, or debug.

This is an example of a machine language program that will add two numbers and find their average. It is in hexadecimal notation instead of binary notation because that is how the computer presented the code to the programmer. The program was run on a VAX/VMS computer, a product of the Digital Equipment Corporation.

```
000     0000A    0000
000     0000F    0008
000     0000B    0008
                 0008
                 0058
                 0000
FF55    CF       FF54  CF    FF53  CF    C1    00A9
        FF24     CF    FF27  CF    D2    C7    00CC
                                                00E4
                                                010D
                                                013D
```

Figure 2.1   A machine language program

The main advantage of machine language is that the execution of the code is very fast and efficient since it is directly executed by the CPU. However, on the downside, machine language is difficult to learn and is far more difficult to edit if errors occur. Moreover, if we want to store some instructions in the memory at some location, then all the instructions after the insertion point would have to be moved down to make room in the memory to accommodate the new instructions. In addition, the code written in machine language is not portable, and to transfer the code to a different computer, it needs to be completely rewritten since the machine language for one computer could be significantly different from that for another computer. Architectural considerations make portability a tough issue to resolve. Table 2.1 lists the advantages and disadvantages of machine language.

Table 2.1   Advantages and disadvantages of machine language

Advantages	Disadvantages
• Code can be directly executed by the computer. • Execution is fast and efficient. • Programs can be written to efficiently utilize memory.	• Code is difficult to write. • Code is difficult to understand by other people. • Code is difficult to maintain. • There is more possibility for errors to creep in. • It is difficult to detect and correct errors. • Code is machine dependent and thus non-portable.

2.2.2 Second Generation: Assembly Language

Second generation programming languages (2GLs) comprise the assembly languages. Assembly languages are symbolic programming languages that use symbolic notations to represent machine language instructions. These languages are closely connected to machine language and the internal architecture of the computer system on which they are used. Since it is close to machine language, assembly language is also a low-level language. Nearly all computer systems have an assembly language available for use.

Assembly language developed in the mid-1950s was a great leap forward. It used symbolic codes, also known as *mnemonic* codes, which are easy-to-remember abbreviations, rather than numbers. Examples of these codes include ADD for add, CMP for compare, and MUL for multiply.

Assembly language programs consist of a series of individual statements or instructions to instruct the computer what to do. Basically, an assembly language statement consists of a label, an operation code, and one or more *operands*.

Labels are used to identify and refer instructions in the program. The operation code (opcode) is a mnemonic that specifies the operation to be performed, such as *move, add, subtract,* or *compare.* The operand specifies the register or the location in the main memory where the data to be processed is located.

However, like machine language, the statement or instruction in assembly language will vary from machine to machine, because the language is directly related to the internal architecture of the computer and is not designed to be machine independent. This makes the code written in assembly language less portable, as the code written to be executed on one machine will not run on machines from a different, or sometimes even the same manufacturer.

Nevertheless, the code written in assembly language will be very efficient in terms of execution time and main memory usage, as the language is similar to computer language.

Programs written in assembly language need a translator, often known as the assembler, to convert them into machine language. This is because the computer will understand only the language of 0s and 1s. It will not understand mnemonics such as ADD and SUB.

The following instructions are part of an assembly language code to illustrate addition of two numbers:

MOV AX,4	Stores the value 4 in the AX register of the CPU
MOV BX,6	Stores the value 6 in the BX register of the CPU
ADD AX,BX	Adds the contents of the AX and BX registers and stores the result in the AX register

Although it is much easier to work with assembly language than with machine language, it still requires the programmer to think on the machine's level. Even today, some programmers use assembly language to write those parts of applications where speed of execution is critical; for example, video games, but most programmers have switched to 3GL or even 4GL to write such codes. Table 2.2 lists the advantages and disadvantages of using assembly language.

Table 2.2 Advantages and disadvantages of assembly language

Advantages	Disadvantages
• It is easy to understand. • It is easier to write programs in assembly language than in machine language. • It is easy to detect and correct errors. • It is easy to modify. • It is less prone to errors.	• Code is machine dependent and thus non-portable. • Programmers must have a good knowledge of the hardware internal architecture of the CPU. • The code cannot be directly executed by the computer.

2.2.3 Third Generation: High-level Language

Third generation programming languages are a refinement of 2GLs. The second generation brought logical structure to software. The third generation was introduced to make the languages more programmer friendly.

The 3GLs spurred the great increase in data processing that occurred in the 1960s and 1970s. In these languages, the program statements are not closely related to the internal characteristics of the computer. Hence, these languages are often referred to as high-level languages.

In general, a statement written in a high-level programming language will expand into several machine language instructions. This is in contrast to assembly languages, where one statement would generate one machine language instruction. 3GLs made programming easier, efficient, and less prone to errors.

High-level languages fall somewhere between natural languages and machine languages. 3GLs include FORTRAN and COBOL, which made it possible for scientists and entrepreneurs to write programs using familiar terms instead of obscure machine instructions.

The widespread use of high-level languages in the early 1960s changed programming into something quite different from what it had been. Programs were written in languages that were more English-like, making them more convenient to use and giving the programmer more time to address a client's problems.

Although 3GLs relieve the programmer of demanding details, they do not provide the flexibility available in low level languages. However, a few high-level languages such as C and FORTH combine some of the flexibility of assembly languages with the power of high-level languages, but these languages are not well suited to programmers at the beginner level.

Some high-level languages were specifically designed to serve a specific purpose (such as controlling industrial robots or creating graphics), whereas other languages were flexible and considered to be general purpose. Most programmers preferred to use general-purpose high-level languages such as BASIC, FORTRAN, Pascal, COBOL, C++, or Java to write the code for their applications.

Again, a translator is needed to translate the instructions written in a high-level language into the computer-executable machine language. Such translators are commonly known as interpreters and compilers. Each high-level language has many compilers, and there is one for each type of computer.

For example, the machine language generated by one computer's C compiler is not the same as the machine language of some other computer. Therefore, it is necessary to have a C compiler for each type of computer on which the C programs are to be executed.

> **Note** Assemblers, linkers, compilers, loaders, and interpreters are all system software, which are discussed in Section 1.13.1.

The 3GLs make it easy to write and debug a program and give a programmer more time to think about its overall logic. Programs written in such languages are portable between machines. For example, a program written in standard C can be compiled and executed on any computer that has a standard C compiler. Table 2.3 provides the advantages and disadvantages of 3GLs.

Table 2.3 Advantages and disadvantages of 3GLs

Advantages	Disadvantages
• The code is machine independent. • It is easy to learn and use the language. • There are few errors. • It is easy to document and understand the code. • It is easy to maintain the code. • It is easy to detect and correct errors.	• Code may not be optimized. • The code is less efficient. • It is difficult to write a code that controls the CPU, memory, and registers.

> **Note** Python, Ruby, and Perl are third generation programming languages that combine some 4GL abilities within a general-purpose 3GL environment.

2.2.4 Fourth Generation: Very High-level Languages

With each generation, programming languages started becoming easier to use and more similar to natural languages. 4GLs are a little different from their prior generation because they are non-procedural. While writing a code using a procedural language, the programmer has to tell the computer how a task is done—add this, compare that, do this if the condition is true, and so on—in a very specific step-by-step manner. In striking contrast, while using a non-procedural language, programmers define what they want the computer to do but they do not supply all the details of how it has to be done.

Although there is no standard rule that defines a 4GL, certain characteristics of such languages include the following:

- The instructions of the code are written in English-like sentences.
- They are non-procedural, so users concentrate on the 'what' instead of the 'how' aspect of the task.
- The code written in a 4GL is easy to maintain.
- The code written in a 4GL enhances the productivity of programmers, as they have to type fewer lines of code to get something done. A programmer supposedly becomes 10 times more productive when he/she writes the code using a 4GL than using a 3GL.

A typical example of a 4GL is the query language, which allows a user to request information from a database with precisely worded English-like sentences. A query language is used as a database user interface and hides the specific details of the database from the user. For example, when working with Structured Query Language (SQL), the programmer just needs to remember a few rules of *syntax* and *logic,* and therefore, it is easier to learn than COBOL or C.

Let us take an example in which a report needs to be generated. The report displays the total number of students enrolled in each class and in each semester. Using a 4GL, the request would look similar to the following:

```
TABLE FILE ENROLMENT
SUM STUDENTS BY SEMESTER BY CLASS
```

Thus, we see that a 4GL is very simple to learn and work with. The same task if written in C or any other 3GL would require multiple lines of code.

The 4GLs are still evolving, which makes it difficult to define or standardize them. The only downside of a 4GL is that it does not make efficient use of a machine's resources. However, the benefit of executing a program quickly and easily far outweighs the extra costs of running it.

2.2.5 Fifth Generation Programming Language

Fifth-generation programming languages (5GLs) are centred on solving problems using the constraints given to a program rather than using an algorithm written by a programmer. Most constraint-based and logic programming languages and some declarative languages form a part of the 5GLs. These languages are widely used in artificial intelligence research. Another aspect of a 5GL is that it contains visual tools to help develop a program. Typical examples of 5GLs include Prolog, OPS5, Mercury, and Visual Basic.

Thus, taking a forward leap, 5GLs are designed to make the computer solve a given problem without the programmer. While working with a 4GL, programmers have to write a specific code to do a work, but with a 5GL, they only have to worry about what problems need to be solved and what conditions need to be met, without worrying about how to implement a routine or an algorithm to solve them.

In general, 5GLs were generally built upon LISP, many originating on the LISP machine, such as ICAD. There are also many frame languages, such as KL-ONE.

In the 1990s, 5GLs were considered the wave of the future, and some predicted that they would replace all other languages for system development (except the low-level languages). During the period ranging from 1982 to 1993, Japan carried out extensive research on and invested a large amount of money into their fifth generation computer systems project, hoping to design a massive computer network of machines using these tools. However, when large programs were built, the flaws of the approach became more apparent. Researchers began to observe that given a set of constraints defining a particular problem, deriving an efficient algorithm to solve it is itself a very difficult problem. All factors could not be automated and some still require the insight of a programmer.

However, today the fifth generation languages are pursued as a possible level of computer language. Software vendors across the globe currently claim that their software meets the visual 'programming' requirements of the 5GL concept.

2.3 PROGRAMMING PARADIGMS

A *programming paradigm* is a fundamental style of programming that defines how the structure and basic elements of a computer program will be built. The style of writing programs and the set of capabilities and limitations that a particular programming language has depends on the programming paradigm it supports. While some programming languages strictly follow a single paradigm, others may draw concepts from more than one. The sweeping trend in the evolution of high-level programming languages has resulted in a shift in programming paradigm. These paradigms, in sequence of their application, can be classified as follows:

- Monolithic programming—emphasizes on finding a solution
- Procedural programming—lays stress on algorithms
- Structured programming—focuses on modules
- Object-oriented programming—emphasizes on classes and objects
- Logic-oriented programming—focuses on goals usually expressed in predicate calculus
- Rule-oriented programming—makes use of 'if-then-else' rules for computation
- Constraint-oriented programming—utilizes invariant relationships to solve a problem

Each of these paradigms has its own strengths and weaknesses and no single paradigm can suit all applications. For example, for designing computation intensive problems, procedure-oriented programming is preferred; for designing a knowledge base, rule-based programming would be the best option; and for hypothesis derivation, logic-oriented programming is used. In this book, we will discuss only first four paradigms. Among these paradigms, object oriented paradigms supersede to serve as the architectural framework in which other paradigms are employed.

2.3.1 Monolithic Programming

Programs written using monolithic programming languages such as assembly language and BASIC consist of global data and sequential code. The global data can be accessed and modified (knowingly or mistakenly) from any part of the program, thereby, posing a serious threat to its integrity.

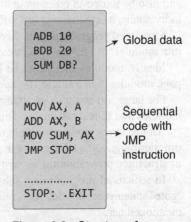

A sequential code is one in which all instructions are executed in the specified sequence. In order to change the sequence of instructions, jump statements or 'goto' statements are used. Figure 2.2 shows the structure of a monolithic program.

As the name suggests, monolithic programs have just one program module as such programming languages do not support the concept of subroutines. Therefore, all the actions required to complete a particular task are embedded within the same application itself. This not only makes the size of the program large but also makes it difficult to debug and maintain.

Figure 2.2 Structure of a monolithic program

For all these reasons, monolithic programming language is used only for very small and simple applications where reusability is not a concern.

2.3.2 Procedural Programming

In procedural languages, a program is divided into *n* number of subroutines that access global data. To avoid repetition of code, each subroutine performs a well-defined task. A subroutine that needs the service provided by another subroutine can call that subroutine. Therefore, with 'jump', 'goto', and 'call' instructions, the sequence of execution of instructions can be altered. Figure 2.3 shows the structure of a procedural language.

FORTRAN and COBOL are two popular procedural programming languages.

Advantages
- The only goal is to write correct programs.
- Programs were easier to write as compared to monolithic programming.

Disadvantages
- Writing programs is complex.
- No concept of reusability.
- Requires more time and effort to write programs.
- Programs are difficult to maintain.
- Global data is shared and therefore may get altered (mistakenly).

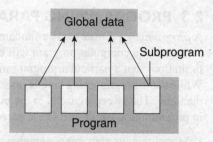

Figure 2.3   Structure of a procedural program

2.3.3 Structured Programming

Structured programming, also referred to as modular programming, was first suggested by mathematicians Corrado Bohm and Guiseppe Jacopini. It was specifically designed to enforce a logical structure on the program to make it more efficient and easier to understand and modify. Structured programming was basically defined to be used in large programs that require a large development team to develop different parts of the same program.

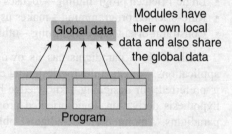

Modules have their own local data and also share the global data

Figure 2.4   Structured program

Structured programming employs a top-down approach in which the overall program structure is broken down into separate modules. This allows the code to be loaded into memory more efficiently and also be reused in other programs. Modules are coded separately and once a module is written and tested individually, it is then integrated with other modules to form the overall program structure (refer to Figure 2.4).

Structured programming is, therefore, based on modularization which groups related statements together into modules. Modularization makes it easier to write, debug, and understand the program.

Ideally, modules should not be longer than a page. It is always easy to understand a series of 10 single-page modules than a single 10-page program.

For large and complex programs, the overall program structure may further require the need to break the modules into subsidiary pieces. This process continues until an individual piece of code can be written easily.

Almost every modern programming language similar to C, Pascal, etc. supports the concepts of structured programming. Even OOP can be thought of as a type of structured programming. In addition to the techniques of structured programming for writing modules, it also focuses on structuring its data.

In structured programming, the program flow follows a simple sequence and usually avoids the use of 'goto' statements. Besides sequential flow, structured programming also supports selection and repetition as mentioned here.

- Selection allows for choosing any one of a number of statements to execute, based on the current status of the program. Selection statements contain keywords such as if, then, end if, or switch, that help to identify the order as a logical executable.
- In repetition, a selected statement remains active until the program reaches a point where there is a need for some other action to take place. It includes keywords such as repeat, for, or do... until. Essentially, repetition instructs the program as to how long it needs to continue the function before requesting further instructions.

Advantages
- The goal of structured programming is to write correct programs that are easy to understand and change.
- Modules enhance programmer's productivity by allowing them to look at the big picture first and focus on details later.

- With modules, many programmers can work on a single, large program, with each working on a different module.
- A structured program takes less time to be written than other programs. Modules or procedures written for one program can be reused in other programs as well.
- Each module performs a specific task.
- Each module has its own local data.
- A structured program is easy to debug because each procedure is specialized to perform just one task and every procedure can be checked individually for the presence of any error. In striking contrast, unstructured programs consist of a sequence of instructions that are not grouped for specific tasks. Their logic is cluttered with details and, therefore, difficult to follow.
- Individual procedures are easy to change as well as understand. In a structured program, every procedure has meaningful names and has clear documentation to identify the task performed by it. Moreover, a correctly written structured program is self-documenting and can be easily understood by another programmer.
- More emphasis is given on the code and the least importance is given to the data.
- Global data may get inadvertently changed by any module using it.
- Structured programs were the first to introduce the concept of functional abstraction.

> **Note**   Functional abstraction allows a programmer to concentrate on what a function (or module) does and not on how it does.

Disadvantages
- Structured programming is not data-centered.
- Global data is shared and therefore may get inadvertently modified.
- Main focus is on functions.

2.3.4 Object Oriented Programming (OOP)

With the increase in size and complexity of programs, there was a need for a new programming paradigm that could help to develop maintainable programs. To implement this, the flaws in previous paradigms had to be corrected. Consequently, OOP was developed. It treats data as a critical element in the program development and restricts its flow freely around the system. We have seen that monolithic, procedural, and structured programming paradigms are task-based as they focus on the actions the software should accomplish. However, the object oriented paradigm is task-based and data-based. In this paradigm, all the relevant data and tasks are grouped together in entities known as objects (refer to Figure 2.5).

For example, consider a list of numbers stored in an array. The procedural or structured programming paradigm considers this list as merely a collection of data. Any program that accesses this list must have some procedures or functions to process this list. For example, to find the largest number or to sort the numbers in the list, we needed specific procedures or functions to do the task. Therefore, the list was a passive entity as it was maintained by a controlling program rather than having the responsibility of maintaining itself.

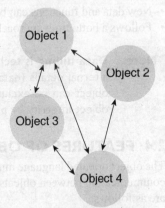

Objects of a program interact by sending messages to each other

Figure 2.5   Object oriented paradigm

However, in the object oriented paradigm, the list and the associated operations are treated as one entity known as an object. In this approach, the list is considered an object consisting of the list, along with a collection of routines for manipulating the list. In the list object, there may be routines for adding a number to the list, deleting a number from the list, sorting the list, etc.

The striking difference between OOP and traditional approaches is that the program accessing this list need not contain procedures for performing tasks; rather, it uses the routines provided in the object. In other words, instead of sorting the list as in the procedural paradigm, the program asks the list to sort itself.

Therefore, we can conclude that the object oriented paradigm is task-based (as it considers operations) as well as data-based (as these operations are grouped with the relevant data).

Figure 2.6 represents a generic object in the object oriented paradigm. Every object contains some data and the operations, methods, or functions that operate on that data. While some objects may contain only basic data types such as characters, integers, and floating types, other objects, on the other hand, may incorporate complex data types such as trees or graphs.

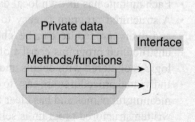

Figure 2.6　Object

Programs that need the object will access the object's methods through a specific interface. The interface specifies how to send a message to the object, that is, a request for a certain operation to be performed.

For example, the interface for the list object may require that any message for adding a new number to the list should include the number to be added. Similarly, the interface might also require that any message for sorting specify whether the sort should be ascending or descending. Hence, an interface specifies how messages can be sent to the object.

> **Note**　OOP is used for simulating real world problems on computers because the real world is made up of objects.

The striking features of OOP include the following:

- The programs are data-centred.
- Programs are divided in terms of objects and not procedures.
- Functions that operate on data are tied together with the data.
- Data is hidden and not accessible by external functions.
- New data and functions can be easily added as and when required.
- Follows a bottom-up approach (discussed in Section 1.16.1) for problem solving.

> **Note**　**Data hiding** is technique widely used in object oriented programming (OOP) to hide the internal details (data members) of an object. Data hiding ensures that data members of an object can be exclusively used only by that object. This is especially important to protect object integrity by preventing unintended or intended changes.

2.4　FEATURES OF OBJECT ORIENTED PROGRAMMING

The object oriented language must support mechanisms to define, create, store, manipulate objects, and allow communication between objects. In this section, we will read about the underlying concepts of OOP. These are as follows:

- Classes
- Objects
- Methods
- Message passing
- Inheritance
- Polymorphism
- Containership
- Reusability
- Delegation
- Data Abstraction and Encapsulation

2.4.1　Classes

Almost every language has some basic data types such as int, float, long, and so on, but not all real world objects can be represented using these built-in types. Therefore, OOP, being specifically designed to solve real world problems, allows its users to create user defined data types in the form of classes.

A *class* is used to describe something in the world, such as occurrences, things, external entities, and so on. A class provides a template or a blueprint that describes the structure and behaviour of a set of similar objects. Once we have the definition for a class, a specific instance of the class can be easily created. For example, consider a class *student*. A student has attributes such as roll number, name, course, and aggregate. The operations that can be performed on its data may include 'getdata', 'setdata', 'editdata', and so on. Figure 2.7 shows the class `Student` with a function `showData()` and attributes namely, `roll_no`, `name`, and `course`. Therefore, we can say that a class describes one or more similar objects.

```
class Student:
def __init__(self, roll_no, name, course):
        self.roll_no = roll_no
        self.name = name
        self.course = course
def showData(self):
        print("ROLL NUMBER : ",self.roll_no)
        print("NAME : ",self.name)
        print("COURSE : ", self.course)
```

Figure 2.7 A sample student class

It must be noted that this data and the set of operations that we have given here can be applied to all students in the class. When we create an instance of a student, we are actually creating an object of class student.

Therefore, once a class is declared, a programmer can create any number of objects of that class.

> **Note** Classes define properties and behaviour of objects.

Therefore, a class is a collection of objects. It is a user-defined data type that behaves same as the built-in data types. This can be realized by ensuring that the syntax of creating an object is same as that of creating an int variable. For example, to create an object (`stud`) of class student, we write

```
student = stud()
```

> **Note** Defining a class does not create any object. Objects have to be explicitly created by using the syntax as follows:
> `object-name = class-name()`

2.4.2 Objects

In the previous section, we have taken an example of student class and have mentioned that a class is used to create instances, known as objects. Therefore, if student is a class, then all the 60 students in a course (assuming there are maximum 60 students in a particular course) are the objects of the student class. Therefore, all students such as Aditya, Chaitanya, Deepti, and Esha are objects of the class.

Hence, a class can have multiple instances.

Every object contains some data and functions (also called methods) as shown in Figure 2.8. These methods store data in variables and respond to the messages that they receive from other objects by executing their methods (procedures).

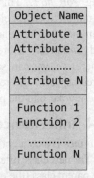

Object Name
Attribute 1
Attribute 2
....
Attribute N
Function 1
Function 2
....
Function N

Figure 2.8 Representation of an object

> **Note** While a class is a logical structure, an object is a physical actuality.

2.4.3 Method and Message Passing

A method is a function associated with a class. It defines the operations that the object can execute when it receives a message. In object oriented language, only methods of the class can access and manipulate the data stored in an instance of the class (or object). Figure 2.9 shows how a class is declared using its data members and member functions.

Every object of the class has its own set of values. Therefore, two distinguishable objects can have the same set of values. Generally, the set of values that the object takes at a particular time is known as the *state* of the object. The state of the object can be changed by applying a particular method. Table 2.4 shows some real world objects along with their data and operations.

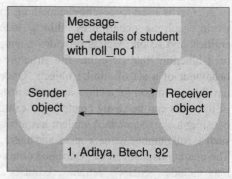

Figure 2.9 Objects sending messages

Table 2.4 Objects with data and functions

Object	Data or attributes	Functions or methods
Person	Name, age, sex	Speak(), walk(), listen(), write()
Vehicle	Name, company, model, capacity, colour	Start(), stop(), accelerate()
Polygon	Vertices, border, colour	Draw(), erase()
Account	Type, number, balance	Deposit(), withdraw(), enquire()
City	Name, population, area, literacy rate	Analyse(), data(), display()
Computer	Brand, resolution, price	Processing(), display(), printing()

Note   An object is an instance of a class which can be uniquely identified by its name. Every object has a state which is given by the values of its attributes at a particular time.

Two objects can communicate with each other through messages. An object asks another object to invoke one of its methods by sending it a message. In Figure 2.9, a sender object is sending a message to the receiver object to get the details of a student. In reply to the message, the receiver sends the results of the execution to the sender.

In the figure, sender has asked the receiver to send the details of student having *roll_no 1*. This means that the sender is passing some specific information to the receiver so that the receiver can send the correct and precise information to the sender. The data that is transferred with the message is called *parameters*. Here, *roll_no 1* is the parameter.

Therefore, we can say that messages that are sent to other objects consist of three aspects—the receiver object, the name of the method that the receiver should invoke, and the parameters that must be used with the method.

2.4.4 Inheritance

Inheritance is a concept of OOP in which a new class is created from an existing class. The new class, often known as a subclass, contains the attributes and methods of the parent class (the existing class from which the new class is created).

The new class, known as subclass or derived class, inherits the attributes and behaviour of the pre-existing class, which is referred to as superclass or parent class (refer to Figure 2.10). The inheritance relationship of subclasses and superclasses generates a hierarchy. Therefore, inheritance relation is also called 'is-a' relation. A subclass not only has all the states and behaviours associated with the superclass but has other specialized features (additional data or methods) as well.

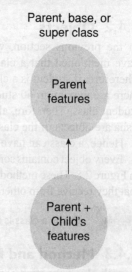

Figure 2.10   Inheritance

The main advantage of inheritance is the ability to reuse the code. When we want a specialized class, we do not have to write the entire code for that class from scratch. We can inherit a class from a general class and add the specialized code for the subclass. For example, if we have a class student with following members:

```
Properties: roll_number, name, course and aggregate
Methods: getdata, setdata
```

We can inherit two classes from the class student, namely, undergraduate students and postgraduate students (refer to Figure 2.11). These two classes will have all the properties and methods of class students and in addition to that, will have even more specialized members.

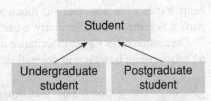

When a derived class receives a message to execute a method, it finds the method in its own class. If it finds the method, then it simply executes it. If the method is not present, it searches for that method in its superclass. If the method is found, it is executed, otherwise, an error message is reported.

Figure 2.11 Example of Inheritance

> **Note** A subclass can inherit properties and methods from multiple parent classes. This is called multiple inheritance.

2.4.5 Polymorphism

Polymorphism, one of the essential concepts of OOP, refers to having several different forms. While inheritance is related to classes and their hierarchy, polymorphism, on the other hand, is related to methods. Polymorphism is a concept that enables the programmers to assign a different meaning or usage to a method in different contexts. In Python, the word 'polymorphism' is often used with inheritance. Polymorphism exists when a number of subclasses is defined which have methods of same name. A function can use objects of any of the polymorphic classes irrespective of the fact that these classes are individually distinct.

Polymorphism can also be applied to operators. For example, we know that operators can be applied only on basic data types that the programming language supports. Therefore, a + b will give the result of adding a and b. If a = 2 and b = 3, then a + b = 5. When we overload the + operator to be used with strings, then Fraction1 + Fraction2 adds two fractional numbers and returns the result.

> **Note** Binding means associating a function call with the corresponding function code to be executed in response to the call.

2.4.6 Containership

Containership is the ability of a class to contain object(s) of one or more classes as member data. For example, class One can have an object of class Two as its data member. This would allow the object of class One to call the public functions of class Two. Here, class One becomes the container, whereas class Two becomes the contained class.

Containership is also called *composition* because as in our example, class One is composed of class Two. In OOP, containership represents a 'has-a' relationship.

2.4.7 Reusability

Reusability means developing codes that can be reused either in the same program or in different programs. Python gives due importance to building programs that are reusable. Reusability is attained through inheritance, containership, and polymorphism.

2.4.8 Delegation

To provide maximum flexibility to programmers and to allow them to generate a reusable code, object oriented languages also support delegation. In composition, an object can be composed of other objects and thus, the object exhibits a 'has-a' relationship.

In delegation, more than one object is involved in handling a request. The object that receives the request for a service, delegates it to another object called its delegate. The property of delegation emphasizes on the ideology that a complex object is made of several simpler objects. For example, our body is made up of brain, heart, hands, eyes, ears, etc. The functioning of the whole body as a system rests on correct functioning of the parts it is composed of. Similarly, a car has a wheel, brake, gears, etc. to control it.

Delegation differs from inheritance in the way that two classes that participate in inheritance share an 'is-a' relationship; however, in delegation, they have a 'has-a' relationship.

> **Note**   Delegation means that one object is dependent on another object to provide functionalities.

Delegation vs Composition

Delegation is closely related to composition i.e., object of one class acts as a data member in another class. However, in composition, the child cannot exist without the context of the parent.

For example, a school has one or more classes. If we remove the school from existence, the classes cease to exist. This is containership. On the other hand, a school also has a number of students, being instances of another entity person. This represents a delegation because even if school does not exist, students will still exist as a person (that is outside of the context of that school).

2.4.9 Data Abstraction and Encapsulation

Data abstraction refers to the process by which data and functions are defined in such a way that only essential details are revealed and the implementation details are hidden. The main focus of data abstraction is to separate the interface and the implementation of a program. For example, as users of television sets, we can switch it on or off, change the channel, set the volume, and add external devices such as speakers and CD or DVD players without knowing the details about how its functionality has been implemented. Therefore, the internal implementation is completely hidden from the external world.

Similarly, in OOP languages, classes provide public methods to the outside world to provide the functionality of the object or to manipulate the object's data. Any entity outside the world does not know about the implementation details of the class or that method.

Data encapsulation, also called data hiding, is the technique of packing data and functions into a single component (class) to hide implementation details of a class from the users. Users are allowed to execute only a restricted set of operations (class methods) on the data members of the class. Therefore, encapsulation organizes the data and methods into a structure that prevents data access by any function (or method) that is not specified in the class. This ensures the integrity of the data contained in the object.

Encapsulation defines three access levels for data variables and member functions of the class. These access levels specify the access rights, explained as follows.

• Any data or function with access level as public can be accessed by any function belonging to any class. This is the lowest level of data protection.
• Any data or function with access level protected can be accessed only by that class or by any class that is inherited from it.
• Any data or function with access level private can be accessed only by the class in which it is declared. This is the highest level of data protection.

> **Note** Creating a new data type using encapsulated items that is well suited for an application is called data abstraction.

2.5 MERITS AND DEMERITS OF OBJECT ORIENTED PROGRAMMING LANGUAGE

OOP offers many benefits to program developers and users. It not only provides a solution for many problems associated with software development and its quality, but also enhances programmer productivity and reduces maintenance cost. Some key advantages of OOP include the following:

- Elimination of redundant code through inheritance (by extending existing classes).
- Higher productivity and reduced development time due to reusability of the existing modules.
- Secure programs as data cannot be modified or accessed by any code outside the class.
- Real world objects in the problem domain can be easily mapped to objects in the program.
- A program can be easily divided into parts based on objects.
- The data-centred design approach captures more details of a model in a form that can be easily implemented.
- Programs designed using OOP are expandable as they can be easily upgraded from small to large systems.
- Message passing between objects simplifies the interface descriptions with external systems.
- Software complexity becomes easily manageable.
- With polymorphism, behaviour of functions, operators, or objects may vary depending upon the circumstances.
- Data abstraction and encapsulation hides implementation details from the external world and provides it a clearly defined interface.
- OOP enables programmers to write easily extendable and maintainable programs.
- OOP supports code reusability to a great extent.

 However, the downside of OOP include the following:

- Programs written using object oriented languages have greater processing overhead as they demand more resources.
- Requires more skills to learn and implement the concepts.
- Beneficial only for large and complicated programs.
- Even an easy to use software when developed using OOP is hard to be built.
- OOP cannot work with existing systems.
- Programmers must have a good command in software engineering and programming methodology.

2.6 APPLICATIONS OF OBJECT ORIENTED PROGRAMMING

No doubt, the concepts of object oriented technology have changed the way of thinking, analyzing, planning, and implementing software. Software or applications developed using this technology are not only efficient but also easy to upgrade. Therefore, programmers and software engineers all over the world have shown their keen interest in developing applications using OOP. As a result, there has been a constant increase in areas where OOP has been successfully implemented. Some of these areas include the following:

- Designing user interfaces such as work screens, menus, windows, and so on
- Real-time systems
- Simulation and modelling
- Compiler design
- Client server system
- Object oriented databases
- Object oriented distributed database
- Artificial intelligence—expert systems and neural networks
- Parallel programming
- Decision control systems
- Office automation systems
- Networks for programming routers, firewalls, and other devices
- Computer-aided design (CAD) systems

- Computer-aided manufacturing (CAM) systems
- Computer animation
- Developing computer games
- Hypertext and hypermedia

2.7 DIFFERENCES BETWEEN POPULAR PROGRAMMING LANGUAGES

Table 2.5 highlights the differences between popular programming languages.

Table 2.5 Comparison between commonly used programming languages

ATTRIBUTE	C	C++	Java	Python	Smalltalk
Cross platform	Good support	Good support	Better support	Better support	Better support
Simple and Concise	Little Difficult	Difficult	Difficult	Easy	Easy
Reusability	Little	Better	Good	Good	Good
Consistent functional constructs	Less	Less	Better	Good	Good
Object oriented	No	Yes	Yes	Yes	Yes
Popularity	High	Good	High	Good; increased in recent times	Little Less
Use	Application, system, general purpose, low-level operations	Application, system	Application, business, client-side, general, mobile development, server-side, web	Application, general, web, scripting, artificial intelligence, scientific computing	Application, general, business, artificial intelligence, education, web
Functional constructs	No	Yes	Yes	Yes	Yes
Procedural	Yes	Yes	Yes	Yes	Yes
Generic	No	Yes	Yes	No	No
Event driven	No	No	Yes	No	Yes
Other paradigms	NA	NA	Concurrent	Aspect oriented	Concurrent, declarative
Program size	Big	Big	Less Big	Small code that requires less memory	Medium
Effort to write programs	More	More	Little Less	Less	Less
Garbage collection	No	No	Yes	Yes	Yes
Standardized	1989, ANSI C89, ISO C90, ISO C99, ISO C11	1198, ISO/IEC 1998, 2003, 2011, 2014	De facto standard	De facto standard	1998, ANSI

Summary

- Programming languages are used to create programs that control the behaviour of a system, to express algorithms, or used as a mode of human communication.
- Every programming language has a vocabulary of syntax and semantics for instructing a computer to perform specific tasks.
- Machine language was used to program the first stored-program computer systems. This is the lowest level of programming language.
- While high-level programming languages are easy for the humans to read and understand, the computer actually understands the machine language, which consists of only numbers.
- Second-generation programming languages comprise the assembly languages which use symbols to represent machine language instructions.
- Assembly languages are symbolic programming languages that use symbolic notation to represent machine-language instructions.
- An assembly language statement consists of a label, an operation code, and one or more operands.
- Once the modules are coded and tested, the object files of all the modules are combined together by the linker to form the final executable file.
- 3GLs (like FORTRAN, COBOL) made it possible for scientists and business people to write programs.

- While working with 4GLs, programmers define only what they want the computer to do, without supplying all the details of how it has to be done.
- 5GLs are centred on solving problems using the constraints given to the program rather than using an algorithm written by a programmer. They are widely used in artificial intelligence research.
- Object oriented programming (OOP) emphasizes on classes and objects.
- Programs written using monolithic programming languages such as assembly language and BASIC consist of global data and sequential code.
- In procedural languages, a program is divided into n number of subroutines that access global data.
- Structured programming employs a top-down approach in which the overall program structure is broken down into separate modules.
- In unstructured programming, programmers write small and simple programs consisting of only one main program.
- OOP treats data as a critical element in the program development and restricts its flow freely around the system.
- A class provides a template or a blueprint that describes the structure and behaviour of a set of similar objects.

Glossary

Data abstraction Creating a new data type using encapsulated items that is well suited for an application.

Data encapsulation A also called data hiding, and is the technique of packing data and functions into a single component (class) to hide implementation details of a class from users.

Functional abstraction A technique that allows a programmer to concentrate on what a function (or module) does and not on how it does.

Inheritance A concept of object oriented programming in which a new class is created from an existing class.

Machine language The lowest level of programming that was used to program the first stored-program computer systems and is the only language that the computer understands.

Method Function associated with a class.

Multiple inheritance A technique that allows a sub class to inherit properties and methods from multiple parent classes.

Object An instance of a class.

Polymorphism A concept that enables programmers to assign a different meaning or usage to a variable, function, or an object in different contexts.

Programming language A language specifically designed to express computations that can be performed the computer.

Programming paradigm A fundamental style of programming that defines how the structure and basic elements of a computer program will be built.

Programming The process of writing a program.

Repetition A technique that allows a selected statement to remain active until the program reaches a point where there is a need for some other action to take place.

Selection A technique that allows for choosing any one of a number of statements to execute, based on the current status of the program.

Sequential code Code in which all the instructions are executed in the specified sequence one by one.

Exercises

Fill in the Blanks

1. Programming languages have a vocabulary of _____ and _____ for instructing a computer to perform specific tasks.
2. Assembly language uses _____ to write programs.
3. An assembly language statement consists of a _____, _____, and _____.
4. The output of an assembler is a _____ file.
5. A typical example of a 4GL is the _____.
6. Examples of a 5GL include _____, _____, and _____.
7. _____ is used to convert assembly-level program into machine language.
8. _____ and _____ are used to translate the instructions written in high-level language into computer-executable machine language.
9. Fifth generation programming languages are widely used in _____.
10. _____ defines the structure of a program.
11. _____ programming emphasizes on classes and objects.
12. Logic-oriented programming focus on _____ expressed in _____.
13. Two examples of languages that support monolithic programming paradigm are _____ and _____.
14. FORTRAN and COBOL are two popular _____ programming languages.
15. Functional abstraction was first supported by _____ programming.
16. An object contains _____ and _____.
17. _____ paradigm supports bottom-up approach of problem solving.
18. _____ provides a template that describes the structure and behaviour of an object.
19. While _____ is a logical structure, _____ is a physical actuality.
20. State defines the _____.
21. The data that is transferred with the message is called _____.
22. A message consists of _____, _____, and _____.
23. Inheritance relation is also called as _____ relation.
24. _____ is related to classes and their hierarchy.
25. Polymorphism is related to _____.
26. Any data or function with access level _____ can be accessed by any function belonging to any class.
27. Programs written in _____ are robust, secure, and reliable.
28. In Python, the word 'polymorphism' is often is used with _____.

State True or False

1. A programming language provides a blueprint to write a program to solve a particular problem.
2. Machine language is the lowest level of language.
3. Machine/assembly language was used in first generation of computers.
4. Assembly language code is machine-dependent.
5. Code written in machine language is not portable.
6. Nonprocedural code that illustrates the 'how' aspect of the task is a feature of 3GL.
7. Constraint-based programming is used for hypothesis derivation.
8. In monolithic paradigm, global data can be accessed and modified from any part of the program.
9. Monolithic program has two modules.
10. Monolithic programs are easy to debug and maintain.
11. Structured programming is based on modularization.
12. Object oriented programming supports modularization.
13. Structured programming heavily used goto statements.
14. Modules enhance the programmer's productivity.
15. A structured program takes more time to be written than other programs.
16. The interface specifies how to send a message to the object.
17. OOP does not support modularization.
18. A class is a user-defined data type.
19. Once a class is declared, a programmer can create maximum 10 objects of that class.
20. Polymorphism means several different forms.
21. Any data or function with access level private can be accessed only by that class or by any class that is inherited from it.
22. OOP helps to develop secure programs.
23. It is difficult to manage software complexity in object oriented programs.
24. Programs written using object oriented languages have greater processing overhead.
25. Fourth-generation programming languages are non-procedural languages.

26. Labels are optional in assembly language.
27. Pascal cannot be used for writing well-structured programs.
28. Assembly language is a low-level programming language.
29. Python is a 4GL.
30. Python support OOP.

Multiple Choice Questions

1. Which is the fastest and the most efficient language?
   (a) Machine level
   (b) Assembly
   (c) High level
   (d) Artificial intelligence

2. FORTRAN, COBOL, and Pascal are examples of which generation language?
   (a) First
   (b) Second
   (c) Third
   (d) Fourth

3. In which generation language does the code comprise instructions written in English-like sentences?
   (a) First
   (b) Second
   (c) Third
   (d) Fourth

4. Which feature is affected by programming paradigm?
   (a) Style of programming
   (b) Capabilities
   (c) Limitations
   (d) All of these

5. C and Pascal belong to which type of programming language?
   (a) Monolithic
   (b) Structured
   (c) Logic-oriented
   (d) Object oriented

6. Which paradigm holds data as a priority?
   (a) Monolithic
   (b) Structured
   (c) Logic-oriented
   (d) Object oriented

7. Two objects can communicate with each other through
   (a) Classes
   (b) Objects
   (c) Methods
   (d) Messages

8. Which concept enables programmers to assign a different meaning or usage to a variable, function, or an object in different contexts?
   (a) Inheritance
   (b) Message passing
   (c) Polymorphism
   (d) Abstraction

9. Which access level allows data and functions to be accessed only by the class in which it is declared?
   (a) Public
   (b) Private
   (c) Protected
   (d) None of these

10. In which of these applications is OOP applied?
    (a) CAD
    (b) CAM
    (c) Compiler design
    (d) All of these

11. Of the following, a 5GL is
    (a) Prolog
    (b) OPSS
    (c) Mercury
    (d) All of these

12. The type of high-level language that uses predicate logic is
    (a) Unstructured
    (b) Procedure oriented
    (c) Logic oriented
    (d) Object oriented

13 The high-level language that is used for numeric, scientific, statistical, and engineering computations is
    (a) C
    (b) Basic
    (c) Java
    (d) FORTRAN

14. The most portable language is
    (a) C
    (b) Basic
    (c) Java
    (d) FORTRAN

15. Which of the following languages does not need any translator?
    (a) Machine language
    (b) 3GL
    (c) Assembly language
    (d) 4GL

16. The language that is used to program the first-stored program computer systems is
    (a) Machine language
    (b) Assembly language
    (c) Pascal
    (d) Fortran

17. The advantages of modularization are
    (a) Reusability
    (b) Enhanced productivity
    (c) Less time to develop
    (d) All of these

18. You can use Python for
    (a) Application programming
    (b) Web programming
    (c) Scientific computing
    (d) All of these

Review Questions

1. What is a programming language?
2. Define programming.
3. State the factors that a user should consider to choose a particular programming language.
4. Write a short note on generation of programming languages.
5. What is machine language? Do we still use it?

6. A code written in machine language is efficient and fast to execute. Comment.
7. How is a third generation programming language better than its predecessors?
8. 4GL code enhances the productivity of the programmers. Justify.
9. What do you understand by the term 'programming paradigm'?
10. Discuss any three programming paradigms in detail.
11. How is structured programming better than monolithic programming?
12. Describe the special characteristics of monolithic programming.
13. Explain how functional abstraction is achieved in structured programming.
14. Write a short note on structured programming.
15. What are the advantages of modularization?
16. How can you categorize high-level languages?

17. Differentiate between a procedural language and an object oriented language.
18. Explain the main features of an object oriented programming language.
19. If given a program to write, how will you select the programming language to write the code?
20. Which programming paradigm is data-based and why?
21. Explain the concepts of OOP.
22. Differentiate between a class and an object.
23. How is a message related with a method?
24. Inheritance helps to make reusable code. Justify.
25. What do you understand by the term 'polymorphism'?
26. Why is data abstraction and encapsulation called the building blocks of OOP?
27. Explain the three levels of data protection.
28. What are the merits and demerits of OOP?
29. Can a program written in a high-level language execute without a linker?

Answers

Fill in the Blanks

1. syntax, semantics
2. mnemonic codes
3. label, an operation code, and one or more operands.
4. Object
5. SQL
6. Lisp, ICAD, KL-ONE
7. Assembler
8. Compiler, interpreter
9. Artificial intelligence research.
10. Programming paradigm
11. Object oriented
12. Goals, predicate
13. Assembly language and BASIC
14. 3GL
15. Structured
16. Data and methods
17. OOP
18. Class
19. Class, object
20. values of its attributes at a particular time
21. parameter
22. the receiver object, the name of the method
that the receiver should invoke, and the parameters that must be used with the method
23. is-a
24. Inheritance
25. Methods
26. Public
27. Python
28. inheritance

State True or False

1. False	2. True	3. True	4. True	5. True	6. False	7. False	8. True	9. False
10. False	11. True	12. True	13. False	14. True	15. False	16. False	17. False	18. True
19. False	20. True	21. False	22. True	23. False	24. True	25. True	26. True	27. False
28. True	29. False	30. True						

Multiple Choice Questions

1. (a) 2. (c) 3. (d) 4. (d) 5. (b) 6. (d) 7. (d) 8. (c) 9. (b) 10. (d) 11. (d) 12. (c)
13. (d) 14. (c) 15. (a) 16. (a) 17. (d) 18. (d)

Basics of Python Programming

3.1 FEATURES OF PYTHON

Python is an exciting and powerful language with the right combination of performance and features that makes programming fun and easy. It is a high-level, interpreted, interactive, object-oriented, and a reliable language that is very simple and uses English-like words. It has a vast library of modules to support integration of complex solutions from pre-built components.

Python is an open-source project, supported by many individuals. It is a platform-independent, scripted language, with complete access to operating system APIs. This allows users to integrate applications seamlessly to create high-powered, highly-focused applications. Python is a complete programming language with the following features.

Simple Python is a simple and a small language. Reading a program written in Python feels almost like reading English. This is in fact the greatest strength of Python which allows programmers to concentrate on the solution to the problem rather than the language itself.

Easy to Learn A Python program is clearly defined and easily readable. The structure of the program is very simple. It uses few keywords and a clearly defined syntax. This makes it easy for just anyone to pick up the language quickly.

Versatile Python supports development of a wide range of applications ranging from simple text processing to WWW browsers to games.

Free and Open Source Python is an example of an *open source software*. Therefore, anyone can freely distribute it, read the source code, edit it, and even use the code to write new (free) programs.

> **Note** Python has been constantly improved by a community of users who have always strived hard to take it to the next level.

High-level Language When writing programs in Python, the programmers don't have to worry about the low-level details like managing memory used by the program, etc. They just need to concentrate on writing solutions of the current problem at hand.

Interactive Programs in Python work in interactive mode which allows interactive testing and debugging of pieces of code. Programmers can easily interact with the interpreter directly at the Python prompt to write their programs.

Portable Python is a portable language and hence the programs behave the same on a wide variety of hardware platforms and has the same interface on all platforms. The programs work on any of the operating systems like Linux, Windows, FreeBSD, Macintosh, Solaris, OS/2, Amiga, AROS, AS/400, BeOS, OS/390, z/OS, Palm OS, QNX, VMS, Psion, Acorn RISC OS, VxWorks, PlayStation, Sharp Zaurus, Windows CE, and even Pocket PC without requiring any changes.

> **Note**   A good Python program must not use any system specific feature.

Object Oriented Python supports object-oriented as well as procedure-oriented style of programming. While object-oriented technique encapsulates data and functionalities within objects, *procedure-oriented* technique, on the other hand, builds the program around procedures or functions which are nothing but reusable pieces of programs. Python is powerful yet a simple language for implementing OOP concepts, especially when compared to languages like C++ or Java.

Interpreted We have already seen the difference between a compiler and a linker in Chapter 1. We know that an interpreted language has a simpler execute cycle and also works faster.

   Python is processed at run-time by the interpreter. So, there is no need to compile a program before executing it. You can simply *run* the program. Basically, Python converts the source code into an intermediate form called *bytecode,* which is then translated into the native language of your computer so that it can be executed. Bytecodes makes the Python code portable since users just have to copy the code and run it without worrying about compiling, linking, and loading processes.

> **Note**   The Python interpreter can run interactively to support program development and testing.

Dynamic Python executes dynamically. Programs written in Python can be copied and used for flexible development of applications. If there is any error, it is reported at run-time to allow interactive program development.

Extensible Since Python is an open source software, anyone can add low-level modules to the Python interpreter. These modules enable programmers to add to or customize their tools to work more efficiently. Moreover, if you want a piece of code not to be accessible for everyone, then you can even code that part of your program in C or C++ and then use them from your Python program.

Embeddable Programmers can embed Python within their C, C++, COM, ActiveX, CORBA, and Java programs to give 'scripting' capabilities for users.

Extensive Libraries Python has a huge library that is easily portable across different platforms. These library functions are compatible on UNIX, Windows, Macintosh, etc. and allows programmers to perform a wide range of applications varying from text processing, maintaining databases, to GUI programming.

   Besides the above stated features, Python has a big list of good features, such as

Easy Maintenance Code written in Python is easy to maintain.

Secure The Python language environment is secure from tampering. Modules can be distributed to prevent altering the source code. Apart from this, additional security checks can be easily added to implement additional security features.

Robust Python programmers cannot manipulate memory directly. Moreover, errors are raised as exceptions that can be catch and handled by the program code. For every syntactical mistake, a simple and easy to interpret message is displayed. All these things makes the language robust.

Multi-threaded Python supports multi-threading, that is executing more than one process of a program simultaneously. It also allows programmers to perform process management tasks.

Garbage Collection The Python run-time environment handles garbage collection of all Python objects. For this, a reference counter is maintained to assure that no object that is currently in use is deleted. An object that is no longer used or has gone out of scope are eligible for garbage collection. This frees the programmers from the worry of memory leak (failure to delete) and dangling reference (deleting too early) problems. However, the programmers can still perform memory management functions by explicitly deleting an unused object.

Limitations of Python

- Parallel processing can be done in Python but not as elegantly as done in some other languages (like JavaScript and Go Lang).
- Being an interpreted language, Python is slow as compared to C/C++. Python is not a very good choice for those developing a high-graphic 3d game that takes up a lot of CPU.
- As compared to other languages, Python is evolving continuously and there is little substantial documentation available for the language.
- As of now, there are few users of Python as compared to those using C, C++ or Java.
- It lacks true multiprocessor support.
- It has very limited commercial support point.
- Python is slower than C or C++ when it comes to computation of heavy tasks and desktop applications.
- It is difficult to pack up a big Python application into a single executable file. This makes it difficult to distribute Python to non-technical users.

> **Note**   BitTorrent, YouTube, Dropbox, Deluge, Cinema 4D, and Bazaar are a few globally-used applications based on Python.

3.2 HISTORY OF PYTHON

Python was developed by Guido van Rossum in the late 80's and early 90's at the National Research Institute for Mathematics and Computer Science in the Netherlands. It has been derived from many languages such as ABC, Modula-3, C, C++, Algol-68, SmallTalk, Unix shell, and other scripting languages. Since early 90's Python has been improved tremendously. Its version 1.0 was released in 1991, which introduced several new functional programming tools. While version 2.0 included list comprehensions and was released in 2000 by the BeOpen Python Labs team. Python 2.7 which is still used today will be supported until 2020. But there will be no 2.8, instead, support team will continue to support version 2.7 and concentrate further development of Python 3. Currently, Python 3.6.4 is already available. The newer versions have better features like flexible string representation, etc.

The difference between 2.x and 3.x versions of Python are discussed in detail Annexure 3.

Although Python is copyrighted, its source code is available under the GNU General Public License (GPL) like that of Perl. Python is currently maintained by a core development team at the institute which is directed by Guido van Rossum.

These days, from data to web development, Python has emerged as a very powerful and popular language. It would be surprising to know that Python is actually older than Java, R, and JavaScript.

Why is it called 'Python'?

Python language was released by its designer, Guido Van Rossum, in February 1991 while working for CWI (also known as Stichting Mathematisch Centrum). At the time he began implementing this language, he was also reading the published scripts from Monty Python's Flying Circus (a BBC comedy series from the 70's). Rossum wanted a name that was short, unique, and slightly mysterious. Since, he was a fan of the show he thought Python would be the perfect name for the new language.

Applications of Python

Since its origin in 1989, Python has grown to become part of a plethora of web-based, desktop-based, graphic design, scientific, and computational applications. With Python being freely available for Windows,

Mac OS X, and Linux/UNIX, its popularity of use is constantly increasing. Some of the key applications of Python include:

Python is a high-level general purpose programming language that is used to develop a wide range of applications including image processing, text processing, web, and enterprise level applications using scientific and numeric data from network.

- *Embedded scripting language*: Python is used as an embedded scripting language for various testing/building/ deployment/monitoring frameworks, scientific apps, and quick scripts.
- *3D Software:* 3D software like Maya uses Python for automating small user tasks, or for doing more complex integration such as talking to databases and asset management systems.
- *Web development:* Python is an easily extensible language that provides good integration with database and other web standards. Therefore, it is a popular language for web development. For example, website *Quora* has a lot of code written in Python. Besides this, *Odoo, a* consolidated suite of business applications and *Google App engine* are other popular web applications based on Python.

For web development, Python has frameworks such as `Django` and `Pyramid`, micro-frameworks such as `Flask` and `Bottle`, and advanced content management systems such as `Plone` and `django CMS`. These frameworks provide libraries and modules which simplifies content management, interaction with database, and interfacing with different internet protocols such as HTTP, SMTP, XML-RPC, FTP, and POP.

- *GUI-based desktop applications:* Simple syntax, modular architecture, rich text processing tools, and the ability to work on multiple operating systems makes Python a preferred choice for developing desktop-based applications. For this, Python has various GUI toolkits like wxPython, PyQt, or PyGtk which help developers create highly functional Graphical User Interface (GUI) including,
- *Image processing and graphic design applications:* Python is used to make 2D imaging software such as `Inkscape`, `GIMP`, `Paint Shop Pro`, and `Scribus`. It is also used to make 3D animation packages, like `Blender`, `3ds Max`, `Cinema 4D`, `Houdini`, `Lightwave`, and `Maya`.
- *Scientific and computational applications:* Features like high speed, productivity, and availability of tools, such as `Scientific Python` and `Numeric Python`, have made Python a preferred language to perform computation and processing of scientific data. 3D modeling software, such as `FreeCAD`, and finite element method software, like `Abaqus`, are coded in Python.

Moreover, `SciPy` is a collection of packages for mathematics, science, and engineering; Pandas is a data analysis and modeling library and `IPython` is a powerful interactive shell that supports ease of editing and recording a work session. In addition to this, `IPython` supports visualizations and parallel computing.

- *Games:* Python has various modules, libraries, and platforms that support development of games. While `PySoy` is a `3D` game engine, `PyGame` on the other hand provides functionality and a library for game development. Games like `Civilization-IV`, `Disney's Toontown Online`, `Vega Strike`, etc. are coded using Python.
- *Enterprise and business applications:* Simple and reliable syntax, modules and libraries, extensibility, and scalability together make Python a suitable coding language for customizing larger applications. For example, `Reddit` which was originally written in Common Lips, was rewritten in Python in 2005. A large part of `Youtube` code is also written in Python.
- *Operating Systems:* Python forms an integral part of Linux distributions. For example, Ubuntu's Ubiquity Installer, and Fedora's and Red Hat Enterprise Linux's Anaconda Installer are written in Python. Gentoo Linux uses Python for Portage, its package management system.
- *Language Development:* Python's design and module architecture is used to develop other languages. For example, `Boo` language uses an object model, syntax, and indentation, similar to Python. `Apple's Swift`, `CoffeeScript`, `Cobra`, and `OCaml` all have syntax similar to Python.

- *Prototyping:* Since Python is very easy to learn and an open source language, it is widely used for prototype development. Moreover, agility, extensibility, and scalability of code written in Python supports faster development from initial prototype.
- *Network Programming:* Python is used for network programming as it has easy to use socket interface, functions for email processing, and support for FTP, IMAP, and other Internet protocols.
- *Teaching:* Python is a perfect language for teaching programming skills at the introductory as well as advanced level.

3.3 THE FUTURE OF PYTHON

Python has a huge user base that is constantly growing. It is a stable language that is going to stay for long. The strength of Python can be understood from the fact that this programming language is the most preferred language of companies, such as Nokia, Google, and YouTube, as well as NASA for its easy syntax. Python has a bright future ahead of it supported by a huge community of OS developers. The support for multiple programming paradigms including object-oriented Python programming, functional Python programming, and parallel programming models makes it an ideal choice for the programmers. Based on the data from Google Trends and other relevant websites, Python is amongst the top five most preferred languages in academics as well industry.

Python is a high-speed dynamic language. Therefore, it works well in applications like photo development and has been embedded in programs such as GIMP and Paint Shop Pro. In fact, the YouTube architect, Cuong Do, has appreciated this language for record speed with which the language allows them to work. The best part is that more and more companies have started using Python for a broader range of applications ranging from social networks, through automation to science calculations.

3.4 WRITING AND EXECUTING FIRST PYTHON PROGRAM

Here onwards, we will be using Python, via the Python console. For that you need to first download Python from www.Python.org. The codes in this book have been developed on Python 3.4.1. But they can also be executed on newer versions like Python 3.5 and 3.6.

Once installed, the Python console can be accessed in several ways. We will discuss only two of them here. First, using the command line and running the Python interpreter directly. Second, using a GUI software that comes installed with Python called Python's Integrated Development and Learning Environment (IDLE), as shown in Figure 3.1.

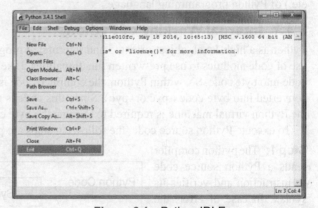

Figure 3.1 Python IDLE

When you run the IDLE, you get a prompt of three right arrows. Type in your instructions at the prompt and press enter. Let us print Hello World!!! on the screen. For this, simply type the following line on the IDLE.

| Example 3.1 | To print a message on the screen |

```
>>> print("Hello World!!!")
Hello World!!!
```

> **Note**   The `>>>` symbol denotes the Python prompt.

Python IDLE works on different platforms (like Windows, Unix, and Mac OS X) in almost the same way. It contains the shell window, an interactive interpreter, debugger, and a multi-window text editor that has features like Python colorizing, smart indent, call tips, and auto completion.

Programmers can even use the REPL editor to write Python programs. The REPL editor is same as IDLE. But, you can think of IDLE as Notepad and REPL as the NotePad++ editor.

Writing Python Programs

In general, the standard way to save and run a Python program is as follows:

Step 1: Open an editor.

Step 2: Write the instructions.

Step 3: Save it as a file with the filename having the extension `.py`.

Step 4: Run the interpreter with the command `python program_name.py` or use IDLE to run the programs.

To execute the program at the *command prompt*, simply change your working directory to `C:\Python34` (or move to the directory where you have saved Python) and then type `python program_name.py`.

If you want to execute the program in Python shell, then just press `F5` key or click on `Run Menu` and then select `Run Module`.

> **Note**   For exiting from the IDLE, click on `File->Exit`, or, press `Ctrl + Q` keys or type `quit()` at the command prompt.

In the next section, we will read about building blocks (such as constants, variables, data types, operators, etc.) of Python programming language.

3.4.1 Internal Working of Python

Python is a high-level, object-oriented and interpreted programming language like Java. It makes extensive use of code modules to use pre-written functionalities. Like other interpreted languages, Python converts the code into byte code. So, within Python, the compiled code is not converted into machine language. It is rather converted into byte code (.pyc or .pyo). Since this code is not understood by the CPU, an interpreter called the Python virtual machine is required to execute the byte codes (refer to Figure 3.2).

To execute Python source code, the following steps are performed:

Step 1: The python compiler reads a Python source code or instruction and verifies its syntax. In case of error, the translation of instructions is immediately halted and the error message is displayed.

Step 2: In case no error is encountered, the Python code is compiled into an intermediate language called "Byte code".

Step 3: Byte code is submitted to the Python

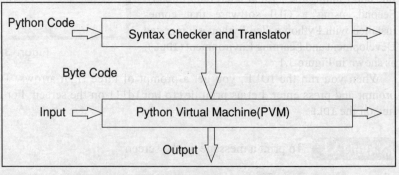

Figure 3.2   Functioning of Python Virtual Machine

Virtual Machine (PVM). PVM is the Python interpreter. It converts the Python byte code into machine-executable code. However, if an error occurs during interpretation, the conversion is halted and an error message is displayed.

3.4.2 Python Tokens

Tokens are the small units of a programming language. Python supports tokens mentioned in Figure 3.3. In this chapter, we will read about literals in detail.

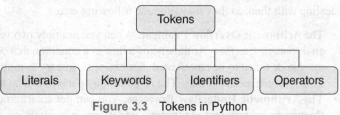

Figure 3.3 Tokens in Python

3.5 LITERAL CONSTANTS

The word "literal" has been derived from literally. The value of a literal constant can be used directly in programs. For example, 7, 3.9, 'A', and "Hello" are literal constants. The number 7 always represents itself and nothing else. Moreover, it is a constant because its value cannot be changed. Hence, it is known as *literal constant*. In this section, we will read about number and string constants in Python.

3.5.1 Numbers

Number as the name suggests, refers to a numeric value. You can use four types of numbers in Python program. These include integers, long integers, floating point, and complex numbers.

- Numbers like 5 or other whole numbers are referred to as *integers*. Bigger whole numbers are called *long integers*. For example, 535633629843L is a long integer. Note that a long integer must have 'l' or 'L' as the suffix.
- Numbers like are 3.23 and 91.5E-2 are termed as *floating point numbers*.
- Numbers of a + bi form (like -3 + 7i) are *complex numbers*.

> **Programming Tip:** You can specify integers in octal as well as hexadecimal number system.

> **Note** The 'E' notation indicates powers of 10. In this case, 91.5E-2 means 91.5 * 10-2.

Types of Integer Literals

There are three types of integer literals–decimal, octal, and hexadecimal integer literal.

Decimal Integer Literal: Any integer literal that does not start with a zero (0) is a decimal integer literal. Example, +17,-26,1234,-89072.

Octal Integer Literal: Any integer literal that starts with digit zero followed by letter o is treated as an octal integer literal in Python. Example, 0o12, 0o7654. Type the following statements in IDLE and see the output.

```
>>> 0o12          >>> -0o12         >>> 0o7654        >>> 0o1789
10                -10               4012              SyntaxError: invalid syntax
Note that decimal equivalent of the octal value is    Digits 8 and 9 are not there
displayed                                              in octal number system
```

Hexadecimal Integer Literal: Any integer literal that starts with digit zero followed by letter x is treated as an octal integer literal in Python. Example, 0x1234, 0xA7B6F.

Remember that commas are never used in numeric literals or numeric values. Therefore, numbers like 3,567 1,23.89 -8,904, are not allowed in Python.

Although, there is no limit to the size of an integer that can be represented in Python, floating-point numbers do have a limited *range* and a limited *precision*. In Python, you can have a floating point number in a range of 10-308 to 10308 with 16 to 17 digits of precision. In fact, large floating point numbers are efficiently represented in scientific notation. For example, `5.0012304*106` (6 digits of precision) can be written as `5.0012304e+6` in scientific notation.

Although floating point numbers are very efficient at handling large numbers, there are some issues while dealing with them as they may produce following errors.

- **The Arithmetic Overflow Problem:** When you multiply two very large floating point numbers you may get an *arithmetic overflow*. Arithmetic overflow is a condition that occurs when a calculated result is too large in magnitude (size) to be represented. For example, just try to multiply `2.7e200 * 4.3e200`. You will get result as `inf`, which means infinity. The result infinity denotes that an arithmetic overflow has occurred.
- **The Arithmetic Underflow Problem:** You can get an arithmetic underflow while doing division of two floating point numbers. Arithmetic underflow is a condition that occurs when a calculated result is too small in magnitude to be represented. For example, just try to divide `3.0e-400/5.0e200`. You will get the result as `0.0`. The value `0.0` indicates that there was an arithmetic underflow in the result.
- **Loss of Precision Problem:** When you divide 1/3 you know that the results is `.33333333…`, where 3 is repeated infinitely. Since any floating-point number has a limited precision and range, the result is just an approximation of the true value.
- Python automatically displays a rounded result to keep the number of digits displayed manageable. For most applications, this slight loss in accuracy is of no practical concern but in scientific computing and other applications in which precise calculations are required, it may be a big issue.

Built-in `format()` Function

Any floating-point value may contain an arbitrary number of decimal places, so it is always recommended to use the built-in `format()` function to produce a string version of a number with a specific number of decimal places. Observe the difference between the following outputs.

```
# Without using format()
>>> float(16/(float(3)))
5.333333333333333
```
```
# Using format()
>>> format(float(16/(float(3))), '.2f')
'5.33'
```

Here, `.2f` in the `format()` function rounds the result to two decimal places of accuracy in the string produced. For very large (or very small) values, 'e' can be used as a *format specifier*.

The `format()` function can also be used to format floating point numbers in scientific notation. Look at the result of the expression given below.

```
>>> format(3**50,'.5e')
'7.17898e+23'
```

The result is formatted in scientific notation with five decimal places of precision. This feature is especially useful when displaying results in which only a certain number of decimal places is needed.

Finally, the `format()` function can also be used to insert a comma in the number as shown below.

```
>>> format(123456,',')
'123,456'
```

Note   The `format()` function produces a numeric string of a floating point value rounded to a specific number of decimal places.

Simple Operations on Numbers

Python can carry out simple operations on numbers. To perform a calculation, simply enter the numbers and the type of operations that needs to be performed on them directly into the Python console, and it will print the answer, as shown in the following examples.

>>>10 + 7 26	>>> 50 + 40 - 35 55	>>> 12 * 10 120	>>> 96 / 12 8.0	>>> (-30 * 4) + 500 380

Note The spaces around the plus and minus signs here are optional. They are just added to make the statement more readable. The code will execute even if you remove the spaces.

In the above example, using a single slash to divide numbers produces a decimal or a float point number. Therefore, internally, 96/12 = 8.0.

Division by Zero Dividing a number by zero in Python generates an error, and no output is produced as shown below.

```
>>>15/0        # generates error
Traceback (most recent call last):
  File "<pyshell#9>", line 1, in <module>
    15/0
ZeroDivisionError: division by zero
```

Thus, we see that the last line of an error message indicates the type of error generated.

Dividing Two Integers We have seen that dividing any two integers produces a floating point number. However, a float is also produced by performing an operation on two floats or on a float and an integer. Observe the following statements. Both these statements when executed results in a floating point number.

```
>>> 5*3.0
15.0
>>> 19 + 3.5
22.5
```

You can easily work with a floating point number and an integer because Python automatically converts the integer to a float. This is known as *implicit conversion* (or type coercion).

Quotient and Remainder When diving two numbers, if you want to know the quotient and remainder, use the floor division (//) and modulo operator (%), respectively. These operators can be used with both floats and integers. Observe the following statements and their output. When we divide 78 by 5 we get a quotient of 15 and a remainder of 3.

>>> 78//5 15	>>> 78 % 5 3	>>> 152.78 // 3.0 50.0	>>> 152.78 % 3.0 2.780000000000001

Exponentiation Besides, +, - , *, and / Python also supports ** operator. The ** operator is used for exponentiation, i.e., raising of one number to the power of another. Consider the statements given below and observe the output.

```
>>> 5**3
125
>>> 121**0.5
11.0
```

3.5.2 Strings

A *string* is a group of characters. If you want to use text in Python, you have to use a string. We have already printed a string in our first program. You can use a string in the following ways in a Python program.

- **Using Single Quotes (')**: For example, a string can be written as `'HELLO'`.
- **Using Double Quotes (")**: Strings in double quotes are exactly same as those in single quotes. Therefore, `'HELLO'` is same as `"HELLO"`.

> **Note**   All spaces and tabs within a string are preserved in quotes (single quote as well as double).

- **Using Triple Quotes (''' ''')**: You can specify multi-line strings using triple quotes. You can use as many single quotes and double quotes as you want in a string within triple quotes.
  An example of a multi-line string can be given as,

```
'''Good morning everyone.
"Welcome to the world of 'Python'."
Happy reading.'''
```

When you print the above string in the IDLE, you will see that the string is printed as it is observing the spaces, tabs, new lines, and quotes (single as well as double).

You can even print a string without using the `print()` function. For this, you need to simply type the string within the quotes (single, double, or triple) as shown below.

`>>> 'Hello'` `'Hello'`	`>>> "HELLO"` `'HELLO'`	`>>> '''HELLO'''` `'HELLO'`

Now, irrespective of the way in which you specify a string, the fact is that all strings are *immutable*. This means that once you have created a string, you cannot change it.

String literal concatenation

Python concatenates two string literals that are placed side by side. Consider the code below wherein Python has automatically concatenated three string literals.

```
>>> print('Beautiful Weather' '.....' 'Seems it would rain')
Beautiful Weather.....Seems it would rain
```

Unicode Strings

Unicode is a standard way of writing international text. That is, if you want to write some text in your native language like Hindi, then you need to have a Unicode-enabled text editor. Python allows you to specify Unicode text by prefixing the string with a u or U. For example,

> **Programming Tip:** There is no char data type in Python.

```
u"Sample Unicode string."
```

> **Note**   The 'U' prefix specifies that the file contains text written in language other than English.

Escape Sequences

Some characters (like `"`, `\`) cannot be directly included in a string. Such characters must be escaped by placing a backslash before them. For example, let us observe what will happen if you try to print `What's your name?`

```
>>> print('What's your name?')
SyntaxError: invalid syntax
```

Can you guess why we got this error? The answer is simple. Python got confused as to where the string starts and ends. So, we need to clearly specify that this single quote does not indicate the end of the string. This indication can be given with the help of an *escape sequence.* You specify the single quote as \' (single quote preceded by a backslash). Let us try again.

```
>>> print('What\'s your name?')
What's your name?
```

> **Note**   An *escape sequence* is a combination of characters that is translated into another character or a sequence of characters that may be difficult or impossible to represent directly.

Similarly, to print a double quotes in a string enclosed within double quotes, you need to precede the double quotes with a backslash as given below.

```
>>> print("The boy replies, \"My name is Aaditya.\"")
The boy replies, "My name is Aaditya."
```

In previous section, we learnt that to print a multi-line string, we use triple quotes. There is another way for doing the same. You can use an escape sequence for the newline character (\n). Characters following the \n are moved to the next line. Observe the output of the following command.

```
>>> print("Today is 15th August. \n India became
independent on this day.")
Today is 15th August.
India became independent on this day.
```

> **Programming Tip:** When a string is printed, the quotes around it are not displayed.

Another useful escape sequence is \t which inserts tab in a string. Consider the command given below to show how the string gets displayed on the screen.

```
>>> print("Hello All. \t Welcome to the world of Python.")
Hello All.    Welcome to the world of Python.
```

Note that when specifying a string, if a single backslash (\) at the end of the line is added, then it indicates that the string is continued in the next line, but no new line is added otherwise. For example,

```
>>> print("I have studied many programming languages. \
But my best favorite language is Python.")

I have studied many programming languages. But my best favorite language is Python.
```

The different types of escape sequences used in Python are summarized in Table 3.1.

Table 3.1   Some of the escape sequences used in Python

Escape Sequence	Purpose	Example	Output
\\	Prints Backslash	print("\\")	\
\'	Prints single-quote	print("\'")	'
\"	Prints double-quote	print("\"")	"

(Contd)

Table 3.1   *(Contd)*

Escape Sequence	Purpose	Example	Output
\a	Rings bell	print("\a")	Bell rings
\f	Prints form feed character	print("Hello\fWorld")	Hello World
\n	Prints newline character	print("Hello\nWorld")	Hello World
\t	Prints a tab	print("Hello\tWorld")	Hello World
\o	Prints octal value	print("\o56")	.
\x	Prints hex value	print("\x87")	+

Raw Strings

If you want to specify a string that should not handle any escape sequences and want to display exactly as specified, then you need to specify that string as a *raw string*.

A raw string is specified by prefixing r or R to the string. Consider the code below that prints the string as it is.

```
>>> print(R "What\'s your name?")
What\'s your name?
```

String Formatting

We have already used the built-in format() function to format floating point numbers. The same function can also be used to control the display of strings. The syntax of format() function is given as,

```
format(value, format_specifier)
```

where, value is the value or the string to be displayed, and format_specifier can contain a combination of formatting options.

Example 3.2   Commands to display 'Hello' left-justified, right-justified, and center-aligned in a field width of 30 characters.

```
>>>format('Hello', '<30')
'                              Hello'
>>> format('Hello','>30')
'          Hello'
>>> format('Hello','^30')
'Hello                              '
```

Here, the '<' symbol means to left justify. Similarly, to right justify the string use the '>'symbol and the '^' symbol to centrally align the string.

We have seen above that format() function uses blank spaces to fill the specified width. But you can also use the format() function to fill the width in the formatted string using any other character as shown below.

```
>>> print('Hello', format('-','-<10'),'World')
('Hello', '----------', 'World')
```

We will learn about string operations later in this chapter.

3.5.3 Slice a String

You can extract subsets of strings by using the slice operator ([ ] and [:]). You need to specify index or the range of index of characters to be extracted. The index of the first character is 0 and the index of the last character is n–1, where n is the number of characters in the string.

If you want to extract characters starting from the end of the string, then you must specify the index as a negative number. For example, the index of the last character is –1. Look at the code given below to understand this concept.

(You can write the program directly on command line or in a new file in IDLE. Small lines of code that we had written so far were written on command line so they started with >>>. But now we will write most of our programs in a new file. There is no compulsion but only for better clarity).

A substring of a string is called a **slice**. You can extract subsets of strings by using the slice operator ([ ] and [:]). You need to specify the index or range of the index of characters to be extracted. The index of the first character is 0 and the index of the last character is n–1, where n is the number of characters in the string.

Index from the start	P	Y	T	H	O	N	Index from the end
	0	1	2	3	4	5	
	–6	–5	–4	–3	–2	–1	

The syntax of slice operation is s[start:end:stride], where start specifies the beginning index of the substring and end is the index of the last character of the string's. *Omitting either start or end index by default takes the start or end of the string. Omitting both means the entire string.*

If you want *to extract characters starting from the end of the string, then you must specify the index as a negative number.* For example, the index of the last character is –1.

Specifying Stride while Slicing Strings: In the slice operation, you can specify a third argument as the *stride.* The stride specifies the number of characters to move forward after the first character is retrieved from the string. By default, the value of stride is 1, which means that every character between two index numbers is retrieved. If the stride is 2, then every second character is accessed, if the stride is 3 then every third character is accessed, and so on.

```
>>> 0x1234          >>> 0xABCD          >>> 0x7B9CF1          >>> 0xTG1F
4660                43981               8101105               SyntaxError: invalid token

Note that decimal equivalent of the hexadecimal value    Digits T and G are not there
is displayed                                             in hexadecimal number system
```

Example 3.3	Program for performing slice operation on strings

```
# String Operations
str = 'Python is Easy !!!'
print(str)
print(str[0])
print(str[3:9])
print(str[4:])
print(str[-1])
print(str[:5])
print(str * 2)
print(str + "ISN'T IT?")
```

```
OUTPUT
Python is Easy !!!
P
hon is

on is Easy !!!
!
Pytho
Python is Easy !!!Python is Easy !!!
Python is Easy !!!ISN'T IT?
```

3.6   VARIABLES AND IDENTIFIERS

Using just literal constants, nothing much can be done in programs. For developing little complex programs, we must store information to manipulate it as and when required. This is where *variables* can help.

Variable, in simple terms, means something that may change. We can store any piece of information in a variable and this information may change. For example, a variable today_temp may have value = 30 today but tomorrow it may be 29 or 31.

Thus, we see that in Python, a variable represents a named location that has a value that can be processed as and when required (like for calculating values).

To be identified easily, each variable is given an appropriate name. Variable names are examples of **identifiers**. *Identifiers,* as the name suggests, are names given to identify something. This something can be a variable, function, class, module, or another object. For naming any identifier, there are some basic rules that you must follow. These rules are:

> **Note**   Python is a case-sensitive language.

- The first character of an identifier must be an underscore ('_') or a letter (upper or lowercase).
- The rest of the identifier name can be underscores ('_'), letters (upper or lowercase), or digits (0-9).
- Identifier names are case-sensitive. For example, myvar and myVar are **not** the same.
- Punctuation characters such as @, $, and % are not allowed within identifiers.

Examples of valid identifier names are sum, __my_var, num1, r, var_20, First, etc.

Examples of invalid identifier names are 1num (starting with a digit), my-var (punctuation and special characters not allowed), %check (first character should be an alphabet or an underscore), Basic Sal (space not allowed), H#R&A (special characters not allowed), etc.

Creating Variables

To create a variable in Python, just assign a value to the identifier using the equal to sign (also known as the assignment operator). For example, the following statements create variables with different values in Python.

```
num = 7
float_num = 12.34
ch = 'A'
str = "ABC"
print(num)
print(float_num)
print(ch)
print(str)
```

```
OUTPUT
7
12.34
A
ABC
```

When we create a variable, Python creates labels referring to those values as shown in Figure 3.4.

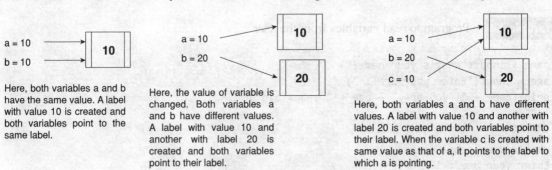

Here, both variables a and b have the same value. A label with value 10 is created and both variables point to the same label.

Here, the value of variable is changed. Both variables a and b have different values. A label with value 10 and another with label 20 is created and both variables point to their label.

Here, both variables a and b have different values. A label with value 10 and another with label 20 is created and both variables point to their label. When the variable c is created with same value as that of a, it points to the label to which a is pointing.

Figure 3.4   Creating Labels

Do you know that Python IDLE remembers variables and their values? Just type the following lines in the command console of IDLE and observe the output.

```
>>> x = 10
>>> y = 20
>>> str1 = "HELLO"
>>> print(str1)
HELLO
>>> print(x * y)
200
```

3.7 DATA TYPES OF IDENTIFIERS

In any programming language, a data type is a classification that specifies which type of value a variable has. It also specifies the type of mathematical, relational, or logical operations that can be applied to it without causing an error. For example, a string data type is used to hold textual data. An integer is a data type that can store whole numbers.

Python has various standard data types that are used to define the operations possible on them and the storage method for each of them. Based on the data type of a variable, the interpreter reserves memory for it and also determine the type of data that can be stored in the reserved memory.

Note Python is a purely object-oriented language. It refers to everything as an object including numbers and strings.

The five standard data types supported by Python include numbers, string, list, tuple, and dictionary. We can even create our own data types in Python (like classes). In this chapter, we will learn about numbers and strings. Other data types will be explored in subsequent chapters.

3.8 INPUT OPERATION

Real world programs need to be interactive. With interactive we mean that you need to take some sort of input or information from the user and work on that input.

To take input from the users, Python makes use of the input() function. The input() function prompts the user to provide some information on which the program can work and give the result. However, we must always remember that the input function takes user's input as a string. So whether you input a number or a string, it is treated as a string only.

Example 3.4   Program to read variables from the user

```
name = input("What's your name?")
age = input("Enter your age : ")
print(name + ", you are " + age + " years old")
```

OUTPUT
```
What's your name? Goransh
Enter your age : 10
Goransh, you are 10 years old
```

Note   In the latest 3.x versions of Python, raw_input() function has been renamed as input().

3.9 COMMENTS

Comments are the non-executable statements in a program. They are just added to describe the statements in the program code. Comments make the program easily readable and understandable by the programmer as well as other users who are seeing the code. The interpreter simply ignores the comments.

In Python, a hash sign (#) that is not inside a string literal begins a comment. All characters following the # and up to the end of the line are part of the comment.

Example 3.5   Program to use comments

```
# This is a comment
print("Hello")  # to display hello
# Program ends here
```

OUTPUT
```
Hello
```

Note that the three comments in the program are not displayed. You can type a comment in a new line or on the same line after a statement or expression.

Note   A program can have any number of comments.

3.10 RESERVED WORDS

In every programming language there are certain words which have a pre-defined meaning. These words which are also known as reserved words or keywords cannot be used for naming identifiers. Table 3.2 shows a list of Python keywords.

Table 3.2 Reserved Words

and	assert	break	class	continue	def	del	elif	else	except
exec	finally	for	from	global	if	import	in	is	lambda
not	or	pass	print	raise	return	try	while	with	yield

Note   All the Python keywords contain lowercase letters only.

3.11 INDENTATION

Whitespace at the beginning of the line is called *indentation. These whitespaces or the indentation are very important in Python.* In a Python program, the leading whitespace including spaces and tabs at the beginning of the logical line determines the indentation level of that logical line.

Programming Tip: Use a single tab for each indentation level.

Note   In most programming languages, indentation has no effect on program logic. It is used to align statements to make the code readable. However, in Python, indentation is used to associate and group statements.

Example 3.6   Program to exhibit indentation errors

```
age = 21
    print("You can vote") # Error! Tab at the start of the line
Traceback (most recent call last):
  File "C:\Python34\Try.py", line 2
    print("You can vote")
    ^
IndentationError: unexpected indent
```

The level of indentation groups statements to form a block of statements. This means that statements in a block must have the same indentation level. Python very strictly checks the indentation level and gives an error if indentation is not correct.

Note   ^ is a standard symbol that indicates where error has occurred in the program.

In the above code, there is a tab at the beginning of the second line. The error indicated by Python tells us that there is an indentation error. Python does not you to arbitrarily start new blocks of statements.
Like other programming languages, Python does not use curly braces ({...}) to indicate blocks of code for class and function definitions or for flow control (discussed later in the book). It uses only indentation to form a block.

Note   All statements inside a block should be at the same indentation level.

3.12 OPERATORS AND EXPRESSIONS

Operators are the constructs that are used to manipulate the value of operands. Some basic operators include +, -, *, and /. In an expression, an operator is used on operand(s) (values to be manipulated). For example, in the expression sum = a + b, a and b are operands and + is the operator.

Python supports different types of operators which are as follows:

- Arithmetic Operators
- Comparison (Relational) Operators
- Assignment Operators
- Logical Operators

- Unary Operators
- Bitwise Operators
- Membership Operators
- Identity Operators

3.12.1 Arithmetic Operators

Some basic arithmetic operators are +, -, *, /, %, **, and //. You can apply these operators on numbers as well as on variables to perform corresponding operations. For example, if a = 100 and b = 200, then look at the Table 3.3 to see the result of operations.

Table 3.3 Arithmetic Operators

Operator	Description	Example	Output
+	Addition: Adds the operands	>>> print(a + b)	300
-	Subtraction: Subtracts operand on the right from the operand on the left of the operator	>>> print(a – b)	-100
*	Multiplication: Multiplies the operands	>>> print(a * b)	20000
/	Division: Divides operand on the left side of the operator with the operand on its right. The division operator returns the quotient.	>>> print(b / a)	2.0
%	Modulus: Divides operand on the left side of the operator with the operand on its right. The modulus operator returns the remainder.	>>> print(b % a)	0

//	Floor Division: Divides the operands and returns the quotient. It also removes the digits after the decimal point. If one of the operands is negative, the result is floored (i.e.,rounded away from zero towards negative infinity).	>>> print(12//5)
		>>> print(12.0//5.0)
		>>> print(-19//5)
		>>> print(-20.0//3)
			2
			2.0
			
			-4
			-7.0

**	Exponent: Performs exponential calculation, that is, raises operand on the right side to the operand on the left of the operator.	>>> print(a**b)	100^{200}

3.12.2 Comparison Operators

Comparison operators also known as *relational operators* are used to compare the values on its either sides and determines the relation between them. For example, assuming a = 100 and b = 200, we can use the comparison operators on them as specified in Table 3.4.

Table 3.4 Comparison Operator

Operator	Description	Example	Output
==	Returns True if the two values are exactly equal.	>>> print(a == b)	False

(Contd)

Table 3.4　(*Contd*)

Operator	Description	Example	Output
!=	Returns True if the two values are not equal.	>>> print(a != b)	True
>	Returns True if the value at the operand on the left side of the operator is greater than the value on its right side.	>>> print(a > b)	False
<	Returns True if the value at the operand on the right side of the operator is greater than the value on its left side.	>>> print(a < b)	True
>=	Returns True if the value at the operand on the left side of the operator is either greater than or equal to the value on its right side.	>>> print(a >= b)	False
<=	Returns True if the value at the operand on the right side of the operator is either greater than or equal to the value on its left side.	>>> print(a <= b)	True

3.12.3　Assignment and In-place or Shortcut Operators

Assignment operator as the name suggests assigns value to the operand. The in-place operators also known as *shortcut operators* that includes +=, -=, *=, /=, %=, //= and **= allow you to write code like num = num + 10 more concisely, as num += 3. Different types of assignment and in-place operators are given in Table 3.5.

Table 3.5　Assignment and in-place Operator

Operator	Description	Example
=	Assign value of the operand on the right side of the operator to the operand on the left.	c = a , assigns value of a to the variable c
+=	Add and assign: Adds the operands on the left and right side of the operator and assigns the result to the operand on the left.	a += b is same as a = a + b
-=	Subtract and assign: Subtracts operand on the right from the operand on the left of the operator and assigns the result to the operand on the left.	a -= b is same as a = a - b
*=	Multiply and assign: Multiplies the operands and assigns result to the operand on the left side of the operator.	a *= b is same as a = a * b
/=	Divide and assign: Divides operand on the left side of the operator with the operand on its right. The division operator returns the quotient. This result is assigned to the operand to the left of the division operator.	a /= b is same as a = a / b
%=	Modulus and assign: Divides operand on the left side of the operator with the operand on its right. The modulus operator returns the remainder which is then assigned to the operand on the left of the operator.	a %= b is same as a = a % b

(*Contd*)

Table 3.5   (*Contd*)

Operator	Description	Example
//=	Floor division: Divides the operands and returns the quotient. It also removes the digits after the decimal point. If one of the operands is negative, the result is floored (rounded away from zero towards negative infinity): the result is assigned to the operand on the left of the operator.	a //= b is same as a = a // b
**=	Exponent and assign: Performs exponential calculation, that is, raises operand on the right side to the operand on the left of the operator and assigns the result in the left operand.	a**= b is same as a = a** b

Note that the in-place operators can also be used on other data types.

Example 3.7   Commands to show the application of the += operator on strings

```
>>> str1 ="Good "
>>> str2 = "Morning"
>>> str1 += str2
>>> print(str1)

Good Morning
```

3.12.4 Unary Operators

Unary operators act on single operands. Python supports unary minus operator. Unary minus operator is strikingly different from the arithmetic operator that operates on two operands and subtracts the second operand from the first operand. When an operand is preceded by a minus sign, the unary operator negates its value.

> **Programming Tip:** Python does not support prefix and postfix increment as well as decrement operators.

For example, if a number is positive, it becomes negative when preceded with a unary minus operator. Similarly, if the number is negative, it becomes positive after applying the unary minus operator. Consider the given example.

```
b = 10
a = -(b);
```

The result of this expression is a = -10, because variable b has a positive value. After applying unary minus operator (-) on the operand b, the value becomes -10, which indicates it as a negative value.

3.12.5 Bitwise Operators

As the name suggests, bitwise operators perform operations at the bit level. These operators include bitwise AND, bitwise OR, bitwise XOR, and shift operators. Bitwise operators expect their operands to be of integers and treat them as a sequence of bits.

Bitwise AND (&)

When we use the bitwise AND operator, the bit in the first operand is ANDed with the corresponding bit in the second operand. The bitwise-AND operator compares each bit of its first operand with the corresponding bit of its second operand. If both bits are 1, the corresponding bit in the result is 1 and 0 otherwise. For example,

```
10101010 & 01010101 = 00000000
```

Bitwise OR (|)

When we use the `bitwise OR` operator, the bit in the first operand is ORed with the corresponding bit in the second operand. The truth table is same as we had seen in `logical OR` operation. The `bitwise-OR` operator compares each bit of its first operand with the corresponding bit of its second operand. If one or both bits are 1, the corresponding bit in the result is 1 and 0 otherwise. For example,

```
10101010 | 01010101 = 11111111
```

Bitwise XOR (^)

When we use the `bitwise XOR` operator, the bit in the first operand is XORed with the corresponding bit in the second operand. That is, the bitwise-XOR operator compares each bit of its first operand with the corresponding bit of its second operand. If one of the bits is 1, the corresponding bit in the result is 1 and 0 otherwise. For example,

```
10101010 ^ 01010101 = 11111111
```

Bitwise NOT (~)

The `bitwise NOT`, or complement, is a unary operation, which performs logical negation on each bit of the operand. By performing negation of each bit, it actually produces the ones' complement of the given binary value. `Bitwise NOT` operator sets the bit to 1, if it was initially 0 and sets it to 0, if it was initially 1. For example,

```
~10101011 = 01010100
```

The truth tables of these bitwise operators are summarized in Table 3.6.

Table 3.6 Truth Tables for Bitwise Operators

A	B	A&B	A	B	A|B	A	B	A^B	A	!A
0	0	0	0	0	0	0	0	0	0	1
0	1	0	0	1	1	0	1	1	1	0
1	0	0	1	0	1	1	0	1		
1	1	1	1	1	1	1	1	0		

3.12.6 Shift Operators

Python supports two bitwise shift operators. They are `shift left (<<)` and `shift right (>>)`. These operations are used to shift bits to the left or to the right. The syntax for a shift operation can be given as follows:

```
operand op num
```

where, the bits in operand are shifted left or right depending on the operator (left if the operator is << and right if the operator is >>) by number of places denoted by num. For example,

```
if we have x = 0001 1101, then
x << 1 gives result = 0011 1010
```

When we apply a left shift, every bit in x is shifted to the left by one place. Therefore, the MSB (most significant bit) of x is lost and the LSB of x is set to 0. Therefore, for example,

```
if we have x = 0001 1101, then
x << 4 gives result = 1010 0000
```

If you observe carefully, you will notice that shifting once to the left multiplies the number by 2. Hence, multiple shifts of 1 to the left, results in multiplying the number by2 over and over again.

On the contrary, when we apply a right shift, every bit in x is shifted to the right by one place. Therefore, the LSB (least significant bit) of x is lost and the MSB of x is set to 0. For example,

```
if we have x = 0001 1101, then
x >> 1 gives result = 0000 1110.
Similarly, if we have x = 0001 1101 then
x << 4 gives result = 0000 0001
```

If you observe carefully, you will notice that shifting once to the right divides the number by 2. Hence, multiple shifts of 1 to the right, results in dividing the number by 2 over and over again.

Note   Bitwise operators cannot be applied to float or double variables.

3.12.7 Logical Operators

Python supports three logical operators—logical AND (&&), logical OR (||), and logical NOT (!). As in case of arithmetic expressions, the logical expressions are evaluated from left to right.

Logical AND

Logical AND operator is used to simultaneously evaluate two conditions or expressions with relational operators. If expressions on both the sides (left and right side) of the logical operator are true, then the whole expression is true. For example,

If we have an expression (a>b) AND (b>c), then the whole expression is true only if both expressions are true. That is, if b is greater than a and c.

Logical OR

Logical OR operator is used to simultaneously evaluate two conditions or expressions with relational operators. If one or both the expressions of the logical operator is true, then the whole expression is true. For example,

If we have an expression (a>b) OR (b>c), then the whole expression is true if either b is greater than a or b is greater than c.

Logical NOT

The logical not operator takes a single expression and negates the value of the expression. Logical NOT produces a zero if the expression evaluates to a non-zero value and produces a 1 if the expression produces a zero. In other words, it just reverses the value of the expression. For example,

```
a = 10, b
b = NOT a;
```
Now, the value of b = 0. The value of a is not zero, therefore, NOT a = 0. The value of !a is assigned to b, hence, the result.

It can be noted that the logical expressions operate in a shortcut (or lazy) fashion and stop the evaluation when it knows the final outcome for sure. For example, in a logical expression involving logical AND, if the first operand is false, then the second operand is not evaluated as it is certain that the result will be false. Similarly, for a logical expression involving logical OR, if the first operand is true, then the second operand is not evaluated as it is certain that the result will be true.

3.12.8 Membership Operators

Python supports two types of membership operators—in and not in. These operators, as the name suggests, test for membership in a sequence such as strings, lists, or tuples that will be discussed in later chapters and are listed below.

in Operator: The operator returns True if a variable is found in the specified sequence and False otherwise. For example, a in nums returns 1, if a is a member of nums.

not in Operator: The operator returns True if a variable is not found in the specified sequence and False otherwise. For example, a not in nums returns 1, if a is not a member of nums.

3.12.9 Identity Operators

Python supports two types of identity operators. These operators compare the memory locations of two objects and are given as follows.

is Operator: Returns True if operands or values on both sides of the operator point to the same object and False otherwise. For example, if a is b returns 1, if id(a) is same as id(b).

is not Operator: Returns True if operands or values on both sides of the operator does not point to the same object and False otherwise. For example, if a is not b returns 1, if id(a) is not same as id(b).

3.12.10 Operators Precedence and Associativity

Table 3.7 lists all operators from highest precedence to lowest. When an expression has more than one operator, then it is the relative priorities of the operators with respect to each other that determine the order in which the expression will be evaluated.

Table 3.7   Operator Precedence Chart

Operator	Description
**	Exponentiation
~, +, -	Complement, unary plus (positive), and minus (negative)
*, /, %, //	Multiply, divide, modulo, and floor division
+, -	Addition and subtraction
>>, <<	Right and left bitwise shift
&	Bitwise 'AND'
^ |	Bitwise exclusive 'OR' and regular 'OR'
<=, <, >, >=	Comparison operators
<>, ==, !=	Equality operators
=, %=, /=, //=, -=, +=, *=, **=	Assignment operators
is, is not	Identity operators
in, not in	Membership operators
not, or, and	Logical operators

Operator precedence table is important as it affects how an expression is evaluated. For example,

```
>>> 10 + 30 * 5
160
```

This is because * has higher precedence than +, so it first multiplies 30 and 5 and then adds 10. The operator precedence table decides which operators are evaluated in what order. However, if you want to change the order in which they are evaluated, you can use parentheses.

> **Note** Parentheses can change the order in which an operator is applied. The operator in the parenthesis is applied first even if there is a higher priority operator in the expression.

Let us try some more codes to see how operator precedence works in our expressions.

```>>> (40 + 20) * 30 / 10``` ```180```	```>>> ((40 + 20) * 30) / 10``` ```180```
```>>> (40 + 20) * (30 / 10)``` ```180```	```>>> 40 + (20 * 30) / 10``` ```100```

Programming Tip: Operators are associated from left to right. This means that operators with same precedence are evaluated in a left to right manner.

Let us take more examples and apply operator precedence on Boolean data types.

```>>>False == False or True```
```True```
```(Because == has a higher```
```precedence than or)```
	```>>>False==(False or True)```
	```False```
	```(Parenthesis has changed```
	```the order of operators)```
		```>>>(False==False) or True```
		```True```

> **Note** Python performs operations in the same order as that of normal mathematics—BEDMAS. That is, Brackets first, then exponentiation, then division, multiplication, and then addition and finally subtraction.

3.13 EXPRESSIONS IN PYTHON

In any programming language, an expression is any legal combination of symbols (like variables, constants, and operators) that represents a value. Every language has its own set of rules that define whether an expression is valid or invalid in that language. In Python, an expression must have at least one operand (variable or constant) and can have one or more operators. On evaluating an expression, we get a value.

Operand is the value on which operator is applied. These operators use constants and variables to form an expression. A * B + C – 5 is an example of an expression, where, +, *, and - are operators; A, B, and C are variables; and 5 is a constant. Some valid expressions in Python are: a x = a / b, y = a * b, z = a^ b, x = a > b, etc. When an expression has more than one operator, then the expression is evaluated using the operator precedence chart.

An example of an illegal expression can be a+, –b, or, <y++. When the program is compiled, it also checks the validity of all expressions. If an illegal expression is encountered, an error message is displayed.

Types of Expressions

Python supports different types of expressions that can be classified as follows.

Based on the position of operators in an expression: These type of expressions include:

- *Infix Expression: It is the most commonly used type of expression in which the operator is placed in between the operands. Example: a = b – c*
- *Prefix Expression: In this type of expression, the operator is placed before the operands. Example: a = –b c*
- *Postfix Expression: In this type of expression, the operator is placed after the operands. Example: a = b c–*

Prefix and postfix expressions are usually used in computers and can be easily evaluated using stacks. You will read about them in data structures.

Based on the data type of the result obtained on evaluating an expression: These type of expressions include:

- *Constant Expressions*: One that involves only constants. Example: 8 + 9 – 2
  Integral Expressions: One that produces an integer result after evaluating the expression. Example:
  ```
  a = 10
  b = 5
  c = a * b
  ```
- *Floating Point Expressions:* One that produces floating point results. Example: a * b / 2
- *Relational Expressions: One that returns either True or False value.* Example: c = a>b
- *Logical Expressions:* One that combines two or more relational expressions and returns a value as *True* or *False*. Example: a>b && y! = 0
- *Bitwise Expressions:* One that manipulates data at bit level. Example: x = y&z
- *Assignment Expressions:* One that assigns a value to a variable. Example: c = a + b or c = 10

3.14 OPERATIONS ON STRINGS

Like numbers, we can also manipulate strings by performing operations on them. In this section, we will read about string concatenation, multiplication, and slicing.

3.14.1 Concatenation

Like numbers, you can also add two strings in Python. The process of combining two strings is called *concatenation*. Two strings whether created using single or double quotes are concatenated in the same way. Look at the codes given in the following example.

Example 3.8 Codes to demonstrate how easily two strings are concatenated

```
>>> print("Missile Man of India" + " - Sir APJ Abdul Kalam")
Missile Man of India - Sir APJ Abdul Kalam
>>> print('Technology ' + ' - Boon or a Bane')
Technology  - Boon or a Bane
>>> print("Prime Minister of India is: " + 'Sh. Narendra Modi')
Prime Minister of India is: Sh. Narendra Modi
```

You can even add numbers as a string. However, adding a string to a number generates an error. These two points may seem the same but they are different. Look at the codes given below.

```
>>> print("Python" + 3.4)
Traceback (most recent call last):
  File "<pyshell#25>", line 1, in <module>

>>> print("Python" + 3.4)
TypeError: Can't convert 'float' object to str implicitly

>>> print("Python" + "3.4")
Python3.4
```

Note that first time we concatenated a string and a number, an error was generated but when we used that number as a string (within quotes), concatenation was done. Now just observe the output of the following statement which concatenates two numbers that are represented as strings.

```
>>> print("12" + "34")
1234
```

3.14.2 Multiplication (or String Repetition)

You cannot add a string and a number but you can definitely multiply a string and a number. When a string is multiplied with an integer *n*, the string is repeated *n* times. Thus, the * operator is also known as string repetition operator. The order of string and integer is not important. Just observe that both the codes given below which produce the same output. However, as a good programming habit, you must write the string first.

> **Programming Tip:** When you multiply a string with a number, the order of the string and the integer doesn't matter, but the string usually comes first.

```
>>> print("Hello " * 5)
Hello Hello Hello Hello Hello
```

```
>>> print(5 * "Hello ")
Hello Hello Hello Hello Hello
```

Remember that you cannot multiply two strings. Also, you cannot multiply a string with a floating point number. Look at the codes given in the following example which illustrates this point.

```
# Multiplying two strings
>>> print("Hello" * "5")
Traceback (most recent call last):
  File "<pyshell#7>", line 1, in <module>
    print("Hello" * "5")
TypeError: can't multiply sequence by
non-int of type 'str'
```

```
# Multiplying a string with a floating
point number
>>> print("Hello" *5.0)
Traceback (most recent call last):  File
"<pyshell#8>", line 1, in <module>
    print("Hello" *5.0)
TypeError: can't multiply sequence by
non-int of type 'float'
```

You can perform string operations on strings as well as on string variables.

Example 3.9   Program that performs addition and multiplication on string variables

```
str = 'Hello '
print(str + '4')
print(str * 5)
```

OUTPUT

```
Hello 4
Hello Hello Hello Hello Hello
```

3.15 OTHER DATA TYPES

In this section, we will take a glimpse of other standard data types in Python.

3.15.1 Tuples

A tuple is similar to the list as it also consists of a number of values separated by commas and enclosed within parentheses. The main difference between lists and tuples is that you can change the values in a list but not in a tuple. This means that while tuple is a read-only data type, the list is not.

Till here, it is fine. But, if you try to write, Tup[2] = 456, that is, to edit the data in a tuple, then an error will be generated.

Example 3.10 Program to demonstrate operations on a tuple

```
Tup = ('a', 'bc', 78, 1.23)
Tup2 = ('d', 78)
print(Tup)
print(Tup[0])        # Prints first element of the Tuple
print(Tup[1:3])      # Prints elements starting from 2nd till 3rd
print(Tup[2:])       # Prints elements starting from 3rd element
print(Tup *2)        # Repeats the Tuple
print(Tup + Tup2)    # Concatenates two Tuples
```

OUTPUT

```
('a', 'bc', 78, 1.23)
a
('bc', 78)
(78, 1.23)
('a', 'bc', 78, 1.23, 'a', 'bc', 78, 1.23)
('a', 'bc', 78, 1.23, 'd', 78)
```

3.15.2 Lists

Lists are the most versatile data type of Python language. A list consist of items separated by commas and enclosed within square brackets ([ ]). For C, C++, or Java programmers, lists are similar to arrays. The only difference in an array and list is that, while array contains values of same data type, a list on the other hand, can have values belonging to different types.

The values stored in a list are accessed using indexes. The index of the first element is 0 and that of the last element is n-1, where n is the total number of elements in the list. Like strings, you can also use the slice, concatenation, and repetition operations on lists.

Example 3.11 Program to demonstrate operation on lists

```
list = ['a', 'bc', 78, 1.23]
list2 = ['d', 78]
print(list)
print(list[0]        # Prints first element of the list
print(list[1:3]      # Prints elements starting from 2nd till 3rd
print(list[2:]       # Prints elements starting from 3rd element
print(list *2)       # Repeats the list
print(list + list2)  # Concatenates two lists
```

OUTPUT
```
['a', 'bc', 78, 1.23]
a
['bc', 78]
[78, 1.23]
['a', 'bc', 78, 1.23, 'a', 'bc', 78, 1.23]
['a', 'bc', 78, 1.23, 'd', 78]
```

3.15.3 Dictionary

Python's dictionaries stores data in key-value pairs. The key values are usually strings and value can be of any data type. The key value pairs are enclosed with curly braces ({ }). Each key-value pair is separated from the other using a colon (:). To access any value in the dictionary, you just need to specify its key in square braces ([ ]). Basically, dictionaries are used for fast retrieval of data.

Note List and dictionary are mutable data types, i.e., their values can be changed.

Example 3.12 Program to demonstrate the use of dictionary

```
Dict = {"Item" : "Chocolate", "Price" : 100}
print(Dict["Item"])
print(Dict["Price"])
```

OUTPUT
```
Chocolate
100
```

3.16 TYPE CONVERSION

In Python, it is just not possible to complete certain operations that involves different types of data. For example, it is not possible to perform "2" + 4 since one operand is an integer and the other is of string type.

```
>>>"20"+"30"        >>> int("2") + int("3")
'2030'              5
```

Another situation in which type conversion is a must is when you want to accept a non-string value (integer or float) as an input. We have read that the input() function returns a string, so we must typecast the input to numbers (integers or floats), to perform calculations on them.

# Without converting the datatype of the input numbers	# Using int for datatype conversion of the input numbers
| ```
x = input("Enter the first number:")
y = input("Enter the second number:")
print(x + y)
``` | ```
x = int(input("Enter the first number:"))
y = int(input("Enter the second number:"))
print(x + y)
``` |
| **OUTPUT** | **OUTPUT** |
| Enter the first number:6
Enter the second number:7
67 | Enter the first number:5
Enter the second number:6
11 |

In such situations, you must perform conversions between data types. Python provides several built-in functions to convert a value from one data type to another. These functions return a new object representing the converted value. Some of them are given in Table 3.8.

Table 3.8 Functions for Type Conversions

Function	Description
int(x)	Converts x to an integer
long(x)	Converts x to a long integer
float(x)	Converts x to a floating point number
str(x)	Converts x to a string
tuple(x)	Converts x to a tuple
list(x)	Converts x to a list
set(x)	Converts x to a set
ord(x)	Converts a single character to its integer value
oct(x)	Converts an integer to an octal string
hex(x)	Converts an integer to a hexadecimal string
chr(x)	Converts an integer to a character
unichr(x)	Converts an integer to a Unicode character
dict(x)	Creates a dictionary if x forms a (key-value) pair

However, before using type conversions to convert a floating point number into an integer number, remember that int() converts a float to an int by truncation (discarding the fractional part) and not by rounding to the nearest whole number. The round() works more appropriately by rounding a floating point number to the nearest integer as shown below.

```
>>> int(2.90)
2
```

```
>>> round(2.90)
3
```

The round() can even take a second optional argument which is usually a number that indicates the number of places of precision to which the first argument should be rounded. For example, round(89.567890,2) returns 89.56.

Note To learn more about a function, you can read its documentation by using the help(). For example, you can write, >>> help(round).

Note that each argument passed to a function has a specific data type. If you pass an argument of the wrong data type to a function, it will generate an error. For example, you cannot find the square root of a string. If you don't know what type of arguments a function accepts, you should use the `help()` before using the function.

Type casting vs Type coercion

In the earlier paragraphs of this section, we have done explicit conversion of a value from one data type to another. This is known as *type casting*. However, in most of the programming languages including Python, there is an implicit conversion of data types either during compilation or during run-time. This is also known *type coercion*. For example, in an expression that has integer and floating point numbers (like $21 + 2.1$ gives 23.1), the compiler will automatically convert the integer into floating point number so that fractional part is not lost.

PROGRAMMING EXAMPLES

Program 3.1 Write a program to enter a number and display its hex and octal equivalent and its square root.

```
num = int(input("Enter a number : "))
print("Hexadecimal of " + str(num) + "  :  " + str(hex(num)))
print("Octal of " + str(num) + "  : " + str(oct(num)))
print("Square root of " + str(num) + " : " + str(num**0.5))
```

OUTPUT

```
Enter a number : 100
Hexadecimal of 100 :   0x64
Octal of 100: 0o144
Square root of 100 : 10.0
```

Program 3.2 Write a program to read and print values of variables of different data types.

```
num = int(input("Enter the value of num : "))
amt = float(input("Enter the value of amt : "))
pi = float(input("Enter the value of pi : "))
code = str(input("Enter the value of code : "))
population_of_India = int(input("Enter the value of population of India : "))
msg = str(input("Enter the value of message : "))
#Print the values of variables
print("NUM = " + str(num) + "\n AMT = " + str(amt) + "\n CODE = " + str(code) + "\n
POPULATION OFINDIA = " + str(population_of_India) + "\n MESSAGE = " + str(msg))
```

OUTPUT

```
Enter the value of num : 55
Enter the value of amt : 879.97
Enter the value of pi : 3.14
Enter the value of code : G
Enter the value of population of India : 7895400000
```

```
Enter the value of message : HELLO
NUM = 55
AMT = 879.97
CODE = G
POPULATION OFINDIA = 7895400000
MESSAGE = HELLO
```

Program 3.3 Write a program to calculate area of a triangle using Heron's formula.

```
(Hint: Heron's formula is given as: area = sqrt(S*(S-a)*(S-b)*(S-c)))
a = float(input("Enter the first side of the triangle : "))
b = float(input("Enter the second side of the triangle : "))
c = float(input("Enter the third side of the triangle : "))
print(a,b,c)
S = (a+b+c)/2
area = (S*(S-a)*(S-b)*(S-c))**0.5
print("Area = " + str(area))
```

OUTPUT

```
Enter the first side of the triangle : 12
Enter the second side of the triangle : 18
Enter the third side of the triangle : 10
12.0 18.0 10.0
Area = 56.5685424949
```

Program 3.4 Write a program to calculate the distance between two points.

```
x1 = (int(input("Enter the x coordinate of the first point : ")))
y1 = (int(input("Enter the y coordinate of the first point : ")))
x2 = (int(input("Enter the x coordinate of the second point : ")))
y2 = (int(input("Enter the y coordinate of the second point : ")))
distance = ((x2-x1)**2+(y2-y1)**2)**0.5
print("Distance = ")
print(distance)
OUTPUT
Enter the x coordinate of the first point : 8
Enter the y coordinate of the first point : 9
Enter the x coordinate of the second point : 10
Enter the y coordinate of the second point : 12
Distance = 3.60555127546
```

Program 3.5 Write a program to perform addition, subtraction, multiplication, division, integer division, and modulo division on two integer numbers.

```
num1 = int(input("Enter two numbers : "))
num2 = int(input("Enter two numbers : "))
add_res = num1+num2
```

```
sub_res = num1+num2
mul_res = num1*num2
idiv_res = num1/num2
modiv_res = num1%num2
fdiv_res = float(num1)/num2
print(str(num1)+" + "+str(num2)+" = "+str(add_res))
print(str(num1)+" - "+str(num2)+" = "+str(sub_res))
print(str(num1)+" * "+str(num2)+" = "+str(mul_res))
print(str(num1)+" / "+str(num2)+" = "+str(idiv_res)+" (Integer Division)")
print(str(num1)+" // "+str(num2)+" = "+str(fdiv_res)+" (Float Division)")
print(str(num1)+" % "+str(num2)+" = "+str(idiv_res)+" (Modulo Division)")
```

OUTPUT

```
Enter two numbers : 5
Enter two numbers : 3
5 + 3 = 8
5 - 3 = 8
5 * 3 = 15
5 / 3 = 1 (Integer Division)
5 // 3 = 1.66666666667 (Float Division)
5 % 3 = 1 (Modulo Division)
```

Program 3.6 Write a program to perform addition, subtraction, division, and multiplication on two floating point numbers.

```
num1 = float(input("Enter two numbers : "))
num2 = float(input("Enter two numbers : "))
add_res = num1+num2
sub_res = num1+num2
mul_res = num1*num2
div_res = num1/num2
print(str(num1)+" + "+str(num2)+" = "+" %.2f"%add_res)
print(str(num1)+" -  "+str(num2)+" = "+" %.2f"%sub_res)
print(str(num1)+" *  "+str(num2)+" = "+" %.2f"%mul_res)
print(str(num1)+" /  "+str(num2)+" = "+" %.2f"%div_res)
```

OUTPUT

```
Enter two numbers : 10.12
Enter two numbers : 56.32
10.12 + 56.32 =  66.44
10.12 -  56.32 =  66.44
10.12 *  56.32 =  569.96
10.12 /  56.32 =  0.18
```

Program 3.7 Write a program that demonstrates the use of relational operators.

```
x = 10
y = 20
```

```
print(str(x)+" < "+str(y)+" = "+str(x<y))
print(str(x)+" == "+str(y)+" = "+str(x==y))
print(str(x)+" != "+str(y)+" = "+str(x!=y))
print(str(x)+" > "+str(y)+" = "+str(x>y))
print(str(x)+" >= "+str(y)+" = "+str(x>=y))
print(str(x)+" <= "+str(y)+" = "+str(x<=y))
```

OUTPUT

```
10 < 20 = True
10 == 20 = False
10 != 20 = True
10 > 20 = False
10 >= 20 = False
10 <= 20 = True
```

Program 3.8 Write a program to calculate area of a circle.

```
radius = float(nput("Enter the radius of the circle : "))
area = 3.14*radius*radius
circumference = 2*3.14*radius
print("AREA = "+str(round(area,2))+"\t CIRCUMFERENCE = "+str(round(circumference,
2)))
```

OUTPUT

```
Enter the radius of the circle : 7.0
AREA = 153.86    CIRCUMFERENCE = 43.96
```

Program 3.9 Write a program to print the digit at one's place of a number.

```
num = int(input("Enter any number : "))
digit_at_ones_place = num%10
print("The digit at ones place of  "+str(num)+" is "+str(digit_at_ones_place))
```

OUTPUT

```
Enter any number : 12345
The digit at ones place of  12345 is 5
```

Program 3.10 Write a program to calculate average of two numbers. Print their deviation.

```
num1 = int(input("Enter the two numbers : "))
num2 = int(input("Enter the two numbers : "))
avg = (num1+num2)/2
dev1 = num1-avg
dev2 = num2-avg
print("AVERAGE = ",avg)
print("Deviation of first num =",dev1)
print("Deviation of second num =",dev2)
```

OUTPUT

```
Enter the two numbers : 7
Enter the two numbers : 10
AVERAGE =  8.5
Deviation of first num = -1.5
Deviation of second num = 1.5
```

Program 3.11 Write a program to convert degrees fahrenheit into degrees celsius.

```python
fahrenheit = float(input("Enter the temperature in fahrenheit : "))
celsius = (0.56)*(fahrenheit-32)
print("Temperature in degrees celsius = ",celsius)
```

OUTPUT

```
Enter the temperature in fahrenheit : 104.3
Temperature in degrees celsius =  40.488
```

Program 3.12 Write a program to calculate the total amount of money in the piggybank, given the coins of Rs 10, Rs 5, Rs 2, and Re 1.

```python
num_of_10_coins = int(input("Enter the number of 10Rs coins in the piggybank : "))
num_of_5_coins = int(input("Enter the number of 5Rs coins in the piggybank : "))
num_of_2_coins = int(input("Enter the number of 2Rs coins in the piggybank : "))
num_of_1_coins = int(input("Enter the number of 1Re coins in the piggybank : "))
total_amt = num_of_10_coins*10+num_of_5_coins*5+num_of_2_coins*2+num_of_1_coins
print("Total amount in the piggybank =",total_amt)
```

OUTPUT

```
Enter the number of 10Rs coins in the piggybank : 6
Enter the number of 5Rs coins in the piggybank : 10
Enter the number of 2Rs coins in the piggybank : 15
Enter the number of 1Re coins in the piggybank : 20
Total amount in the piggybank = 160
```

Program 3.13 Write a program to calculate the bill amount for an item given its quantity sold, value, discount, and tax.

```python
qty = float(input("Enter the quantity of item sold : "))
val = float(input("Enter the value of item : "))
discount = float(input("Enter the discount percentage : "))
tax = float(input("Enter the tax : "))
amt = qty*val
discount_amt = (amt*discount)/100
sub_total = amt-discount_amt
tax_amt = (sub_total*tax)/100
total_amt = sub_total + tax_amt
print("**********BILL***********")
```

```
print(" Quantity sold : \t ",qty)
print("Price per item : \t",val)
print("\n \t \t  ---------------")
print("Amount : \t\t",amt)
print("Discount : \t\t-",discount_amt)
print("   \t \t ------------------")
print("Discounted Total : \t",sub_total)
print("Tax : \t\t\t + ",tax_amt)
print("   \t \t    ------------------")
print("Total amount to be paid ",total_amt)
```

OUTPUT

```
Enter the quantity of item sold : 80
Enter the value of item : 100
Enter the discount percentage :  10
Enter the tax :  14
**********BILL***********
 Quantity sold :      80.0
Price per item :     100.0
           ---------------
Amount :            8000.0
Discount :         - 800.0
          ------------------
Discounted Total :  7200.0
Tax :              +1008.0
          ------------------
Total amount to be paid  8208.0
```

Program 3.14 Write a program to calculate a student's result based on two examinations, 1 sports event, and 3 activities conducted. The weightage of activities = 30 per cent, sports = 20 per cent, and examination = 50 per cent.

```
ACTIVITIES_WEIGHTAGE = 30.0
SPORTS_WEIHTAGE = 20.0
EXAMS_WEIGHTAGE = 50.0
EXAMS_TOTAL = 200.0
ACTIVITIES_TOTAL = 60.0
SPORTS_TOTAL = 50.0
exam_score1 = int(input("Enter the marks in first examination (out of 100) : "))
exam_score2 = int(input("Enter the marks in second examination(out of 100) : "))
sports_score = int(input("Enter the score obtained in sports activities (out of 50)
 : "))
activities_score1 = int(input("Enter the marks in first activity (out of 20) : "))
activities_score2 = int(input("Enter the marks in second activity (out of 20) : "))
activities_score3 = int(input("Enter the marks in third activity (out of 20) : "))
exam_total = exam_score1 + exam_score2
activities_total = activities_score1 + activities_score2 + activities_score3
```

```
exam_percent = float(exam_total * EXAMS_WEIGHTAGE / EXAMS_TOTAL)
sports_percent = float(sports_score * SPORTS_WEIHTAGE / SPORTS_TOTAL)
activities_percent = float(activities_total * ACTIVITIES_WEIGHTAGE / ACTIVITIES_
TOTAL)
total_percent = exam_percent + sports_percent + activities_percent
print("\n\n ********************** RESULT*************************")
print("\n Total percent in examination :", exam_percent)
print("\n Total percent in activities :",activities_percent)
print("\n Total percent in sports", sports_percent)
print("\n --------------------------------------------------------")
print("\n Total percentage", total_percent)
```

OUTPUT

```
Enter the marks in first examination (out of 100) : 95
Enter the marks in second examination(out of 100) : 92
Enter the score obtained in sports activities (out of 50) : 47
Enter the marks in first activity (out of 20) : 18
Enter the marks in second activity (out of 20) : 17
Enter the marks in third activity (out of 20) : 19
 ********************** RESULT*************************
Total percent in examination : 46.75
Total percent in activities : 27.0
Total percent in sports 18.8
 --------------------------------------------------------
Total percentage 92.55
```

Program 3.15 Write a program to convert a floating point number into the corresponding integer.

```
a = float(input("Enter any floating point number = "))
print("The integer variant of ")+str(a)+(" = ")+str(int(a))
```

OUTPUT

```
Enter any floating point number = 56.78
The integer variant of 56.78 = 56
```

Program 3.16 Write a program to convert an integer into the corresponding floating point number.

```
a = int(input("Enter any integer = "))
print("The floating point variant of ")+str(a)+(" = ")+str(float(a))
```

OUTPUT

```
Enter any integer = 123
The floating point variant of 123 = 123.0
```

Summary

- Python is a high-level, interpreted, interactive, object-oriented, and a reliable language that is very simple and uses English-like words.
- Python is an open source project, supported by many individuals. It is a platform-independent, scripted language, with complete access to operating system API's.
- Programmers can embed Python within their C, C++, COM, ActiveX, CORBA, and Java programs to give 'scripting' capabilities for users.
- The Python run-time environment handles garbage collection of all Python objects.
- Unicode is a standard way of writing international text.
- If you want to specify a string that should not handle any escape sequences and want to display exactly as specified, then you need to specify that string as a *raw string*.
- Based on the data type of a variable, the interpreter reserves memory for it and also determines the type of data that can be stored in the reserved memory.
- In Python, you can reassign variables as many times as you want to change the value stored in them.
- The level of indentation groups statements to form a block of statements.
- Trying to reference a variable that has not been assigned any value causes an error.
- A variable of Boolean type can have only one of the two values—True or False.
- The input() function prompts the user to provide some information on which the program can work and give the result.
- Comments are the non-executable statements in a program. They are just added to describe the statements in the program code.
- You can extract subsets of strings by using the slice operator ([ ] and [:]).

Glossary

Comments Non-executable statements in a program added to describe the statements in the program code.
Expressions A combination of values, variables, and operators that performs a specific task.
Identifiers Names given to identify something.
Indentation Whitespace at the beginning of the line.
Operators Constructs used to manipulate the value of operands.

Removing a variable Deleting the reference from the name to the value of the variable.
Reserved Words Words that have a pre-defined meaning in a programming language.
String A group of characters.
Variables Parts of your computer's memory where information is stored.

Exercises

Fill in the Blanks

1. Python converts the source code into an intermediate form called _____.
2. Python supports _____ that is executing more than one process of a program simultaneously.
3. A _____ is maintained to assure that no object that is currently in use is deleted.
4. Garbage collection frees the programmers from the worry of _____ and _____ problems.
5. Python is embedded in programs like _____ and _____.
6. Literals of the form a + bi are called _____.
7. 123.45E-9 is equal to _____.

8. _____ converts an integer to a floating point number.
9. The _____ operator returns the quotient after division.
10. _____ are reserved memory locations that stores values.
11. To find x^y, you will use _____ operator.
12. _____ is a group of characters.
13. _____ is a standard way of writing international text.
14. _____ are parts of your computer's memory where information is stored.

15. R"Hi" indicates that the string a _____ string.
16. Variable names can contain only _____, _____, and _____.
17. _____ of a variable gives an indication of what type of value will be stored in it.
18. Python refers to everything as an _____ including numbers and strings.
19. A variable is automatically declared when _____.
20. A program in Python is stored with a _____ extension.
21. To print Hello, on screen, you will write _____ ("Hello").
22. If, (_____ 7 * −3) + 9 = 30, the fill up the missing character.
23. What should be written in the blank to generate ZeroDivisionError in case of (25+36)/ (−8+_____)?
24. If (2+_____)**2 = 25.
25. To prompt the user for an input, _____ function is used.

26. To print "Python is fun", fill up the blanks.
    print("Python" + '_____ + "_____")
27. A statement block is formed by the level of _____.
28. _____ operators act on single operands.
29. _____ operator performs logical negation on each bit of the operand.
30. If expressions on both the sides of the logical operator are true, then the whole expression is _____.
31. _____ can change the order in which an operator is applied.
32. Fill in the blanks to declare a variable, add multiply 2 to it, and print its value.
    >>>num = 12; x_____ = 2;
    print_____
33. Boolean values in Python are _____ and _____.
34. >>>70 != 80 gives output as _____.
35. 89%0 = _____

State True or False

1. Python uses English-like words.
2. Python is a proprietary programming language.
3. You can call functions of the operating system from a program written in Python.
4. You can make games in Python.
5. A good Python program must use any system specific feature.
6. It is possible to code a part of your program in C or C++ and then use them in a Python program.
7. Code written in Python is difficult to maintain.
8. An object that is currently being used is eligible for garbage collection.
9. Programmers should explicitly delete an unused object.
10. Python has been derived from C.
11. Python supports only object oriented programming paradigm.
12. In Python, integers can be specified in octal as well as hexadecimal number system.
13. All spaces and tabs within a string are preserved in quotes.

14. Each variable has a unique name.
15. You cannot multiply a string with a floating point number.
16. You cannot use single quotes and double quotes in a string within triple quotes.
17. You can print a string without using the print function.
18. char is a valid data type in Python.
19. If you want to specify a string that should not handle any escape sequences, then you need to specify it as a unicode string.
20. Python is a case-insensitive language.
21. Variable names can start with numbers.
22. A variable can be assigned a value only once.
23. Python variables do not have specific types.
24. Keywords cannot be used for naming identifiers.
25. Relational operators are used to compare the values on its either sides.
26. In-place operators can be applied on strings.
27. You can add as well as multiply two strings.

Multiple Choice Questions

1. Identify the words which best describes Python.
   (a) Interpreted   (b) reliable
   (c) simple   (d) All of these
2. Select the integer literal.
   (a) 10.345   (b) 9
   (c) '9'   (d) "9"

3. Which of these will not be stored as a float?
   (a) 23.0   (b) 1/3
   (c) 15   (d) ABC
4. Which operator gives the remainder after division?
   (a) /   (b) //
   (c) %   (d) *

5. Python allows you to specify Unicode text by prefixing the string with which character?
   - (a) U
   - (b) R
   - (c) S
   - (d) A

6. What is the output of this code?
   ```
   >>> print("print '''print hello'''''")
   ```
   - (a) print '''print hello'''print("print hello")
   - (b) An error message
   - (c) 'print print hello'
   - (d) print "print print hello"

7. Which of the following is a valid string literal?
   - (a) "Computer"
   - (b) 'Computer'
   - (c) '''Computer'''
   - (d) All of these

8. Which line of code produces an error?
   - (a) "one" + "2"
   - (b) '5' + 6
   - (c) 3 + 4
   - (d) "7" + 'eight'

9.
   ```
   >>>spam = "eggs"
   >>>print(spam*3)
   ```
   - (a) Spamspamspam
   - (b) eggseggseggs
   - (c) "spamspamspam"
   - (d) spam*3

10. What is the output of this code?
    ```
    >>>int("30" + "40")
    ```
    - (a) "70"
    - (b) "3040"
    - (c) 3040
    - (d) ("30" + "40")

11. What is the output of this code?
    ```
    >>> float("123" * int(input("Enter a number:")))
    Enter a number: 3
    ```
    - (a) "123123123"
    - (b) "369.0"
    - (c) 123123123.0
    - (d) 369.0

12. Identify the correct variable name
    - (a) this_is_a_variable = 7
    - (b) 123abc – 10.22
    - (c) ThisBook = "Python"
    - (d) %name = "xyz"

13. Which of these is a valid variable name in Python?
    - (a) This is a variable
    - (b) This_Is_A_VARIABLE
    - (c) This-is-a-variable
    - (d) ^var

14. A variable can be removed using which _____ keyword.
    - (a) remove
    - (b) clear
    - (c) del
    - (d) delete

15. To specify more than one statements in a single line, use a _____ to separate the statements.
    - (a) ,
    - (b) ;
    - (c) :
    - (d) /

16. The input() function takes user's input as a
    - (a) integer
    - (b) float
    - (c) string
    - (d) character

17. Comments start with which symbol?
    - (a) "
    - (b) //
    - (c) #
    - (d) *

18. Bitwise operator can be applied on which data type?
    - (a) integer
    - (b) float
    - (c) string
    - (d) list

19. Which operator treats operand as a sequence of bits?
    - (a) Relational
    - (b) Arithmetic
    - (c) Bitwise
    - (d) Logical

20. Which operator is also known as string repetition operator?
    - (a) +
    - (b) *
    - (c) &
    - (d) ^

21. If, x = 5; y = ___ ; and print(x+y) gives 12, then y is
    - (a) 7
    - (b) =
    - (c) 7
    - (d) "7"

22. Which of the following results in True?
    - (a) >>>9=9 and 1==1
    - (b) >>>3==5 and 7==3
    - (c) >>>7!=1 and 5==5
    - (d) >>4<1 and 1>6

23. Which of the following results in False?
    - (a) >>>9=9 or 1==1
    - (b) >>>3==4 or 7==7
    - (c) >>>7!=1 or 5==5
    - (d) >>4<1 or 1>6

24. Identify the correct arithmetic expression in Python
    - (a) 11(12+13)
    - (b) (5*6)(7+8)
    - (c) 4*(3-2)
    - (d) 5***3

25.
    ```
    >>> print (format(56.78901, '.3f'))
    ```
    - (a) 56.789
    - (b) 5.6789
    - (c) 0.56789
    - (d) 56789

26. The following statement will produce ___ lines of output.
    ```
    print('Good\n Morning \n World\n ---Bye')
    ```
    - (a) 1
    - (b) 2
    - (c) 3
    - (d) 4

27. Identify the expression that may result in arithmetic overflow.
    - (a) a*b
    - (b) a**b
    - (c) a/b
    - (d) a+b

Review Questions

1. Describe the features of Python.
2. Python has developed as an open source project. Justify this statement.
3. What are literals? Explain with the help of examples.
4. What is implicit conversion? Give an example.
5. List the various operators supported in Python.

6. Explain the significance of escape sequences with the help of relevant examples

7. What are identifiers? List the rules to name an identifier

8. Write a short note on data types in Python

9. Python variables do not have specific types. Justify this statement with the help of an example

10. Differentiate between physical and logical line

11. What are comments? Explain their utility

12. Write a short note on operators supported in Python.

13. With the help of an example explain the concept of string concatenation.

14. Why is * called string repetition operator? Give an example.

15. What is slicing operator? How can you extract a substring from a given string?

16. What is type conversion? Explain the need for type conversion with the help of relevant examples.

17. The statement print "Hello # World" will be executed or not? If yes, justify its output.
    (*Hint: The # inside a string, so it is just considered as a character and not as comment.*)

18. Differentiate between = and ==
    (*Hint: The = is used to assign value but the == is used to test if two things have the same value.*)

19. Is it necessary to put a space between operators and operands?

20. What is wrong in the statement: 1_Singer = 'Sonu Nigam'?

21. Which data type will you use to represent the following data values?
    (a) Number of days in a year
    (b) The circumference of a rectangle
    (c) You father's salary
    (d) Distance between moon and the earth
    (e) Name of your best friend
    (f) Whether you would go for the party?

22. Differentiate between integer and floating point numbers.

23. Express the following floating point numbers in scientific notation:
    (a) 123.45
    (b) 0.005678
    (c) 9.2014

24. Identify the valid numeric literals in Python.
    (a) 5678   (b) 5,678
    (c) 5678.0   (d) 0.5678
    (e) 0.56+10

25. Which of the following expressions would result in overflow or underflow error?

    (a) `1.23e + 150*4.56e + 100`
    (b) `6.78e - 100/4.67e + 200`

26. Identify valid string literals in Python.
    (a) `"Hello"`   (b) `'hello'`
    (c) `"Hello"`   (d) `'Hello there'`
    (e) `' '`

27. Identify valid assignment statements.
    (a) `= b + 1`   (b) `a = a + 1`
    (c) `a + b = 10`   (d) `a + 1 = 1`

28. Evaluate the following arithmetic expressions using the rules of operator precedence in Python.
    (a) `4 + 5*10`   (b) `6 + 7*2 + 5`
    (c) `20//4*2`   (d) `5*6**3`
    (e) `24//6//3`   (f) `4**2**3`
    (g) `100 - (15*3)`   (h) `50%7`
    (i) `-(100/6) + 5`

29. Identify the expressions which will involve coercion and the ones which will involve explicit type conversion.
    (a) `5.0+2`   b. `6.5*3.0`
    (c) `7.0 + float(8)`   d. `6.2*5.0`
    (e) `5.7 + int(9.0)`

30. Write the following values in the exponential notation.
    (a) `1230.4567`
    (b) `0.00000056009`
    (c) `7000809.000000000003`

31. Evaluate the following expressions:
    (a) `True and False`
    (b) `(100<0) and (100>20)`
    (c) `True or False`
    (d) `(100<0) or (100>20)`
    (e) `not(True) and False`
    (f) `not (100<0) or (100>20)`
    (g) `not(True and False)`
    (h) `not (100<0 or 100>20)`
    (i) `not True and False`
    (j) `100<0 and not 100>20`
    (k) `not True and False or True`
    (l) `not (100<0 or 100<200)`

32. Give an appropriate Boolean expression for each of the following.
    (a) Check if variable v is greater than or equal to 0, and less than 10.
    (b) Check if variable v is less than 10 and greater than or equal to 0, or it is equal to 20.
    (c) Check if either the name 'Radha' or 'Krishnan' appears in a list of names assigned to variable `last_names`.
    (d) Check if the name 'Radha' appears and the name 'Krishnan' does not appear in a list of last names assigned to variable `last_names`.

Programming Problems

1. Write a program to enter two integers and then perform all arithmetic operations on them.
2. Repeat the program in Question 1 using floating point numbers.
3. Write a program to perform string concatenation.
4. Write a program to demonstrate printing a string within single quotes, double quotes, and triple quotes.
5. Write a program to print the ASCII value of a character.
6. Write a program to read a character in uppercase and then print it in lowercase.
7. Write a program to swap two numbers using a temporary variable.
8. Write a program to demonstrate implicit conversion.
9. Write a program to demonstrate explicit conversion.
10. Write a program to read the address of a user. Display the result by breaking it in multiple lines.
11. Write a program to read two floating point numbers. Add these numbers and assign the result to an integer. Finally display the value of all the three variables.
12. Write a program to calculate simple interest and compound interest.
13. Write a program that prompts users to enter two integers x and y. The program then calculates and displays x^y.
14. Write a program that prompts user to enter his first name and last name and then displays a message "Greetings!!! First name Last name".
15. Write a program to calculate salary of an employee given his basic pay (to be entered by the user), HRA = 10 per cent of basic pay, TA = 5 per cent of basic pay. Define HRA and TA as constants and use them to calculate the salary of the employee.
16. Write a program to prepare a grocery bill. For that enter the name of the items purchased, quantity in which it is purchased, and its price per unit. Then display the bill in the following format.

```
*************** B I L L ****************
Item Name        Item Quantity      Item Price


*************************************
Total Amount to be paid
*************************************
```

17. Momentum is calculated as, e = mc², where m is the mass of the object and c is its velocity. Write a program that accepts an object's mass (in kilograms) and velocity (in meters per second) and displays its momentum.
18. Write a program that calculates number of seconds in a day.
19. Write a program that prompts the user to enter the first name and the last name. Then display the following message.
```
Hello firstname lastname
Welcome to Python!
```

Find the Output

1. `>>> 250 + 130 - 70`
2. `>>> (32 + 5.2 - 3) * 10`
3. `>>> 100%(45//2)`
4. `>>> 'Python is an interesting language'`
5. `>>> "Python is an interesting language"`
6. `>>>'''Hi … \n`
   `How are you?'''`
7. `>>>print("Python \n is  \n Fun!!!")`
8. `>>>print("Great !!!!"*3)`
9. `>>>4*'2'`
10. `>>>print(3*'7')`
11. `>>>x = 10`
    `>>>x *= 3`
    `>>>print(x)`
12. `>>>x = "Hello, "`
    `>>>x+ = "World!!!"`
    `>>>print(x)`
13. `days = "Mon Tue Wed Thu Fri Sat Sun"`
    `months = "Jan\nFeb\nMar\nApr\nMay\nJun\nJul\`
    `nAug"`
    `print("Days are : "+ days)`
    `print("Months are: "+ months)`
    `print(""" There's a new dream today.`
    `I'll tell you some other day.`
    `Come on, let's enjoy. """)`
14. `# print(1234)`
15. `>>>num1 = 2`
    `>>>num2 = 3`
    `>>>del num1`
    `>>>num2 = 4`
    `>>>num1 = 5`
    `>>>print(num1 * num2)`
16. `>>> num1 = "7"`
    `>>> num1 += "10"`

```
>>> num2 = int(num1) + 3
>>> print(float(num2))
```
17.
```
>>> word = input("Enter a word :")
Enter a word :Hello
>>> print(word + 'World')
```
18.
```
>>> num1 = 9
>>> num2 = num1 + 5
```

```
>>> num2 = int(str(num2) + "4")
>>> print(num2)
```
19. `abs(10-20)`
20. `print(abs(10-20) * 3))`

Find the Error

1. `>>>1+'2'+3+'4'`
2. `>>>'17'*'87'`
3. `>>>'pythonisfun'*7.0`
4.
```
num = 10
print(num)
```
5.
```
sal = 4567.89
print('$' + sal)
```

6.
```
a = 10
b = 20
sum = a + b + c
print(sum)
```

Answers

Fill in the Blanks

1. bytecode
2. multi-threading
3. reference counter
4. memory leak, dangling reference
5. GIMP, Paint Shop Pro.
6. complex numbers
7. `123.45 * 10-9`
8. Implicit conversion
9. `//`
10. Variables
11. `**`
12. String
13. Unicode
14. Variables
15. raw
16. letters, numbers, and underscores.
17. Data type
18. object
19. a value is assigned to it
20. `.py`
21. `print("Hello")`
22. `-`
23. 8
24. 3
25. `input()`
26. `is', fun"`
27. Indentation
28. Unary
29. Bitwise NOT
30. `true`
31. Parentheses
32. `*, num`
33. `True, False`
34. `True`
35. `Error`

State True or False

1. True   2. False   3. True   4. True   5. False   6. True   7. False   8. False   9. True   10. True
11. False   12. True   13. True   14. True   15. True   16. False   17. True   18. False   19. False   20. False
21. False   22. False   23. True   24. True   25. True   26. True   27. False

Multiple Choice Questions

1. (d)   2. (b)   3. (c)   4. (c)   5. (a)   6. (a)   7. (d)   8. (b)   9. (b)   10. (c)   11. (c)   12. (c)
13. (b)   14. (c)   15. (b)   16. (c)   17. (c)   18. (a)   19. (c)   20. (b)   21. (a)   22. (a)   23. (d)   24. (c)
25. (a)   26. (d)   27. (b)

CHAPTER 4

Decision Control Statements

KEY Concepts

- If, If-Else, Nested If Statement • If-elif Statement • While and For Loop • The range() Function • Nested Loop • Break, Continue, and Pass Statement • The else Statement used with Loops

4.1 INTRODUCTION TO DECISION CONTROL STATEMENTS

A *control statement* is a statement that determines the control flow of a set of instructions, i.e., it decides the sequence in which the instructions in a program are to be executed. A control statement can either comprise of one or more instructions. The three fundamental methods of control flow in a programming language are *sequential, selection, and iterative control*.

Till now we have learnt that the code in a Python program is executed sequentially from the first line of the program to its last line. That is, the second statement is executed after the first, the third statement is executed after the second, so on and so forth. This method is known as sequential control flow.

However, in some cases we want to either execute only a selected set of statements (i.e., selection control) or execute a set of statements repeatedly (i.e., iterative control). Thus, the decision control statements can alter the flow of a sequence of instructions. Such type of conditional processing provided by the decision control statements extends the usefulness of programs. It allows the programmers to build a program that determine which statements of the code should be executed and which should be ignored. Figure 4.1 shows the categorization of decision control statements. We will be discussing selection control and iterative control statements in this chapter.

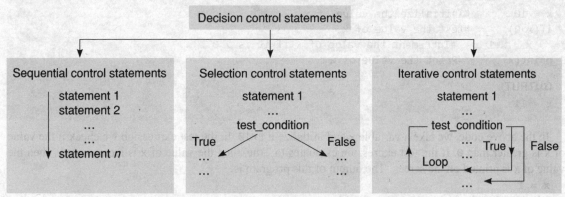

Figure 4.1   Types of decision control statements

4.2 SELECTION/CONDITIONAL BRANCHING STATEMENTS

The decision control statements usually jumps from one part of the code to another depending on whether a particular condition is satisfied or not. That is, they allow you to execute statements selectively based on certain decisions. Such type of decision control statements are known as *selection control statements* or *conditional branching statements*. Python language supports different types of conditional branching statements which are as follows:

- `If statement`
- `If-else statement`
- `Nested if statement`
- `If-elif-else statement`

4.2.1 `if` Statement

The `if` statement is the simplest form of decision control statement that is frequently used in decision making. An `if` statement is a selection control statement based on the value of a given Boolean expression. The general form of a simple `if` statement is shown in Figure 4.2.

The `if` structure may include

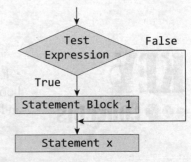

```
Syntax of if Statement

if test_expression:
    statement1
    ......
    statement n
statement x
```

Figure 4.2 `if` statement construct

1 statement or n statements enclosed within the `if` block. First, the `test expression` is evaluated. If the test expression is True, the statement of `if` block (statement 1 to n) are executed, otherwise these statements will be skipped and the execution will jump to statement x.

Programming Tip: Properly indent the statements that are dependent on the previous statements.

The statement in an `if` construct is any valid statement and the `test expression` is any valid expression that may include logical operators. Note that a **header** in Python is a specific keyword followed by a colon. In the above figure, the `if` statement has a header, `"if test_expression:"` having keyword `if`. The group of statements following a header is called a **suite**. After the header, all instructions (or statements) are indented at the same level. While four spaces is commonly used for each level of indentation, any number of spaces may be used.

Note   Header and its suite are together known as a *clause*.

Example 4.1   Program to increment a number if it is positive

```
x = 10        #Initialize the value of x
if(x>0):      #test the value of x
    x = x+1      #Increment the value of x if it is > 0
print(x)      #Print the value of x

OUTPUT
x = 11
```

In the above code, we take a variable x and initialize it to 10. In the test expression we check if the value of x is greater than 0. If the test expression evaluates to True, then the value of x is incremented. Then the value of x is printed on the screen. The output of this program is:

    x = 1

Observe that the print statement will be executed even if the test expression is False. Python uses indentation to form a block of code. Other languages such as C and C++ use curly braces to accomplish this.

PROGRAMMING EXAMPLES

Program 4.1 **Write a program to determine whether a person is eligible to vote.**

```
age = int(input("Enter the age : "))
if(age>=18):
    print("You are eligible to vote")
```

OUTPUT

```
Enter the age : 35
You are eligible to vote
```

Program 4.2 **Write a program to determine the character entered by the user.**

```
char = input("Press any key : ")
if(char.isalpha()):
    print("The user has entered a character")
if(char.isdigit()):
    print("The user has entered a digit")
if(char.isspace()):
    print("The user entered a white space character")
```

OUTPUT

```
Press any key : 7
The user has entered a digit
```

4.2.2 `if-else` Statement

We have studied that using `if` statement plays a vital role in conditional branching. Its usage is very simple. The test expression is evaluated and if the result is `True`, the statement(s) followed by the expression is executed, else if the expression is `False`, the statement is skipped by the compiler.

But what if you want a separate set of statements to be executed when the expression returns a zero value? In such cases, we use an `if-else` statement rather than using simple `if` statement. The general form of a simple `if-else` statement is shown in Figure 4.3.

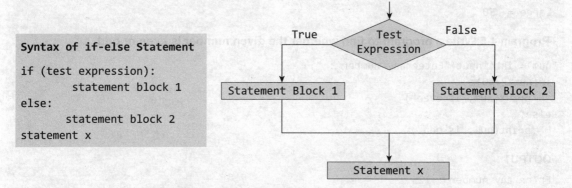

Syntax of if-else Statement

```
if (test expression):
        statement block 1
else:
        statement block 2
statement x
```

Figure 4.3 `if-else` statement construct

In the aforementioned syntax, we have written a statement block. A statement block may include one or more statements. According to the `if-else` construct, first the test expression is evaluated. If the expression is True, statement block 1 is executed and statement block 2 is skipped. Otherwise, if the expression is False, statement block 2 is executed and statement block 1 is ignored. Now in any case after the statement block 1 or 2 gets executed, the control will pass to statement x. Therefore, statement x is executed in every case.

Note   If and else statements are used to determine which option in a series of possibilities is True.

Program 4.3 Write a program to determine whether a person is eligible to vote or not. If he is not eligible, display how many years are left to be eligible.

```
age = int(input("Enter the age : "))
if(age>=18):
    print("You are eligible to vote")
else:
        yrs = 18 - age
        print("You have to wait for another " + str(yrs) +" years to cast your vote")
```

OUTPUT
```
Enter the age : 10
You have to wait for another 8 years to cast your vote
```

Program 4.4 Write a program to find larger of two numbers.

```
a = int(input("Enter the value of a : "))
b = int(input("Enter the value of b : "))
if(a>b):
    large = a
else:
    large = b
print("Large = ",large)
```

OUTPUT
```
Enter the value of a : 50
Enter the value of b : 30
Large =  50
```

Program 4.5 Write a program to find whether the given number is even or odd.

```
num = int(input("Enter any number : "))
if(num%2==0):
    print(num,"is even")
else:
    print(num,"is odd")
```

OUTPUT
```
Enter any number : 125
125 is odd
```

Program 4.6 Write a program to enter any character. If the entered character is in lowercase then convert it into uppercase and if it is an uppercase character, then convert it into lowercase.

```
ch = input("Enter any character : ")
if(ch >= 'A' and ch <='Z'):
    ch = ch.lower()
    print("The entered character was in uppercase. In lowercase it is : " + ch)
else:
    ch = ch.upper()
    print("The entered character was in lowercase. In uppercase it is : " + ch)
```

OUTPUT

```
Enter any character : c
The entered character was in lowercase. In uppercase it is : C
```

Program 4.7 A company decides to give bonus to all its employees on Diwali. A 5% bonus on salary is given to the male workers and 10% bonus on salary to the female workers. Write a program to enter the salary of the employee and sex of the employee. If the salary of the employee is less than ₹ 10,000 then the employee gets an extra 2% bonus on salary. Calculate the bonus that has to be given to the employee and display the salary that the employee will get.

```
ch = input("Enter the sex of the employee (m or f) : ")
sal = int(input("Enter the salary of the employee : "))
if (ch=='m'):
    bonus = 0.05*sal
else :
    bonus = 0.10*sal
amt_to_be_paid = sal+bonus
print(" Salary = ",sal)
print(" Bonus = ",bonus)
print(" ******************************")
print("Amount to be paid : ",amt_to_be_paid)
```

OUTPUT

```
Enter the sex of the employee (m or f) : f
Enter the salary of the employee : 50000
 Salary =  50000
 Bonus =  5000.0
******************************
Amount to be paid :  55000.0
```

Program 4.8 Write a program to find whether a given year is a leap year or not.

```
year = int(input("Enter any year : "))
if((year%4==0 and year %100!=0) or (year%400 == 0)):
    print("Leap Year")
```

```
else:
    print("Not a Leap Year")
```

4.2.3 Nested if Statements

A statement that contains other statements is called a *compound statement*. To perform more complex checks, if statements can be nested, that is, can be placed one inside the other. In such a case, the inner if statement is the statement part of the outer one. Nested if statements are used to check if more than one condition is satisfied. Consider the code given below to understand this concept.

> **Note**   if statements can be nested resulting in multi-way selection.

> **Example 4.2**   Program that prompts the user to enter a number and then print its interval

```
num = int(input("Enter any number from 0-30: "))
if(num>=0 and num<10):
    print("It is in the range 0-10")
if(num>=10 and num<20):w
    print("It is in the range 10-20")
if(num>=20 and num<30):
    print("It is in the range 20-30")
```

OUTPUT

```
Enter any number from 0-30: 25
It is in the range 20-30
```

> **Note**   You can do the same program using if-else and if-elif-else statements.

4.2.4 if-elif-else Statement

Python supports if-elif-else statements to test additional conditions apart from the initial test expression. The if-elif-else construct works in the same way as a usual if-else statement. If-elif-else construct is also known as *nested-if construct*. Its syntax is given in Figure 4.4.

Programming Tip: Do not use floating point numbers for checking for equality in the test expression.

> **Note**   The elif (short for else if) statement is a shortcut to if and else statements. A series of if and elif statements have a final else block, which is executed if none of the if or elif expressions is True.

Note that it is not necessary that every if statement should have an else block as Python supports simple if statements also. After the first test expression or the first if branch, the programmer can have as many elif branches as he wants depending on the expressions that have to be tested. A series of if-elif statements can have a final else block, which is called if none of the if or elif expressions is True.

Programming Tip: Python does not have switch statement. You can use an if...elif...else statement to do the same thing.

Syntax of if-elif-else Statement

```
if ( test expression 1)
    statement block 1
elif ( test expression 2)
    statement block 2
..........................
elif (test expression N)
    statement block N
else
    Statement Block X
Statement Y
```

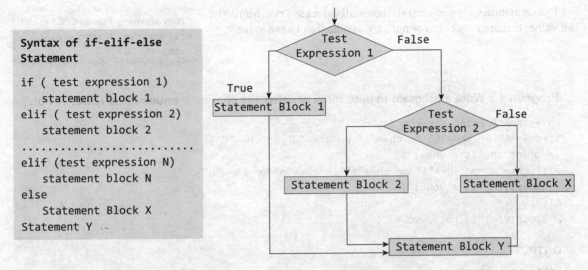

Figure 4.4 `if-elif-else` statement construct

Note The `elif` and `else` parts are optional.

Example 4.3 Program to test whether a number entered by the user is negative, positive, or equal to zero

```
num = int(input("Enter any number : "))
if(num==0):
    print("The value is equal to zero")
elif(num>0):
    print("The number is positive")
else:
    print("The number is negative")
```

OUTPUT
```
Enter any number : -10
The number is negative
```

Note The colons are placed after the `if-else` and the `elif` statements.

In the program to test whether a number is positive or negative, note that if the first test expression evaluates a True value, then rest of the statements in the code will be ignored and after executing the `print` statement that displays "The value is equal to zero", the control will jump to `return 0` statement.

Programming Tip: Keep the logical expressions simple and short. For this, you may use nested `if` statements.

Note Use the AND/ OR operators to form a compound relation expression. In Python, the following expression is invalid.

    if (60 ≤ marks ≤ 75):
The correct way to write is,
    if ((marks ≥ 60) and (marks ≤ 75):

Python assumes any non-zero and non-null values as `True`. Similarly, all values that are either zero or null, are assumed as `False` value.

Programming Tip: In C/C++, `elif` statement is same as `elseif` statement.

Program 4.9 Write a program to determine whether the character entered is a vowel or not.

```python
ch = input("Enter any character : ")
if(ch=="A" or ch=="E" or ch=="I" or ch=="O" or ch=="U"):
    print ch,"is a vowel")
elif(ch=="a" or ch=="e" or ch=="i" or ch=="o" or ch=="u"):
    print(ch,"is a vowel")
else:
    print(ch,"is not a vowel")
```

OUTPUT

```
Enter any character : h
h is not a vowel
```

Program 4.10 Write a program to find the greatest number from three numbers.

```python
num1 = int(input("Enter the first number : "))
num2 = int(input("Enter the second number : "))
num3 = int(input("Enter the third number : "))
if(num1>num2):
    if(num1>num3):
        print(num1,"is greater than",num2,"and",num3)
    else:
        print(num3,"is greater than",num1,"and",num2)
elif(num2>num3):
    print(num2,"is greater than",num1,"and",num3)
else:
    print("The three numbers are equal")
```

OUTPUT:

```
Enter the first number : 13
Enter the second number : 43
Enter the third number : 25
43 is greater than 13 and 25
```

Program 4.11 Write a program that prompts the user to enter a number between 1–7 and then displays the corresponding day of the week.

```python
num = int(input("Enter any number between 1 to 7 : "))
if(num==1): print("Sunday")
elif(num==2): print("Monday")
elif(num==3): print("Tuesday")
elif(num==4): print("Wednesday")
```

Programming Tip: Unlike C/C++, Python uses and, not, or keywords in Boolean expressions. It does not allow symbols &&, ||, ! Boolean logic in `if` statements.

```python
elif(num==5): print("Thursday")
elif(num==6): print("Friday")
elif(num==7): print("Saturday")
else :
print("Wrong input")
```

OUTPUT

```
Enter any number between 1 to 7 : 5
Thursday
```

Program 4.12 Write a program to calculate tax given the following conditions:

```
If income is less than 1,50, 000 then no tax
If taxable income is 1,50,001 - 300,000 then charge 10% tax
If taxable income is 3,00,001 - 500,000 then charge 20% tax
If taxable income is above 5,00,001 then charge 30% tax
```

```python
MIN1 = 150001
MAX1 = 300000
RATE1 = 0.10
MIN2 = 300001
MAX2 = 500000
RATE2 = 0.20
MIN3 = 500001
RATE3 = 0.30

income = int(input("Enter the income : "))
taxable_income = income - 150000
if(taxable_income <= 0):
    print("No tax")
elif(taxable_income>=MIN1 and taxable_income<MAX1):
    tax = (taxable_income - MIN1) * RATE1
elif(taxable_income>=MIN2 and taxable_income<MAX2):
    tax = (taxable_income - MIN2) * RATE2
else:
    tax = (taxable_income-MIN3)*RATE3
print("TAX = ",tax)
```

OUTPUT

```
Enter the income : 2000000
TAX =  404999.7
```

Program 4.13 Write a program to take input from the user and then check whether it is a number or a character. If it is a character, determine whether it is in uppercase or lowercase.

```python
ch = input("Enter the character : ")
if(ch>="A" and ch<="Z"):
```

```
   print("Uppercase character was entered")
elif(ch>='a' and ch<='z'):
   print("Lowercase character was entered")
elif(ch>='0' and ch<='9'):
   print("A number was entered")
```

> **Programming Tip:** Use Boolean logic to check for complicate or multiple conditions in the `if` statement.

OUTPUT

```
Enter any character : C
Uppercase character was entered
```

Program 4.14 Write a program to enter the marks of a student in four subjects. Then calculate the total and aggregate, and display the grade obtained by the student. If the student scores an aggregate greater than 75%, then the grade is Distinction. If aggregate is 60>= and <75, then the grade is First Division. If aggregate is 50>= and <60, then the grade is Second Division. If aggregate is 40>= and <50, then the grade is Third Division. Else the grade is Fail.

```
marks1 = int(input("Enter the marks in Mathematics : "))
marks2 = int(input("Enter the marks in Science : "))
marks3 = int(input("Enter the marks in Social Science : "))
marks4 = int(input("Enter the marks in Computers : "))
total = marks1+marks2+marks3+marks4
avg = float(total)/4
print("Total = ",total,"\t Aggregate = ",avg)
if(avg>=75):
   print("Distinction")
elif(avg>=60 and avg<75):
   print("First Division")
elif(avg>=50 and avg<60):
   print("Second Division")
elif(avg>=40 and avg<50):
   print("Third Division")
else:
   print("Fail")
```

OUTPUT

```
Enter the marks in Mathematics : 90
Enter the marks in Science : 91
Enter the marks in Social Science : 92
Enter the marks in Computers : 93
Total =  366     Aggregate =  91.5
Distinction
```

Program 4.15 Write a program to calculate roots of a quadratic equation.

```
a = int(input("Enter the values of a : "))
```

```
b = int(input("Enter the values of b : "))
c = int(input("Enter the values of c : "))
D = (b*b)-(4*a*c)
deno = 2*a
if(D>0):
    print("REAL ROOTS")
    root1 = (-b + D**0.5)/deno
    root2 = (-b - D**0.5)/deno
    print("Root1 = ",root1,"\tRoot2 = ",root2)
elif(D==0):
    print "EQUAL ROOTS"
    root1 = -b/deno
    print("Root1 and Root2 = ",root1)
else:
    print("IMAGINARY ROOTS")
```

> **Programming Tip:** While forming the conditional expression, try to use positive statements rather than using compound negative statements.

OUTPUT:

```
Enter the values of a, b and c : 3 4 5
IMAGINARY ROOTS
```

Comparing Floating Point Numbers

Never test floating point numbers for exact equality. This is because floating point numbers are just approximations, so it is always better to test floating point numbers for 'approximately equal' rather than testing for exactly equal.

We can test for approximate equality by subtracting the two floating point numbers (that are to be tested) and comparing their absolute value of the difference against a very small number such as epsilon.

4.3 BASIC LOOP STRUCTURES/ITERATIVE STATEMENTS

Python supports basic loop structures through iterative statements. *Iterative statements* are decision control statements that are used to repeat the execution of a list of statements. Python language supports two types of iterative statements — *while* loop and *for* loop. In this section, we will discuss both of them.

4.3.1 while Loop

The while loop provides a mechanism to repeat one or more statements while a particular condition is True. Figure 4.5 shows the syntax and general form of representation of a while loop.

Note in the while loop, the condition is tested before any of the statements in the statement block is executed. If the condition is True, only then the statements will be executed otherwise if the condition is False, the control will jump to statement y, that is the immediate statement outside the while loop block.

In the flowchart, it is clear that we need to constantly update the condition of the while loop. It is this condition which determines when the loop will end. The while loop will execute as long as the condition is True. Note That if the condition is never updated and the condition never becomes False, then the computer will run into an infinite loop which is never desirable.

> **Programming Tip:** Iterative statements are used to repeat the execution of a list of statements, depending on the value of an integer expression.

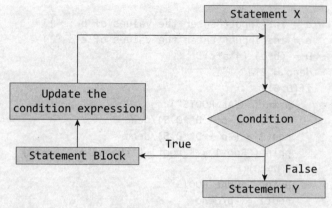

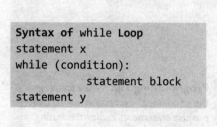

Figure 4.5   The while loop construct

A while loop is also referred to as a top-checking loop since control condition is placed as the first line of the code. If the control condition evaluates to False, then the statements enclosed in the loop are never executed. Look at the following example code.

Example 4.4   Program to print first 10 numbers using a while loop

```
i = 0
while(i<=10):
    print(i,end=" ")
    i = i+1
```

OUTPUT

```
0 1 2 3 4 5 6 7 8 9 10
```

Note that initially i = 0 and is less than 10, that is, the condition is True, so in the while loop the value of i is printed and the condition is updated so that with every execution of the loop, the condition becomes more approachable.

For printing values in the same line, use end with a separator. You can specify any separator like tab (\t), space, comma, etc., with end. Consider the following example.

Note   In simple terms, end specifies the values which have to be printed after the print statement has been executed.

Example 4.5   Program to separate two values printed on the same line using a tab

```
i = 0
while(i<=10):
    print(i, end = '\t')
    i+=1
```

OUTPUT

```
0       1       2       3       4       5       6       7       8       9       10
```

> **Note** If you use end = "", then there will be no space between two values. There is no difference in the way you write the end statement as end = '' or end = "".

Let us now look at some more programming examples that illustrates the use of while loop.

Program 4.16 Write a program to calculate the sum and average of first 10 numbers.

```
i = 0
s = 0
while(i<=10):
    s = s+i
    i=i+1
avg = float(s)/10
print("The sum of first 10 numbers is :",s)
print("The average of first 10 numbers is :",avg)
```

> **Programming Tip:** Check that the relational operator is not mistyped as an assignment operator.

OUTPUT

```
The sum of first 10 numbers is : 55
The average of first 10 numbers is : 5.5
```

Program 4.17 Write a program to print 20 horizontal asterisks(*).

```
i = 1
while(i<=20):
    print("*",end="")
    i = i+1
```

OUTPUT

```
********************
```

Program 4.18 Write a program to calculate the sum of numbers from m to n.

```
m = int(input("Enter the value of m : "))
n = int(input("Enter the value of n : "))
s = 0
while(m<=n):
    s = s+m
    m = m+1
print("SUM = ",s)
```

OUTPUT

```
Enter the value of m : 3
Enter the value of n : 9
SUM =  42
```

Program 4.19 Write a program to read the numbers until -1 is encountered. Also count the negative, positives, and zeroes entered by the user.

```
negatives = positives = zeroes = 0
print("Enter -1 to exit...")
while(1):
    num = int(input("Enter any number : "))
    if(num==-1):
        break
    if(num==0):
        zeroes = zeroes+1
    elif(num>0):
        positives = positives+1
    else:
        negatives = negatives+1
print("Count of positive numbers entered : ",positives)
print("Count of negative numbers entered : ",negatives)
print("Count of zeroes entered : ",zeroes)
```

OUTPUT

```
Enter -1 to exit...
Enter any number : 7
Enter any number : 9
Enter any number : 1
Enter any number : 3
Enter any number : -3
Enter any number : -6
Enter any number : -7
Enter any number : 4
Enter any number : 5
Enter any number : 0
Enter any number : -1
Count of positive numbers entered :  6
Count of negative numbers entered :  3
Count of zeroes entered :  1
```

Program 4.20 Write a program to read the numbers until -1 is encountered. Find the average of positive numbers and negative numbers entered by the user.

```
neg_count = 0
neg_s = 0
pos_count = 0
pos_s = 0
print("Enter -1 to exit...")
num = int(input("Enter the number : "))
while(num!=-1):
    if(num<0):
        neg_count=neg_count+1
        neg_s=neg_s+num
```

Programming Tip: if statement is run once if condition is True, and never if it is False.
A while statement is similar, except that it can be run more than once.

```
    else:
        pos_count=pos_count+1
        pos_s=pos_s+num
    num = int(input("Enter the number : "))
neg_avg = float(neg_s)/neg_count
pos_avg = float(pos_s)/pos_count
print("The average of negative numbers is : ",neg_avg)
print("The average of positive numbers is : ",pos_avg)
```

OUTPUT

```
Enter -1 to exit...
Enter the number : 7
Enter the number : -2
Enter the number : 9
Enter the number : -8
Enter the number : -6
Enter the number : -4
Enter the number : 10
Enter the number : -1
The average of negative numbers is :  -5.0
The average of positive numbers is :  8.66666666667
```

Program 4.21 Write a program to find whether the given number is an Amstrong number or not.

Hint: An **Armstrong number** of three digits is an integer such that the sum of the cubes of its digits is equal to the **number** itself. For example, 371 is an **Armstrong number** since 3**3 + 7**3 + 1**3 = 371.

```
n = int(input("Enter the number : "))
s = 0
num = n
while(n>0):
    r = n%10
    s = s+(r**3)
    n = n/10
if(s==num):
    print("The number is Armstrong")
else:
    print("The number is not Armstrong")
```

OUTPUT

```
Enter the number : 432
432 is not an Armstrong number
```

Program 4.22 Write a program to enter a decimal number. Calculate and display the binary equivalent of this number.

```
decimal_num = int(input("Enter the decimal number: "))
binary_num = 0
i = 0
while(decimal_num!=0):
    remainder = decimal_num%2
    binary_num = binary_num+remainder*(10**i)
    decimal_num = decimal_num/2
    i = i+1
print("The binary equivalent =",binary_num)
```

> **Assignment:** WAP to convert a decimal number into octal and hexadecimal. *Hint:* Instead of dividing by 2, divide by 8 and 16 respectively.

OUTPUT

```
Enter the decimal number : 7
The binary equivalent = 111
```

Program 4.23 Write a program to enter a binary number and convert it into decimal number.

```
binary_num = int(input("Enter the binary number : "))
decimal_num = 0
i = 0
while(binary_num!=0):
    remainder = binary_num%10
    decimal_num = decimal_num+remainder*(2**i)
    binary_num = binary_num/10
    i = i+1
print("The decimal equivalent is",decimal_num)
```

OUTPUT

```
Enter the binary number : 1101
The decimal equivalent is 13
```

Program 4.24 Write a program to read a character until a * is encountered. Also count the number of uppercase, lowercase, and numbers entered by the users.

```
ch = input("Enter any character : ")
num_count = 0
up_count = 0
low_count = 0
if(ch>='0' and ch <= '9'):
    num = num+1
elif(ch>='a'' and ch<='z'):
    low_count = low_count+1
elif(ch>='A' and ch<='Z'):
    up_count = up_count+1
while(ch!='*'):
    ch = input("Enter any character : ")
    if(ch>='0' and ch <= '9'):
```

> **Programming Tip:** Statement inside while loop are repeatedly executed, until condition is True. Once it becomes False, the next section of code is executed.

```
        num_count = num_count+1
    elif(ch>='a' and ch<='z'):
        low_count = low_count+1
    elif(ch>='A' and ch<='Z'):
        up_count = up_count+1
print("Number of lowercase characters are : ",low_count)
print("Number of uppercase characters are : ",up_count)
print("Number of numerals are : ",num_count)
```

OUTPUT

```
Enter any character : O
Enter another character. Enter * to exit. x
Enter another character. Enter * to exit. F
Enter another character. Enter * to exit. o
Enter another character. Enter * to exit.R
Enter another character. Enter * to exit. d
Enter another character. Enter * to exit. *
Total count of lowercase characters entered = 3
Total count of uppercase characters entered =3
Total count of numbers entered = 0
```

> **Programming Tip:** Placing a semi-colon after the while and for loop in not a syntax error. So it will not be reported by the compiler. However, it is considered to be a logical error as it changes output of the program.

Program 4.25 Write a program to enter a number and then calculate the sum of its digits.

```
sumOfDigits = 0
num = int(input("Enter the number : "))
while(num!=0):
    temp=num%10
    sumOfDigits = sumOfDigits+temp
    num=num/10
print("The sum of digits is :",sumOfDigits)
```

OUTPUT

```
Enter the number : 123
The sum of digits = 6
```

Program 4.26 Write a program to calculate GCD of two numbers.

```
num1 = int(input("Enter the two numbers : "))
num2 = int(input("Enter the two numbers : "))
if(num1>num2):
    dividend = num1
    divisor = num2
else:
    dividend = num2
    divisor = num1
while(divisor!=0):
```

```
    remainder = dividend%divisor
    dividend = divisor
    divisor = remainder
print("GCD of",num1,"and",num2,"is",dividend)
```

OUTPUT

```
Enter the first number : 64
Enter the second number : 14
GCD of 64 and 14 is = 2
```

Program 4.27 Write a program to print the reverse of a number.

```
num = int(input("Enter the number : "))
print("The reversed number is :",)
while(num!=0):
    temp = num%10
    print(temp, end="  ")
    num = num/10
```

OUTPUT

```
Enter the number : 123
The reversed number is : 3 2 1
```

Program 4.28   Write a program using a while loop that asks the user for a number, and prints a countdown from that number to zero.

```
n = int(input("Enter the value of n : "))
while n>=0:
    print(n, end = ' ')
    n = n-1
```

OUTPUT

```
Enter the value of n : 10
10 9 8 7 6 5 4 3 2 1 0
```

Thus, we see that while loop is very useful for designing interactive programs in which the number of times the statements in the loop to be executed is not known in advance. The program will execute until the user wants to stop by entering -1.

> **Programming Tip:** To stop an infinite loop, either press Ctrl + C keys or press the close button of the Python shell window (i.e., IDLE) the IDLE.

Example 4.6   The following code calculates the average of first 10 numbers, but since the condition never becomes False, the output is *not* generated. Hence, the intended task will not be performed.

```
i = 0
sum = 0
```

```
avg = 0.0
while(i<=10):
        sum = sum + i
avg = sum/10
print("\n The sum of first 10 numbers = ", sum)
print("\n The average of first 10 numbers = ", avg)
```

Now look at the code given below which the computer will hang up in an infinite loop.

Note   The infinite loop is a loop which never stops running. Its condition is always True.

4.3.2 for Loop

Like the while loop, the for loop provides a mechanism to repeat a task until a particular condition is True. The For loop is usually known as a determinate or definite loop because the programmer knows exactly how many times the loop will repeat. The number of times the loop has to be executed can be determined mathematically checking the logic of the loop.

Programming Tip: There is a difference in for loop syntax. Python syntax uses the range function which makes the loop simpler, more expressive, and less prone to error(s).

The for...in statement is a looping statement used in Python to iterate over a sequence of objects, i.e., go through each item in a sequence. Here, by sequence we mean just an ordered collection of items.

The flow of statements in a for loop can be given as in Figure 4.6.

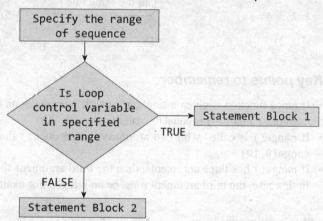

Syntax of for Loop
for loop_contol_var in sequence: statement block

Figure 4.6   for loop construct

When a for loop is used, a range of sequence is specified (only once). The items of the sequence are assigned to the loop control variable one after the other. The for loop is executed for each item in the sequence. With every iteration of the loop, a check is made to identify whether the loop control variable has been assigned all the values in the range. If all the values have been assigned, the statement block of the loop is executed else, the statements comprising the statement block of the for loop are skipped and the control jumps to the immediate statement following the for loop body.

Every iteration of the loop must make the loop control variable closer to the end of the range. So, with every iteration, the loop variable must be updated. Updating the loop variable makes it point to the next item in the sequence.

Note   The for loop is widely used to execute a single or a group of statements a limited number of times.

The range() Function

The range() is a built-in function in Python that is used to iterate over a sequence of numbers. The syntax of range() is

```
range(beg, end, [step])
```

The range() produces a sequence of numbers starting with beg (inclusive) and ending with one less than the number end. The step argument is optional (that is why it is placed in brackets). By default, every number in the range is incremented by 1 but we can specify a different increment using step. It can be both negative and positive, but not zero.

Note   Step can be either a positive value or negative but it cannot be equal to zero.

Example 4.7   Programs to print first n numbers using the range() in a for loop

```
for i in range(1, 5):
    print(i, end= " ")

OUTPUT
1 2 3 4
```
Print numbers in the same line

```
for i in range(1, 10, 2):
    print(i, end= " ")

OUTPUT
1 3 5 7 9
```
beg   step   end

Key points to remember

- If range function is given a single argument, it produces an object with values from 0 to argument-1. For example: range(10) is equal to writing range(0, 10)
- If range() is called with two arguments, it produces values from the first to the second. For example, range(0,10)
- If range() has three arguments, then the third argument specifies the interval of the sequence produced. In this case, the third argument must be an integer. For example, range(1,20,3)

```
for i in range(10):
    print (i, end= ' ')

OUTPUT
0 1 2 3 4 5 6 7 8 9
```

```
for i in range(1,15):
    print (i, end= ' ')

OUTPUT
1 2 3 4 5 6 7 8 9 10 11 12 13 14
```

```
for i in range(1,20,3):
    print (i, end= ' ')

OUTPUT
1 4 7 10 13 16 19
```

4.3.3 Selecting an Appropriate Loop

Loops can be of different types such as entry-controlled (also known as pre-test), exit-controlled (also known as post-test), counter-controlled, and condition controlled (or sentinel-controlled) loops.

Pre-test and Post-test loops

While in an entry-controlled loop, condition is tested before the loop starts, an exit-controlled loop, tests the condition after the loop is executed. If the condition is not met in entry-controlled loop, then the loop will never execute. However, in case of post-test, the body of the loop is executed unconditionally for the first time.

If your requirement is to have a pre-test loop, then choose a `for` loop or a `while` loop. Look at Table 4.1 which shows a comparison between a pre-test loop and a post-test loop.

Table 4.1 Comparison between pre-test and post-test loops

Feature	Pre-test loop	Post-test loop
Initialization	1	2
Number of tests	N+1	N
Statements executed	N	N
Loop control variable update	N	N
Minimum iterations	0	1

Condition-controlled and Counter-controlled loops

When we know in advance the number of times the loop should be executed, we use a counter-controlled loop. The counter is a variable that must be initialized, tested, and updated for performing the loop operations. Such a counter-controlled loop in which the counter is assigned a constant or a value is also known as a *definite repetition loop*.

When we do not know in advance the number of times the loop will be executed, we use a condition-controlled (or sentinel-controlled or indefinite loop) loop. In such a loop, a special value called the *sentinel value* is used to change the loop control expression from True to False. For example, when data is read from the user, the user may be notified that when they want the execution to stop, they may enter -1. This value is called a sentinel value. A condition-controlled loop is often useful for indefinite repetition loops as they use a True/ False condition to control the number of times the loop is executed.

If your requirement is to have a counter-controlled loop, then choose `for` loop, else, if you need to have a sentinel-controlled loop then go for a `while` loop. Although a sentinel-controlled loop can be implemented using `for` loop but `while` loop offers better option. Table 4.2 shows the comparison between the counter-controlled and condition-controlled loops.

Table 4.2 Comparison between condition-controlled and counter-controlled loops

Attitude	Counter-controlled loop	Condition controlled loop
Number of execution	Used when number of times the loop has to be executed is known in advance.	Used when number of times the loop has to be executed is not known in advance.
Condition variable	In counter-controlled loops, we have a counter variable.	In condition-controlled loops, we use a sentinel variable.
Value and limitation of variable	The value of the counter variable and the condition for loop execution, both are strict.	The value of the counter variable and the condition for loop execution, both are strict.

(Contd)

Table 4.2   *(Contd)*

Attitude	Counter-controlled loop	Condition controlled loop

Example	`i = 0`
	`while(i<=10):`
	    `print(i, end = " ")`
	    `i+=1`
		`i = 1`
		`while(i>0):`
		    `print(i, end = " ")`
		    `i+=1`
		    `if(i==10):`
		        `break`

Program 4.29 Write a program using for loop to calculate the average of first n natural numbers.

```
n = int(input("Enter the value of n : "))
avg = 0.0
s = 0
for i in range(1,n+1):
    s = s+i
avg = s/i
print("The sum of first",n,"natural numbers is",s)
print("The average of first",n,"natural numbers is",avg)
```

OUTPUT

```
Enter the value of n : 10
The sum of first n natural numbers = 55
n The average of first n natural numbers = 5.500
```

Program 4.30 Write a program to print the multiplication table of n, where n is entered by the user.

```
n = int(input("Enter any number : "))
print("Multiplication table of",n)
print("*********************************")
for i in range(1,11):
    print(n,"X",i,"=",n*i)
```

OUTPUT

```
Enter any number : 2
Multiplication table of 2
***********************
2 X 0 = 0
2 X 1 = 2
...
2 X 10 = 20
```

Program 4.31 Write a program using for loop to print all the numbers from m–n thereby classifying them as even or odd.

```
m = int(input("Enter the value of m : "))
n = int(input("Enter the value of n : "))
for i in range(m,n+1):
    if(i%2==0):
        print(i,"is even number")
    else:
        print(i,"is odd number")
```

OUTPUT

```
Enter the value of m : 5
Enter the value of n : 12
5 is odd number
6 is even number
7 is odd number
8 is even number
9 is odd number
10 is even number
11 is odd number
12 is even number
```

Program 4.32 Write a program using for loop to calculate factorial of a number.

```
num = int(input("Enter the number : "))
if(num==0):
    fact = 1
fact = 1
for i in range(1,num+1):
    fact = fact*i
print("Factorial of",num,"is",fact)
```

OUTPUT

```
Enter the number : 5
Factorial of is : 120
```

Program 4.33 Write a program to classify a given number as prime or composite.

```
number = int(input('Enter number : '))
isComposite = 0
for i in range(2,number):
    if(number%i == 0):
        isComposite = 1
        break
if(isComposite == 1):
    print("Number is Composite")
else :
    print("Number is prime")
```

OUTPUT

```
Enter the number : 5
5 is a prime number
```

Program 4.34 Write a program using while loop to read the numbers until -1 is encountered. Also, count the number of prime numbers and composite numbers entered by the user.

```python
total_prime = 0
total_composite = 0

while(1):
    num = int(input("Enter no. "))
    if(num == -1):
        break
    is_composite = 0
    for i in range(2,num):
        if(num%i == 0):
            is_composite = 1
            break
    if(is_composite):
        total_composite+=1
    else:
        total_prime+=1
print("total composite : ",total_composite)
print("total prime : ",total_prime)
```

OUTPUT

```
Enter no. 4
Enter no. 6
Enter no. 7
Enter no. 8
Enter no. 9
Enter no. 10
Enter no. 11
Enter no. 35
Enter no. 76
Enter no. 39
Enter no. -1
total composite :  8
total prime :  2
```

Program 4.35 Write a program to calculate pow(x,n).

```python
num = int(input("Enter the number : "))
n = int(input("Till which power to calculate?"))
```

```
result = 1
for i in range(n):
    result = result*num
print(num,"raised to the power",n,"is",result)
```

OUTPUT

```
Enter the number : 2
Till which power to calculate : 5
2 raised to the power 5 is 32
```

Program 4.36 Write a program that displays all leap years from 1900–2101.

```
print("Leap Years from 1900-2101 are : ")
for i in range(1900,2101):
    if(i%4==0):
        print(i,end=' ')
```

OUTPUT

```
Leap Years from 1900-2101 are :

1900 1904 1908 1912 1916 1920 1924 1928 1932 1936 1940 1944 1948 1952 1956 1960
1964 1968 1972 1976 1980 1984 1988 1992 1996 2000 2004 2008 2012 2016 2020 2024
2028 2032 2036 2040 2044 2048 2052 2056 2060 2064 2068 2072 2076 2080 2084 2088
2092 2096 2100
```

Program 4.37 Write a program to sum the series—1+ 1/2 +... +1/n.

```
n = int(input("Enter the number : "))
s = 0.0
for i in range(1,n+1):
    a = 1.0/i
    s = s+a
print("The sum of 1,1/2...1/"+str(n)+" is "+str(s))
```

OUTPUT

```
Enter the number : 5
The sum of 1,1/2...1/5 is 2.28333333333
```

Program 4.38 Write a program to sum the series—$1/1^2 + 1/2^2 + ... 1/n^2$.

```
n = int(input("Enter the number : "))
s = 0.0
for i in range(1,n+1):
    a = 1.0/(i**2)
    s = s+a
print("The sum of series is",s)
```

OUTPUT

```
Enter the number : 5
The sum of series is 1.46361111111
```

Program 4.39 Write a program to sum the series—1/2 + 2/3 + . . . +n/(n+1).

```
n = int(input("Enter the number : "))
s = 0.0
for i in range(1,n+1):
    a = float(i)/(i+1)
    s = s+a
print("The sum of 1/2+2/3...n/(n+1) is",s)
```

OUTPUT

```
Enter the number : 5
The sum of 1/2+2/3...n/(n+1) is 3.55
```

Program 4.40 Write a program to sum the series—1/1 + 2^2/2 + 3^3/3 +. . . +n^2/n.

```
n = int(input("Enter the value of n : "))
s = 0.0
for i in range(1,n+1):
    a = float(i**i)/i
    s = s+a
print("The sum of the series is",s)
```

OUTPUT

```
Enter the value of n : 5
The sum of the series is 701.0
```

Program 4.41 Write a program to calculate sum of cubes of numbers from 1–n.

```
n = int(input("Enter the value of n : "))
s = 0
for i in range(1,n+1):
    a = i**3
    s = s+a
print("The sum of cubes is",s)
```

Programming Tip: It is a logical error to skip the updating of loop control variable in the while loop. Without an update statement, the loop will become an infinite loop.

OUTPUT

```
Enter the value of n : 5
The sum of cubes is 225
```

Program 4.42 Write a program to sum of squares of even numbers.

```
n = int(input("Enter the number : "))
s = 0
for i in range(1,n+1):
```

```
    if(i%2==0):
        term = i**2
    else:
        term = 0
    s = s+term
print("The sum of squares of even number less than",n,"is",s)
```

OUTPUT

```
Enter the number : 10
The sum of squares of even number less than 10 is 220
```

Program 4.43 Write a program using for loop to calculate the value of an investment. Input an initial value of investment and annual interest, and calculate the value of investment over time.

```
initVal = float(input("Enter the initial value : "))
ROI = float(input("Enter the rate of interest : "))
yrs = int(input("Enter the number of years for which investment has to be done : "))
futureVal = initVal
print("\tYear \t\t Value")
print("------------------")
for i in range(1,yrs+1):
    futureVal = futureVal * (1+ROI/100.0)
    print(i," \t\t ",futureVal)
```

OUTPUT

```
Enter the investment value : 20000
Enter the rate of interest: 12
Enter the number of years for which investment has to be done : 5
YEAR            VALUE
------------------
1           22400.00
2           25088.00
3           28098.56
4           31470.38
5           35246.83
```

Program 4.44 Write a program to generate calendar of a month given the start_day and the number of days in that month.

```
startDay = int(input("Enter the start day of month (1-7) : "))
num_of_days = int(input("Enter number of days : "))
print("Sun Mon  Tues  Wed  Thurs  Fri  Sat")
print("-------------------------------------------")
for i in range(startDay-1):
    print(end = "        ")
```

```
i = startDay-1
for j in range(1,num_of_days+1):
    if(i>6):
        print()
        i = 1
    else:
        i = i+1
    print(str(j) +"    ", end = " ")
```

OUTPUT

```
Enter the start day of month (1-7) : 5
Enter number of days : 31
Sun  Mon  Tues Wed  Thurs Fri  Sat
-----------------------------------
                    01    02    03
04   05   06   07   08    09    10
11   12   13   14   15    16    17
18   19   20   21   22    23    24
25   26   27   28   29    30    31
```

4.4 NESTED LOOPS

Python allows its users to have nested loops, that is, loops that can be placed inside other loops. Although this feature will work with any loop like while loop as well as for loop, but it is most commonly used with the for loop, because this is easiest to control. A for loop can be used to control the number of times a particular set of statements will be executed. Another outer loop could be used to control the number of times that a whole loop is repeated.

Loops can be nested to any desired level. However, the loops should be properly indented to identify which statements are contained within each for statement. To see the benefit of nesting loops, we will see some programs that exhibits the use of nested loops.

Program 4.45 Write a program to print the following pattern.

```
Pass 1- 1 2 3 4 5
Pass 2- 1 2 3 4 5
Pass 3- 1 2 3 4 5
Pass 4- 1 2 3 4 5
Pass 5- 1 2 3 4 5

for i in range(1,6):
    print("PASS",i,"-  ",end=' ')
    for j in range(1,6):
        print(j, end=' ')
    print()
```

Program 4.46 Write a program to print the following pattern.

```
**********
**********
**********
**********
**********
for i in range(5):
    print()
    for j in range(5):
        print("*",end=' ')
```

Program 4.47 Write a program to print the following pattern.

```
*
**
***
****
*****
for i in range(1,6):
    print()
    for j in range(i):
        print("*", end=' ')
```

Program 4.48 Write a program to print the following pattern.

```
1
1 2
1 2 3
1 2 3 4
1 2 3 4 5
for i in range(1,6):
    print()
    for j in range(1,i+1):
        print(j, end=' ')
```

Program 4.49 Write a program to print the following pattern.

```
1
22
333
4444
55555
for i in range(1,6):
    print()
    for j in range(1,i+1):
        print(i, end=' ')
```

Program 4.50 Write a program to print the following pattern.

```
0
12
345
6789
```

```python
count = 0
for i in range(1,5):
    print()          #prints a new line
    for j in range(1,i+1):
        print(count, end=' ')
        count = count+1
```

Program 4.51 Write a program to print the following pattern.

```
    1
   12
  123
 1234
12345
```

```python
N = 5
for i in range(1,N+1):
    for k in range(N,i,-1):
        print(" ", end=' ')
    for j in range(1,i+1):
        print(j, end=' ')
    print()
```

Program 4.52 Write a program to print the following pattern.

```
        1
      1 2 1
    1 2 3 2 1
  1 2 3 4 3 2 1
1 2 3 4 5 4 3 2 1
```

```python
N = 5
for i in range(1,N+1):
    for k in range(N,i,-1):
        print(" ", end=' ')
    for j in range(1,i+1):
        print(j, end=' ')
    for l in range(i-1,0,-1):
        print(l, end=' ')
    print()
```

Program 4.53 Write a program to print the following pattern.

```
    1
   2 2
  3 3 3
 4 4 4 4
5 5 5 5 5
```

```
N = 5
for i in range(1,N+1):
    for k in range(N,i,-1):
        print("", end=' ')
    for j in range(1,i+1):
        print(i, end=' ')
    print()
```

4.5 THE break STATEMENT

The break statement is used to terminate the execution of the nearest enclosing loop in which it appears. The break statement is widely used with for loop and while loop. When compiler encounters a break statement, the control passes to the statement that follows the loop in which the break statement appears. Its syntax is quite simple, just type keyword break as shown below.

> **Programming Tip:** Using break or continue statement outside a loop causes an error.

```
break
```

Example 4.8   Program to demonstrate the break statement

```
i = 1
while i <= 10:
        print(i, end=" ")
        if i==5:
                break
        i = i+1
print("\n Done")
```

OUTPUT

```
1 2 3 4 5
Done
```

Note that the code is meant to print first 10 numbers using a while loop, but it will actually print only numbers from 0 to 4. As soon as i becomes equal to 5, the break statement is executed and the control jumps to the statement following the while loop.

Hence, the break statement is used to exit a loop from any point within its body, bypassing its normal termination expression. When the break statement is encountered inside a loop, the loop is immediately terminated, and program control is passed to the next statement following the loop. Figure 4.7 shows the transfer of control when the break statement is encountered.

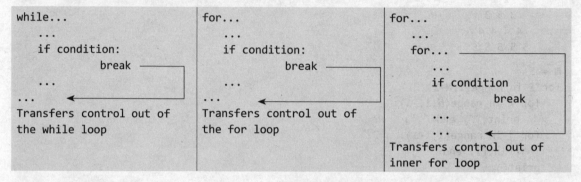

Figure 4.7   The break statement

Note   break statement terminates the loop and transfers execution to the statement immediately following the loop.

4.6 THE continue STATEMENT

Like the break statement, the continue statement can only appear in the body of a loop. When the compiler encounters a continue statement, then the rest of the statements in the loop are skipped and the control is unconditionally transferred to the loop-continuation portion of the nearest enclosing loop. Its syntax is quite simple, just type keyword continue as shown below.

Programming Tip: When the compiler encounters a continue statement, then the rest of the statements in the loop are skipped and the control is unconditionally transferred to the loop-continuation portion of the nearest enclosing loop.

```
continue
```

Again like the break statement, the continue statement cannot be used without an enclosing for or a while loop. When the continue statement is encountered in the while and for loop, the control is transferred to the code that tests the controlling expression. However, if placed with a for loop, the continue statement causes a branch to the code that updates the loop variable.

Example 4.9   Program to demonstrate the continue statement

```
for i in range(1,11):
    if(i==5):
        continue
    print(i, end=" ")
print("\n Done")
```

OUTPUT

```
1 2 3 4 6 7 8 9 10
Done
```

Note that the code is meant to print numbers from 0 to 10. But as soon as i becomes equal to 5, the continue statement is encountered, so rest of the statement(s) in the for loop are skipped. In the output, there is no 5 is missing 5 could not be printed as continue caused early increment of i and skipping of statement that printed the value of i on screen). Figure 4.8 illustrates the use of continue statement in loops.

```
while(...) ◄─────────────────────┐
    ...                          │
    If condition:                │
    continue  ───────────────────┘
    ...
...
Transfers control to the condition
expression of the while loop
```

```
for(...)◄────────────────┐
    ...                  │
    if condition:        │
        continue ────────┘
    ...
...
Transfers control to the condition
expression of the for loop
```

```
for(...)
    ...
    for(...)◄────────────────┐
        ...                  │
        if condition:        │
            continue ────────┘
    ...
...
Transfers control to the condition
expression of the inner for loop
```

Figure 4.8   The continue statement

Hence, we conclude that the continue statement is somewhat the opposite of the break statement. It forces the next iteration of the loop to take place, skipping any code in between itself and the test condition of the loop. The continue statement is usually used to restart a statement sequence when an error occurs.

Note	The continue statement is used to stop the current iteration of the loop and continues with the next one.

Look at the following codes that demonstrate the use of break and continue statements.

Program 4.54 Write a program to calculate square root of a number. Demonstrate the use of break and continue statements.

```
import math
total_prime = 0
total_composite = 0

while(1):
    num = int(input("Enter no. "))
    if(num == 999):
        break
    elif num < 0:
        print("Square root of negative numbers cannot be calculated")
        continue
```

```
    else:
        print("Square root of ", num, " = ", math.sqrt(num))
```

OUTPUT

```
Enter no. 100
Square root of  100  =  10.0
Enter no. 81
Square root of  81  =  9.0
Enter no. 64
Square root of  64  =  8.0
Enter no. -1
Square root of negative numbers cannot be calculated
Enter no. 999
```

Program 4.55 Write a program that prompts users to enter numbers. The process will repeat until user enters -1. Finally, the program prints the count of prime and composite numbers entered.

```
prime_count = 0
comp_count = 0
n = int(input("Enter the number : "))
while(n!=-1):
    flag = 0
    for i in range(2,n):
        if(n%i==0):
            flag = 1
            break
    if(flag==0):
        prime_count=prime_count+1
    else:
        comp_count=comp_count+1
    n = int(input("Enter the number : "))
print("Number of prime numbers is : ",prime_count)
print("Number of composite numbers is : ",comp_count)
```

```
Enter the number : 9
Enter the number : 8
Enter the number : 7
Enter the number : 6
Enter the number : 5
Enter the number : 4
Enter the number : 3
Enter the number : 2
Enter the number : 10
Enter the number : 11
Enter the number : 12
Enter the number : 98
```

```
Enter the number : 87
Enter the number : 67
Enter the number : -1
Number of prime numbers is :  6
Number of composite numbers is :  8
```

Program 4.56 Using a `for` loop, write a program that prints out the decimal equivalents of 1/2, 1/3, 1/4,...,1/10.

```
for i in range(1,10):
    print("1/", i, " = %f" %(1.0/i))
```

OUTPUT

```
1/ 1  = 1.000000
1/ 2  = 0.500000
1/ 3  = 0.333333
1/ 4  = 0.250000
1/ 5  = 0.200000
1/ 6  = 0.166667
1/ 7  = 0.142857
1/ 8  = 0.125000
1/ 9  = 0.111111
```

4.7 THE pass STATEMENT

The pass statement is used when a statement is required syntactically but no command or code has to be executed. It specifies a *null operation* or simply No Operation (NOP) statement. Nothing happens when the pass statement is executed. Syntax of pass statement is simple, just type the keyword pass as shown below.

Programming Tip: The pass statement is used when a statement is required syntactically but otherwise no statement is required logically.

```
pass
```

Example 4.10 Program to demonstrate pass statement

```
for letter in "HELLO":
        pass      #The statement is doing nothing
        print("Pass : ", letter)
print("Done")
```

OUTPUT

```
Pass :  H
Pass :  E
Pass :  L
Pass :  L
Pass :  O
Done
```

The pass statement is used as a placeholder. For example, if we have a loop that is not implemented yet, but we may wish to write some code in it in the future. In such cases pass statement can be written because we cannot have an empty body of the loop. Though the pass statement will not do anything but it will make the program syntactically correct. This is shown in the code below. When you run this code, there will be no output on the screen.

```
for letter in "HELLO":
```

Difference between comment and pass statements   In Python programming, pass is a null statement. The difference between a comment and pass statement is that while the interpreter ignores a comment entirely, pass is not ignored. Comment is not executed but pass statement is executed but nothing happens.

Difference between *break*, *continue*, and *pass*

The break statement terminates the execution of the nearest enclosing loop in which it appears.

The continue statement skips the rest of the statements in the loop and transfers the control unconditionally to the loop-continuation portion of the nearest enclosing loop.

The pass statement is a do-nothing statement in a loop. It is just added to make the loop syntactically correct. That is, a pass statement is written as we cannot have an empty body of the loop.

4.8 THE else STATEMENT USED WITH LOOPS

We have studied if-else block in this chapter. Unlike C and C++, in Python you can have the *else* statement associated with a loop statements. If the **else** statement is used with a *for* loop, the *else* statement is executed when the loop has completed iterating. But when used with the *while* loop, the *else* statement is executed when the condition becomes False. For example, look at the code given below which illustrates this concept.

Example 4.11   Programs to demonstrate else statement with loops

```
for letter in "HELLO":
        print(letter, end=" ")
else:
        print("\nDone")


OUTPUT
H E L L O
Done
```

```
i = 1
while(i<0):
        print(i)
        i = i - 1
else:
        print(i, "is not negative so
loop did not execute")


OUTPUT
1 is not negative so loop did not execute
```

Summary

- if and else statements are used to determine which option in a series of possibilities is True.
- Nested if statements are used to check if more than one conditions are satisfied.

- A series of if elif statements have a final else block, which is executed if none of the if or elif expressions is True.

- Never test floating point numbers for exact equality. This is because floating pint numbers are just approximations, so it is always better to test floating point numbers for 'approximately equal' rather than testing for exactly equal.
- Python language supports two types of iterative statements—while loop and for loop.
- In the while loop, the condition is tested before any of the statements in the statement block is executed.
- We must update the condition of the while loop to prevent it from becoming an infinite loop.
- while loop is very useful for designing interactive programs in which the number of times the statements in the loop has to be executed is not known in advance.

- For loop is usually known as a determinate or definite loop because the programmer knows exactly how many times the loop will repeat.
- range() is a built-in function in Python that is used to iterate over a sequence of numbers.
- Using break or continue statement outside a loop causes an error.
- When the compiler encounters a continue statement then the rest of the statements in the loop are skipped and the control is unconditionally transferred to the loop-continuation portion of the nearest enclosing loop.
- Pass statement is used when a statement is required syntactically but no command or code has to be executed.

Glossary

Conditional branching statements Statements that helps to jump from one part of the program to another depending on whether a particular condition is satisfied or not.

Continue statement When the compiler encounters a continue statement then the rest of the statements in the loop are skipped and the control is unconditionally transferred to the loop-continuation portion of the nearest enclosing loop.

Dangling else problem Problem encountered with nesting of if-else statements which is created when there is no matching else for every if statement. This is solved in Python by indenting the nested if statements.

for loop The mechanism used to repeat a task until a particular condition is True. The for loop is usually known as a determinate or definite loop because the programmer knows exactly how many times the loop will repeat.

if-else-if statement Decision control statement that works in the same way as a normal if statement. It is also known as nested if construct.

if-else statement Decision control statement in which first the test expression is evaluated. If the expression is True, if block is executed and else block is skipped. Otherwise, if the expression is False, else block is executed and if block is ignored.

if statement Simplest form of decision control statement that is frequently used in decision making.

Infinite loop A loop which never stops running. Its condition is always True.

Iterative statements Statements used to repeat the execution of a list of statements.

Nested loops Loops that can be placed inside other loops.

while loop The mechanism used to repeat one or more statements while a particular condition is True.

Exercises

Fill in the Blanks

1.
```
x = 100
y = 200
__x>y__
        print("In if")
_____
        print("In else")
```
2. _____ is a short form of "else if" statement.
3. Fill the blanks to print Welcome on the screen.
```
x = 15
y = 500
```
```
if x>100 __ y>100:
___("Welcome")
```
4. >>>not 1==1 gives the answer _____.
5.
```
i = 1
while i > 0:
print("loop")
```
The above loop is an example of _____.
6. Fill in the blanks to create a loop that increments the value of x by 2 and prints the even values from 0–100.
```
    x = 0
```

```
___x <= ___
___(x)
x += 2
```

7. Python uses _____ to form a block of code.
8. A series of `if-elif` statements have a final _____ block, which is executed if none of the `if` or `elif` expressions is `True`.
9. Python assumes any non-zero and non-null values as _____.
10. _____ statements are used to repeatedly execute one or more statements in a block.
11. If the condition in the `while` loop never becomes `False`, then it will result in an _____.
12. _____ loop can be used when the number of times the statements in loop has to be executed is not known in advance.
13. _____ loop is called a definite loop.

14. When a `for` loop is used, a _____ of sequence is specified.
15. _____ is a built-in function that is used to iterate over a sequence of numbers.
16. If your requirement is to have a counter-controlled loop, then choose _____ loop.
17. To specify an empty body of a `for` loop, you will use _____ statement.
18. Fill in the blanks to create a `for` loop that prints only the odd values in the range:
```
____ i in range(0,20,):
print(___)
```
19. A _____ statement contains other statements.
20. _____ begin with a keyword and end with a colon.

State True or False

1. Indentation identifies a statement block.
2. You cannot use logical operators in `if` statement condition.
3. Statements in `if-else` block should be properly aligned.
4. You can use floating point numbers for checking for equality in the test expression.
5. It is necessary that every `if` statement should have an `else` block.
6. `elif` and `else` blocks are optional.
7. While forming the conditional expression, we should use positive statements rather than using compound negative statements.
8. The `while` loop is used to repeat one or more statements while a particular condition is `False`.
9. If the control condition evaluates to False, then the statements enclosed in the loop are never executed.
10. Every alternate item of the sequence is assigned to the loop control variable one after the other.

11. The step argument in `range()` can be zero.
12. A sentinel-controlled loop can be implemented using `for` loop.
13. Loops can be nested to any desired level.
14. You can use `break` or `continue` statements outside loop.
15. `pass` is a null statement.
16. You can have the `else` statement associated with loop statements.
17. In a `while` loop, if the body is executed n times, then the test expression is executed n+1 times.
18. The number of times the loop control variable is updated is equal to the number of times the loop iterates.
19. In a `while` loop, the loop control variable is initialized in the body of the loop.
20. All `if` statements must contain either an else statement.
21. Statements within a suite can be indented a different amount.

Multiple Choice Questions

1. Which part of if statement should be indented?
   (a) The first statement
   (b) All the statements
   (c) Statements within the `if` block
   (d) None of these
2. How many numbers will be printed?
```
i = 5
while i>=0:
    print(i)
    i=i-1
```

   (a) 5   (b) 6
   (c) 4   (d) 0
3. How many numbers will be printed?
```
i = 10
while True:
print(i)
i = i - 1
if i<=7:
break
```

(a) 1   (b) 2
(c) 3   (d) 4

4. Which statement ends the current iteration of the loop and continues with the next one?
   (a) `break`   (b) `continue`
   (c) `skip`   (d) `pass`

5. Which of the following is placed after the if condition?
   (a) `;`   (b) `.`
   (c) `:`   (d) `,`

6. Which statement is used to terminate the execution of the nearest enclosing loop in which it appears?
   (a) `pass`   (b) `break`
   (c) `continue`   (d) `jump`

7. Which statement is used to stop the current iteration of the loop and continues with the next one?
   (a) `pass`   (b) `break`
   (c) `continue`   (d) `jump`

8. Which statement indicates a NOP?
   (a) `pass`   (b) `break`
   (c) `continue`   (d) `jump`

9. What would happen if we replace the `break` statement in the code with a `'continue'`?
   (a) It will stop executing
   (b) It would run forever
   (c) You will have to press Ctrl + C
   (d) There would be no change

10. How many lines will be printed by this code?
    ```
    while False:
        print("Hello")
    ```
    (a) 1   (b) 0
    (c) 10   (d) countless

Review Questions

1. Write a short note on conditional branching statements supported by Python.
2. When should we used nested `if` statements? Illustrate your answer with the help of an example.
3. It is necessary for every `if` block to be accompanied with an `else` block. Comment on this statement with the help of an example.
4. `for` loop is usually known as a determinate or definite loop. Justify the statement with the help of an example.
5. Explain the syntax of `for` loop.
6. With the help of an example, explain the utility of `range()`.
7. Differentiate between counter-controlled loops and sentinel-controlled loops.
8. Explain the utility of `break` statement with the help of an example.
9. Explain the utility of `continue` statement with the help of an example.
10. Differentiate between `pass` and `continue` statement.
11. What happens when the `else` clause is associated with a loop?
12. Identify the definite and indefinite loop.

`num = input("Enter a number: ")` `while num != 0:` `num =` `input("Enter a number: ")`	`num = input("Enter a number: ")` `num = 0` `while num<10:` `print(2**num)`

13. Change the indentation to make the code syntactically correct.
    ```
    if condition1:
    statement1
    elif condition2:
    statement2
    elif condition3:
    statement3
    elif condition4:
    statement4
    ```

Programming Problems

1. Write a program to input two numbers and check whether they are equal or not.
2. Write a program that prompts users to enter a character (O, A, B, C, F). Then using `if-elif-else` construct display *Outstanding, Very Good, Good, Average,* and *Fail* respectively.
3. Write a program that determines whether an alphabet, digit or a whitespace was entered.
4. Write a program that determines whether a digit, uppercase, or a lowercase character was entered.
5. Write a program that counts the number of lowercase characters, uppercase characters, and digits entered by the user.
6. Write a program that prompts user to enter a number. If the number is equal to 99, print "Congratulations". If the number is less than 99, print—enter again and aim higher-else print enter again a lower number. The program should run until the user guesses the correct number that is 99.

7. Write a program to demonstrate the use of nested `if` structure.

8. Write a program that displays first 10 natural numbers using for loop.

9. Write a program to find whether a given year is leap year or not.

10. Write a program that finds average of first n numbers using for loop.

11. Write a program to sum the series $1^2/1 + 2^2/2 + 3^2/3 + ... + n^2/n$.

12. Write a program that prints a number, its square, and cube repeatedly in the range `(1,n)`.

13. Write a program that prompts the user to enter a string. The program calculates and displays the length of the string until the user enters `"QUIT"`.
(*Hint: Use a while loop*)

14. Write a program that prompts the user to enter five words. If the length of any word is less than 6 characters, then it asks the user to enter it again. However, if the word is of 6 or more characters, then it displays it on the screen.

15. Write a program that determines whether a student is eligible for PG course or not. To be eligible, the student must have obtained more than `80%` in X and XII examination, and `70%` plus marks in Graduation. If the student changes his stream (Science, Commerce, or Arts), then deduct `5%` from his Graduation score.

16. Write a program that displays `Oxford University Press` as
a. `oxford university press`
b. `OXFORD UNIVERSITY PRESS`
c. `oXFORD uNIVERSITY pRESS`

17. Write a program that prompts users to enter numbers. Once the user enters -1, it displays the count, sum, and average of even numbers and that of odd numbers.

18. Write a program to read a floating point number and an integer. If the value of the floating point number is greater than `4.14,` then add `10` to the integer.

19. Enter two integers as dividend and divisor. If the divisor is greater than zero then divide the dividend by the divisor. Assign their result to an integer variable rem and their quotient to a floating point number quo.

20. Write a program to print the prime factors of a number.

21. Write a program to test if a given number is a power of 2.
(*Hint: A number x is a power of 2 if x != 0 and x & (x - 1)) == 0*)

22. Write a program to print the Floyd's triangle.

23. Write a program to read two numbers. Then find out whether the first number is a multiple of the second number.

24. Write a program to display the `sin(x)` value where x ranges from `0` to `360` in steps of `15`.

25. Write a program to display the `cos(x)` and `tan(x)` value where x ranges from `0` to `360` in steps of `15`.

26. Write a program to calculate electricity bill based on following information.

Consumption Unit	Rate of Charge
0 – 150	₹ 3 per unit
151 – 350	₹ 100 plus ₹ 3.75 per unit exceeding 150 units
301 – 450	₹ 250 plus ₹ 4 per unit exceeding 350 units
451 – 600	₹ 300 plus ₹ 4.25 per unit exceeding 450 units
Above 600	₹ 400 plus ₹ 5 per unit exceeding 600 units

27. Write a program to read an angle from the user and then displays its quadrant.

28. Write a program that accepts the current date and the date of birth of the user. Then calculate the age of the user and display it on the screen. Note that the date should be displayed in the format specified as—dd/mm/yy.

29. Write a program that displays all the numbers from 1-100 that are not divisible 2 as well as by 3.

30. Write a program to calculate parking charges of a vehicle. Enter the type of vehicle as a character (like c for car, b for bus, etc.) and number of hours, then calculate charges as given below:
Truck/bus – 20 ₹ per hour
Car – 10 ₹ per hour
Scooter/ Cycle/ Motor cycle – 5 ₹ per hour

31. Modify the above program to calculate the parking charges. Read the hours and minutes when the vehicle enters the parking lot. When the vehicle is leaving, enter its leaving time. Calculate the difference between the two timings to calculate the number of hours and minutes for which the vehicle was parked. Finally, calculate the charges based on following rules and then display the result on the screen.

Vehicle Name	Rate till 3 hours	Rate after 3 hours
Truck/bus	20	30
Car	10	20
Cycle/ Motor cycle/ Scooter	5	10

32. Write a program to print a table of sine and cos functions for the interval from `0`-`360` degrees in increments of `15`.

33. Write a program to read month of the year as an integer. Then display the name of the month.

34. Write a program to print the sum of all odd numbers from 1 to 100.

35. Write a program that prints whether every number in a range is prime or composite.

36. Write an interactive program to read an integer. If it is positive then display the corresponding binary representation of that number. The user must enter 999 to stop. In case the user enters a negative number, then ignore that input and ask the user to re-enter any different number.

37. Write a program that accepts any number and prints the number of digits in that number.

38. Write a program that prints numbers from 20 to 1 (counts downwards).

39. The following for loops are written to print numbers from 1 to 10. Are these loops correct? Justify your answer.

for i in range(10): print(i)	for i in range(10): num = i+1 print(num)	for i in range(10): print(i) i = i+1

40. Write a program to generate the following pattern.
```
* * * * *
*       *
*       *
*       *
* * * * *
```

41. Write a program to generate the following pattern.
```
$ * * * *
* $     *
*   $   *
*     $ *
* * * * $
```

42. Write a program to generate the following pattern.
```
$ * * * $
* $   $ *
*   $   *
* $   $ *
$ * * * $
```

43. Write programs to implement the following sequence of numbers.
```
1, 8, 27, 64,...
-5, -2, 0, 3, 6, 9, 12,...
-2, -4, -6, -8, -10, -12,...
1, 4, 7, 10, …
```

44. Write a program that reads integers until the user wants to stop. When the user stops entering numbers, display the largest of all the numbers entered.

45. Write a program to print the sum of the following n^{th} series.
   - $-x + x^2 - x^3 + x^4 +...$
   - $1 + (1+2) + (1+2+3) +...$
   - $1 - x + x^2/2! - x^3/3! +...$

46. Write a program to print the following pattern
```
*
* *
* * *
* * * *
* * * * *
* * * *
* * *
* *
*
```

47. Write a program to print the following pattern.
```
1
2 1 2
3 2 1 2 3
```

48. Write a program to read a 5 digit number and then display the number in the following formats... for example, the if the user entered 12345, the result should be

12345	1
2345	12
345	123
45	1234
5	12345

49. A video library rents new videos for ₹ 75 a day, and old movies for ₹ 50 a day. Write a program to calculate the total charge for a customer's video rentals. The program should prompt the user for the number of each type of video and output the total cost.

50. An employee's total weekly pay is calculated by multiplying the hourly wage and number of regular hours plus any overtime pay which in turn is calculated as total overtime hours multiplied by 1.5 times the hourly wage. Write a program that takes as inputs the hourly wage, total regular hours, and total overtime hours, and prints an employee's total weekly pay.

51. Write a simple Python program that displays the following powers of 2, one per line: $2^1, 2^2, 2^3, 2^4, 2^5, 2^6, 2^7, 2^8$.

52. Write a program that converts grams to kilograms and meters to centimeters.

Find the Output

```
1. years = 200
   if(years == 100):
               print( "Century")
   elif(years == 75):
               print ("Platinum Jublee")
   elif(years == 50):
               print ("Half Century")
   elif(years == 25):
               print ("Silver Jublee")
   elif(years == 10):
               print ("Decade")
   else:
               print ("Nothing")
2. num = 100
   if num > 30:
         print("30")
   if num<50:
         print("50")
   if num==7:
         print("70")
3. x = 100
   if x == 50:
         print("Yeah")
   else:
         print("Try Again")
4. num = 100
   if (num + 1) > 100:
       if (num * 2) >= 200:
           print("You win")
       else:
           print("Try Again")
   a. You Win      b. Try Again
   c. There is no output
5. num = 70
   if num == 50:
       print( "50")
   elif num == 10:
       print( "10")
   elif num == 70:
       print( "70")
   else:
       print( "Number is not 50, 10 or 70")
   print("Number is not 50, 10 or 70")
```

```
6. if(10 == 10) and (10+20>30):
             print("Done")
   else:
             print("Do It")
7. >>>not 10>70
8. if not True:
           print("10")
   elif not(10+10 == 30):
           print("20")
   else:
           print("30")
9. if 10 + 30 == 60:
           print("Best")
   else:
           print("Worst")
10. a = 10
    b = 20
    if not 10 + 10 == b or a == 40 and 70== 80:
            print("Yes")
    elif a != b:
            print("No")
11. i=1
    while i<=6:
            print(i, end = " ")
    i=i+1
    print("Done")
12. i=0
    while i<10:
        i = i + 1
        if(i == 5):
          print( "\n Continue")
          continue
        if(i==7):
          print("\n Breaking")
          break
        print( i, end = " ")
    print( "\n Done")
13. for i in range(5):
            print("hello!", end = " ")
14. for i in range(10):
            if not i%2==0:
                print(i+1)
```

Find the Error

```
1. num = 100
   if num > 100:
       print(num)
2. while i in range(0,5):
       print(i)
```

```
3. for i in range(0,15,3)
       print(i)
4. while i < 10:
       print(i)
       i+=1
```

```
5.  i = 0
    while i < 10;
        print(i)
        i+=1
```

```
6.  num = 3
    if num > 0:
        print("POSITIVE.")
    print("This is always printed.")
```

Answers

Fill in the Blanks

1. if, :, else:
2. elif
3. or, print
4. False
5. Infinite Loop
6. while, 100:, print
7. indentation
8. else
9. True
10. Iterative
11. infinite loop
12. while
13. for
14. range
15. range()
16. for
17. pass
18. for, 2*i+1
19. compound
20. Headers

State True or False

1. True   2. False   3. True   4. False   5. False   6. True   7. True   8. False   9. True   10. False
11. False   12. True   13. True   14. False   15. True   16. True   17. True   18. True   19. False   20. False
21. False

Multiple Choice Questions

1. (c)   2. (b)   3. (c)   4. (b)   5. (c)   6. (b)   7. (c)   8. (a)   9. (b)   10. (b)

1

Simple Calculator

A *simple calculator* performs basic tasks such as addition, subtraction, multiplication, and division. Let us write a program that takes two numbers as input from the user. It also displays a menu of operations that the user is allowed to perform. Prompt the user to enter the desired operation and then apply the operation on the numbers.

```python
# Program to make a simple calculator
import math
print("\t____CALCULATOR_____")

def sum(a,b):
    a+=b
    return a

def sub(a,b):
    if a > b:
        a-=b
        return a
    else :
        b-=a
        return b

def mul(a,b):
    a*=b
    return a

def div(a,b):
    q=a/b
    r=a%b
    print("\nThe quotient is : %s" %q)
    print("\nThe remainder is : %s" %r)

def sqr(a):
    x= math.sqrt(a)
    return x

while(True):
    print("\n\nChoose the operation you want to perform: ")
    print("\n\t1.ADDITION")
```

```
print("\n\t2.SUBTRACTION")
print("\n\t3.MULTIPLICATION")
print("\n\t4.DIVISION")
print("\n\t5.SQUARE ROOT")
print("\n\t6.EXIT")

choice = int(input('>'))

if choice==1 :
    print("\n\nEnter the two numbers: ")
    num1 = int(input('>'))
    num2 = int(input('>'))
    s=sum(num1,num2)
    print("The sum is : %s" %s)

elif choice == 2 :
    print("\n\nEnter the two numbers: ")
    num1 = int(input('>'))
    num2 = int(input('>'))
    m=sub(num1,num2)
    print("\nThe difference is: %s" %m)

elif choice == 3 :
    print("\n\nEnter the two numbers: ")
    num1 = int(input('>'))
    num2 = int(input('>'))
    p=mul(num1,num2)
    print("\nThe prodct is: %s" %p)

elif choice == 4:
    print("\n\nEnter the two numbers: ")
    num1 = int(input('>'))
    num2 = int(input('>'))
    div(num1,num2)

elif choice == 5 :
    print("\n\nEnter the number: ")
    num1 = int(input('>'))
    r=sqr(num1)
    print("\nThe square root is : %s" %r)

else:
    print("\nYou chose to exit.Bye......")
    break
```

OUTPUT

```
_____CALCULATOR_____
Choose the operation you want to perform:

    1. ADDITION
```

```
        2. SUBTRACTION

        3. MULTIPLICATION

        4. DIVISION

        5. SQUARE ROOT

        6. EXIT
>5

Enter the number:
>25

The square root is : 5.0

Choose the operation you want to perform:

        1. ADDITION

        2. SUBTRACTION

        3. MULTIPLICATION

        4. DIVISION
        5. SQUARE ROOT
        6. EXIT
>6

You chose to exit.Bye......
```

CASE STUDY

2

Generating a Calendar

If you are a C or C++ programmer, then you know displaying the calendar of a particular year is a tedious job. You would have to write at least 75 lines of code to do the job. But Python has a calendar module with pre-defined functions which makes this task very-very simple. The program given below prints the calendar of an arbitrary year as entered by the user.

```
# Program to print the Calendar of any given year

import calendar
y = int(input("Enter the year: "))
m = 1
print("\n******** CALENDAR *******")
Cal = calendar.TextCalendar(calendar.SUNDAY)
# An instance of TextCalendar class is created and calendar. SUNDAY means that you
want to start displaying the calendar from Sunday
i=1
while i<=12:
    Cal.prmonth(y,i)
    i+=1
#prmonth() is a function of the class that prints the calendar for given month and year
```

OUTPUT

Enter the year: 2017

******** CALENDAR *******

```
    January 2017
Su Mo Tu We Th Fr Sa
 1  2  3  4  5  6  7
 8  9 10 11 12 13 14
15 16 17 18 19 20 21
22 23 24 25 26 27 28
29 30 31

    February 2017
Su Mo Tu We Th Fr Sa
          1  2  3  4
 5  6  7  8  9 10 11
12 13 14 15 16 17 18
19 20 21 22 23 24 25
26 27 28
```

```
      March 2017                    August 2017
Su Mo Tu We Th Fr Sa          Su Mo Tu We Th Fr Sa
          1  2  3  4                  1  2  3  4  5
 5  6  7  8  9 10 11           6  7  8  9 10 11 12
12 13 14 15 16 17 18          13 14 15 16 17 18 19
19 20 21 22 23 24 25          20 21 22 23 24 25 26
26 27 28 29 30 31             27 28 29 30 31

      April 2017                  September 2017
Su Mo Tu We Th Fr Sa          Su Mo Tu We Th Fr Sa
                   1                           1  2
 2  3  4  5  6  7  8           3  4  5  6  7  8  9
 9 10 11 12 13 14 15          10 11 12 13 14 15 16
16 17 18 19 20 21 22          17 18 19 20 21 22 23
23 24 25 26 27 28 29          24 25 26 27 28 29 30
30

       May 2017                   October 2017
Su Mo Tu We Th Fr Sa          Su Mo Tu We Th Fr Sa
 1  2  3  4  5  6              1  2  3  4  5  6  7
 7  8  9 10 11 12 13           8  9 10 11 12 13 14
14 15 16 17 18 19 20          15 16 17 18 19 20 21
21 22 23 24 25 26 27          22 23 24 25 26 27 28
28 29 30 31                   29 30 31

      June 2017                  November 2017
Su Mo Tu We Th Fr Sa          Su Mo Tu We Th Fr Sa
             1  2  3                    1  2  3  4
 4  5  6  7  8  9 10           5  6  7  8  9 10 11
11 12 13 14 15 16 17          12 13 14 15 16 17 18
18 19 20 21 22 23 24          19 20 21 22 23 24 25
25 26 27 28 29 30             26 27 28 29 30

      July 2017                  December 2017
Su Mo Tu We Th Fr Sa          Su Mo Tu We Th Fr Sa
                   1                          1  2
 2  3  4  5  6  7  8           3  4  5  6  7  8  9
 9 10 11 12 13 14 15          10 11 12 13 14  15 16
16 17 18 19 20 21 22          17 18 19 20 21  22 23
23 24 25 26 27 28 29          24 25 26 27 28  29 30
30 31                         31
```

CHAPTER 5
Functions and Modules

KEY ●●● Concepts

- Defining, Redefining, and Calling Functions • Variable Scope and Lifetime • return Statement • Required, Keyword, Default, and Variable Arguments • Lambda and Recursive Functions • Documentation Strings, Modules, and Packages • Standard Library, globals(), locals(), and reload()

5.1 INTRODUCTION

A *function* is a block of organized and reusable program code that performs a single, specific, and well-defined task. Python enables its programmers to break up a program into functions, each of which can be written more or less independently of the others. Therefore, the code of one function is completely insulated from the codes of the other functions.

Every function interfaces to the outside world in terms of how information is transferred to it and how results generated by the function are transmitted back from it. This interface is basically specified by the function name. For example, we have been using functions such as input() to take input from the user, print() to display some information on the screen, and int() to convert the user entered information into int datatype.

Let us consider Figure 5.1 which explains how a function func1() is called to perform a well-defined task. As soon as func1() is called, the program control is passed to the first statement in the function. All the statements in the function are executed and then the program control is passed to the statement following the one that called the function.

In the Figure 5.2 we see that func1() calls function named func2(). Therefore, func1() is known as the *calling function* and func2() is known as the *called function*. The moment the compiler encounters a function call, instead of executing the next statement in the calling function, the control jumps to the statements that are a part of the called

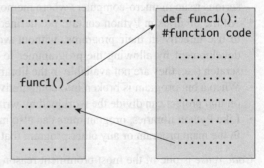

Figure 5.1 Calling a function

function. After the called function is executed, the control is returned back to the calling program.

It is not necessary that the func1() can call only one function, it can call as many functions as it wants and as many times as it wants. For example, a function call placed within for loop or while loop may call the same function multiple times until the condition holds true.

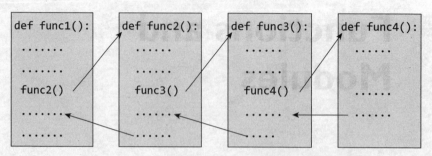

Figure 5.2 Function calling another function

> **Note** Every function encapsulates a set of operations and when called it returns the information to the calling program.

5.1.1 Need for Functions

Let us analyze the reasons for segmenting a program into manageable chunks of code.

- Dividing the program into separate well defined functions facilitates each function to be written and tested separately. This simplifies the process of program development. Figure 5.3 shows that the *Function A* calls other functions for dividing the entire code into smaller sections (or functions).

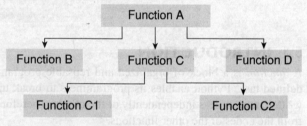

Figure 5.3 Top–down approach of solving a problem

- Understanding, coding, and testing multiple separate functions are far easier than doing the same for one huge function.
- If a big program has to be developed without the use of any function, then there will be a large number of lines in the code and maintaining that program will be a big mess. Also , the large size of the program is a serious issue in micro-computers where memory space is limited.
- All the libraries in Python contain pre-defined and pre-tested functions which the programmers are free to use directly in their programs, without worrying about their code details. This speeds up program development by allowing the programmer to concentrate only on the code that has to be written from scratch (i.e., they are not available in the libraries).
- When a big program is broken into comparatively smaller functions, then different programmers working on that project can divide the workload by writing different functions.
- Like Python libraries, programmers can also make their own functions and use them from different points in the main program or any other program that needs its functionalities.

Code reuse is one of the most prominent reason to use functions. Large programs usually follow the **DRY** principle, that is, *Don't Repeat Yourself* principle. Once a function is written, it can be called multiple times within the same or by a different program wherever its functionality is required. Correspondingly, a bad repetitive code abides by the **WET** principle, i.e., *Write Everything Twice, or We Enjoy Typing*.

Consider a program that executes a set of instructions repeatedly n times, though not continuously. In such case, the instructions had to be repeated continuously for n times they can better be placed within a loop. But if these instructions have to be executed abruptly from anywhere within the program code, then instead of writing these instructions everywhere they are required, a better way is to place these instructions in a function and call that function wherever required. Figure 5.4 explains this concept.

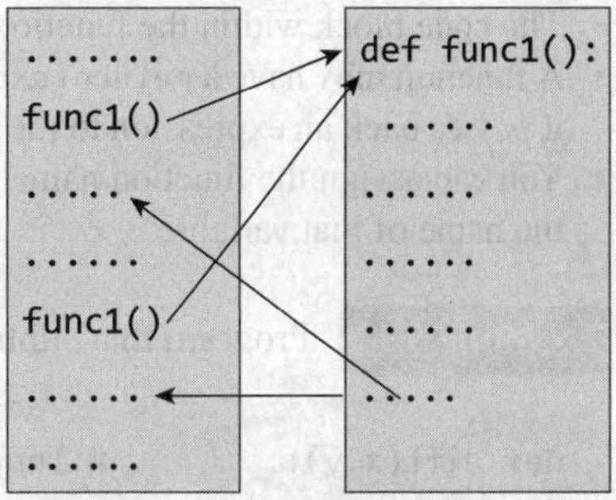

> **Note** Functions provide better modularity for your application and a high degree of code reuse.

Figure 5.4 Function func1() called twice from the main module

5.2 FUNCTION DEFINITION

Any function can be compared to a black box (that is used for an entity having unknown implementation) that takes in input, processes it and then spits out the result. However, we may also have a function that does not take any inputs at all, or that does not return anything at all. While using functions we will be using the terminology given below.

- A function, *f* that uses another function *g*, is known as the *calling function* and *g* is known as the *called function*.
- The inputs that the function takes are known as *arguments/parameters*.
- When a called function returns some result back to the calling function, it is said to *return* that result.
- The calling function may or may not pass *parameters* to the called function. If the called function accepts arguments, the calling function will pass parameters, else not.
- *Function declaration* is a declaration statement that identifies a function with its name, a list of arguments that it accepts, and the type of data it returns.
- *Function definition* consists of a function header that identifies the function, followed by the body of the function containing the executable code for that function.

> **Note** Besides using built-in functions, users can also write their own functions. Such functions are called user defined functions.

Python gives functions first class treatment and gives them equal status with other objects. There are two basic types of functions, built-in functions and user defined ones. The built-in functions comes as a part of the Python language. For examples, `dir()`, `len()`, or `abs()`. The user defined functions, on the other hand, are functions created by users in their programs using the `def` keyword.

> **Programming Tip:** Function naming follows the same rules of writing identifiers in Python.

As a Python programmer, you can write any number of functions in your program. However, to define a function, you must keep the following points in mind.

- Function blocks starts with the keyword `def`.
- The keyword is followed by the function name and parentheses (( )). The function name is used to uniquely identify the function.
- After the parentheses a colon (:) is placed.
- Parameters or arguments that the function accepts are placed within parentheses. Through these parameters values are passed to the function. They are optional. In case no values are to be passed, nothing is placed within the parenthesis.
- The first statement of a function can be an optional statement—the documentation string of the function or *docstring* describe what the function does. We will discuss this later in the book.

- The code block within the function is properly indented to form the block code.
- A function may have a return[expression] statement. That is, the return statement is optional. If it exits, it passes back an expression to the caller. A return statement with no arguments is the same as return None.
- You can assign the function name to a variable. Doing this will allow you to call the same function using the name of that variable.

Example 5.1   Program that subtracts two numbers using a function

```
def diff(x,y):        # function to subtract two numbers
        return x-y
a = 20
b = 10
operation = diff      # function name assigned to a variable
print(operation(a,b)) # function called using variable name
```

OUTPUT

```
10
```

Note   The words before parentheses specifies the function name, and the comma-separated values inside the parentheses are function arguments.

When a function is defined, space is allocated for that function in the memory. A function definition comprises of two parts:

- Function header
- Function body

The syntax of a function definition can be given as:

```
def function_name(variable1, variable2,..)        ← Function Header
    documentation string
    statement block                    ← Function Body
    return [expression]
```

Programming Tip: The indented statements form *body* of the function.

Example 5.2   To write a function that displays a string repeatedly

```
def func():
        for i in range(4):
                print("Hello World")
func()      #function call
```

Programming Tip: The parameter list in the function definition as well as function declaration must match with each other.

OUTPUT

```
Hello World
Hello World
Hello World
Hello World
```

In the aforementioned code, name of the function is func. It takes no arguments, and prints "Hello World" four times. The function is first defined before being called. The statements in the function are executed only when the function is called.

Note Before calling a function, you must define it just as you assign variables before using them.

5.3 FUNCTION CALL

Defining a function means specifying its name, parameters that are expected, and the set of instructions. Once the basic structure of a function is finalized, it can be executed by calling it.

> **Programming Tip:** It is a logic error if the arguments in the function call are placed in a wrong order.

The function call statement invokes the function. When a function is invoked, the program control jumps to the called function to execute the statements that are a part of that function. Once the called function is executed, the program control passes back to the calling function. The syntax of calling a function that does not accept parameters is simply the name of the function followed by parenthesis, which is given as,

```
function_name()
```

Function call statement has the following syntax when it accepts parameters.

```
function_name(variable1, variable2, …)
```

When the function is called, the interpreter checks that the correct number and type of arguments are used in the function call. It also checks the type of the returned value (if it returns a value to the calling function).

Note List of variables used in function call is known as the actual parameter list. The actual parameter list may be variable names, expressions, or constants.

5.3.1 Function Parameters

A function can take parameters which are nothing but some values that are passed to it so that the function can manipulate them to produce the desired result. These parameters are normal variables with a small difference that the values of these variables are defined (initialized) when we call the function and are then passed to the function.

Parameters are specified within the pair of parentheses in the function definition and are separated by commas.

Key points to remember while calling the function

- The function name and the number of arguments in the function call must be same as that given in the function definition.
- If by mistake the parameters passed to a function are more than that it is specified to accept, then an error will be returned.

Example 5.3 Program to demonstrate the mismatch between function parameters and arguments

```
def func(i, j):
        print("Hello World", i, j)
```

```
func(5)
```

OUTPUT

```
TypeError: func() takes exactly 2 arguments (1 given)
```

- If by mistake the parameters passed to a function are less than that it is specified to accept, then an error will be returned.

> **Programming Tip:** You can call a function from another function or directly from the Python prompt.

Example 5.4 Program to demonstrate the mismatch between function parameters and arguments

```
def func(i):
        print("Hello World", i)
func(5, 5)
```

OUTPUT

```
TypeError: func() takes exactly 1 argument (2 given)
```

- Names of variables in function call and header of function definition may vary.

Example 5.5 Program to demonstrate mismatch of name of function parameters and arguments

```
def func(i):               # function definition header accepts a variable with name i
    print("Hello World", i)
j = 10
func(j)                    # Function is called using variable j
```

OUTPUT
```
Hello World 10
```

- If the data type of the argument passed does not match with that expected in the function, then an error is generated.

Example 5.6 Program to demonstrate mismatch between data types of function parameters and arguments

```
def func(i):
    print("Hello World" + i)
func(5)
```

OUTPUT

```
TypeError: cannot concatenate 'str' and 'int' objects
```

- Arguments may be passed in the form of expressions to the called function. In such a case, arguments are first evaluated and converted to the type of formal parameter and then the body of the function gets executed.

Example 5.7 Program to demonstrate that the arguments may be passed in the form of expressions to the called function.

```
def func(i):
        print("Hello World", i)
func(5+2*3)
```

OUTPUT
```
Hello World 11
```

- The parameter list must be separated with commas.
- If the function returns a value then it may be assigned to some variable in the calling program. For example,

```
variable_name = function_name(variable1, variable2, ...);
```

Let us now try a program using a function.

Example 5.8 Program to add two integers using functions

```
def total(a,b):      # function accepting parameters
    result = a+b
    print("Sum of ", a, " and ", b, " = ", result)

a = int(input("Enter the first number : "))
b - int(input("Enter the second number : "))
total(a,b) #function call with two arguments
```

OUTPUT
```
Enter the first number : 10
Enter the second number : 20
Sum of 10 and 20 = 30
```

In the function `total()` used in the above program, we have declared a variable `result` just like any other variable. Variables declared within a function are called *local variables*. We will read more about it in the next section.

5.4 VARIABLE SCOPE AND LIFETIME

In Python, you cannot just access any variable from any part of your program. Some of the variables may not even exist for the entire duration of the program. In which part of the program you can access a variable and in which parts of the program a variable exists depends on how the variable has been declared. Therefore, we need to understand these two things:

- **Scope of the variable** Part of the program in which a variable is accessible is called its *scope*.
- **Lifetime of the variable** Duration for which the variable exists is called its *lifetime*.

5.4.1 Local and Global Variables

Global variables are those variables which are defined in the main body of the program file. They are visible throughout the program file. As a good programming habit, you must try to avoid the use of global variables because they may get altered by mistake and then result in erroneous

> **Programming Tip:** Trying to access local variable outside the function produces an error.

output. But this does not mean that you should not use them at all. As a golden rule, use only those variables or objects that are meant to be used globally, like functions and classes, should be put in the global section of the program (i.e., above any other function or line of code).

Correspondingly, a variable which is defined within a function is *local* to that function. A local variable can be accessed from the point of its definition until the end of the function in which it is defined. It exists as long as the function is executing. Function parameters behave like local variables in the function. Moreover, whenever we use the assignment operator (=) inside a function, a new local variable is created (provided a variable with the same name is not defined in the local scope).

> **Example 5.9** Program to understand the difference between local and global variables

```
num1 = 10    # global variable
print("Global variable num1 = ", num1)
def func(num2):          # num2 is function parameter
        print("In Function - Local Variable num2 = ",num2)
        num3 = 30        #num3 is a local variable
        print("In Function - Local Variable num3 = ",num3)
func(20)       #20 is passed as an argument to the function
print("num1 again = ", num1)       #global variable is being accessed
#Error- local variable can't be used outside the function in which it is defined
print("num3 outside function = ", num3)
```

OUTPUT

```
Global variable num1 = 10
In Function - Local Variable num2 = 20
In Function - Local Variable num3 = 30
num1 again =  10
num3 outside function =
Traceback (most recent call last):
  File "C:\Python34\Try.py", line 12, in <module>
    print("num3 outside function = ", num3)
NameError: name 'num3' is not defined
```

> **Programming Tip:** Variables can only be used after the point of their declaration

The following Table 5.1 lists the differences between global and local variables.

Table 5.1 Comparison Between Global and Local Variables

Global Variables	Local Variables
1. They are defined in the main body of the program file.	1. They are defined within a function and is *local* to that function.
2. They can be accessed throughout the program file.	2. They can be accessed from the point of its definition until the end of the block in which it is defined.
3. Global variables are accessible to all functions in the program.	3. They are not related in any way to other variables with the same names used outside the function.

5.4.2 Using the Global Statement

To define a variable defined inside a function as global, you must use the global statement. This declares the local or the inner variable of the function to have module scope. Look at the code given below and observe its output to understand this concept.

Example 5.10 Program to demonstrate the use of global statement

```
var = "Good"
def show():
        global var1
        var1 = "Morning"
        print("In Function var is - ", var)
show()
print("Outside function, var1 is - ", var1)        #accessible as it is global
variable
print("var is - ", var)
```

OUTPUT

```
In Function var is -  Good
Outside function, var1 is -  Morning
var is -  Good
```

> **Programming Tip:** All variables have the scope of the block.

Key points to remember

- You can have a variable with the same name as that of a global variable in the program. In such a case a new local variable of that name is created which is different from the global variable. For example, look at the code in the following example and observe its output.

Example 5.11 Program to demonstrate name clash of local and global variable

```
var = "Good"
def show():
```

```
        var = "Morning"
        print("In Function var is - ", var)
show()
print("Outside function, var is - ", var)
```

OUTPUT

```
In Function var is -  Morning
Outside function, var is -  Good
```

- If we have a global variable and then create another global variable using the global statement, then changes made in the variable will be reflected everywhere in the program. This concept is illustrated in the code given below.

Example 5.12   Program to demonstrate modifying a global variable

```
var = "Good"
def show():
        global var
        var = "Morning"
        print("In Function var is - ", var)
show()
print("Outside function, var is - ", var)
var = "Fantastic"
print("Outside function, after modification, var is - ", var)
```

> **Programming Tip:** You cannot assign value to a variable defined outside a function without using the global statement.

OUTPUT

```
In Function var is -  Morning
Outside function, var is -  Morning
Outside function, after modification, var is -  Fantastic
```

- In case of nested functions (function inside another function), the inner function can access variables defined in both outer as well as inner function, but the outer function can access variables defined only in the outer function. The following code explains this concept.

> **Programming Tip:** Arguments are specified within parentheses. If there is more than one argument, then they are separated using comma.

Example 5.13   Program to demonstrate access of variables in inner and outer functions

```
def outer_func():
        outer_var = 10
        def inner_func():
                inner_var = 20
                print("Outer Variable = ", outer_var)
                print("Inner Variable = ", inner_var)
        inner_func()
```

```
      print("Outer Variable = ", outer_var)
      print("Inner Variable = ", inner_var)  #not accessible
outer_func()    #function call
```

OUTPUT

```
Outer Variable =  10
Inner Variable =  20
Outer Variable =  10
Traceback (most recent call last):
  File "C:\Python34\Try.py", line 10, in <module>
  File ""C:\Python34\Try.py", line 9, in outer_func
NameError: name 'inner_var' is not defined
```

- If a variable in the inner function is defined with the same name as that of a variable defined in the outer function, then a new variable is created in the inner function. Look at the code given below to understand this concept.

Example 5.14 Program to demonstrate name clash variables in case of nested functions

```
def outer_func():
        var = 10
        def inner_func():
                var = 20
                print("Inner Variable = ", var)
        inner_func()
        print("Outer Variable = ", var)

outer_func()
```

OUTPUT

```
Inner Variable =  20
Outer Variable =  10
```

Note   In the above program, even if we use global statement we would get the same result as global statement is applicable for the entire program and not just for outer function.

5.4.3 Resolution of Names

As discussed in the previous section, *scope* defines the visibility of a name within a block. If a local variable is defined in a block, its scope is that particular block. If it is defined in a function, then its scope is all blocks within that function.

When a variable name is used in a code block, it is resolved using the nearest enclosing scope. If no variable of that name is found, then a NameError is raised. In the code given below, str is a global string because it has been defined before calling the function.

Programming Tip: Try to avoid the use of global variables and global statement.

Example 5.15 Program that demonstrates using a variable defined in global namespace

```
def func():
        print(str)
str = "Hello World !!!"
func()
```

OUTPUT

```
Hello World !!!
```

You cannot define a local variable with the same name as that of global variable. If you want to do that, you must use the global statement. The code given below illustrates this concept.

Example 5.16 Program that demonstrates using a local variable with same name as that of global

```
def f():
        print(str) #global
        str = "Hello World!"  #local
        print(str)
str = "Welcome to Python Programming!"
f()
```

OUTPUT

```
UnboundLocalError: local variable 'str'
referenced before assignment
```

```
def f():
        global str
        print(str)
        str = "Hello World!"
        print(str)
str = "Welcome to Python Programming!"
f()
```

OUTPUT

```
Welcome to Python Programming!
Hello World!
```

5.5 THE return STATEMENT

In all our functions written above, no where we have used the return statement. But you will be surprised to know that every function has an implicit return statement as the last instruction in the function body. This implicit return statement returns nothing to its caller, so it is said to return None, where None means nothing. But you can change this default behavior by explicitly using the return statement to return some value back to the caller. The syntax of return statement is,

> **Programming Tip:** A return statement with no arguments is the same as return None.

```
return [expression]
```

The expression is written in brackets because it is optional. If the expression is present, it is evaluated and the resultant value is returned to the calling function. However, if no expression is specified then the function will return None.

Note   A function may or may not return a value.

The return statement is used for two things.

- Return a value to the caller
- To end and exit a function and go back to its caller

Example 5.17   Program to write a function without a `return` statement and try to print its return value. As mentioned earlier, such a function should return `None`.

```
def display(str):
    print(str)
x = display("Hello World") #assigning return value to another variable
print(x)
#print return value without assigning it to another variable
print(display("Hello Again"))
```

OUTPUT
```
Hello World
None
Hello Again
None
```

It should be noted that in the output `None` is returned from the function. The return value may or may not be assigned to another variable in the caller.

Example 5.18   Program to write another function which returns an integer to the caller

```
def cube(x):
    return (x*x*x)
num = 10
result = cube(num)
print("Cube of ", num, " = ", result)
```

OUTPUT
```
Cube of 10 = 1000
```

Note   The return statement cannot be used outside of a function definition.

Key points to remember
- The return statement must appear within the function.
- Once you return a value from a function, it immediately exits that function. Therefore, any code written after the return statement is never executed. The program given in the following example illustrates this concept.

Example 5.19   Program to demonstrate flow of control after the `return` statement

```
def display():
    print("In Function")
    print("About to execute return statement")
    return
    print("This line will never be displayed")
```

```
display()
print("Back to the caller")
```

OUTPUT
```
In Function
About to execute return statement
Back to the caller
```

5.6 FRUITFUL FUNCTIONS

A fruitful function is one in which there is a return statement with an expression. This means that a fruitful function returns a value that can be utilized by the calling function for further processing.

> **Programming Tip:** In a fruitful function, make sure that every possible path through the program has a return statement, especially when the function has return statements in decision control statements.

5.6.1 The return Statement

In all our functions written above, no where we have used the return statement. But you will be surprised to know that every function has an implicit return statement as the last instruction in the function body. This implicit `return` statement returns nothing to its caller, so it is said to return None, where None means nothing. But you can change this default behavior by explicitly using the return statement to return some value back to the caller. The syntax of return statement is,

> **Programming Tip:** A return statement with no arguments is the same as return None.

```
return [expression]
```

The expression is written in brackets because it is optional. If the expression is present, it is evaluated and the resultant value is returned to the calling function. However, if no expression is specified then the function will return None.

> **Note** A function may or may not return a value.

The return statement is used for two things.

- Return a value to the caller
- To end and exit a function and go back to its caller

Example 5.20 Program to write a function without a return statement and try to print its return value. As mentioned earlier, such a function should return None.

```
def display(str):
    print(str)
x = display("Hello World") #assigning return value to another variable
print(x)
#print return value without assigning it to another variable
print(display("Hello Again"))
```

OUTPUT
```
Hello World
None
Hello Again
None
```

It should be noted that in the output None is returned from the function. The return value may or may not be assigned to another variable in the caller.

Example 5.21 Program to write another function which returns an integer to the caller.

```
def cube(x):
    return (x*x*x)
num = 10
result = cube(num)
print("Cube of ", num, " = ", result)
```

OUTPUT
```
Cube of 10 = 1000
```

Note The return statement cannot be used outside of a function definition.

Key points to remember

- The return statement must appear within the function.
- Once you return a value from a function, it immediately exits that function. Therefore, any code written after the return statement is never executed. The program given in the following example illustrates this concept.

Example 5.22 Program to demonstrate flow of control after the return statement

```
def display():
    print("In Function")
    print("About to execute return statement")
    return
    print("This line will never be displayed")
display()
print("Back to the caller")
```

OUTPUT
```
In Function
About to execute return statement
Back to the caller
```

5.6.2 Parameters

We have already discussed in the previous section, the technique to define and call a function. In this section, we will go a step forward and learn some more ways of defining a function. All these features make Python a wonderful language. Some of these features include

- Required arguments
- Keyword arguments
- Default arguments
- Variable-length arguments

Required Arguments

We have already been using this type of formal arguments. In the *required arguments*, the arguments are passed to a function in correct positional order. Also, the number of arguments in the function call should exactly match with the number of arguments specified in the function definition.

Look at three different versions of `display()` given below and observe the output. The function displays the string only when number and type of arguments in the function call matches with that specified in the function definition, otherwise a `TypeError` is returned.

```def display(): print("Hello") display("Hi")``` **OUTPUT** `TypeError: display() takes no arguments (1 given)`	```def display(str): print(str) display()``` **OUTPUT** `TypeError: display() takes exactly 1 argument (0 given)`	```def display(str): print(str) str ="Hello" display(str)``` **OUTPUT** `Hello`

Keyword Arguments

When we call a function with some values, the values are assigned to the arguments based on their position. Python also allows functions to be called using keyword arguments in which the order (or position) of the arguments can be changed. The values are not assigned to arguments according to their position but based on their name (or keyword).

> **Programming Tip:** Having a required argument after keyword arguments will cause error.

Keyword arguments when used in function calls, helps the function to identify the arguments by the parameter name. This is especially beneficial in two cases.

- First, if you skip arguments.
- Second, if in the function call you change the order of parameters. That is, in any order different from that specified in the function definition.

In both the cases mentioned above, Python interpreter uses keywords provided in the function call to match the values with parameters.

Example 5.23 Program to demonstrate keyword arguments

```
def display(str, int_x, float_y):
    print("The string is : ",str)
    print("The integer value is : ", int_x)
    print("The floating point value is : ", float_y)
display(float_y = 56789.045, str = "Hello", int_x = 1234)
```

OUTPUT

```
The string is:  Hello
The integer value is:  1234
The floating point value is:  56789.045
```

Example 5.24 Consider another program for keyword arguments in which during function call we use assignment operator to assign values to function parameters using other variables (instead of values).

```
def display(name, age, salary):
    print("Name : ", name)
    print("Age : ", age)
    print("Salary : ", salary)
n = "Aadi"
a = 35
s = 123456
display(salary = s, name = n, age = a)
```

OUTPUT

```
Name :  Aadi
Age :  35
Salary :  123456
```

Key points to remember

- All the keyword arguments passed should match one of the arguments accepted by the function.
- The order of keyword arguments is not important.
- In no case an argument should receive a value more than once.

Note   Keyword arguments makes the program code easier to read and understand.

Default Arguments

Python allows users to specify function arguments that can have default values. This means that a function can be called with fewer arguments than it is defined to have. That is, if the function accepts three parameters, but function call provides only two arguments, then the third parameter will be assigned the default (already specified) value.

The default value to an argument is provided by using the assignment operator (=). Users can specify a default value for one or more arguments.

Note   A default argument assumes a default value if a value is not provided in the function call for that argument.

Example 5.25 Program that uses default arguments

```
def display(name, course = "BTech"):
    print("Name : " + name)
    print("Course : ", course)
display(course = "BCA", name = "Arav") # Keyword Arguments
display(name = "Reyansh")              # Default Argument for course

OUTPUT
Name : Arav
Course :  BCA
Name : Reyansh
Course :  BTech
```

In the above code, the parameter name does not have a default value and is therefore mandatory. That is, you must specify a value for this parameter during the function call. But, parameter, course has already been given a default value, so it is optional. If a value is provided, it will overwrite the default value and in case a value is not specified during function call, the one provided in the function definition as the default value will be used.

Key points to remember

- You can specify any number of default arguments in your function.
- If you have default arguments, then they must be written after the non-default arguments. This means that non-default arguments cannot follow default arguments. Therefore, the line of code given in the following example will produce an error.

Example 5.26 Program to demonstrate default arguments

```
def display(name, course = "BTech", marks):   #error
    print("Name : " + name)
    print("Course : ", course)
    print("Marks : ", marks)
display(name = "Reyansh", 90)

OUTPUT
SyntaxError: non-default argument follows default argument
```

Programming Tip: All the arguments to the right of the default argument must also have default values.

Note A positional argument is assigned based on its position in the argument list but a keyword argument is assigned based on parameter name.

Variable-length Arguments

In some situations, it is not known in advance how many arguments will be passed to a function. In such cases, Python allows programmers to make function calls with arbitrary (or any) number of arguments.

When we use arbitrary arguments or variable-length arguments, then the function definition uses an asterisk (*) before the parameter name. Syntax for a function using variable arguments can be given as,

```
def functionname([arg1, arg2,.... ] *var_args_tuple ):
    function statements
    return [expression]
```

Example 5.27 Program to demonstrate the use of variable-length arguments

```
def func(name, *fav_subjects):
    print("\n", name, " likes to read ")
    for subject in fav_subjects:
        print(subject, end=" ")
func("Goransh", "Mathematics", "Android Programming")
func("Richa", "C", "Data Structures", "Design and Analysis of Algorithms")
func("Krish")
```

OUTPUT
```
Goransh  likes to read  Mathematics Android Programming
Richa likes to read  C Data Structures Design and Analysis of Algorithms
Krish  likes to read
```

In the above program, in the function definition, we have two parameters—one is name and the other is variable-length parameter fav_subjects. The function is called three times with 3, 4, and 1 parameter(s) respectively. The first value is assigned to name and the other values are assigned to parameter fav_subjects. Everyone can have any number of favorite subjects and some can even have none. So when the third call is made, fav_subjects has no value and hence the for loop will not execute as there is no subject available in fav_subjects.

Key points to remember

- The arbitrary number of arguments passed to the function basically form a tuple (data structure discussed later in this book) before being passed into the function.
- Inside the called function, for loop is used to access the arguments.
- The variable-length arguments if present in the function definition should be the last in the list of formal parameters.
- Any formal parameters written after the variable-length arguments must be keyword-only arguments.

Note A function cannot be used on the right side of an assignment statement. Therefore writing, *total(a, b) = s;* is invalid.

5.7 LAMBDA FUNCTIONS OR ANONYMOUS FUNCTIONS

Lambda or anonymous functions are so called because they are not declared as other functions using the def keyword. Rather, they are created using the lambda keyword. Lambda functions are throw-away functions, i.e. they are just needed where they have been created and can be used anywhere a function is required. The lambda feature was added to Python due to the demand from LISP programmers.

Note   Lambda is simply the name of a letter 'L' in the Greek alphabet.

Lambda functions contain only a single line. Its syntax can be given as,

```
lambda arguments: expression
```

The arguments contain a comma separated list of arguments and the expression is an arithmetic expression that uses these arguments. The function can be assigned to a variable to give it a name.

Example 5.28   Program that adds two numbers using the syntax of lambda function

```
sum = lambda x, y: x + y
print("Sum = ", sum(3, 5))

OUTPUT
Sum = 8
```

In the above code, the lambda function returns the sum of its two arguments. In the above program, lambda x, y: x + y is the lambda function. x and y are the arguments, and x + y is the expression that gets evaluated and returned. Note that the lambda function has no name. It returns a function object which is assigned to the identifier sum. Moreover,

```
lambda x, y: x + y
```

is same as writing,

```
def sum(x,y):
    return x+y
```

Note   You can use lambda functions wherever function objects are required.

Key points to remember

Programming Tip: Lambda functions are not equivalent to inline functions in C/ C++.

- Lambda functions have no name.
- Lambda functions can take any number of arguments.
- Lambda functions can return just one value in the form of an expression.
- Lambda function definition does not have an explicit **return** statement but it always contains an expression which is returned.
- They are a one-line version of a function and hence cannot contain multiple expressions.
- They cannot access variables other than those in their parameter list.
- Lambda functions cannot even access global variables.
- You can pass lambda functions as arguments in other functions. Look at the code given in the following example to see how this is possible.

Example 5.29 Program to find smaller of two numbers using `lambda` function

```
def small(a,b):              # a regular function that returns smaller value
    if(a<b):
        return a
    else:
        return b
sum = lambda x, y : x+y      # lambda function to add two numbers
diff = lambda x, y : x-y     # lambda function to subtract two numbers
#pass lambda functions as arguments to the regular function
print("Smaller of two numbers = ", small(sum(-3, -2), diff(-1, 2)))
```

Programming Tip: If you find lambda functions difficult, better use normal functions for clarity.

OUTPUT
```
Smaller of two numbers = -5
```

- Lambda functions are used along with built-in functions like `filter()`, `map()`, `reduce()`, etc. We will discuss these functions in later chapters.
- You can use lambda functions in regular functions.

Example 5.30 Program to use a `lambda` function with an ordinary function

```
def increment(y):
    return (lambda x: x+1)(y)
a = 100
print("a = ", a)
print("a after incrementing = ")
b = increment(a)
print(b)
```

OUTPUT
```
a = 100
a after incrementing = 101
```

In the aforementioned code, the regular function increment accepts a value in y. It then passes y to a lambda function. The lambda function increments its value and finally the regular function returns the incremented value to the caller.

- You can use a lambda function without assigning it to a variable. This is shown below.

# lambda function assigned to variable twice	# lambda function not assigned to any variable twice

`twice = lambda x: x*2`
`print(twice(9))`
 	
OUTPUT
`18`
	`print ((lambda x: x*2) (9))`
	`(twice(9))`
	
	OUTPUT
	`18`

Argument passed to lambda function

Argument passed to lambda function

You can pass lambda arguments to a function. This is shown in the code given below.

Example 5.31   Program that passes `lambda` function as an argument to a function

```
def func(f, n):
    print(f(n))

twice = lambda x: x * 2
thrice = lambda x: x * 3

func(twice, 4)
func(thrice, 3)
```

OUTPUT
```
8
9
```

- You can define a lambda that receives no arguments but simply returns an expression. Look at the code given in the following example.

Example 5.32   Program that uses a `lambda` function to find the sum of first 10 natural numbers

```
x = lambda: sum(range(1, 11))
# Invoke lambda expression that accepts no arguments but returns a value in y
print(x())
```

OUTPUT
```
55
```

> **Programming Tip:** The print() returns None.

In the above code, we have assigned a variable x to a lambda expression and then invoked the lambda function with empty parentheses (without arguments).

- You can call a lambda function from another lambda unction. In such a case, the lambda function is said to be a nested function. However, use of nested lambda functions must be avoided. The program code given below demonstrates this concept.

Example 5.33   Program to add two numbers using `lambda` function

```
add = lambda x, y: x + y      #lambda function that adds two numbers
#lambda function that calls another lambda function to generate the result
multiply_and_add = lambda x, y, z: x * add(y,z)
print(multiply_and_add(3,4,5))
```

OUTPUT
```
27
```

| Note | With nested lambdas, recursion can occur and may also result in a RuntimeError: maximum recursion depth exceeded error. |

- The time taken by a lambda function to perform a computation is almost similar to that take taken by a regular function.

Higher Orders Functions

Higher Orders Functions are functions that perform operations on other functions. These operations may include taking one or more functions as an argument or returning a function as the result. It may be doing both of these things but definitely a function cannot do both to qualify as a high order function.

5.8 FUNCTION COMPOSITION IN PYTHON

Function composition combines two functions in such a way that the result of one function is passed as an argument to the other function. It can be denoted as $f(g(x))$, where x is an argument to the function $g()$ and the result of $g(x)$ is an argument to the function $f()$. The result of function composition is finally given as the result of function $f()$.

Example 5.34 Use function composition to increment a number and then square it.

```python
import functools
def square(x):
    return(x * * 2)
def inc(x):
    return(x + 1)
inc_and_square = compose(square, inc)
res = inc_and_square(9)
print(res)
```

OUTPUT

```
100
```

In this way, you can compose n functions. First, compose the first two functions, then compose the newly created function with the next one, and so on.

5.9 DOCUMENTATION STRINGS

Docstrings (documentation strings) serve the same purpose as that of comments, as they are designed to explain code. However, they are more specific and have a proper syntax. As you can see below, they are created by putting a multiline string to explain the function. To understand the concept of documentation strings, let us first revisit the syntax of defining a function.

```python
def functionname(parameters):
    "function_docstring"
    function statements
    return [expression]
```

As per the syntax, the first statement of the function body can optionally be a string literal which is also known as documentation string, or *docstring*. Docstrings are important as they help tools to automatically generate online or printed documentation. It also helps users and readers of the code to interactively browse through code. As a good programming habit, you must have a habit of including docstrings.

Key points to remember

- As the first line, it should always be short and concise highlighting the summary of the object's purpose.
- It should not specify information like the object's name or type.
- It should begin with a capital letter and end with a period.
- Triple quotes are used to extend the docstring to multiple lines. This docstring specified can be accessed through the __doc__ attribute of the function.
- In case of multiple lines in the documentation string, the second line should be blank, to separate the summary from the rest of the description. The other lines should be one or more paragraphs describing the object's calling conventions, its side effects, etc.
- The first non-blank line after the first line of the documentation string determines the amount of indentation for the entire documentation string.
- Unlike comments, docstrings are retained throughout the runtime of the program. So, users can inspect them during program execution.

Example 5.35 Program to show a multi-line docstring

```
def func():
    """The program just prints a message.
    It will display Hello World !!!   """
    print("Hello World !!!")
print(func.__doc__)
```

OUTPUT
```
Hello world!!!
The program just prints a message.
    It will display Hello World !!!
```

5.10 GOOD PROGRAMMING PRACTICES

While writing large and complex programs, you must take care of some points that will help you to develop readable, effective, and efficient code. For Python, **PEP 8** has emerged as the coding style guide that most projects adhere to promote a very readable and eye pleasing coding style. Some basic points that you should follow are:

- Instead of tabs, use 4 spaces for indentation.
- Insert blank lines to separate functions and classes, and statement blocks inside functions.
- Wherever required, use comments to explain the code.
- Use document strings that explains the purpose of the function.
- Use spaces around operators and after commas.

- Name of the classes should be written as ClassName (observe the capital letters, another example can be StudentInfo). We will read about classes in subsequent chapters.
- Name of the functions should be in lowercase with underscores to separate words. For example, display_info() and get_data().
- Do not use non-ASCII characters in function names or any other identifier.

PROGRAMMING EXAMPLES

Program 5.1 Write a program using functions to check whether two numbers are equal or not.

```
def check_relation(a,b):
    if(a==b):
        return 0
    if(a>b):
        return 1
    if(a<b):
        return -1

a = 3
b = 5
res = check_relation(a,b)
if(res==0):
    print("a is equal to b")
if(res==1):
    print("a is greater than b")
if(res==-1):
    print("a is less than b")
```

Programming Tip: Function should be defined before it is called.

OUTPUT

```
a is less than b
```

Program 5.2 Write a program to swap two numbers.

```
def swap(a,b):
    a,b = b,a
    print("After swap : ")
    print("First number = ",a)
    print("Second number = ",b)

a = input("\n Enter the first number : ")
b = input("\n Enter the second number : ")
print("Before swap : ")
print("First number = ",a)
print("Second number = ",b)
swap(a,b)
```

OUTPUT

```
Enter the first number : 29
Enter the second number : 56
Before swap :
First number =  29
Second number =  56
After swap :
First number =  56
Second number =  29
```

Program 5.3 Write a program to return the full name of a person.

```
def name(firstName, lastName):
    separator = ' '
    n = firstName + separator + lastName
    return n
print(name('Janak', 'Raj'))
```

OUTPUT

```
Janak Raj
```

Program 5.4 Write a program to return the average of its arguments.

```
def avg(n1, n2):
    return (n1+n2)/2.0
n1 = int(input("Enter the first number : "))
n2 = int(input("Enter the second number : "))
print("AVERAGE = ", avg(n1,n2))
```

OUTPUT

```
Enter the first number : 5
Enter the second number : 7
AVERAGE =  6.0
```

Program 5.5 Write a program using functions and return statement to check whether a number is even or odd.

```
def evenodd(a):
    if(a%2==0):
            return 1
    else:
            return -1
a = int(input("Enter the number : "))
flag = evenodd(a)
if(flag==1):
    print("Number is even")
```

```
if(flag==-1):
      print("Number is odd")
```

OUTPUT

```
Enter the number : 1091
Number is odd
```

Program 5.6 Write a program to convert time into minutes.

```
def convert_time_in_min(hrs,minute):
      minute = hrs*60+minute
      return minute
h = int(input("Enter the hours : "))
m = int(input("Enter the minutes : "))
m = convert_time_in_min(h,m)
print("Minutes =",m)
```

OUTPUT

```
Enter the hours and minutes : 6
Enter the hours and minutes : 34
Minutes = 394
```

Program 5.7 Write a program to calculate simple interest. Suppose the customer is a senior citizen. He is being offered 12 per cent rate of interest; for all other customers, the ROI is 10 per cent.

```
def interest(p,y,s):
    if(s=='y'):
        SI = float((p*y*12)/100)
    else:
        SI = float((p*y*10)/100)
    return SI
p = float(input("Enter the principle amount : "))
y = float(input("Enter the number of years : "))
senior = input("Is customer senior citizen(y/n) : ")
print("Interest :",interest(p,y,senior))
```

OUTPUT

```
Enter the principle amount : 200000
Enter the number of years : 3
Is customer senior citizen(y/n) : n
Interest : 60000.0
```

Program 5.8 Write a program to calculate the volume of a cuboid using default arguments.

```python
def volume(l,w=3,h=4):
    print("Length :",l,"\tWidth :",w,"\tHeight :",h)
    return l*w*h

print("Volume :",volume(4,6,2))
print("Volume :",volume(4,6))
print("Volume :",volume(4))
```

OUTPUT

```
Volume : Length : 4        Width : 6        Height : 2
48
Volume : Length : 4        Width : 6        Height : 4
96
Volume : Length : 4        Width : 3        Height : 4
48
```

Program 5.9 Write a program that computes P(n,r).

```python
def fact(n):
    f = 1
    if(n==0 or n==1):
        return 1
    else:
        for i in range(1,int(n+1)):
            f = f*i
    return f

n = int(input("Enter the value of n : "))
r = int(input("Enter the value of r : "))
result = float(fact(n))/float(fact(r))
print("P(",str(n),"/",str(r),") = ",str(result))
```

OUTPUT

```
Enter the value of n : 9
Enter the value of r : 4
P( 9 / 4 ) =  15120.0
```

Program 5.10 Write a program to sum the series 1/1! + 4/2! + 27/3! + ...

```python
def fact(n):
    f = 1
    if(n==0 or n==1):
        return 1
    else:
        for i in range(1,int(n+1)):
```

```
                f = f*i
     return f

n = int(input("Enter the value of n : "))
s = 0.0
for i in range(1,n+1):
     s = s+(float(i**i)/fact(i))
print("Result :",s)
```

OUTPUT
```
Enter the value of n : 5
Result : 44.2083333333
```

Program 5.11 Write a program that uses docstings and variable-length arguments to add the values passed to the function.

```
def add(*args):
    '''Function returns the sum of values passed to it'''
    sum = 0
    for i in args:
        sum  += i
    return sum

print(add.__doc__)
print("SUM = ",add(25, 30, 45, 50))
```

OUTPUT
```
Function returns the sum of values passed to it
SUM - 150
```

Program 5.12 Write a program that greets a person.

```
def greet(name, mesg):
   """This function
   welcomes the person passed whose name
   is passed as a
   parameter"""

   print("Welcome, " + name + ". " + mesg)

mesg = "Happy Reading. Python is Fun !"
name = input("\n Enter your name : ")
greet(name, mesg)
```

OUTPUT
```
Enter your name : Goransh
Welcome, Goransh. Happy Reading. Python is Fun !
```

Program 5.13 Write a program to print the following pattern using default arguments.

```
%%%%%
^^^^^^
^^^^^^^^^^
^^^^^^^^^^^^^^^
^^^^^^^^^^^^^^^
def pattern(c='%',n=6,r=1):
    for i in range(r):
        print()
        for j in range(n):
            print(c, end = ' ')
c = input("Enter the character to be displayed : ")
n = int(input("Enter the number of rows : "))
m = int(input("Enter the number of columns : "))
pattern()
pattern(c)
pattern(c,n)
pattern(c,n,m)
```

5.11 RECURSIVE FUNCTIONS

A *recursive function* is defined as a function that calls itself to solve a smaller version of its task until a final call is made which does not require a call to itself. Every recursive solution has two major cases, which are as follows:

- *base case*, in which the problem is simple enough to be solved directly without making any further calls to the same function.
- *recursive case,* in which first the problem at hand is divided into simpler sub-parts. Second, the function calls itself but with sub-parts of the problem obtained in the first step. Third, the result is obtained by combining the solutions of simpler sub-parts.

Thus, we see that recursion utilized divide and conquer technique of problem solving. *Divide and conquer technique* is a method of solving a given problem by dividing it into two or more smaller instances. Each of these smaller instances is recursively solved, and the solutions are combined to produce a solution for the original problem. Therefore, recursion is used for defining large and complex problems in terms of a smaller and more easily solvable problem. In a recursive function, a complicated problem is defined in terms of simpler problems and the simplest problem is given explicitly.

> **Programming Tip:** Every recursive function must have at least one base case. Otherwise, the recursive function will generate an infinite sequence of calls thereby resulting in an error condition known as an infinite stack.

To understand recursive functions, let us take an example of calculating factorial of a number. To calculate n!, what we have to do is multiply the number with factorial of number that is 1 less than that number. In other words, n! = n X (n-1)!

Let us say we need to find the value of 5!...

5! = 5 X 4 X 3 X 2 X 1

= 120

This can be written as

5! = 5 X 4!, where
4!= 4 X 3!

Therefore,

5! = 5 X 4 X 3!

Similarly, we can also write,

5! = 5 X 4 X 3 X 2!

Expanding further

5! = 5 X 4 X 3 X 2 X 1!
We know, 1! = 1

PROBLEM	SOLUTION
5!	5 X 4 X 3 X 2 X 1!
= 5 X 4!	= 5 X 4 X 3 X 2 X 1
= 5 X 4 X 3!	= 5 X 4 X 3 X 2
= 5 X 4 X 3 X 2!	= 5 X 4 X 6
= 5 X 4 X 3 X 2 X 1!	= 5 X 24
	= 120

Figure 5.5 Recursive factorial function

Therefore, the series of problem and solution can be given as shown in Figure 5.5.

Now if you look at the problem carefully, you can see that we can write a recursive function to calculate the factorial of a number. Note that we have said every recursive function must have a base case and a recursive case. For the factorial function,

- **Base case** is when n=1, because if n = 1, the result is known to be 1 as 1! = 1.
- **Recursive case** of the factorial function will call itself but with a smaller value of n, this case can be given as

$$factorial(n) = n \times factorial(n-1)$$

Example 5.36 Program to calculate the factorial of a number recursively

```
def fact(n):
    if(n==1 or n==0):
        return 1
    else:
        return n*fact(n-1)
n = int(input("Enter the value of n : "))
print("The factorial of",n,"is",fact(n))
```

OUTPUT
```
Enter the value of n : 6
The factorial of 6 is 720
```

From the aforementioned example, let us analyze the basic steps of a recursive program.

Step 1: Specify the base case which will stop the function from making a call to itself.

Step 2: Check to see whether the current value being processed matches with the value of the base case. If yes, process and return the value.

Step 3: Divide the problem into a smaller or simpler sub-problem.

Step 4: Call the function on the sub-problem.

Step 5: Combine the results of the sub-problems.

Step 6: Return the result of the entire problem.

> **Note**   The base case of a recursive function acts as the terminating condition. So, in the absence of an explicitly defined base case, a recursive function would call itself indefinitely.

5.11.1 Greatest Common Divisor

The greatest common divisor of two numbers (integers) is the largest integer that divides both the numbers. We can find GCD of two numbers recursively by using the Euclid's algorithm that states:

```
GCD(a,b) =  ┌  b, if b divides a
            │
            └  GCD(b, a mob b) otherwise
```

   GCD() can be implemented as a recursive function because if b does not divide a, then we call the same function (GCD) with another set of parameters that are smaller and simpler than the original ones. (Here we assume that a > b. However if a < b, then interchange a and b in the formula given above).

Working:
Assume a = 62 and b = 8
```
GCD(62, 8)
      rem = 62 % 8 = 6
      GCD(8, 6)
            rem = 8 % 6 = 2
            GCD(6, 2)
                  rem = 6 % 2 = 0
            Return 2
      Return 2
Return 2
```

> **Program 5.14 Write a program to calculate GCD using recursive functions.**
>
> ```python
> def GCD(x,y):
>       rem = x%y
>       if(rem==0):
>             return y
>       else:
>             return GCD(y,rem)
>
>
> n = int(input("Enter the first number : "))
> m = int(input("Enter the second number : "))
> print("The GCD of numbers is", GCD(n,m))
> ```
>
> **OUTPUT**
> ```
> Enter the first number :  50
> Enter the second number :  5
> The GCD of numbers is 5
> ```

5.11.2 Finding Exponents

We can find a solution to find exponent of a number using recursion. To find x^y, the base case would be when $y=0$, as we know that any number raise to the power 0 is 1. Therefore, the general formula to find x^y can be given as

$$EXP(x,y) = \begin{cases} 1, & \text{if } y == 0 \\ x * EXP(x^{y-1}) & \text{otherwise} \end{cases}$$

Working:
```
exp_rec(2, 4) = 2 * exp_rec( 2, 3)
      exp_rec(2, 3) =  2 * exp_rec( 2, 2)
          exp_rec(2, 2) - 2 * exp_rec( 2, 1)
              exp_rec(2, 1)  = 2 * exp_rec( 2, 0)
                  exp_rec( 2, 0) = 1
              exp_rec( 2, 1) = 2 * 1 = 2
          exp_rec( 2, 2) = 2 * 2 = 4
      exp_rec( 2, 3) = 2 * 4 = 8
exp_rec( 2, 4) = 2 * 8 = 16
```

Program 5.15 Write a program to calculate exp(x,y) using recursive functions.
```
def exp_rec(x,y):
     if(y==0):
            return 1
     else:
            return (x*exp_rec(x,y-1))
n = int(input("Enter the first number : "))
m = int(input("Enter the second number : "))
print("Result = ", exp_rec(n,m))
```

OUTPUT
```
Enter the first number : 5
Enter the second number : 3
Result = 125
```

Note Recursive functions can become infinite if you don't specify the base case.

5.11.3 The Fibonacci Series

The Fibonacci series can be given as:

0   1   1   2   3   5   8   13   21   34   55……

That is, the third term of the series is the sum of the first and second terms. On similar grounds, fourth term is the sum of second and third terms, so on and so forth. Now we will design a recursive solution to find the nth term of the Fibonacci series. The general formula to do so can be given as

```
FIB(n) =    1, if n<=2

            FIB (n - 1) + FIB (n - 2), otherwise
```

As per the formula, `FIB(1)` =1 and `FIB(2)` = 1. So we have two base cases. This is necessary because every problem is divided into two smaller problems. (Refer Figure 5.6)

Working:
If n = 7.

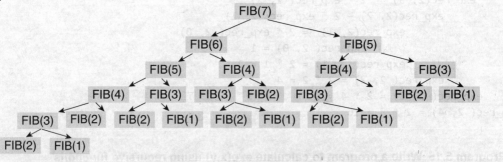

Figure 5.6   Recursion structure of FIB function

Note   Recursion can also be indirect. That is, one function can call a second function which in turn calls the first, which again calls the second, and so on. This can occur with any number of functions.

Program 5.16 Write a program to print the Fibonacci series using recursion.

```python
def fibonacci(n):
    if(n<2):
        return 1
    return (fibonacci(n-1)+fibonacci(n-2))


n = int(input("Enter the number of terms : "))
for i in range(n):
    print("Fibonacci(",i,") = ",fibonacci(i))
```

OUTPUT

```
Enter the number of terms : 5
Fibonacci( 0 ) = 1
Fibonacci( 1 ) = 1
Fibonacci( 2 ) = 2
Fibonacci( 3 ) = 3
Fibonacci( 4 ) = 5
```

Infinite Recursion

Let us consider the recursive program given below and observe the output.

```python
def func(n, count=0):
    if n==0:
        return count
    else:
        return func(n, count+1)
print("Number of times recursive function was invoked = ", func(100))
```

OUTPUT

```
Traceback (most recent call last):
File "C:\Python34\Try.py", Line 6, in <module>
File "C:\Python34\Try.py", line 5, in func
File "C:\Python34\Try.py", line 5, in func
.
.
.
.
.
File "C:\Python34\Try.py", line 2, in func
RuntimeError: maximum recursion depth exceeded in comparison
```

In the above code, recursion never reaches the base case and therefore, goes on making recursive call forever. Such a recursive call is called *infinite recursion*. To limit the side effects that can be caused by infinite recursion, Python reports a run-time error message when the maximum recursion depth is reached.

Recursion depth means the number of times a function is called. Python has specified maximum recursion depth to a value that is highly unlikely to be ever reached by any recursive function.

Note that usually Python allows not more than 1000 recursive calls thereby setting a limit in case of infinite recursion.

5.11.4 Tail Recursion

Tail recursive functions look similar to non-tail recursive functions but are considered to be better than them as tail-recursion can be optimized by the compiler. Compilers use a system stack to store pertinent information (like parameter values) during each recursive call. This means that a non-tail-recursive function has greater **stack depth** (i.e, maximum amount of stack space used at any time during compilation). On the contrary, compilers easily optimize tail-recursive functions as in the last statement, there is nothing left to do in the current function, so saving the current function's stack frame is of no use.

Non-Tail Recursive	Tail Recursive

`def factorial(n):`
`    if n == 0: return 1`
`    else: return factorial(n-1) * n`
	`def tail_factorial(n, prod=1):`
	`    if n == 1:`
	`        return prod`
	`    else:`
	`        return tail_factorial(n-1,`
	`prod * n)`

In the above two codes, which are almost similar, a minute difference can be observed in the last line. In the non-tail version, the compiler every time saves the number with which the returned result will be multiplied but in the tail-call version, the compiler just has to make another function call and there is no need to save variables and state used in the current function.

Since a head recursive function consumes a lot of computer resources, it is often limited to making a maximum 980 calls. A tail-recursive function, on the other hand, can go even beyond that.

Example 5.37

```python
def fib(i, current = 0, next = 1):
  if i == 0:
    return current
  else:
    return fib(i - 1, next, current + next)
print(fib(50))
```

OUTPUT

12586269025

5.11.5 Recursion vs Iteration

Recursion is more of a top-down approach to problem solving in which the original problem is divided into smaller sub-problems. On the contrary, iteration follows a bottom-up approach that begins with what is known and then constructing the solution step-by-step.

Recursion is an excellent way of solving complex problems especially when the problem can be defined in recursive terms. For such problems a recursive code can be written and modified in a much simpler and clearer manner.

However, recursive solutions are not always the best solutions. In some cases recursive programs may require substantial amount of run-time overhead. Therefore, when implementing a recursive solution, there is a trade-off involved between the time spent in constructing and maintaining the program and the cost incurred in running time and memory space required for the execution of the program.

Whenever a recursive function is called, some amount of overhead in the form of a run-time stack is always involved. Before jumping to the function with a smaller parameter, the original parameters, the local variables, and the return address of the calling function are all stored on the system stack. Therefore, while using recursion a lot of time is needed to first push all the information on the stack when function is called and then time is again involved in retrieving the information stored on the stack once the control passes back to the calling function.

To conclude, one must use recursion only to find solution to a problem for which no obvious iterative solution is known. To summarize the concept of recursion, let us briefly discuss the pros and cons of recursion.

Pros The benefits of using a recursive program are:

- Recursive solutions often tend to be shorter and simpler than non-recursive ones.
- Code is clearer and easier to use.
- Recursion uses the original formula to solve a problem.

- It Follows a divide and conquer technique to solve problems.
- In some (limited) instances, recursion may be more efficient.

Cons The limitations of using a recursive program are:

- For some programmers and readers, recursion is a difficult concept.
- Recursion is implemented using system stack. If the stack space on the system is limited, recursion to a deeper level will be difficult to implement.
- Aborting a recursive process in midstream is slow and sometimes nasty.
- Using a recursive function takes more memory and time to execute as compared to its non-recursive counterpart.
- It is difficult to find bugs, particularly when using global variables.

Conclusion The advantages of recursion pays off for the extra overhead involved in terms of time and space required.

Program 5.17 Write a program to count number of times a recursive function is called.

```
def func(n, count=0):
    if n==0:
        return count
    else:
        return func(n-1, count+1)
print("Number of times recursive function was invoked = ", func(100))
```

OUTPUT

```
Number of times recursive function was invoked =  100
```

Note　Recursive functions make the code look clean and elegant.

5.12 MODULES

In the previous section, we have seen that functions help us to reuse a particular piece of code. Modules goes a step ahead. It allows you to reuse one or more functions in your programs, even in the programs in which those functions have not been defined.

Putting simply, module is a file with a .py extension that has definitions of all functions and variables that you would like to use even in other programs. The program in which you want to use functions or variables defined in the module will simply import that particular module (or .py file).

Note　Modules are pre-written pieces of code that are used to perform common tasks like generating random numbers, performing mathematical operations, etc.

The basic way to use a module is to add import module_name as the first line of your program and then writing module_name.var to access functions and values with the name var in the module. Let us first use the standard library modules.

Example 5.38   Program to print the `sys.path` variable

```
import sys
print("\n PYTHONPATH = \n", sys.path)
```

OUTPUT
```
PYTHONPATH =
['C:\\Python34', 'C:\\Python34\\Lib\\idlelib', 'C:\\Windows\\system32\\python34.
zip', 'C:\\Python34\\DLLs', 'C:\\Python34\\lib', 'C:\\Python34', 'C:\\Python34\\
lib\\site-packages']
```

In the above code, we import the `sys` module (short form of system) using the import statement to use its functionality related to the Python interpreter and its environment.

When the `import sys` statement is executed, Python looks for the `sys.py` module in one of the directories listed in its `sys.path` variable. If the file is found, then the statements in the module is executed.

Module Loading and Execution

A module imported in a program must be located and loaded into memory before it can be used. Python first searches for the modules in the current working directory. If the module is not found there, it then looks for the module in the directories specified in the `PYTHONPATH` environment variable. If the module is still not found or if the `PYTHONPATH` variable is not defined, then a Python installation-specific path (like `C:\Python34\Lib`) is searched. If the module is not located even there, then an error `ImportError` exception is generated.

Till now, we have saved our modules in the same directory as that of the program importing it. But, if you want the module to be available to other programs as well, then the module should be either saved in the directory specified in the `PYTHONPATH`, or stored in the Python installation Lib directory.

Once a module is located, it is loaded in memory. A compiled version of the module with file extension `.pyc` is generated. Next time when the module is imported, this `.pyc` file is loaded, rather than the `.py` file, to save the time of recompiling. A new compiled version of a module is again produced whenever the compiled version is out of date (based on the dates when the `.pyc` file was created/modified). Even the programmer can force the Python shell to reload and recompile the `.py` file to generate a new `.pyc` file by using the `reload()` function.

5.12.1 The from...import statement

A module may contain definition for many variables and functions. When you import a module, you can use any variable or function defined in that module. But if you want to use only selected variables or functions, then you can use the `from...import` statement. For example, in the aforementioned program you are using only the path variable in the `sys` module, so you could have better written from `sys` import path.

Example 5.39   Program to show the use of `from...import` statement

```
from math import pi
print("PI = ", + pi)
```

OUTPUT
```
PI = 3.141592653589793
```

To import more than one item from a module, use a comma separated list. For example, to import the value of `pi` and `sqrt()` from the math module you can write,

```
from math import pi, sqrt
```

However, to import all the identifiers defined in the `sys` module, you can use the `from sys import *` statement. However, you should avoid using the `import *` statement as it confuses variables in your code with variables in the external module.

Note   This imports * statement imports all names except those beginning with an underscore (_).

You can also import a module with a different name using the **as** keyword. This is particularly more important when a module either has a long or confusing name.

Example 5.40   Program to show the use of `'as'` keyword

```
from math import sqrt as square_root
print(square_root(81))
```

OUTPUT
```
9.0
```

Python also allows you to pass command line arguments to your program. This can be done using the `sys` module. The `argv` variable in this module keeps a track of command line arguments passed to the `.py` script as shown below.

```
import sys
print(sys.argv)
```

To execute this program code, go to Command Prompt (in Windows) and write,

```
C:\Python34> python main.py Hello World
```

Thereafter, you will get the output as,

```
['main.py', 'Hello', 'World']
```

Program 5.18 Write a program to add two numbers that are given using command line arguments.

```
import sys
a = int(sys.argv[1])
b = int(sys.argv[2])
sum = a+b
print("SUM = ", sum)
```

OUTPUT
```
C:\Python34\python sum.py 3 4
SUM = 7
```

sys.exit() You can use sys.exit([*arg*]) to exit from Python. Here, arg is an optional argument which can either be an integer giving the exit status or another type of object. If it is an integer, zero signifies successful termination and any non-zero value indicates an error or abnormal termination of the program. Most systems require the value of arg to be in the range 0-127, and therefore produces undefined results otherwise. None is same as passing zero. If another type of object is passed, it results in an exit code of 1. Generally, sys.exit("Error Message") is a quick way to exit a program when an error occurs.

Example 5.41 Program to demonstrate sys.exit

```
import sys
print("HELLO WORLD")
sys.exit(0)
```

OUTPUT
```
HELLO WORLD
```

5.12.2 Name of Module

Every module has a name. You can find the name of a module by using the __name__ attribute of the module.

Example 5.42 Program to print the name of the module in which your statements is written

```
print("Hello")
print("Name of this module is : ", __name__)
```

OUTPUT
```
Hello
Name of this module is :  __main__
```

Observe the output and always remember that the for every standalone program written by the user the name of the module is __main__.

5.12.3 Making Your Own Modules

You can easily create as many modules as you want. In fact, you have already been doing that. Every Python program is a module, that is, every file that you save as .py extension is a module. The code given in the following example illustrates this concept.

First write these lines in a file and save the file as MyModule.py

```
def display():        #function definition
    print("Hello")
    print("Name of called module is : ", __name__)

str = "Welcome to the world of Python !!!    #variable definition
```

Then, open another file (main.py) and write the lines of code given as follows:

```
import MyModule
print("MyModule str = ", MyModule.str)        #using variable defined in MyModule
MyModule.display()                             #using function defined in MyModule
print("Name of calling module is : ", __name__)
```

When you run this code, you will get the following output.

```
MyModule str =  Welcome to the world of Python !!!
Hello
Name of called module is :  MyModule
Name of calling module is :  __main__
```

> **Note**   Modules should be placed in the same directory as that of the program in which it is imported.
> It can also be stored in one of the directories listed in sys.path.

Note that we have been using the dot operator to access members (variables or functions) of the module. Assuming that MyModule had many other variables or functions definition, we could have specifically imported just str and display() by writing the import statement as

```
from MyModule import str, display
```

Example 5.43   Program that defines a function large in a module which will be used to find larger of two values and called from code in another module

```
# Code in MyModule
def large(a,b):
    if a>h:
        return a
    else:
        return b


# Code in Find.py

import MyModule
print("Large(50, 100) = ", MyModule.large(50,100))
print("Large('B', 'c') = ", MyModule.large('B', 'c'))
print("Large('HI', 'BI') = ", MyModule.large('HI','BI'))

OUTPUT
Large(50, 100) =  100
Large('B', 'c') =  c
Large('HI', 'BI') =  HI
```

5.12.4 The `dir()` Function

`dir()` is a built-in function that lists the identifiers defined in a module. These identifiers may include functions, classes, and variables. The `dir()` works as given in the following example.

Example 5.44   Program to demonstrate the use of `dir()` function

```
def print_var(x):
    print(x)
x = 10
print_var(x)
print(dir())
```

OUTPUT

```
10
['__builtins__', '__doc__', '__file__', '__name__', '__package__', 'print_var', 'x']
```

If you mention the module name in the `dir()` function, it will return the list of the names defined in that module. For example,

```
>>> dir(MyModule)
['__builtins__', '__doc__', '__file__', '__name__', '__package__', 'display', 'str']
```

If no name is specified, the `dir()` will return the list of names defined in the current module.
Just import the `sys` package and try to `dir` its contents. You will see a big list of identifiers. However, the `dir(sys)` does not list the names of built-in functions and variables. To see the list of those, write `dir(__builtin__)` as they are defined in the standard module `__builtin__`. This is shown below.

Example 5.45   Program to print all identifiers in the `dir()` function

```
import __builtin__
print(dir(__builtin__))
```

OUTPUT

```
['ArithmeticError', 'AssertionError', 'AttributeError', 'BaseException',
'BufferError', 'BytesWarning', 'DeprecationWarning', 'EOFError', 'Ellipsis',
'EnvironmentError', 'Exception', 'False', 'FloatingPointError', 'FutureWarning',
'GeneratorExit', 'IOError', 'ImportError', 'ImportWarning', 'IndentationError',
'IndexError', 'KeyError', 'KeyboardInterrupt', 'LookupError', 'MemoryError',
'NameError', 'None', 'NotImplemented', 'NotImplementedError', 'OSError',
'OverflowError', 'PendingDeprecationWarning', 'ReferenceError', 'RuntimeError',
'RuntimeWarning', 'StandardError', 'StopIteration', 'SyntaxError',
'SyntaxWarning', 'SystemError', 'SystemExit', 'TabError', 'True', 'TypeError',
'UnboundLocalError', 'UnicodeDecodeError', 'UnicodeEncodeError', 'UnicodeError',
'UnicodeTranslateError', 'UnicodeWarning', 'UserWarning', 'ValueError', 'Warning',
```

```
'WindowsError', 'ZeroDivisionError', '__debug__', '__doc__', '__import__', '__
name__', '__package__', 'abs', 'all', 'any', 'apply', 'basestring', 'bin', 'bool',
'buffer', 'bytearray', 'bytes', 'callable', 'chr', 'classmethod', 'cmp', 'coerce',
'compile', 'complex', 'copyright', 'credits', 'delattr', 'dict', 'dir', 'divmod',
'enumerate', 'eval', 'execfile', 'exit', 'file', 'filter', 'float', 'format',
'frozenset', 'getattr', 'globals', 'hasattr', 'hash', 'help', 'hex', 'id', 'input',
'int', 'intern', 'isinstance', 'issubclass', 'iter', 'len', 'license', 'list',
'locals', 'long', 'map', 'max', 'memoryview', 'min', 'next', 'object', 'oct',
'open', 'ord', 'pow', 'print', 'property', 'quit', 'range', 'raw_input', 'reduce',
'reload', 'repr', 'reversed', 'round', 'set', 'setattr', 'slice', 'sorted',
'staticmethod', 'str', 'sum', 'super', 'tuple', 'type', 'unichr', 'unicode',
'vars', 'xrange', 'zip']
```

Note By convention, modules are named using lowercase letters and optional underscore characters.

5.12.5 **The Python Module**

We have seen that a *Python module* is a file that contains some definitions and statements. When a Python file is executed directly, it is considered the *main module* of a program. Main modules are given the special name __main__ and provide the basis for a complete Python program. The main module may *import* any number of other modules which may in turn import other modules. But the main module of a Python program cannot be imported into other modules.

5.12.6 **Modules and Namespaces**

A *namespace* is a container that provides a named context for identifiers. Two identifiers with the same name in the same scope will lead to a name clash. In simple terms, Python does not allow programmers to have two different identifiers with the same name. However, in some situations we need to have same name identifiers. To cater to such situations, namespaces is the keyword. Namespaces enable programs to avoid potential *name clashes* by associating each identifier with the namespace from which it originates.

```
# module1
def repeat_x(x):
    return x*2

# module2
def repeat_x(x):
    return x**2

import module1
import module2
result = repeat_x(10)      # ambiguous reference for identifier repeat_x
```

In the above example, module1 and module2 are imported into the same program. Each module has a function repeat_x(), which return very different results. When we call the repeat_x() from the main module, there will be a name clash as it will be difficult to determine which of these two functions should be called. Namespaces provide a means for resolving such problems.

In Python, each module has its own namespace. This namespace includes the names of all items (functions and variables) defined in the module. Therefore, two instances of repeat_x(), each defined in their own module, are distinguished by being fully qualified with the name of the module in which each is defined as, module1.repeat_x and module2.repeat_x. This is illustrated as follows:

```
import module1
import module2
result1 = module1.repeat_x(10)    # refers to repeat_x in module1
result2 = module2.repeat_x(10)    # refers to repeat_x in module2
```

Local, Global, and Built-in Namespaces

During a program's execution, there are three main namespaces that are referenced—the built-in namespace, the global namespace, and the local namespace. The *built-in namespace,* as the name suggests contains names of all the built-in functions, constants, etc. that are already defined in Python. The *global namespace* contains identifiers of the currently executing module and the *local namespace* has identifiers defined in the currently executing function (if any).

When the Python interpreter sees an identifier, it first searches the local namespace, then the global namespace, and finally the built-in namespace. Therefore, if two identifiers with the same name are defined in more than one of these namespaces, it becomes masked, as shown in the following example.

Example 5.46   Program to demonstrate name clashes in different namespaces

```
def max(numbers):        # global namespace
    print("USER DEFINED FUNCTION MAX.....")
    large = -1        # local namespace
    for i in numbers:
        if i>large:
            large = i
    return large
numbers = [9,-1,4,2,7]
print(max(numbers))
print("Sum of these numbers = ", sum(numbers))  #built-in namespace

OUTPUT
USER DEFINED FUNCTION MAX.....
9
Sum of these numbers =   21
```

In the aforementioned program, we have used function max() which is defined in the global namespace of the program. Local identifier, large is defined in a function. So it is accessible only in that function. Note that we have also used the function sum(). We have not given any definition of this function, so Python automatically uses the built-in version of the function.

Module Private Variables

In Python, all identifiers defined in a module are public by default. This means that all identifiers are accessible by any other module that imports it. But, if you want some variables or functions in a module to be privately used within the module, but not to be accessed from outside it, then you need to declare those identifiers as private.

In Python, identifiers whose name starts with two underscores (__) are known as private identifiers. These identifiers can be used only within the module. In no way, they can be accessed from outside the module. Therefore, when the module is imported using the `import * form modulename`, all the identifiers of a module's namespace is imported except the private ones (ones beginning with double underscores). Thus, private identifiers become inaccessible from within the importing module.

Advantages of Modules Python modules provide all the benefits of modular software design. These modules provide services and functionality that can be reused in other programs. Even the standard library of Python contains a set of modules. It allows you to logically organize the code so that it becomes easier to understand and use.

Key points to remember

- A modules can import other modules.
- It is customary but not mandatory to place all import statements at the beginning of a module.
- A module is loaded only once, irrespective of the number of times it is imported.

5.13 PACKAGES IN PYTHON

A *package* is a hierarchical file directory structure that has modules and other packages within it. Like modules, you can very easily create packages in Python.

Remember that, every package in Python is a directory which must have a special file called __init__.py. This file may not even have a single line of code. It is simply added to indicate that this directory is not an ordinary directory and contains a Python package. In your programs, you can import a package in the same way as you import any module.

For example, to create a package called `MyPackage,` create a directory called `MyPackage` having the module `MyModule` and the __init__.py file. Now, to use `MyModule` in a program, you must first import it. This can be done in two ways.

```
import MyPackage.MyModule
```

or

```
from MyPackage import MyModule
```

The __init__.py is a very important file that also determines which modules the package exports as the `API`, while keeping other modules internal, by overriding the __all__ variable as shown below.

```
__init__.py:
__all__ = ["MyModule"]
```

Key points to remember

- Packages are searched for in the path specified by `sys.path`.
- __init__.py file can be an empty file and may also be used to execute initialization code for the package or set the __all__ variable.

- The import statement first checks if the item is defined in the package. If it is unable to find it, an ImportError exception is raised.
- When importing an item using syntax like import item.subitem.subitem, each item except the last must be a package. That is, the last item should either be a module or a package. In no case it can be a class or function or variable defined in the previous item.
- Packages have an attribute __path__ which is initialized with a list having the name of the directory holding the __init__.py file. The __path__ attribute can be modified to change the future searches for modules and sub-packages contained in the package.

Program 5.19 Write a program that prints absolute value, square root, and cube of a number.

```
import math

def cube(x):
    return x**3

a = -100
print("a = ", a)
a = abs(a)
print("abs(a) = ", a)
print("Square Root of ",a, " = ", math.sqrt(a))
print("Cube of ",a, " = ", cube(a))
```

OUTPUT

```
a =  -100
abs(a) =  100
Square Root of  100  =  10.0
Cube of  100  =  1000000
```

> **Programming Tip:** * imports all objects from a module.

Program 5.20 Write a program to generate 10 random numbers between 1 to 100.

```
import random

for i in range(10):
        value = random.randint(1,100)
        print(value)
```

OUTPUT

```
66 68 14 7 76 8 70 43 60 70
```

5.14 STANDARD LIBRARY MODULES

Python supports three types of modules—those written by the programmer, those that are installed from external sources, and those that are pre-installed with Python. Modules that are pre-installed in Python are together known as the *standard library*. Some useful modules in the standard library are string, re, datetime, math,

> **Programming Tip:** Most of the modules in Standard Library of Python are available on all platforms, but others are Windows or Unix specific.

random, os, multiprocessing, subprocess, socket, email, json, doctest, unittest, pdb, argparse, and sys. You can use these modules for performing tasks like string parsing, data serialization, testing, debugging and manipulating dates, emails, command line arguments, etc.

> **Note** Some of the modules in the Standard Library are written in Python, and others are written in C.

5.15 Globals(), Locals(), AND Reload()

The globals() and locals() functions are used to return the names in the global and local namespaces (In Python, each function, module, class, package, etc. owns a "**namespace**" in which variable names are identified and resolved). The result of these functions is of course, dependent on the location from where they are called. For example,

- If locals() is called from within a function, names that can be accessed locally from that function will be returned.
- If globals() is called from within a function, all the names that can be accessed globally from that function is returned.

  Both the functions return names using dictionary. These names can be extracted using the keys() function. Dictionary data structure and key() will be discussed later in this book.

- Reload() When a module is imported into a program, the code in the module is executed only once. If you want to re-execute the top-level code in a module, you must use the reload() function. This function again imports a module that was previously imported. The syntax of the reload() function is gives as,

```
reload(module_name)
```

Here, module_name is the name of the module that has to be reloaded.

Program 5.21 Write a program to display the date and time using the Time module.

```
import time
localtime = time.asctime(time.localtime(time.time()) )
print("Local current time :", localtime)
```

OUTPUT

```
Local current time : Sun Dec 11 21:01:45 2016
```

Program 5.22 Write a program that prints the calendar of a particular month.

```
import calendar
print(calendar.month(2017, 1))
```

OUTPUT

```
    January 2017
Mo Tu We Th Fr Sa Su
                   1
 2  3  4  5  6  7  8
 9 10 11 12 13 14 15
16 17 18 19 20 21 22
23 24 25 26 27 28 29
30 31
```

Program 5.23 Write a program that uses the getpass module to prompt the user for a password, without echoing what they type to the console.

```
import getpass
password = getpass.getpass(prompt='Enter the password : ')
if password == 'oxford':
    print('Welcome to the world of Python Programming. ')
else:
    print('Incorrect password... Sorry, you cannot read our book.')
```

OUTPUT

```
Enter the password : oxford
Welcome to the world of Python Programming.
```

5.16 FUNCTION REDEFINITION

We have already learnt in the previous chapters that in Python, we can redefine a variable. That is you can change the value and even the type of value that the variable is holding. For example, in one line you can write x = 5.6 and in the other line you can redefine x by writing x = "Hello". Similar to redifining variables, you can also redefine functions in Python.

Programming Tip: Trying to import a module that is not available causes an ImportError.

Example 5.47 Program to demonstrate function redefinition

```
import datetime
def showMessage(msg):
    print(msg)
showMessage("Hello")
def showMessage(msg):
    now = datetime.datetime.now()
    print(msg)
    print(str(now))
showMessage("Current Date and Time is : ")
```

OUTPUT

```
Hello
Current Date and Time is :  2016-10-10 11:45:53.063000
```

In the above code, we have a function showMessage() which is first defined to simply display a message that is passed to it. After the function call, we have redefined the function to print the message as well as the current date and time.

Python Package Index (PyPI)

In Python, many third-party modules are stored in the **Python Package Index** (PyPI). To install them, you can use a program called *pip*. However, new versions of Python have these modules installed by default. Once you have these modules, installing libraries from PyPI becomes very easy. Simply, go to the command line (for Windows it will be the Command Prompt), and enter *pip install library_name*. Once the library is installed, import it in your program and use it in your code.

Using **pip** is the standard way of installing libraries on most operating systems, but some libraries have prebuilt binaries (executable files) for Windows which can be installed with a GUI the same way you would install other programs.

SUMMARY

- Understanding, coding, and testing multiple separate functions are far easier than doing the same for one huge function.
- Large programs usually follow the **DRY** principle, that is, *Don't Repeat Yourself* principle. Once a function is written it can be called multiple times wherever its functionality is required.
- A bad repetitive code abides by the **WET** principle, i.e; *Write Everything Twice, or We Enjoy Typing.*
- A function, f() that uses another function g(), is known as the *calling function* and g() is known as the *called function*.
- When a called function returns some result back to the calling function, it is said to *return* that result.
- Defining a function means specifying its name, parameters that are expected, and the set of instructions. Once the structure of a function is finalized, it can be executed by calling it.
- In nested functions, the inner function can access variables defined in both outer as well as inner function,

- but the outer function can access variables defined only in the outer function.
- Once you return a value from a function, it immediately exits that function. Therefore, any code written after the return statement is never executed.
- Keyword arguments when used in function calls, helps the function to identify the arguments by the parameter name.
- When the number of arguments passed to a function is not known in advance, then use arbitrary (or any) number of arguments in the function header.
- Docstrings (documentation strings) serve the same purpose as that of comments, as they are designed to explain code.
- The base case of a recursive function acts as the terminating condition.
- The globals() and locals() functions are used to return the names in the global and local namespaces.

GLOSSARY

Arguments/parameters The inputs that the function takes.
Function A piece of code that perform a well-defined task.
Function declaration A declaration statement that identifies a function with its name, a list of arguments that it accepts, and the type of data it returns.
Global variables Variables which are defined in the main body of the program file. They are visible throughout the program file.
Lifetime of the variable Duration for which the variable exists.

Module A file with a .py extension that has definitions of all functions and variables that you would like to use even in other programs.
Package A hierarchical file directory structure that has modules and other packages within it.
Recursive function A function that calls itself to solve a smaller version of its task until a final call is made which does not require a call to itself.
Scope of the variable Part of the program in which a variable is accessible.

EXERCISES

Fill In the Blanks

1. In `range(0, 100, 5)` name of the function is _____ and it has _____ arguments.
2. _____ error is caused by importing an unknown module.
3. _____ consists of a function header followed by function.
4. User-defined functions are created by using the _____ keyword.
5. The _____ is used to uniquely identify the function.
6. _____ describe what the function does.
7. Fill in the blanks to define a function named display.

   ```
   ___ display()__
   print("Hello World")
   ```

8. After the called function is executed, the control is returned back to the _____.
9. A return statement with no arguments is the same as return _____.
10. Before calling a function, you must _____ it.
11. _____ variable can be accessed from the point of its definition until the end of the function in which it is defined.
12. To define a variable defined inside a function as global, _____ statement is used.
13. Every function has an implicit _____ statement as the last instruction in the function body.
14. Any formal parameters written after the variable-length arguments must be _____ arguments.
15. _____ are not declared as other functions using the `def` keyword.
16. This docstring specified can be accessed through the _____ attribute of the function.
17. You can find the name of a module by using the _____ attribute of the module.
18. _____ is a built-in function that lists the identifiers defined in a module.
19. Every package in Python is a directory which must have a special file called _____.
20. Packages have an attribute _____ which is initialized with a list having the name of the directory holding the `__init__.py` file.
21. Fill in the blanks to define a function that takes two arguments and prints their sum.

    ```
    ___ mult(x,y)__
    print(x*__)
    ```

22. Fill in the blanks to define a function that prints "Positive", if its parameter is greater than 0 and "Negative" otherwise.

    ```
    ___ pos_neg(x):
        if x>0:
            _____ ("Positive")
        ___
            print("Negative")
    ```

23. Fill in the blanks to define a function that compares the lengths of its arguments and returns the longest one.

    ```
    def max_len(x, y):
        if len(x)>=__(y):
            ___x
        else:
            ___y
    ```

24. Fill in the blanks to pass the function cube as an argument to the function "test".

    ```
    ___ cube(x):
    return x*x*x
    def do(func,x)__
        print(func(x))
    do(_____, 2)
    ```

25. To import the `sqrt` and `cos` function from the `math` module, write _____.
26. Python's preinstalled modules forms the _____.
27. Fill in the blanks to calculate x*(x+1) using lambda function and call it for the number 10.

    ```
    res = (_____x: x__(x+1))__
    print(res)
    ```

28. The _____ command is used to force the reloading of a given module.
29. _____, _____, and _____ namespaces may exist during the execution of any given Python program.

State True Or False

1. Docstring can contain multiple lines of text.
2. Every function can be written more or less independently of the others.
3. When a function call is encountered, the control jumps to the calling function.
4. A function can call only one function.
5. Code reuse is one of the most prominent reason to use functions.
6. Large programs usually follow the WET principle.
7. We can have a function that does not take any inputs at all.
8. The calling function may or may not pass *parameters* to the called function.
9. The return statement is optional.
10. Python does not allow you to assign the function name to a variable.
11. Names of variables in function call and header of function definition may vary.
12. Arguments may be passed in the form of expressions to the called function.
13. You can have a variable with the same name as that of a global variable in the program.
14. You should make extensive use of global variables and global statements.
15. The return statement can be used outside of a function definition.
16. Any code written after the return statement is never executed.
17. The order of keyword arguments is not important.
18. Default arguments should always be written after the non-default arguments.
19. You can specify only one default argument in your function.
20. The variable-length arguments if present in the function definition should be first in the list of formal parameters.
21. A function cannot be used on the left side of an assignment statement.
22. Lambda functions are throw-away functions.
23. Lambda functions can be used wherever function objects are required.
24. Lambda functions cannot access global variables.
25. Lambda function performs better than regular functions.
26. A recursive function takes more memory and time to execute as compared to its non-recursive counterpart.
27. It is mandatory to place all import statements at the beginning of a module.
28. With the `"import modulename"` statement, any item from the imported module must be prefixed with the module name.
29. All Python Standard Library modules must be imported before any programmer-defined modules.
30. If a particular module is imported more than once in a Python program, the interpreter will load the module only once.
31. A function can be called from anywhere within a program.
32. A statement can call more than one function.
33. Function calls may contain arguments that are function calls.
34. All functions that returns a value must accept at least one parameter.

Multiple Choice Questions

1. DRY principle makes the code
   (a) Reusable (b) Loop forever
   (c) Bad and repetitive (d) Complex
2. How many times will the `print()` execute in the code given below?
```
def display():
  print('a')
  print('b')
  return
print('c')
print('d')
```
   (a) 1 (b) 2
   (c) 3 (d) 4
3. What is the output of this code?
```
import random as r
print(random.randmint(1, 10))
```
   (a) An error occurs (b) 1
   (c) 10 (d) any random value
4. How would you refer to the `sqrt` function if it was imported by writing like this—
```
from math import sqrt as square_root
math. _____
```
   (a) `square_root` (b) `math.sqrt`
   (c) `sqrt` (d) `square_root`
5. The code will print how many numbers?
```
def display(x):
    for i in range(x):
        print(i)
    return
display(10)
```
   (a) 0 (b) 1
   (c) 9 (d) 10

6. Which statement invokes the function?
   (a) Function definition   (b) Function call
   (c) Function header   (d) __doc__
7. If number of arguments in function definition and function call does not match, then which type of error is returned?
   (a) NameError   (b) ImportError
   (c) TypeError   (d) NumberError
8. _____ of a variable determines the part of the program in which it is accessible
   (a) Scope   (b) Lifetime
   (c) Data Type   (d) Value
9. Arbitrary arguments have which symbol in the function definition before the parameter name?
   (a) &   (b) #
   (c) %   (d) *
10. Modules are files saved with _____ extension
    (a) .py   (b) mod
    (c) mdl   (d) imp
11. This imports * statement import all names in the module except those beginning with _____

(a) %   (b) $
(c) _   (d) !
12. PyPI stands for _____.
    (a) Python Project Index   (b) Python Package Installer
    (c) Python Package Index   (d) Package Python Installer
13. How would you refer to the randint function if it was imported by writing like this __
    from random import randint as r_int?
    (a) random.rnd_int   (b) r_int
    (c) randint.r_int   (d) randint
14. Identify the correct way of calling a function named display() that prints Hello on the screen.
    (a) print(display)
    (b) displayHello
    (c) result = display()
    (d) displayHello()

Review Questions

1. Define function and give its advantages.
2. Can a function call another function? Justify your answer with the help of an example.
3. What do you understand by the term arguments? How do we pass them to a function?
4. What are user-defined functions? With the help of an example illustrate how you can have such functions in your program.
5. The return statement is optional. Justify this statement with the help of an example.
6. Differentiate between local and global variables.
7. Define a function that calculates the sum of all numbers from 0 to its argument.
8. Arguments may be passed in the form of expressions to the called function. Justify this testament with the help of an example.
9. When you can have a variable with the same name as that of a global variable in the program, how is the

name resolved in Python? Explain with the help of a program.
10. With the help of an example, explain the concept of accessibility of variables in nested functions.
11. Explain the use of return statement.
12. Explain the utility of keyword arguments.
13. What are docstrings?
14. Draw a comparison between recursive and iterative technique for problem solving.
15. What are modules? How do you use them in your programs?
16. What are variable-length arguments? Explain with the help of a code.
17. Write short notes on
    (a) Keyword arguments
    (b) Default arguments
    (c) Lambda functions
18. What are packages in python?

Programming Problems

1. Write a program that finds the greatest of three given numbers using functions. Pass the numbers as arguments.
2. Write a program that prints the time taken to execute a program in Python.
3. Write a function that returns the absolute value of a number.

4. Write a program that uses lambda function to multiply two numbers.
5. Write a program that passes lambda function as an argument to another function to compute the cube of a number.

6. Write a function `is_prime()` that returns a `1` if the argument passed to it is a prime a number and a `0` otherwise.
7. Write a function that accepts an integer between `1` and `12` to represent the month number and displays the corresponding month of the year (For example, if `month = 1`, then display JANUARY).
8. Write a function `is_leap_year` which takes the year as its argument and checks whether the year is a leap year or not and then displays an appropriate message on the screen.
9. Write a program to concatenate two strings using recursion.
10. Write a program to read an integer number. Print the reverse of this number using recursion.
11. Write a program to swap two variables that are defined as global variables.
12. Write a program to compute `F(x, y)` where

    `F(x, y) = F(x-y, y) + 1 if y ≤ x`

13. Write a program to compute `F(n, r)` where `F(n, r)` can be recursively defined as

    `F(n, r) = F(n-1, r) + F(n-1, r-1) .`

14. Write a program to compute `lambda(n)` for all positive values of n where, `lambda(n)` can be recursively defined as

    `lambda(n) = lambda(n/2) + 1 if n > 1`

15. Write a program to compute `F(M,N)`, where `F(M,N)` can be recursively defined as

    `F(M,N) = 1 if M = 0 or M ≥ N ≥ 1`

    and `F(M,N) = F(M-1,N) + F(M-1, N-1)`, otherwise .

16. Write a menu driven program using functions to perform calculator operations such as adding, subtracting, multiplying, and dividing two integers.
17. Write a program using a function that calculates the hypotenuse of a right-angled triangle.
18. Write a function that accepts a number n as input and returns the average of numbers from `1` to n.
19. Write a program to find the biggest of three integers using functions.
20. Write a program to calculate the area of a triangle using a function.
21. Write a program using a function to calculate x to the power of y, where y can be either negative or positive.

22. Write a program using the function (C (n,r)) to calculate the compound interest for the given principal, rate of interest, and number of years.
23. Write a program using a function that returns the surface area and volume of a sphere.
24. Write a program to reverse a string using recursion.
25. Write a program to reverse a string without using recursion.
26. Write a program to calculate `exp(x,y)` using recursion.
27. Write a program to calculate `exp(x,y)` without using recursion.
28. Write a program to print the Fibonacci series using recursion.
29. Write a program to print the Fibonacci series without using recursion.
30. Write a function that converts temperature given in Celsius into Fahrenheit.
31. Write a function to draw the following pattern on the screen.

    ```
    ********
    !      !
    !      !
    !      !
    ********
    ```

32. Write a function to print a table of binomial coefficients which is given by the formula:

    `B(m, x) = m!/ (x! (m-x)!) where m > x`
    (*Hint*: B (m,0) = 1, B(0,0) = 1 and B(m,x) = B(m, x-1) * [(m − x + 1)/x])

33. Write a function called `printStatus` that is passed status code 'S', 'M', 'D', or 'U' and returns the string 'Separated', 'Married', 'Divorced', or 'Unmarried', respectively. In case an inappropriate letter is passed, print an appropriate message. Also include a `docstring` with your function.
34. Write a function that accepts three integers, and returns `True` if any of the integers is `0`, otherwise it returns `False`.
35. Write a function that accepts three integers, and returns `True` if they are sorted, otherwise it returns `False`.
36. Write a function that accepts two positive numbers n and m where m<=n, and returns numbers between `1` and n that are divisible by m.
37. Write a function that displays `"Hello name"`, for any given name passed to it.

Find the Output

```
1. num = 10
   def show():
       var = 20
       print("In Function var is - ", num)

       show()
   print("Outside function, var is - ", num)
```

```
2.  def f():
        s = "Hello World!"
        print(s)

    s = "Welcome to Python Programming"
    f()
    print(s)
3.  def f():
        global var
        print(varr)
        var = 10
        print(var)
    var = 100
    f()
4.  def display (str):
        print(str+"!")
    display ("Hello World")
5.  def sqr(x):
        print(x*x)
    sqr(10)
6.  def mul_twice(x,y):
        print(x*y)
        print(x*y)
    mul_twice(5, 10)
7.  def func():
        global x
        print("x =", x)
        x = 100
        print('x is now = ', x)
    x = 10
    func()
    print('x =', x)
8.  def func1():
        var = 3
        func2(var)
    def func2(var):
        print(var)
    func1()
9.  def func(x):
        print 'x = ', x
        x = 100
        print('In Function, x after
        modification = ', x)
    x = 50
    func(x)
    print('Outside Function, x = ', x)
10. def display( str ):
        print(str)
        return

    display("Hello World !!")
    display("Welcome to Python Programming")
```

```
11. def sum( num1, num2 ):
        total = num1 + num2
        print("Inside function, Total = ",
        total)
        return total
    total = sum( 10, 20 )
    print("Outside the function, Total = ",
    total)
12. def min(x,y):
        if x<y:
            return x
        else:
            return y
    print(min(4, 7))
13. def add(x, y):
        sum = x + y
        return sum
        print("This won't be printed")
    print(add(10,20))
14. def display(str):
        "This prints a passed string into
        this function"
        print(str)
        return
    display(str = "Welcome")
15. def say(message, repeat_it = 2):
        print(message * repeat_it)
    say('Hello')
    say('Hello', 5)
16. def func(x, y = 100, z = 1000):
        print('x = ', x, 'y = ', y, 'and z =
        ', z)
    func(5, 15, 25)
    func(35, z = 55)
    func(y = 70, x = 200)
17. def greet(*names):
        for name in names:
            print("Hello",name)
    greet("Aryan","Nikita","Chaitanya")
18. def func(arg1, *var):
        "This prints arbitrary arguments"
        print(arg1)
        for i in var:
        print(i)
        return

    func("Score is : ", 10, 20, 30)
    func( "\n Average Score = ", 20)
19. expo_3 = lambda x: x ** 3
    print(expo_3(5))
20. add_five = lambda n: n + 5
    mult_add_five = lambda n: add_five(n * 10)
    print(mult_add_five(9))
```

```
21. def func():
        """Do nothing.

        Nothing doing.
        """
        pass
    print(func.__doc__)
22. def C_to_F(c):
            return c * 9/5 + 32
    print(C_to_F(37))
23. def pow(x, y=3):
      r = 1
      for i in range(y):
        r = r * x
        return r
    print(pow(5))
    print(pow(2, 5))
24. def display(name, deptt, sal):
            print("Name: ", name)
            print("Department: ", deptt)
            print("Salary: ", sal)

    display(sal = 100000, name="Tavisha", deptt
    = "IT")
    display(deptt = "HR", name="Dev", sal =
    50000)
25. def display(mesg):
            return mesg + "!"
    print_str = display
```

```
    str = print_str("Hello")
    print(str)
26. from random import randint as r
    for i in range(10):
            value = r(1,100)
                print(value)
27. print((lambda x:x**2+5*x+6)(-3))
28. double =lambda x:x*2
    sub=lambda x,y:x-y
    print(sub(double(5),9))
29. def is_even(x):
        if x==0:
            return True
        else:
            return is_odd(x-1)


    def is_odd(x):
        return not is_even(x)


    print(is_even(22))
30. def display(x):
        for i in range(x):
            print(i)
            return
    display(5)
```

Find the Error

```
1. def func():
            print("Hello World")
2. var1 = "Good"
   def show():
            var2 = "Morning"
        print(var1)
        print(var2)
   show()
   print(var1)
   print(var2)
3. def f():
        print(var)
        var = 10
        print(var)
   var = 100
   f()
4. def f():
      var = 100
        print(var)
```

```
   f()
   print(var)
5. def func(var):
            var+=1
            var *= 2
            print(var)
   func(9)
   print(var)
6. def func1():
      var = 3
      func2()
   def func2():
      print(var)
   func1()
7. def display(x,y):
      print(x+y)
   display(10)
8. def func(a, b):
       print(a)
```

```
        print(b)
    func(b=10, 20)
9.  def func1():
        print("func1()")
    func1()
    func2()
    def func2():
        print("func2()")
10. import math as m
    print(math.sqrt(25))
    a. Error  b.  25 c.  5  d.  625
```

```
11. def factorial(x):
        return x*factorial(x-1)
        print(factorial(6))
12. def sum_to(x):
        return x+sum_to(x-1)
        print(sum_to(5))
```

Answers

Fill in the Blanks

1. range, 3
2. ImportError
3. Function definition
4. def
5. function name
6. docstring
7. def, :
8. calling program
9. None
10. define
11. local
12. global
13. return
14. keyword-only
15. Lambda functions
16. __doc__
17. __name__
18. dir()
19. __init__.py
20. __path__
21. def, :, y
22. def, print, else:
23. len, return, return
24. def, :, cube
25. from math import sqrt, cos
26. Standard Library
27. lambda, *, (10)
28. reload()
29. Built-in, global, local

State True or False

1. True 2. True 3. False 4. False 5. True 6. False 7. True 8. True 9. True 10. False
11. True 12. True 13. True 14. False 15. False 16. True 17. True 18. True 19. False 20. False
21. False 22. True 23. True 24. True 25. False 26. True 27. False 28. True 29. False 30. True
31. True 32. True 33. True 34. False

Multiple Choice Questions

1. (a) 2. (b) 3. (a) 4. (d) 5. (d) 6. (b) 7. (c) 8. (a) 9. (d) 10. (a) 11 (c) 12. (c)
13. (b) 14. (c)

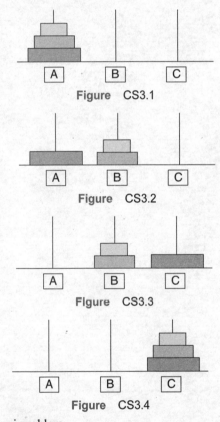

CASE STUDY
3

Tower of Hanoi

The tower of Hanoi is one of the main applications of recursion. It says, 'if you can solve n–1 cases, then you can easily solve the nth case'. Look at Figure CS3.1 which shows three rings mounted on pole A.

The problem is to move all these rings from pole A to pole C while maintaining the same order. The main issue is that the smaller disk must always come above the larger disk.

We will be doing this using a spare pole. In our case, A is the source pole, C is the destination pole, and B is the spare pole. To transfer all the three rings from A to C, we will first shift the upper two rings (n–1 rings) from the source pole to the spare pole. We move the first two rings from pole A to B as shown in Figure CS3.2.

Now that n–1 rings have been removed from pole A, the nth ring can be easily moved from the source pole (A) to the destination pole (C). Figure CS3.3 shows this step.

The final step is to move the n–1 rings from the spare pole (B) to the destination pole (C). This is shown in Figure CS3.4.

To summarize, the solution to our problem of moving n rings from A to C using B as spare can be given as:

Base case: if n = 1
Σ Move the ring from A to C using B as spare

Recursive case:
Σ Move n – 1 rings from A to B using C as spare
Σ Move the one ring left on A to C using B as spare
Σ Move n – 1 rings from B to C using A as spare.

The following code implements the solution of the tower of Hanoi problem.

Figure   CS3.1

Figure   CS3.2

Figure   CS3.3

Figure   CS3.4

```python
# Program to implement tower of Hanoi
def hanoi(n, A, B, C):
    if n > 0:
        hanoi(n - 1, A, C, B)
        if A:
            C.append(A.pop())
        hanoi(n - 1, B, A, C)
```

```
A = [1,2,3,4]
C = []
B = []
hanoi(len(A),A,B,C)
print(A, B, C)
```

OUTPUT

[] [] [1, 2, 3, 4]

Shuffling a Deck of Cards

Let us write a small code that will form a deck of cards and then shuffle it. In the program, we will use the product() function contained in the itertools module to create a deck of cards. The product() function performs the Cartesian product of the two sequence. Here, the two sequence are—numbers from 1 to 13 and the four suits. So, in all there are 13 * 4 = 52 combinations to form the deck. Each combination that forms a card is stored as a tuple. For example, deck[0] = (1,'Spade').

Once the deck is formed, it is shuffled using the shuffle() function in the random module and then five cards are drawn and their combination is displayed to the user. Every time you run the program, you will get a different output.

```
# Program to shuffle a deck of cards
import itertools, random
# Form a deck of cards
deck = list(itertools.product(range(1,14),['Spade','Heart','Diamond','Club']))
# Shuffle the cards
random.shuffle(deck)
# Draw five cards
print("Your combination of cards is :")
for i in range(5):
    print(deck[i][0], "of", deck[i][1])
```

OUTPUT
```
Your combination of cards is :
11 of Heart
2 of Spade
13 of Club
7 of Club
4 of Club
```

Python Strings Revisited

KEY
●●● Concepts

• Concatenating, Appending, Multiplying Strings • String Formatting Operator • Built-in String Methods and Functions • Slice, subscript, in and not in Operators • Comparing and Iterating Strings • The String Module

6.1 INTRODUCTION

The Python string data type is a sequence made up of one or more individual characters, where a character could be a letter, digit, whitespace, or any other symbol. Python treats strings as contiguous series of characters delimited by single, double or even triple quotes. Python has a built-in string class named "str" that has many useful features. We can simultaneously declare and define a string by creating a variable of string type. This can be done in several ways which are as follows:

```
name = "India"              graduate = 'N'
country = name              nationality = str("Indian")
```

Here, name, graduate, country, and nationality are all string variables.

We have already seen in Chapter 3 that string literals can be enclosed by either triple, double or single quotes. Escape sequences work with each type of string literals. A multiple-line text within quotes must have a backslash \ at the end of each line to escape the new line.

Indexing: Individual characters in a string are accessed using the subscript ([ ]) operator. The expression in brackets is called an *index*. The index specifies a member of an ordered set and in this case it specifies the character we want to access from the given set of characters in the string.

The index of the first character is 0 and that of the last character is n-1 where n is the number of characters in the string. If you try to exceed the bounds (below 0 or above n-1), then an error is raised.

Traversing a String: A string can be traversed by accessing character(s) from one index to another. For example, the following program uses indexing to traverse a string from the first character to the last.

| Example 6.1 | Program to demonstrate string traversal using indexing |

```
message = "Hello!"
index = 0
for i in message:
  print("message[", index, "] = ", i)
index += 1
```

OUTPUT

```
message[ 0 ] = H
message[ 1 ] = e
message[ 2 ] = l
message[ 3 ] = l
message[ 4 ] = o
message[ 5 ] = !
```

We see that there are 6 characters in the message, if we try to access 7th character by writing, `print(message[7])`, then the `IndexError: string index out of range` error will be generated. Index can either be an integer or an expression that evaluates to an integer.

| Example 6.2 | Program to demonstrate an expression used as an index of a string |

```
str = "Hello, welcome to the world of Python"
i = 2
print(str[i])   # index is an integer
print(str[i*3+1])   # index is an expression that evaluates to an integer
```

OUTPUT

```
l
w
```

Therefore, when you try to execute the following code, an error will be generated.

```
str = "Hello, welcome to the world of Python"
print(str['o'])
TypeError: string indices must be integers, not str
```

Also note that even the whitespace characters, exclamation mark and any other symbol (like ?, <, >, *, @, #, $, %, etc.) that forms a part of the string would be assigned its own index number.

6.2 CONCATENATING, APPENDING, AND MULTIPLYING STRINGS

The word concatenate means to join together. Python allows you to concatenate two strings using the + operator as shown in the following example.

Example 6.3   Program to concatenate two strings using + operator

```
str1 = "Hello "
str2 = "World"
str3 = str1 + str2
print("The concatenated string is : ", str3)
```

OUTPUT

```
The concatenated string is :  Hello World
```

Append mean to add something at the end. In Python you can add one string at the end of another string using the += operator as shown below.

Example 6.4   Program to append a string using += operator

```
str = "Hello, "
name = input("\n Enter your name : ")
str += name
str += ". Welcome to Python Programming."
print(str)
```

OUTPUT

```
Enter your name : Arnav
Hello, Arnav. Welcome to Python Programming.
```

You can use the * operator to repeat a string *n* number of times.

Example 6.5   Program to repeat a string using * operator

```
str = "Hello"
print(str * 3)
```

OUTPUT

```
HelloHelloHello
```

The str() function is used to convert values of any other type into string type. This helps the programmer to concatenate a string with any other data which is otherwise not allowed.

`str1 = "Hello"`
`var = 7`
`str2 = str1 + var`
`print(str2)`
	`str1 = "Hello"`
	`var = 7`
	`str2 = str1 + str(var)`
	`print(str2)`

OUTPUT	OUTPUT

<pre>Traceback (most recent call last):
  File "C:\Python34\Try.py", line 3,
  in <module>
    str2 = str1 + var
TypeError: cannot concatenate 'str'
and 'int' objects</pre>
	<pre>Hello7</pre>

The print statement prints one or more literals or values in a new line. If you don't want to print on a new line then, add end statement with a separator like whitespace, comma, etc. as shown below.

<pre>print("Hello")
print("World")</pre>
	<pre>print("Hello", end = ' ')
	print("World")</pre>

OUTPUT	**OUTPUT**

<pre>Hello
World</pre>
	<pre>Hello World</pre>

A raw string literal which is prefixed by an `'r'` passes all the characters as it is. They are not processed in any special way, not even the escape sequences. Look at the output of the code carefully to understand this difference.

Example 6.6   Program to print a raw string

```
print("\n Hello")
print(r"\n World")
```

OUTPUT

```
Hello
\n World
```

Note   The `'u'` prefix is used to write Unicode string literals.

6.3 STRINGS ARE IMMUTABLE

Python strings are immutable which means that once created they cannot be changed. Whenever you try to modify an existing string variable, a new string is created.

Every object in Python is stored in memory. You can find out whether two variables are referring to the same object or not by using the `id()`. The `id()` returns the memory address of that object. As both `str1` and `str2` points to same memory location, they both point to the same object.

Example 6.7   Program to demonstrate string references using the `id()` function

```
str1 = "Hello"
print("Str1 is : ", str1)
print("ID of str1 is : ", id(str1))

str2 = "World"
print("Str2 is : ", str2)
```

```
print("ID of str1 is : ", id(str2))
str1 += str2
print("Str1 after concatenation is : ", str1)
print("ID of str1 is : ", id(str1))
str3 = str1
print("str3 = ", str3)
print("ID of str3 is : ", id(str3))
```

OUTPUT
```
Str1 is :  Hello
ID of str1 is :  45093344
Str2 is :  World
ID of str1 is :  45093312
Str1 after concatenation is :  HelloWorld
ID of str1 is :  43861792
str3 =  HelloWorld
ID of str3 is :  43861792
```

From the output, it is very clear that str1 and str2 are two different string objects with different values and have a different memory address. When we concatenate str1 and str2, a new string is created because strings are immutable in nature. You can check this fact by observing the current and previous address of str1.

Finally, we create a new string variable str3 and initialize it with str1. Since they both point to the same value, their address is exactly same. Now can you guess the output of the following code:

```
str = "Hi"
str[0] = 'B'
print(str)
```

Yes, the code will result in an error— TypeError: 'str' object does not support item assignment simply because strings are immutable. If you want to make any kind of changes you must create a new string as shown below.

```
str = "Hi"
new_str = "Bi"
print("Old String = ",str)
print("New String = ",new_str)
```

OUTPUT
```
Old String =  Hi
New String =  Bi
```

> **Note** We cannot delete or remove characters from a string. However, we can delete the entire string using the keyword del.

6.4 STRING FORMATTING OPERATOR

If you are a C programmer, then you are already familiar with % sign. This string formatting operator is one of the exciting features of Python. The % operator takes a format string on the left (that has %d, %s, etc.) and the corresponding

> **Programming Tip:** A tuple is made of values separated by commas inside parentheses.

values in a tuple (will be discussed in subsequent chapter) on the right. The format operator, % allows users to construct strings, replacing parts of the strings with the data stored in variables. The syntax for the string formatting operation is:

```
"<FORMAT>" % (<VALUES>)
```

The statement begins with a *format* string consisting of a sequence of characters and *conversion specifications*. Conversion specifications start with a % operator and can appear anywhere within the string. Following the format string is a % sign and then a set of values, one per conversion specification, separated by commas and enclosed in parenthesis. If there is a single value then parenthesis is optional. Just observe the code given below carefully.

Example 6.8 Program to use format sequences while printing a string

```
name = "Aarish"
age = 8
print("Name = %s and Age = %d" %(name, age))
print("Name = %s and Age = %d" %("Anika", 6))

OUTPUT
Name = Aarish and Age = 8
Name = Anika and Age = 6
```

In the output we can see that %s has been replaced by a string and %d has been replaced by an integer value. The values to be substituted are provided at the end of the line—in brackets prefixed by %. You can either supply these values directly or by using variables. Table 6.1 lists other string formatting characters.

Note that the number and type of values in the tuple should match the number and type of format sequences or conversion specifications in the string, otherwise an error is returned.

```
>>> '%d %f %s' % (100, 23.89)
TypeError: not enough arguments for format string
Traceback (most recent call last):
File "<pyshell#0>", line 1, in <module>
"%f" %"abc"
TypeError: float argument required, not str
```

In the first case, number of arguments don't match and in the second case the type of argument didn't match. Hence, the error.

The following Table 6.1 lists some format characters used for printing different types of data.

Table 6.1 Formatting Symbols

Format Symbol	Purpose
%c	Character
%d or %i	Signed decimal integer
%s	String
%u	Unsigned decimal integer

(Contd)

Table 6.1   (*Contd*)

Format Symbol	Purpose
%o	Octal integer
%x or %X	Hexadecimal integer (x for lower case characters a–f and X for upper case characters A–F)
%e or %E	Exponential notation
%f	Floating point number
%g or %G	Short numbers in floating point or exponential notation

To further understand the power of formatting strings, execute the code given below and observe the output, how weird and unorganized it looks.

Example 6.9   Program to display powers of a number without using formatting characters

```
i = 1
print("i\ti**2\ti**3\ti**4\ti**5\ti**6\ti**7\ti**8\ti**9\ti**10")
while i <= 10:
    print(i, '\t', i**2, '\t', i**3, '\t', i**5, '\t', i**10, '\t', i**20)
    i += 1
```

OUTPUT

i	i**2	i**3	i**4	i**5	i**6	i**7	i**8	i**9	i**10
1	1	1	1	1	1				
2	4	8	32	1024	1048576				
3	9	27	243	59049	3486784401				
4	16	64	1024	1048576	1099511627776				
5	25	125	3125	9765625	95367431640625				
6	36	216	7776	60466176	3656158440062976				
7	49	343	16807	282475249	79792266297612001				
8	64	512	32768	1073741824	1152921504606846976				
9	81	729	59049	3486784401	12157665459056928801				
10	100	1000	100000	10000000000	100000000000000000000				

The program prints a table that prints powers of numbers from 1 to 10. Tabs are used to align the columns of values. We see that as the digits increases the columns becomes misaligned. Let's look at a different version of this program which gives a very clean and clear output.

Example 6.10   Program to display powers of a number using formatting characters

```
i = 1
print("%-4s%-5s%-6s%-8s%-13s%-15s%-17s%-19s%-21s%-23s" % \
    ('i', 'i**2', 'i**3', 'i**4', 'i**5', 'i**6', 'i**7', 'i**8', 'i**9', 'i**10'))
while i <= 10:
print("%-4d%-5d%-6d%-8d%-13d%-15d%-17d%-19d%-21d%-23d" % (i, i**2, i**3, i**4,
i**5, i**6, i**7, i**8, i**9, i**10))
    i += 1
```

OUTPUT

i	i**2	i**3	i**4	i**5	i**6	i**7	i**8	i**9	i**10
1	1	1	1	1	1	1	1	1	1
2	4	8	16	32	64	128	256	512	1024
3	9	27	81	243	729	2187	6561	19683	59049
4	16	64	256	1024	4096	16384	65536	262144	1048576
5	25	125	625	3125	15625	78125	390625	1953125	9765625
6	36	216	1296	7776	46656	279936	1679616	10077696	60466176
7	49	343	2401	16807	117649	823543	5764801	40353607	282475249
8	64	512	4096	32768	262144	2097152	16777216	134217728	1073741824
9	81	729	6561	59049	531441	4782969	43046721	387420489	3486784401
10	100	1000	10000	100000	1000000	10000000	100000000	1000000000	10000000000

In the above code, we have set the width of each column independently using the string formatting feature of Python. The - after each % in the conversion string indicates left justification. The numerical values specify the minimum length. Therefore, %-15d means it is a left justified number that is at least 15 characters wide.

Note	You don't need to type semi-colon at the end of each line in Python because Python treats each line of code as a separate statement.

6.4.1 Additional String Formatting Operator Examples

```
>>> '%d' % 10
'10'
>>> '%d' % 0b111  # binary number converted into integer
'7'
>>> "%s" % 'HELLO'
'HELLO'
>>> "%s %s" % ('HELLO', 'WORLD')
'HELLO WORLD'

>>> "%x" % 17   # Converts an integer into hexadecimal value
'11'
>>> "%03d" %9  #zero padding used
'009'
>>> "%-5d" % 9    # left adjusted
'9    '
>>> '% d' % 9     # space used
' 9'
```

```
>>> '%+d' % 9        # sign flag used
'+9'
>>> '%+d' % -9
'-9'
>>> '%f' % 1.23
'1.230000'
>>> '%.1f' % 1.23
'1.2'
>>> '%.2f' % 1.23
'1.23'
>>> '%.3f' % 1.23
'1.230'
>>> '%d' % 1.23   # floating point converted to integer
'1'
>>> '%f' % 123    # Integer converted to floating point
'1230.000000'
>>> '%e' % 1234567890
'1.234568e+09'
>>> 'XYZ %c' % 65
'XYZ A'
```

6.5 BUILT-IN STRING METHODS AND FUNCTIONS

Strings are an example of Python *objects*. As discussed earlier, an object is an entity that contains both data (the actual string itself) as well as functions to manipulate that data. These functions are available to any *instance* (variable) of the object.

Python supports many built-in methods to manipulate strings. A method is just like a function. The only difference between a function and method is that a method is invoked or called on an object. For example, if the variable str is a string, then you can call the upper() method as str.upper() to convert all the characters of str in uppercase. Table 6.2 discusses some of the most commonly used string methods.

Table 6.2 Commonly Used String Methods

Function	Usage	Example
capitalize()	This function is used to capitalize first letter of the string.	str = "hello" print(str.capitalize()) **OUTPUT** Hello
center(width, fillchar)	Returns a string with the original string centered to a total of width columns and filled with fillchar in columns that do not have characters.	str = "hello" print(str.center(10, '*')) **OUTPUT** **hello***

(Contd)

Table 6.2 (*Contd*)

Function	Usage	Example
count(str, beg, end)	Counts number of times str occurs in a string. You can specify beg as 0 and end as the length of the message to search the entire string or use any other value to just search a part of the string.	str = "he" message = "helloworldhellohello" print(message. count (str,0, len (message))) **OUTPUT** 3
endswith (suffix, beg, end)	Checks if string ends with suffix; returns True if so and False otherwise. You can either set beg = 0 and end equal to the length of the message to search entire string or use any other value to search a part of it.	message = "She is my best friend" print(message.endswith("end", 0,len(message))) **OUTPUT** True
startswith (prefix, beg, end)	Checks if string starts with prefix; if so, it returns True and False otherwise. You can either set beg = 0 and end equal to the length of the message to search entire string or use any other value to search a part of it.	str = "The world is beautiful" print(str.startswith ("Th",0, len(str))) **OUTPUT** True
find(str, beg, end)	Checks if str is present in string. If found it returns the position at which str occurs in string, otherwise returns -1. You can either set beg = 0 and end equal to the length of the message to search entire string or use any other value to search a part of it.	message = "She is my best friend" print(message. find("my",0, len (message))) **OUTPUT** 7
index(str, beg, end)	Same as find but raises an exception if str is not found.	message = "She is my best friend" print(message.index("mine", 0, len(message))) **OUTPUT** ValueError: substring not found
rfind(str, beg, end)	Same as find but starts searching from the end.	str = "Is this your bag?" print(str.rfind("is", 0, len(str))) **OUTPUT** 5
rindex(str, beg, end)	Same as rindex but start searching from the end and raises an exception if str is not found.	str = "Is this your bag?" print(str.rindex("you", 0, len(str))) **OUTPUT** 8

(*Contd*)

Table 6.2   (*Contd*)

Function	Usage	Example
isalnum()	Returns True if string has at least 1 character and every character is either a number or an alphabet and False otherwise.	message = "JamesBond007" print(message.isalnum()) **OUTPUT** True
isalpha()	Returns True if string has at least 1 character and every character is an alphabet and False otherwise.	message = "JamesBond007" print(message.isalpha()) **OUTPUT** False
isdigit()	Returns True if string contains only digits and False otherwise.	message = "007" print(message.isdigit()) **OUTPUT** True
islower()	Returns True if string has at least 1 character and every character is a lowercase alphabet and False otherwise.	message = "Hello" print(message.islower()) **OUTPUT** False
isspace()	Returns True if string contains only whitespace characters and False otherwise.	message = " " print(message.isspace()) **OUTPUT** True
isupper()	Returns True if string has at least 1 character and every character is an upper case alphabet and False otherwise.	message = "HELLO" print(message.isupper()) **OUTPUT** True
len(string)	Returns the length of the string.	str = "Hello" print(len(str)) **OUTPUT** 5
ljust(width[, fillchar])	Returns a string left-justified to a total of width columns. Columns without characters are padded with the character specified in the fillchar argument.	str = "Hello" print(str.ljust(10, '*')) **OUTPUT** Hello*****
rjust(width[, fillchar])	Returns a string right-justified to a total of width columns. Columns without characters are padded with the character specified in the fillchar argument.	str = "Hello" print(str.rjust(10, '*')) **OUTPUT** *****Hello

(*Contd*)

Table 6.2 (*Contd*)

Function	Usage	Example
zfill (width)	Returns string left padded with zeros to a total of width characters. It is used with numbers and also retains its sign (+ or -).	str = "1234" print(str.zfill(10)) **OUTPUT** 0000001234
lower()	Converts all characters in the string into lowercase.	str = "Hello" print(str.lower()) **OUTPUT** hello
upper()	Converts all characters in the string into uppercase.	str = "Hello" print(str.upper()) **OUTPUT** HELLO
lstrip()	Removes all leading whitespace in string.	str = " Hello" print(str.lstrip()) **OUTPUT** Hello
rstrip()	Removes all trailing whitespace in string.	str = "Hello " print(str.lstrip()) **OUTPUT** Hello
strip()	Removes all leading and trailing whitespace in string.	str = " Hello " print(str.strip()) **OUTPUT** Hello
max(str)	Returns the highest alphabetical character (having highest ASCII value) from the string str.	str = "hello friendz" print(max(str)) **OUTPUT** z
min(str)	Returns the lowest alphabetical character (lowest ASCII value) from the string str.	str = "hello friendz" print(min(str)) **OUTPUT** d
replace(old, new [, max])	Replaces all or max (if given) occurrences of old in string with new.	str = "hello hello hello" print(str.replace("he", "FO")) **OUTPUT** FOlloFOlloFOllo

> **Programming Tip:** The empty parentheses means that this method takes no argument.

(*Contd*)

Table 6.2　(*Contd*)

Function	Usage	Example

title()	Returns string in title case.	```str = "The world is beautiful"```
		```print(str.title())```
		
		OUTPUT
		```The World Is Beautiful```

swapcase()	Toggles the case of every character (uppercase character becomes lowercase and vice versa).	```str = "The World Is Beautiful"```
		```print(str.swapcase())```
		
		OUTPUT
		```tHE wORLD iS bEAUTIFUL```

split(delim)	Returns a list of substrings separated by the specified delimiter. If no delimiter is specified then by default it splits strings on all whitespace characters.	```str = "abc,def, ghi,jkl"```
		```print(str.split(','))```
		
		OUTPUT
		```['abc', 'def', ' ghi', 'jkl']```

join(list)	It is just the opposite of split. The function joins a list of strings using the delimiter with which the function is invoked.	```print('-'.join(['abc', 'def', 'ghi', 'jkl']))```
		
		OUTPUT
		```abc-def-ghi-jkl```

isidentifier()	Returns True if the string is a valid identifier.	```str = "Hello"```
		```print(str.isidentifier())```
		
		OUTPUT
		```True```

enumerate(str)	Returns an enumerate object that lists the index and value of all the characters in the string as pairs.	```str = "Hello WOrld"```
		```print(list(enumerate(str)))```
		
		OUTPUT
		```[(0, 'H'), (1, 'e'), (2, 'l'), (3, 'l'), (4, 'o'), (5, ' '), (6, 'W'), (7, 'O'), (8, 'r'), (9, 'l'), (10, 'd')]```

Note that the strip() when used with a string argument will strip (from both ends) any combination of the specified characters in the string as shown below.

Example 6.11　To demonstrate strip method on a string object

```
str = "abcdcbabcdcbabcdabcdbcabcdcba"
print(str.strip('abc'))
```

OUTPUT
```
dcbabcdcbabcdabcdbcabcd
```

Let us discuss two more important functions—format() and splitlines().

- The format() function used with strings is a very versatile and powerful function used for formatting strings. Format strings have curly braces {} as placeholders or replacement fields which gets replaced. We can even use positional arguments or keyword arguments to specify the order of fields that have to be replaced. Consider the code given in the following example and carefully observe the sequence of fields in the output and then compare the sequence as given in the arguments of the format() function.

Example 6.12 Program to demonstrate format() function

```
str1 = "{}, {} and {}".format('Sun','Moon','Stars')
print("\n The default sequence of arguments is : " + str1)
str2 = "{1}, {0} and {2}".format('Sun','Moon','Stars')
print("\n The positional sequence of arguments (1, 0 and 2) is : " + str2)
str3 = "{c}, {b} and {a}".format(a='Sun',b='Moon',c='Stars')
print("\n The keyword sequence of arguments is : " + str3)
```

OUTPUT

```
The default sequence of arguments is : Sun, Moon and Stars
The positional sequence of arguments (1, 0 and 2) is : Moon, Sun and Stars
The keyword sequence of arguments is : Stars, Moon and Sun
```

- The splitlines() returns a list of the lines in the string. This method uses the newline characters like \r or \n to split lines. Line breaks are not included in the resulting list unless keepends is given as True. The syntax of splitlines() is given as,

```
str.splitlines([keepends])
```

In the syntax, keepends is optional. Look at the code given below and observe its output, both when keepends is specified as True and when keepends is not specified at all.

```
print('Sun and \n\n Stars, Planets \r and Moon\r\n'.splitlines())
print('Sun and \n\n Stars, Planets \r and Moon\r\n'.splitlines(True))
```

OUTPUT

```
['Sun and ', '', ' Stars, Planets ', ' and Moon']
['Sun and \n', '\n', ' Stars, Planets \r', ' and Moon\r\n']
```

Note The isX string methods are used to validate user input.

6.6 SLICE OPERATION

A substring of a string is called a *slice*. The slice operation is used to refer to sub-parts of sequences (we will read about them in subsequent chapters) and strings. You can take subset of a string from the original string by using [] operator also known as *slicing operator*. Before reading about the slice operation, let us first consider the index of characters in a string as shown in Figure 6.1.

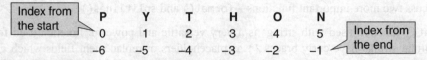

Figure 6.1 Indices in a string

The syntax of slice operation is s[start:end], where start specifies the beginning index of the substring and end-1 is the index of the last character. Now let us take an example, if we have a string str = "PYTHON" then the index of characters starting from first character and from the last character can be given as shown in the Figure 6.1. Look at the slice operations given below and observe the output on vis-a-vis our string.

> **Programming Tip:** Calling a method is also known as method invocation.

| Note | Omitting either start or end index by default takes start or end of the string. Omitting both means the entire string. |

Example 6.13 Program to demonstrate slice operation on string objects

```
str = "PYTHON"
print("str[1:5] = ", str[1:5])   #characters starting at index 1 and extending up
to but not including index 5
print("str[:6] = ", str[:6])     # defaults to the start of the string
print("str[1:] = ", str[1:])     # defaults to the end of the string
print("str[:] = ", str[:])       # defaults to the entire string
print("str[1:20] = ", str[1:20]) # an index that is too big is truncated down to
length of the string
```

OUTPUT

```
str[1:5] =  YTHO
str[:6] =  PYTHON
str[1:] =  YTHON
str[:] =  PYTHON
str[1:20] =  YTHON
```

> **Programming Tip:** Python does not have any separate data type for characters. They are represented as a single character string.

Python gives you the flexibility to either access a string from the first character or from the last character. If we access the string from the first character then we use a zero based index, but when doing it backward the index starts with -1.

| Note | Python uses negative numbers to access the characters at the end of the string. Negative index numbers count back from the end of the string. |

Example 6.14 Program to understand how characters in a string are accessed using negative indexes

```
str = "PYTHON"
print("str[-1] = ", str[-1])   # last character is accessed
print("str[-6] = ", str[-6])   # first character is accessed
```

```
print("str[-2:] = ", str[-2:]) # second last and the last characters are accessed
print("str[:-2] = ", str[:-2]) # all characters upto but not including second last
character
print("str[-5:-2] = ", str[-5:-2]) # characters from second upto second last are
accessed
```

OUTPUT

```
str[-1] =  N
str[-6] =  P
str[-2:] =  ON
str[:-2] =  PYTH
str[-5:-2] =  YTH
```

By observing the outputs of the two codes mentioned in Examples 6.13 and 6.14, we can draw following inferences:

- Elements are accessed from left towards right.
- For any index n, s[:n] + s[n:] = s. This is true even if n is a negative number. So, we can say that the slice operation s[:n] and s[n:] always partition the string into two parts such that all characters are conserved.

Note When using negative index numbers, start with the lower number first as it occurs earlier in the string.

6.6.1 Specifying Stride While Slicing Strings

In the slice operation, you can specify a third argument as the stride, which refers to the number of characters to move forward after the first character is retrieved from the string. The default value of stride is 1. Hence, in all the above examples where the value of stride is not specified, its default value of 1 is used which means that every character between two index numbers is retrieved. The code given below illustrates this difference.

Example 6.15 Program to use slice operation with stride

```
str = "Welcome to the world of Python"
print("str[2:10] = ", str[2:10])     # default stride is 1
print("str[2:10:1] = ", str[2:10:1])  # same as stride = 1
print("str[2:10:2] = ", str[2:10:2])  # skips every alternate character
print("str[2:13:4] = ", str[2:13:4])  # skips every fourth character
```

OUTPUT

```
str[2:10] = lcome to
str[2:10:1] = lcome to
str[2:10:2] = loet
str[2:13:4] = le
```

Note that even the whitespace characters are skipped as they are also a part of the string. If you omit the first two arguments and only specify the third one, then the entire string is used in steps (as given by the third argument). This is shown in the following example.

Example 6.16   Program to demonstrate splice operation with just last (positive) argument

```
str = "Welcome to the world of Python"
print("str[::3] = ", str[::3])
```

OUTPUT
```
str[::3] = WceohwloPh
```

You can also specify a negative value for the third argument. This is especially useful to print the original string in reverse order by setting the value of stride to −1 as shown below.

Example 6.17   Program to demonstrate splice operation with just last (negative) argument

```
str = "Welcome to the world of Python"
print("str[::-1] = ", str[::-1])
```

OUTPUT
```
str[::-1] = nohtyP fo dlrow eht ot emocleW
```

In this example, we have considered the entire original string, reversed it through the negative stride and with a stride of -3, we have skipped every third letter of the reversed string.

Example 6.18   Program to print the string in reverse thereby skipping every third character

```
str = "Welcome to the world of Python"
print("str[::-3]", str[::-3])
```

OUTPUT
```
str[::-3] = nt  r ttml
```

6.7 ord() AND chr() FUNCTIONS

The ord() function returns the ASCII code of the character and the chr() function returns character represented by a ASCII number. Consider the following examples.

ch = 'R' print(ord(ch))	print(chr(82))	print(chr(112))	print(ord('p'))
OUTPUT	**OUTPUT**	**OUTPUT**	**OUTPUT**
82	R	p	112

6.8 in AND not in OPERATORS

in and not in operators can be used with strings to determine whether a string is present in another string. Therefore, the in and not in operator are also known as membership operators.

```
str1 = "Welcome to the world of Python
!!!"
str2 = "the"
if str2 in str1:
    print("Found")
else:
    print("Not Found")
```

OUTPUT

Found

```
str1 = "This is a very good book"
str2 = "best"
if str2 not in str1:
    print("The book is very good but it
may not be the best one.")
else:
    print ("It is the best book.")
```

OUTPUT

The book is very good but it may not be
the best one.

You can also use the in and not in operators to check whether a character is present is in a word. For example, observe the commands and their outputs given below.

| >>> 'u' in "stars"
 False | >>> 'v' not in "success"
 True | >>> 'vi' in "victory"
 True |

While using the in and not in operators, remember that a string is a substring of itself as shown below.

| >>> "world" in "world"
 True | >>> 'a' in 'a'
 True |

6.9 COMPARING STRINGS

Python allows you to compare strings using relational (or comparison) operators such as > , < , < = , etc. Some of these operators along with their description and usage are given in Table 6.3.

Table 6.3 String Comparison Operators and their Description

Operator	Description	Example
==	If two strings are equal, it returns True.	>>> "AbC" == "AbC" True

!= or <>	If two strings are not equal, it returns True.	>>> "AbC" != "Abc"
		 True
		 >>> "abc" <> "ABC"
		 True

>	If the first string is greater than the second, it returns True.	>>> "abc" > "Abc" True
<	If the second string is greater than the first, it returns True.	>>> "abC" < "abc" True
>=	If the first string is greater than or equal to the second, it returns True.	>>> "aBC" >= "ABC" True
<=	If the second string is greater than or equal to the first, it returns True.	>>> "ABc" <= "ABc" True

These operators compare the strings by using the lexicographical order i.e. using ASCII value of the characters. The ASCII values of A–Z is 65–90 and ASCII code for a-z is 97-122. This means that book is greater than Book because the ASCII value of 'b' is 98 and 'B' is 66. Let us try more examples.

`>>> "TED" == "ted"` `False`	`>>> "talk" > "talks"` `False`	`>>> "Main" < "main"` `True`
`>>> "True" >= "False"` `True`	`>>> "like" != "likes"` `True`	`>>> "tend" <= "tent"` `True`

> **Note**   String values are ordered using lexicographical (dictionary) ordering. The lexicographical order is similar to the alphabetical order that is used with a dictionary (which is discussed in Chapter 8), except that all the uppercase letters come before all the lowercase letters. For example, 'Arman' is less than 'Ben' as the ASCII value for 'A' is 65, and 'B' is 66.

6.10 ITERATING STRING

String is a sequence type (sequence of characters). You can iterate through the string using `for` loop as shown in the code given below.

Example 6.19   Program to iterate a given string using `for` loop

```
str = "Welcome to Python"
for i in str:
print(i, end=' ')
```

OUTPUT
```
W e l c o m e   t o   P y t h o n
```

In the above code, the `for` loop executes for every character in `str`. The loop starts with the first character and automatically ends when the last character is accessed. You can also iterate through the string using `while` loop by writing the following code.

Example 6.20   Program to iterate a given string using `while` loop

```
message = " Welcome to Python "
index = 0
while index < len(message):
    letter = message[index]
    print(letter, end=' ')
    index += 1
```

OUTPUT
```
W e l c o m e   t o   P y t h o n
```

In the above program the loop traverses the string and displays each letter. The loop condition is `index < len(message)`, so the moment index becomes equal to the length of the string, the condition evaluates to `False`, and the body of the loop is not executed. As we said earlier, index of the last character is `len(message) – 1`.

Another point to observe carefully is that *you can iterate through a string either using an index or by using each character in the string*. For example, both the codes given below perform the same job of copying one string into another using the `for` loop but the way you iterate is different—through character or index of the character.

```
# Uses character to iterate
def copy(str):
    new_str = ''
    for i in str:
        new_str += i
    return new_str

str = input("\n Enter a string : ")
print("\n The copied string is : ",
copy(str))
```

OUTPUT

```
Enter a string : Python
The copied string is :  Python
```

```
# Uses index of character to iterate
def copy(str):
    new_str = ''
    for i in range(len(str)):
        new_str += str[i]
     return new_str

str = input("\n Enter a string : ")
print("\n The copied string is : ",
copy(str))
```

OUTPUT

```
Enter a string : Python
The copied string is :  Python
```

PROGRAMMING EXAMPLES

Program 6.1 Write a program to print the following pattern.

```
A
AB
ABC
ABCD
ABCDE
ABCDEF
for i in range(1,7):
        ch = 'A'
        print()
        for j in range(1,i+1):
            print(ch, end=' ')
            ch = chr(ord(ch)+1)
```

Program 6.2 Write a program that takes user's name and PAN card number as input. Validate the information using isX function and print the details.

```
while(1):
    name = input("\n Enter your name : ")
    if name.isalpha() == False:
        print("Invalid Name, Sorry you cannot proceed.")
        break
    else:
        pan_card_no = input("\n Enter your PAN card number : ")
        if pan_card_no.isalnum() == False:
            print("Invalid PAN card Number, Sorry you cannot proceed.")
            break
    print("Please check, "+name+", your PAN card number is : "+pan_card_no)
    break
```

OUTPUT

```
Enter your name : OM
Enter your PAN card number : ABCDE1234F
Please check, OM, your PAN card number is : ABCDE1234F
```

Program 6.3 Write a program that encrypts a message by adding a key value to every character. (Caesar Cipher)

Hint: Say, if key = 3, then add 3 to every character

```python
message = "HelloWorld"
index = 0
while index < len(message):
    letter = message[index]
    print(chr(ord(letter) + 3), end=' ')
    index += 1
```

OUTPUT

```
K h o o r Z r u o g
```

Program 6.4 Write a program that uses split() to split a multiline string.

```python
letter = '''Dear Students,
I am pleased to inform you that,
there is a workshop on Python in college tomorrow.
Everyone should come and
there will also be a quiz in Python, whosoever wins
will win a Gold Medal.'''

print(letter.split('\n'))
```

OUTPUT

```
['Dear Students,', 'I am pleased to inform you that, ', 'there is a workshop on
Python in college tomorrow.', 'Everyone should come and', 'there will also be a
quiz in Python, whosoever wins', 'will win a Gold Medal.']
```

Program 6.5 Write a program to generate an Abecedarian series.

Hint: Abecedarian refers to a series or list in which the elements appear in alphabetical order

```python
str1 = "ABCDEFGH"
str2 = "ate"
for letter in str1:
    print((letter + str2), end=' ')
```

OUTPUT

```
Aate    Bate    Cate    Date    Eate    Fate    Gate    Hate
```

Program 6.6 Write a program that accepts a string from user and redisplays the same string after removing vowels from it.

```python
def remove_vowels(s):
    new_str = ""
    for i in s:
        if i in "aeiouAEIOU":
            pass
        else:
            new_str += i
    print("The string without vowels is : ", new_str)
str = input("\n Enter a string : ")
remove_vowels(str)
```

OUTPUT

```
Enter a string : The food is very tasty
The string without vowels is :   Th fd s vry tsty
```

Program 6.7 Write a program that finds whether a given character is present in a string or not. In case it is present it prints the index at which it is present. Do not use built-in find functions to search the character.

```python
def find_ch(s, c):
    index = 0
    while(index < len(s)):
        if s[index] == c:
            print(c, "found in string at index : ", index)
            return
        else:
            pass
        index += 1
    print (c, " is not present in the string")

str = input("\n Enter a string : ")
ch = input("\n Enter the character to be searched : ")
find_ch(str, ch)
```

Programming Tip: Index numbers allow us to access specific characters within a string.

OUTPUT

```
Enter a string : God is Great
Enter the character to be searched : r
r found in string at index :   8
```

Program 6.8 Write a program that emulates the `rfind` function.

```python
def rfind_ch(s, c):
    index = len(s)-1
    while index>=0:
```

```
            if s[index] == c:
                return index
            index = index - 1
        return -1
str = input("\n Enter a string : ")
ch = input("\n Enter the character to be searched : ")
index = rfind_ch(str, ch)
if index != -1:
        print(ch, " is found at location ", index)
    else:
        print(ch, "is not present in the string")
```

> **Programming Tip:** The start and end parameters in find() and rfind() are optional.

OUTPUT

```
Enter a string : Let us study Python
Enter the character to be searched : s
s  is found at location  7
```

Program 6.9 Write a program that counts the occurrences of a character in a string. Do not use built-in count function.

```
def count_ch(s, c):
    count = 0
    for i in s:
        if i == c:
            count += 1
    return count
str = input("\n Enter a string : ")
ch = input("\n Enter the character to be searched : ")
count = count_ch(str, ch)
print("In ", str, ch, " occurs ", count, " times")
```

OUTPUT

```
Enter a string : Lovely Flowers
Enter the character to be searched : e
In  Lovely Flowers e  occurs  2  times
```

Program 6.10 Modify the above program so that it starts counting from the specified location.

```
def count_ch(s, c, beg = 0):
    count = 0
    index = beg
    while index < len(s):
        if s[index] == c:
            count += 1
        index += 1
    return count
str = input("\n Enter a string : ")
```

```
ch = input("\n Enter the character to be searched : ")
count = count_ch(str, ch)
print("In ", str, ch, " occurs ", count, " times from beginning to end")
loc = int(input("\n From which position do you want to start counting : "))
count = count_ch(str, ch, loc)
print("In ", str, ch, " occurs ", count, " times from position", loc, " to end")
```

OUTPUT

```
Enter a string : Good Going
Enter the character to be searched : o
In  Good Going o  occurs  3  times from beginning to end
From which position do you want to start counting : 2
In  Good Going o  occurs  2  times from position 2  to end
```

Program 6.11 Write a program to reverse a string.

```
def reverse(str):
    new_str = ''
    i = len(str)-1
    while i>=0:
        new_str += str[i]
        i -= 1
    return new_str

str = input("\n Enter a string : ")
print("\n The reversed string is : ", reverse(str))
```

OUTPUT

```
Enter a string : Python
The reversed string is :  nohtyP
```

Program 6.12 Write a program to parse an email id to print from which email server it was sent and when.

```
info = 'From priti.rao@gmail.com Sun Oct 16 20:29:16 2016'

start = info.find('@') + 1        # Extract characters after @ symbol
end = info.find(".com") + 4       # Extract till m, find returns index of m.
mailserver = info[start:end]      # Extract characters

start = end + 1                   # Ignore whitespace
end = len(info) - 1               # Extract till last character
date_time = info[start:end]

print("The email has been sent through " + mailserver)
print("It was sent on " + date_time)
```

OUTPUT

```
The email has been sent through gmail.com
It was sent on Sun Oct 16 20:29:16 2016
```

6.11 THE STRING MODULE

The string module consists of a number of useful constants, classes, and functions (some of which are deprecated). These functions are used to manipulate strings.

String constants Some constants defined in the string module are:

string.ascii_letters: Combination of ascii_lowercase and ascii_uppercase constants.

string.ascii_lowercase: Refers to all lowercase letters from a-z.

string.ascii_uppercase: Refers to all uppercase letters, A-Z.

string.digits: Refers to digits from 0-9.

string.hexdigits: Refers to hexadecimal digits, 0-9, a-f, and A-F.

string.lowercase: A string that has all the characters that are considered lowercase letters.

string.octdigits: Refers to octal digits, 0-7.

string.punctuation: String of ASCII characters that are considered to be punctuation characters.

string.printable: String of printable characters which includes digits, letters, punctuation, and whitespace.

string.uppercase: A string that has all the characters that are considered uppercase letters.

string.whitespace: A string that has all characters that are considered whitespace like space, tab, linefeed, return, form-feed, and vertical tab.

Example 6.21 Program that uses different methods (upper, lower, split, join, count, replace, and find) on string object

```
str = "Welcome to the world of Python"
print("Uppercase - ", str.upper())
print("Lowercase - ", str.lower())
print("Split - ", str.split())
print("Join - ", '-'.join(str.split()))
print("Replace - ", str.replace("Python", "Java"))
print("Count of o - ", str.count('o') )
print("Find of - ", str.find("of"))
```

OUTPUT
```
Uppercase -  WELCOME TO THE WORLD OF PYTHON
Lowercase -  welcome to the world of python
Split -  ['Welcome', 'to', 'the', 'world', 'of', 'Python']
Join -  Welcome-to-the-world-of-Python
Replace -  Welcome to the world of Java
Count of o -  5
Find of -  21
```

Programming Tip: A method is called by appending its name to the variable name using the period as a delimiter.

To see the contents of the string module, use the dir() with the module name as an argument as shown below.

```
>>> dir(string)
['ChainMap', 'Formatter', 'Template', '_TemplateMetaclass', '__builtins__', '__cached__', '__doc__', '__file__', '__loader__', '__name__', '__package__', '__spec__', '_re', '_string', 'ascii_letters', 'ascii_lowercase', 'ascii_uppercase', 'capwords', 'digits', 'hexdigits', 'octdigits', 'printable', 'punctuation', 'whitespace']
```

To know the details of a particular item, you can use the `type` command. The function `type()` takes as an argument the module name followed by the dot operator and the item name.

Example 6.22 Program that displays the type of an item in the `string` module

```
import string
print(type(string.digits))
```
OUTPUT
```
<class 'str'>
```

```
import string
print(type(string.ascii_letters))
```
OUTPUT
```
<class 'str'>
```

From the output we can see that the type function returns the type of the item in the string module. Just type the following lines and observe the output.

Example 6.23 Program that displays the type of an item in the `string` module

```
import string
print(string.digits)
```

OUTPUT
```
0123456789
```

```
import string
print(string.ascii_letters)
```

OUTPUT
```
abcdefghijklmnopqrstuvwxyzABCDEFGHIJKLMNOPQRSTUVWXYZ
```

When you try to print what makes the part of digits in a string in Python, all digits from 0-9 are returned. Same is the case with `ascii_letters`. You can yourself try the rest of the constants defined in the `string` module. However, to find the details of a particular function, you can print its documentation using the *docstring* through __doc__ attribute as shown below.

Example 6.24 Program to print the docstring of an item in `string` module

```
import string
print(string.__builtins__.__doc__)
```

OUTPUT
```
dict() -> new empty dictionary
dict(mapping) -> new dictionary initialized from a mapping object's
    (key, value) pairs
dict(iterable) -> new dictionary initialized as if via:
    d = {}
    for k, v in iterable:
        d[k] = v
dict(**kwargs) -> new dictionary initialized with the name=value pairs
    in the keyword argument list.  For example:  dict(one=1, two=2)
```

You can even use the `help()` to print the details of a particular item in the string module as shown below.

Example 6.25   Program using `help()`

```
str = "Hello"
print(help(str.isalpha))
```

OUTPUT

```
Help on built-in function isalpha:
isalpha(...)
    S.isalpha() -> bool
        Return True if all characters in S are alphabetic
    and there is at least one character in S, False otherwise.
None
```

> **Programming Tip:** Passing '\n' in split() allows us to split the multiline string stored in the string variable.

Working with Constants in String Module

You can use the constants defined in the string module along with the `find()` function to classify characters. For example, if `find(lowercase, ch)` returns a value except `-1`, then it means that ch must be a lowercase character. An alternate way to do the same job is to use the `in` operator or even the comparison operation. All three ways are shown below.

```
# First Way
import string
print(string.find(string.
lowercase, 'g') != -1)
```

OUTPUT

True

```
# Second Way
import string
print('g' in string.
lowercase)
```

OUTPUT

True

```
# Third Way
import string
ch = 'g'
print('a' <= ch <= 'z')
```

OUTPUT

True

> **Note**   Type() shows the type of an object and the dir()shows the available methods.

Another very useful constant defined in the string module is *whitespace*. When you write, `print (string.whitespace)` then all the characters that moves the cursor ahead without printing anything are displayed. These whitespace characters include space, tab, and newline characters.

You can even use the `dir()` with a string object or a string variable as shown below.

```
str = "Hello"
print(dir(str))
```

OUTPUT

```
['__add__', '__class__', '__contains__', '__delattr__', '__doc__', '__eq__',
'__format__', '__ge__', '__getattribute__', '__getitem__', '__getnewargs__', '__
getslice__', '__gt__', '__hash__', '__init__', '__le__', '__len__', '__lt__', '__
mod__', '__mul__', '__ne__', '__new__', '__reduce__', '__reduce_ex__', '__repr__',
'__rmod__', '__rmul__', '__setattr__', '__sizeof__', '__str__', '__subclasshook__',
'_formatter_field_name_split', '_formatter_parser', 'capitalize', 'center', 'count',
'decode', 'encode', 'endswith', 'expandtabs', 'find', 'format', 'index', 'isalnum',
'isalpha', 'isdigit', 'islower', 'isspace', 'istitle', 'isupper', 'join', 'ljust',
'lower', 'lstrip', 'partition', 'replace', 'rfind', 'rindex', 'rjust', 'rpartition',
```

```
'rsplit', 'rstrip', 'split', 'splitlines', 'startswith', 'strip', 'swapcase',
'title', 'translate', 'upper', 'zfill']
```

Copying and Pasting Strings with the Pyperclip Module

The pyperclip module in Python has copy() and paste() functions that can send text to and receive text from the computer's clipboard. Copying the output of your program to the clipboard makes it easy to paste it to an email, word processor, or some other software.

However, this module does not come with Python and you need to explicitly install it. Once the module is installed, you can type the following commands in IDLE or at the command prompt.

```
import pyperclip
pyperclip.copy('Welcome to the world of Python !!!')
pyperclip.paste()
'Welcome to the world of Python !!!'
```

Note After copying your Python text, if you copy something outside of your program, then the contents of the clipboard will change and the paste() function will return it.

6.12 REGULAR EXPRESSIONS

Regular expressions are a powerful tool for various kinds of string manipulation. These are basically a special text string that is used for describing a search pattern to extract information from text such as code, files, log, spreadsheets, or even documents.

Regular expressions are a *domain specific language* (DSL) that is present as a library in most of the modern programming languages, besides Python. A *regular expression* is a special sequence of characters that helps to match or find strings in another string. In Python, regular expressions can be accessed using the **re** module which comes as a part of the Standard Library. In this section, we will discuss some important methods in the **re** module.

Programming Tip: An exception re.error is raised if any error occurs while compiling or using regular expressions.

6.12.1 The match() Function

As the name suggest, the match() function matches a pattern to a string with optional flags. The syntax of match() function is,

```
re.match(pattern, string, flags=0)
```

The function tries to match the pattern (which specifies the regular expression to be matched) with a string (that will be searched for the pattern at the beginning of the string). The flag field is optional. Some values of flags are specified in the Table 6.4. To specify more than one flag, you can use the bitwise OR operator as in re.I | re.M. If the re.match() function finds a match, it returns the match object and None otherwise.

Table 6.4   Different values of flags

Flag	Description
re.I	Case sensitive matching
re.M	Matches at the end of the line
re.X	Ignores whitespace characters
re.U	Interprets letters according to Unicode character set

Example 6.26 Program to demonstrate the use of `match()` function

```
import re
string = "She sells sea shells on the sea shore"
pattern1 = "sells"
if re.match(pattern1, string):
    print("Match Found")
else:
    print(pattern1, "is not present in the string")
pattern2 = "She"
if re.match(pattern2, string):
    print("Match Found")
else:
    print(pattern2, "is not present in the string")
```

OUTPUT
```
sells is not present in the string
Match Found
```

In the above program, 'sells' is present in the string but still we got the output as match not found. This is because the `re.match()` function finds a match only at the beginning of the string. Since, the word 'sells' is present in the middle of the string, hence the result.

Note On success, match() function returns an object representing the match, else returns None.

6.12.2 The search() Function

In the previous function, we saw that even when the pattern was present in the string, None was returned because the match was done only at the beginning of the string. So, we have another function, i.e. `search()`, in the re module that searches for a pattern anywhere in the string. The syntax of the `search()` function can be given as,

Programming Tip: While using regular expressions, always use raw strings.

```
re.search(pattern, string, flags=0)
```

The syntax is similar to the `match()` function. The function searches for first occurrence of *pattern* within a *string* with optional *flags*. If the search is successful, a *match* object is returned and None otherwise.

Example 6.27 Program to demonstrate the use of `search()` function

```
import re
string = "She sells sea shells on the sea shore"
pattern = "sells"
if re.search(pattern, string):
    print("Match Found")
```

```
else:
    print(pattern, "is not present in the string")
```

OUTPUT

```
Match Found
```

> **Note** The re.search() finds a match of a pattern anywhere in the string.

6.12.3 The sub() Function

The sub() function in the re module can be used to search a pattern in the string and replace it with another pattern. The syntax of sub() function can be given as,

```
re.sub(pattern, repl, string, max=0)
```

According to the syntax, the sub() function replaces all occurrences of the pattern in string with repl, substituting all occurrences unless any max value is provided. This method returns a modified string.

Example 6.28 Program to demonstrate the use of sub() function

```
import re
string = "She sells sea shells on the sea shore"
pattern = "sea"
repl = "ocean"
new_string = re.sub(pattern, repl, string, 1)
print(new_string)
```

OUTPUT

```
She sells ocean shells on the sea shore
```

In the above program, note that only one occurrence was replaced and not all because we had provided 1 as the value of max.

6.12.4 The findall() and finditer() Functions

The findall() function is used to search a string and returns a list of matches of the pattern in the string. If no match is found, then the returned list is empty. The syntax of match() function can be given as,

```
matchList = re.findall(pattern, input_str, flags=0)
```

Example 6.29 Program to demonstrate the use of findall() function

```
import re
pattern = r"[a-zA-Z]+ \d+"
matches = re.findall(pattern, "LXI 2013, VXI 2015, VDI 20104, Maruti Suzuki Cars in
```

```
India")
for match in matches:
    print(match, end = " ")
```

OUTPUT
```
LXI 2013  VXI 2015  VDI 20104
```

> **Note**   The re.findall() function returns a list of all substrings that match a pattern.

In the above code, the regular expression, pattern = r"[a-zA-Z]+ \d+", finds all patterns that begin with one or more characters followed by a space and then followed by one or more digits.

The finditer() function is same as findall() function but instead of returning match objects, it returns an iterator. This iterator can be used to print the index of match in the given string.

Example 6.30   Program to demonstrate the use of finditer() function

```
import re
pattern = r"[a-zA-Z]+ \d+"
matches = re.finditer(pattern, "LXI 2013, VXI 2015, VDI 20104, Maruti Suzuki Cars
availble with us")
for match in matches:
    print("Match found at starting index : ", match.start())
    print("Match found at ending index : ", match.end())
    print("Match found at starting and ending index : ", match.span())
```

OUTPUT
```
Match found at starting index :  0
Match found at ending index :  8
Match found at starting and ending index :  (0, 8)
Match found at starting index :  10
Match found at ending index :  18
Match found at starting and ending index :  (10, 18)
Match found at starting index :  20
Match found at ending index :  29
Match found at starting and ending index :  (20, 29)
```

Note that the start() function returns the starting index of the first match in the given string. Similarly, we have end() function which returns the ending index of the first match. Another method, span() returns the starting and ending index of the first match as a tuple.

> **Note**   The match object returned by search(), match(), and findall() functions have start() and end() methods, that returns the starting and ending index of the first match.

6.12.5 Flag Options

The search(), findall(), and match() functions of the module take options to modify the behavior of the pattern match. Some of these flags are:

re.I or re.IGNORECASE—Ignores case of characters, so "Match", "MATCH", "mAtCh", etc are all same

re.S or re.DOTALL—Enables dot (.) to match newline character. By default, dot matches any character other than the newline character.

re.M or re.MULTILINE—Makes the ^ and $ to match the start and end of each line. That is, it matches even after and before line breaks in the string. By default, ^ and $ matches the start and end of the whole string.

re.L or re.LOCALE—Makes the flag \w to match all characters that are considered letters in the given current locale settings.

re.U or re.UNICODE—Treats all letters from all scripts as word characters.

6.12.6 Using Verbose in Regular Expression

The flag, re.VERBOSE, allows users to write regular expressions that look nicer. Such expressions are easy to read and understand as you can visually separate logical sections of the pattern and add comments in it.

For example, if you are writing a code to validate an email address, then using regular expression, it will be,

```python
email = re.compile(r'^([a-z0-9_\.-]+)@([0-9a-z\.-]+)\.([a-z\.]{2, 6})$',
            re.IGNORECASE)
```

This expression can be a little confusing as it is messy. The code given below uses re.VERBOSE to make every single part of the expression clear and easily understandable.

```python
import re
def email_checker(email):

    emailexp =re.compile(r"""
                        ^([a-z0-9_\.-]+)           # local Part
                        @                          # single @ sign
                         ([0-9a-z\.-]+)            # Domain name
                        \.                         # single Dot .
                         ([a-z]{2,6})$             # Top level Domain
                        """,re.VERBOSE | re.IGNORECASE)

    res = emailexp.fullmatch(email)
    #If match is found, the string is valid
    if res:
        print("{} is Valid. Details are as follow:".format(email))

        #prints first part/personal detail of Email Id
        print("Local:{}".format(res.group(1)))

        #prints Domain Name of Email Id
        print("Domain:{}".format(res.group(2)))

        #prints Top Level Domain Name of Email Id
        print("Top Level domain:{}".format(res.group(3)))
        print()

    else:
        #If match is not found,string is invalid
```

```
        print("{} is Invalid".format(email))

email_checker("info@jruma.com")
email_checker("jruma@gmail.com@")
email_checker("info@.com")
```

OUTPUT

```
info@jruma.com is Valid. Details are as follows:
Local:info
Domain:jruma
Top Level domain:com

jruma@gmail.com@ is Invalid
info@.com is Invalid
```

6.13 METACHARACTERS IN REGULAR EXPRESSION

Metacharacters make regular expressions more powerful than normal string methods. They allow you to create regular expressions to represent concepts like "one or more repetitions of a vowel".

Python allows users to specify metacharacters (like +, ?, ., *, ^, $, (), [], {}, |, \) in regular expressions. Table 6.5 lists some metacharacters and their purpose.

Table 6.5 Metacharacters and their Description and Usage

Metacharacter	Description	Example	Remarks
^	Matches at the beginning of the line.	^Hi	It will match Hi at the start of the string.
$	Matches at the end of the line.	Hi$	It will match Hi at the end of the string.
.	Matches any single character except the newline character.	Lo.	It will match Lot, Log, etc.
[...]	Matches any single character in brackets.	[Hh]ello	It will match "Hello" or "hello".
[^...]	Matches any single character not in brackets.	[^aeiou]	It will match anything other than a lowercase vowel.
re*	Matches 0 or more occurrences of regular expression.	[a-z]*	It will match zero or more occurrence of lowercase characters.
re+	Matches 1 or more occurrence of regular expression.	[a-z]+	It will match one or more occurrence of lowercase characters
re?	Matches 0 or 1 occurrence of regular expression.	Book?	It will match "Book" or "Books".
re{n}	Matches exactly n number of occurrences of regular expression.	42{1}5	It will match 425.

(Contd)

Table 6.5 (*Contd*)

Metacharacter	Description	Example	Remarks
re{n,}	Matches n or more occurrences of regular expression.	42{1,}5	It will match 42225 or any number with more than one 2s between 4 and 5.
re{n,m}	Matches at least n and at most m occurrences of regular expression.	42{1,3}5	It will match 425, 4225, 42225.
a|b	Matches either a or b.	"Hello" | "Hi"	It will match Hello or Hi.
\w	Matches word characters.	re.search(r'\w', 'xx123xx')	Match will be made.
\W	Matches non-word characters.	if(re.search(r'\W', '@#$%')): print("Done")	Done
\s	Matches whitespace, equivalent to [\t\n\r\f].	if(re.search(r'\s',"abcdsd")): print("Done")	Done
\S	Matches non-whitespace, equivalent to [^\t\n\r\f].	if(re.search(r'\S'," abcdsd")): print("Done")	Done
\d{n}	Matches exactly n digits.	\d{2}	It will match exactly 2 digits.
\d{n,}	Matches n or more digits.	\d{3,}	It will match 3 or more digits.
\d{n,m}	Matches n and at most m digits.	\d{2,4}	It will match 2,3 or 4 digits.
\D	Matches non-digits.	(\D+\d)	It will match Hello 5678, or any string starting with no digit followed by digits(s).
\A	Matches beginning of the string.	\AHi	It will match Hi at the beginning of the string.
\Z	Matches end of the string.	Hi\Z	It will match Hi at the end of the string.

\G	Matches point where last match finished.	import re
		if(re.search(r'\Gabc','abcba cabc')):
		    print("Done")
		else:
		    print("Not Done")
			Not Done

\b	Matches word boundaries when outside brackets. Matches backspace when inside brackets.	\bHi\b	It will match Hi at the word boundary.
\B	Matches non-word boundaries.	\bHi\B	Hi should start at word boundary but end at a non-boundary as in High
\n, \t, etc.	Matches newlines, tabs, etc.	re.search(r'\t', '123 \t abc ')	Match will be made.

6.13.1 **Character Classes**

When we put the characters to be matched inside square brackets, we call it a character class. For example, [aeiou] defines a character class that has a vowel character.

> **Programming Tip:** Placing a ^ at the start of a character class causes it to match any character other than the ones included.

Example 6.31 Program that checks if the string has at least one vowel

```
import re
pattern=r"[aeiou]"
if re.search(pattern,"clue"):
    print("Match clue")
if re.search(pattern,"bcdfg"):
    print("Match bcdfg")
```

OUTPUT
```
Match clue
```

Key points to remember

- Other metacharacters like $ and . have no meaning within character classes. Moreover, the metacharacter ^ has no meaning unless it is the first character in a class.
- Metacharacters like *, +, ?, {, and } specify numbers of repetitions.
- * matches 0 or more occurrences of the regular expression.

Example 6.32 Program to demonstrate the use of metacharacter *

```
import re
pattern=r"hi(de)*"
if re.search(pattern, "hidededede"):
    print("Match hidededede")
if re.search(pattern, "hi"):
    print("Match hi")    # zero or more de match
```

OUTPUT
```
Match hidededede
Match hi
```

- + matches one or more occurrences of the regular expression.

Example 6.33 Program to demonstrate the use of metacharacter +

```
import re
pattern=r"hi(de)+"
if re.search(pattern, "hidededede"):
    print "Match hidededede"
if re.search(pattern, "hi"):
    print "Match hi"    # at least one de required for match
```

OUTPUT
```
Match hidededede
```

- The metacharacter ? means zero or one repetitions.

Example 6.34 Program to demonstrate the use of metacharacter ?

```
import re
pattern=r"hi(de)?"
if re.search(pattern, "hidededede"):
      print("Match hidededede")
if re.search(pattern, "hi"):
      print("Match hi")     # matches 0 or 1 occurrence
```

OUTPUT
```
Match hidededede
Match hi
```

- Curly braces represent the number of repetitions between two numbers. The regular expression {m,n} means m to n repetitions of the expressions. Hence {0,1} is the same as ?. if m is missing, then it is taken to be zero and if n is missing, it is taken to be infinity.

Example 6.35 Program to demonstrate the use of {m,n} regular expression

```
import re
pattern = r"2{1,4}$"
if re.match(pattern,"2"):
    print("Match 2")
if re.match(pattern,"222"):
    print("Match 222")
if re.match(pattern,"22222"):
    print("Match 22222")     # does not match because only max 4 2's will match
```

> **Programming Tip:** metacharacter '+' means {1,}.

OUTPUT
```
Match 2
Match 222
```

Some More Examples
- The pattern ^pr.y$ means that the string should start with pr, then follow with any single character, (except a newline character) and end with y. so the string could be pray or prey.
- The character class [a-z] matches any lowercase character.
- The character class [A-F] matches any uppercase character from A to F.
- The character class [0-9] matches any digit.
- The character class [A-Za-z] defines multiple ranges in one class. It matches a letter of any case.
- The multiple ranges pattern = r"[A-Z][A-Z][0-9]" will match all strings with length 3, where first and second characters are any uppercase character and the third is any digit.

- The metacharacter | means either of the two. For example, pattern r"pr(a|e)y", will match both pray as well as prey.
- The expression match = re.search(r'\d\s*\d\s*\d', 'ab12   3cd') will be matched.
- \s (whitespace) includes newlines characters. To match a run of whitespace that may include a newline character, use \s*.
- [^abc] means any character except "a", "b", or "c" but [a^bc] means an "a", "b", "c", or a "^".

6.13.2 Groups

A group is created by surrounding a part of the regular expression with *parentheses*. You can even give group as an argument to the metacharacters such as * and ?.

Example 6.36   Program to demonstrate the use of groups

```
import re
pattern = r"gr(ea)*t"   # group of ea created
if re.match(pattern,"great"):
    print("Match ea")
if re.match(pattern, "greaeaeaeaeaeaeaat"):
    print("Match greaeaeaeaeaeaeaat")
```

OUTPUT
```
Match ea
Match greaeaeaeaeaeaeaat
```

The content of groups in a match can be accessed by using the group() function. For example, group(0) or group() returns the whole match.
group(n), where n is greater than 0, returns the nth group from the left.
group() returns all groups up from 1.

Example 6.37   Program to demonstrate the use of various group functions

```
import re
pattern = r"Go(od)Go(in)gPy(th)on"
match = re.match(pattern, "GoodGoingPythonGoodGoingPythonGoodGoingPython")
if match:
    print(match.group())
    print(match.group(0))
    print(match.group(1))
    print(match.group(2))
    print(match.groups())
```

OUTPUT
```
GoodGoingPython
GoodGoingPython
od
in
('od', 'in', 'th')
```

Note Python allows you to even nest the groups.

Python supports two useful types of groups—*named group* and *non-capturing group*.

- **Named groups** have the format (?P<name>...), where name is the name of the group, and ... is the content. They are just like normal groups but are accessed by their name as well as by number.
- **Non-capturing groups** having the format (?:...) are not accessible by the group method, so they can be added to an existing regular expression without breaking the numbering.

Example 6.38 Program to demonstrate the use of named and non-capturing groups

```python
import re
pattern = r"Go(?P<FIRST>od)Go(?:in)gPy(th)on"
match = re.match(pattern, "GoodGoingPythonGoodGoingPythonGoodGoingPython")
if match:
    print(match.group("FIRST"))
    print(match.group(1))
    print(match.group(2))
    print(match.groups())   # (in) is not accessed by group method
```

OUTPUT
```
od
od
th
('od', 'th')
```

Now try the following program and observe the output.

Example 6.39 Program to demonstrate the use of metacharacters and groups

```python
import re
match = re.search("([0-9]+).*: (.*)", "Phone number: 12345678, DOB: October 17,
2000")
print(match.group())
print(match.group(1))
print(match.group(2))
print(match.group(1,2))
```

OUTPUT
```
12345678, DOB: October 17, 2000
12345678
October 17, 2000
('12345678', 'October 17, 2000')
```

6.13.3 Application of Regular Expression to Extract Email

We can use regular expressions to extract date, time, email address, etc. from the text. For example, we know that an email address has username which consist of character(s) and may include dots or dashes. The username is followed by @ sign and the domain name. The domain name may also include characters, dashes, and dots. Consider the following email address given below.

```
Info-books@oxford-india.com
```

Now, the regular expression representing the structure of email address can be given as,

```
Pattern = r"[\w.-]+@[\w.-]+"
```

where, [\w.-]+ matches one or more occurrences of character(s), dot, or dash.

Example 6.40 Program to extract an email address from a text

```
import re
pattern = r"[\w.-]+@[\w.-]+"
string = "Please send your feedback at info@oxford.com"
match=re.search(pattern, string)
if match:
    print("Email to : ", match.group())
else:
    print("No Match")
```

OUTPUT
```
Email to :  info@oxford.com
```

Note If the string has multiple addresses, use the re.findall() method instead of re.search() to extract all email addresses.

Program 6.13 Write a program that uses a regular expression to match strings which starts with a sequence of digits (at least one digit) followed by a blank and after this arbitrary characters.

```
import re
pattern = r"^[0-9]+ .*"
string = "12 abc"
match = re.search(pattern, string)
if match:
    print("Match")
```

OUTPUT
```
Match
```

Program 6.14 Write a program to extract each character from a string using a regular expression.

```
import re
result=re.findall(r'.','Good Going')
print(result)
```

> **Programming Tip:** To ignore space use \w instead of \.

OUTPUT

```
['G', 'o', 'o', 'd', ' ', 'G', 'o', 'i', 'n', 'g']
```

Program 6.15 Write a program to extract each word from a string using a regular expression.

```
import re
result=re.findall(r'\w+','Good Going Python')
print(result)
```

OUTPUT

```
['Good', 'Going', 'Python']
```

Program 6.16 Write a program to print the first word of the string.

```
import re
result=re.findall(r'^\w+','Good Going Python')
print(result)
```

OUTPUT

```
['Good']
```

Program 6.17 Write a program to print the last word of the string.

```
import re
result=re.findall(r'\w+$','Good Going Python')
print(result)
```

OUTPUT

```
['Python']
```

Program 6.18 Write a program to print the characters in pairs.

```
import re
result=re.findall(r'\w\w','Good Going Python')
print(result)
```

OUTPUT

```
['Go', 'od', 'Go', 'in', 'Py', 'th', 'on']
```

Program 6.19 Write a program to print only the first two characters of every word.

```python
import re
result=re.findall(r'\b\w\w','Good Going Python')
print(result)
```

OUTPUT

```
['Go', 'Go', 'Py']
```

Program 6.20 Write a program to extract a date from a given string.

```python
import re
result = re.findall(r'\d{2}-\d{2}-\d{4}','Hello, my name is Srishti and my date of
joining is 11-15-1999 and have experience of more than 17 years')
print("Date of Appointment is : ", result)
```

OUTPUT

```
Date of Appointment is :  ['11-15-1999']
```

Program 6.21 Write a program to extract the year from a given string.

```python
import re
result = re.findall(r'\d{2}-\d{2}-(\d{4})','Hello, my name is Srishti and my date
of joining is 11-15-1999 and have experience of more than 17 years')
print("Year of joining is : ", result)
```

> **Programming Tip:** To print words that begins with consonant use ^.

OUTPUT

```
Year of joining is :  ['1999']
```

Program 6.22 Write a program that prints only those words that starts with a vowel.

```python
import re
result = re.findall(r'\b[aeiouAEIOU]\w+','Hello, my name is Srishti and my date of
joining is 11-15-1999 and have experience of more than 17 years')
print(result)
```

OUTPUT

```
['is', 'and', 'of', 'is', 'and', 'experience', 'of']
```

Program 6.23 Write a program that validates a mobile phone number. The number should start with 7, 8, or 9 followed by 9 digits.

```python
import re
List = ['7838456789', '1234567890', '9876543210', '8901234567', '4567890123']
for i in List:
    result = re.findall(r'[7-9]{1}[0-9]{9}',i)
    if result:
        print(result, end = " ")
```

OUTPUT

```
['7838456789'] ['9876543210'] ['8901234567']
```

Program 6.24 Write a program that replaces , , ; , - from a string with a blank space character.

```
import re
result = re.sub(r'[;,-]',' ','Hello! My name- is Srishti.; My date-of-joining is
11-15-1999 and have experience of, more than 17 years;')
print(result)
```

OUTPUT

```
Hello! My name  is Srishti.  My date of joining is 11 15 1999 and have experience
of  more than 17 years
```

Program 6.25 Write a program that uses a regular expression to pluralize a word.

```
import re
def pluralize(noun):
    if re.search('[sxz]$', noun):
        return re.sub('$', 'es', noun)
    elif re.search('[^aeioudgkprt]h$', noun):
        return re.sub('$', 'es', noun)
    elif re.search('[^aeiou]y$', noun):
        return re.sub('y$', 'ies', noun)
    else:
        return noun + 's'
List = ["bush", "fox", "toy", "cap"]
for i in List:
    print(i, '-', pluralize(i))
```

OUTPUT

```
bush - bushes
fox - foxes
toy - toys
cap - caps
```

Summary

- The Python string data type is a sequence made up of one or more individual characters, where a character could be a letter, digit, whitespace, or any other symbol.
- The in operator checks if one character or string is contained in another string.
- The whitespace characters, exclamation mark, and any other symbol (like ?, <,>,*, @, #, $, %, etc.) that

- forms a part of the string would be assigned its own index number.
- Concatenate means to join together and append means to add something at the end.
- A raw string literal which is prefixed by an 'r' passes all the characters as it is.

- Python strings are immutable which means that once created they cannot be changed.
- The number and type of values in the tuple should match the number and type of format sequences or conversion specifications in the string, otherwise an error is returned.
- Strings are an example of Python objects.
- in and not in operators can be used with strings to determine whether a string is present in another string.

Therefore, the in and not in operator are also known as membership operators.

- The string module consist of a number of useful constants, classes, and functions. These functions are used to manipulate strings.

GLOSSARY

Dot notation Use of the dot operator (.) to access functions inside a module.
Empty string A string that has no characters and has a length = 0.
Format operator % Operator that takes a format string and a tuple to generate a string that includes values of the tuple formatted as specified by the format string.
Format sequence Sequence of characters in a format string, like %d, that specifies how a value should be formatted.
Format string String used with the % or format operator that contains format sequences.
Immutable The property of a sequence whose items cannot be assigned.

Index A variable or value used to access a member of an ordered set.
Invocation A statement that calls a method.
Method A function that is called on an object using dot notation.
Sequence An ordered set of values in which each value is identified by an integer index.
Slice A part of a string obtained by specifying a range of indices.
Traversing a string Accessing each character in the string, one at a time.
Whitespace Characters that move the cursor without printing visible characters.

EXERCISES

Fill in the Blanks

1. String is a sequence made up of one or more _____.
2. A multiple-line text within quotes must have a _____ at the end of each line.
3. Individual characters in a string are accessed using the _____ operator.
4. _____ error is generated when index out of bounds is accessed.
5. _____ means to join together.
6. The _____ function is used to convert values of any other type into string type.
7. The _____ returns the memory address of that object.
8. Conversion specifications start with a _____ operator.
9. A method is invoked or called on an _____.
10. _____ function checks if the string ends with suffix.
11. _____ function toggles the case of every character.
12. The _____ returns a list of the lines in the string.
13. Omitting both ends in the slice operation means selecting the _____.
14. If we access the string from the first character then we use a _____ based index but when doing it backward the index starts with _____.
15. _____ function returns the ASCII code of the character.
16. _____ and _____ operators are known as membership operators.
17. _____ function is used to know the details of a particular item.
18. _____ function displays the methods in a module.
19. Fill in the blanks to print the starting and ending positions of the match.

```
import _____
pattern=r"good"
match=re.
search(pattern,"greatgoodjobdonegood")
print(match._____)
print(match._____)
```

20. Fill in the blanks to replace all 2s in the string with 8s.
```
import _____
number = "07287249832"
pattern = r"2"
print re.___(pattern,"__",_____)
```

21. _____ is a pattern to create a pattern that matches strings having 4 characters and the last character being an exclamation mark.

22. [abc][def] will match a string with _____ characters. The first character can be _____ and second can be any of _____.

23. Fill in the blanks to create a pattern that matches strings containing one or more 21s.
```
r"(21)__$"
```

24. 'color' and 'colour' both will be matched if the regular expression is _____.

25. The expression '([^aeiou][aeiou][^aeiou])+' would match _____.

26. _____ string will match the regular expression "[01]+0$".

27. The dot character is preceded by a backslash to _____.

28. The _____ meta character matches 0 or more occurrences of the regular expression.

State True or False

1. Character in a string could a letter, digit, whitespace, or any other symbol.
2. Python treats strings as contiguous series of characters delimited by single or double quotes but not triple quotes.
3. Python has a built-in string class as well as a string module that has many methods.
4. Index can either be an integer or an expression that evaluates to a floating point number.
5. In a string, all whitespace characters are also assigned an index value.
6. Raw strings do not process escape sequences.
7. 'r' is used as a prefix for Unicode strings.
8. We cannot delete or remove characters from a string.
9. The % operator takes a format string on the right and the corresponding values in a tuple on the left.
10. Conversion specifications start with a % operator and can appear anywhere within the string.
11. The number and type of values in the tuple should match the number and type of format sequences or conversion specifications in the string.
12. The - after each % in the conversion string indicates right justification.

13. You can access a string using negative indexes.
14. odr() function returns character represented by an ASCII number.
15. A string is a substring of itself.
16. Strings are compared based on ASCII values of their characters.
17. Regular expressions can be used to verify an email address.
18. '....' would match any string with only dots.
19. `re.match(r"^gr.y$","stingray")` will result in a match.
20. `re.search(r"[A-Z][A-Z][0-9]","E3")` will result in a match.
21. `re.match(r"ice(-)?cream", "icecream")` will match.
22. `(123|456)\1` will match "123" or "456", followed by the same thing.
23. `re.search(r"\b(cat)\b", "We scattered.")` will match.
24. The `re.match()` finds a match of a pattern anywhere in the string.
25. [^abc] and [a^bc] means the same thing.

Multiple Choice Questions

1. The index of the first character in the string is _____.
   (a) 0   (b) 1
   (c) n-1   (d) n
2. The index of the last character in the string is _____.
   (a) 0   (b) 1
   (c) n-1   (d) n

3. Which error is generated when the index is not integer?
   (a) IndexError   (b) NameError
   (c) TypeError   (d) BoundError
4. Which of the following word best means to add something at the end?

(a) Concatenate   (b) Append

(c) Join   (d) Add

5. In Python a string is appended to another string by using which operator?

(a) +   (b) *

(c) []   (d) +=

6. Which operator is used to repeat a string n number of times?

(a) +   (b) *

(c) []   (d) +=

7. The print statement prints one or more literals or values followed by a_____.

(a) Newline character   (b) Tab

(b) Whitespace   (d) Exclamation

8. Which error is generated when a character in a string variable is modified?

(a) IndexError   (b) NameError

(c) TypeError   (d) BoundError

9. You can delete the entire string using which keyword?

(a) del   (b) erase

(c) remove   (d) delete

10. Which operator takes a format string on the left and the corresponding values in a tuple on the right?

(a) +   (b) *

(b) []   (d) %

11. Which character is used for hexadecimal integers in the format string?

(a) u   (b) x

(c) d   (d) s

12. When using find(), if str is not present in the string then what is returned?

(a) 0   (b) -1

(c) n-1   (d) ValueError

13. "Cool" becomes "COOL", which two functions must have been applied?

(a) strip() and upper()

(b) strip() and lower()

(c) strip() and capitalize()

(d) lstrip() and rstrip()

14. In the split(), if no delimiter is specified, then by default it splits strings on which characters?

(a) whitespace   (b) comma

(c) newline   (d) colon

15. The splitlines(), splits lines in strings on which characters?

(a) whitespace   (b) comma

(c) newline   (c) colon

16. By default, the value of stride is _____

(a) 0   (b) -1

(c) 1   (d) n-1

17. To print the original string in reverse order, you can set the stride as _____

(a) 0   (b) -1

(c) 1   (d) n-1

18. Identify the correct result from the following

(a) ord('10') = 50   (b) chr(72) = 'H'

(c) chr(55) = 9   (d) ord('z') = 123

19. Which of these patterns would not match the string "Good Morning" when used with match()?

(a) Good   (b) Morning

(c) Go   (d) Good Morn

20. [a^]* would match, all strings with

(a) Zero or more repetition of any character

(b) Zero or more repetition of a

(c) Zero or more repetition of ^

(d) both b and c

21. What would group(3) be of a match of 9(08) (7(65)43)2(1)?

(a) 08   (b) 7

(c) 65   (d) 76543

22. Which regular expression is not equivalent to the others?

(a) (a|b|c|d|e)   (b) [abcde]

(c) [a-f]   (d) none of these

23. How many groups are there in regular expression (ab)(c(d(e)f))(g)?

(a) 4   (b) 1

(c) 3   (d) 5

Review Questions

1. With the help of an example, explain how we can create string variables in Python.

2. With the help of an example, explain how we can concatenate a string and a floating point data.

3. Python strings are immutable. Comment on this statement.

4. Write a short note on format operator.

5. What will happen when the strip() is used with a string argument?

6. Explain the use of format() with the help of an example.

7. What is slice operation? Explain with an example.

8. With the help of an example explain the significance of membership operators.

9. Differentiate between the following.

(a) a method and a function

(a) find() and index()

(a) find() and rfind()

10. If `str = 'Welcome to the world of Python Programming'`, answer the following,
    (a) Write an instruction to print the tenth character of the string.
    (a) Write an instruction that prints the index of the first occurrence of the letter 'o' in the string.

Programming Exercises

1. Modify the `find_ch()` function so that it starts finding the character from the specified position in the string.
2. Write a program to calculate the length of a string.
3. Write a Python program to get a string made of the first 2 and the last 2 characters from a given a string. If the string length is less than 2, return instead the empty string.
4. Write a Python program to get a string from a given string where all occurrences of its first character have been changed to `'$'`, except the first character itself.
5. Write a Python program to get a single string from two given strings, separated by a space and swap the first two characters of each string.
6. Write a Python program to add `'ing'` at the end of a given string (length should be at least 3). If the given string already ends with `'ing'` then add `'ly'` instead. If the string length of the given string is less than 3, leave it unchanged.
7. Write a program to find the first appearance of the substring `'not'` and `'poor'` from a given string, if `'bad'` follows the `'poor'`, replace the whole `'not'...'poor'` substring with `'good'`. Return the resulting string.
8. Write a function that takes a list of words and returns the length of the longest one.
9. Write a program to remove the nth index character from a non-empty string.
10. Write a program to change a given string to a new string where the first and last characters have been exchanged.
11. Write a program to remove the characters which have odd index values of a given string.
12. Write a program to count the occurrences of each word in a given sentence.
13. Write a program that accepts a comma separated sequence of words as input and prints the unique words in sorted form (alphanumerically).
14. Write a function to insert a string in the middle of a string.
15. Write a function to get a string made of 4 copies of the last two characters of a specified string (length must be at least 2).

11. With the help of relevant examples, explain at least 5 metacharacters that are frequently used in regular expressions.
12. Write an expression using metacharacters that will match all strings with length 5, where first character is an uppercase character and the last is any digit.

16. Write a function to get a string made of its first three characters of a specified string. If the length of the string is less than 3, then return the original string.
17. Write a function to get the first half of a specified string of even length.
18. Write a function to reverses a string if its length is a multiple of 4.
19. Write a function to convert a given string to all uppercase if it contains at least 2 uppercase characters in the first 4 characters.
20. Write a program to sort a string lexicographically.
21. Write a program to remove newline characters from text.
22. Write a program to check whether a string starts with specified characters.
23. Write a program to remove existing indentation from all of the lines in a given text.
24. Write a program to add a prefix text to all of the lines in a string.
25. Write a program to set the indentation of the first line.
26. Write a program to print floating numbers upto 2 decimal places.
27. Write a program to print floating numbers upto 2 decimal places with sign.
28. Write a program to print floating numbers with no decimal places.
29. Write a program to print integers with zeros on the left of specified width.
30. Write a program to print integers with `'*'` on the right of specified width.
31. Write a program to display a number with comma separator.
32. Write a program to format a number with percentage.
33. Write a program to display a number in left, right, and center aligned of width `10`.
34. Write a program to strip a set of characters from a string.
35. Write a program to create a mirror of the given string. For example, `"abc" = "cba"`.
36. Write a program that removes all the occurrences of a specified character from a given string.

37. Write a program to check whether a string is a palindrome or not.
38. Write a program to remove all the occurrences of a given word from the string.
39. Write a program to concatenate two strings in a third string. Do not use + operator.
40. Write a program to append a string to another string. Do not use += operator.
41. Write a program to swap two strings.
42. Write a program to insert a string in another string.
43. Write a program to delete a string from another string.
44. Write a program to replace a string with another string. Do not use the replace().
45. Write a program that removes leading and trailing spaces from a string.
46. Write a program to read a name and then display it in abbreviated form, like `Janak Raj Thareja` should be displayed as `JRT`.
47. Write a program to read a name and then display it in abbreviated form, like `Janak Raj Thareja` should be displayed as `J.R. Thareja`.
48. Write a program to count the number of characters, words, and lines in the given text.
49. Write a program to count the number of digits, upper case characters, lower case characters, and special characters in a given string.

50. Write a program to extract the first n characters of a string.
51. Write a program to copy n characters of a string from the `m`th position in another string. Do not use the slice operation.
52. Write a program to delete the last character of a string.
53. Write a program to delete the first character of a string.
54. Write a program to encrypt a string using substitution Cipher.
55. Write a program that encrypts a string using multiplicative cipher. Generate the key randomly.
56. Write the command to print "hello world" as "Hello world".
57. Write the command to print "hello world" as "Hello World".
58. Write the command to print "hElLo WoRlD" as "HeLlO wOrLd".
59. Write the command to print "hello world" as "Hello Friends".
60. Write a program that uses regular expression to match strings which starts with an upper case character followed by a digit and a '-'.
61. Write a program that replaces '-' from a string with a '/'.

Find The Output

1. ```
s = "Welcome"
print(s[1:3])
```
2. ```
s = "Welcome"
print(s[ : 6])
```
3. ```
s = "Welcome"
print(s[4 :])
```
4. ```
s = "Welcome"
print(s[1:-1])
```
5. ```
str = "Welcome"
print("come" in str)
```
6. ```
str = "Welcome"
print("come" not in str)
```
7. ```
"free" == "freedom"
```
8. ```
"man" != "men"
```
9. ```
str = "Welcome to Python"
print(str.isalnum())
```
10. ```
"Hello".isalpha()
```
11. ```
"14-10-2106".isdigit()
```
12. ```
print("hello".islower())
```
13. ```
"\t".isspace()
```
14. ```
str = "Hello"
print(str.startswith("he"))
```

15. ```
str = "Hello, welcome to the world of Python"
print(str.find("o"))
```
16. ```
str = "Hello, welcome to the world of Python"
print(str.find("if"))
```
17. ```
str = "Hello, welcome to the world of Python"
print(str.rfind("of"))
```
18. ```
str = "Hello, welcome to the world of Python"
print(str.count("o"))
```
19. ```
"us" not in "success"
```
20. ```
"mi" in "ours"
```
21. ```
for i in 'Python':
    print(2 * i, end=' ')
```
22. ```
import string
print(string.find("abcdabcdabcd", "cd", 3))
```
23. ```
import string
print(string.find("abcdabcdabcdabcdabcd",
"cd",7, 13))
```
24. ```
a = 10
b = 20
print("3**4 = %d and %d * %d = %f" % (3**4,
a, b, a * b))
```

25. ```python
    print("%d %f %s" % (7, 15, 28))
    print("%-.2f" % 369)
    print("%-10.2f%-10.2f" % (91, 23.456))
    print("%5.2f  %5.2f  $%5.2f" % (9, 1.2, 55.78))
    ```
26. ```python
    str1 = 'Welcome!'
    str2 = 'to Python'
    str3 = str1[:2] + str2[len(str2) - 2:]
    print(str3)
    ```
27. ```python
    print("She sells sea shells on the sea shore.".find("sea", 3, -6))
    ```
28. ```python
    len("She sells sea shells on the sea shore.")
    ```
29. ```python
    str = "Welcome to the world of Python"
    print(str[:10].find("t"))
    ```
30. ```python
    str = "Welcome to the world of Python"
    start = 3
    end = 10
    print(str[start:end])
    ```
31. ```python
    str = "Hello"
    print(str.startswith('h'))
    print(str.lower().startswith('h')
    ```
32. ```python
    'In %d years I have saved %g %s.' % (3, 4.5, 'lakh rupees')
    ```
33. ```python
    ', '.join(['Sun', 'Stars', 'Planets'])
    ```
34. ```python
    '   '.join(['Welcome', 'to', 'the', 'world', 'of', 'Python!'])
    ```
35. ```python
    'Hello'.join(['Welcome', 'to', 'the', 'world', 'of', 'Python!'])
    ```
36. ```python
    "Good morning students".split()
    ```
37. ```python
    'WelcomeHellotoHellotheHelloworld
    HelloofHelloPython!'.split('Hello')
    ```
38. ```python
    import re
    pattern = r"[a-zA-Z]+ \d+"
    matches = re.findall(pattern, "June 24, August 9, Dec 12")
    for match in matches:
        print(match, end=' ')
    ```
39. ```python
    import re
    pattern = r"good"
    if re.match(pattern,"greatgood
    jobdonegoodgood"):
        print("Match")
    else:
        print("No match")
    if re.search(pattern,"greatgoodjobdone
    goodgood"):
        print("Match")
    else:
        print("No match")
    print(re.findall(pattern,"greatgoodjob
    donegoodgood")
    ```
40. ```python
    import re
    string = "Good Morning, Welcome to the world
    of Python..."
    pattern = r"Morning"
    print(re.sub(pattern,"Evening", string))
    ```
41. ```python
    import re
    pattern=r"[^aeiou]"
    if re.search(pattern,"clue"):
        print("Match clue")
    if re.search(pattern,"bcdfg"):
        print("Match bcdfg")
    if re.search(pattern,"CLUE"):
        print("Match CLUE")
    ```
42. ```python
    import re
    print(re.sub(r"([a-zA-Z]+)(\d+)", r"\2 of
    \1",
    "Jan 16, June 05, Septmenber 15, Dec 04"))
    ```
43. ```python
    import re
    if re.search(r"P[ye][td]hon","Python is a
    wonderful language"):
        print("Match")
    if re.search(r"Python\.$","I like Python."):
        print("Good")
    print(re.search(r"Python\.$","I like Python as
    well as Java."))
    if re.search("[0-9]+", "PNo. : 25227568,
    Date: February 17, 2017"):
        print("Number OK")
    ```
44. ```python
    import re
    test = "Date of Examination : Sun Mar 26
    09:30:00 2017"
    pattern = r"\b(?P<hours>\d\d):(?P<minutes>\
    d\d):(?P<seconds>\d\d)\b"
    match = re.search(pattern, test)
    print(match.group('hours'), end=' ')
    print(match.group('minutes'), end=' ')
    print(match.group('seconds'), end=' ')
    print(match.span('seconds'))
    ```
45. ```python
    import re
    match = re.findall("[gP]\w+", "good going,
    welcome to Python 3.6.0")
    print(match)
    ```
46. ```python
    import re
    match = re.split(r'o','Good Going, Welcome to
    Python')
    print(match)
    match = re.split(r'i','Good Going, Welcome to
    Python',maxsplit=3)
    print(match)
    ```

```
47. import re
    List = ["Log Lot", "Leg Lead", "Lo Lo", "Kin
    Pin"]
    for i in List:
```

```
    match = re.match("(L\w+)\W(L\w+)", i)
    if match:
        print(match.group(), end=' ')
```

Find The Error

```
1. str = "Hello world"
   str[6] = 'W'
   print(str)
```
```
   print(str)
   str = 'Python'
   print(str)
```

2. "%s %s %s %s" % ('Welcome', 'to', 'Python')

3. "%s %s %s" % ('East', 'West', 'North', 'South')

4. "%d %f %f" % (10, 20, 'Hello')

```
5. str = 'abcdefgh'
   str[5] = 'a'
```

```
6. str = "Hello World"
   del str[2]
   print(str)
```

Answers

Fill in the Blanks

1. characters
2. backslash (\)
   subscript ([ ])
4. IndexError
5. concatenate
6. str()
7. id()
8. %

9. object
10. endswith()
11. swapcase()
12. splitlines()
13. entire string
14. zero, -1
15. ord()
16. in and not in

17. type()
18. dir()
19. re, start(), end()
20. re, sub, "8", number
21. pattern = r"[A-Z]
    [A-Z][0-9][!]"
22. 2, a b or c, d e or f
23. +

24. colo?r
25. denpat (just an example)
26. 01100 (just an example)
27. to escape the dot
    character.
28. *

State True or False

1. True   2. False   3. True   4. False   5. True   6. True   7. False   8. True   9. False
10. True   11. True   12. False   13. True   14. False   15. True   16. True   17. True   18. False
19. False   20. True   21. True   22. False   23. False   24. False   25. False

Multiple Choice Questions

1. (a)   2. (c)   3. (c)   4. (b)   5. (d)   6. (b)   7. (a)   8. (c)   9. (a)   10. (d)   11. (b)   12. (b)
13. (a)   14. (a)   15. (c)   16. (c)   17. (b)   18. (b)   19. (c)   20. (b)   21. (c)   22. (c)   23. (d)

CHAPTER 7 File Handling

• Files, their Types and File Paths • Opening and Closing Files
• Reading, Writing, and Appending Data • File, Directory, and
OS Module Methods

7.1 INTRODUCTION

A file is a collection of data stored on a secondary storage device like hard disk. Till now, we had been processing data that was entered through the computer's keyboard using the input(). But this task can become very tedious especially when there is a huge amount of data to be processed. A better solution, therefore, is to combine all the input data into a file and then design a Python program to read this data from the file whenever required.

When a program is being executed, its data is stored in *random access memory* (RAM). Though RAM can be accessed faster by the CPU, it is also **volatile**, which means that when the program ends, or the computer shuts down, all the data is lost. If you want to use the data in future, then you need to store this data on a permanent or non-volatile storage media such as the hard disk, USB drive, DVD, etc.

Data on non-volatile storage media is stored in named locations on the media called **files**. You can think of working with files as working with a notebook. To use a notebook, you must first open it. Once the notebook is opened, you can read the contents that you had previously written in it or write some new content into it. After using the notebook, you close it. The same concept can be applied to files. We first open a file, read or write to it, and then finally close it.

A file is basically used because real life applications involve large amounts of data and in such situations the console oriented I/O operations pose two major problems:

• First, it becomes cumbersome and time consuming to handle huge amount of data through terminals.
• Second, when doing I/O using terminal, the entire data is lost when either the program is terminated or computer is turned off. Therefore, it becomes necessary to store data on a permanent storage (the disks) and read whenever necessary, without destroying the data.

In order to use files, we have to learn file input and output operations, that is, how data is read or written to a file. Although file I/O operations is almost same as terminal I/O, the only difference is that when doing file I/O, the user must specify the name of the file from which data should be read/written.

7.2 FILE PATH

Files that we use are stored on a storage medium like the hard disk in such a way that they can be easily retrieved as and when required. Most file systems that are used today stores files in a tree (or *hierarchical*) structure. At the top of the tree is one (or more) root nodes. Under the root node, there are other files and folders (or directories) and each folder can in turn contain other files and folders. Even these folders can contain other files and folders and this can go on to an almost limitless depth. The type of file is indicated by its extension. Consider the tree structure given in Figure 7.1.

Every file is identified by its path that begins from the root node or the root folder. In Windows, C:\ (also known as C drive) is the root folder but you can also have a path that starts from other drives like D:\, E:\, etc. The file path is also known as *pathname*. For

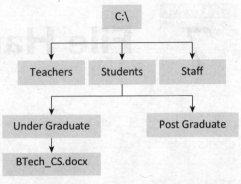

Figure 7.1 Files and Folders

> **Programming Tip:** Folder names and file names are case sensitive in Windows but they are case insensitive in Linux.

example, in the Figure 7.1, the file BTech_CS.docx file is stored in the C:\. C: drive has a folder Students which in turn has a sub-folder (folder within a folder) named Graduate. The sub-folder Graduate has the desired file. So the path of this file can be written as,

```
C:\Students\Under Graduate\BTech_CS.docx
```

> **Note**   The characters after the dot form the extension of the file. For example, .docx indicates that the file is a Word document.

Note that the character used to separate the folder names (also called the *delimiter*) is specific to the file system. For example, Solaris OS uses the forward slash (/) while Microsoft Windows uses the backslash slash (\).

> **Note**   A relative path is specified relative to the program's current working directory.

Relative Path and Absolute Path

A file path can be either *relative* or *absolute*. While an absolute path always contains the root and the complete directory list to specify the exact location the file, relative path on the other hand, needs to be combined with another path in order to access a file. That is, relative pathnames starts with respect to the current working directory and therefore lacks the leading slashes. For example, C:\Students\Under Graduate\ BTech_CS.docx is the absolute path as all of the information needed to locate the file is contained in the path but Under Graduate\BTech_CS.docx is a relative path as only a part of the complete path is specified.

Note that when a relative file path, is specified, the relative path is joined with the current directory to create an absolute file path. Therefore, in our example, if the current working directory is C:\Students, then the relative path, Under Graduate\BTech_CS.docx, is equivalent to using its absolute path.

> **Note**   If you use a relative file path from the wrong directory, then either the wrong file will be accessed or no file will be accessed if no file of the specified name exists in the given path.

7.3 TYPES OF FILES

Like C and C++, Python also supports two types of files—text files and binary files.

7.3.1 ASCII Text Files

A *text file* is a stream of characters that can be sequentially processed by a computer in forward direction. For this reason a text file is usually opened for only one kind of operation (reading, writing, or appending) at any given time. Because text files can process characters, they can only read or write data one character at a time. In Python, a text stream is treated as a special kind of file.

> **Programming Tip:** The contents of a binary file are not human readable. If you want that data stored in the file must be human-readable, then store the data in a text file.

Depending on the requirements of the operating system and on the operation that has to be performed (read/write operation) on the file, the newline characters may be converted to or from carriage-return/linefeed combinations. Besides this, other character conversions may also be done to satisfy the storage requirements of the operating system. However, these conversions occur transparently to process a text file.

In a text file, each line contains zero or more characters and ends with one or more characters that specify the end of line. Each line in a text file can have maximum of 255 characters. When data is written to a text file, each newline character is converted to a carriage return/line feed character. Similarly, when data is read from a text file, each carriage return/line feed character is converted to newline character.

Another important thing is that when a text file is used, there are actually two representations of data—internal or external. For example, an `integer` value will be represented as a number that occupies 2 or 4 bytes of memory internally but externally the `integer` value will be represented as a string of characters representing its decimal or hexadecimal value.

> **Note**   In a text file, each line of data ends with a newline character. Each file ends with a special character called the end-of-file (EOF) marker.

7.3.2 Binary Files

A *binary file* is a file which may contain any type of data, encoded in binary form for computer storage and processing purposes. It includes files such as word processing documents, PDFs, images, spreadsheets, videos, zip files, and other executable programs. Like a text file, a binary file is a collection of bytes. A binary file is also referred to as a *character stream* with following two essential differences.

- A binary file does not require any special processing of the data and each byte of data is transferred to or from the disk unprocessed.
- `Python` places no constructs on the file, and it may be read from, or written to, in any manner the programmer wants.

While text files can be processed sequentially, binary files, on the other hand, can be either processed sequentially or randomly depending on the needs of the application. In Python, to process a file randomly, the programmer must move the current file position to an appropriate place in the file before reading or writing data. For example, if a file is used to store records (using structures) of students, then to update a particular record, the programmer must first locate the appropriate record, read the record into memory, update it, and finally write the record back to disk at its appropriate location in the file.

> **Note**   Binary files store data in the internal representation format. Therefore, an integer value will be stored in binary form as 2 byte value. The same format is used to store data in memory as well as in file. Like text file, binary file also ends with an EOF market.

In a text file, an integer value 123 will be stored as a sequence of three characters—1, 2, and 3. As each character takes 1 byte, therefore, to store the integer value 123, we need 3 bytes. However, in a binary file, the `integer` value 123 will be stored in 2 bytes in the binary form. This clearly indicates that binary files takes less space to store the same piece of data and eliminates conversion between internal and external representations and are thus more efficient than the text files.

Thus, we see that text files contain only basic characters and do not store any information about the color, font, and size of the text. Examples of text files include files with .txt or .py extension. These files can be opened with Windows Notepad. These files can be easily read and the contents of the file are treated as an ordinary string value. Binary files, on the other hand, cannot be read by text editors like Notepad. If you open a binary file in Notepad, you will see some scrambles, and absurd data.

> **Note**   Binary files are mainly used to store data beyond text such as images, executables, etc.

7.4 OPENING AND CLOSING FILES

Python has many in-built functions and methods to manipulate files. These functions and methods basically work on a file object.

7.4.1 The open() Function

Before reading from or writing to a file, you must first open it using Python's built-in open() function. This function creates a file object, which will be used to invoke methods associated with it. The syntax of open() is:

```
fileObj = open(file_name [, access_mode])
```

Here,

file_name is a string value that specifies name of the file that you want to access.

access_mode indicates the mode in which the file has to be opened, i.e., read, write, append, etc. Table 7.1 lists other possible values of access mode argument.

The open() function returns a file object. This file object will be used to read, write, or perform any other operation on the file. It works like a file handle.

You can also print the details of file object as shown in the code given below.

```
file = open("File1.txt", "rb")
print(file)
```

OUTPUT
```
<open file 'File1.txt', mode 'rb' at 0x02A850D0>
```

> **Note**   Access mode is an optional parameter and the default file access mode is read (r).

Note that a file handle is different from a file. Try to understand it by using an analogy of *TV* and the *TV remote control*. You can use the remote control to switch channels, change the volume, etc. But whatever changes you try to do using remote control are actually applied on the TV. So your file handle or the file object acts as a remote control of your file (TV). Whatever changes you want to perform on the file is actually carried out through the file object.

Table 7.1 Access Modes

Mode	Purpose
r	This is the default mode of opening a file which opens the file for reading only. The file pointer is placed at the beginning of the file.
rb	This mode opens a file for reading only in binary format. The file pointer is placed at the beginning of the file.

(Contd)

Table 7.1 (*Contd*)

Mode	Purpose
r+	This mode opens a file for both reading and writing. The file pointer is placed at the beginning of the file.
rb+	This mode opens the file for both reading and writing in binary format. The file pointer is placed at the beginning of the file.
w	This mode opens the file for writing only. When a file is opened in w mode, two things can happen. If the file does not exist, a new file is created for writing. If the file already exists and has some data stored in it, the contents are overwritten.
wb	Opens a file in binary format for writing only. When a file is opened in this mode, two things can happen. If the file does not exist, a new file is created for writing. If the file already exists and has some data stored in it, the contents are overwritten.
w+	Opens a file for both writing and reading. When a file is opened in this mode, two things can happen. If the file does not exist, a new file is created for reading as well as writing. If the file already exists and has some data stored in it, the contents are overwritten.
wb+	Opens a file in binary format for both reading and writing. When a file is opened in this mode, two things can happen. If the file does not exist, a new file is created for reading as well as writing. If the file already exists and has some data stored in it, the contents are overwritten.
a	Opens a file for appending. The file pointer is placed at the end of the file if the file exists. If the file does not exist, it creates a new file for writing.
ab	Opens a file in binary format for appending. The file pointer is at the end of the file if the file exists. If the file does not exist, it creates a new file for writing.
a+	Opens a file for both reading and appending. The file pointer is placed at the end of the file if the file exists. If the file does not exist, it creates a new file for reading and writing.
ab+	Opens a file in binary format for both reading and appending. The file pointer is placed at the end of the file if the file exists. If the file does not exist, a new file is created for reading and writing.

7.4.2 The File Object Attributes

Once a file is successfully opened, a *file* object is returned. Using this file object, you can easily access different types of information related to that file. This information can be obtained by reading values of specific attributes of the file. Table 7.2 list attributes related to file object.

Table 7.2   File Object Attributes

Attribute	Information Obtained
fileObj.closed	Returns True if the file is closed and False otherwise
fileObj.mode	Returns access mode with which file has been opened
fileObj.name	Returns name of the file

Example 7.1   Program to open a file and print its attribute values

```
file = open("File1.txt", "wb")
print("Name of the file: ", file.name)
print("File is closed.", file.closed)
```

```
print("File has been opened in ", file.mode, "mode")
```

OUTPUT
```
Name of the file:  File1.txt
File is closed. False
File has been opened in wb mode
```

7.4.3 The close() Method

The `close()` method as the name suggests is used to close the file object. Once a file object is closed, you cannot further read from or write into the file associated with the file object. While closing the file object the `close()` flushes any unwritten information (means transfers the data to file that was supposed to be written in the file but has not yet been transferred). Although, Python automatically closes a file when the reference object of a file is reassigned to another file, but as a good programming habit you should always explicitly use the `close()` method to close a file. The syntax of `close()` is,

```
fileObj.close()
```

The `close()` method frees up any system resources such as file descriptors, file locks, etc. that are associated with the file. Moreover, there is an upper limit to the number of files a program can open. If that limit is exceeded then the program may even crash or work in an unexpected manner. Thus, you can waste lots of memory if you keep many files open unnecessarily and also remember that open files always stand a chance of corruption and data loss.

Once the file is closed using the `close()` method, any attempt to use the file object will result in an error.

Example 7.2   Program to access a file after it is closed

```
file = open("File1.txt", "wb")
print("Name of the file: ", file.name)
print("File is closed.", file.closed)
print("FIle is now being closed.. You cannot use the File Object")
file.close()
print("File is closed.", file.close())
print(file.read())
```

OUTPUT
```
Name of the file:  File1.txt
File is closed. False
FIle is now being closed.. You cannot use the File Object
File is closed. True
Traceback (most recent call last):
  File "C:\Python34\Try.py", line 7, in <module>
    print(file.read())
ValueError: I/O operation on closed file
```

Note   Python has a garbage collector to clean up unreferenced objects but still it is our responsibility to close the file and release the resources consumed by it.

7.5 READING AND WRITING FILES

The `read()` and `write()` are used to read data from file and write data to files respectively. In this section, we will study both these functions to manipulate data our data through files.

7.5.1 `write()` and `writelines()` Methods

The `write()` method is used to write a string to an already opened file. Of course this string may include numbers, special characters, or other symbols. While writing data to a file, you must remember that the `write()` method does not add a newline character (`'\n'`) to the end of the string. The syntax of `write()` method is:

```
fileObj.write(string);
```

As per the syntax, the string that is passed as an argument to the `write()` is written into the opened file.

Example 7.3 Program that writes a message in the file, `File1.txt`

```
file = open("File1.txt", "w")
file.write("Hello All, hope you are enjoying learning Python")
file.close()
print("Data Written into the file.......")
```

OUTPUT

```
Data Written into the file......."
```

Now, if you open the `File1.txt`, you will see that it has the contents, `"Hello All, hope you are enjoying learning Python"` written in it. The file is created in the same directory where your program file (`.py` file) is stored, that is in the `C:\Python34` folder.

Note The `write()` method returns `None`.

The `writelines()` method is used to write a list of strings.

Example 7.4 Program to write to a file using the `writelines()` method

```
file = open("File1.txt", "w")
lines = ["Hello World, ", "Welcome to the world of Python", "Enjoy Learning
Python"]
file.writelines(lines)
file.close()
print("Data written to file........")
```

OUTPUT

```
Data written to file........
```

7.5.2 `append()` Method

Once you have stored some data in a file, you can always open that file again to write more data or append data to it. To append a file, you must open it using `'a'` or `'ab'` mode depending on whether it is a text file or a binary file. Note that if you open a file in `'w'` or `'wb'` mode and then start writing data into it, then its existing contents would be overwritten. So always open the file in `'a'` or `'ab'` mode to add more data to existing data stored in the file.

Appending data is especially essential when creating a log of events or combining a large set of data into one file. The code given below appends data to our `File1.txt` file.

Example 7.5   Program to append data to an already existing file

```
file = open("File1.txt", "a")
file.write("\n Python is a very simple yet powerful language")
file.close()
print("Data appended to file........")
```

OUTPUT
```
Data appended to file........"
```

Note   If you open a file in append mode then the file is created if it did not exist.

7.5.3 The read() and readline() Methods

The `read()` method is used to read a string from an already opened file. As said before, the string can include alphabets, numbers, characters, or other symbols. The syntax of `read()` method is given as,

```
fileObj.read([count])
```

In the above syntax, count is an optional parameter which if passed to the `read()` method specifies the number of bytes to be read from the opened file. The `read()` method starts reading from the beginning of the file and if *count* is missing or has a negative value, then it reads the entire contents of the file (i.e., till the end of file).

Example 7.6   Program to print the first `10` characters of the file `File1.txt`

```
file = open("File1.txt", "r")
print(file.read(10))
file.close()
```

OUTPUT
```
Hello All,
```

Note that if you try to open a file for reading that does not exist, then you will get an error, as shown below.

```
file1 = open("file2.txt","r")
print(file2.read())
```

OUTPUT
```
Traceback (most recent call last):
  File "C:\Python34\Try.py", line 1, in <module>
    file1 = open("file2.txt","r")
IOError: [Errno 2] No such file or directory: 'file2.txt'
```

> **Note** read() method returns newline as '\n'.

The readline() method is used to read a single line from the file. The method returns an empty string when the end of the file has been reached. Note that a blank line is represented by \n and the readline() method returns a string containing only a single newline character when a blank line is encountered in the file.

Example 7.7 Consider adding a few more lines in the file File1.txt and read its contents using the readline() method. The following are the contents of the file which will be also used in Examples 7.8, 7.9, 7.10, and 7.13.

```
# File1.txt
Hello All,

Hope you are enjoying learning Python
We have tried to cover every point in detail to avoid confusion
Happy Reading
```

```
file = open("File1.txt", "r")
print("First Line : ", file.readline())
print("Second Line : ", file.readline())
print("Third Line : ", file.readline())
file.close()
```

> **Programming Tip:** Binary files are more efficient than text files so we have opened the files using rb and wb access modes. You could have also opened using r or w access mode to work with text files.

OUTPUT
```
First Line :  Hello All,
Second Line :
Third Line :  Hope you are enjoying learning Python
```

> **Note** After reading a line from the file using the readline() method, the control automatically passes to the next line. That is why, when you call the readline() again, the next line in the file is returned.

The readlines() method is used to read all the lines in the file. The code for doing so is given below.

Example 7.8 Program to demonstrate readlines() function

```
file = open("File1.txt", "r")
print(file.readlines())
file.close()
```

OUTPUT
```
['Hello All,\r\n', '\r\n', 'Hope you are enjoying learning Python\r\n', '\r\n', 'We have tried to cover every point in detail to avoid confusion\r\n', '\r\n', 'Happy Reading\r\n']
```

The list() method is also used to display entire contents of the file. You just need to pass the file object as an argument to the list() method.

Example 7.9 Program to display the contents of the file `File1.txt` using the `list()` method.

```python
file = open("File1.txt", "r")
print(list(file))
file.close()
```

OUTPUT

```
['Hello All,\r\n', '\r\n', 'Hope you are enjoying learning Python\r\n', '\r\n', 'We
have tried to cover every point in detail to avoid confusion\r\n', '\r\n', 'Happy
Reading\r\n']
```

The last and probably a very fast, simple, and efficient way to display a file is to loop over the file object to print every line in it. This is shown in the code given below.

Example 7.10 Program to display the contents of a file

```python
file = open("File1.txt", "r")
for line in file:
    print(line)
file.close()
```

OUTPUT

```
Hello All,

Hope you are enjoying learning Python

We have tried to cover every point in detail to avoid confusion

Happy Reading
```

Note All reading methods return an empty string when end-of-file (EOF) is reached. That is, if you have to read the entire file and then again call `readline()`, an empty string would be returned.

7.5.4 Opening Files using with Keyword

It is good programming habit to use the `with` keyword when working with file objects. This has the advantage that the file is properly closed after it is used even if an error occurs during read or write operation or even when you forget to explicitly close the file. This difference is clearly evident from the code given as follows using the contents of `file1.txt`. This file is also used in Examples 7.11 and 7.12.

```
Hello World
Welcome to the world of Python Programming.
```

```python with open("file1.txt", "rb") as file: for line in file: print(line) print("Let's check if the file is closed : ", file.close()) ```	```python file = open("file1.txt", "rb") for line in file: print(line) print("Let's check if the file is closed : ", file.close()) ```
OUTPUT	**OUTPUT**
Hello World	Hello World

Welcome to the world of Python Programming. Let's check if the file is closed : True	Welcome to the world of Python Programming. Let's check if the file is closed : False

In the first code, the file is opened using the `with` keyword. After the file is used in the `for` loop, it is automatically closed as soon as the block of code comprising of the `for` loop is over. But when the file is opened without the `with` keyword, it is not closed automatically. You need to explicitly close the file after using it.

Note   Calling `close()` on a file object that is already closed does not raise any error but fails silently as shown below.

```
with open("file1.txt","r") as file:
    print(file.read())        # file is already closed after the last line is read
file.close()                  # attempt to close a file that is already closed
```

OUTPUT
```
Hello World

Welcome to the world of Programming
```

Note   When you open a file for reading, or writing, the file is searched in the current working directory. If the file exists somewhere else then you need to specify the path of the file.

7.5.5 Splitting Words

Python allows you to read line(s) from a file and splits the line (treated as a string) based on a character. By default, this character is space but you can even specify any other character to split words in the string.

Example 7.11   Program to split the line into a series of words and use space to perform the split operation

```
with open("file1.txt", "r") as file:
    line = file.readline()
    words = line.split()
    print(words)
```

OUTPUT
```
['Hello', 'World,', 'Welcome', 'to', 'the', 'world', 'of', 'Python', 'Programming']
```

Example 7.12   Program to perform split operation whenever a comma is encountered

```
with open("file1.txt", "r") as file:
    line = file.readline()
    words = line.split(',')
    print(words)
```

OUTPUT
```
['Hello World', 'Welcome to the world of Python Programming\n']
```

7.5.6 Opening Files Using Command Line Arguments

Python has a **sys** module through which users can access command-line arguments in their programs. The **sys.argv** specifies the list of command-line arguments and len(sys.argv) gives the number of command-line arguments. The sys.argv[0] is the name of the program (Python script name). The program given below uses command line argument to open a file and display its contents.

```
import sys
with open(sys.argv[1]) as filename:
        for line in filename:
                print(line)
```

OUTPUT (Run this program in Windows Command Prompt)

```
C:\Python38>python Try.py File3.txt
Good Morning to all of
Welcome to the world
of
Python Programming
enjoy to the fullest
GOOD MORNING TO ALL OF
WELCOME TO THE WORLD
OF
PYTHON PROGRAMMING
ENJOY TO THE FULLEST
C:\Python38>
```

PROGRAMMING EXAMPLES

Program 7.1 Write a program that opens two files using command line arguments. Copy the contents of the first file into the second while transforming all upper case characters into lower ones.

```
import sys
file_name = open(sys.argv[2], "w")
with open(sys.argv[1]) as filename:
        for line in filename:
                file_name.write(line.lower())
print("Files Copied")
```

OUTPUT

```
(Run as C:\Python34>python Try.py File3.txt New_File.txt)
Files Copied
C:\Python34>
```

7.5.7 Some Other Useful File Methods

Table 7.3 discusses some additional file methods.

Table 7.3 File Methods

Method	Description	Example

fileno()	Returns the file number of the file (which is an integer descriptor)	`file = open("File1.txt", "w")`
		`print(file.fileno())`
		
		OUTPUT
		`3`

flush()	Flushes the write buffer of the file stream	`file = open("File1.txt", "w")` `file.flush()`

isatty()	Returns True if the file stream is interactive and False otherwise	`file = open("File1.txt", "w")`
		`file.write("Hello")`
		`print(file.isatty())`
		
		OUTPUT
		`False`

readline(n)	Reads and returns one line from file. n is optional. If n is specified then atmost n bytes are read	`file = open("Try.py", "r")`
		`print(file.readline(10))`
		
		OUTPUT
		`file = ope`

truncate(n)	Resizes the file to n bytes	`file = open("File.txt", "w")`
		`file.write("Welcome to the world of programming....")`
		`file.truncate(5)`
		`file = open("File.txt", "r")`
		`print(file.read())`
		
		OUTPUT
		`Welco`

rstrip()	Strips off whitespaces including newline characters from the right side of the string read from the file.	`file = open("File.txt")`
		`line = file.readline()`
		`print(line.rstrip())`
		
		OUTPUT
		`Greetings to All !!!`

7.6 FILE POSITIONS

With every file, the file management system associates a pointer often known as *file pointer* that facilitates the movement across the file for reading and/ or writing data. The file pointer specifies a location from where the current read or write operation is initiated. Once the read/write operation is completed, the pointer is automatically updated.

Python has various methods that tells or sets the position of the file pointer. For example, the `tell()` method tells the current position within the file at which the next read or write operation will occur. It is specified as number of bytes from the beginning of the file. When you just open a file for reading, the file pointer is positioned at location 0, which is the beginning of the file.

The `seek(offset[, from])` method is used to set the position of the file pointer or in simpler terms, move the file pointer to a new location. The `offset` argument indicates the number of bytes to be moved and the `from` argument specifies the reference position from where the bytes are to be moved. Table 7.4 specifies the value of `from` argument and its corresponding interpretation. Note that the `from` value 2 is especially important when working with MP3 files that stores tags at the end of the file, so you directly issue a command to move the file pointer to a position 128 bytes from the end of the files.

Table 7.4   From and its Position

From	Reference Position
0	From the beginning of the file
1	From the current position of the file
2	From the end of the file

Example 7.13   Program that tells and sets the position of the file pointer

```python
file = open("File1.txt", "rb")
print("Position of file pointer before reading is : ", file.tell())
print(file.read(10))
print("Position of file pointer after reading is : ", file.tell())
print("Setting 3 bytes from the current position of file pointer")
file.seek(3,1)
print(file.read())
file.close()
```

OUTPUT

```
Position of file pointer before reading is : 0
Hello All,
Position of file pointer after reading is : 10
Setting 3 bytes from the current position of file pointer
pe you are enjoying learning Python
```

Note   In Python, you don't need to import any library to read and write files. Just create a file object and call the open function to read/write to the file.

7.6.1 Seek a Position in a File

The `seek()` function accepts one or two arguments. When a single argument is specified, the byte position within the file where the jump has to be made is given. In case of two arguments, the `seek()` function can specify the location from which byte to start relative to the beginning, the current position, or the end of the file. The possible values could be `os.SEEK_SET`, `os.SEEK_CUR` and `os.SEEK_END` to set the file position from beginning, or to current cursor position or relative to end of the file, respectively.

For example,

```python
import os
with open('File1.txt', 'rb') as file:
    # Jump to beginning of file
    file.seek(0)    # Equivalent to writing file.seek(0, os.SEEK_SET)

    # Read 10 bytes, moving cursor forward
    print(file.read(10))
    # Move 5 bytes backwards from current position (towards beginning)
```

```
file.seek(-2, os.SEEK_CUR)
# Re-read the three bytes
print(file.read(3))
# Go to the end of the file
file.seek(0, os.SEEK_END)
# Read last two bytes of the file
file.seek(-2, os.SEEK_CUR)
print(file.read(2))
```

Program 7.2 Write a program that copies first 10 bytes of a binary file into another.

```
with open("File1.txt", "rb") as file1:
    with open("file2.txt","wb") as file2:
            buf = file1.read(10)
            file2.write(buf)
print("File Copied")
```

OUTPUT

```
File Copied
```

Program 7.3 Write a program that copies one Python script into another in such a way that all comment lines are skipped and not copied in the destination file.

```
with open("First.py", "rb") as file1:
    with open("Second.py","wb") as file2:
        while True:
            buf = file1.readline()
            if len(buf)!=0:
                if buf[0] -- '#':
                    continue
                else:
                    file2.write(buf)
            else:
                break
print("File Copied")
```

OUTPUT

```
File Copied
```

Program 7.4 Write a program that accepts filename as an input from the user. Open the file and count the number of times a character appears in the file.

```
filename = input("Enter the filename : ")
with open(filename) as file:
    text = file.read()
```

```
        letter = input("Enter the character to be searched : ")
        count = 0
        for char in text:
            if char == letter:
                    count += 1
print(letter, "appears ", count, " times in file")
```

OUTPUT

```
Enter the filename : File1.txt
Enter the character to be searched : a
a appears 7 times in file
```

Program 7.5 Write a program that reads data from a file and calculates the percentage of vowels and consonants in the file.

```
filename = input("Enter the filename : ")
with open(filename) as file:
    text = file.read()
    count_vowels = 0
    count_consonants = 0
    for char in text:
        if char in "aeiou":
            count_vowels += 1
        else:
            count_consonants += 1
print("Number of vowels = ", count_vowels)
print("Number of consonants = ", count_consonants)
print("Total Length of File = ", len(text))
print("Percentatge of vowels in the file = ", ((count_vowels)*100)/len(text),"%")
print("Percentatge of consonants in the file = ", ((count_consonants)*100)/
len(text), "%")
```

OUTPUT

```
Enter the filename : File1.txt
Number of vowels =  31
Number of consonants =  77
Total Length of File =  108
Percentatge of vowels in the file =  28 %
Percentatge of consonants in the file =  71 %
```

7.7 RENAMING AND DELETING FILES

The os module in Python has various methods that can be used to perform file-processing operations like renaming and deleting files. To use the methods defined in the os module, you should first import it in your program and then call any related functions.

The rename() Method: The rename() method takes two arguments, the current filename and the new filename. Its syntax is,

> **Programming Tip:** The *file* object provides functions to manipulate files.

```
os.rename(old_file_name, new_file_name)
```

Example 7.14 Program to rename file "File1.txt" to "Students.txt"

```
import os
os.rename("File1.txt", "Students.txt")
print("File Renamed")

OUTPUT
File Renamed
```

You can check whether the above code renamed the right file by checking in the C:\Python34 directory. Now, there is no file named File1.txt but it does have a file named Students.txt.

The remove() Method: This method can be used to delete file(s). The method takes a filename (name of the file to be deleted) as an argument and deletes that file. Its syntax is:

```
os.remove(file_name)
```

Example 7.15 Program to delete a file named File1.txt

```
import os
os.remove("File1.txt")
print("File Deleted")

OUTPUT
File Deleted
```

Let us now check the contents of the directory. The file name File1.txt no longer exists.

7.8 DIRECTORY METHODS

As we all know a directory is a collection of files where each file may be of a different format. Python has various methods in the os module that help programmers to work with directories. These methods allow users to create, remove, and change directories.

The mkdir() Method: The mkdir()method of the os module is used to create directories in the current directory. The method takes the name of the directory (the one to be created) as an argument. The syntax of mkdir() is,

```
os.mkdir("new_dir_name")
```

Example 7.16   Program to create a new directory New Dir in the current directory

```
import os
os.mkdir("New Dir")
print("Directory Created")
```

OUTPUT

```
Directory Created
```

Just check the contents of C:\Python34 directory. You will find a new directory named New Dir.

The getcwd() Method: The getcwd() method is used to display the current working directory (cwd). We have already read that, all files and folders whose path does not exist in the root folder are assumed to be present in the current working directory. So to know your cwd is quite important at times and for this getcwd() method is used. The syntax of getcwd() is,

> **Programming Tip:** You must use escape sequence when using the backward slash.

```
os.getcwd()
```

The chdir() Method: The chdir() method is used to change the current directory. The method takes the name of the directory which you want to make the current directory as an argument. Its syntax is

```
os.chdir("dir_name")
```

Example 7.17   Program that changes the current directory to our newly created directory—New Dir.

```
import os
print("Current Working Directory is : ", os.getcwd())
os.chdir("New Dir")
print("After chdir, the current Directory is now...... ",
end = ' ')
print(os.getcwd())
```

> **Programming Tip:** os object methods provide methods to process files as well as directories.

OUTPUT

```
Current Working Directory is : C:\Python34
After chdir, the current Directory is now......  C:\Python34\New Dir
```

Note that an error will be displayed if you try to change to a directory that does not exist. For example, if we had mistakenly written New Dir as New Dit, then we will get the following error message.

```
Traceback (most recent call last):
  File "C:\Python34\Try.py", line 3, in <module>
    os.chdir("New Dit")
WindowsError: [Error 2] The system cannot find the file specified: 'New Dit'
```

The `rmdir()` Method: The `rmdir()` method is used to remove or delete a directory. For this, it accepts the name of the directory to be deleted as an argument. However, before removing a directory, it should be absolutely empty and all the contents in it should be removed. The syntax of `remove()` method is,

```
os.rmdir("dir_name")
```

For example, the code given below will remove our newly created directory—`New Dir`. In case, the specified directory is not in the current working directory, you should always specify the complete path of the directory as otherwise the method would search for that directory in the current directory only.

Example 7.18 Program to demonstrate the use of `rmdir()` function

```
import os
os.rmdir("New Dir")
print("Directory Deleted...... ")
```

OUTPUT
```
Directory Deleted......
```

> **Programming Tip:** To remove a non-empty directory, use the `rmtree()` method defined inside the `shutil.` module.

Just check the `C:\Python34` folder, the `New Dir` directory no longer exists in it. If you try to delete a non-empty directory, then you will get `OSError: [WinError 145] The directory is not empty`. If you still want to delete the non-empty directory, use the `rmtree()` method defined in the `shutil` module as shown below.

```
import shutil
shutil.rmtree("Dir1")
```

The `makedirs()` Method: The method `makedirs()` is used to create more than one folder. For example, if you pass string `C:\Python34\Dir1\Dir2\Dir3` as an argument to `makedirs()` method, then Python will create folder `Dir1` in `Python34` folder, `Dir2` in `Dir1` folder, and `Dir3` in the `Dir2` folder. The implementation of `makedirs()` method is shown in the code given below.

```
import os
os.makedirs("C:\\Python34\\Dir1\Dir2\\Dir3")
```

Note that we have put `\\` slashes in the string so that the first slash acts as an escape sequence. You can check the execution of this code by checking the contents of `Python34` folder in which you will now find a folder named `Dir1` which in turn has a folder `Dir2` containing another folder `Dir3`.

The `os.path.join()` Method: We have read that in Windows, path names are written using the backslash but in Unix, Linux, OS X, and other operating systems they are specified using the forward slash character. To make your program portable you must cater to both the ways of representing file path. To make your work easier, Python `os` module has a `join()` method. When you pass a string value of file and folder names that makes up the path, then `os.path.join()` method will return a string with a file path that has correct path separators.

> **Programming Tip:** If you use a method defined in a module without importing that module, then you will get a NameError.

Example 7.19   Program that uses `os.path.join()` method to form a valid file path

```
import os
print(os.path.join("c:", "students", "under graduate", "BTech.docx"))
```

OUTPUT
```
c:\students\under graduate\BTech.docx
```

It can be noted here that since the above code is executed on Windows, therefore, the output has backward slashes. If the same code was run on another operating system (like Linux), you would have got forward slashes.

Thus, we see that the `os.path.join()` method is used to create strings for file names. The file names can then be passed to other file related functions (like to open the file).

Example 7.20   Program to print the absolute path of a file using `os.path.join`

```
import os
path = "d:\\="
filename = "First.txt"
abs_path = os.path.join(path, filename)
print("ABSOLUTE FILE PATH = ", abs_path)
file = open(abs_path, "w")
file.write("Hello")
file.close()
file = open(abs_path, "r")
print(file.read())
```

OUTPUT
```
ABSOLUTE FILE PATH =  d:\First.txt
Hello
```

In the above program, we use the `join()` method to form the file path and then pass the file path as an argument to `open()`. We first open the file in write mode to write some text in it, close the file, and then again open to read its content.

7.8.1 Methods from the os Module

The `os.path.abspath()` Method: This method uses the string value passed to it to form an absolute path. Thus, it is another way to convert a relative path to an absolute path.

Example 7.21   Program to demonstrate the use of `os.path.abspath()` method

```
import os
print(os.path.abspath("Python\\Strings.docx"))
```

OUTPUT
```
C:\Python34\Python\Strings.docx
```

In the above code, the string `Python\\Strings.docx` is joined with the current working directory to form an absolute path.

The os.path.isabs(path) Method: This method accepts a file path as an argument and returns True if the path is an absolute path and False otherwise.

Example 7.22 Program to demonstrate the use of os.path.isabs() method

```
import os
print("os.path.isabs(\"Python\\Strings.docx\") = ",
os.path.isabs("Python\\Strings.docx"))
print("os.path.isabs(\"C:\\Python34\\Python\\Strings.docx\") = ",
os.path.isabs("C:\Python34\Python\\Strings.docx"))

OUTPUT
os.path.isabs("Python\Strings.docx") =  False
os.path.isabs("C:\Python34\Python\Strings.docx") =  True
```

The os.path.relpath(path, start) Method: This method accepts a file path and a start string as an argument and returns a relative path that begins from the start. If start is not given, the current directory is taken as start.

Example 7.23 Program to demonstrate the use of os.path.relpath() method

```
import os
print("os.path.relpath(\"C:\\Python\\Chapters\\First
Draft\\Strings.docx\") = ", os.path.relpath("C:\Python\Chapters\First
Draft\Strings.docx", "C:\Python"))

OUTPUT
path.relpath("C:\Python\Chapters\First Draft\Strings.docx")= Chapters\First Draft\
Strings.docx
```

The os.path.dirname(path) Method: This method returns a string that includes everything specified in the path (passed as argument to the method) that comes before the last slash.

The os.path.basename(path) Method: This method returns a string that includes everything specified in the path (passed as argument to the method) that comes after the last slash.

Example 7.24 Program to demonstrate the use of dirname() and basename() methods

```
import os
print("os.path.dirname(\"C:\\Python\\Chapters\\First
Draft\\Strings.docx\") = ", os.path.dirname("C:\Python\
Chapters\First
Draft\Strings.docx"))
```

Programming Tip: Do not combine paths using string concatenation (+). Rather, use os.path. join() method.

```
print("os.path.basename(\"C:\\Python\\Chapters\\First
Draft\\Strings.docx\") = ", os.path.basename("C:\Python\Chapters\First
Draft\Strings.docx"))
```

OUTPUT
```
os.path.dirname("C:\Python\Chapters\First Draft\Strings.docx") =
C:\Python\Chapters\First Draft
os.path.basename("C:\Python\Chapters\First Draft\Strings.docx") =
Strings.docx
```

The os.path.split(path) Method: This method accepts a file path and returns its directory name as well as the basename. So it is equivalent to using two separate methods, os.path.dirname() and os.path.basename().

Example 7.25   Program to demonstrate the use of os.path.split() method

```
import os
print("os.path.split(\"C:\\Python\\Chapters\\First
Draft\\Strings.docx\") = ", os.path.split("C:\Python\Chapters\First
Draft\Strings.docx"))
```

OUTPUT
```
os.path.split("C:\Python\Chapters\First Draft\Strings.docx") =
    ('C:\\Python\\Chapters\\First Draft', 'Strings.docx')
```

The os.path.getsize(path) Method: This method returns the size of the file specified in the path argument.

The os.listdir(path) Method: This method returns a list of filenames in the specified path.

Example 7.26   Program to demonstrate the use of os.path.getsize() and os.listdir() methods

```
import os
print("os.path.getsize(\"C:\\Python34\\Try.py\") = ",
os.path.getsize("C:\Python34\Try.py"))
print("os.listdir(\"C:\\Python34\") = ", os.listdir("C:\Python34"))
```

OUTPUT
```
os.path.getsize("C:\Python34\Try.py") =  174
os.listdir("C:\Python34") =  ['Dir1', 'DLLs', 'Doc', 'File1.txt', 'include', 'Lib',
'libs', 'LICENSE.txt', 'MyModule.py', 'MyModule.pyc', 'NEWS.txt', 'python.exe',
'pythonw.exe', 'README.txt', 'Scripts', 'tcl', 'Tools', 'Try.py', 'w9xpopen.exe']
```

The os.path.exists(path) Method: The method as the name suggests accepts a path as an argument and returns True if the file or folder specified in the path exists and False otherwise.

The os.path.isfile(path) Method: The method as the name suggests accepts a path as an argument and returns True if the path specifies a file and False otherwise.

The os.path.isdir(path) Method: The method as the name suggests accepts a path as an argument and returns True if the path specifies a an existing directory and False otherwise.

Get File Extension: To obtain the file extension of a file, we can use the os.path.splitext() function. This functions, splits a file path to get the file's extension. The function returns a tuple containing the filename and the extension as given below.

```
import os

print(os.path.splitext('File1.txt'))
```

OUTPUT
```
('File1', '.txt')
```

Example 7.27 Program to demonstrate the use of some methods defined in the os module

```
import os
print("os.path.exists(\"C:\\Python34\\Dir1\") = ",
os.path.exists("C:\Python34\Dir1"))

print("os.path.isfile(\"C:\\Python34\\Dir1\") = ",
os.path.isfile("C:\Python34\Dir1"))

print("os.path.isdir(\"C:\\Python34\\Dir1\") = ",
os.path.isdir("C:\Python34\Dir1"))

print("os.path.isfile(\"C:\\Python34\\Try.py\") = ",
os.path.isfile("C:\Python34\Try.py"))

print("os.path.isdir(\"C:\\Python34\\Try.py\") = ",
os.path.isdir("C:\Python34\Try.py"))
```

OUTPUT
```
os.path.exists("C:\Python34\Dir1") =  True
os.path.isfile("C:\Python34\Dir1") =  False
os.path.isdir("C:\Python34\Dir1") =  True
os.path.isfile("C:\Python34\Try.py") =  True
os.path.isdir("C:\Python34\Try.py") =  False
```

Program 7.6 Write a program that counts the number of tabs, spaces, and newline characters in a file.

```
filename = input("Enter the filename : ")
with open(filename) as file:
    text = file.read()
    count_tab = 0
```

```
    count_space = 0
    count_nl = 0
    for char in text:
        if char == '\t':
                count_tab += 1
        if char == ' ':
                count_space += 1
        if char == '\n':
                count_nl += 1
print("TABS = ", count_tab)
print("SPACES = ", count_space)
print("NEW LINES = ", count_nl)
```

OUTPUT
```
Enter the filename : File1.txt
```

Program 7.7 Write a program that computes the total size of all the files in `C:\Python34` folder.

```
import os
totalSize = 0
for file in os.listdir("C:\Python34"):
    totalSize += os.path.getsize(os.path.join("C:\Python34",file))
print("Total size of all the files in C:\\Python34 folder = ", totalSize)
```

OUTPUT
```
Total size of all the files in C:\Python34 folder =   799866
```

Program 7.8 Write a program to check if flash drive is connected to your computer.

```
import os
print("os.path.exists(\"G:\\") = ", os.path.exists("G:\\"))
```

OUTPUT
```
os.path.exists("G:\\") =  True
```

Program 7.9 Write a program that reads a file line by line. Each line read from the file is copied to another file with line numbers specified at the beginning of the line.

```
file1 = open("file1.txt","r")
file2 = open("File.txt","w")
num = 1
for line in file1:
    file2.write(str(num) + " : " + line)
    num = num + 1
file1.close()
file2.close()
```

Program 7.10 Write a program that generates a Quiz and uses two files—Questions.txt and Answers.txt. The program opens Questions.txt and reads a question and displays the question with options on the screen. The program then opens the Answer.txt file and displays the correct answers.

```
file1 = open("Questions.txt", "r")
file2 = open("Answers.txt", "r")
ques = file1.read()
qlines= ques.split('\n')
for lines in qlines:
    print(lines)
ans = file2.read()
alines= ans.split('\n')
print("CORRECT ANSWERS")
for lines in alines:
    print(lines)
```

OUTPUT

```
Who is the Prime Minister of India?
1. Narendra Modi     2. Shivraj Patil
Who is the President of USA?
1. Hilary Clinton    2. Donald Trump

CORRECT ANSWERS
1
2
```

Program 7.11 Write a program that fetches data from a specified url and prints it on screen.

```
import urllib.request
x = urllib.request.urlopen('https://www.google.com/')
print(x.read())
```

OUTPUT

```
The contents of google.com is printed
```

Program 7.12 Write a program that fetches data from a specified url and writes it in a file.
Hint: Use the urllib2 module that handles the url

```
import urllib.request

url = 'https://www.google.com/search?q=python'
headers = {}
headers['User-Agent'] = "Mozilla/5.0 (X11; Linux i686) AppleWebKit/537.17 (KHTML,
like Gecko) Chrome/24.0.1312.27 Safari/537.17"
Request = urllib.request.Request(url, headers = headers)
Response = urllib.request.urlopen(Request)
Data = Response.read()
File = open('URL_File.txt','w')
File.write(str(Data))
```

```
File.close()
print("Contents written in the file......")
```

OUTPUT

Contents written in the file......

7.8.2 Get File Permissions

To know about permissions of a particular file, we can use the os.stat() function as shown below.

```
import os
stats = os.stat('File1.txt')
print(stats.st_mode)
```

OUTPUT

33206

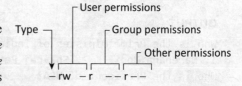

To understand this output, we need to capture the details. There are four parts to the mode. The first character specifies the *file type*. A dash (-) in this position means that it is a *regular file* (nothing special about it). If the file is a directory, then 'd' is written here.

Value at the other positions specifies permissions in three sets: the *user* (who owns the file), *group*, and *other* (*for all other users except the owner and those in the specified group*) permissions. For example, the rw- characters denote user permissions, r-- are the group permissions, and r-- are permissions for others. Here, r means that the file is readable, w means that the file is writable and x denotes that the file is executable (i.e, you can run it as a program).

Every combination of rwx bits is known as permission bits. As per this example, the user has permission to read and write in the file, a particular group of users has the permission to just read the file and all other users (not included in the first two categories) can also just read the file.

7.8.3 Set File Permissions (CHMOD)

To change permissions of a file, the os.chmod() function is used. To set the desired permissions, we can use the Bitwise OR operator. Some important values for permissions are given in the stat package and can be used as:

```
# import stat
stat.S_IRUSR # Read, user
stat.S_IWUSR # Write, user
stat.S_IXUSR # Execute, user

stat.S_IRGRP # Read, group
stat.S_IWGRP # Write, group
stat.S_IXGRP # Execute, group

stat.S_IROTH # Read, other
stat.S_IWOTH # Write, other
stat.S_IXOTH # Execute, other
```

```
stat.S_IRWXU # Read, write, and execute for user
stat.S_IRWXG # Read, write, and execute for group
stat.S_IRWXO # Read, write, and execute for other
```

For example, to set all permissions for the user only, all the user permissions can be bitwise ORed by writing
S_IRUSR | S_IWUSR | SIXUSR.

```
import os
import stat
os.chmod('File1.txt', stat.S_IRWXU | stat.S_IRWXG | stat.S_IRWXO)
```

Example 7.28 Write a program to copy a file using shutil module.

```
To copy a file from Python code, we can use the shutil.copy() function as given
below:

import shutil
shutil.copy('File1.txt', 'File1_copy.txt')
```

> **Programming Tip:** To move a file, we can use the shutil.move() function

7.8.4 Change Ownership (CHOWN)

shutil.chown() and os.chown() are used to change ownership of a file. The code given below is used to change the ownership of a particular user (by using user id or user name) or a group of users (by specifying the name or id of the group).

```
from shutil import chown

chown('File1.txt', user='john')
chown(' File1.txt', group='tiger')
#to give root permissions to user and group, we can write,
chown(' File1.txt', user='root', group='root')
chown(' File1.txt', user=0, group=0)  # root uids
```

7.8.5 Get File Timestamp

The os.stat() function is used to get information about a file including its timestamps. It returns st_atime (last access time), st_mtime (last modify time) and st_ctime (create time), all in seconds. The code given below prints these timings:

```
import os

stats = os.stat(' File1.txt')
print(stats.st_atime)
print(stats.st_mtime)
print(stats.st_ctime)
print(type(stats.st_mtime))  # <class 'float'>
```

We can do the same job by using the datetime package. Output obtained from this package is more readable and thus usable.

```python
import datetime
date_object = datetime.datetime.
fromtimestamp(stats.st_ctime)
print(date_object)
print(date_object.strftime('%Y-%m-%d-%H:%M'))
```

7.8.6 Set File Timestamp

The os.utime() function is used to update the timestamp of a file. For example, the code given below updates the timestamp of File1.txt by setting it to the current time.

```python
import os
import datetime
os.utime('File1.txt')
```

Similarly, to specify the timestamp to set the access time and modify time in seconds, we can give these values in a tuple by writing,

```python
time_in_seconds = datetime.datetime.now().timestamp)
os.utime(File1.txt', times=(time_in_seconds, time_in_seconds))
```

7.8.7 SYMLINK

We know that a *symlink* or a *Symbolic Link* refers to a shortcut to another file. Technically, it is a file that points to another file. In Python, we can use the os.path.islink() function to find out if a file is a symbolic link or not. The code given below demonstrates the use of this function.

```python
import os
print(os.path.islink('File1.txt'))
```

We can even create a symbolic link from our Python code by using the os.symlink() function as shown below.

```python
import os
os.symlink('File1.txt', 'SL_File1.txt')
```

Note that to check the hard links of a file, the os.stat() function will be used. The hard link is the exact replica of the actual file it is pointing to. Every file has at least one hard link. The number of hard links can then be printed by using the st_nlink attribute of the result as shown in the code given below.

```python
import os
stats = os.stat('File1.txt')
# Number of hard links
print(stats.st_nlink)
```

Correspondingly, to create a hard link, we use the `os.link()` function.

```
import os
os.link('File1.txt', 'HL_File1.txt')
```

Example 7.29 Write a program to download web pages through the web and write in a file.

We can download a web page in Python using the requests module. However, remember that downloading web pages containing server-side scripts (like PHP, ASP) will not work as those are encrypted web pages and the requests module works only with non-encrypted web pages such as HTML.

```
import requests
import re
url = 'https://www.python.org/doc/essays/blurb/'
r = requests.get(url, allow_redirects=True)
filename = "content.txt"
open(filename, 'wb').write(r.content)
```

Summary

- A permanent or non-volatile storage media like the hard disk, USB drive, DVD, etc. is used to store data for future use.
- At the top of the tree is one (or more) root nodes. Under the root node, there are other files and folders (or directories) and each folder can in turn contain other files and folders.
- Every file is identified by its path that begins from the root node or the root folder.
- A file path can be either *relative* or *absolute*. While an absolute path always contains the root and the complete directory list to specify the exact location the file, relative path on the other hand, needs to be combined with another path in order to access a file.
- Each file ends with a special character called the end-of-file (EOF) marker.
- A binary file is a file which may contain any type of data, encoded in binary form for computer storage and processing purposes.
- `open()` function creates a file object, which will be used to invoke methods associated with it.

- The `close()` method is used to close the file object. Once a file object is closed, you cannot further read from or write into the file associated with the file object.
- Python has a garbage collector to clean up unreferenced objects but still it is our responsibility to close the file and release the resources consumed by it.
- To append a file, you must open it using `'a'` or `'ab'` mode depending on whether it is a text file or a binary file.
- The `read()` method is used to read a string from an already opened file.
- The file pointer specifies a location from where the current read or write operation is initiated.
- The `tell()` method tells the current position within the file at which the next read or write operation will occur. It is specified as number of bytes from the beginning of the file.
- The `getcwd()` method is used to display the current working directory.

Glossary

Delimiter One or more characters used to specify the boundary between different parts of text.

Directory Collection of files, also called a folder. A directory can have other files and directories within it.

File A stream of information that is usually stored on a permanent storage media like hard drive, floppy disk, CD-ROM, etc.

File handle An object that allows you to manipulate/read/write/close the file.

File path A sequence of directory names that specifies the exact location of a file.

Non-volatile memory Memory that can store data even when the power supply to the computer system is switched off. Hard drives, flash drives, and rewritable compact disks (CD-RW) are each examples of non-volatile memory.

Text file A file having printable characters organized into lines separated by newline characters.

Volatile memory Memory that loses data as soon as the computer system is switched off. RAM is an example of volatile memory.

Exercises

Fill In The Blanks

1. _____ function is used to access files
2. Fill in the blanks to read a file using the with keyword.
   ```
   ___open("File.txt")__file:
   data = file.read()
   ```
3. Fill in the blanks to open a file called "abc.bin" in binary read mode.
   ```
   File = open(_____,_____)
   ```
4. How many characters would be printed by this code (one character is one byte)?
   ```
   file=open("FILE.txt","r")
   for i in range(100):
       print(file.read(10))
   file.close()
   ```
5. Fill in the blanks to open a file, read its content, and print its length.
   ```
   file=_____("File.txt","r")
   text = file._____()
   print (_____(text))
   file.close()
   ```
6. Fill in the blanks to open a file for reading using the with statement.
   ```
   _____open("File.txt")__file:
   print(file._____())
   ```
7. Most file systems that are used today stores files in a _____ structure.
8. Every file is identified by its path that begins from the _____.
9. In Windows, _____ is the root folder.
10. A relative path is specified relative to the program's _____.
11. _____ pathnames starts with respect to the current working directory.
12. Each file ends with a special character called the _____.
13. open() function returns a _____.
14. The _____ method frees up any system resources such as file descriptors, file locks, etc.
15. Any attempt to use the file object will result in a _____.
16. The write() method returns _____.
17. If you try to open a file for reading that does not exist, then you will get _____.
18. The readline() method returns _____ when the end of the file has been reached.
19. If you do not want the new file to be created in the current working directory, then you must specify the _____.
20. The _____ specifies a location from where the current read or write operation is initiated.
21. _____ method tells the current position within the file at which the next read or write operation will occur.
22. When you open a file for reading, the file pointer is positioned at _____.
23. _____ method is used to delete a file.
24. If you try to change to a directory that does not exist, _____ will be generated.
25. If you try to delete a non-empty directory, then you will get _____.
26. To remove a non-empty directory, use the _____ method defined inside the _____ module.
27. The method _____ is used to create more than one folder.
28. _____ method is used to create strings for filenames.
29. The _____ method uses the string value passed to it to form an absolute path.

State True or False

1. When a program is being executed, its data is stored in ROM.
2. RAM is an example of non-volatile memory.
3. You can have only one root in all the file systems.
4. Delimiters may vary from one operating system to another.
5. Folder names and file names are case insensitive in Windows.
6. Absolute path always contains the root.
7. The contents of a binary file are human readable.
8. Text files includes files like word processing documents, PDFs, images, spreadsheets, videos, zip files, and other executable programs.
9. Binary files are more efficient than text files.
10. `*.py` files are binary files.
11. When you open a file for appending that does not exist, then a new file is created.
12. You can open any number of files without any sort of restriction.
13. The `read()` method starts reading from the beginning of the file.
14. If count is missing or has a negative value in the `read()` method then, no contents are read from the file.
15. The `readline()` method is used to read all the lines in the file.
16. The `tell()` method moves the file pointer to a new location.
17. Before removing a directory, it should be absolutely empty.
18. `os.path.abs()` method accepts a file path as an argument and returns `True` if the path is an absolute path and `False` otherwise.
19. The `cwd()` method is used to display the current working directory.

Multiple Choice Questions

1. Identify the right way to close a file
   - (a) `File.close()`
   - (b) `close(File)`
   - (c) `close("File")`
   - (d) `File.closed`
2. If the `File.txt` has `10` lines written in it, what will be the result?
   `len(open("File.txt").readlines())`
   - (a) `1`
   - (b) `0`
   - (c) `10`
   - (d) `2`
3. If a file opened in `'w'` mode does not exist, then
   - (a) nothing will happen
   - (b) file will be created
   - (c) data will be written to a file that has name a similar to the specified name
   - (d) error will be generated
4. Identify the right way to write `"Welcome to Python"` in a file?
   - (a) `write(file," Welcome to Python")`
   - (b) `write("Welcome to Python",file)`
   - (c) `file.write("Welcome to Python")`
   - (d) `"Welcome to Python".write(file)`
5. What will happen when a file is opened in write mode and then immediately closed?
   - (a) File contents are deleted
   - (b) Nothing happens
   - (c) A blank line is written to the file
   - (d) An error occurs
6. A file is stored in _____ memory.
   - (a) primary
   - (b) secondary
   - (c) cache
   - (d) volatile
7. _____ is an example of volatile memory
   - (a) RAM
   - (b) DVD
   - (c) Hard disk
   - (d) Pen drive
8. In the path `C:\Students\Under Graduate\BTech_CS.docx`, _____ is the sub-folder
   - (a) `C:`
   - (b) Students
   - (c) `BTech_CS`
   - (d) Under Graduate
9. Identify the delimiter in the Solaris file system
   - (a) `/`
   - (b) `\`
   - (c) `:`
   - (d) `|`
10. The default access mode is _____
    - (a) `r`
    - (b) `w`
    - (c) `rb`
    - (d) `wb`
11. By default, a new file is created in which directory
    - (a) root directory
    - (b) current working directory
    - (c) Python directory
    - (d) D drive
12. Which method is used to read a single line from the file?
    - (a) `read()`
    - (b) `readline()`
    - (c) `readlines()`
    - (d) `reads()`
13. Which method is used to display entire contents of the file
    - (a) `read()`
    - (b) `readlines()`
    - (c) `list()`
    - (d) all of these

14. In the seek() method, what will be the value of from if you want to specify number of bytes from the current location of the file pointer?
    - (a) 0
    - (b) 1
    - (c) 2
    - (d) 3

15. Which method returns a string that includes everything specified in the path?
    - (a) os.path.dirname(path)
    - (b) os.path.basename(path)
    - (c) os.path.relpath()
    - (d) os.path.abs()

Review Questions

1. What are files? Why do we need them?
2. Explain the significance of root node?
3. Differentiate between absolute and relative file path.
4. Differentiate between a file and folder.
5. Differentiate between text and binary files.
6. Explain the utility of open() function.
7. What are different access modes in which you can open a file?
8. With the help of an example explain any three attributes of file object.
9. Is it mandatory to call the close() method after using the file?
10. Explain the syntax of read() method.
11. Give the significance of with keyword.
12. Write a short note on different methods to read data from a file.
13. With the help of suitable examples explain different ways in which you can write data in a file.
14. Discuss some directory methods present in the os module.

Programming Problems

1. Write a program that reads text from a file and writes it into another file but in the reverse order.
   (*Hint: Make the first line in the original file as the last line in the copied file.*)
2. Write a program that reads a file and prints only those lines that has the word 'print'.
3. Write a program that has several lines. Each line begins with a line number. Now read this file line by line and copy the line in another file but do not copy the numbers.
4. Write a program that reads text from a file and writes it into another file but in the reverse order.
   (*Hint: Make the first line in the original file as the last line in the copied file.*)
5. Write a program to compare two files.
6. Write a program to copy one file into another. Copy one character at a time.
7. Write a program to read and write the details of a student in a file.
8. Write a program to count the number of records stored in file employee.
9. Write a program to edit a record stored in 'employee'.txt file.
10. Write a program to read a file that contains small case characters. Then write these characters into another file with all lowercase characters converted into uppercase.
11. Write a program to merge two files into a third file. The names of the files must be entered using command line arguments.
12. Write a menu driven program that reads details of a faculty. Provide options to add a new record, delete a record, update an existing record, and display all or a particular record. (*Hint: To delete a record, make a temporary file. Copy all the records except the one to be deleted. Then, rename the temporary file as the main file.*)
13. Write a menu driven program that maintains a file DIRECTORY that stores the name and telephone number of a person. The program must allow users to add new contacts, search a contact based on name, search a contact based on phone number, update the number, update the name, and delete a contact.
14. Write a program that reads a file and copies its contents in another file. While copying, replace all full stops with commas.
15. Write a program that exchanges the contents of two files.
16. Write a program that writes data to a file in such a way that each character after a full stop is capitalized and all numbers are written in brackets.

Fill in the Blanks and Identify the Usage of the Lines

1. `File = open("File.txt", "r")`
   The above statement _____ a text file.
2. `file.read()`
   The above statement _____ a text file.
3. `print(file.readline())`
   The above statement _____ a text file.
4. `print(file.readlines())`
   The above statement _____ a text file.
5. `file.write("Welcome")`
   The above statement _____ a text file.
6. `file = open("File.txt", "w")`
   The above statement _____ a text file.
7. `file.writelines(lines)`
   The above statement _____ a text file.
8. `file = open("File.txt", "a")`
   The above statement _____ a text file.
9. `file.close()`
   The above statement _____ a text file.
10. `file.read(10)`
    The above statement _____ a text file.
11. `file.seek(file.tell()-10)`
    The above statement _____ a text file.
12. `file = open("File.txt", "r+b")`
    The above statement _____
13. `file.seek(-10,2)`
    The above statement _____
14. `file.seek(20,1)`
    The above statement _____
15. `file.seek(30,0)`
    The above statement _____

Find the Output

1. ```
import os
Files = ['BTech.txt', 'BCA.csv', 'BSc.docx']
for file in Files:
  print(os.path.join('C:\\Users\\
  Students', file))
```
2. ```
with open("File.txt", "w") as file:
  file.write("Greetings to All !!! \n
  Welcome to the world of programming\n")
with open("File.txt") as file:
  print(file.read())
```
3. ```
file=open("File.txt","r")
file.read()
text = file.read())
print(len(text))
file.close()
```
4. ```
str="Welcome to Python Programming"
file=open("File.txt","w")
n =file.write(str)
print(n)
file.close()
```
5. What will be written in the file?
   1. `file.write("Oxford" + " University" + "Press")`
   2. `file.write(str(len("Oxford University Press")))`
   3. `file.write("Clue".replace('C', 'B')`
   4. `file.write("HELLO".lower())`

Find the Error

1. ```
with open("File.txt") as file
  file.write("Hello World")
with open(File.txt) as f:
data = f.read()
print(data)
```
2. ```
filename = "File.txt"
file = open("filename", "r")
for line in file:
  print(line, end = ' ')
```
3. ```
filename = "File.txt"
file = open(filename, "r")
while True:
  print(file.readline())
```
4. ```
file = open("File.txt", "a")
write("Hello World again")
```

Answers

Fill in the Blanks

1. open()
2. with, as
3. "abc.bin", "rb"
4. 10
5. open, read, len
6. with, as, read
7. tree (or hierarchical)
8. root node or the root folder.
9. C:\ (also known as C drive)
10. current working directory
11. Relative
12. end-of-file (EOF) marker
13. file object
14. close()
15. ValueError
16. None
17. IOError
18. an empty string
19. path
20. file pointer
21. tell()
22. location 0
23. remove()
24. WindowsError
25. OSError
26. rmtree(),shutil
27. mkdirs()
28. os.path.join()
29. os.path.abspath()

State True or False

1. False
2. False
3. False
4. True
5. False
6. True
7. False
8. False
9. True
10. False
11. True
12. False
13. True
14. False
15. False
16. False
17. True
18. False
19. False

Multiple Choice Questions

1. (a) 2. 10 3. (b) 4. (c) 5. (a) 6. (b) 7. (a) 8. (d) 9. (a) 10. (a) 11. (b) 12. (b) 13. (d) 14. (b) 15. (a)

5

Creating a Hash File (or a message digest of a file)

Hashing is the process of transforming a string of characters of arbitrary length into a usually shorter fixed-length string that represents the original string. The output of the hash function is called *message digest*. Hashing is used in many encryption algorithms.

The hash or message digest is generated by a mathematical formula in such a way that it is extremely unlikely that some other text will produce the same hash value. Hashes are very important in security systems. They ensure that transmitted messages have not been tampered with. Consider the steps given below which helps to ensure that the message is not modified during transmission.

Step 1: The sender creates a hash of the message.

Step 2: The hash is encrypted using an encryption algorithm.

Step 3: The sender transmits the hash as well as the original message.

Step 4: The receiver receives the message and hash and decrypts both the message and the hash.

Step 5: The sender takes original message and again generates another hash from the received message.

Step 6: If the received hash is same as hash generated, indicates that the message was transmitted intact.

Thus, we see that hashing is widely used in cryptography. There are many hashing functions like MD5, SHA-1, etc. However, we will create hash using the SHA-1 hashing algorithm which generates a hash value which is 160 bits long.

In the program given below, instead of taking the entire file all at once, we have taken chunks of data. This is especially important when files are very large to fit in memory all at once. Processing data in small chunks (of 1024 bytes, here) makes efficient utilization of memory. The file to be hashed has been opened in the read in binary mode as binary files are more efficient than text files. In Python, hash functions are available in the hashlib module. The file is read in the while loop and on reaching the end, an empty byte is obtained. The program finally prints the message digest in hexadecimal representation using the hexdigest() method.

```
# Program to create a hash file
import hashlib
def hash_file(filename):
    hash = hashlib.sha1()       # make a hash object
    with open(filename,'rb') as file:
        chunk = 0
        while chunk != b":
            chunk = file.read(1024)
            hash.update(chunk)
```

```
    return hash.hexdigest()
text = hash_file("Body.txt")
print("Hash of file is : ",text)
```

OUTPUT

Hash of file is :   24134bdf497ce78a0903dfdb69d0019283faa8c3

6

Mail Merge Program

You must have already tried the Mail Merge feature of MS Word which is used to send the same letter to a large number of people. With this feature, you just have to type the contents that has to be sent to a number of people in one file. In another file, type the names of all the receivers of the email. Then merge both these files in such a way as if it was specifically written for an individual. Consider the files given below which have been used to illustrate how mail merge is practically realized through Python.

Note that to perform mail merge, we have created three files—Names.txt that stores names of the receivers, Body.txt that stores the content or body of the mail (or message) to be sent and the main program file which is basically a Python script that opens both the files and merges them.

In the code for the mail merge, we open both the files in reading mode and iterate over each name using a for loop. New files with name "[Name].txt" are created, where [Name] is the name of the receiver as specified in the file storing all the names of the receivers. The strip() method has been used to clean up leading and trailing whitespaces. This is especially important because while reading a line from the file, the newline '\n' character is also read. Finally, the write() method is used to write the body (contents of the mail) into the new [Name].txt files.

```
# Contents of Names.txt
Reema
Goransh

# Contents of Body.txt
Greetings !!!
This is to invite you to attend the National Conference at IIT Delhi on 29th August
2017.

Looking forward for your participation.

Registration Fess : Rs. 1000

Thanks and Regards,

Conference Convener

# Program for Mail Merge
with open("Names.txt",'r') as Names:
    with open("Body.txt",'r') as Body:
        text = Body.read()
        for name in Names:
```

```
            msg = "Hello "+ name + text
            with open(name.strip()+".txt",'w') as File:
                File.write(msg)
```

OUTPUT

```
#Contents of Reema.txt
Hello Reema
Greetings !!!
This is to invite you to attend the National Conference at IIT Delhi on 29th August
2017.

Looking forward for your participation.
Registration Fees : Rs. 1000
Thanks and Regards,
Conference Convener
```

```
#Contents of Goransh.txt
Hello Goransh
Greetings !!!
This is to invite you to attend the National Conference at IIT Delhi on 29th August
2017.
Looking forward for your participation.
Registration Fees : Rs. 1000

Thanks and Regards,

Conference Convener
```

Finding Resolution of an Image

JPEG (Joint Photographic Experts Group) is one of the most widely used compression techniques for image compression. Most of the image file formats have headers stored in the initial few bytes to retain some useful information about the file.

In the following program, we will find out the resolution of JPEG image by reading the information stored in the header.

```
# Program to find the resolution of an image

def find_res(filename):

    with open(filename,'rb') as img_file:    # open image in binary mode
        # height of image is at 164th position
        img_file.seek(163)
        # read the 2 bytes
        a = img_file.read(2)
        # calculate height
        height = (a[0] << 8) + a[1]
        # read next 2 bytes which stores the width
        a = img_file.read(2)
        # calculate width
        width = (a[0] << 8) + a[1]
    print("IMAGE RESOLUTION IS : ",width,"x",height)
find_res("C:\Python34\Icon.jpg")
```

OUTPUT
```
IMAGE RESOLUTION IS :  4352 x 769
```

In this program, we opened the image in binary mode as all non-text files must be open in this mode. In a JPEG file, the height of the image is stored in the header at 164th position followed by width of the image. Both this information are two bytes long. This two bytes information is converted into a number using the bitwise shift operator (<<) and finally, the resolution of the image is displayed.

Note The above program will run only for JPEG images as every file format uses a slightly different way to store the same information.

8 Data Structures

• Creating, Accessing, Updating, and Cloning Lists • List Methods and Functions • Functional Programming • Creating, Accessing, Updating, and Deleting Tuples • Working with Sets and Dictionaries • Nested Lists, Sets, Tuples, and Dictionaries • List and Dictionary Comprehensions

8.1 SEQUENCE

A *data structure* is a group of data elements that are put together under one name. Data structure defines a particular way of storing and organizing data in a computer so that it can be used efficiently.

> **Note** All data structures discussed in this chapter are compound data structure as they are made of simple elements. For example, if we have defined a list as List = [1,2,3,4,5], then List is a compound data structure having integers 1, 2, 3, 4, and 5, which are the simple or basic elements.

Sequence is the most basic data structure in Python. In the sequence data structure, each element has a specific index. This index value starts from zero and is automatically incremented for the next element in the sequence. In Python, sequence is the generic term for an ordered set. For example, we have already studied strings which are a sequence of characters. In this chapter, we will learn about lists and tuples, which are also a type of sequence.

Python has some basic built-in functions that help programmers to manipulate elements that form a part of a sequence. These functions include finding the length of a sequence, finding the largest and smallest elements in a sequence, etc. Other operations that can be performed on a sequence include indexing, slicing, adding, multiplying, and checking for membership.

8.2 LISTS

List is a versatile data type available in Python. It is a sequence in which elements are written as a list of comma-separated values (items) between square brackets. The key feature of a list is that it can have elements that belong to different data types. Let us create lists by writing different comma-separated values between square brackets.

The syntax of defining a list can be given as,

```
List_variable = [val1, val2,...]
```

`>>> list_A = [1,2,3,4,5]`
`>>> print(list_A)`
`[1, 2, 3, 4, 5]`
	`>>> list_B = ['A', 'b', 'C', 'd', 'E']`
	`>>> print(list_B)`
	`['A', 'b', 'C', 'd', 'E']`

`>>> list_C = ["Good", "Going"]`
`>>> print(list_C)`
`['Good', 'Going']`
	`>>> list_D = [1, 'a', "bcd"]`
	`>>> print(list_D)`
	`[1, 'a', 'bcd']`

Note   List is mutable which means that value of its elements can be changed.

8.2.1 Access Values in Lists

Similar to strings, lists can also be sliced and concatenated. To access values in lists, square brackets are used to slice along with the index or indices to get value stored at that index. If you can recollect from the last chapter, the syntax for the slice operation is given as,

```
seq = List[start:stop:step]
```

For example,

```
seq = List[::2]  # get every other element, starting with index 0
seq = List[1::2] # get every other element, starting with index 1
```

Example 8.1   Program to demonstrate the slice operations used to access the elements of the list

```
num_list = [1,2,3,4,5,6,7,8,9,10]
print("num_list is : ", num_list)
print("First element in the list is ", num_list[0])
print("num_list[2:5] = ", num_list[2:5])
print("num_list[::2] = ", num_list[::2])
print("num_list[1::3] = ", num_list[1::3])

OUTPUT
num_list is :  [1, 2, 3, 4, 5, 6, 7, 8, 9, 10]
First element in the list is  1
num_list[2:5] =  [3, 4, 5]
num_list[::2] =  [1, 3, 5, 7, 9]
num_list[1::3] =  [2, 5, 8]
```

8.2.2 Updating Values in Lists

Once created, one or more elements of a list can be easily updated by giving the slice on the left-hand side of the assignment operator. You can also append new values in the list and remove existing value(s) from the list using the append() method and del statement respectively as shown in the following code.

Example 8.2 Program to illustrate updating values in a list

```
num_list = [1,2,3,4,5,6,7,8,9,10]
print("List is : ", num_list)
num_list[5] = 100
print("List after udpation is : ", num_list)
num_list.append(200)
print("List after appending a value is ", num_list)
del num_list[3]
print("List after deleting a value is ", num_list)
```

> **Programming Tip:** append() and insert() methods are list methods. They cannot be called on other values such as strings or integers.

OUTPUT
```
List is :  [1, 2, 3, 4, 5, 6, 7, 8, 9, 10]
List after udpation is :  [1, 2, 3, 4, 5, 100, 7, 8, 9, 10]
List after appending a value is  [1, 2, 3, 4, 5, 100, 7, 8, 9, 10, 200]
List after deleting a value is  [1, 2, 3, 5, 100, 7, 8, 9, 10, 200]
```

Note If you know exactly which element(s) to delete, use the del statement, otherwise use the remove() method to delete the unknown elements.

Example 8.3 Programs to illustrate deletion of numbers from a list using del statements

```
num_list = [1,2,3,4,5,6,7,8,9,10]   # a list is defined
del num_list[2:4]          # deletes numbers at index 2 and 3
print(num_list)
```

OUTPUT
```
[1, 2, 5, 6, 7, 8, 9, 10]
```

```
num_list = [1,2,3,4,5,6,7,8,9,10]   # a list is defined
del num_list[:]         # deletes all the numbers from the list
print(num_list)         # an empty list is printed
```

OUTPUT
```
[]
```

Can you now imagine what will happen if you write del num_list? Yes, the entire variables will be deleted. If you make any attempt to use this variable after the del statement, then an error will be generated. This is very much evident from the code given in the following example.

Example 8.4   Program to illustrate deletion of a list

```
num_list = [1,2,3,4,5,6,7,8,9,10]
del num_list
print(num_list)
```

> **Programming Tip:** When using slice operation, an IndexError is generated if the index is outside the list.

OUTPUT

```
Traceback (most recent call last):
  File "C:\Python34\Try.py", line 3, in <module>
    print(num_list)
NameError: name 'num_list' is not defined
```

To insert items from another list or sequence at a particular location, you can use the *slice operation*. This will result in the creation of a list within another list. The program given below demonstrates this concept.

Example 8.5   Program to insert a list in another list using the slice operation

```
num_list = [1, 9,11,13,15]
print("Original List : ", num_list)
num_list[2] = [3,5,7]
print("After inserting another list, the updated list is : ", num_list)
```

OUTPUT

```
Original List :  [1, 9, 11, 13, 15]
After inserting another list, the updated list is :  [1, 9, [3, 5, 7], 13, 15]
```

8.2.3 Nested Lists

Nested list means a list within another list. We have already said that a list has elements of different data types which can include even a list. For example, in the following code, list1 is a list that has another list at index 3.

Example 8.6   Program to illustrate nested list

```
list1 = [1, 'a', "abc", [2,3,4,5], 8.9]
i=0
while i<(len(list1)):
    print("List1[",i,"] = ",list1[i])
    i+=1
```

OUTPUT

```
List1[0] =  1
List1[1] =  a
List1[2] =  abc
List1[3] =  [2, 3, 4, 5]
List1[4] =  8.9
```

Remember that you can specify an element in the nested list by using a set of indices. For example, to print the second element of the nested list, we will write `print(list[3][1])`. The first index specifies the starting location of the nested list in the main list and the second index specifies the index of the element within the nested list.

8.2.4 Cloning Lists

If you want to modify a list and also keep a copy of the original list, then you should create a separate copy of the list (not just the reference). This process is called *cloning*. The slice operation is used to clone a list.

Example 8.7 Program to create a copy as well as the clone of the original list

```
list1 = [1,2,3,4,5,6,7,8,9,10]
list2 = list1                    #copies a list using reference
print("List1 = ", list1)
print("List2 = ", list2)    #both lists point to the same list
list3 = list1[2:6]
print("List3 = ", list3)     #list is a clone of list1

OUTPUT
List1 =  [1, 2, 3, 4, 5, 6, 7, 8, 9, 10]
List2 =  [1, 2, 3, 4, 5, 6, 7, 8, 9, 10]
List3 =  [3, 4, 5, 6]
```

8.2.5 Basic List Operations

Lists behave in the similar way as strings when operators like + (concatenation) and * (repetition) are used. It works similar in case of operations discussed in Table 8.1.

Table 8.1 Operations on Lists

Operation	Description	Example	Output
len	Returns length of list	`len([1,2,3,4,5,6,7,8,9,10])`	10
concatenation	Joins two lists	`[1,2,3,4,5] + [6,7,8,9,10]`	`[1, 2, 3, 4, 5, 6, 7, 8, 9, 10]`
repetition	Repeats elements in the list	`"Hello", "World"*2`	`['Hello', 'World', 'Hello', 'World']`
in	Checks if the value is present In the list	`'a' in ['a','e', 'i','o','u']`	True
not in	Checks if the value is not present In the list	`3 not in [0,2,4,6,8]`	True
max	Returns maximum value in the list	`>>> num_list = [6,3,7,0,1,2,4,9]` `>>> print(max(num_list))`	9
min	Returns minimum value in the list	`>>> num_list = [6,3,7,0,1,2,4,9]` `>>> print(min(num_list))`	0
sum	Adds the values in the list that has numbers	`num_list = [1,2,3,4,5,6,7,8,9,10]` `print("SUM = ", sum(num_list))`	SUM = 55

(Contd)

Table 8.1 *(Contd)*

Operation	Description	Example	Output
all	Returns True if all elements of the list are true (or if the list is empty)	`>>> num_list = [0,1,2,3]` `>>> print(all(num_list))`	`False`

any	Returns True if any element of the list is true. If the list is empty, returns False	`>>> num_list =`
		`[6,3,7,0,1,2,4,9]`
		`>>> print(any(num_list))`
			`True`

list	Converts an iterable (tuple, string, set, dictionary) to a list	`>>> list1 = list("HELLO")` `>>> print(list1)`	`['H', 'E', 'L', 'L', 'O']`

sorted	Returns a new sorted list. The original list is not sorted.	`>>> list1 = [3,4,1,2,7,8]`
		`>>> list2 = sorted(list1)`
		`>>> print(list2)`
			`[1, 2, 3, 4, 7, 8]`

Let us try to see some more examples to understand how indexing, slicing, and other operations are performed on lists.

```
>>> list_A = ["Hello", "World", "Good", "Morning"]
>>> print(list_A[2])   # index starts at 0
Good
>>> print(list_A[-3]) # 3rd elemnt from the end
World
>>> print(list_A[1:]) # prints all elements starting
from index 1
['World', 'Good', 'Morning']
```

Programming Tip: An error is generated if you try to delete an element from the list that is not present in the list.

8.2.6 List Aliasing

When we assign one variable/object to the other, both of them actually point to the same variable or object in memory. For example, when we assign one list object to another list object, both the objects point to the same list in a computer's memory. In such a case, the reference diagram looks can be given as,

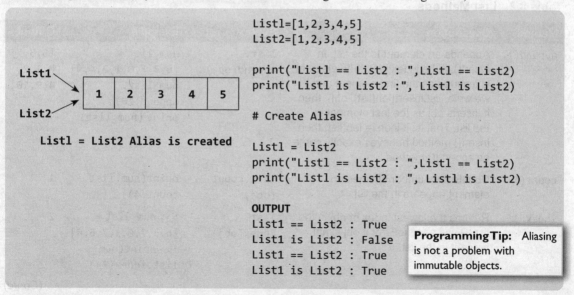

```
List1=[1,2,3,4,5]
List2=[1,2,3,4,5]

print("List1 == List2 : ",List1 == List2)
print("List1 is List2 :", List1 is List2)

# Create Alias

List1 = List2
print("List1 == List2 : ",List1 == List2)
print("List1 is List2 : ", List1 is List2)

OUTPUT
List1 == List2 : True
List1 is List2 : False
List1 == List2 : True
List1 is List2 : True
```

Programming Tip: Aliasing is not a problem with immutable objects.

In the above code, since the same list has two different names, List1 and List2 are **aliased**. Now, changes made in List1 will be reflected in List2 as well and vice versa. Although aliasing can be useful, it can sometime produce unexpected and undesirable results. Therefore, it is safer to avoid aliasing when working with mutable objects.

8.2.7 List Cloning

If you want to modify a list and also keep a copy of the original list, then you should create a separate copy of the list (not just the reference). This process is called *cloning*. The slice operation is used to clone a list.

Example 8.8   Program to create a copy as well as the clone of the original list

```
list1 = [1,2,3,4,5,6,7,8,9,10]
list2 = list1                #copies a list using reference
print("List1 = ", list1)
print("List2 = ", list2)     #both lists point to the same list
list3 = list1[2:6]
print("List3 = ", list3)     #list is a clone of list1

OUTPUT
List1 =  [1, 2, 3, 4, 5, 6, 7, 8, 9, 10]
List2 =  [1, 2, 3, 4, 5, 6, 7, 8, 9, 10]
List3 =  [3, 4, 5, 6]
```

8.2.8 List Methods

Python has various methods to help programmers work efficiently with lists. Some of these methods are summarized in Table 8.2.

> **Programming Tip:** Array elements can be removed using pop() or remove() method. While pop() returns the deleted value, remove() does not return. Moreover, pop() takes either no parameter or the index value as its parameter. But, remove() takes the element value itself as the parameter. If you give the index value in the parameter slot, it will throw an error.

Table 8.2   List Methods

Method	Description	Syntax	Example	Output
append()	Appends an element to the list. In insert(), if the index is 0, then element is inserted as the first element and if we write, list.insert(len(list), obj), then it inserts obj as the last element in the list. That is, if index= len(list) then insert() method behaves exactly same as append() method.	list.append(obj)	num_list = [6,3,7,0,1,2,4,9] num_list.append(10) print (num_list)	[6,3,7, 0,1,2, 4,9,10]
count()	Counts the number of times an element appears in the list.	list.count(obj)	print(num_list.count(4))	1
index()	Returns the lowest index of obj in the list. Gives a ValueError if obj is not present in the list.	list.index(obj)	>>> num_list = [6,3,7,0,3,7,6,0] >>> print(num_list.index(7))	2

(Contd)

Table 8.2 *(Contd)*

Method	Description	Syntax	Example	Output

insert()	Inserts obj at the specified index in the list.	list. insert(index, obj)	>>> num_list = [6,3,7,0,3,7,6,0]
			>>> num_list. insert(3, 100)
			>>> print(num_list)
				[6,3,7, 100,0, 3,7,6, 0]

pop()	Removes the element at the specified index from the list. Index is an optional parameter. If no index is specified, then removes the last object (or element) from the list.	list. pop([index])	num_list = [6,3,7,0,1,2,4,9] print(num_list. pop()) print(num_list)	9 [6, 3, 7, 0, 1, 2, 4]

remove()	Removes or deletes obj from the list. ValueError is generated if obj is not present in the list. If multiple copies of obj exists in the list, then the first value is deleted.	list. remove(obj)	>>> num_list = [6,3,7,0,1,2,4,9]
			>>> num_list. remove(0)
			>>> print(num_list)
				[6,3,7, 1,2,4, 9]

reverse()	Reverse the elements in the list.	list. reverse()	>>> num_list = [6,3,7,0,1,2,4,9]
			>>> num_list. reverse()
			>>>print(num_list)
				[9, 4, 2, 1, 0, 7, 3, 6]

sort()	Sorts the elements in the list.	list.sort()	>>> num_list = [6,3,7,0,1,2,4,9]
			>>> num_list. sort()
			>>> print(num_list)
				[0, 1, 2, 3, 4, 6, 7, 9]

extend()	Adds the elements in a list to the end of another list. Using + or += on a list is similar to using extend().	list1. extend(list2)	>>> num_list1 = [1,2,3,4,5]
			>>> num_list2 = [6,7,8,9,10]
			>>> num_list1. extend(num_list2)
			>>>print(num_list1)
				[1, 2, 3, 4, 5, 6, 7, 8, 9, 10]

Key points to remember
- insert(), remove(), and sort() methods only modify the list and do not return any value. If you print the return values of these methods, you will get None. This is a design principle that is applicable to all mutable data structures in Python. The code given below illustrates this point.

Example 8.9   To print the return values

```
>>> num_list = [100, 200, 300, 400]
>>> print(num_list.insert(2, 250))
```

Programming Tip: It is safer to avoid aliasing when you are working with mutable objects.

OUTPUT

None

- When one list is assigned to another list using the assignment operator (=), then a new copy of the list is not made. Instead, assignment makes the two variables point to the one list in memory. This is also known as *aliasing*.

Example 8.10   Program that uses the assignment operator to assign one list to another list variable

```
num_list1 = [1,2,3,4,5]
num_list2 = num_list1
print(num_list2)
```

OUTPUT

[1, 2, 3, 4, 5]

In the above code, the two lists, num_list1 and num_list2, point to the same memory location but are identified using two different names. This means that the two lists are **aliased**. Since lists are mutable, changes made with one alias affect the other.

Note   An *alias* is a second name for a piece of data. In Python, aliasing happens whenever one variable's value is assigned to another variable.

- The sort() method uses ASCII values to sort the values in the list. This means that uppercase letter comes before lowercase letters and numbers comes even before the uppercase letters. The functionality of the sort() method is clearly evident from the code given below.

Example 8.11   Program to show the sort() mentioned

```
list1 = ['1', 'a', "abc", '2', 'B', "Def"]
list1.sort()
print(list1)
```

OUTPUT

[1, 2, 'B', 'Def', 'a', 'abc']

- Items in a list can also be deleted by assigning an empty list to a slice of elements as shown below.

Example 8.12 Program to delete items using empty list

```
list = ['p','r','o','g','r','a','m']
list[2:5] = []
print(list)
```

OUTPUT

```
['p', 'r', 'a', 'm']
```

8.2.9 Using Lists as Stack

Stack is an important data structure which stores its elements in an ordered manner. We will explain the concept of stacks using an analogy. You must have seen a pile of plates where one plate is placed on top of another as shown in Figure 8.1. Now, when you want to remove a plate, you remove the topmost plate first. Hence, you can add and remove an element (i.e. a plate) only at/from one position which is the topmost position.

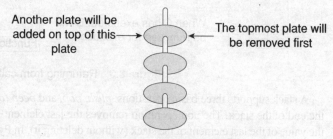

Figure 8.1 A stack of plates

Stack is a linear data structure which uses the same principle, i.e., the elements in a stack are added and removed only from one end. Hence, a stack is called a **LIFO** (Last-In-First-Out) data structure, as the element that was inserted last is the first one to be taken out.

Now the question is, where do we need stacks in computer science? The answer is in function calls. Consider an example, where we are executing function A. In the course of its execution, function A calls another function B. Function B in turn calls another function C, which calls function D. In order to keep track of the returning point of each active function, a special stack called system stack or call stack is used. Whenever a function calls another function, the calling function is pushed onto the top of the stack. This is because after the called function gets executed, the control is passed back to the calling function. Look at Figure 8.2 which shows this concept.

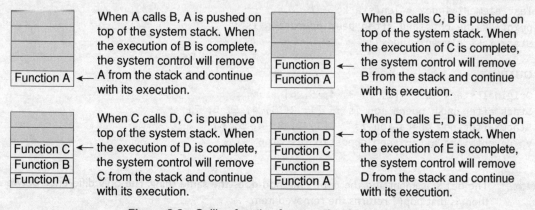

Figure 8.2 Calling function from another function

Now, when function E is executed, function D will be removed from the top of the stack and executed. Once function D gets completely executed, function C will be removed from the stack for execution. The whole procedure will be repeated until all the functions get executed. Let us look at the stack after each function is executed. This is shown in Figure 8.3. The system stack ensures a proper execution order of functions. Therefore, stacks are frequently used in situations where the order of processing is very important, especially when the processing needs to be postponed until other conditions are fulfilled.

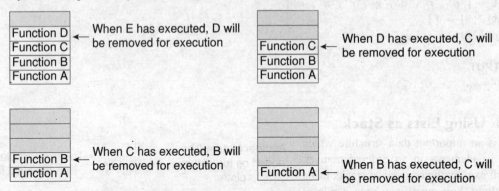

Figure 8.3   Returning from called functions

A stack supports three basic operations: *push, pop*, and *peep (or peek)*. The push operation adds an element at the end of the stack. The pop operation removes the last element from the stack. And, the peep operation returns the value of the last element of the stack (without deleting it). In Python, the list methods make it very easy to use a list as a stack. For example, to push an element in the stack, you will use the append() method, to pop an element use the pop() method, and for peep operation use the slicing operation as illustrated in the program given below.

Example 8.13   Program to illustrate operations on a stack

```
stack = [1,2,3,4,5,6]
print("Original stack is : ", stack)
stack.append(7)
print("Stack after push operation is : ", stack)
stack.pop()
print("Stack after pop operation is : ", stack)
last_element_index = len(stack) - 1
print("Value obtained after peep operation is : ",
stack[last_element_index])
```

OUTPUT
```
Original stack is :  [1, 2, 3, 4, 5, 6]
Stack after push operation is :  [1, 2, 3, 4, 5, 6, 7]
Stack after pop operation is :  [1, 2, 3, 4, 5, 6]
Value obtained after peep operation is :  6
```

Note   The del statement and the pop() method does the same thing. The only difference between them is that pop() returns the removed item.

8.2.10 Using Lists as Queues

Queue is an important data structure which stores its elements in an ordered manner. For example, consider the analogies given below.

- People moving on an escalator. The people who got on the escalator first will be the first one to step out of it.
- People waiting for a bus. The first person standing in the line will be the first one to get into the bus.
- People standing outside the ticketing window of a cinema hall. The first person in the line will get the ticket first and thus will be the first one to move out of it.
- Luggage kept on conveyor belts. The bag which was placed first will be the first to come out at the other end.
- Cars lined at a toll bridge. The first car to reach the bridge will be the first to leave.

In all these examples, we see that the element at the first position is served first. Same is the case with queue data structure. A queue is a **FIFO** (First-In-First-Out) data structure in which the element that is inserted first is the first one to be taken out. The elements in a queue are added at one end and removed from the other end. In computer systems, the operating system makes full use of queues for the following tasks.

- To maintain waiting lists for a single shared resource like printer, disk, CPU, etc.
- To transfer data asynchronously (data not necessarily received at same rate as sent) between two processes (IO buffers), e.g., pipes, file IO, and sockets.
- As buffers on MP3 players and portable CD players, iPod playlist, etc.
- Handling interrupts. When programming a real-time system that can be interrupted, for example, by a mouse click, it is necessary to process the interrupts immediately; before proceeding with the current job. If the interrupts have to be handled in the order of arrival, then a FIFO queue is the appropriate data structure.
- Queues are also used in the playlist of jukebox to add songs to the end and play from the front of the list.

Queue supports three basic operations—*insert, delete,* and *peep (or peek)*. In Python, you can easily implement a queue by using the append() method to insert an element at the end of the queue, pop() method with an index 0 to delete the first element from the queue, and slice operation to print the value of the last the element in the queue. The program given below illustrates this concepts.

Example 8.14 Program to show the implementation of a queue using list data structure

```
queue = [1,2,3,4,5,6]
print("Original queue is : ", queue)
queue.append(7)
print("Queue after insertion is : ", queue)
queue.pop(0)
print("Queue after deletion is : ", queue)
print("Value obtained after peep operation is : ", queue[(len(queue) - 1)])
```

OUTPUT

```
Original queue is :  [1, 2, 3, 4, 5, 6]
Queue after insertion is :  [1, 2, 3, 4, 5, 6, 7]
Queue after deletion is :  [2, 3, 4, 5, 6, 7]
Value obtained after peep operation is :  7
```

8.2.11 List Comprehensions

Till now, we know that to create an empty list, we need to write, List = []. Just check how a list of cubes is created in the program given below.

Example 8.15   Program to make a list of cubes

```
cubes = []   # an empty list
for i in range(11):
    cubes.append(i**3)
print("Cubes of numbers from 1-10 : ", cubes)
```

OUTPUT

```
Cubes of numbers from 1-10 :   [0, 1, 8, 27, 64, 125, 216, 343, 512, 729, 1000]
```

Note   You can also create an empty list by using the built-in list type object. For example, by writing L = list(), an empty list L is created.

Python also supports computed lists called *list comprehensions* having the following syntax.

```
List = [expression for variable in sequence]
```

Where, the expression is evaluated once, for every item in the sequence.

List comprehensions help programmers to create lists in a concise way. This is mainly beneficial to make new lists where each element is the obtained by applying some operations to each member of another sequence or iterable. List comprehension is also used to create a subsequence of those elements that satisfy a certain condition.

Note   An iterable is an object that can be used repeatedly in subsequent loop statements, say for example, for loop.

Example 8.16   Program to combine three lines of code into one

```
>>> cubes = [i**3 for i in range(11)]
>>> print(cubes)
```

OUTPUT

```
[0, 1, 8, 27, 64, 125, 216, 343, 512, 729, 1000]
```

You can also use the list comprehension to combine the elements of two lists. For example, observe the code given below.

Example 8.17   Program to combine and print elements of two list using list comprehension

```
print([(x, y) for x in [10,20,30] for y in [30,10,40] if x != y])
```

OUTPUT

```
[(10, 30), (10, 40), (20, 30), (20, 10), (20, 40), (30, 10), (30, 40)]
```

In the code, two values, one from each list is used to create a new list only if the two values are not same.

8.2.12 Looping in Lists

Python's for and in constructs are extremely useful especially when working with lists. The for var in list statement is an easy way to access each element in a list (or any other sequence). For example, in the following code, the for loop is used to access each item in the list.

```
for i in list:
    print(i)
```

Example 8.18 Program to find the sum and mean of elements in a list

```
num_list = [1,2,3,4,5,6,7,8,9,10]
sum = 0
for i in num_list:
    sum += i
print("Sum of elements in the list = ", sum)
print("Average of elements in the list = ",
float(sum/float(len(num_list))))
```

OUTPUT

```
Sum of elements in the list =  55
Average of elements in the list =  5.5
```

Python offers multiple ways to access a list. Some of them are discussed in this section.

- **Using the enumerate() function:** This is used when you want to print both index as well as an item in the list. The enumerate() function returns an enumerate object which contains the index and value of all the items of the list as a tuple.

Example 8.19 Program to illustrate the use of enumerate() to print an individual item and its index in the list

```
num_list = [1,2,3,4,5]
for index, i in enumerate(num_list):
    print(i, " is at index : ", index)
```

OUTPUT

```
1  is a t index :  0
2  is a t index :  1
3  is a t index :  2
4  is a t index :  3
5  is a t index :  4
```

- **Using the range() function:** If you need to print index, then you can use the range() function as shown in the code given below.

Example 8.20   Program to print the index of values in a list

```
num_list = [1,2,3,4,5]
for i in range(len(num_list)):
    print("index : ", i)
```

> **Programming Tip:** The index must be an integer. If you specify a non-integer number as the index, then TypeError will be generated

OUTPUT
```
index :  0
index :  1
index :  2
index :  3
index :  4
```

- **Using an iterator:** You can create an iterator using the built-in `iter()` function. The iterator is used to loop over the elements of the list. For this, the iterator fetches the value and then automatically points to the next element in the list when it is used with the `next()` method.

Example 8.21   Program to print the elements in the list using an iterator

```
num_list = [1,2,3,4,5]
it = iter(num_list)
for i in range(len(num_list)):
    print("Element at index ", i, " is : ", next(it))
```

OUTPUT
```
Element at index  0  is :  1
Element at index  1  is :  2
Element at index  2  is :  3
Element at index  3  is :  4
Element at index  4  is :  5
```

> **Note**   An iterator is often used to wrap an iterable and return each item of interest. All iterators are iterable, but all iterables are *not* iterators. An iterator can only be used in a single `for` loop, whereas an iterable can be used repeatedly in subsequent `for` loops.

Example 8.22   Write a program to generate prime numbers with the help of an algorithm given by the Greek Mathematician named Eratosthenes.

```
def SieveOfEratosthenes(n):

    # Create a boolean array "prime[0..n]" and initialize
    # all entries it as true. A value in prime[i] will
    # finally be false if i is Not a prime, else true.
```

```
    prime = [True for i in range(n + 1)]
    num = 2
    while (num * num <= n):

        # If prime[num] is not changed, then it is a prime
        if (prime[num] == True):

            # Update all multiples of p
            for i in range(num ** 2, n + 1, num):
                prime[i] = False
        num += 1
    prime[0]= False
    prime[1]= False
    # Print all prime numbers
    for num in range(n + 1):
        if prime[num]:
            print(num, end = "  ")

n = 50
print( "Prime numbers smaller than ",n, " are : ")
SieveOfEratosthenes(n)
OUTPUT
Prime numbers smaller than  50  are :
2  3  5  7  11  13  17  19  23  29  31  37  41  43  47
```

8.3 FUNCTIONAL PROGRAMMING

Functional programming decomposes a problem into a set of functions. The map(), filter(), and reduce() functions which we will discuss in this section form a part of functional programming tools that work on all list items. However, it is recommended to use list comprehensions instead of these functions where possible.

8.3.1 filter() Function

The filter() function constructs a list from those elements of the list for which a function returns True. The syntax of the filter() function is given as,

```
filter(function, sequence)
```

As per the syntax, the filter() function returns a sequence that contains items from the sequence for which the function is True. If *sequence* is a string, Unicode, or a tuple, then the result will be of the same type; otherwise, it is always a list.

Example 8.23   Program to create a list of numbers divisible by 2 or 4 using list comprehension

```
def check(x):
    if (x % 2 == 0 or x % 4 == 0):
        return 1
# call check() for every value between 2 to 21
```

Programming Tip: Do not add or remove elements from the list during iteration.

```
evens = list(filter(check, range(2, 22)))
print(evens)
```

OUTPUT
```
[2, 4, 6, 8, 10, 12, 14, 16, 18, 20]
```

From the output of the above program, we see that the filter() function returns True or False. Functions that return a *boolean* value are called *predicates*. Only those values in the range that are divisible by 2 or 4 are included in the newly created list.

8.3.2 map() Function

The map() function applies a particular function to every element of a list. Its syntax is same as the filter function.

```
map(function, sequence)
```

After applying the specified function on the sequence, the map() function returns the modified list. The map() function calls function(item) for each item in the sequence and returns a list of the return values.

Example 8.24   Program that adds 2 to every value in the list

```
def add_2(x):
    x += 2
    return x
num_list = [1,2,3,4,5,6,7]
print("Original List is : ", num_list)
new_list = list(map(add_2, num_list))
print("Modified List is : ", new_list)
```

OUTPUT
```
Original List is :  [1, 2, 3, 4, 5, 6, 7]
Modified List is :  [3, 4, 5, 6, 7, 8, 9]
```

Note that in the above code, the map() function calls add_2() which adds 2 to every value in the list. You can even pass more than one sequence in the map() function. But in this case, remember two things.

- First, the function must have as many arguments as there are sequences.
- Second, each argument is called with the corresponding item from each sequence (or None if one sequence is shorter than another).

Example 8.25   Program to pass more than one sequence to the map() function

```
def add(x,y):
    return x+y
list1 = [1,2,3,4,5]
```

```
list2 = [6,7,8,9,10]
list3 = list(map(add, list1, list2))
print("Sum of ", list1, " and ", list2, " = ", list3)
```

OUTPUT

```
Sum of  [1, 2, 3, 4, 5]  and  [6, 7, 8, 9, 10]  =  [7, 9, 11, 13, 15]
```

8.3.3 reduce() Function

The reduce() function with syntax as given below returns a single value generated by calling the function on the first two items of the sequence, then on the result and the next item, and so on.

```
reduce(function, sequence)
```

Example 8.26　Program to calculate the sum of values in a list using the reduce() function (Refer Figure 8.4)

```
import functools #functools is a module that contains the function reduce()
def add(x,y):
    return x+y
num_list = [1,2,3,4,5]
print("Sum of values in list = ")
print(functools.reduce(add, num_list))
```

OUTPUT

```
Sum of values in list =  15
```

Figure 8.4　reduce() function

Key points to remember

- If there is only one item in the sequence, then its value is returned.
- If the sequence is empty, an exception is raised.
- Creating a list in a very extensive range will generate a MemoryError or OverflowError. For example,

```
List = [5*i for i in range(100**100)]
```

When you execute the above statement, you will get the system overflow problem. Python window will stop responding and you will have to press Ctrl+C to come out of this state.

PROGRAMMING EXAMPLES

Program 8.1 Write a program that creates a list of numbers from 1–20 that are either divisible by 2 or divisible by 4 without using the filter function.

```
div_2_4 = []
for i in range(2, 22):
```

```
    if(i%2 == 0 or i%4 == 0):
        div_2_4.append(i)
print(div_2_4)
```

OUTPUT

```
[2, 4, 6, 8, 10, 12, 14, 16, 18, 20]
```

Program 8.2 Write a program using filter function to a list of squares of numbers from 1–10. Then use the for...in construct to sum the elements in the list generated.

```
def square(x):
    return(x**2)
squares = []
squares = list(filter(square, range(1, 11)))
print("List of squares in the range 1-10 = ", squares)
sum = 0
for i in squares:
    sum += i
print("Sum of squares in the range 1-10 = ", sum)
```

OUTPUT

```
List of squares in the range 1-10 =  [1, 4, 9, 16, 25, 36, 49, 64, 81, 100]
Sum of squares in the range 1-10 =   385
```

Program 8.3 Write a program the defines a list of countries that are a member of BRICS. Check whether a country is a member of BRICS or not.

```
country = ["Brazil", "India", "China", "Russia", "Sri Lanka"]
is_member = input("Enter the name of country : ")
if is_member in country:
    print(is_member, "has also joined BRICS")
else:
    print(is_member, " is not a member of BRICS")
```

OUTPUT

```
Enter the name of country : Pakistan
Pakistan is not a member of BRICS
```

Program 8.4 Write a program to create a list of numbers in the range 1 to 10. Then delete all the even numbers from the list and print the final list.

```
num_list = []
for i in range(1, 11):
    num_list.append(i)
print("Original List : ", num_list)
for index, i in enumerate(num_list):
    if(i%2==0):
```

```
        del num_list[index]
print("List after deleting even numbers : ",num_list)
```

OUTPUT

```
Original List :  [1, 2, 3, 4, 5, 6, 7, 8, 9, 10]
List after deleting even numbers :  [1, 3, 5, 7, 9]
```

Program 8.5 Write a program to print index at which a particular value exists. If the value exists at multiple locations in the list, then print all the indices. Also, count the number of times that value is repeated in the list.

```
num_list = [1,2,3,4,5,6,5,4,3,2,1]
num = int(input("Enter the value to be searched : "))
i=0
count = 0
while i<len(num_list):
    if num == num_list[i]:
        print(num, " found at location", i)
        count += 1
    i += 1
print(num, " appears ", count, " times in the list")
```

OUTPUT

```
Enter the value to be searched : 4
4  found at location 3
4  found at location 7
4  appears  2  times in the list
list_words = []
```

Program 8.6 Write a program that creates a list of words by combining the words in two individual lists.

```
list_words = []
for x in ["Hello ", "World "]:
    for y in ["Python", "Programming"]:
        word = x + y
        list_words.append(word)
print("List combining the words in two individual lists is : ", list_words)
```

OUTPUT

```
List combining the words in two individual lists is :  ['Hello Python', 'Hello
Programming', 'World Python', 'World Programming']
```

Program 8.7 Write a program that forms a list of first character of every word in another list.

```
list1 = ["Hello", "Welcome", "To", "The", "World", "Of", "Python"]
letters = []
```

```
for word in list1:
    letters.append(word[0])
print(letters)
```

OUTPUT

```
['H', 'W', 'T', 'T', 'W', 'O', 'P']
```

Program 8.8 Write a program to remove all duplicates from a list.

```
num_list = [1,2,3,4,5,6,7,6,5,4]
print("Original List : ", num_list)
i=0
while i<len(num_list):
    num = num_list[i]
    for j in range(i+1, len(num_list)):
        val = num_list[j]
        if val == num:
            num_list.pop(j)
    i = i + 1
print("List after removing duplicates : ", num_list)
```

OUTPUT

```
Original List :  [1, 2, 3, 4, 5, 6, 7, 6, 5, 4]
List after removing duplicates :  [1, 2, 3, 4, 5, 6, 7]
```

Program 8.9 Write a program to create a list of numbers in the specified range in particular steps. Reverse the list and print its values.

```
num_list = []
m = int(input("Enter the starting of the range : "))
n = int(input("Enter the ending of the range : "))
o = int(input("Enter the steps in the range : "))
for i in range(m,n, o):
    num_list.append(i)
print("Original List :", num_list)
num_list.reverse()
print("Reversed List : ", num_list)
```

OUTPUT

```
Enter the starting of the range : 2
Enter the ending of the range : 30
Enter the steps in the range : 3
Original List : [2, 5, 8, 11, 14, 17, 20, 23, 26, 29]
Reversed List :  [29, 26, 23, 20, 17, 14, 11, 8, 5, 2]
```

Program 8.10 Write a program that creates a list of 10 random integers. Then create two lists—Odd List and Even List that has all odd and even values in the list respectively.

```
import random
num_list = []
for i in range(10):
    val = random.randint(1, 100)
    num_list.append(val)
print("Original List : ", num_list)
even_list = []
odd_list = []
for i in range(len(num_list)):
    if(num_list[i] % 2 == 0):
        even_list.append(num_list[i])
    else:
        odd_list.append(num_list[i])
print("Even Numbers List = ", even_list)
print("Odd Numbers List = ", odd_list)
```

OUTPUT

```
Original List : [93, 27, 9, 68, 68, 88, 14, 33, 64, 21]
Even Numbers List = [68, 68, 88, 14, 64]
Odd Numbers List = [93, 27, 9, 33, 21]
```

Program 8.11 Write a program to create a list of first 20 odd numbers using the shortcut method.

```
odd = [2*i + 1 for i in range(20)]
print(odd)
```

OUTPUT

```
[1, 3, 5, 7, 9, 11, 13, 15, 17, 19, 21, 23, 25, 27, 29, 31, 33, 35, 37, 39]
```

Program 8.12 Write a program that passes a list to a function that scales each element in the list by a factor of 10. Print the list values at different stages to show that changes made to one list is automatically reflected in the other list.

```
def change(list1):
    for i in range(len(list1)):
        list1[i] = list1[i] * 10
    print("After change in function, List is : ", list1)
num_list = [1,2,3,4,5,6]
print("Original List is : ", num_list)
change(num_list)
print("List after change is : ", num_list)
```

OUTPUT

```
Original List is :  [1, 2, 3, 4, 5, 6]
After change in function, List is :  [10, 20, 30,
40, 50, 60]
List after change is :  [10, 20, 30, 40, 50, 60]
```

> **Programming Tip:** Creating a list in a very extensive range will result in a **OverflowError**. This can be corrected by using generators.

Program 8.13 Write a program that has a list of both positive and negative numbers. Create another list using `filter()` that has only positive values.

```
def is_positive(x):
    if x>=0:
        return x
num_list = [10, -20, 30, -40, 50, -60, 70, -80, 90, -100]
List = []
List = list(filter(is_positive, num_list))
print("Positive Values List = ",List)
```

OUTPUT

```
Positive Values List =  [10, 30, 50, 70, 90]
```

Program 8.14 Write a program that converts strings of all uppercase characters into strings of all lowercase characters using the `map()` function.

```
def to_lower(str):
    return str.lower()
list1 = ["HELLO", "WELCOME", "TO", "PYTHON"]
list2 = list(map(to_lower,list1))
print("List in lowercase characters is : ", list2)
```

OUTPUT

```
List in lowercase characters is :  ['hello', 'welcome', 'to', 'python']
```

Program 8.15 Write a program using `map()` function to create a list of squares of numbers in the range 1–10.

```
def squares(x):
    return x*x
sq_list = list(map(squares, range(1,11)))
print("List of squares from 1-10 : ", sq_list)
```

OUTPUT

```
List of squares from 1-10 :  [1, 4, 9, 16, 25, 36, 49, 64, 81, 100]
```

Program 8.16 Write a program to combine values in two lists using list comprehension. Combine only those values of a list that are multiples of values in the first list.

```
print([(x, y) for x in [10,20,30,50] for y in [35,40,55,60] if y % x == 0 or x%y == 0])
```

OUTPUT

```
[(10, 40), (10, 60), (20, 40), (20, 60), (30, 60)]
```

Program 8.17 Write a program that converts a list of temperatures in Celsius into Fahrenheit.

```
def convert_to_F(Temp_C):
    return ((float(9)/5)*Temp_C + 32)
Temp_in_C = (36.5, 37, 37.5,39)
Temp_in_F = list(map(convert_to_F, Temp_in_C))
print("List of temperatures in Celsius : ", Temp_in_C)
print("List of temperatures in Fahrenheit : ", Temp_in_F)
```

OUTPUT

```
List of temperatures in Celsius :  (36.5, 37, 37.5, 39)
List of temperatures in Fahrenheit :  [97.7, 98.60000000000001, 99.5, 102.2]
```

Program 8.18 Write a program to find largest value in a list using reduce() function.

```
import functools
def max_ele(x,y):
    return x>y
num_list = [4,1,8,2,9,3,0]
print("Largest value in the list is : ", functools.reduce(max, num_list))
```

OUTPUT

```
Largest value in the list is :  9
```

Program 8.19 Write a program that has a list of functions that scales a number by a factor of 2, 3, and 4. Call each function in the list on a given number.

```
L = [lambda x: x * 2,lambda x: x * 3, lambda x: x * 4]
for f in L:
    print(f(5))
print("\n Multiplying the value of 100 by 2 we get : ",(L[0](100)))
```

OUTPUT

```
10 15 20
Multiplying the value of 100 by 2 we get :  200
```

Program 8.20 Write a program to generate in the Fibonacci sequence and store it in a list. Then find the sum of the even-valued terms.

```
a = 0
b = 1
n = int(input("Enter the number of terms : "))
i=2
```

```
List = [a,b]
while i<n:
    s = a + b
    List.append(s)
    a = b
    b = s
    i += 1
print(List)
i=0
sum = 0
while i<n:
    sum += List[i]
    i += 2
print("SUM = ", sum)
```

OUTPUT

```
Enter the number of terms : 10
[0, 1, 1, 2, 3, 5, 8, 13, 21, 34]
SUM =  33
```

Program 8.21 Write a program to add two matrices (using nested lists).

```
X = [[2,5,4],
    [1 ,3,9],
    [7 ,6, 2]]
Y = [[1,8,5],
    [7,3,6],
    [4,0,9]]
result = [[0,0,0],
         [0,0,0],
         [0,0,0]]
for i in range(len(X)):
    for j in range(len(X[0])):
        result[i][j] = X[i][j] + Y[i][j]
for r in result:
    print(r)
```

OUTPUT

```
[3, 13, 9]
[8, 6, 15]
[11, 6, 11]
```

Program 8.22 Write a program to find the median of a list of numbers.

```
List = []
n = int(input("Enter the number of elements to be inserted in the list : "))
for i in range(n):
```

```
   print("Enter number ", i + 1, " : ")
   num = int(input())
   List.append(num)
print("Sorted List is......")
List = sorted(List)
print(List)
i = len(List) - 1
if n%2 != 0:
   print("MEDIAN = ", List[i//2])
else:
   print("MEDIAN = ", (List[i//2] + List[i+1//2])/2)
```

OUTPUT

```
Enter the number of elements to be inserted in the list : 6
Enter number  1  :  2
Enter number  2  :  9
Enter number  3  :  1
Enter number  4  :  7
Enter number  5  :  4
Enter number  6  :  8
Sorted List is......
[1, 2, 4, 7, 8, 9]
MEDIAN =  6.5
```

Program 8.23 Write a program to calculate distance between two points.

```
import math
p1 = []
p2 = []
x1 = int(input("Enter the x co-ordinate of starting point : "))
y1 = int(input("Enter the y co-ordinate of starting point : "))
x2 = int(input("Enter the x co-ordinate of ending point : "))
y2 = int(input("Enter the y co-ordinate of ending point : "))
p1.append(x1)
p1.append(x2)
p2.append(x2)
p2.append(y2)
distance = math.sqrt( ((p1[0]-p2[0])**2)+((p1[1]-p2[1])**2) )
print("DISTANCE = %f" %distance)
```

OUTPUT

```
Enter the x co-ordinate of starting point : 2
Enter the y co-ordinate of starting point : 4
Enter the x co-ordinate of ending point : 7
Enter the y co-ordinate of ending point : 9
DISTANCE = 5.385165
```

Program 8.24 Write a program to circulate the values of N variables.

```
def circulate(L, n):
print("Circulating the elements of list")
for i in range(0,n):
val = L.pop(0)
L.append(val)
print(L)
n = int(input("Enter number of values:"))
L = []
for i in range(0,n):
val = int(input("Enter a value:"))
L.append(val)
circulate(L,n)
```

OUTPUT

```
Enter number of values:5
Enter a value:1
Enter a value:2
Enter a value:3
Enter a value:4
Enter a value:5
Circulating the elements of list
[2,3,4,5,1]
[3,4,5,1,2]
[4,5,1,2,3]
[5,1,2,3,4]
[1,2,3,4,5]
```

8.4 TUPLE

Like lists, tuple is another data structure supported by Python. It is very similar to lists but differs in two things.

- First, a tuple is a sequence of *immutable* objects. This means that while you can change the value of one or more items in a list, you cannot change the values in a tuple.
- Second, tuples use parentheses to define its elements whereas lists use square brackets.

8.4.1 Creating Tuple

Creating a tuple is very simple and almost similar to creating a list. For creating a tuple, generally you need to just put the different comma-separated values within a parentheses as shown below.

Tup1 = (val 1, val 2,...), where val (or values) can be an integer, a floating number, a character, or a string. Consider the following examples and observe their outputs.

Example 8.27 Programs to show how to create the different types of tuples

```
Tup1 = ()    # Creates an empty tuple
print(Tup1)
```

```
OUTPUT
()
```

```
Tup1 = (5)    # Creates a tuple with a single element
print(Tup1)
```

```
OUTPUT
5
```

```
Tup1 = (1,2,3,4,5)    # Creates a tuple of integers
print(Tup1)
Tup2 = ('a','b','c','d')     # Creates a tuple of characters
print(Tup2)
Tup3 = ("abc","def","ghi")  #Creates a tuple of strings
print(Tup3)
Tup4 = (1.2,2.3,3.4,4.5)  #Creates a tuple of floating point numbers
print(Tup4)
Tup5 = (1,"abc",2.3,'d')  #Creates a tuple of mixed values
print(Tup5)
```

```
OUTPUT
(1, 2, 3, 4, 5)
('a', 'b', 'c', 'd')
('abc', 'def', 'ghi')
(1.2, 2.3, 3.4, 4.5)
(1, 'abc', 2.3, 'd')
```

Key points to remember

- Any set of multiple, comma-separated values written without an identifying symbol like brackets [ ] (because it specifies a list) and parentheses ( ) (for tuples), etc., are treated as tuples by default. Some examples of such tuples are given below.

```
# Tuple with parentheses
print('a', "bcd", 2, 4.6)

OUTPUT
a bcd 2 4.6
```

```
# Default tuple without parentheses
a,b = 10, 20
print(a,b)

OUTPUT
10 20
```

- If you want to create a tuple with a single element, then you must add a comma after the element. In the absence of a comma, Python treats the element as an ordinary data type.

Example 8.28   Programs to demonstrate the necessity of having a comma in the tuple

```
Tup = (10,) # comma after first element
print(type(Tup))

OUTPUT
<type 'tuple'>
```

```
Tup = (10) # comma missing
print(type(Tup))

OUTPUT
<type 'int'>
```

8.4.2 Utility of Tuples

In real-world applications, tuples are extremely useful for representing records or structures as we call in other programming languages. These structures store related information about a subject together. The information belongs to different data types. For example, a tuple that stores information about a student can have elements like roll_no, name, course, total_marks, avg, etc. If you carefully observe, these individual elements can have different data types. For example, roll_no can be an integer or an alphanumeric value, name and course will of course be string, and total_marks and avg can be floating point numbers.

Some built-in functions return a tuple. For example, the divmod() function returns two values—quotient as well as the remainder after performing the divide operation.

Example 8.29   Program to illustrate the use of divmod() function

```
quo, rem = divmod(100,3)
print("Quotient = ",quo)
print("Remainder = ", rem)

OUTPUT
Quotient =  33
Remainder =  1
```

8.4.3 Accessing Values in a Tuple

Like other sequences (strings and lists) covered so far, indices in a tuple also starts at 0. You can even perform operations like slice, concatenate, etc. on a tuple. For example, to access values in tuple, slice operation is used along with the index or indices to obtain value stored at that index.

Example 8.30   Program to illustrate the use of slice operation to retrieve value(s) stored in a tuple

```
Tup1 = (1,2,3,4,5,6,7,8,9,10)
print("Tup[3:6] = ", Tup1[3:6])
print("Tup[:8] = ", Tup1[:4])
print("Tup[4:] = ", Tup1[4:])
print("Tup[:] = ", Tup1[:])
```

```
OUTPUT
Tup[3:6] =  (4, 5, 6)
Tup[:8] =  (1, 2, 3, 4)
Tup[4:] =  (5, 6, 7, 8, 9, 10)
Tup[:] =  (1, 2, 3, 4, 5, 6, 7, 8, 9, 10)
```

8.3.4 Updating Tuple

We have already learnt that tuple is immutable and so, the value(s) in the tuple cannot be changed. You can only extract values from a tuple to form another tuple.

Example 8.31   Program to extract values from a tuple

```
Tup1 = (1,2,3,4,5)
Tup2 = (6,7,8,9,10)
Tup3 = Tup1 + Tup2
print(Tup3)

OUTPUT
(1, 2, 3, 4, 5, 6, 7, 8, 9, 10)
```

8.4.5 Deleting Elements in Tuple

Since tuple is an immutable data structure, you cannot delete value(s) from it. Of course, you can create a new tuple that has all elements in your tuple except the ones you don't want (those you wanted to be deleted). Observe the code given in the following example and note the error generated.

Example 8.32   Program to illustrate that tuples are immutable

```
Tup1 = (1,2,3,4,5)
del Tup1[3]
print(Tup1)

OUTPUT
Traceback (most recent call last):
  File "C:\Python34\Try.py", line 2, in <module>
    del Tup1[3]
TypeError: 'tuple' object doesn't support item deletion
```

However, you can always delete the entire tuple by using the del statement. This is done in the code given below.

Example 8.33 Program to delete a tuple

```
Tup1 = (1,2,3,4,5)
del Tup1
print(Tup1)
```

OUTPUT

```
Traceback (most recent call last):
  File "C:\Python34\Try.py", line 3, in <module>
    print Tup1
NameError: name 'Tup1' is not defined
```

Note that this exception is raised because you are now trying to print a tuple that has already been deleted.

8.4.6 Basic Tuple Operations

Like strings and lists, you can also perform operations like concatenation, repetition, etc. on tuples. The only difference is that a new tuple should be created when a change is required in an existing tuple. Table 8.3 summarizes some operations on tuples.

Table 8.3 Operations on Tuples

Operation	Expression	Output
Length	len((1,2,3,4,5,6))	6
Concatenation	(1,2,3) + (4,5,6)	(1, 2, 3, 4, 5, 6)
Repetition	('Good..')*3	'Good..Good..Good..'
Membership	5 in (1,2,3,4,5,6,7,8,9)	True
Iteration	for i in (1,2,3,4,5,6,7,8,9,10): print(i,end=' ')	1,2,3,4,5,6,7,8,9,10
Comparison (Use >, <, ==)	Tup1 = (1,2,3,4,5) Tup2 = (1,2,3,4,5) print(Tup1>Tup2)	False
Maximum	max(1,0,3,8,2,9)	9
Minimum	min(1,0,3,8,2,9)	0
Convert to tuple (converts a sequence into a tuple)	tuple("Hello") tuple([1,2,3,4,5])	('H', 'e', 'l', 'l', 'o') (1, 2, 3, 4, 5)

8.4.7 Tuple Assignment

Tuple assignment is a very powerful feature in Python. It allows a tuple of variables on the left side of the assignment operator to be assigned values from a tuple given on the right side of the assignment operator. Each value is assigned to its respective variable.

In case, an expression is specified on the right side of the assignment operator, first that expression is evaluated and then assignment is done. This feature makes tuple assignment quite versatile. Look at the code given below.

Example 8.34 Program to show the different ways of tuple assignment

```
# an unnamed tuple of values assigned to values of another unnamed tuple
(val1, val2, val3) = (1,2,3)
print(val1, val2, val3)
Tup1 = (100, 200, 300)
(val1, val2, val3) = Tup1     # tuple assigned to another tuple
print(val1, val2, val3)
# expressions are evaluated before assignment
(val1, val2, val3)= (2+4, 5/3 + 4, 9%6)
print(val1, val2, val3)

OUTPUT
1 2 3
100 200 300
6 5.666667 3
```

Note that while assigning values to a tuple, you must ensure that number of values on both the sides of the assignment operator are same otherwise, an error will be generated as shown below.

```
(val1, val2, val3) = (1,2)
print(val1, val2, val3)

OUTPUT
Traceback (most recent call last):
  File "C:\Python34\Try.py", line 1, in <module>
    (val1, val2, val3) = (1,2)
ValueError: need more than 2 values to unpack (expected 3, got 2)
```

8.4.8 Tuples for Returning Multiple Values

We have learnt that a function can return only a single value. But at times, we need to return more than one value from a function. In such situations, it is preferable to group together multiple values and return them together.

Example 8.35 Program to return the highest as well as the lowest values in the list

```
def max_min(vals):
    x = max(vals)
    y = min(vals)
    return (x,y)
vals = (99, 98, 90, 97, 89, 86, 93, 82)
(max_marks, min_marks) = max_min(vals)
print("Highest Marks = ", max_marks)
print("Lowest Marks = ", min_marks)
```

Programming Tip: You can't delete elements from a tuple. Methods like remove() or pop() do not work with a tuple.

OUTPUT

```
Highest Marks =  99
Lowest Marks =  82
```

Note   Unlike lists, tuples do not support remove(), pop(), append(), sort(), reverse(), and insert() methods.

8.4.9 Nested Tuples

Python allows you to define a tuple inside another tuple. This is called a *nested tuple*. Consider the program code given below. We have a list of students who have topped in their respective courses. We store the name, course, and aggregate of three students as tuples inside the tuple Toppers.

Example 8.36   Program to demonstrate the use of nested tuples

```
Toppers = (("Arav", "BSc",92.0), ("Chaitanya", "BCA", 99.0),
("Dhruvika", "Btech", 97))
for i in Toppers:
    print(i)
```

OUTPUT

```
('Arav', 'BSc', 92.0)
('Chaitanya', 'BCA', 99.0)
('Dhruvika', 'Btech', 97)
```

• You can even specify a list within a tuple. The code is given below.

Example 8.37   Program to print the name of the topper and her marks in 4 subjects wherein the marks are specified as a list in the tuple Topper

```
Topper = ("Janvi",[94, 95, 96, 97])
print("Class Topper : ", Topper[0])
print("Highest Scores in 4 Subjects : ", Topper[1:])
```

OUTPUT

```
Class Topper :  Janvi
Highest Scores in 4 Subjects :  ([94, 95, 96, 97],)
```

8.4.10 Checking the Index: index() Method

The index of an element in the tuple can be obtained by using the index() method. If the element being searched is not present in the list, then error is generated. The syntax of index() is given as,

```
list.index(obj)
```

where, obj is the object to be found out.

Consider the examples given below.

Example 8.38 Program to demonstrate the use of `index()` method

```
Tup = (1,2,3,4,5,6,7,8)
print(Tup.index(4))
```

OUTPUT

```
3
```

Example 8.39 Program to print the location at which an element is present in the list using the `index()` method

```
students = ("Bhavya", "Era", "Falguni","Huma")
index = students.index("Falguni")
print("Falguni is present at location : ", index)
index = students.index("Isha")
print("Isha is present at location : ", index)
```

OUTPUT

```
Falguni is present at location :  2
Traceback (most recent call last):
  File "C:\Python34\Try.py", line 4, in <module>
    index = students.index("Isha")
ValueError: tuple.index(x): x not in tuple
```

8.4.11 Counting the Elements: count()Method

The count() method is used to return the number of elements with a specific value in a tuple.

Example 8.40 Program to count the number of times letter `'x'` appears in the specified string

```
tup = "abcdxxxabcdxxxabcdxxx"
print("x appears ", tup.count('x'), " times in ", tup)
```

OUTPUT

```
x appears  9  times in  abcdxxxabcdxxxabcdxxx
```

8.4.12 List Comprehension and Tuples

We have already studied list comprehension to create a new list in the earlier sections of this chapter. You can use the same concept to manipulate the values in one tuple to create a new tuple.

Example 8.41 Consider the program given below passes a tuple as an argument to a function `double()`. The function scales each value in the tuple by a factor of two and places the scaled values in another tuple.

```
def double(T):
    return ([i*2 for i in T])
Tup = 1,2,3,4,5
print("Original Tuple : ", Tup)
print("Double Values: ",double(Tup))
```

OUTPUT

```
Original Tuple :  (1, 2, 3, 4, 5)
Double Values:  [2, 4, 6, 8, 10]
```

Note If a sequence is specified without parenthesis, it is treated to be a tuple by default.

8.4.13 Variable-length Argument Tuples

Many built-in functions like max(), min(), sum(), etc. use variable-length arguments since these functions themselves do not know how many arguments will be passed to them. Variable-length arguments tuple is a striking feature in Python. It allows a function to accept a variable (different) number of arguments. This is especially useful in defining functions that are applicable to a large variety of arguments. For example, if you have a function that displays all the parameters passed to it, then even the function does not know how many values it will be passed. In such cases, we use a variable-length argument that begins with a '*' symbol. Any argument that starts with a '*' symbol is known as *gather* and specifies a variable-length argument.

Example 8.42 Program to manipulate efficiently each value that is passed to the tuple using variable-length arguments

```
def display(*args):
    print(args)
Tup = (1,2,3,4,5,6)
display(Tup)
```

OUTPUT

```
((1, 2, 3, 4, 5, 6),)
```

The opposite of gather is *scatter*. So, in case you have a function that accepts multiple arguments but not a tuple, then the tuple is scattered to pass individual elements. Look at the code given below which demonstrates this concept.

Example 8.43 Programs to illustrate scatter in terms of Tuple

```
Tup = (56, 3)
quo, rem = divmod(Tup)
print(quo, rem)
```

```
Tup = (56, 3)
#values are now scattered and passed
quo, rem = divmod(*Tup)
print(quo, rem)
```

OUTPUT	OUTPUT	

Traceback (most recent call last):
  File "C:\Python34\Try.py", line 2, in
<module>
   quo, rem = divmod(Tup)
TypeError: divmod expected 2 arguments,
got 1
	18 2	**Programming Tip:** If a negative value is used for the step, the slice is done backwards.

In the first code, only Tup was passed (a single argument) but the divmod() expects two arguments, hence, the error occurs. While in the second code, the symbol * denotes that there may be more than one argument. So Python, extracts the values (scatters them) to obtain two values on which the operation can be applied.

8.4.14 The zip() Function

zip() is a built-in function that takes two or more sequences and "zips" them into a list of tuples. The tuple thus, formed has one element from each sequence. The code given below illustrates this concept.

Example 8.44 Program to show the use of zip() function

```
Tup = (1,2,3,4,5)
List1 = ['a','b','c','d','e']
print(list((zip(Tup, List1))))
```

OUTPUT

```
[(1, 'a'), (2, 'b'), (3, 'c'), (4, 'd'), (5, 'e')]
```

From the output, we see that the result of zip() function is a list of tuples where each tuple contains a character from the list and an integer from the tuple. In the above example, there are equal number of values in the list and tuple. But if the two sequences have different length, then the result has the length of the shorter one as illustrated in the code given below.

Example 8.45 Program to use zip() function on variable-length sequences

```
Tup = (1,2,3)
List1 = ['a','b','c','d','e']
print(list(zip(Tup, List1)))
```

OUTPUT

```
[(1, 'a'), (2, 'b'), (3, 'c')]
```

- You can even print the elements in a tuple using the for statement as shown below.

Example 8.46 Program to print elements in a tuple using for loop

```
Tup = ((1, 'a'), (2, 'b'), (3, 'c'))
for i, char in Tup:
    print(i, char)
```

Programming Tip: Slicing can be done on tuples.

OUTPUT

```
1 a
2 b
3 c
```

- To traverse the elements of a sequence and also print their indices, use the built-in function enumerate().

Example 8.47   Program that uses enumerate() function to print elements as well as their indices

```
for index, element in enumerate('ABCDEFG'):
    print(index, element)
```

OUTPUT

```
0 A
1 B
2 C
3 D
4 E
5 F
6 G
```

Key points to remember

- Tuples can be converted into lists, and vice versa using the built-in tuple() function that takes a list and returns a tuple with the same elements. Similarly, the list() function takes a tuple and returns a list.
- You cannot divide or subtract tuples. If you try to do so you will get a TypeError with "unsupported operand type".
- Since tuples are immutable, they do not support methods like sort() and reverse(), as these methods modify existing lists. However, Python has a built-in function sorted() which takes any sequence as a parameter and returns a new list with the same elements but in a different order. For example, the code given in the following example illustrates this concept.

Programming Tip: Tuples are faster than lists, but they cannot be changed.

Example 8.48   Program to sort a tuple of values

```
Tup = (5,1,0,2,8,3,9)
print(sorted(Tup))
```

OUTPUT

```
[0, 1, 2, 3, 5, 8, 9]
```

If you write,
```
tup = ("abc","def")
x,y = tup
print(x, y)
```

```
abc def
```

then syntactically, it works as assigning x with value `tup[0]` and y with value `tup[1]`.

- You can use string formatting feature to print values in the Tuple. This is shown in the code given below.

Example 8.49 Program to illustrate string formatting function with tuple

```
Tup = ("Heena", 89, 82,4)
print("%s got %d marks in CSA and her aggregate was
%.2f" %(Tup[0], Tup[1], Tup[2]))
```

> **Programming Tip:** Reassigning a value in a tuple causes a TypeError.

OUTPUT

```
Heena got 89 marks in CSA and her aggregate was 82.00
```

8.4.15 Advantages of Tuple over List

Although tuples are similar to lists, there are some advantages of implementing a tuple over a list. Some of these advantages are listed below.

- Tuples are used to store values of different data types. Lists can however, store data of similar data types.
- Since tuples are immutable, iterating through tuples is faster than iterating over a list. This means that a tuple performs better than a list.
- Tuples can be used as key for a dictionary but lists cannot be used as keys. We will learn about dictionaries in the next section.
- Tuples are best suited for storing data that is write-protected (you can read the data but cannot write to it).
- Tuples can be used in place of lists where the number of values is known and small.
- If you are passing a tuple as an argument to a function, then the potential for unexpected behavior due to aliasing gets reduced.
- Multiple values from a function can be returned using a tuple.
- Tuples are used to format strings.

Program 8.25 Write a program to swap two values using tuple assignment.

```
val1 = 10
val2 = 20
print "val1 = ",val1, " val2 = ",val2
(val1,val2) = (val2,val1)
print("val1 = ",val1, " val2 = ",val2)
```

OUTPUT

```
val1 =  10  val2 =  20
val1 =  20  val2 =  10
```

Program 8.26 Write a program using a function that returns the area and circumference of a circle whose radius is passed as an argument.

```
PI = 3.14
def cal_a_r(r):
    return (PI*r*r, 2*PI*r)
radius = float(input("Enter the radius : "))
(area, circumference) = cal_a_r(radius)
print("Area of the circle with radius", radius, " = ", area)
print("Circumference of the circle with radius ", radius, " = ", circumference)
```

OUTPUT

```
Enter the radius : 7
Area of the circle with radius 7.0  =  153.86
Circumference of the circle with radius  7.0  =  43.96
```

Program 8.27 Write a program that has a nested list to store toppers details. Edit the details and reprint the details.

```
Toppers = (("Arav", "BSc",92.0), ("Chaitanya", "BCA",
99.0), ("Dhruvika", "Btech", 97))
for i in Toppers:
    print(i)
choice = input("Do you want to edit the details : ")
if choice == 'y':
    name = input("Enter the name of the students whose details are to be
edited : ")
    new_name = input("Enter the correct name : ")
    new_course = input("Enter the correct course : ")
    new_aggr = input("Enter the correct aggregate : ")
    i = 0
    new_Toppers = ()
    while i<len(Toppers):
        if Toppers[i][0] == name:
            new_Toppers += (new_name, new_course, new_aggr)
        else:
            new_Toppers += Toppers[i]
        i+=1
for i in new_Toppers:
    print(i,end = ' ')
```

> **Programming Tip:** You cannot add elements to a tuple. Methods like append() or extend() does not work with tuple.

OUTPUT

```
('Arav', 'BSc', 92.0)
('Chaitanya''Chiatanya', 'BCA', 99.0)
('Dhruvika', 'Btech', 97)
Do you want to edit the details : y
Enter the name of the students whose details are to be edited : Chaitanya
Enter the correct name : Chaitanya
Enter the correct course : BCA
```

```
Enter the correct aggregate : 100
Arav BSc 92.0 Chaitanya BCA 100 Dhruvika Btech 97
```

Program 8.28 Write a program that scans an email address and forms a tuple of user name and domain.

```
addr = 'abc@gmail.com'
user_name, domain_name = addr.split('@')
print ("User Name : ", user_name)
print("Domain Name : ", domain_name)
```

OUTPUT

```
User Name :  abc
Domain Name :  gmail.com
```

Program 8.29 Write a program that has a list of numbers (both positive as well as negative). Make a new tuple that has only positive values from this list.

```
Tup = (-10,1,2,-9,3,4,-8,5,6)
newTup = ()
for i in Tup:
    if i>0:
        newTup += (i,)
print(newTup)
```

OUTPUT

```
(1, 2, 3, 4, 5, 6)
```

Program 8.30 Write a program that accepts different number of arguments and return sum of only the positive values passed to it.

```
def sum_pos(*args):
    tot = 0
    for i in args:
        if i>0:
            tot += i
    return tot
print("sum_pos(1,-9,2,-8,3,-7,4,-6,5) = ", sum_pos(1,-9,2,-8,3,-7,4,-6,5))
```

OUTPUT

```
sum_pos(1,-9,2,-8,3,-7,4,-6,5) =  15
```

Program 8.31 Write a program that has two sequences. First which stores some questions and second stores the corresponding answers. Use the zip() function to form a valid question answer series.

```
Ques = ["Roll_No", "Name", "Course"]
Ans = [7, "Saesha", "BSc"]
for q,a in zip(Ques, Ans):
```

```
    print("What is your", q, "?")
    print("My", q, "is : ", a)
```

> **Programming Tip:** If the index specified in the tuple slice is too big, then an IndexError exception is raised.

OUTPUT

```
What is your Roll_No ?
My Roll_No is :  2
What is your Name ?
My Name is :   Saesha
What is your Course ?
My Course is :  BSc
```

8.5 SETS

Sets is another data structure supported by Python. Basically, sets are same as lists but with a difference that sets are lists with no duplicate entries. Technically, a set is a mutable and an unordered collection of items. This means that we can easily add or remove items from it.

8.5.1 Creating a Set

A set is created by placing all the elements inside curly brackets {}, separated by comma or by using the built-in function set(). The syntax of creating a set can be given as,

```
set_variable = {val1, val2, ...}
```

For example, to create a set you can write,

```
>>> s = {1,2.0,"abc"}
>>> print( s )
set([1, 2.0,'abc'])
```

A set can have any number of items and they may be of different data types. For example, the code given below creates a set using the set() function. The code converts a list of different types of values into a set.

Example 8.50 Program to convert a list of values into a set

```
s = set([1,2,'a','b',"def",4.56])
print(s)
```

> **Programming Tip:** If we add the same element multiple times in a set, they are removed because a set cannot have duplicate values.

OUTPUT

```
set(['a', 1, 2, 'b', 4.56, 'def'])
```

The program given below demonstrates different ways of creating sets, that is, sets being created by using a list, tuples or string.

Example 8.51 Program to create a set

```
List1 = [1,2,3,4,5,6,5,4,3,2,1]
print(set(List1))    # list is converted into a set
```

```
Tup1 = ('a','b','c','d','b','e','a')
print(set(Tup1))# tuple is converted into a set
str = "abcdefabcdefg"
print(set(str))    # string is converted into a set
# forms a set of words
print(set("She sells sea shells on the sea shore".split()))
```

OUTPUT

```
set([1, 2, 3, 4, 5, 6])
set(['a', 'c', 'b', 'e', 'd'])
set(['a', 'c', 'b', 'e', 'd', 'g', 'f'])
set(['on', 'shells', 'shore', 'She', 'sea', 'sells', 'the'])
```

Like in case of mathematical sets, Python sets are also a powerful tool as they have the ability to calculate differences and intersections between other sets. Figures 8.5(a–d) given below demonstrate various set operations.

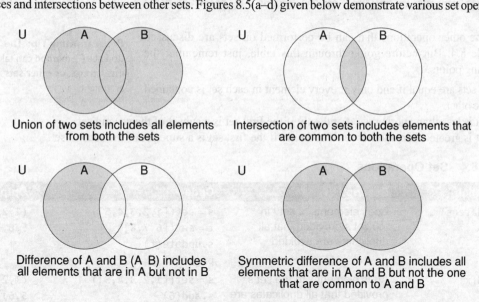

Union of two sets includes all elements from both the sets

Intersection of two sets includes elements that are common to both the sets

Difference of A and B (A B) includes all elements that are in A but not in B

Symmetric difference of A and B includes all elements that are in A and B but not the one that are common to A and B

Figure 8.5 Set operations

Example 8.52 Program to find intersection, union, and symmetric difference between two sets

```
Coders = set(["Arnav","Goransh","Mani","Parul"])
Analysts = set(["Krish","Mehak","Shiv","Goransh","Mani"])
print("Coders : ", Coders)
print("Analysts : ", Analysts)
print("People working as Coders as well as Analysts :
", Coders.intersection(Analysts))
print("People working as Coders or Analysts :
", Coders.union(Analysts))
print("People working as Coders but not Analysts :
```

```
", Coders.difference(Analysts))
print("People working as Analysts but not Coders :
", Analysts.difference(Coders))
print("People working in only one of the groups :
", Coders.symmetric_difference(Analysts))
```

OUTPUT

```
Coders : {'Arnav', 'Mani', 'Goransh', 'Parul'}
Analysts : {'Shiv', 'Mani', 'Krish', 'Goransh', 'Mehak'}
People working as coders as well as Analysts : {'Mani', 'Goransh'}
People working as Coders or Analysts : {'Goransh', 'Parul', 'Krish', 'Mehak',
'Shiv', 'Arnav', 'Mani'}
People working as Coders but not Analysts : {'Arnav', 'Parul'}
People working as Analysts but not Coders : {'Shiv', 'Krish', 'Mehak'}
People working in only one of the groups : {'Krish', 'Mehak', 'Shiv', 'Arnav', 'Parul'}
```

Some other operations that can be performed on sets are discussed in Table 8.4. But before going through this table, just remember the following points.

> **Programming Tip:** The update() method can take tuples, lists, strings, or other sets as its argument.

- Two sets are equal if and only if every element in each set is contained in the other.
- A set is less than another set if and only if the first set is a subset of the second set.
- A set is greater than another set if and only if the first set is a superset of the second set.

Table 8.4 Set Operations

Operation	Description	Code	Output
s.update(t)	Adds elements of set t in the set s provided that all duplicates are avoided	s = set([1,2,3,4,5]) t = set([6,7,8]) s.update(t) print(s)	(1,2,3,4, 5,6,7,8)
s.add(x)	Adds element x to the set s provided that all duplicates are avoided	s = set([1,2,3,4,5]) s.add(6) print(s)	(1,2,3,4, 5,6)
s.remove(x)	Removes element x from set s. Returns KeyError if x is not present	s = set([1,2,3,4,5]) s.remove(3) print(s)	(1,2,4,5)
s.discard(x)	Same as remove() but does not give an error if x is not present in the set	s = set([1,2,3,4,5]) s.discard(3) print(s)	(1,2,4,5)
s.pop()	Removes and returns any arbitrary element from s. KeyError is raised if s is empty	s = set([1,2,3,4,5]) s.pop() print(s)	(2,3,4,5)
s.clear()	Removes all elements from the set	s = set([1,2,3,4,5]) s.clear() print(s)	set()

(Contd)

Table 8.4 (*Contd*)

Operation	Description	Code	Output
`len(s)`	Returns the length of set	`s = set([1,2,3,4,5])` `print(len(s))`	5
`x in s`	Returns True is x is present in set s and False otherwise	`s = set([1,2,3,4,5])` `print(3 in s)`	True
`x not in s`	Returns True is x is not present in set s and False otherwise	`s = set([1,2,3,4,5])` `print(6 not in s)`	True

`s.issubset(t)` or `s<=t`	Returns True if every element in set s is present in set t and False otherwise	`s = set([1,2,3,4,5])`
		`t = set([1,2,3,4,5,6,7,8,9,10])`
		`print(s<=t)`
			True

`s.issuperset(t)` or `s>=t`	Returns True if every element in t is present in set s and False otherwise	`s = set([1,2,3,4,5])`
		`t = set([1,2,3,4,5,6,7,8,9,10])`
		`print(s.issuperset(t))`
			False

`s.union(t)` or `s|t`	Returns a set s that has elements from both sets s and t	`s = set([1,2,3,4,5])`
		`t = set([1,2,3,4,5,6,7,8,9,10])`
		`print(s|t)`
			(1,2,3,4,5,6,7,8,9,10)

`s.intersection(t)` or `s&t`	Returns a new set that has elements which are common to both the sets s and t	`s = set([1,2,3,4,5])`
		`t = set([1,2,3,4,5,6,7,8,9,10])`
		`z = s&t`
		`print(z)`
			(1,2,3,4,5)

`s.intersection_update(t)`	Returns a set that has elements which are common to both the sets s and t	`s = set([1,2,10,12])`
		`t = set([1,2,3,4,5,6,7,8,9,10])`
		`s.intersection_update(t)`
		`print(s)`
			(1,2,10)

`s.difference(t)` or `s-t`	Returns a new set that has elements in set s but not in t	`s = set([1,2,10,12])`
		`t = set([1,2,3,4,5,6,7,8,9,10])`
		`z = s-t`
		`print(z)`
			(12)

`s.difference_update(t)`	Removes all elements of another set from this set	`s = set([1,2,10,12])`
		`t = set([1,2,3,4,5,6,7,8,9,10])`
		`s.difference_update(t)`
		`print(s)`
			(12)

`s.symmetric_difference(t)` or `s^t`	Returns a new set with elements either in s or in t but not both	`s = set([1,2,10,12])`
		`t = set([1,2,3,4,5,6,7,8,9,10])`
		`z = s^t`
		`print(z)`
			(3,4,5,6,7,8,9,12)

(*Contd*)

Table 8.4   (*Contd*)

Operation	Description	Code	Output
s.copy()	Returns a copy of set s	s = set([1,2,10,12]) t = set([1,2,3,4,5,6,7,8,9, 10]) print(s.copy())	(1,2,12,10)
s.isisjoint(t)	Returns True if two sets have a null intersection	s = set([1,2, 3]) t = set([4,5,6]) print(s.isdisjoint(t))	True
all(s)	Returns True if all elements in the set are True and False otherwise	s = set([0,1,2,3,4]) print(all(s))	False
any(s)	Returns True if any of the elements in the set is True. Returns False if the set is empty	s = set([0,1,2,3,4]) print(any(s))	True
enumerate(s)	Returns an enumerate object which contains index as well as value of all the items of set as a pair	s = set(['a','b','c','d']) for i in enumerate(s): print(i,end=' ')	(0, 'a') (1, 'c') (2, 'b') (3, 'd')
max(s)	Returns the maximum value in a set	s = set([0,1,2,3,4,5]) print(max(s))	5
min(s)	Returns the minimum value in a set	s = set([0,1,2,3,4,5]) print(min(s))	0
sum(s)	Returns the sum of elements in the set	s = set([0,1,2,3,4,5]) print(sum(s))	15
sorted(s)	Return a new sorted list from elements in the set. It does not sorts the set as sets are immutable.	s = set([5,4,3,2,1,0]) print(sorted(s))	[0,1,2,3, 4,5]
s == t and s != t	s == t returns True if the two set are equivalent and False otherwise. s!=t returns True if both sets are not equivalent and False otherwise	s = set(['a','b','c']) t = set("abc") z = set(tuple('abc')) print(s == t) print(s!=z)	True False

Key points to remember

- A set cannot contain other mutable objects (like lists). Therefore, the following code will give an error when executed.

```
s = {10,20,[30,40]}
Traceback (most recent call last):
  File "C:\Python34\Try.py", line 1, in <module>
    s = {10,20,[30,40]}
TypeError: unhashable type: 'list'
```

- To make an empty list you write, List1 = [], to make an empty tuple you write Tup = (), but to make an empty set you cannot write s = {}, because Python will make this as a dictionary. Therefore, to create an empty set use the set() as shown below.

```
>>> s = set()              >>> t = {}
>>> print(s)               >>> print(type(t))
set()                      <class 'dict'>
print(type(s))
<class 'set'>
```

- Since sets are unordered, indexing have no meaning.
- Set operations do not allow users to access or change an element using indexing or slicing. This is illustrated by code given below.

Example 8.53   Program to illustrate updating of a set

```
s = {1,2,3,4,5}
print(s[0])
```

OUTPUT
```
Traceback (most recent call last):
  File "C:\Python34\Try.py", line 2, in <module>
    print(s[0])
TypeError: 'set' object does not support indexing
```

Note   A set can be created from a list but a set cannot contain a list.

- You can iterate through each item in a set using a for loop as shown in the code given below.

Example 8.54   Program to iterate through a set

```
s = set("Hello All, Good Morning")
for i in s:
    print(i,end = ' ')
```

OUTPUT
```
A   e d G i H M l o , g r n
```

- The copy() method makes a shallow copy of the set. This means that all the objects in the new set are references to the same objects as the original set.

Note   To add a single element in the set use the add() method and to add multiple elements in the set, use the update() method.

Program 8.32 Write a program that generates a set of prime numbers and another set of odd numbers. Demonstrate the result of union, intersection, difference, and symmetric difference operations on these sets.

```python
odds = set([x*2+1 for x in range(1,10)])
print(odds)
primes = set()
for i in range(2, 20):
    j = 2
    flag = 0
    while j<i/2:
        if i%j == 0:
            flag = 1
        j+=1
    if flag == 0:
        primes.add(i)
print(primes)
print("UNION : ",odds.union(primes))
print("INTERSECTION : ", odds.intersection(primes))
print("SYMMETRIC DIFFERENCE : ", odds.symmetric_difference(primes))
print("DIFFERENCE : ", odds.difference(primes))
```

OUTPUT

```
{3, 5, 7, 9, 11, 13, 15, 17, 19}
{2, 3, 4, 5, 7, 11, 13, 17, 19}
UNION :  {2, 3, 4, 5, 7, 9, 11, 13, 15, 17, 19}
INTERSECTION :  {3, 5, 7, 11, 13, 17, 19}
SYMMETRIC DIFFERENCE :  {2, 4, 9, 15}
DIFFERENCE :  {9, 15}
```

Program 8.33 Write a program that creates two sets. One of even numbers in range 1-10 and the other has all composite numbers in range 1–20. Demonstrate the use all(), issuperset(), len(), and sum() functions on the sets.

```python
evens = set([x*2 for x in range(1,10)])
print("EVENS : ", evens)
composites = set()
for i in range(2, 20):
    j = 2
    flag = 0
    while j<=i/2:
        if i%j == 0:
            composites.add(i)
        j+=1
print("COMPOSITES : ", composites)
print("SUPERSET : ", evens.issuperset(composites))
print("ALL : ", all(evens))
print("LENGTH OF COMPOSITES SET : ", len(composites))
print("SUM OF ALL NUMBERS IN EVENS SET : ", sum(evens))
```

OUTPUT

```
EVENS :  {2, 4, 6, 8, 10, 12, 14, 16, 18}
COMPOSITES :  {4, 6, 8, 9, 10, 12, 14, 15, 16, 18}
SUPERSET :  False
ALL :  True
LENGTH OF COMPOSITES SET :  10
SUM OF ALL NUMBERS IN EVENS SET :  90
```

Program 8.34 Write a program that creates two sets—squares and cubes in range 1–10. Demonstrate the use of update(), pop(), remove(), add() and clear() functions.

```
squares = set([x**2 for x in range(1,10)])
cubes = set([x**3 for x in range(1,10)])
print("SQUARES : ", squares)
print("CUBES : ", cubes)
squares.update(cubes)
print("UPDATE : ", squares)
squares.add(11*11)
squares.add(11*11*11)
print("ADD : ", squares)
print("POP : ", squares.pop())
squares.remove(1331)
print("REMOVE : ", squares)
squares.clear()
print("CLEAR : ", squares)
```

OUTPUT

```
SQUARES :  {64, 1, 4, 36, 9, 16, 49, 81, 25}
CUBES :  {64, 1, 512, 8, 343, 216, 729, 27, 125}
UPDATE :  {64, 1, 512, 4, 36, 8, 9, 16, 49, 81, 729, 343, 216, 25, 27, 125}
ADD :  {64, 1, 512, 121, 4, 36, 8, 9, 16, 49, 81, 1331, 729, 343, 216, 25, 27, 125}
POP :  64
REMOVE :  {1, 512, 121, 4, 36, 8, 9, 16, 49, 81, 729, 343, 216, 25, 27, 125}
CLEAR :  set()
```

Program 8.35 Write a program that has a list of countries. Create a set of the countries and print the names of the countries in sorted order.

```
countries = ['India', 'Russia', 'China', 'Brazil', 'England']
C_set = sorted(set(countries))
print(C_set)
```

OUTPUT

```
['Brazil', 'China', 'England', 'India', 'Russia']
```

8.5.2 Set Comprehensions

Set comprehensions are similar to list comprehensions. The key difference between them is that set comprehensions use curly brackets { } while list comprehensions have square brackets. Table given below shows the comparison between list and set comprehension.

Table 8.5

Set Comprehension	List Comprehension
Uses curly braces to create a set.	Uses a square bracket to create a list.
All members are unique. No duplicates.	Contains duplicate values.
Returns a set	Returns a list

For example, the code given below creates a set comprising only even numbers that are present in the input list. Since we are creating s set, all the duplicate values are discarded.

```
List1 = [1, 1, 2, 3, 3, 4, 5, 5, 6, 7, 7]
set1 = set()
# Using loop for constructing output set
for var in list:
    if var % 2 = = 0:
        set1.add(var)
print("Output Set using for loop:", set1)

OUTPUT

Output Set using for loop: {2, 4, 6}
```

```
List1 = [1, 1, 2, 3, 3, 4, 5, 5, 6, 7, 7]
set1 = {var for var in list1 if var % 2 =
    = 0}
print("Output Set using Set
Comprehension:", set1)

OUTPUT

Output Set using Set Comprehension:
{2, 4, 6}
```

The codes given above show the formation of the desired set using two ways- by iterating through list elements using for loop and using set comprehensions. The major difference between the two techniques is that set comprehensions are more efficient as they do not allocate memory for the whole list. Rather, they generate each value one by one

The syntax of set comprehension can be given as,

```
{expression(variable) for variable in input_set [predicate][, …]}
```

where,

expression is optional. If present, it specifies which members from the input set/list will be incorporated in the new set.

variable is a required parameter that specifies the members of an input set.

input_set is a required parameter that gives the input set.

predicate is an optional parameter that is used as an expression acting as a filter on members of the input set.

[, …]] is optional and is used for nested comprehension.

Program 8.36 Write a program to remove ',' and '.' with a blank space in a string. Make a set of unique words using comprehension.

```
phrase = "She sells, sea shells on the sea shore. Sea shells on the sea shore
are really beautiful"
words = phrase.lower().replace('.', '').replace(',', '').split()
```

```
unique_words = {word for word in words}
print(unique_words)
```

OUTPUT

```
{'shells', 'shore', 'are', 'beautiful', 'she', 'sea', 'the', 'on', 'really',
'sells'}
```

Program 8.37 Write a program using set comprehension to form a set of words with less than three characters.

```
phrase = "The cat is in the hut. The bug is under the table. You must buy a
pair of new shoes before the annual day"
words = phrase.lower().split()
unique_words = {word for word in words if len(word) < 3}
print(unique_words)
```

OUTPUT

```
{'of', 'a', 'in', 'is'}
```

Nested Set Comprehensions

Like list and dictionary comprehensions, set comprehensions can also be nested within another. However, there is one important point to note here. In nested sets, the inner sets have to be frozen sets or an error will be generated. A frozen set is just like a set, but while a frozen set is not mutable, an ordinary set is. Using a frozen set is necessary, as mutable objects cannot be accessed with hash-based memory lookups. To make a frozen set, we can use the frozenset() function as shown in the code given below.

```
phrase = "The cat is in the hut. The bug is under the table. You must buy a pair of
new shoe before the annual day"
words = phrase.lower().replace('.', '').replace(',', '').split()
vowels = ['a', 'e', 'i', 'o', 'u']
consonants = {frozenset({letter for letter in word if letter not in vowels}) for word
in words}
print(consonants)
```

OUTPUT

```
{frozenset({'t', 'c'}), frozenset({'y'}), frozenset({'f'}), frozenset({'b', 'l',
't'}), frozenset({'h', 't'}), frozenset({'n', 'w'}), frozenset({'b', 'r', 'f'}),
frozenset({'s', 'm', 't'}), frozenset({'n', 'r', 'd'}), frozenset({'d', 'y'}),
frozenset({'h', 's'}), frozenset(), frozenset({'n', 'l'}), frozenset({'s'}),
frozenset({'n'}), frozenset({'b', 'y'}), frozenset({'r', 'p'}), frozenset({'b',
'g'})}
```

Remember that sets within lists or dictionaries do not require frozen sets.

8.6 DICTIONARIES

Dictionary is a data structure in which we store values as a pair of key and value. Each key is separated from its value by a colon (:), and consecutive

> **Programming Tip:** Using a mutable object as a dictionary key causes a TypeError.

items are separated by commas. The entire items in a dictionary are enclosed in curly brackets({}). The syntax for defining a dictionary is

```
dictionary_name = {key_1: value_1, key_2: value_2, key_3: value_3}
```

If there are many keys and values in dictionaries, then we can also write just one key-value pair on a line to make the code easier to read and understand. This is shown below.

```
dictionary_name = {key_1: value_1,
                   key_2: value_2,
                   key_3: value_3,
                   }
```

While, keys in the dictionary must be unique and be of any immutable data type (like strings, numbers, or tuples), there is no stringent requirement for uniqueness and type of values. That is, value of a key can be of any type. Remember that *dictionaries are not sequences, rather they are mappings*. **Mappings** are collections of objects that store objects by key instead of by relative position.

Note   Dictionary keys are case-sensitive. Two keys with the same name but in different case are not the same in Python.

8.6.1 Creating a Dictionary

The syntax to create an empty dictionary can be given as,

```
dictionary_variable = []
```

The syntax to create a dictionary with key-value pairs is:

```
dictionary_variable = {key1 : val1, key2 : val2, ...}
```

• To create an empty dictionary, just write the following line of code.

```
Dict = {}
print(Dict)
```

OUTPUT
```
{}
```

• A dictionary can be also created by specifying key-value pairs separated by a colon in curly brackets as shown below. Note that one key value pair is separated from the other using a comma.

```
Dict = {'Roll_No' : '16/001', 'Name' : 'Arav', 'Course' : 'BTech'}
print(Dict)
```

OUTPUT
```
{'Roll_No': '16/001', 'Name': 'Arav', 'Course': 'BTech'}
```

- To create a dictionary with one or more key-value pairs you can also use the `dict()` function. The `dict()` creates a dictionary directly from a sequence of key value pairs. For example, the line of code given below creates a dictionary using a list of key-value pairs.

> **Programming Tip:** Hash table is an array whose indexes are obtained using a hash function on the keys. A hash function distributes the keys evenly in the array and minimizes collisions.

```
print(dict([('Roll_No', '16/001'), ('Name','Arav'), ('Course','BTech')]))
```

OUTPUT

```
{'Roll_No': '16/001', 'Name': 'Arav', 'Course': 'BTech'}
```

- Dictionary comprehensions is another way of creating a dictionary. A *dictionary comprehension* is a syntactic construct which creates a dictionary based on existing dictionary. The syntax can be given as,

```
D = {expression for variable in sequence [if condition]}
```

According to the syntax, we place the dictionary comprehension within curly brackets. It has three parts – for loop, condition, and expression. First, the `for` loop is used to go through the sequence. The `if` condition is optional and if specified, only those values in the sequence are evaluated using the expression which satisfy the condition.

> **Note**   The expression generates elements of dictionary from items in the sequence that satisfy the condition.

Example 8.55   Program to create `10` key-value pairs where key is a number in the range `1–10` and the value is twice the number

```
Dict = {x : 2*x for x in range(1,10)}
print(Dict)
```

OUTPUT

```
{1: 2, 2: 4, 3: 6, 4: 8, 5: 10, 6: 12, 7: 14, 8: 16, 9: 18}
```

8.6.2 Accessing Values

To access values in a dictionary, square brackets are used along with the key to obtain its value.

Example 8.56   Program to access values stored in a dictionary

```
Dict = {'Roll_No' : '16/001', 'Name' : 'Arav', 'Course' : 'BTech'}
print("Dict[ROll_NO] = ", Dict['Roll_No'])
print("Dict[NAME] = ", Dict['Name'])
print("Dict[COURSE] = ", Dict['Course'])
```

OUTPUT

```
Dict[ROll_NO] =  16/001
Dict[NAME] =  Arav
Dict[COURSE] =  BTech
```

Note that if you try to access an item with a key, which is not specified in the dictionary, a KeyError is generated. For example,

```
Dict = {}
print("Dict[MARKS] = ", Dict['Marks'])
```

> **Programming Tip:** Collision means two or more keys pointing to the same location.

then, we will get the output as,

```
Traceback (most recent call last):
  File "C:\Python34\Try.py", line 2, in <module>
    print "Dict[MARKS] = ", Dict['Marks']
KeyError: 'Marks'
```

8.6.3 Adding and Modifying an Item in a Dictionary

To add a new entry or a key-value pair in a dictionary, just specify the key-value pair as you had done for the existing pairs. The syntax to add an item in a dictionary is given as,

```
dictionary_variable[key] = val
```

Example 8.57   Program to add a new item in the dictionary

```
Dict = {'Roll_No' : '16/001', 'Name' : 'Arav', 'Course' : 'BTech'}
print("Dict[ROll_NO] = ", Dict['Roll_No'])
print("Dict[NAME] = ", Dict['Name'])
print("Dict[COURSE] = ", Dict['Course'])
Dict['Marks'] = 95      # new entry
print("Dict[MARKS] = ", Dict['Marks'])
```

> **Programming Tip:** Trying to index a key that isn't part of the dictionary returns a KeyError.

```
OUTPUT
Dict[ROll_NO] =  16/001
Dict[NAME] =  Arav
Dict[COURSE] =  BTech
Dict[MARKS] =  95
```

8.6.4 Modifying an Entry

To modify an entry, just overwrite the existing value as shown in the following example.

Example 8.58   Program to modify an item in the dictionary

```
Dict = {'Roll_No' : '16/001', 'Name' : 'Arav', 'Course' : 'BTech'}
print("Dict[ROll_NO] = ", Dict['Roll_No'])
print("Dict[NAME] = ", Dict['Name'])
print("Dict[COURSE] = ", Dict['Course'])
Dict['Marks'] = 95      # new entry
print("Dict[MARKS] = ", Dict['Marks'])
```

```
Dict['Course'] = 'BCA'
print("Dict[COURSE] = ", Dict['Course']) #entry updated
```

OUTPUT
```
Dict[ROll_NO] =  16/001
Dict[NAME] =  Arav
Dict[COURSE] =  BTech
Dict[MARKS] =  95
Dict[COURSE] =  BCA
```

Note Dictionary is an associative array also known as hashes since any key of the dictionary can be associated or mapped to a value.

8.6.5 Deleting Items

You can delete one or more items using the del keyword. To delete or remove all the items in just one statement, use the clear() function. Finally, to remove an entire dictionary from the memory, we can again use the del statement as del Dict_name. The syntax to use the del statement can be given as,

```
del dictionary_variable[key]
```

Example 8.59 Program to demonstrate the use of del statement and clear() function

```
Dict = {'Roll_No' : '16/001', 'Name' : 'Arav', 'Course' : 'BTech'}
print("Dict[ROll_NO] = ", Dict['Roll_No'])
print("Dict[NAME] = ", Dict['Name'])
print("Dict[COURSE] = ", Dict['Course'])
del Dict['Course']    # deletes a key-value pair
print("After deleting course : ", Dict)
Dict.clear()         # deletes all entries
print("After clear(), Dictionary has no items : ", Dict)
del Dict             # deletes the variable Dict from memory
print("Dict does not exist.......")
print(Dict)
```

> **Programming Tip:** Only immutable objects can be used as keys to dictionaries.

OUTPUT
```
Dict[ROll_NO] =  16/001
Dict[NAME] =  Arav
Dict[COURSE] =  BTech
After deleting course :  { 'Roll_No': '16/001', 'Name': 'Arav'}
After clear(), Dictionary has no items :  {}
Dict does not exist.......
Traceback (most recent call last):
  File "C:\Python34\Try.py", line 11, in <module>
    print(Dict)
NameError: name 'Dict' is not defined
```

- You can also use the pop() method to delete a particular key from the dictionary. The syntax of the pop() method is given as,

```
dict.pop(key [, default])
```

As the name suggests, the pop() method removes an item from the dictionary and returns its value. If the specified key is not present in the dictionary, then the default value is returned. Since default is optional, if you do not specify the default value and the key is also not present in the dictionary, then a KeyError is generated. Another method dict.popitem() randomly pops and returns an item from the dictionary. The use of these methods are illustrated in the program given below.

Example 8.60   Program to randomly pop() or remove an element from a dictionary

```
Dict = {'Roll_No' : '16/001', 'Name' : 'Arav', 'Course' : 'BTech'}
print("Name is : ", Dict.pop('Name'))    # returns Name)
print("Dictionary after popping Name is : ", Dict)
print("Marks is :", Dict.pop('Marks', -1))    # returns default value
print("Dictionary after popping Marks is : ", Dict)
print("Randomly popping any item : ",Dict.popitem())
print("Dictionary after random popping is : ", Dict)
print("Aggregate is :", Dict.pop('Aggr'))    # generates error
print("Dictionary after popping Aggregate is : ", Dict)
```

OUTPUT
```
Name is :  Arav
Dictionary after popping Name is :  {'Course': 'BTech', 'Roll_No': '16/001'}
Marks is : -1
Dictionary after popping Marks is :  {'Course': 'BTech', 'Roll_No': '16/001'}
Randomly popping any item :  ('Course', 'BTech')
Dictionary after random popping is :  {'Roll_No': '16/001'}
Traceback (most recent call last):
  File "C:\Python34\Try.py", line 8, in <module>
    print("Aggregate is :", Dict.pop('Aggr'))
KeyError: 'Aggr'
```

Key points to remember

- Keys must have unique values. Not even a single key can be duplicated in a dictionary. If you try to add a duplicate key, then the last assignment is retained. This is shown in the example given below.

Example 8.61   Program to illustrate the use of duplicate keys in a dictionary

```
Dict = {'Roll_No' : '16/001', 'Name' : 'Arav', 'Course' : 'BTech', 'Name' :
'Kriti'}
print("Dict[ROll_NO] = ", Dict['Roll_No'])
print("Dict[NAME] = ", Dict['Name'])
```

```
print("Dict[COURSE] = ", Dict['Course'])
```

OUTPUT

```
Dict[ROll_NO] =  16/001
Dict[NAME] =  Kriti
Dict[COURSE] =  BTech
```

- In a dictionary, keys should be strictly of a type that is immutable. This means that a key can be of strings, number, or tuple type but it cannot be a list which is mutable. In case you try to make your key of a mutable type, then a TypeError will be generated as shown below.

Example 8.62 Program to illustrate the use of mutable keys in a dictionary

```
Dict = {'Roll_No' : '16/001', 'Name' : 'Arav', 'Course' : 'BTech'}
print("Dict[ROll_NO] = ", Dict['Roll_No'])
print("Dict[NAME] = ", Dict['Name'])
print("Dict[COURSE] = ", Dict['Course'])
```

OUTPUT

```
Dict[ROll_NO] =  16/001
Dict[NAME] =  Arav
Dict[COURSE] =  BTech
```

> **Programming Tip:** In Python "None" is a special value like null or nil which means no value.

- Tuples can be used as keys only if they contain immutable objects like strings, numbers, or other tuples. If a tuple used as key contains any mutable object either directly or indirectly, then an error is generated. This is shown in the code given in the following example.

Example 8.63 Program to use tuple as keys

```
Dict = {(1,2),([4,5,6])}
print(Dict)
```

OUTPUT

```
Traceback (most recent call last):
  File "C:\Python34\Try.py", line 1, in <module>
    Dict = {(1,2),([4,5,6])}
TypeError: unhashable type: 'list'
```

- The in keyword can be used to check whether a single key is present in the dictionary.

Example 8.64 Program to check single key in a dictionary

```
Dict = {'Roll_No' : '16/001', 'Name' : 'Arav', 'Course' : 'BTech'}
if 'Course' in Dict:
```

```
    print(Dict['Course'])
```

OUTPUT

BTech

> **Programming Tip:** A KeyError occurs on an invalid access of a key like when a key that is used is not present in the dictionary.

8.6.6 Sorting Items in a Dictionary

The keys() method of dictionary returns a list of all the keys used in the dictionary in an arbitrary order. The sorted() function is used to sort the keys as shown below.

Example 8.65 Program to sort keys of a dictionary

```
Dict = {'Roll_No' : '16/001', 'Name' : 'Arav', 'Course' : 'BTech'}
print(sorted(Dict.keys()))
```

OUTPUT

['Course', 'Name', 'Roll_No']

8.6.7 Looping over a Dictionary

You can loop over a dictionary to access only values, only keys, and both using the for loop as shown in the code given below.

Example 8.66 Program to access items in a dictionary using for loop

```
Dict = {'Roll_No' : '16/001', 'Name' : 'Arav', 'Course' : 'BTech'}
print("KEYS : ", end = ' ')
for key in Dict:
    print(key, end = ' ')    # accessing only keys
print("\nVALUES : ", end = ' ')
for val in Dict.values():
    print(val, end = ' ')    # accessing only values
print("\nDICTIONARY : ", end = ' ')
for key, val in Dict.items():
    print(key, val, "\t", end = ' ')  # accessing keys and values
```

OUTPUT

```
KEYS :  Roll_No Course Name
VALUES :  16/001 BTech Arav
DICTIONARY :  Roll_No 16/001   Course BTech      Name Arav
```

8.6.8 Nested Dictionaries

You can also define a dictionary inside another dictionary. The program given below demonstrates this concept.

Example 8.67 Program to illustrate nested dictionary (i.e., use of one dictionary inside another)

```
Students = {'Shiv' : {'CS':90, 'DS':89, 'CSA':92},
            'Sadhvi' : {'CS':91, 'DS':87, 'CSA':94},
            'Krish' : {'CS':93, 'DS':92, 'CSA':88}}
for key, val in Students.items():
    print(key, val)
```

OUTPUT

```
Sadhvi {'CS': 91, 'CSA': 94, 'DS': 87}
Krish {'CS': 93, 'CSA': 88, 'DS': 92}
Shiv {'CS': 90, 'CSA': 92, 'DS': 89}
```

8.6.9 Built-in Dictionary Functions and Methods

Table 8.6 discusses some methods and functions that can be used on dictionaries in Python.

Table 8.6 Methods and Functions of Dictionaries

Operation	Description	Example	Output
len(Dict)	Returns the length of dictionary. That is, number of items (key-value pairs)	Dict1 = {'Roll_No' : '16/001', 'Name' : 'Arav', 'Course' : 'BTech'} print(len(Dict1))	3
str(Dict)	Returns a string representation of the dictionary	Dict1 = {'Roll_No' : '16/001', 'Name' : 'Arav', 'Course' : 'BTech'} print(str(Dict1))	{'Name': 'Arav', 'Roll_No': '16/001', 'Course': 'BTech'}
Dict.clear()	Deletes all entries in the dictionary	Dict1 = {'Roll_No' : '16/001', 'Name' : 'Arav', 'Course' : 'BTech'} Dict1.clear() print(Dict1)	{}
Dict.copy()	Returns a shallow copy of the dictionary, i.e., the dictionary returned will not have a duplicate copy of Dict but will have the same reference	Dict1 = {'Roll_No' : '16/001', 'Name' : 'Arav', 'Course' : 'BTech'} Dict2 = Dict1.copy() print("Dict2 : ", Dict2) Dict2['Name'] = 'Saesha' print("Dict1 after modification : ", Dict1)	Dict2 : {'Course': 'BTech', 'Name': 'Arav', 'Roll_No': '16/001'} Dict1 after modification: {'Course': 'BTech',

(Contd)

Table 8.6 *(Contd)*

Operation	Description	Example	Output
		print("Dict2 after modification : ",Dict2)	'Name': 'Arav', 'Roll_No': '16/001'} Dict2 after modification: {'Course': 'BTech', 'Name': 'Saesha', 'Roll_No': '16/001'}
Dict.fromkeys(seq[,val])	Create a new dictionary with keys from seq and values set to val. If no val is specified then, None is assigned as default value	Subjects = ['CSA', 'C++', 'DS', 'OS'] Marks = dict.fromkeys(Subjects,-1) print(Marks)	{'OS': -1, 'DS': -1, 'CSA': -1, 'C++': -1}
Dict.get(key)	Returns the value for the key passed as argument. If the key is not present in dictionary, it will return the default value. If no default value is specified then it will return None	Dict1 = {'Roll_No' : '16/001', 'Name' : 'Arav', 'Course' : 'BTech'} print(Dict1.get('Name'))	Arav
Dict.has_key(key)	Returns True if the key is present in the dictionary and False otherwise	Dict1 = {'Roll_No' : '16/001', 'Name' : 'Arav', 'Course' : 'BTech'} print('Marks' in Dict1)	False
Dict.items()	Returns a list of tuples (key-value pair)	Dict1 = {'Roll_No' : '16/001', 'Name' : 'Arav', 'Course' : 'BTech'} print(Dict1.items())	[('Course', 'BTech'), ('Name', 'Arav'), ('Roll_No', '16/001')]
Dict.keys()	Returns a list of keys in the dictionary	Dict1 = {'Roll_No' : '16/001', 'Name' : 'Arav', 'Course' : 'BTech'} print(Dict1.keys())	['Course', 'Name', 'Roll_No']
Dict.setdefault(key, value)	Sets a default value for a key that is not present in the dictionary	Dict1 = {'Roll_No' : '16/001', 'Name' : 'Arav', 'Course' : 'BTech'}	Arav has got marks = 0

(Contd)

Table 8.6 (*Contd*)

Operation	Description	Example	Output
		Dict1. setdefault('Marks',0) print(Dict1['Name'], "has got marks = ", Dict1. get('Marks'))	
Dict1.update(Dict2)	Adds the key-value pairs of Dict2 to the key-value pairs of Dict1	Dict1 = {'Roll_No' : '16/001', 'Name' : 'Arav', 'Course' : 'BTech'} Dict2 = {'Marks' : 90, 'Grade' : 'O'} Dict1.update(Dict2) print(Dict1)	{'Grade':'O', 'Course': 'BTech', 'Name': 'Arav', 'Roll_No': '16/001', 'Marks': 90}
Dict.values()	Returns a list of values in dictionary	Dict1 = {'Roll_No' : '16/001', 'Name' : 'Arav', 'Course' : 'BTech'} print(Dict1.values())	['BTech', 'Arav', '16/001']
Dict.iteritems()	Used to iterate through items in the dictionary	Dict = {'Roll_No' : '16/001', 'Name' : 'Arav', 'Course' : 'BTech'} for i,j in Dict.iteritems(): print(i, j)	Course BTech Name Arav Roll_No 16/001
in and not in	Checks whether a given key is present in dictionary or not	Dict = {'Roll_No' : '16/001', 'Name' : 'Arav', 'Course' : 'BTech'} print('Name' in Dict) print('Marks' in Dict)	True False

8.6.10 Difference Between a List and a Dictionary

There are two main differences between a list and a dictionary.

- First, a list is an ordered set of items. But, a dictionary is a data structure that is used for matching one item (key) with another (value).
- Second, in lists, you can use indexing to access a particular item. But, these indexes should be a number. In dictionaries, you can use any type (immutable) of value as an index. For example, when we write Dict['Name'], Name acts as an index but it is not a number but a string.
- Third, lists are used to look up a value whereas a dictionary is used to take one value and look up another value. For this reason, dictionary is also known as a *lookup table*.

In fact, the main advantage of a dictionary is that you don't need to search for a value one by one in the entire set of values, you can find a value instantly.

- Fourth, the key-value pair may not be displayed in the order in which it was specified while defining the dictionary. This is because Python uses complex algorithms (called hashing) to provide fast access to the items stored in the dictionary. This also makes dictionary preferable to use over a list of tuples.

8.6.11 String Formatting with Dictionaries

Python also allows you to use string formatting feature with dictionaries. So you can use %s, %d, %f, etc. to represent string, integer, floating point number, or any other data.

Example 8.68   Program that uses string formatting feature to print the key-value pairs stored in the dictionary

```
Dict = {'Sneha' : 'BTech', 'Mayank' : 'BCA'}
for key, val in Dict.items():
    print("%s is studying %s" % (key,val))
```

OUTPUT
```
Sneha is studying BTech
Mayank is studying BCA
```

8.6.12 When to use which Data Structure?

- Use lists to store a collection of data that does not need random access.
- Use lists if the data has to be modified frequently.
- Use a set if you want to ensure that every element in the data structure must be unique.
- Use tuples when you want that your data should not be altered.

8.6.13 List vs Tuple vs Dictionary vs Set

- *Tuples are lists which cannot be edited.* While tuples are immutable, lists on the other hand are mutable. Hence, they can be easily edited. *Tuples have fixed size*, so you cannot add or delete items from it. But you can easily add or delete elements in a list. Look at the codes given below which demonstrates the concept.

```
# Editing and Inserting value in
List
sports = ['cricket', 'tennis']
print(sports)
sports.append('baseball')
print(sports)
sports[2] = 'basketball'
print(sports)
```

OUTPUT
```
['cricket', 'tennis']
['cricket', 'tennis', 'baseball']
['cricket', 'tennis', 'basketball']
```

```
# Editing and Inserting value in
Tuple
sports = ('cricket', 'tennis')
print(sports)
# Does not support the append method
# sports.append('baseball')
sports[2] = 'basketball'
print(sports)
```

OUTPUT
```
('cricket', 'tennis')
Traceback (most recent call last):
  File "C:\Python34\Try.py", line 5, in
<module>
    sports[2] = 'basketball'
TypeError: 'tuple' object does not
support item assignment
```

- Due to the mutability difference, *tuples are easier on memory and processor in comparison to lists*. This means that you can easily achieve performance optimization by using tuples, wherever possible. Moreover, tuples are best used as heterogeneous collections while lists are best used as homogenous collections (where heterogeneous means that the items contained in a tuple may belong to different types or concepts).
- Sets are used to store unordered values and *do not have index*. Unlike tuples and lists, sets can *have no duplicate data*. However, like lists and unlike tuples, you can use the `add()` function to add an element to a set and the `update()` function to edit the elements in the set.

Example 8.69 Program to add an item in a set

```
sports = set(['cricket', 'tennis'])
print(sports)
sports.add('baseball')
print(sports)
```

OUTPUT

```
{'cricket', 'tennis'}
{'cricket', 'tennis', 'baseball'}
```

- Dictionary is used to store key-value pairs. Its underlying concept and usage is absolutely different from that of list, tuple, or set. Dictionaries are best data structure for frequent lookup operations. Consider the code given below.

Example 8.70 Program that uses a dictionary to return the name of the employee of an organization when his project name is given

```
Dict = {'ProjectA' : 'Manav', 'ProjectB' : 'Raghav', 'ProjectC' : 'Harsh',
'ProjectD' : 'Vineet'}
print(Dict['ProjectC'])
```

OUTPUT

```
Harsh
```

Program 8.38 Write a program that has a dictionary of states and their codes. Add another state in the pre-defined dictionary, print all the items in the dictionary, and try to print code for a state that does not exist. Set a default value prior to printing.

```
states = {'Delhi' : 'DL', 'Haryana' : 'HR', 'Maharashtra' : 'MH', 'Rajasthan' : 'RJ'}
states['Tamil Nadu'] = 'TN'      # add another state
states.setdefault('Karnataka','Sorry, no idea')
print("Code for Rajasthan is : ", states['Rajasthan'])
print("-" * 5, "CODES", "-" * 5)
for i in states.items():
    print(i)
print("Code for Karnataka : ", states.get('Karnataka'))
```

OUTPUT

```
Code for Rajasthan is :  RJ
----- CODES -----
('Karnataka', 'Sorry, no idea')
('Haryana', 'HR')
('Delhi', 'DL')
('Rajasthan', 'RJ')
('Maharashtra', 'MH')
('Tamil Nadu', 'TN')
Code for Karnataka :  Sorry, no idea
```

Program 8.39 Write a program that creates a dictionary of radius of a circle and its circumference.

```
print("Enter -1 to exit....")
Circumference = {}
while True:
    r = float(input("Enter raidus : "))
    if r == -1:
        break
    else:
        Dict = {r:2*3.14*r}
        Circumference.update(Dict)
print(Circumference)
```

OUTPUT

```
Enter -1 to exit....
Enter raidus : 5
Enter raidus : 7
Enter raidus : 8
Enter raidus : -1
{8.0: 50.24, 5.0: 31.400000000000002, 7.0: 43.96}
```

Program 8.40 Write a program that creates two dictionaries. One that stores conversion values from meters to centimeters and the other that stores values from centimeters to meters.

```
m_cm = {x : x*100 for x in range(1,11)}
temp = m_cm.values()
cm_m = {x : x/100 for x in temp}
print("Meters : Centimeters", m_cm)
print("Centimeters : Meters", cm_m)
```

OUTPUT

```
Meters : Centimeters {1: 100, 2: 200, 3: 300, 4: 400, 5: 500, 6: 600, 7: 700,
8: 800, 9: 900, 10: 1000}
```

Centimeters : Meters {800: 8, 100: 1, 200: 2, 300: 3, 400: 4, 1000: 10, 500: 5, 600: 6, 900: 9, 700: 7}

Program 8.41 Write a program that has a set of words in English language and their corresponding words in Hindi. Define another dictionary that has a list of words in Hindi and their corresponding words in Urdu. Take all words from English language and display their meanings in both the languages.

```
E_H = {'Friend' : 'Mitr', 'Teacher' : 'Shikshak', 'Book' : 'Pustak',
'Queen' : 'Rani'}
H_U = {'Mitr' : 'Dost', 'Shikshak' : 'Adhyapak', 'Pustak' : 'Kitab',
'Rani' : 'Begum'}
for i in E_H:
    print(i, "in Hindi means", E_H[i], "and in Urdu means", H_U[E_H[i]])
```

OUTPUT

```
Book in Hindi means Pustak and in Urdu means Kitab
Teacher in Hindi means Shikshak and in Urdu means Adhyapak
Friend in Hindi means Mitr and in Urdu means Dost
Queen in Hindi means Rani and in Urdu means Begum
```

Program 8.42 Write a program that calculates fib(n) using a dictionary.

```
Dict = {0: 0, 1: 1}
def fib(n):
    if n not in Dict:
        val = fib(n-1) + fib(n-2)
        Dict[n] = val
    return Dict[n]
n - int(input("Enter the value of n : "))
print("Fib(", n, ") = ", fib(n))
```

OUTPUT

```
Enter the value of n : 10
Fib( 10 ) = 55
```

Program 8.43 Write a program that creates a dictionary of cubes of odd numbers in the range 1–10.

```
Dict = {x:x**3 for x in range(10) if x%2==1}
print(Dict)
```

OUTPUT

```
{1: 1, 3: 27, 9: 729, 5: 125, 7: 343}
```

Program 8.44 Write a program that prompts the user to enter a message. Now count and print the number of occurrences of each character.

```
def count(message):
    letter_counts = {}
    for letter in message:
        letter_counts[letter] = letter_counts.get(letter, 0) + 1
    print(letter_counts)
message = input("Enter a message : ")
count(message)
```

OUTPUT

```
Enter a message : Good Morning Friends
{' ': 2, 'e': 1, 'd': 2, 'G': 1, 'F': 1, 'i': 2, 'M': 1, 'o': 3, 'n': 3, 'g': 1,
's': 1, 'r': 2}
```

Program 8.45 Write a program to store a sparse matrix as a dictionary.

```
matrix = [[0,0,0,1,0],
          [2,0,0,0,3],
          [0,0,0,4,0]]
Dict = {}
print("Sparse Matrix")
for i in range(len(matrix)):
    print("\n")
    for j in range(len(matrix[i])):
        print(matrix[i][j], end = ' ')
        if matrix[i][j]!=0:
            Dict[(i,j)] = matrix[i][j]
print("\n\nSparse Matrix can be efficiently represented as Dictionary : ")
print(Dict)
```

OUTPUT

```
Sparse Matrix
0 0 0 1 0
2 0 0 0 3
0 0 0 4 0
Sparse Matrix can be efficiently represented as Dictionary :
{(0, 3): 1, (2, 3): 4, (1, 0): 2, (1, 4): 3}
```

Program 8.46 Write a program that inverts a dictionary. That is, it makes key of one dictionary value of another and vice versa.

```
Dict = {'Roll_No' : '16/001', 'Name' : 'Arav', 'Course' : 'BTech'}
inverted = {}
for key, val in Dict.items():
    inverted[val] = key
print("Dict : ", Dict)
print("Inverted Dict : ", inverted)
```

OUTPUT

```
Dict :  {'Course': 'BTech', 'Name': 'Arav', 'Roll_No': '16/001'}
Inverted Dict :  {'BTech': 'Course', 'Arav': 'Name', '16/001': 'Roll_No'}
```

Program 8.47 Write a program that has dictionary of names of students and a list of their marks in 4 subjects. Create another dictionary from this dictionary that has name of the students and their total marks. Find out the topper and his/her score.

```
Marks = {'Neha' : [97,89,94, 90], 'Mitul' : [92,91,94,87], 'Shefali' : [67,99, 88,90]}
tot=0
Tot_Marks = Marks.copy()
for key, val in Marks.items():
    tot = sum(val)
    Tot_Marks[key] = tot
print(Tot_Marks)
max = 0
Topper = ''
for key, val in Tot_Marks.items():
    if val>max:
        max = val
            Topper = key
print("Topper is : ", Topper, "with marks = ", max)
```

OUTPUT

```
{'Neha': 370, 'Mitul': 364, 'Shefali': 344}
Topper is :  Neha with marks =  370
```

Program 8.48 Write a program that print a histogram of frequencies of characters occurring in a message.

```
msg = 'Hello All, Good Morning... Welcome to the World of Python'
msg = msg.lower()
Dict = dict()
for word in msg:
    if word not in Dict:
        Dict[word] = 1
    else:
        Dict[word] = Dict[word] + 1
print(Dict)
for key, val in Dict.items():
    print(key, '\t', '*' * val)
```

OUTPUT

```
{'a': 1, ' ': 9, 'c': 1, 'e': 4, 'd': 2, 'g': 2, 'f': 1, 'i': 1, 'h': 3, 'm': 2,
'l': 6, 'o': 9, ',': 1, '.': 3, 'r': 2, 't': 3, 'w': 2, 'y': 1, 'n': 3, 'p': 1}
```

```
a  *
   *********
c  *
e  ****
d  **
g  **
f  *
i  *
h  ***
m  **
l  ******
o  *********
,  *
.  ***
r  **
t  ***
w  **
y  *
n  ***
p  *
```

Program 8.49 Write a program that prompts the user to enter a filename. Open the file and print the frequency of each word in it.

```python
filename = input('Enter the file name: ')
file = open(filename)
counts = dict()
for line in file:
    words = line.split()
    for word in words:
        if word not in counts:
            counts[word] = 1
        else:
            counts[word] += 1
print(counts)
```

OUTPUT

```
Enter the file name: File1.txt
{'a': 1, 'and': 1, '#': 1, 'language': 1, 'Python': 1, 'of': 1, 'is': 1, 'Welcome':
1, 'Programming': 1, 'to': 1, 'interesting': 1, 'very': 1, 'world': 1, 'the': 1,
'Reading': 1, 'Hello': 1, 'simple': 1, 'Happy': 1}
```

Program 8.50 Write a program to count the numbers of characters in the string and store them in a dictionary data structure.

```python
str = "Good Morning World"
len = len(str)
```

```
Dict = {str:len}
print(Dict)
```

OUTPUT

```
{'Good Morning World': 18}
```

Program 8.51 Write a program that combines the lists to a dictionary.

```
keys = ['Name', 'Age', 'Marital Status']
values = ["Om", 38, "Married"]
details = zip(keys, values)
Dict = dict(details)
print(Dict)
```

OUTPUT

```
{'Name': 'Om', 'Age': 38, 'Marital Status': 'Married'}
```

Summary

- Slice operation can be performed on strings, tuples, and lists.
- If you want to modify a list and also keep a copy of the original list, then you should create a separate copy of the list (not just the reference). This process is called *cloning*.
- The sort() method uses ASCII values to sort the values in the list.
- List comprehensions help programmers to create lists in a concise way.
- The enumerate() function is used when you want to print both index as well as an item in the list.
- The filter() function constructs a list from those elements of the list for which a function returns True.

- The function map() applies a particular function to every element of a list.
- You cannot edit, insert, or delete values from a tuple. But you can always perform operations like concatenation, repetition, etc., on tuples.
- If a sequence is specified without parenthesis, it is treated to be a tuple by default.
- Variable-length arguments allows a function to accept a variable (different) number of arguments.
- zip() is a built-in function that takes two or more sequences and "zips" them into a list of tuples.
- Tuples can be used as key for a dictionary but lists cannot be used as keys.
- A *set* is a mutable and an unordered collection of items.

Glossary

Data structure An organization of data to make it easier to use.

Dictionary A collection of key-value pairs that maps from keys to values. While keys can be of any immutable type, there is no such restriction on its associated value which can be of any type.

Dictionary comprehension A syntactic construct which creates a dictionary based on an existing dictionary.

Hash function A function used to compute the location for a key.

Immutable data Data which cannot be modified. Assigning values to elements or slices of immutable data results in a run-time error.

Key Data that is mapped to a value in a dictionary. Keys are unique data items that are used to look up values in a dictionary.

Key-value pair A pair of items in a dictionary. Key is used to lookup for a value stored in the dictionary.

List A mutable data structure that can have elements that belong to different data types.

Lookup A dictionary operation that takes a key and finds the corresponding value.

Mutable data value Data which can be modified.

Nested loops A loop inside another loop. The inner loop runs to completion each time the outer loop runs.

Tuple An immutable data structure that stores related items together.

Exercises

Fill in the Blanks

1. _____ defines a particular way of storing and organizing data in a computer.
2. When using slice operation, _____ is generated if the index is outside the list.
3. `[10,20] < [20,10]` will return _____.
4. `insert()`, `remove()`, and `sort()` returns _____.
5. The `sort()` method uses _____ values to sort the values in the list.
6. _____ help programmers to create lists in a concise way.
7. _____ is used to print both index as well as an item in the list.
8. _____ can be used to loop over the elements of the list.
9. The _____ function applies a particular function to every element of a list.
10. If there is only one item in the sequence, `map()` function will return _____.
11. Any argument that starts with a _____ is known as _____ and specifies a variable-length argument.
12. _____ function takes two or more sequences and "zips" them into a list of tuples.
13. To add a single element in the set, use the _____ method and to add multiple elements in the set, use the _____ method.
14. Fill in the blanks to create a list and print its second element.
    ```
    List = ___10, 20, 30, 40]
    print(list[___])
    ```
15. Fill in the blanks to create a list, reassign its third element, and print the list.
    ```
    List = [1,2,3,4,5__
    List[__] = 30
    print(__)
    ```
16. Fill in the blanks to print "Hello" if the list contains 'H'.
    ```
    Letters = ['W', 'G', 'H']
    __ 'H'__ Letters:
        print("_____")
    ```

17. Fill in the blanks to add `'G'` to the end of the list and print the list's length.
    ```
    Letters.____('G')
    print(__ ___)
    ```
18. Fill in the blanks to print the letters in the list.
    ```
    Letters = ['H', 'E', 'L', 'L','O']
    __ i __Letters__
    print(i)
    ```
19. Fill in the blanks to print the second element of the list, if it contains odd number of elements.
    ```
    List =[10, 20, 30, 40, 50]
    If ___(list)%2__0__
        print(List[__])
    ```
20. If `tup = ("abc", "def", "ghi", "jkl")`, `tup[-1]` will print _____.
21. Fill in the blanks to print `"Hi"`, if the key 90 is present in the dictionary named `"Dict"`.
    ```
    if _____
    print("Hi")
    ```
22. Fill in the blanks to create a list, dictionary, and tuple.
    ```
    List=__"abc", "def"__
    Dict=__1:"abc", 2:"def"__
    Tup=__"abc","def"__
    ```
23. Fill in the banks to print the first two elements of the list.
    ```
    List=[1,2,3,4,5,6]
    print(list[0_])
    ```
24. `List = [i*2 for i in range(__)]` will create a list of even numbers between 0 and 18
25. Fill in the blanks to create a list of multiples of 3 from 0 to 30.
    ```
    List = __i for i in range(30) __ i%__==0]
    ```
26. If `print((lambda x:x**2+3*x+7)(-7))`, will print _____
27. Fill in the blanks to create a set, add the letter "xyz" and print its length.
    ```
    words = __"abc","def","ghi"__
    words.__("jkl")
    print(__(words))
    ```

28. Fill in the blanks to remove all items from the list that are greater than _____ from the list.
```
List = [10,20,50,55,80,30,100,70]
print(list(____(lambda x:x__55,____)))
```

29. ```
List =[15,20,25,30, 35, 40]
print(list(___(_____x: x%__!=0, List)))
```

30. The range of index values for a list of 10 elements will be _____.

## State True or False

1. The index value starts from zero.
2. List is an immutable data structure.
3. A tuple can be sliced.
4. It is possible to edit, add, and delete elements from a list.
5. It is possible to edit, add, and delete elements from a tuple.
6. Slice operation can be used to insert items from another list or sequence at a particular location
7. The slice operation is used to clone a list.
8. When a list is assigned to another using the assignment operator, then a new copy of the list is made.
9. Items in a list can be deleted by assigning an empty list to a slice of elements.
10. If you specify a non-integer number as the index, then IndexError will be generated.
11. The filter() function returns a Boolean value.
12. The map() function returns a list of values.
13. If the sequence is empty, map() function will raise an exception.
14. You cannot perform operations like concatenation, repetition, etc. on tuples.
15. It is possible to specify a list within a tuple.
16. If a sequence is specified without parenthesis, it is treated to be a list by default.
17. Lists are faster than tuples.
18. Tuples can be used as key for a dictionary but lists cannot be used as keys.
19. It is possible to compare two sets.
20. A set can be created from a list but a set cannot contain a list.
21. Keys in the dictionary must be of any mutable data type.
22. Dictionary keys are case-insensitive.

## Multiple Choice Questions

1. If List = [1,2,3,4,5] then List[5] will result in _____
   (a) 4          (b) 3
   (c) 2          (d) Error
2. If List = [1,2,3,4,5] and we write List[3] = List[1], then what will be List[3]
   (a) 1          (b) 3
   (c) 2          (d) 4
3. type(x) will print
   (a) <class 'list'>   (b) <class 'tuple'>
   (c) <class 'int'>    (d) Error
4. If tup = ("abc", "def", "ghi", "jkl"), then tup("def") will return
   (a) 1          (b) 2
   (c) 0          (d) Error
5. print((0, 10, 20) < (0, 30, 40)) will print
   (a) True       (b) False
   (c) Equal      (d) Error
6. If Dict = {1:2, 3:4, 4:11, 5:6, 7:8}, then print(Dict[Dict[3]]) will print
   (a) 2          (b) 8
   (c) 11         (d) 6
7. If List = [1,2,3,4,5,6,7,8,9,10], then print List[8:4:-1] will give
   (a) [2,3,4,5]      (b) [9,8,7,6]
   (c) [6,7,8,9]      (d) [5,4,3,2]
8. If List = min([sum([10,20]),max(abs(-30),4)]), then List = _____
   (a) 10         (b) 20
   (c) 30         (d) 4
9. Which slice operation will reverse the list?
   (a) Lists[-1:]      (b) numbers[::-1]
   (c) numbers[:-1:]   (d) List[9:8:1]
10. If List = (12,8,7,5), then print(max(min(List [:2]),abs(-6))) will print
    (a) 12         (b) 8
    (c) 7          (d) 5
11. Which function constructs a list from those elements of the list for which a function returns True?
    (a) Filter()       (b) map()
    (c) reduce()       (d) enumerate()
12. Which data structure allows you to return multiple values from a function?
    (a) List           (b) Tuple
    (c) Dictionary     (d) Set
13. Which data structure does not allow duplicate values?
    (a) List           (b) Tuple
    (c) Dictionary     (d) Set
14. Which data structure does not support indexing?
    (a) List           (b) Tuple
    (c) Dictionary     (d) Set
```

Review Questions

1. Give the properties of lists.
2. Discuss different in ways in which you can create a list.
3. Explain the use of del statement to delete values from a list. Also differentiate between del and remove().
4. With the help of an example explain the concept of nested lists.
5. With the help of an example, explain the concept of list comprehension.
6. It is possible use the list comprehension to combine the elements of two lists. Justify with the help of an example.
7. With the help of an example explain the significance of enumerate() function.
8. How can you return more than one value from a function. Explain with the help of a program.
9. What do you understand by variable-length arguments?

10. With the help of program illustrate the gather and scatter technique of passing and using function arguments.
11. How are tuples a useful data structure?
12. What do you understand by the term dictionary comprehension?
13. Write a short note on the following functions:
    (a) Filter()
    (b) Map()
    (c) Reduce()
14. Differentiate between:
    (a) append() and insert() methods of list
    (b) pop() and remove() methods of list
    (c) del() and pop() methods of list
    (d) remove(), pop(), and discard() methods of sets

Programming Problems

1. Use list comprehension to construct the following lists
   (a) ['1a', '2a', '3a', '4a'].
   (b) ['ab', 'ac', 'ad', 'bb', 'bc', 'bd'].
   (c) ['ab', 'ad', 'bc'], from the list created above (using slice operation)
   (d) Multiples of 10
2. Make a list of five random numbers.
3. Make a list of first ten letters of the alphabet, then using the slice operation do the following operations.
   (a) Print the first three letters from the list
   (b) Print any three letters from the middle
   (c) Print the letters from any particular index to the end of the list
4. Write a program that converts a list of characters into their corresponding ASCII values using map() function.
5. Write a program using reduce() function to calculate the sum of first 10 natural numbers.
6. Write a program that uses filter() function to filter out only even numbers from a list.
7. Write a program that uses map() to print the double value of each element in a list.
8. Write a program that creates a list ['a', 'b', 'c'], then create a tuple from that list. Now, do the opposite. That is, create the tuple ('a', 'b', 'c'), and then create a list from it.
9. Create a tuple that has just one element which in turn may have three elements 'a', 'b', and 'c'. Print the length of this tuple.
10. Create a dictionary of products purchased and their MRPs. Calculate the bill and display to the customer.

11. Write a program that prompts user to enter a string and returns in alphabetical order, a letter and its frequency of occurrence in the string. (Ignore case).
12. Write a program that has a dictionary of your friends name (as keys) and their birthdays. Print the items in the dictionary in a sorted order. Prompt the user to enter a name and check if it is present in the dictionary. If the name does not exist, then ask the user to enter DOB. Add the details in the dictionary.
13. Write a program that displays a menu and its price. Take the order from the customer. Check if the ordered product is in the menu. In case it is not there, the customer should be asked to reorder and if it is present, then product should be added in the bill.
14. Write a program that prints the maximum and minimum value in a dictionary.
15. Write a program to get a dictionary from an object's fields.
16. Write a program to remove duplicates from a dictionary.
17. Write a program to check whether a dictionary has some key-value pairs stored in it or not.
18. Write a program to implement a user-defined stack.
19. Write a program to implement a user-defined queue.
20. Write a program that prints the maximum value of the second half of the list.
21. Write a program that finds the sum of all the numbers in a list using a while loop.
22. Write a program that finds sum of all even numbers in a list.
23. Write a program that reverse a list using a loop.

24. Write a program to find whether a particular element is present in the list using a loop.
25. Write a program that prompts the user to enter an alphabet. Print all the words in the list that starts with that alphabet.
26. Write a program that prints all consonants in a string using list comprehension.
27. Write a program that has a predefined list. Create a copy of this list in such a way that only those values that are in `valid_tuple` are added in the new list.
28. Write a program that prompts a number from user and adds it in a list. If the value entered by user is greater than `100`, then add `"EXCESS"` in the list.
29. Write a program that counts the number of times a value appears in the list. Use a loop to do the same.
30. Write a program to insert a value in a list at the specified location using `while` loop.
31. Write a program that creates a list of numbers from `1-50` that are either divisible by `3` or divisible by `6`.
32. Write a program using filter function to a list of cubes of numbers from `1-10`.

33. Write a program to create a list of numbers in the range 1 to 20. Then delete all the numbers from the list that are divisible by 3.
34. Write a program to find the sum of all values in a list using `reduce()` function.
35. Write a program to transpose two matrices.
36. Write a program that accepts different number of arguments and return the maximum value passed to it.
37. Write a program to make a quiz. Use `zip()` function to extract question into and answer into two separate lists.
38. Make two sets of random integers and apply all set operations on them.
39. Using dictionary comprehension, create a dictionary of numbers and their squares in the range `(1-10)`.
40. Write a program that displays information about an employee. Use nested dictionary to do the task.
41. Give an expression to form a set of squares of numbers present in an input list consisting of some random values in the range 1-20.

Find the Output

1.
```
from math import pi
list = [str(round(pi, val)) for val in
range(1, 5)]
print(list)
```
2.
```
colors = ['red', 'blue', 'green']
print(colors[2])
print(len(colors))
```
3.
```
list = ['abc', 'def', 'ghi', 'jkl']
print(list[1:-1])
list[0:2] = 'xyz'
print(list)
```
4.
```
list = ['abc', 'def', 'ghi', 'jkl', [1,2,3,4,5]]
print(list[4][2])
```
5.
```
list = ['p','r','o','g','r','a','m','m','i','n','g']
print(list[2:5])
print(list[:-5])
print(list[5:])
print(list[:])
```
6.
```
even = [2,4,6]
print(even + [10, 12, 14])
print(even*2)
even.insert(1,0)
print(even)
del even[2]
print(even)
```
7.
```
list = ['p','r','o','g','r','a','m']
list.remove('p')
print(list)
```

```
print(list.pop(1))
print(list)
print(list.pop())
print(list)
```
8.
```
list = [9,4,3,8,0,2,3,6]
print(list.index(3))
print(list.count(8))
list.sort()
print(list)
list.reverse()
print(list)
print(0 in list)
```
9.
```
list = [2 ** x for x in range(5)]
print(list)
```
10.
```
countries = ['India', 'Sri Lanka', 'New
Zealand', 'Japan', 'Russia']
for index, country in enumerate(countries):
print("The country, " + country + ", is at
position " + str(index) + ".")
```
11.
```
list = [(1, 2), [3, 4], '56', 78, 9.0]
print(list[0], type(list[0]))
print(list[2:3], type(list[0:1]))
print(list[2], type(list[2]))
```
12.
```
words = 'Welcome to the world of Programming'.
split()
msg = [[word.upper(), word.lower(), len(word)]
for word in words]
for i in msg:
    print(i)
```

```
13. item = [x+y for x in 'cup' for y in 'pen']
    print(item)
14. print([x+y for x in 'cup' for y in 'pen' if
    x != 't' and y != 'o' ])
15. list =[ [1,2]*3 ] *4
    print(list)
16. list = [10, 20, 30, 40, 50, 60, 70, 80, 90]
    print(list[-4:-1])
    print(list[-1:-4])
    print(list[-5:])
    print(list[-6:-2:2])
    print(list[::-1])
17. list = [[10, 20, [30, 40, [50, 60]]]]
    print(list[0])
    print(list[0][2])
    print(list[0][2][2])
    print(list[0][0])
    print(list[0][2][1])
    print(list[0][2][2][0])
18. List = [100, 90, 80, 70, 60, 50]
    List[2] = List[1] - 20
    if 30 in List:
        print(List[3])
    else:
        print(List[4])
19. List = list(range(2, 20, 3))
    print(List[5])
20. List = [-5, -3, 0, 3, 6]
    print([x*2 for x in List])
    print([x for x in List if x >= 0])
21. print([(x, x*2) for x in range(5)])
22. List = [[1,2,3], [4,5,6], [7,8,9]]
    print([val for x in List for val in x])
23. DC = [-100, 0, 32, 40, 100]
    DF = map(lambda temp: (9.0/5)*temp + 32, DC)
    print(DF)
24. List = [1,2,3,4,5,6,7,8,9,10]
    print(list(filter(lambda x: x % 4 == 0,
    List)))
    print(list( map(lambda x: x * 2 + 5, List))
    print(reduce(lambda x, y: x + y, List))
25. Tup = ("abc", "def")
    (key, value) = Tup
    print(key, value)
26. Tup = (1,2,3)
    Add_Tup = Tup + Tup
    print(Add_Tup)
    Mul_Tup = Tup * 3
    print(Mul_Tup)
27. msg = "HelloWorld"
    pairs = []
```

```
    for i in range(1, len(msg), 2):
        first = msg[i - 1]
        second = msg[i]
        pairs.append((first, second))
    for item in pairs:
        print(item)
28. Tup  = (1, 'abc')
    List = [1, 'abc']
    print(Tup == List)
    print(Tup == tuple(List))
    print(list(Tup) == List)
    print((1, 2) + (3, 4))
29. list = ['Good', 'Morning']
    y, x = list
    print(x, y)
30. A = ('Chinu', 30, 'Female')
    B = ('Varun', 32, 'Male')
    for i in [A, B]:
        print('%s is a %d year old %s' %i)
31. Tup = ('Good',)
    for i in range(4):
        Tup = (Tup,)
        print(Tup)
32. Tup1='a','bcd',12.34
    Tup2=Tup1,(5,6,7,8)
    print(Tup2)
33. Tup = (1, 2, [3, 4])
    Tup[2][0] = 5
    print(Tup)
34. Tup = ("Good Morning")
    print(Tup.index('M'), end = ' ')
    print(Tup.index('n', 5))
    print(Tup.index('r',4,8))
35. IT_studs = set(['Dev', 'Era', 'Francis',
    'Geet'])
    Elec_studs = set(['Geet', 'Harman', 'Susan',
    'Janak'])
    CS_studs = set(['Era', 'Francis', 'Susan',
    'Krishnav'])
    students = IT_studs | Elec_studs | CS_studs
    print("Students : ", students)
    IT_Elec_studs = IT_studs & Elec_studs
    CS_studs.add('Loveya')
    print("Is Students Superset of IT : ",
    students.issuperset(IT_studs))
    CS_studs.update(Elec_studs)
    print("CS Students : ", CS_studs)
36. x = {1, 2, 3, 4, 5}
    y = {4, 5, 6, 7, 8}
    print(x.difference(y))
    print(y.symmetric_difference(x))
```

```
    x.difference_update(y)
    print(x)
37. x = set()
    x.add("abc")
    x.add("def")
    x.update(["ghi","jkl"])
    print(x)
38. Dict = {"India":"New Delhi", "Nepal":
    "Kathmandu"}
    Dict1 = {"USA":"Washington DC"}
    Dict.update(Dict1)
    print(Dict)
39. Dict={"India":"NewDelhi","Nepal":"Kathmandu",
    "USA":"WashingtonDC"}
    del Dict["Nepal"]
    for key,val in Dict.items():
    print(key,val)
40. Dict = {"India":"New Delhi",
    "Nepal":"Kathmandu","USA":"WashingtonDC"}
    print(Dict.get("Russia"))
    print(Dict.get("Pakistan", "No Idea"))
41. Studs = {'Mitanshi', 'Harshita', 'Pritika'}
    Toppers = {}.fromkeys(Studs, 0)
    print(Toppers)
    Toppers['Mitanshi'] = 97
    Toppers['Harshita'] = 92
    Toppers['Pritika'] = 89
    Toppers.setdefault('Nisha', -1)
    print(Toppers)
42. Toppers = {}
    Toppers['Mitanshi'] = 97
    Toppers['Harshita'] = 92
    Toppers['Pritika'] = 89
    print('Harshita got ' + str(Toppers.
    get('Harshita')) + ' marks.')
43. rec = {'Name': {'First': 'Chaitanya',
    'Last': 'Raj'},
       'Marks': [80, 76, 84],
       'Course': 'BTech'}
```

```
    print(rec['Name'])
    print(rec['Name']['Last'])
    print(rec['Marks'])
    rec['Marks'].append(72)
    print(rec)
44. List = [-10,20,-30,40,-50]
    if all([abs(i)<30 for i in List]):
        print("Hi")
    else:
        print("Bye")

45. def add_two(x):
    return x+2
    List = [10,20,30,40,50]
    result = list(map(add_two,List))
    print(result)
46. List = [13,26,39,52,64]
    print(list(filter(lambda x:x%2==1,List)))
47. str = "abcdefghijklmno"
    for i in range(0, len(str), 2):
        print(str[i], end = " ")
48. print([ord(ch) for ch in 'PYTHON'])
49. >>> {s for s in [1, 2, 1, 0]}
    set([0, 1, 2])
50. >>> {s**2 for s in [1, 2, 1, 0]}
    set([0, 1, 4])
51. >>> {s**2 for s in range(10)}
    set([0, 1, 4, 9, 16, 25, 36, 49, 64, 81])
52. sentence = "These five women stalwarts are
    Rani of Jhansi, Rani of Kittur, Rani Abbakka,
    Sultana Razia and Kalpana Chawla. "
    chars = sentence.split()
    set1 - {word for word in chars}
    print(set1)
    {'Jhansi,',   'women',   'are',   'Abbakka,',
    'Kittur,',      'stalwarts',      'Kalpana',
    'Chawla.', 'Rani', 'These', 'of', 'Sultana',
    'five', 'and', 'Razia'}
```

Find the Error

```
1. list = ['abc', 'def', 'ghi', 'jkl']
   print(list[2.0])
2. even = [2,4,6]
   del even
   print(even)
3. list = [(1, 2), [3, 4], '56', 78, 9.0]
   list.remove('abc')
4. msg = "Hello"
   msg.append("World")
   print(msg)
```

```
5. tup = ("abc", "def", "ghi", "jkl")
   tup.append("mno")
6. tup.remove("abc")
7. Tup = ('abc', 'def', 'ghi','jkl')
   Tup[2] = 'xyz'
8. x, y = 10, 20, 30
9. x = {1, 2, 3, 4, 5}
   x.add([6,7,8])
   print(x)
```

```
10.  Dict = {[02,89, 85]:"PCM"}
     print(Dict)
11.  Dict       =       {"India":"New    Delhi",
     "Nepal":"Kathmandu"}
     print(Dict["USA"])
```

```
12.  Dict = {}
     print(Dict[0])
13.  Tup1 = (9,8,7,6,5)
     Tup2 = (1,2,3,4,5)
     print(Tup1 - Tup2)
```

Answers

Fill in the blanks

1. Data structure
2. IndexError
3. True
4. None
5. ASCII
6. List comprehensions
7. enumerate() function
8. iter function
9. map()
10. that value

11. * symbol, gather
12. zip()
13. add(), update()
14. [, 1
15.], 2, List
16. if, in, Hello
17. append, len, (, Letters,)
18. for, in,:
19. len, !=,:, 1
20. jkl

21. 90, in, Dict
22. [], {}, ()
23. :2
24. 10
25. [, if, 3
26. 35
27. {,}, add, len
28. filter, >, List
29. filter, lambda, 2
30. 0-10

State True or False

1. True   2. False   3. True   4. True   5. False   6. True   7. False   8. False   9. True   10. False
11. True   12. True   13. True   14. False   15. True   16. False   17. False   18. True   19. True   20. True
21. False   22. False

Multiple Choice Questions

1. (d)   2. (c)   3. (c)   4. (d)   5. (a)   6. (c)   7. (b)   8. (c)   9. (b)   10. (b)   11. (a)   12. (b)
13. (d)   14. (d)

Classes and Objects

• Class and Objects • Class and Instance Variables • Public and Private Variables • Special Methods • Built-in Attributes and Functions • Garbage Collection • Class Method and Static Method

9.1 INTRODUCTION

In all our programs till now, we have been using the procedure-oriented technique in which our program is written using functions or blocks of statements which manipulate data. However, another and in fact, a better style of programming is called object oriented programming in which data and functions are combined to form a class.

Compared with other programming languages, Python has a very short and simple way to define and use classes. The class mechanism supported by Python is actually a mixture of that found in C++ and Modula-3. As discussed in Chapter 2, Python supports all the standard features of Object Oriented Programming. In this chapter, we will study about these features in detail.

9.2 CLASSES AND OBJECTS

Classes and objects are the two main aspects of object oriented programming. In fact, a class is the basic building block in Python. A **class** creates a new type and object is an instance (or variable) of the class. Classes provides a blueprint or a template using which objects are created. In fact, *in Python, everything is an object or an instance of some class.* For example, all integer variables that we define in our program are actually instances of class int. Similarly, all string variables are objects of class string. Recall that we had used string methods using the variable name followed by the dot operator and the method name. We have already studied that we can find out the type of any object using the type() function.

> **Note** The Python Standard Library is based on the concept of classes and objects.

9.2.1 Defining Classes

Python has a very simple syntax of defining a class. This syntax can be given as,

```
class class_name:
    <statement-1>
    <statement-2>
        .
        .
        .
    <statement-N>
```

> **Programming Tip:** A class can be defined in a function or with an `if` statement.

From the syntax, we see that class definition is quite similar to function definition. It starts with a keyword class followed by the class_name and a colon (:). The statement in the definition can be any of these—sequential instructions, decision control statements, loop statements, and can even include function definitions. Variables defined in a class are called *class variables* and functions defined inside a class are called *class methods*. Class variables and class methods are together known as *class members*. The class members can be accessed through class objects. Class methods have access to all the data contained in the instance of the object.

Class definitions can appear anywhere in a program, but they are usually written near the beginning of the program, after the import statements. Note that when a class definition is entered, a new namespace is created, and used as the local scope. Therefore, all assignments to local variables go into this new namespace.

> **Note**   A class creates a new local namespace where all its attributes (data and functions) are defined.

9.2.2 Creating Objects

Once a class is defined, the next job is to create an object (or instance) of that class. The object can then access class variables and class methods using the dot operator (.). The syntax to create an object is given as,

```
object_name = class_name()
```

Creating an object or instance of a class is known as *class instantiation*. From the syntax, we can see that class instantiation uses function notation. Using the syntax, an empty object of a class is created. Thus, we see that in Python, to create a new object, call a class as if it were a function. The syntax for accessing a class member through the class object is

> **Programming Tip:** Python does not require the new operator to create an object.

```
object_name.class_member_name
```

Example 9.1   Program to access class variable using class object

```
class ABC:
    var = 10     # class variable
obj = ABC()
print(obj.var)   # class variable is accessed using class object

OUTPUT
10
```

> **Programming Tip:** self in Python works in the same way as the "this" pointer in C++.

In the above program, we have defined a class ABC which has a variable var having a value of 10. The object of the class is created and used to access the class variable using the dot operator. Thus, we can think of a class as a *factory* for making objects.

9.2.3 Data Abstraction and Hiding through Classes

In Chapter 2, we had learnt that data abstraction refers to the process by which data and functions are defined in such a way that only essential details are provided to the outside world and the implementation details are hidden. In Python and other object oriented programming languages, classes provide methods to the outside world to provide the functionality of the object or to manipulate the object's data. Any entity outside the world does not know about the implementation details of the class or that method.

Data encapsulation, also called data hiding, organizes the data and methods into a structure that prevents data access by any function (or method) that is not specified in the class. This ensures the integrity of the data contained in the object.

Encapsulation defines different access levels for data variables and member functions of the class. These access levels specifies the access rights, for example,

- Any data or function with access level *public* can be accessed by any function belonging to any class. This is the lowest level of data protection.
- Any data or function with access level *private* can be accessed only by the class in which it is declared. This is the highest level of data protection. In Python, private variables are prefixed with a double underscore (__). For example, __var is a private variable of the class.

Note Functions defined inside a class are called class methods.

9.3 CLASS METHOD AND SELF ARGUMENT

Class methods (or functions defined in the class) are exactly same as ordinary functions that we have been defining so far with just one small difference. Class methods must have the first argument named as self. This is the first argument that is added to the beginning of the parameter list. Moreover, you do not pass a value for this parameter when you call the method. Python provides its value automatically. The self argument refers to the object itself. That is, the object that has called the method. This means that even if a method that takes no arguments, it should be defined to accept the self. Similarly, a function defined to accept one parameter will actually take two—self and the parameter, so on and so forth.

Since, the class methods uses self, they require an object or instance of the class to be used. For this reason, they are often referred to as *instance methods*.

Note If you have a method which takes no arguments, then you still have to define the method to have a self argument.

Consider the program given below which has one class variable and one class method. Observe that the class method accepts no values but still has self as an argument. Both the class members are accessed through the object of the class.

Example 9.2 Program to access class members using the class object

```
class ABC():
    var = 10
    def display(self):
        print("In class method.....")
obj = ABC()
print(obj.var)
obj.display()
```

> **Programming Tip:** You can give any name for the self parameter, but you should not do so.

OUTPUT
```
10
In class method.....
```

Key points to remember

- The statements inside the class definition must be properly indented.
- A class that has no other statements should have a pass statement at least.
- Class methods or functions that begins with double underscore (__) are special functions with a predefined and a special meaning.

9.4 THE __init__() METHOD (THE CLASS CONSTRUCTOR)

The __init__() method has a special significance in Python classes. The __init__() method is automatically executed when an object of a class is created. The method is useful to initialize the variables of the class object. Note the __init__() is prefixed as well as suffixed by double underscores. The __init__() method can be declared as, def __init__(self, [args...]). Look at the program given below that uses the __init__() method.

Example 9.3   Program illustrating the use of __init__() method

```
class ABC():
    def __init__(self,val):
        print("In class method.....")
        self.val = val
        print("The value is : ", val)
obj = ABC(10)
```

OUTPUT
```
In class method.....
The value is :  10
```

In the program, the __init__() method accepts one argument val. Like any other class method the first argument has to be self. In the __init__() method we define a variable as self.val which has exactly the same name as that specified in the argument list. Though the two

> **Programming Tip:** The __init__() method is same as constructor in C++ and Java.

variables have the same name, they are entirely different variables. The self.val belongs to the newly created object. Note that we have just created an object in the main module and no where have we called the __init__() method. This is because the __init__() method is automatically involved when the object of the class is created.

> **Note**   It is a good programming habit to initialize all attributes in the __init__() method. Although values can be initialized in other methods also but it is not recommended.

9.5 CLASS VARIABLES AND OBJECT VARIABLES

We have seen that a class can have variables defined in it. Basically, these variables are of two types—class variables and object variables. As the name suggests, class variables are owned by the class and object variables are owned by each object. What this specifically means can be understood by using the following points.

- If a class has n objects, then there will be n separate copies of the object variable as each object will have its own object variable.
- The object variable is not shared between objects.
- A change made to the object variable by one object will not be reflected in other objects.

- If a class has one class variable, then there will be one copy only for that variable. All the objects of that class will share the class variable.
- Since there exists a single copy of the class variable, any change made to the class variable by an object will be reflected in all other objects.

> **Note** Class variables and object variables are ordinary variables that are bound to the class's and object's namespace respectively.

Example 9.4 Program to differentiate between class and object variables

```
class ABC():
    class_var = 0    # class variable
    def __init__(self,var):
        ABC.class_var += 1
        self.var = var  # object variable
        print("The Object value is : ", var)
        print("The value of class variable is : ", ABC.class_var)
obj1 = ABC(10)
obj2 = ABC(20)
obj3 = ABC(30)
```

OUTPUT

```
The Object value is :  10
The value of class variable is :  1
The Object value is :  20
The value of class variable is :  2
The Object value is :  30
The value of class variable is :  3
```

> **Programming Tip:** Class variable must be prefixed by the class name and dot operator.

In the above program, we have a class variable `class_var` which is shared by all three objects of the class. It is initialized to zero and each time an object is created, the `class_var` is incremented by 1. Since, the variable is shared by all objects, changes made to `class_var` by one object is reflected in other objects as well. Note that class variable is accessed using the class name followed by the dot operator as the variable belongs to the class.

Then we have object variable which is unique for every object. When an object is created and the `__init__()` method is called, the object variable is initialized. The object variable belongs to only a particular object.

> **Note** Class variables are usually used to keep a count of number of objects created from a class.

We have already seen that one use of class variables or class attributes is to count the number of objects created. Another important use of such variables is to define constants associated with a particular class or provide default attribute values. For example, the code given in the following example uses the class variable to specify a default value for the objects. Now, each individual object may either change it or retain the default value.

Example 9.5 Program illustrating the modification of an instance variable

```python
class Number:
    even = 0    # default value
    def check(self, num):
        if num%2 == 0:
            self.even = 1
    def Even_Odd(self, num):
        self.check(num)
        if self.even == 1:
            print(num, "is even")
        else:
            print(num, "is odd")
n = Number()
n.Even_Odd(21)
```

OUTPUT

```
21 is odd
```

> **Programming Tip:** Class attributes are defined at the same indentation level as that of class methods.

Name Clashes: Note that in the above program, we had a class variable even with value 0. We had set an attribute of the object which has the same name as the class attribute. So here, we are actually *overriding* the class attribute with an instance attribute. The instance (or the object) attribute will take precedence over the class attribute. If we create two objects of Number, then both the objects will have their own copy of even. Changes made in one object will not be reflected in the other. But this is not true for a mutable type attribute. Remember that, if you modify a mutable object in one place, the change will be reflected in all other places as well. This difference is reflected in the program given below.

Note Overriding means that the first definition is not available anymore.

Example 9.6 Program modifying a mutable type attribute

```python
class Number:
    evens = []
    odds = []
    def __init__(self, num):
        self.num = num
        if num%2 == 0:
            Number.evens.append(num)
        else:
            Number.odds.append(num)
N1 = Number(21)
N2 = Number(32)
N3 = Number(43)
N4 = Number(54)
N5 = Number(65)
```

```
print("Even Numbers are : ", Number.evens)
print("Odd Numbers are : ", Number.odds)
```

OUTPUT
```
Even Numbers are :  [32, 54]
Odd Numbers are :  [21, 43, 65]
```

In the aforementioned program, we have defined two lists as class variables which are of mutable types. The class variable is being shared among all objects. So any change made by any of the object will be reflected in the final list. So, whether you write, Number.evens, self.evens, N1.evens, N2.evens, N3.evens, N4.evens, or N5.evens, it will all print the same list.

Note A variable defined inside the class is known as class attribute or simply attribute.

9.6 THE __del__() METHOD

In the previous section, we saw the __init__() method which initializes an object when it is created. Similar to the __init__() method, we have the __del__() method which does just the opposite work. The __del__() method is automatically called

Programming Tip: __del__() method is analogous to destructors in C++ and Java.

when an object is going out of scope. This is the time when an object will no longer be used and its occupied resources are returned back to the system so that they can be reused as and when required. You can also explicitly do the same using the del keyword.

Example 9.7 Program to illustrate the use of __del__() method

```
class ABC():
    class_var = 0     # class variable
    def __init__(self,var):
        ABC.class_var += 1
        self.var = var   # object variable
        print("The Object value is : ", var)
        print("The value of class variable is : ", ABC.class_var)
    def __del__(self):
        ABC.class_var -= 1
        Print("Object with value %d is going out of scope"%self.var)
obj1 = ABC(10)
obj2 = ABC(20)
obj3 = ABC(30)
del obj1
del obj2
del obj3
```

Programming Tip: In C++ and Java, all members are private by default but in Python, they are public by default

OUTPUT
```
The Object value is :  10
```

```
The value of class variable is :   1
The Object value is :   20
The value of class variable is :   2
The Object value is :   30
The value of class variable is :   3
Object with value 10 is going out of scope
Object with value 20 is going out of scope
Object with value 30 is going out of scope
```

Thus, we see that the __del__() is invoked when the object is about to be destroyed. This method might be used to clean up any resources used by it.

9.7 OTHER SPECIAL METHODS

In this section, we will read about some other functions that have a special meaning in Python. These functions include:

- **__repr__():** This method has built-in function with syntax repr(object). It returns a string representation of an object. The function works on any object, not just class instances.
- **__cmp__():** This method is called to compare two class objects. In fact, the function can even compare any two Python objects by using the equality operator (==). For class instances, the __cmp__() method can be defined to write the customized comparison logic.
- **__len__():** This method function has a built-in function that has the syntax len(object). It returns the length of an object.

Example 9.8   Program to illustrate the use of special methods in Python classes

```python
class ABC():
    def __init__(self, name, var):
        self.name = name
        self.var = var
    def __repr__(self):
        return repr(self.var)
    def __len__(self):
        return len(self.name)
    def __cmp__(self, obj):
        return self.var - obj.var
obj = ABC("abcdef", 10)
print("The value stored in object is : ", repr(obj))
print("The length of name stored in object is : ", len(obj))
obj1 = ABC("ghijkl", 1)
val = obj.__cmp__(obj1)
if val == 0:
    print("Both values are equal")
elif val == -1:
    print("First value is less than second")
else:
    print("Second value is less than first")
```

OUTPUT
```
The value stored in object is :  10
The length of name stored in object is :  6
Second value is less than first
```

Python has a lot of other special methods that let classes act like numbers so that you can perform arithmetic operations like add, subtract, etc. on them. All those methods cannot be discussed here but other special methods are:

- The __call__() method: The method lets a class act like a function so that its instance can be called directly in obj(arg1,arg2,...).
- The __lt__(), __le__(), __eq__(), __ne__(), __gt__(), and __ge__(): These methods are used to compare two objects.
- The __hash__() method: It is used to calculate a hash for the object. The hash will decide a placing of objects in data structures such as sets and dictionaries.
- The __iter__() method: This method is used for iteration over objects, for example, for loops.
- The __getitem__() method: This method is used for indexing. It can be declared as, def __getitem__ (self, key)
- The __setitem__() method: This method is used to assign an item to indexed values. It can be declared as, def __setitem__(self, key, value)

Example 9.9 Program to demonstrate the use of __getitem__() and __setitem__() methods

```python
class Numbers:
        def __init__(self,myList):
                self.myList = myList

        def __getitem__(self,index):
                return self.myList[index]
        def __setitem__(self,index, val):
                self.myList[index] = val
NumList = Numbers([1,2,3,4,5,6,7,8,9])
print(NumList[5])
NumList[3] = 10
print(NumList.myList)
```

OUTPUT
```
6
[1, 2, 3, 10, 5, 6, 7, 8, 9]
```

Note Trying to access an attribute of an instance that is not defined or a method that is undefined causes an **AttributeError**.

9.8 PUBLIC AND PRIVATE DATA MEMBERS

Public variables are those variables that are defined in the class and can be accessed from anywhere in the program, of course using the dot operator. Here, anywhere from the program means that the public variables can be accessed from within the class as well as from outside the class in which it is defined.

Private variables, on the other hand, are those variables that are defined in the class with a double score prefix (__). These variables can be accessed only from within the class and from nowhere outside the class.

Example 9.10 Program to illustrate the difference between public and private variables

```
class ABC():
    def __init__(self, var1, var2):
        self.var1 = var1
        self.__var2 = var2
    def display(self):
        print("From class method, Var1 = ", self.var1)
        print("From class method, Var2 = ", self.__var2)
obj = ABC(10, 20)
obj.display()
print("From main module, Var1 = ", obj.var1)
print("From main module, Var2 = ", obj.__var2)

OUTPUT

From class method, Var1 = 10
From class method, Var2 = 20
From main module, Var1 = 10
From main module, Var2 =

Traceback (most recent call last):
  File "C:\Python34\Try.py", line 11, in <module>
    print("From main module, Var2 = ", obj.__var2)
AttributeError: ABC instance has no attribute '__var2'
```

As a good programming habit, you should never try to access a private variable from anywhere outside the class. But if for some reason, you need to do it, then you can access the private variable using the following syntax,

```
objectname._classname__privatevariable
```

So, to remove the error from the above code, you could have written the last statement as

```
print("From main module, Var2 = ", obj._ABC__var2)
```

9.9 PRIVATE METHODS

Remember that, private attributes should not be accessed from anywhere outside the class. Like private attributes, you can even have private methods in your class. Usually, we keep those methods as private which have implementation details. So like private attributes, you should also not use a private method from anywhere outside the class. However, if it is very necessary to access them from outside the class, then they are accessed with a small difference. A private method can be accessed using the object name as well as the class name from outside the class. The syntax for accessing the private method in such a case would be,

```
objectname._classname__privatemethodname
```

Example 9.11   Program to illustrate the use of a private method

```
class ABC():
    def __init__(self, var):
        self.__var = var
    def __display(self):
        print("From class method, Var = ", self.__var)
obj = ABC(10)
obj._ABC__display()
```

OUTPUT
```
From class method, Var =  10
```

Note   Like private attributes, Python also allows you to have private methods to discourage people from accessing parts of a class that have implementation details.

9.10 CALLING A CLASS METHOD FROM ANOTHER CLASS METHOD

You can call a class method from another class method by using the self. This is shown in the program given below.

Example 9.12   Program to call a class method from another method of the same class

```
class ABC():
    def __init__(self, var):
        self.var = var
    def display(self):
        print("Var is = ", self.var)
    def add_2(self):
        self.var += 2
        self.display()
obj = ABC(10)
obj.add_2()
```

OUTPUT
```
Var is = 12
```

Key points to remember
• Like functions and modules, class also has a documentation string, which can be accessed using className.__doc__. The lines of code given below specifies the docstring.

```
class ABC:
    '''This is a docstring. I have created a new class'''
pass
```

• Class methods can reference global names in the same way as ordinary functions.

Example 9.13 Program to show how a class method calls a function defined in the global namespace

```
def scale_10(x):
    return x*10
class ABC():
    def __init__(self, var):
        self.var = var
    def display(self):
        print("Var is = ", self.var)
    def modify(self):
        self.var = scale_10(self.var)
obj = ABC(10)
obj.display()
obj.modify()
obj.display()
```

OUTPUT

```
Var is =  10
Var is =  100
```

Note A class is never used as a global scope.

• Unlike in C++ and Java, Python allows programmers to add, remove, or modify attributes of classes and objects at any time.

Example 9.14 Program to add variables to a class at run-time

```
class ABC():
    def __init__(self, var):
        self.var = var
    def display(self):
        print("Var is = ", self.var)
obj = ABC(10)
obj.display()
obj.new_var = 20  # variable added at run-time
print("New Var = ", obj.new_var)
obj.new_var = 30  # modifying newly added variable
print("New Var after modification = ", obj.new_var)
del obj.new_var   # newly created variable is deleted
print("New Var after deletion = ", obj.new_var)
```

OUTPUT

```
Var is =  10
New Var =  20
New Var after modification =  30
```

```
New Var after deletion =
Traceback (most recent call last):
  File "C:\Python34\Try.py", line 13, in <module>
  print("New Var after deletion = ", obj.new_var)
AttributeError: ABC instance has no attribute 'new_var'
```

9.11 BUILT-IN FUNCTIONS TO CHECK, GET, SET, AND DELETE CLASS ATTRIBUTES

Python has some built-in functions that can also be used to work with attributes (variables defined in class). You can use these functions to check whether a class has a particular attribute or not, get its value if it exists, set a new value, or even delete that attribute. These built-in functions include the following.

`hasattr(obj,name)`: The function is used to check if an object possesses the attribute or not.

`getattr(obj, name[, default])`: The function is used to access or get the attribute of object. Since `getattr()` is a built-in function and not a method of the class, it is not called using the dot operator. Rather, it takes the object as its first parameter. The second parameter is the name of the variable as a string, and the optional third parameter is the default value to be returned if the attribute does not exist. If the attribute name does not exist in the object's namespace and the default value is also not specified, then an exception will be raised. Note that `getattr(obj, 'var')` is same as writing `obj.var`. However, you should always try to use the latter variant.

`setattr(obj,name,value)`: The function is used to set an attribute of the object. If attribute does not exist, then it would be created. The first parameter of the `setattr()` function is the object, the second parameter is the name of the attribute, and the third is the new value for the specified attribute.

`delattr(obj,name)`: The function deletes an attribute. Once deleted, the variable is no longer a class or object attribute.

Example 9.15 Program to demonstrate the use of `getattr()`, `seattr()`, and `delattr()` functions

```
class ABC():
    def __init__(self, var):
        self.var = var
    def display(self):
        print("Var is = ", self.var)
obj = ABC(10)
obj.display()
print("Check if object has attribute var .....", hasattr(obj,'var'))
getattr(obj,'var')
setattr(obj,'var', 50)
print("After setting value, var is : ", obj.var)
setattr(obj,'count',10)
print("New variable count is created and its value is : ", obj.count)
delattr(obj,'var')
print("After deleting the attribute, var is : ", obj.var)
```

OUTPUT

```
Var is =  10
```

```
Check if object has attribute var ..... True
After setting value, var is :  50
New variable count is created and its value is :  10
After deleting the attribute, var is :
Traceback (most recent call last):
  File "C:\Python34\Try.py", line 15, in <module>
    print "After deleting the attribute, var is : ", obj.var
AttributeError: ABC instance has no attribute 'var'
```

9.12 BUILT-IN CLASS ATTRIBUTES

Every class defined in Python has some built-in attributes associated with it. Like other attributes, these attributes can also be accessed using dot operator.

.__dict__: The attributes gives a dictionary containing the class's or object's (with whichever it is accessed) namespace.

.__doc__: The attribute gives the class documentation string if specified. In case the documentation string is not specified, then the attribute returns None.

.__name__: The attribute returns the name of the class.

.__module__: The attribute gives the name of the module in which the class (or the object) is defined.

.__bases__: The attribute is used in inheritance (discussed in Chapter 10) to return the base classes in the order of their occurrence in the base class list. As for now, it returns an empty tuple.

Example 9.16   Program to demonstrate the use of built-in class attributes

```
class ABC():
    def __init__(self, var1, var2):
        self.var1 = var1
        self.var2 = var2
    def display(self):
        print("Var1 is = ", self.var1)
        print("Var2 is = ", self.var2)
obj = ABC(10, 12.34)
obj.display()
print("object.__dict__ - ", obj.__dict__)
print("object.__doc__ - ", obj.__doc__)
print("class.__name__ - ", ABC.__name__)
print("object.__module__ - ", obj.__module__)
print("class.__bases__ - ", ABC.__bases__)
```

OUTPUT

```
Var1 is =  10
Var2 is =  12.34
obj.__dict__ - {'var1': 10, 'var2': 12.34}
obj.__doc__ - None
```

```
class.__name__ -  ABC
obj.__module__ -  __main__
class.__bases__ -  ()
```

Note   The **__repr__()** special method is used for string representation of the instance.

9.13 GARBAGE COLLECTION (DESTROYING OBJECTS)

Python performs automatic garbage collection. This means that it deletes all the objects (built-in types or user defined like class objects) automatically that are no longer needed and that have gone out of scope to free the memory space. The process by which Python periodically reclaims unwanted memory is known as *garbage collection.*

Python's garbage collector runs in the background during program execution. It immediately takes action (of reclaiming memory) as soon as an object's reference count reaches zero.

Let us recall that an object's reference count increases when we create its aliases. That is, when we assign an object a new name or place it within a list, tuple, or dictionary. Similarly, the object's reference count becomes zero when it is deleted with `del` statement. Moreover, each time the object's reference is reassigned, or its reference goes out of scope, its reference count decreases.

Note   When an object's reference count reaches zero, Python recollects the memory used by it.

Consider the following examples which illustrate the way in which reference count changes for a given object.

> **Programming Tip:** Object of a class can be deleted using `del` statement.

```
var1 = 10       # Create object var1
var2 = var1     # Increase ref. count  of var1 - object assignment
var3 = [var2]   # Increase ref. count  of var1 - object used in a list
var2 - 50       # Decrease ref. count  of var1 - reassignment
var3[0] = -1    # Decrease ref. count  of var1 - removal from list
del var1        # Decrease ref. count  of var1 - object deleted
```

PROGRAMMING EXAMPLES

Program 9.1 Write a program that uses class to store the name and marks of students. Use list to store the marks in three subjects.

```
class Students:
    def __init__(self, name):
        self.name = name
        self.marks = []
    def enterMarks(self):
        for i in range(3):
            m = int(input("Enter the marks of %s in subject %d : "%(self.name,i+1)))
            self.marks.append(m)
```

```
    def display(self):
        print(self.name," got ", self.marks)
s1 = Students("Anisha")
s1.enterMarks()
s2 = Students("Jignesh")
s2.enterMarks()
s1.display()
s2.display()
```

OUTPUT

```
Enter the marks of Anisha in subject 1 : 89
Enter the marks of Anisha in subject 2 : 88
Enter the marks of Anisha in subject 3 : 87
Enter the marks of Jignesh in subject 1 : 78
Enter the marks of Jignesh in subject 2 : 90
Enter the marks of Jignesh in subject 3 : 87
Anisha  got  [89, 88, 87]
Jignesh  got  [78, 90, 87]
```

Program 9.2 Write a program with class Employee that keeps a track of the number of employees in an organization and also stores their name, designation, and salary details.

```
class Employee:
    empCount = 0
    def __init__(self, name, desig, salary):
        self.name = name
        self.desig = desig
        self.salary = salary
        Employee.empCount += 1

    def displayCount(self):
        print("There are %d employees" % Employee.empCount)

    def displayDetails(self):
        print("Name : ", self.name,  ", Designation : ", self.desig, ", Salary :
        ", self.salary)
e1 = Employee("Farhan", "Manager", 100000)
e2 = Employee("Mike", "Team Leader", 90000)
e3 = Employee("Niyam", "Programmer", 80000)
e4 = Employee("Ojas", "Office Assistant", 60000)
e4.displayCount()
print("Details of second employee - \n ")
e2.displayDetails()
```

OUTPUT

```
There are 4 employees
Details of second employee -
Name :  Mike , Designation :  Team Leader , Salary :  90000
```

Program 9.3 Write a program that has a class `Person` storing name and date of birth (DOB) of a person. The program should subtract the DOB from today's date to find out whether a person is eligible to vote or not.

```
import datetime
class Person():
    def __init__(self, name, dob):
        self.name = name
        self.dob = dob
    def check(self):
        today = datetime.date.today()
        age = today.year - self.dob.year
        if today < datetime.date(today.year, self.dob.month, self.dob.day):
            age -= 1
        if age>=18:
            print(self.name, ", Congratulations... You are eligible to vote.")
        else:
            print(self.name, ", Sorry... You should be at least 18 years of age to
cast your vote.")
P = Person("Saesha", datetime.date(1998, 12, 11))
P.check()
```

OUTPUT

```
Saesha , Congratulations... You are eligible to vote.
```

Program 9.4 Write a program that has a class `Circle`. Use a class variable to define the value of constant PI. Use this class variable to calculate area and circumference of a circle with specified radius.

```
class Circle:
    PI = 3.14159
    def __init__(self, radius):
        self.radius = radius
    def area(self):
        return Circle.PI*self.radius*self.radius
    def circumference(self):
        return 2*Circle.PI*self.radius
C = Circle(7.5)
print("AREA = ", C.area())
print("CIRCUMFERENCE = ", C.circumference())
```

OUTPUT

```
AREA =  176.7144375
CIRCUMFERENCE =  47.12385
```

Program 9.5 Write a program that has a class student that stores roll number, name, and marks (in three subjects) of the students. Display the information (roll number, name, and total marks) stored about the student.

```python
class student:
    __marks = []
    def set_data(self,r,n,m1,m2,m3):
        student.__rollno = r
        student.__name = n
        student.__marks.append(m1)
        student.__marks.append(m2)
        student.__marks.append(m3)
    def display_data(self):
        print("Student Details")
        print("Roll Number :",student.__rollno)
        print("Name :",student.__name)
        print("Marks :",self.total())
    def total(self):
        m = student.__marks
        return m[0]+m[1]+m[2]

r = int(input("Enter the roll number : "))
n = input("Enter the name : ")
m1 = int(input("Enter the marks in first subject : "))
m2 = int(input("Enter the marks in first subject : "))
m3 = int(input("Enter the marks in first subject : "))
s1 = student()
s1.set_data(r,n,m1,m2,m3)
s1.display_data()
```

OUTPUT

```
Enter the roll number : 123
Enter the name : Shivan
Enter the marks in first subject : 89
Enter the marks in first subject : 90
Enter the marks in first subject : 92
Student Details
Roll Number : 123
Name : Shivan
Marks : 271
```

Program 9.6 Write a class Rectangle that has attributes Length and Breadth and a method area which returns the area of the rectangle.

```python
class Rectangle:
    def get_data(self):
        Rectangle.length = int(input("Enter the length : "))
        Rectangle.breadth = int(input("Enter the breadth : "))
```

```
    def show_data(self):
        print("Length =",Rectangle.length,"\t Breadth =",Rectangle.breadth)
    def area(self):
        print("Area =",Rectangle.length*Rectangle.breadth)

rect = Rectangle()
rect.get_data()
rect.show_data()
rect.area()
```

OUTPUT

```
Enter the length : 10
Enter the breadth : 5
Length = 10          Breadth = 5
Area = 50
```

Program 9.7 Write a program that has a class fraction with attributes numerator and denominator. Enter the values of the attributes and print the fraction in simplified form.

```
class fraction:
    def get_data(self):
        self.__num = int(input("Enter the numerator : "))
        self.__deno = int(input("Enter the denominator : "))
        if(self.__deno == 0):
            print("Fraction not possible")
            exit()

    def display_data(self):
        self.__simplify()
        print(self.__num,"/",self.__deno)

    def __simplify(self):
        print("The simplified fraction is :")
        common_divisor = self.__GCD(self.__num,self.__deno)
        self.__num = self.__num/common_divisor
        self.__deno = self.__deno/common_divisor

    def __GCD(self, a, b):
        if(b==0):
            return a
        else:
            return self.__GCD(b, a%b)

f = fraction()
f.get_data()
f.display_data()
```

OUTPUT
```
Enter the numerator : 20
Enter the denominator : 100
The simplified fraction is : 1.0 / 5.0
```

Program 9.8 Write a program that has a class store which keeps a record of code and price of each product. Display a menu of all products to the user and prompt him to enter the quantity of each item required. Generate a bill and display the total amount.

```python
class store:
    __item_code = []
    __price = []

    def get_data(self):
        for i in range(5):
            self.__item_code.append(int(input("Enter the code of item : ")))
            self.__price.append(int(input("Enter the price : ")))

    def display_data(self):
        print("ITEM CODE \t PRICE")
        for i in range(5):
            print(self.__item_code[i],"\t\t",self.__price[i])

    def calculate_bill(self, quant):
        total_amount = 0
        for i in range(5):
            total_amount = total_amount+self.__price[i]*quant[i]
        print("***********BILL****************")
        print("ITEM \t PRICE \t QUANTITY \t SUBTOTAL")
        for i in range(5):
            print(self.__item_code[i],"\t",self.__price[i],"\t",quant[i],"\t
            t",quant[i]*self.__price[i])
        print("*******************************")
        print("Total =", total_amount)

s = store()
s.get_data()
s.display_data()
q = []
print("Enter the quantity of each item : ")
for i in range(5):
    q.append(int(input()))
s.calculate_bill(q)
```

OUTPUT
```
Enter the code of item : 123
Enter the price : 9876
Enter the code of item : 345
```

```
Enter the price : 8765
Enter the code of item : 456
Enter the price : 7654
Enter the code of item : 567
Enter the price : 6543
Enter the code of item : 890
Enter the price : 5436
ITEM CODE      PRICE
123            9876
345            8765
456            7654
567            6543
890            5436
Enter the quantity of each item :
1
2
1
3
2
************BILL***************
ITEM    PRICE    QUANTITY    SUBTOTAL
123     9876     1           9876
345     8765     2           17530
456     7654     1           7654
567     6543     3           19629
890     5436     2           10872
*******************************

Total = 65561
```

Program 9.9 Write a program that has a class Numbers with values stored in a list. Write a class method to find the largest value.

```python
''' Program to use a constructor to create an array and find the largest element
from that array '''
class Numbers:
    def __init__(self):
        self.values = []

    def find_max(self):
        max = ''
        for i in self.values:
            if(i > max):
                max = i
        print('Maximum element : %r' %max)

    def insert_element(self):
        value = input('Enter value : ')
        self.values.append(value)
```

```
x = Numbers()
ch = 'y'
while(ch == 'y'):
    x.insert_element()
    ch = input('Do you wish to enter more elements?')
x.find_max()
```

OUTPUT

```
Enter value : hi
Do you wish to enter more elements?y
Enter value : bye
Do you wish to enter more elements?y
Enter value : cheer
Do you wish to enter more elements?y
Enter value : smile
Do you wish to enter more elements?n
Maximum element : 'smile'
```

Program 9.10 Write a class that stores a string and all its status details such as number of uppercase characters, vowels, consonants, spaces, etc.

```
class String:
    def __init__(self):
        self.vowels = 0
        self.spaces = 0
        self.consonants = 0
        self.uppercase = 0
        self.lowercase = 0
        self.string = str(input("Enter string : "))

    def count_uppercase(self):
        for letter in self.string:
            if(letter.isupper()):
                self.uppercase+=1

    def count_lowercase(self):
        for letter in self.string:
            if(letter.islower()):
                self.lowercase+=1

    def count_vowels(self):
        for letter in self.string:
            if(letter in ('a','e','i' ,'o','u')):
                self.vowels+=1
            elif(letter in ('A','E','I','O','U')):
                self.vowels+=1

    def count_spaces(self):
        for letter in self.string:
```

```
            if(letter == ' '):
                self.spaces+=1
    def count_consonants(self):
        for letter in self.string:
            if(letter not in ('a','e','i','o','u','A','E','I','O','U',' ')):
                self.consonants+=1

    def compute_stat(self):
        self.count_uppercase()
        self.count_lowercase()
        self.count_vowels()
        self.count_spaces()
        self.count_consonants()

    def show_stat(self):
        print('Vowels : %d'%self.vowels)
        print('Consonants : %d' %self.consonants)
        print('Spaces : %d' %self.spaces)
        print('Uppercase : %d' %self.uppercase)
        print('Lowercase : %d' %self.lowercase)
s = String()
s.compute_stat()
s.show_stat()
```

OUTPUT

```
Enter string : This program must show statistics for this string
Vowels : 11
Consonants : 31
Spaces : 7
Uppercase : 1
Lowercase : 41
```

Program 9.11 Write a program that uses datetime module within a class. Enter manufacturing date and expiry date of the product. The program must display the years, months, and days that are left for expiry.

```
import datetime
class Product:
    def __init__(self):
        self.manufacture = datetime.datetime.strptime(input("Enter manufacturing
date (mm/dd/yyyy): "),'%m/%d/%Y')
        self.expiry = datetime.datetime.strptime(input("Enter expiry date (mm/dd/
yyyy): "),'%m/%d/%Y')

    def time_to_expire(self):
        today = datetime.datetime.now()
        if(today > self.expiry):
```

```
                print('Product has already expired.')
            else:
                time_left = self.expiry.date() - datetime.datetime.now().date()
                print('Time left : ',time_left)

    def show(self):
        print('Expiry : ',self.expiry)
        print('Manufacturing : ',self.manufacture)
x = Product()
x.time_to_expire()
```

OUTPUT

```
Enter manufacturing date (mm/dd/yyyy): 1/1/2013
Enter expiry date (mm/dd/yyyy): 1/1/2017
Time left :  232 days, 0:00:00
```

Program 9.12 Write a program to deposit or withdraw money in a bank account.

```
class Account:
    def __init__(self):
        self.balance = 0
        print('New Account Created.')

    def deposit(self):
        amount = float(input('Enter amount to deposit : '))
        self.balance+=amount
        print('New Balance : %f' %self.balance)

    def withdraw(self):
        amount = float(input('Enter amount to withdraw : '))
        if(amount > self.balance):
            print('Insufficient balance')
        else:
            self.balance-=amount
            print('New Balance : %f' %self.balance)

    def enquiry(self):
        print('Balance : %f' %self.balance)

account = Account()
account.deposit()
account.withdraw()
account.enquiry()
```

OUTPUT

```
New Account Created.
Enter amount to deposit : 1000
New Balance : 1000.000000
```

```
Enter amount to withdraw : 25.23
New Balance : 974.770000
Balance : 974.770000
```

Program 9.13 Write a menu driven program that keeps record of books and journals available in a library.

```python
class Book:
    def __init__(self):
        self.title = ""
        self.author = ""
        self.price = 0

    def read(self):
        self.title = input("Enter Book Title : ")
        self.author = input("Enter Book Author : ")
        self.price = float(input("Enter Book Price : "))

    def display(self):
        print("Title : ",self.title)
        print("Author : ",self.author)
        print("Price : ",self.price)
        print("\n")

my_books = []
ch = 'y'
while(ch == 'y'):
    print('''
    1. Add New Book
    2. Display Books
    ''')
    choice = int(input("Enter choice : "))
    if(choice == 1):
        book = Book()
        book.read()
        my_books.append(book)
    elif(choice == 2):
        for i in my_books:
            i.display()
    else:
        print("Invalid Choice")

    ch = input("Do you want to continue..")
print("Bye!")
```

OUTPUT

```
1. Add New Book
2. Display Books
```

```
Enter choice : 1
Enter Book Title : OOPS with C++
Enter Book Author : Balaguruswamy
Enter Book Price : 385
Do you want to continue..y

    1. Add New Book
    2. Display Books

Enter choice : 1
Enter Book Title : Computer Networks
Enter Book Author : Forouzan
Enter Book Price : 550
Do you want to continue..y
    1. Add New Book
    2. Display Books

Enter choice : 1
Enter Book Title : Computer Fundamentals
Enter Book Author : P.K. Sinha
Enter Book Price : 250
Do you want to continue..y
    1. Add New Book
    2. Display Books

Enter choice : 2
Title :  OOPS with C++
Author :  Balaguruswamy
Price :  385.0

Title :  Computer Networks
Author :  Forouzan
Price :  550.0

Title :  Computer Fundamentals
Author :  P.K. Sinha
Price :  250.0

Do you want to continue..n
Bye!
```

> **Programming Tip:** The ideal way is to define the classes in a separate file, and then import them in the main program file using `import` statement.

9.14 CLASS METHODS

Till now, we have seen that methods defined in a class are called by an instance of a class. These methods automatically take `self` as the first argument. *Class methods* are little different from these ordinary methods. First, they are called by a class (not by instance of the class). Second, the first argument of the `classmethod` is `cls`, not the `self`.

Class methods are widely used for factory methods, which instantiate an instance of a class, using different parameters from those usually passed to the class constructor. The program code given in the following example illustrates this concept.

> **Note**   Class methods are marked with a `classmethod` decorator.

Example 9.17   Program to demonstrate the use of `classmethod`

```
class Rectangle:
        def __init__(self,length, breadth):
                self.length = length
                self.breadth = breadth

        def area(self):
                return self.length * self.breadth
        @classmethod
        def Square(cls,side):
                return cls(side,side)
S = Rectangle.Square(10)
print("AREA = ", S.area())
```

OUTPUT

```
AREA = 100
```

9.15 STATIC METHODS

Static methods are a special case of methods. Any functionality that belongs to a class, but that does not require the object is placed in the static method. Static methods are similar to class methods. The only difference is that a static method does not receive any additional arguments. They are just like normal functions that belong to a class.

> **Programming Tip:** A static method is marked with the `staticmethod` decorator.

Remember that, a static method does not use the `self` variable and is defined using a built-in function named `staticmethod`. Python has a handy syntax, called a *decorator*, to make it easier to apply the `staticmethod` function to the method function definition. The syntax for using the `staticmethod` decorator is given as,

```
@staticmethod

def name(args...):

    statements
```

A static method can be called either on the class or on an instance. When it is called with an instance, the instance is ignored except for its class.

> **Note**   A decorator is a syntactic convenience that takes in a function, adds some functionality to it and then returns it. The syntax of a decorator uses the @ character as a prefix to the function. Using decorators is also called *metaprogramming* because a part of the program tries to modify another part of the program at compile time.

Example 9.18   Program to illustrate `static` method

```
class Choice:
        def __init__(self, subjects):
                self.subjects = subjects
```

```
        @staticmethod
        def validate_subject(subjects):
                if "CSA" in subjects:
                        print("This option is no longer available.")
                else:
                        return True
subjects = ["DS","CSA","FoC","OS","ToC"]
if all(Choice.validate_subject(i) for i in subjects):
        ch = Choice(subjects)
        print("You have been allotted the subjects : ", subjects)
```

OUTPUT

This option is no longer available.

Note   A static method does not depend on the state of the object.

__new__() **Method:** This is a static method which is called to create a new instance of class cls. It takes the class of which an instance was requested as its first argument. The remaining arguments are those passed to the object constructor expression (the call to the class). This method returns the new object instance of cls.

The __new__() method allows subclasses of immutable types (like integer, string, or tuple) to customize instance creation. It is also commonly overridden in custom metaclasses in order to customize class creation.

The __new__() and __init__() methods together are used for constructing objects.

Summary

- Classes and objects are the two main aspects of object oriented programming.
- Classes provides a blueprint or a template using which objects are created.
- Class methods have access to all the data contained in the instance of the object.
- Class definitions can appear anywhere in a program, but they are usually written near the beginning of the program, after the import statements.
- Class methods must have the first argument named as self.

- The __init__() method is automatically executed when an object of a class is created. The method is useful to initialize the variables of the class object.
- The __del__() method is automatically called when an object is going out of scope.
- Public variables are those variables that are defined in the class and can be accessed from anywhere in the program.
- Class methods are used for factory methods, which instantiate an instance of a class. It uses different parameters from those usually passed to the class constructor.

Glossary

Attribute Data items that makes up an instance.

Class A user-defined prototype for an object that defines a set of attributes (class variables and instance variables) and methods that are accessed via dot notation.

Class variable A variable defined within a class that is shared by all instances of a class.

Data member A variable (class variable or instance variable) defined within the class that holds data associated with a class and its objects.

Instance Object of a class.

Instance variable A variable that is defined inside a class method and belongs only to the current instance of the class.

Instantiation The process of creating an instance of a class.

Method Function defined in a class definition and is invoked on instances of that class.

Namespace A mapping from names to objects in such a way that there is no relation between names in different namespaces.

Object Instance and object are used interchangeably.

Object oriented language A language that supports object oriented features like classes, inheritance, operator overloading, etc.

Object oriented programming A style of programming in which data and the operations that manipulate it are together encapsulated inside a single entity called class.

Exercises

Fill in the Blanks

1. _____ and _____ are the two main aspects of object oriented programming.
2. _____ methods are passed to the calling class.
3. Class must be defined after the _____ statement.
4. The parameter names for the calling class is _____.
5. _____ is the automatic process by which unnecessary objects are deleted to free memory.
6. _____ variable must be prefixed by the class name and dot operator.
7. The _____ function is a built-in function that returns the length of an object.
8. The _____ method is used for indexing.
9. To access the document string of a class, you will write _____.
10. Fill in the blanks to make display() a class method.

```
class ABC:
    def __init__(self,name):
        self.name=name
    _____
    ____ display(cls):
        print("Good Morning")
```

11. Fill in the blanks to create a class that has an __init__() method to assign the "name" attribute. Then create an object of the class.

```
___ ABC:
    def ____(self,name):
        self_____=name
P = ABC("Neem__
```

12. Fill in the blanks to create a class with a method display().

```
class ABC_
    def _init_(self,name):
        self.name=name
    ___ display(___):
        print("Hello"+____.name)
A = ABC("Mudika")
A.display()
```

13. Fill in the blanks to make the var attribute strongly private.

```
class ABC:
    __var = 10
    def display(self)_____
        print(___.__var)
A = ABC()
A.display()
```

State True or False

1. Class is an instance of the object.
2. Classes provides a blueprint or a template using which objects are created.
3. The parameter name for the calling instance of the class is cls.
4. A class can be defined in a function or in an if statement.
5. A method defined in a class cannot have loops.
6. No value is passed for the self parameter when the class method is called.
7. Every class method accepts at least one parameter.
8. The first argument of the __init__() method must be cls.
9. The object variable is shared between objects.
10. A change made to the object variable by one object will not be reflected in other objects.

11. Any change made in the class variable by an object will be reflected to all other objects.
12. By default, all variables are private in Python.
13. The __repr__() method works only on class objects.
14. Private variables are defined in the class and can be accessed from anywhere in the program.
15. You can access a private variable from outside the class but by using the class name.
16. You can define private methods in a class.
17. Class methods cannot reference global names in the same way as ordinary functions.
18. You can add attributes to an instance outside the class.
19. A static method does not depend on the state of the object.

Multiple Choice Questions

1. Which of the following creates a new type?
   (a) Class   (b) object
   (c) attribute   (d) method

2. Which type of error is caused by trying to access unknown attributes?
   (a) `ValueError`   (b) `NameError`
   (c) `AttributeError`   (d) `Type Error`

3. Select which of the following can be a static method
   (a) `def func(self,x,y):`
   (b) `def func(x,y):`
   (c) `def func(cls,x,y):`
   (d) `def func(@static,x,y):`

4. Class members are accesses through which operator?
   (a) %   (b) :   (c) *   (d) .

5. Which method is automatically executed when an object of a class is created?
   (a) `__init__()`   (b) `__del__()`
   (c) `__call__()`   (d) `__repr__()`

6. In which method should all variables be initialized?
   (a) `__init__()`   (b) `__del__()`
   (c) `__call__()`   (d) `__repr__()`

7. If a class has one class variable, then how many copies will be created for that variable?
   (a) 0   (b) 1
   (c) n   (d) infinite

8. Which variables are usually used to keep a count of number of objects created from a class?
   (a) class   (b) object
   (c) ordinary   (d) temporary

9. Which method is automatically invoked when an object is about to be destroyed?
   (a) `__init__()`   (b) `__del__()`
   (c) `__call__()`   (d) `__repr__()`

10. Which special method returns a string representation of an object?
    (a) `__init__()`   (b) `__del__()`
    (c) `__call__()`   (d) `__repr__()`

11. Which method lets a class act like a function?
    (a) `__init__()`   (b) `__del__()`
    (c) `__call__()`   (d) `__repr__()`

12. Which error is generated when an attempt is made to access an undefined method?
    (a) `ValueError`   (b) `NameError`
    (c) `AttributeError`   (d) `Type Error`

Review Questions

1. What is a class? How do you define it?
2. What are class members? How can you access them?
3. Differentiate between class variables and instance variables.
4. Write a short note on special class methods.
5. What is class instantiation? How is it done?
6. What does the `self` argument signify in the class methods?
7. With the help of an example explain the significance of the `__init__()` method.
8. What difference will you observe when the class variable is of mutable and immutable type?
9. Explain the significance of `__del__()` and `__repr__()` methods.
10. Differentiate between public and private variables.
11. Write a short note on built-in functions that are used with objects.
12. Write a short note on different built-in attributes associated with a class.
13. What do you understand by the term garbage collection?
14. With the help of examples explain the concept of `classmethods` and `staticmethods`.

Programming Problems

1. Write a program that has a class `Point` with attributes as the `X` and `Y` co-ordinates. Make two objects of this class and find the midpoint of both the points.
2. Write a program that has a class `Cars`. Create two objects and set `car1` to be a red convertible with price ₹10 lakhs and name `Pugo`, and `car2` to be a blue sedan named `Mavo` worth ₹6 lakhs.
3. Write a program that uses a class attribute to define some default titles for faculty in a college. Display the name along with title and department of the college.
4. Add a method `reflect_x` to class `Point`, which returns a new point which is the reflection of the point about the x-axis. For example, `Point(7,8)`. `reflect_x` is `Point(7,-8)`.

5. Write a static method that checks whether all words in a list starts with a vowel.
6. Make a class `triangle`. Enter its three sides and calculate its area.
7. Write a menu driven program to read, display, simplify, add, and subtract two fractions.
8. Write a menu driven program to read, display, add and subtract two complex numbers.
9. Write a menu driven program to read, display, add, and subtract two distances.
10. Write a menu driven program to read, display, add, and subtract two time objects.
11. Write a menu driven program to read, display, add, and subtract two height objects.
12. Write a program to read two `POINTS` and calculate the distance between them.
13. Write a class that has a list of integers as data members and read(), display(), find_largest(), find_smallest(), sum(), and find_mean() as its member functions
14. Make a class `Book` with members, title, author, publisher, and `ISBN` number. The functions of the class should read and display the data.
15. Write a program that swaps two members of a class.

16. Write a program to find mean of two numbers belonging to two different objects of the same class.
17. Write a program that has a class `student` with data members—roll_no and marks in three subjects. Make at least four objects of this class. Use one or more functions that finds total of each student and then sorts the student's records in descending order based on their marks.
18. Write a menu driven program to read, add, and subtract two polynomials.
19. Write a program that uses a time structure within a class. Enter any time and your favorite show's time. The program must display how much time is left for it to start.
20. Write a menu driven program to add or delete items from your inventory of stationary items. You can use a dictionary to store item and the brand.
21. Write a menu driven program to read, add, subtract, multiply, divide, and transpose two matrices.
22. Write a program that displays the details of a cricket player. The details must include his name, matched played, run rate, wickets taken, maiden overs, overs played, number of centuries, and half centuries, etc.

Find the Output

1.
```python
class Employee:
    deptt = 'IT'
    def __init__(self, name):
        self.name = name
E1 = Employee('Raghav')
print(E1.name, end=" ")
print(E1.deptt)
```
2.
```python
class Car:
    def __init__(self, company, model):
        self.company = company
        self.model = model
Dzire = Car('Maruti', 'Swift Dzire ZX')
print(Dzire.model)
```
3.
```python
class Car:
    company = "Maruti"
    def __init__(self, model, year = 2016):
        self.model = model
        self.year = year
    def display(self):
        print("Company - %s, Model - %s, Year - %d" %(self.company, self.model, self.year))
Dzire = Car('Swift Dzire ZX')
Dzire.display()
```
4.
```python
class ABC():
    def __init__(self, var):
        self.__var = var
    def display(self):
        print("From class method, Var = ", self.__var)
obj = ABC(10)
obj.display()
```
5.
```python
class Person():
    def __init__(self, name):
        self.__name = name
    def __display(self):
        print("Good Morning ", self.__name)
    def greet(self):
        self.__display()
obj = Person("Roy")
obj.greet()
```
6.
```python
class ABC:
    __var=7
    def display(self):
        print(self.__var)
a = ABC()
a.display()
print(a._ABC__var)
```

Find the Error

1. ```
class Car:
    def __init__(self, company, model):
        self.company = company
        self.model = model
Dzire = Car('Maruti', 'Swift Dzire ZX')
print(Dzire.model)
print(Dzire.mfg_years)
```

2. ```
class Car:
    def __init__(self, company, model):
        self.company = company
        self.model = model
    def display(self):
        print("Company - %s, Model - %s"
%(self.company, self.model))
Dzire = Car('Maruti', 'Swift Dzire ZX')
del Dzire
Dzire.display()
```

3. ```
class Car:
    def __init__(self, company, model):
        self.company = company
        self.model = model
    def display(self):
        print("Company - %s, Model - %s"
%(self.company, self.model))
Dzire = Car('Maruti', 'Swift Dzire ZX')
del Dzire.model
Dzire.display()
```

4. ```
class Car:
    def __init__(self, company, model):
        self.company = company
        self.model = model
    def display(self):
        print("Company - %s, Model - %s"
%(self.company, self.model))
Dzire = Car('Maruti', 'Swift Dzire ZX')
del Dzire.display
Dzire.display()
```

5. ```
class Car:
    def __init__(self, company, model):
        self.company = company
        self.model = model
    def display(self):
        print("Company - %s, Model - %s"
%(self.company, self.model))
Dzire = Car('Maruti', 'Swift Dzire ZX')
del Dzire
Dzire.display()
```

6. ```
class ABC():
    def __init__(self, var):
        self.__var = var
    def display(self):
        print("From class method, Var = ",
self.var)
obj = ABC(10)
obj.display()
print("From main module, Var = ", obj.__var)
```

7. ```
class ABC():
    def __init__(self, var):
        self.__var = var
    def __display(self):
        print("From class method, Var = ",
self.__var)
obj = ABC(10)
obj.__display()
```

# Answers

## Fill in the Blanks

1. classes, objects
2. @classmethod
3. import
4. cls
5. Garbage collection
6. class
7. len
8. __getitem__()
9. className.__doc__
10. @classmethod, def
11. class, __init__,.name,")
12. :, def, self, self
13. __, :, ABC, __, var

## State True or False

1. False 2. True 3. False 4. True 5. False 6. True 7. True 8. False 9. False 10. True
11. True 12. False 13. False 14. False 15. True 16. True 17. False 18. True 19. True

## Multiple Choice Questions

1. (a) 2. (c) 3. (b) 4. (d) 5. (a) 6. (a) 7. (b) 8. (a) 9. (b) 10. (d) 11. (c) 12. (c)
```

10 Inheritance

- Inheritance and its Types • Method Overriding • Containership
- Abstract Class and Interface • Metaclass

10.1 INTRODUCTION

Reusability is an important feature of OOP. Reusing an existing piece of code has manifolds benefits. It not only saves effort and cost required to build a software product, but also enhances its reliability. Now, no longer it will be required to re-write, re-debug, and re-test the code that has already been tested and being used in existing software.

To support reusability, Python supports the concept of re-using existing classes. For this, Python allows its programmers to create new classes that re-use the pre-written and tested classes. The existing classes are adapted as per user's requirements so that the newly formed classes can be incorporated in current software application being developed.

The technique of creating a new class from an existing class is called *inheritance*. The old or existing class is called the *base class* and the new class is known as the *derived class* or *subclass*. The derived classes are created by first inheriting the data and methods of the base class and then adding new specialized data and functions in it. In this process of inheritance, the base class remains unchanged. The concept of inheritance is therefore, frequently used to implement the 'is-a' relationship. For example, teacher is-a person, student is-a person; while both teacher and student are a person in the first place, both also have some distinguishing features. So all the common traits of teacher and student are specified in the Person class and specialized features are incorporated in two separate classes—Teacher and Student. Similarly, a dentist or a surgeon is a doctor and doctor is a person. Figure 10.1 illustrates the concept of inheritance which follows a top–down approach to problem solving. In **top-down** approach, generalized classes are designed first and then specialized classes are derived by inheriting/extending the generalized classes.

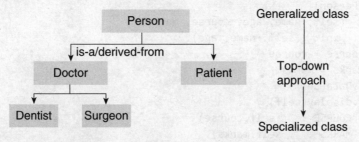

Figure 10.1   is-a relationship between classes

> **Note**   The derived class inherits all the capabilities of the base class and adds refinements and extensions of its own.

Remember that, when we make functions, we first write the individual functions and then call them from our main module. So we are building our program using small-small pieces (individual functions). This approach is called *bottom-up approach*. But in case of class hierarchy, we are first designing base classes and then from those classes, specialized classes are created as we go down the hierarchy. This is a top-down approach. In bottom-up approach, the main deliverable is at the top of the hierarchy but in a top-down approach, the main deliverable is at the bottom.

10.2 INHERITING CLASSES IN PYTHON

The syntax to inherit a class can be given as,

```
class DerivedClass(BaseClass):
    body_of_derived_class
```

Note that instead of writing the `BaseClass`, you can even specify an expression like `modulename.BaseClass`. This is especially useful when the base class is defined in a different module. Let us look at the following example.

Example 10.1   Program to demonstrate the use of inheritance

```
class Person:
    def __init__(self, name, age):
        self.name = name
        self.age = age
    def display(self):
        print("NAME : ", self.name)
        print("AGE : ", self.age)
class Teacher(Person):
    def __init__(self, name, age, exp, r_area):
        Person.__init__(self, name, age)
        self.exp = exp
        self.r_area = r_area
    def displayData(self):
        Person.display(self)
        print("EXPERIENCE : ", self.exp)
        print("RESEARCH AREA : ", self.r_area)
class Student(Person):
    def __init__(self, name, age, course, marks):
        Person.__init__(self, name, age)
        self.course = course
        self.marks = marks
    def displayData(self):
        Person.display(self)
        print("COURSE : ", self.course)
        print("MARKS : ", self.marks)
```

```
print("*********TEACHER**********")
T = Teacher("Jaya", 43, 20, "Recommender Systems")
T.displayData()
print("*********STUDENT**********")
S = Student("Mani", 20, "BTech", 78)
S.displayData()
```

OUTPUT

```
*********TEACHER**********
NAME :  Jaya
AGE :  43
EXPERIENCE :  20
RESEARCH AREA :  Recommender Systems

*********STUDENT**********
NAME :  Mani
AGE :  20
COURSE :  BTech
MARKS :  78
```

In the aforementioned program, classes `Teacher` and `Student` are both inherited from class `Person`. Therefore, the inherited classes have all the features (attributes and methods) of the base class. Note that a derived class is instantiated in the same way as any other class is. To create an object of the derived class, just write the derived class name followed by an empty brackets as in `DerivedClassName()`.

> **Note** When we use the `.__base__` attribute with class name, the base (or the parent) class of the specified class is returned. Therefore, `print(Student.__bases__)` will print (`<class '__main__.Person'>,`)

10.2.1 Polymorphism and Method Overriding

Polymorphism, in simple terms, refers to having several different forms. It is one of the key features of OOP. It enables the programmers to assign a different meaning or usage to a variable, function, or an object in different contexts. While inheritance is related to classes and their hierarchy, polymorphism, on the other hand, is related to methods. When polymorphism is applied to a function or method depending on the given parameters, a particular form of the function can be selected for execution. In Python, method overriding is one way of implementing polymorphism.

Relationship Between Inheritance and Polymorphism

Polymorphism, an essential concept of OOP, means having several different forms. While inheritance is related to classes and their hierarchy, polymorphism, on the other hand, is related to methods. Polymorphism allows the programmers to assign a different meaning or usage to a method in different contexts. In Python, the word Polymorphism when used with inheritance means defining a number of subclasses that have methods of same name. A function can use objects of any of the polymorphic classes irrespective of the fact that these classes are individually distinct. Thus, in Python, one way of providing polymorphism is method overriding in which a derived class method has methods of same name as specified in the base class but giving it a new meaning.

In the program (Example 10.1) given under Section 10.2, notice that __init__() method was defined in all the three classes. When this happens, the method in the derived class overrides that in the base class. This means that __init__() in Teacher and Student gets preference over the __init__() method in the Person class. Thus, ***method overriding*** is the ability of a class to change the implementation of a method provided by one of its ancestors. It is an important concept of OOP since it exploits the power of inheritance.

Observe another thing that when we override a base class method, we extend the functionality of the base class method. This is done by calling the method in the base class method from the derived class method and also adding additional statements in the derived class method.

Instead of writing Person.__init__(self, name, age), you could have also written super().__init__(self, name, age). Here, super() is a built-in function that denotes the base class. So when you invoke a method using the super() function, then the parent version of the method is called.

> **Note**   In Python, every class is inherited from the base class object.

Note that in case of multiple inheritance (a class derived from more than one base class), you need to invoke the super() function in __init__() method of every class. This would be clear by looking at the program given below and observing its output.

Example 10.2   Program to demonstrate the issue of invoking __init__() in case of multiple inheritance.

```
class Base1(object):
    def __init__(self):
        print("Base1 Class")
class Base2(object):
    def __init__(self):
        print("Base2 Class")
class Derived(Base1, Base2):
    pass
D = Derived()
```

OUTPUT

```
Base1 Class
```

In the above method, an object of derived class is made. Since there is no __init__() method in the derived class, the __init__() method of the first base class gets called. But since, there is no call to super() function in the __init__() method of Base1 class, no further __init__() method is invoked. This problem has been recitified in the code given in the following example.

Example 10.3   Program to demonstrate the call of super() from __init__() of a base class

```
class Base1(object):
    def __init__(self):
        print("Base1 Class")
        super(Base1, self).__init__()
class Base2(object):
    def __init__(self):
```

```
        print("Base2 Class")
class Derived(Base1, Base2):
    pass
D = Derived()
```

OUTPUT

```
Base1 Class
Base2 Class
```

Example 10.4 Program to call the __init__() methods of all the classes

```
class Base1(object):
    def __init__(self):
        print("Base1 Class")
        super(Base1, self).__init__()
class Base2(object):
    def __init__(self):
        print("Base2 Class")
class Derived(Base1, Base2):
    def __init__(self):
        super(Derived, self).__init__()
        print("Derived Class")
D = Derived()
```

OUTPUT

```
Base1 Class
Base2 Class
Derived Class
```

Two more built-in functions isinstance() and issubclass() are very useful in Python to check instances. The isinstance() function returns True if the object is an instance of the class or other classes derived from it. Similarly, the issubclass() checks for class inheritance as shown in the following example. Just try the following statements and observe the output.

Example 10.5 Program to demonstrate isinstance() and issubclass(). (Note that the following code is in continuation to Example 10.1 where we had defined classes—Person, Teacher, and Student).

```
print("T is a Teacher : ", isinstance(T,Teacher))
print("T is a Person : ", isinstance(T,Person))
print("T is an integer : ", isinstance(T,int))
print("T is an object : ", isinstance(T,object))
print("Person is a subclass of Teacher : ", issubclass(Person,Teacher))
print("Teacher is a subclass of Person : ", issubclass(Teacher,Person))
print("Boolean is a subclass of int : ", issubclass(bool,int))
```

OUTPUT
```
T is a Teacher :  True
T is a Person :  True
T is an integer :  False
T is an object :  True
Person is a subclass of Teacher :  False
Teacher is a subclass of Person :  True
Boolean is a subclass of int :  True
```

10.3 TYPES OF INHERITANCE

Python supports different variants of inheritance such as single, multiple, multi-level, and multi-path inheritances. While, in single inheritance, a class can be derived from a single base class, in multiple inheritance, on the other hand, a class can be derived from more than one base class. Besides these, Python has other types of inheritance which will be discussed in this section.

10.3.1 Multiple Inheritance

When a derived class inherits features from more than one base class (Figure 10.2), it is called *multiple inheritance*. The derived class has all the features of both the base classes and in addition to them, can have additional new features. The syntax for multiple inheritance is similar to that of single inheritance and can be given as:

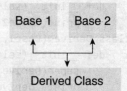

```
class Base1:
    statement block
class Base2:
    statement block
class Derived(Base1, Base2):
    statement block
```

Features of both the base classes plus its own

Figure 10.2   Multiple inheritance

In the multiple inheritance scenario, any specified attribute is first searched in the current (or the derived) class. If it is not found there, the search continues into parent classes using depth-first technique, that is, in left-right fashion without searching same class twice. Let us take an example to better understand this concept.

Note   If the specified attribute is not found in the derived class, the search proceeds to look in the base class. This rule is applied recursively if the base class itself is derived from some other class.

Example 10.6   Program to demonstrate multiple inheritance

```
class Base1(object):         # First Base Class
  def __init__(self):
    super(Base1, self).__init__()
    print("Base1 Class")
class Base2(object):         # Second Base Class
  def __init__(self):
```

```
    super(Base2, self).__init__()
    print("Base2 Class")
class Derived(Base1, Base2):    # Derived Class derived from Base1 and Base2
  def __init__(self):
    super(Derived, self).__init__()
    print("Derived Class")
D = Derived()
```

OUTPUT

```
Base2 Class
Base1 Class
Derived Class
```

The order of output may confuse you. But do not worry, it's all because of MRO (that works on depth-first traversal) which will be discussed shortly. For now, just understand that the order of class hierarchy can be given as—Derived -> Base1 -> Object and Derived -> Base2 -> Object.

When we create an instance of the derived class, the following things happen.

Step 1: The __init__() method of Derived class is called.

Step 2: The __init__() method of Base1 class is invoked (according to MRO) from the __init__() method of Derived class.

Step 3: The __init__() method of Base2 class is invoked (according to MRO) from the __init__() method of Base1 class.

Step 4: From the __init__() method of Base2, the __init__() method of Object is invoked which does nothing. Finally, Base2 class gets printed on the screen and the control is returned to the __init__() method of Base1 class.

Step 5: Base1 class gets printed and the control is transferred back to the __init__() method of Derived class.

Step 6: Derived class gets printed on the screen and hence the result.

10.3.2 Multi-level Inheritance

The technique of deriving a class from an already derived class is called *multi-level inheritance*. In Figure 10.3, Base Class acts as the base for *Derived Class 1* which in turn acts as a base for *Derived Class 2*. The *Derived Class 1* has features of *Base Class* plus its own features. The *Derived Class 1* is known as the *intermediate base class* as this class provides a link for inheritance between the *Base Class* and the *Derived Class 2*. The chain of classes—Base Class -> Derived Class 1 -> Derived Class 2 is known as the *inheritance path*. In multi-level inheritance, number of levels can go up to any number based on the requirement. The syntax for multi-level inheritance can be given as,

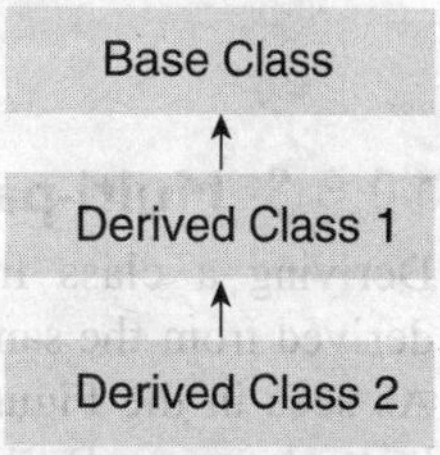

```
class Base:
    pass
class Derived1(Base):
    pass
class Derived2(Derived1):
    Pass
```

Base Class

↑

Derived Class 1

↑

Derived Class 2

Features of base class, derived class, plus its own

Figure 10.3 Multi-level inheritance

In multi-level inheritance scenario, any specified attribute is first searched in the current class (*Derived Class 2*). If it is not found there, then the *Derived Class 1* is searched, if it is not found even there then the *Base Class* is searched. If the attribute is still not found, then finally the object class is checked. This order is also called *linearization* of *Derived Class 2*. Correspondingly, the set of rules used to find this linearization order is called *Method Resolution Order (MRO)*.

> **Programming Tip:** All methods in Python are effectively virtual.

The MRO ensures that a class appears before its parent classes. However, in case of multiple inheritance, the MRO is the same as a tuple of base classes. You can check the MRO of a class by either using the __mro__ attribute or the mro() method. While the __mro__ attribute returns a tuple, the mro() method returns a list.

> **Note** Python has MRO and an algorithm C3 to keep a track of classes and their hierarchy.

Example 10.7 Program to demonstrate multi-level inheritance

```
class Person:                 # Base class
    def name(self):
        print('Name...')
class Teacher(Person):        # Class derived from Person
    def Qualification(self):
        print('Qualification...Ph.D must')
class HOD(Teacher):    # Class derived from Teacher, now hierarchy is Person-
>Teacher->HOD
    def experience(self):
        print('Experience......at least 15 years')
hod = HOD()
hod.name()
hod.Qualification()
hod.experience()
```

OUTPUT

```
Name...
Qualification...Ph.D must
Experience......at least 15 years
```

10.3.3 Multi-path Inheritance

Deriving a class from other derived classes that are in turn derived from the same base class is called *multi-path inheritance*. As seen in the Figure 10.4, the derived class has two immediate base classes— *Derived Class 1* and *Derived Class 2*. Both these base classes are themselves derived from the *Base Class*, thereby forming a grandparent, parent, and child form of a relationship. The derived class inherits the features of the *Base Class* (grandparent) via two separate paths. Therefore, the *Base Class* is also known as the *indirect base class*.

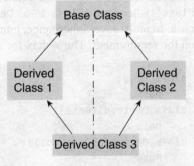

Figure 10.4 Multi-path inheritance

Example 10.8 Program to demonstrate multi-path inheritance

```
class Student:
    def name(self):
        print('Name...')
class Academic_Performance(Student):
    def Acad_score(self):
        print('Academic Score...90% and above')
class ECA(Student):
    def ECA_score(self):
        print('ECA Score......60% and above')
class Result(Academic_Performance, ECA):
    def Eligibility(self):
        print("*******Minimum Eligibility to Apply*******")
        self.Acad_score()
        self.ECA_score()

R = Result()
R. Eligibility()
```

OUTPUT
```
*******Minimum Eligibility to Apply*******
Academic Score...90% and above
ECA Score......60% and above
```

Problem in Multi-Path Inheritance (Diamond Problem)

The derived class inherits the members of the base class (grandparent) twice, via parent1 (*Derived Class 1*) and via parent 2 (*Derived Class 2*). This results in ambiguity because a duplicate set of members is created. This ambiguous situation must be avoided.

Thus, we see that diamond relationships exist when at least one of the parent classes can be accessed through multiple paths from the bottommost class. Diamond relationship is very common in Python as all classes inherit from the object and in case of multiple inheritance there is more than one path to reach the object. To prevent base classes from being accessed more than once, the dynamic algorithm (C3 and the MRO) linearizes the search order in such a way that the left-to-right ordering specified in each class is preserved and each parent is called only once (also known as monotonic).

10.4 COMPOSITION OR CONTAINERSHIP OR COMPLEX OBJECTS

Complex objects are objects that are built from smaller or simpler objects. For example, a car is built using a metal frame, an engine, some tyres, a transmission, a steering wheel, and several other parts. Similarly, a computer system is made up of several parts such as CPU, motherboard, memory, and so on. This process of building complex objects from simpler ones is called *composition or containership.*

In object-oriented programming languages, object composition is used for objects that have a has-a relationship to each other. For example, a car has-a metal frame, has-an engine, etc., and a personal computer has-a CPU, a motherboard, and other components.

Until now, we have been using classes that have data members of built-in type. While this worked well for simple classes, for designing classes that simulate real world applications, programmers often need data members that belong to other simpler classes.

Remember that in *composition,* the two objects are quite strongly linked. This means that one object can be thought of as exclusively *belonging* to the other object. If the owner object ceases to exist, the owned object will also cease to exist.

> **Note**   In composition, complex classes have data members belonging to other simpler classes.

Benefits
- Each individual class can be simple and straightforward.
- A class can focus on performing one specific task.
- The class is easier to write, debug, understand, and be usable by other programmers.
- While simpler classes can perform all the operations, the complex class can be designed to coordinate the data flow between simpler classes.
- It lowers the overall complexity of the complex object because the main task of the complex object would then be to delegate tasks to the sub-objects, who already know how to do them.

Scope of Use
Although there is no well-defined rule to state when a programmer must use composition, as a rule of thumb, each class should be built to accomplish a single task. The task should be to either perform some part of manipulation or be responsible for coordinating other classes but cannot perform both tasks. Following are some points which you should remember while deciding whether to use composition or inheritance.
- Try to limit the use of multiple inheritance as it makes the program complex to read, underst, and and debug.
- Composition should be used to package code into modules that are used in many different unrelated pieces of codes.
- Inheritance should be used only when there are clearly related reusable pieces of code that fits under a single common concept or if you are specifically asked to use it.

> **Note**   If the link between two objects is weak, and neither object has exclusive ownership of the other, then it is not composition. It is rather called *aggregation.*

> **Example 10.9**   Program that uses complex objects

```
class One:
    def set(self,var):
        self.var = var
    def get(self):
        return self.var
class Two:
    def __init__(self, var):
        self.o = One()    # object of class One is created
    # method of class One is invoked using its object in class Two
        self.o.set(var)
    def show(self):
        print("Number = ", self.o.get())
T = Two(100)
T.show()
```

OUTPUT
```
Number = 100
```

Note that in the aforementioned program, class Two has an object of class One as its data member. To access a member of One, we must use objects of both the classes as in self.o.get(). Thus, we see that composition is generally used when the features of an existing class is needed inside the new class, but not its interface. For this, existing class's object is embedded in the new class. The programmer will use the interface of the new class but implementation details of the original class.

A comparison between containership and inheritance is given in Table 10.1.

Table 10.1 Comparison between Inheritance and Containership

Inheritance	Containership
• Enables a class to inherit data and functions from a base class by extending it.	• Enables a class to contain objects of different classes as its data member.
• The derived class may override the functionality of base class.	• The container class cannot alter or override the functionality of the contained class.
• The derived class may add data or functions to the base class.	• The container class cannot add anything to the contained class.
• Inheritance represents a "is-a" relationship.	• Containership represents a "has-a" relationship.
• Example: A Student is a Person.	• Example: class One has a class Two.

10.5 ABSTRACT CLASSES AND INTERFACES

In some OOP languages like C++ and Java, it is possible to create a class which cannot be instantiated. This means that that you cannot create objects of that class. Such classes could only be inherited and then an object of the derived class was used to access the features of the base class. Such a class was known as the abstract class.

An abstract class corresponds to an abstract concept. For example, a polygon may refer to a rectangle, triangle, or any other closed figure. Therefore, an abstract class is a class that is specifically defined to lay a foundation for other classes that exhibits a common behaviour or similar characteristics. It is primarily used only as a base class for inheritance.

Programming Tip: Instantiating an object of an abstract class causes an error.

Since an abstract class is an incomplete class, users are not allowed to create its object. To use such a class, programmers must derive it keeping in mind that they would only be either using or overriding the features specified in that class.

Therefore, we see that an abstract class just serves as a *template* for other classes by defining a list of methods that the classes must implement. It makes no sense to instantiate an abstract class because all the method definitions are empty and must be implemented in a subclass.

The abstract class is thus an *interface* definition. In inheritance, we say that a class *implements* an interface if it inherits from the class which specifies that interface. In Python, we use the NotImplementedError to restrict the instantiation of a class. Any class that has the NotImplementedError inside method definitions cannot be instantiated. Consider the program given in the following example which creates an abstract class Fruit. Two other classes, Mango and Orange are derived from Fruit that implements all the methods defined in Fruit. Then we create the objects of the derived classes to access the methods defined in these classes.

Example 10.10 Program to illustrate the concept of abstract class

```python
class Fruit:
    def taste(self):
        raise NotImplementedError()
    def rich_in(self):
        raise NotImplementedError()
    def colour(self):
        raise NotImplementedError()
class Mango(Fruit):
    def taste(self):
        return "Sweet"
    def rich_in(self):
        return "Vitamin A"
    def colour(self):
        return "Yellow"
class Orange(Fruit):
    def taste(self):
        return "Sour"
    def rich_in(self):
        return "Vitamin C"
    def colour(self):
        return "Orange"
Alphanso = Mango()
print(Alphanso.taste(), Alphanso.rich_in(), Alphanso.colour())
Org = Orange()
print(Org.taste(), Org.rich_in(), Org.colour())
```

Programming Tip: Super falls apart if the methods of subclasses do not take the same arguments.

OUTPUT

```
Sweet Vitamin A Yellow
Sour Vitamin C Orange
```

10.6 METACLASS

A metaclass is the class of a class. While a class defines how an instance of the class behaves, a metaclass, on the other hand, defines how a class behaves. Every class that we create in Python is an instance of a metaclass (refer Figure 10.5).

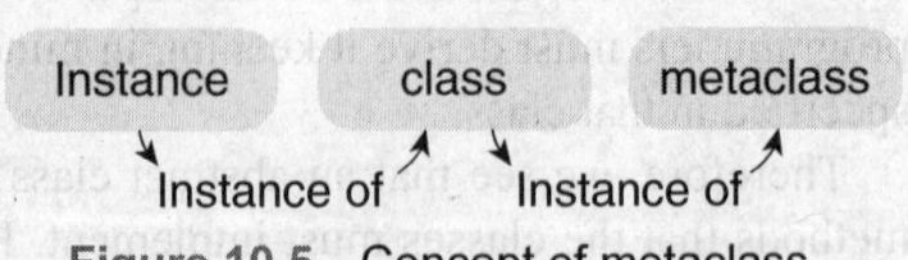

Instance → class → metaclass
Instance of   Instance of

Figure 10.5 Concept of metaclass

For example, *type* is a metaclass in Python. It is itself a class, and it is its own type. Although, you cannot make an exact replica of something like type, but Python does allow you to create a metaclass by making a subclass type.

A *metaclass* is most commonly used as a class factory. As we create an instance of the class by calling the class, Python creates a new class by calling the metaclass. By defining __init__() and __new__() methods in the metaclass, you can do a lot of extra things (while creating a class) like registering the new class with some registry, or replacing the class completely.

Programming Tip: In Python, a new class is created by calling the metaclass.

Python allows you to define normal methods on the metaclass which are like classmethods, as they can be called on the class without an instance. However, there is a difference between them as that they cannot be called on an instance of the class. Python also allows you to define the normal magic methods, such as __add__(), __iter__(), and __getattr__(), to implement or change how the class behaves.

Substitutability

Substitutability is a principle in object oriented programming that states that, in a computer program, if S is a subtype of T, then objects of type T may be replaced with objects of type S. In other words, an object of type T may be substituted with an object of a subtype S without changing any desirable property of type T.

Liskov has given a *substitution* principle also known as the **Liskov substitution principle (LSP)** which defines a subtyping relation, called **(strong) behavioural subtyping**. It is a semantic rather than syntactic relation.

PROGRAMMING EXAMPLES

Program 10.1 Write a program that has a class Point. Define another class Location which has two objects (Location and Destination) of class Point. Also define a function in Location that prints the reflection of Destination on the x axis.

```python
class Point:
    def __init__(self, x, y):
        self. x = x
        self.y = y
    def get(self):
        return (self.x,self.y)
class Location:
    def __init__(self,x1,y1,x2,y2):
        self.Source = Point(x1,y1)
        self.Destination = Point(x2,y2)
    def show(self):
        print("Source = ", self.Source.get())
        print("Destination = ", self.Destination.get())
    def reflection(self):
        self.Destination.x = -self.Destination.x
        print("Reflection Point on x Axis is : ", self.Destination.x, self.
Destination.y)
L = Location(1,2,3,4)
L.show()
L.reflection()
```

OUTPUT

```
Source =  (1, 2)
Destination =  (3, 4)
Reflection Point on x Axis is :  -3 4
```

Program 10.2 Write a program that has classes such as Student, Course, and Department. Enroll a student in a course of a particular department.

```python
class Student:
    def __init__(self, name, rollno, course, year):
```

```
            self.name = name
            self.rollno = rollno
            self.course = Course(course, year)
    def show(self):
        print(self.name, self.rollno)
        print(self.course.get())
class Course:
    def __init__(self, name, year):
        self.name = name
        self.year = year
    def get(self):
        return(self.name, self.year)
class Deptt:
    def __init__(self, name):
        self.name = name
        self.courses = []
    def get(self):
        return(name, courses)
    def add_courses(self,name):
        self.courses.append(name)
    def show_courses(self):
        print("Courses offered in this department are : ",self.courses)
D1 = Deptt("Mathematics")
D2 = Deptt("Computer Science")
D1.add_courses("BA(H)")
D1.add_courses("BSc(H)")
D2.add_courses("BCA")
D2.add_courses("BTech")
print("*** Dear Students, the list of courses offered in their respective
departments is given below.. Kindly choose any one course*************")
D1.show_courses()
D2.show_courses()
S = Student("Harman", 1234, "BCA", 2017)
S.show()
```

OUTPUT

```
*** Dear Students, the list of courses offered in their respective departments is
given below.. Kindly choose any one course*************
Courses offered in this department are :  ['BA(H)', 'BSc(H)']
Courses offered in this department are :  ['BCA', 'BTech']
Harman 1234
('BCA', 2017)
```

Program 10.3 Write a program that has an abstract class Polygon. Derive two classes Rectangle and Triangle from Polygon and write methods to get the details of their dimensions and hence calculate the area.

```
class Polygon:
    def get_data(self):
        raise NotImplementedError()
    def area(self):
        raise NotImplementedError()
class Rectangle(Polygon):
    def get_data(self):
        self.length = float(input("Enter the Length of the Rectangle : "))
        self.breadth = float(input("Enter the Breadth of the Rectangle : "))
    def area(self):
        return self.length * self.breadth;
class Triangle(Polygon):
    def get_data(self):
        self.base = float(input("Enter the Base of the Triangle : "))
        self.height = float(input("Enter the Height of the Triangle : "))
    def area(self):
        return 0.5*self.base * self.height;
R = Rectangle()
R.get_data()
print("Area of Rectangle : ", R.area())
T = Triangle()
T.get_data()
print("Area of Triangle : ", T.area())
```

OUTPUT

```
Enter the Length of the Rectangle : 70
Enter the Breadth of the Rectangle : 30
Area of Rectangle :  2100.0
Enter the Base of the Triangle : 50
Enter the Height of the Triangle : 100
Area of Triangle :  2500.0
```

Program 10.4 Write a program with class Bill. The users have the option to pay the bill either by cheque or by cash. Use the inheritance to model this situation.

```
class Bill:
    def __init__(self, items, price):
        self.total = 0;
        self.items = items
        self.price = price
        for i in self.price:
            self.total += i
    def display(self):
        print("\n ITEM \t\t\t PRICE")
        for i in range(len(self.items)):
                print(self.items[i], "\t", self.price[i])
        print("**********************")
```

```python
        print("TOTAL = ", self.total)
class Cash_Payment(Bill):
    def __init__(self, items,  price, deno, value) :
        Bill.__init__(self,items, price)
        #self.n = n;
        self.deno = deno
        self.value = value
    def show_Cash_Payment_Details(self):
        Bill.display(self)
        for i in range(len(deno)):
            print(deno[i], "*", value[i], " = ", deno[i] * value[i])
class Cheque_Payment(Bill):
    def __init__(self, items, price, cno, name) :
        Bill.__init__(self, items, price)
        self. cno = cno
        self.name = name
    def show_Check_Payment_Details(self):
        Bill.display(self)
        print("CHEQUE NUMBER : ", self.cno)
        print("BANK NAME : ", self.name)
items = ["External Hard Disk", "RAM", "Printer", "Pen Drive"]
price = [5000, 2000, 6000, 800]
option = int(input("Would you like to pay by cheque or cash (1/2): "))
if(option==1):
    name = input("Enter the name of the bank : ")
    cno = input("Enter the cheque number : ")
    Cheque = Cheque_Payment(items, price, cno, name)
    Cheque.show_Check_Payment_Details()
else:
    deno = [10, 20,50, 100, 500, 2000]
    value = [1,1,1,20,4,5]
    CP = Cash_Payment(items, price, deno, value)

    CP.show_Cash_Payment_Details()
```

OUTPUT

```
Would you like to pay by cheque or cash (1/2): 1
Enter the name of the bank : ICICI
Enter the cheque number : 12345
ITEM                PRICE
External Hard Disk 5000
RAM                 2000
Printer             6000
Pen Drive           800
*********************
TOTAL =   13800
```

```
CHEQUE NUMBER :  12345
BANK NAME :  ICICI
```

Program 10.5 Write a program that has a class Person. Inherit a class Faculty from Person which also has a class Publications.

```python
class Person:
    def __init__(self, name, age, sex):
        self.name = name
        self.age = age
        self.sex = sex
    def display(self):
        print("NAME : ", self.name)
        print("AGE : ", self.age)
        print("SEX : ", self.sex)
class Publications:
    def __init__(self, no_RP, no_Books, no_Art):
        self.no_RP = no_RP
        self.no_Books = no_Books
        self.no_Art = no_Art
    def display(self):
        print("Number of Research papers Published : ", self.no_RP)
        print("Number of Books Published : ", self.no_Books)
        print("Number of Articles Published : ", self.no_Art)
class Faculty(Person):
    def __init__(self, name, age, sex, desig, dept,no_RP, no_Books, no_Art):
        Person.__init__(self, name, age, sex)
        self.desig = desig
        self.dept = dept
        self.Pub = Publications(no_RP, no_Books, no_Art)
    def display(self):
        Person.display(self)
        print("DESIGNATION : ", self.desig)
        print("DEPARTMENT : ", self.dept)
        self.Pub.display()
F = Faculty("Pooja", 38, "Female", "TIC", "Computer Science", 22, 1, 3)
F.display()
```

OUTPUT

```
NAME :  Pooja
AGE :  38
SEX :  Female
DESIGNATION :  TIC
DEPARTMENT :  Computer Science
Number of Research papers Published :  22
Number of Books Published :  1
Number of Articles Published :  3
```

Summary

- Inheritance helps to reuse code.
- The derived classes are created by first inheriting the data and methods of the base class and then adding new specialized data and functions in it.
- In this process of inheritance, the base class remains unchanged.
- The concept of inheritance is used to implement the `"is a"` relationship.
- Inheritance follows a top-down approach to problem solving.
- In top-down Design approach, generalized classes are designed first and then specialized classes are derived by inheriting/extending the generalized classes.
- Method in the derived class overrides that in the base class.
- `super()` is a built-in function that denotes the base class.
- In Python, every class is inherited from the base class object.

- The `isinstance()` function returns `True` if the object is an instance of the class or other classes derived from it. The `issubclass()` checks for class inheritance.
- When a class inherits another with the same attributes or methods, it overrides them.
- The MRO ensures that a class appears before its parent classes.
- MRO of a class can be checked by either using the `__mro__` attribute or the `mro()` method. While the `__mro__` attribute returns a tuple, the `mro()` method returns a list.
- If the link between two objects is weak, and neither object has exclusive ownership of the other, then it is not composition. It is rather called *aggregation*.
- An abstract class is an incomplete class, so users are not allowed to create its object.
- The `NotImplementedError` is used to restrict the instantiation of a class.

Glossary

Abstract class A class that is specifically defined to lay a foundation for other classes that exhibits a common behaviour or similar characteristics. It is primarily used only as a base class for inheritance.

Base class The old or existing class is called the *base class*.

Complex objects Objects built from smaller or simpler objects.

Containership The process of building complex objects from simpler ones is called *composition or containership*.

Derived class The new class obtained from an existing class is known as the *derived class* or *subclass*.

Inheritance The technique of creating a new class from an existing class is called *inheritance*.

Multi-level inheritance The technique of deriving a class from an already derived class is called multi-level inheritance.

Multi-path inheritance Deriving a class from other derived classes that are in turn derived from the same base class is called *multi-path inheritance*.

Multiple inheritance When a derived class inherits features from more than one base class, it is called *multiple inheritance*.

EXERCISES

Fill in the Blanks

1. The technique of creating a new class from an existing class is called _____.
2. The old or existing class is called the _____.
3. The new class obtained from an existing class is known as the _____.
4. The _____ class inherits all the capabilities of the _____ class.
5. `super()` is a built-in function that denotes the _____ class.
6. In case of multiple inheritance, _____ function is invoked in `__init__()` method of every class.
7. When a derived class inherits features from more than one base class, it is called _____.
8. `MRO` of a class can be checked by either using the _____ or the _____.
9. While the `__mro__` attribute returns a _____, the `mro()` method returns a _____.

10. The process of building complex objects from simpler ones is called _____.
11. _____ class is specifically defined to lay a foundation for other classes that exhibits a common behaviour or similar characteristics.
12. An abstract class serves as a _____ for other classes.

13. The _____ is used to restrict the instantiation of a class.
14. `issubclass(list,object)` will result in _____.
15. `isinstance({"Name":"Girish","Course": "MBA"}, set)` returns _____.

State True or False

1. Inheritance supports reusability of code.
2. To support re-usability, Python supports the concept of re-using existing classes.
3. The derived class has less features than the base class.
4. When a class is derived from the base class, the base class also gets modified.
5. In inheritance, specialized classes are designed before generalized classes.
6. The derived class inherits all the capabilities of the base class and adds refinements and extensions of its own.
7. Methods in the base class overrides that in the derived class.

8. If there is no `__init__()` method in the derived class, the `__init__()` method of the last base class gets called.
9. The MRO ensures that a class appears before its parent classes.
10. Deriving a class from other derived classes that are in turn derived from the same base class is called *multi-level inheritance*.
11. Abstract class is used only as a base class for inheritance.
12. An abstract class is an incomplete class
13. Any class that has the `NotImplementedError` inside method definitions can be instantiated.
14. `isinstance(1.2,object)` will return `False`.
15. `isinstance([1,2,3,4], list)` will return `True`.

Multiple Choice Questions

1. The concept of inheritance is used to implement which relationship?
   (a) `is-a`   (b) `was-a`
   (c) `has-a`   (d) `in-a`
2. Inheritance follows which approach to problem solving?
   (a) Bottom-up   (b) Top-down
   (c) Bottom-down   (d) Top-up
3. Which function returns `True` if the object is an instance of the class or other classes derived from it?
   (a) `isobject()`   (b) `issubclass()`
   (c) `isinstance()` (d) `issuperclass()`
4. Which function checks for class inheritance?
   (a) `isobject()`   (b) `issubclass()`
   (c) `isinstance()` (d) `issuperclass()`
5. The technique of deriving a class from an already derived class is called _____
   (a) single inheritance
   (b) multiple inheritance

   (c) multi-level inheritance
   (d) multi-path inheritance
6. In OOP languages, object composition is used for objects that have a _____ relationship to each other.
   (a) `is-a`   (b) `was-a`
   (c) `has-a`   (d) `in-a`
7. If the link between two objects is weak, then it is called
   (a) aggregation   (b) composition
   (c) inheritance   (d) containership
8. You cannot create objects of which type of class?
   (a) base   (b) derived
   (c) abstract   (d) intermediate
9. The correct way of inheriting a Derived class from the Base class is
   (a) `class Base(Derived):`
   (b) `class Derived(Base):`
   (c) `class (Base)Derived:`
   (d) `class (Derived)Base:`

Review Questions

1. What is inheritance?
2. How does inheritance allow users to reuse code?
3. Differentiate between base class and derived class.

4. With the help of an example explain the significance of `super()` function.
5. Give the syntax of multiple inheritance.

6. Explain with an example, what will happen when an object of derived class is made and there is no __init__() method in the derived class.

7. What will happen when a class inherits from another class with the same attributes or methods? Will it override them?

8. If the specified attribute is not present in the current class then where will the search be made? Explain the concept in terms of multiple inheritance.

9. What is multi-level inheritance?

10. Define the term intermediate class and inheritance path in case of multi-level inheritance.

11. What do you understand by linearization and MRO?

12. What is an indirect base class?

13. What is diamond problem?

14. What are complex objects? Give the significance of having them in our programs.

15. In composition, the objects are strongly linked. Justify this statement

16. Differentiate between the following:
    (a) simple, multiple, and multi-level inheritance
    (b) inheritance and composition
    (c) containership and aggregation

17. What are abstract classes?

Programming Problems

1. Write an abstract class Vehicle. Derive three classes Car, Motorcycle and Truck from it. Define appropriate methods and print the details of the vehicle.

2. Define a class Employee. Display the personal and salary details of five employees using single inheritance.

3. Define a class Student with data members as rollno and name. Derive a class Fees from Student that has a data member fees and functions to submit fees and generate receipt. Derive another class Result from Student that displays the marks and grade obtained by the student.

4. Define a class Employee with data members as empno, name, and designation. Derive a class Qualification from Employee that has data members UG, PG, and experience. Create another class Salary which is derived from both these classes to display the details of the employee and compute their increments based on their experience and educational qualification.

5. Write a program that has a class Student to store the details of students in a class. Derive another class Toppers from the Student that stores records of only top three students of the class.

6. Write a program that has a class Person. Derive a class Baseball_Player from Person and display all the details of a famous baseball player.

7. Write a program that extends the class Shape to calculate the area of a circle and a cone. (*Hint: To calculate area of a circle only one variable is required so when creating object, pass the other variable with value 1*)

8. Write a program that extends the class Result so that the final result of the Student is evaluated based on the marks obtained in tests, activities, and sports.

9. Write a program that extends the Employee class so that it stores two more data members—DOB and Date of Hiring. The Date must be defined as a separate class.

10. Write a program that has a class Train with data members—no_of_seats_1 st, no_of_seats_2 Tier, and no_of_seats_3Tier —and member functions to set and display data. Derive a class Reservation that has data members— seats_booked_1 st, seats_booked_2Tier, and seats_booked_3Tier—, and functions to book and cancel tickets, and display status.

11. Write a program that has a class Distance with members—kms and metres. Derive classes School and Office which store the distance from your house to school and office along with other details.

12. Write a program that extends the class Employee. Derive a class Manager from Employee so that it lists all the details of the manager as well as the details of employees working under that manager.

13. Write a program for a publishing company that markets both printed books and audio-visual lectures stored on CDs. Write a class Publication that stores title and price. Derive a class book which has an additional member as no_pages and a class Lecture with member play_time.

Find the Output

1.
```python
print(isinstance("Python",object))
```

2.
```python
class Parent:
    def func(self):
        print("PARENT func()")
class Child(Parent):
    pass
P = Parent()
C = Child()
P.func()
C.func()
```

3.
```python
class Parent:
    def func(self):
        print("PARENT func()")
class Child(Parent):
    def func(self):
        print("CHILD func()")
P = Parent()
C = Child()
P.func()
C.func()
```

4.
```python
class Parent(object):
    def func(self):
        print("PARENT func()")
class Child(Parent):
    def func(self):
        print("CHILD, BEFORE PARENT func()")
        super(Child, self).func()
        print("CHILD, AFTER PARENT func()")
P = Parent()
C = Child()
P.func()
C.func()
```

5.
```python
class Parent:
    def func1(self):
        print("PARENT func1()")
    def func2(self):
        print("PARENT func1()")
    def func3(self):
        print("PARENT func3()")
class Child(Parent):
    def func1(self):
        print("CHILD func1()")
    def altered(self):
        print("CHILD, BEFORE PARENT func3()")
        super(Child, self).func3()
        print("CHILD, AFTER PARENT func3()")
P = Parent()
C = Child()
P.func2()
C.func2()
```

```python
P.func1()
C.func1()
P.func3()
C.func3()
```

6.
```python
class Base(object):
    def func1(self):
        print("BASE func1()")
    def func2(self):
        print("BASE func2()")
    def func3(self):
        print("BASE func3()")
class Derived(object):
    def __init__(self):
        self.base = Base()
    def func2(self):
        self.base.func2()
    def func1(self) :
        print("CHILD func1()")
    def func3(self):
        print("CHILD, BEFORE OTHER altered()")
        self.base.func3()
        print("CHILD, AFTER OTHER func3()")
C = Derived()
C.func2()
C.func1()
C.func3()
```

7.
```python
class Base:
    bVar = 10
    def __init__(self):
        print("Calling parent constructor")
    def func1(self):
        print('Calling parent method')
    def setVar(self, var):
        Base.bVar = var
    def getVar(self):
        print("Base Variable :", Base.bVar)
class Derived(Base):
    def __init__(self):
        print("Calling Derived Constructor")
    def func2(self):
        print('Calling Derived method')
D = Derived()
D.func2()
D.func1()
D.setVar(20)
D.getVar()
```

8.
```python
class Base:
    def func(self):
        print('Calling base method')
class Derived(Base):
```

```
        def func(self):
            print('Calling Derived method')
    D = Derived()
    D.func()
9.  class One(object):
        def __init__(self):
            print("init of One")
    class Two(object):
        def __init__(self):
            print("init of Two")
    class Three(One):
        def __init__(self):
            print("init of Three")
            super(Three, self).__init__()
    class Four(Three, Two):
        def __init__(self):
            print("init of Four")
            super(Four, self).__init__()
    F = Four()
10. class Vehicle:
        def __init__(self, name, color):
            self.__name = name
            self.__color = color
        def get(self):
            return (self.__name, self.__color)
        def set(self, name, color):
            self.__name = name
            self.__color = color
    class Car(Vehicle):
        def __init__(self, name, color, model):
            Vehicle.__init__(self,name, color)
            self.__model = model
        def getDescription(self):
            return self.get(), self.__model
    C = Car("Ecosport", "Red", "2016")
    print(C.getDescription())
11. class BaseClass1():
        def method_base1(self):
            print("Base 1 method called")
    class BaseClass2():
        def method_base2(self):
            print("Base 2 method called")
    class DerivedClass(BaseClass1, BaseClass2):
        def derived_method(self):
            print("child method")
    D = DerivedClass()
    D.method_base1()
    D.method_base2()
```

```
12. class Parent():
        def __init__(self):
            self.__x = 1
        def show(self):
            print("Show from Parent : ",
                self.__X)
    class Child(Parent):
        def __init__(self):
            self.__y = 1
        def show(self):
            print("Show from Child", self.__y)
    C = Child()
    C.show()
13. class A:
        def method1(self):
            print('Hello...')
    class B(A):
        def method2(self):
            print('\t World...')
    class C(B):
        def method3(self):
            print('\t\t Good Morning...')
    c = C()
    c.method1()
    c.method2()
    c.method3()
14. class A:
        def display(self):
            print('Hello...')
    class B(A):
        def display(self):
            print('\t World...')
    class C(B):
        def display(self):
            print('Good Morning...')
    c = C()
    c.display()
15. class Country:
        def __init__(self, name):
            self.name = name
        def capital(self):
            raise NotImplementedError
            ("Subclass must implement abstract
            method")
    class India(Country):
        def capital(self):
            return 'New Delhi'
```

```
class USA(Country):
    def capital(self):
        return 'Washington DC'
countries = [India('India'), USA('USA')]
for country in countries:
    print(country.name + ': ' + country.
    capital())
```

16.
```
class One:
    def method1(self):
        print("ONE")
class Two(One):
    def method2(self):
        print("TWO")
class Three(Two):
    def method3(self):
        print("THREE")
```

```
T=Three()
T.method1()
T.method2()
T.method3()
```

17.
```
class One:
    def method(self):
        print("ONE")
class Two(One):
    def method(self):
        print("TWO")
class Three(Two):
    def method3(self):
        print("THREE")
T=Three()
T.method()
```

Find the Error

1.
```
class One:
    def __init__(self):
        print("init of One")
        super(One, self).__init__()
class Two:
    def __init__(self):
        print("init of Two")
        super(Two, self).__init__()
class Three(One):
    def __init__(self):
        print("init of Three")
        super(Three, self).__init__()
class Four(Three, Two):
    def __init__(self):
        print("init of Four")
        super(Four, self).__init__()
if __name__ == '__main__':
    Four()
```

2.
```
class One(object):
    def save(self):
        super(One, self).save()
class Two(object):
    def save(self):
        super(Two, self).save()
class Three(One):
    def save(self):
        super(Three, self).save()
class Four(Three, Two):
    pass
```

```
if __name__ == '__main__':
    Four().save()
```

3.
```
class One:
    def method1(self):
        print("ONE")
class Two(One):
    def method2(self):
        print("TWO")
class Three(Two):
    def method3(self):
        print("THREE")
T=Three()
T.method()
```

4.
```
class One:
    def method1():
        print("ONE")
class Two(One):
    def method2():
        print("TWO")
T=Two()
T.method2()
```

5.
```
class One:
    def __method(self):
        print("ONE")
class Two(One):
    def __method(self):
        print("TWO")
T=Two()
T.method()
```

Answers

Fill in the Blanks

1. inheritance
2. base class
3. derived class
4. derived, base
5. base
6. super()

7. multiple inheritance.
8. __mro__ attribute or the mro() method
9. tuple, list
10. composition or containership
11. Abstract

12. template
13. NotImplementedError
14. True
15. False

State True or False

1. True 2. True 3. True 4. False 5. False 6. True 7. False 8. False 9. True 10. False
11. True 12. True 13. False 14. False 15. True

Multiple Choice Questions

1. (a) 2. (b) 3. (c) 4. (b) 5. (c) 6. (c) 7. (a) 8. (c) 9. (a)

CHAPTER 11

Operator Overloading

KEY Concepts

Basic Concepts of Operator Overloading • Advantages • Overloading Arithmetic and Logical Operators • Reverse Adding • Overriding __getitem__(), __setitem__(), in operator, and __call__() • Overloading Miscellaneous Functions

11.1 INTRODUCTION

Till now, we have seen that Python is an interesting and easy language. You can build classes with desired attributes and methods. But just think, if you want to add two Time values, where Time is a user-defined class, then how good it would be if we write T3 = T1 + T2, where T1, T2, and T3 are all objects of the class Time. As of now, we need to write the same statement as T3 = T1.add(T2).

Basically, the meaning of operators like +, =, *, /, >, <, etc. are pre-defined in any programming language. Programmers can use them directly on built-in data types to write their programs. But, for user-defined types like objects, these operators do not work. Therefore, Python allows programmers to redefine the meaning of operators when they operate on class objects. This feature is called operator overloading. *Operator overloading* allows programmers to extend the meaning of existing operators so that in addition to the basic data types, they can be also applied to user-defined data types.

You already have a clue of operator overloading. Just give a thought, if you write 5 + 2, then the integers are added, when you write str1 + str2, two strings are concatenated, when you write List1 + List2, the two lists are merged, so on and so forth. Thus, we see that the same operator behaves differently with different types.

11.1.1 Concept of Operator Overloading

With operator overloading, a programmer is allowed to provide his own definition for an operator to a class by overloading the built-in operator. This enables the programmer to perform some specific computation when the operator is applied on class objects and to apply a standard definition when the same operator is applied on a built-in data type.

This means that while evaluating an expression with operators, Python looks at the operands around the operator. If the operands are of built-in types, Python calls a built-in routine. In case, the operator is being applied on user-defined operand(s), the Python compiler checks to see if the programmer has an overloaded operator function that it can call. If such a function whose parameters match the type(s) and number of the operands exists in the program, the function is called, otherwise a compiler error is generated.

Another form of Polymorphism

Like function overloading, operator overloading is also a form of compile-time polymorphism. Operator overloading, is therefore less commonly known as operator *ad hoc polymorphism* since different operators have different implementations depending on their arguments. Operator overloading is generally defined by the language, the programmer, or both.

> **Note**   Ad hoc polymorphism is a specific case of polymorphism where different operators have different implementations depending on their arguments.

11.1.2 Advantage of Operator Overloading

We can easily write our Python programs without the knowledge of operator overloading, but the knowledge and use of this feature can help us in many ways. Some of them are:

* With operator overloading, programmers can use the same notations for user-defined objects and built-in objects. For example, to add two complex numbers, we can simply write C1 + C2.
* With operator overloading, a similar level of syntactic support is provided to user-defined types as provided to the built-in types.
* In scientific computing where computational representation of mathematical objects is required, operator overloading provides great ease to understand the concept.
* Operator overloading makes the program clearer. For example, the statement

(C1.mul(C2).div(C1.add(C2)) can be better written as C1 * C2 / C1 + C2

11.2 IMPLEMENTING OPERATOR OVERLOADING

Just consider the code given below which is trying to add two complex numbers and observe the result.

Example 11.1   Program to add two complex numbers without overloading the + operator

```
class Complex:
    def __init__(self):
        self.real = 0
        self.imag = 0
    def setValue(self, real, imag):
        self.real = real
        self.imag = imag
    def display(self):
        print("(", self.real, " + ", self.imag, "i)")
C1 = Complex()
C1.setValue(1,2)
C2 = Complex()
C2.setValue(3,4)
C3 = Complex()
C3 = C1 + C2
C3.display()
```

OUTPUT

```
Traceback (most recent call last):
```

```
   File "C:\Python34\Try.py", line 15, in <module>
     C3 = C1 + C2
 TypeError: unsupported operand type(s) for +: 'instance' and 'instance'
```

So, the reason for this error is simple. + operator does not work on user-defined objects. Now, to do the same concept, we will add an operator overloading function in our code. For example, look at the code given below which has the overloaded add function specified as __add__().

Example 11.2 Program to overload the + operator on a complex object

```
class Complex:
    def __init__(self):
        self.real = 0
        self.imag = 0
    def setValue(self, real, imag):
        self.real = real
        self.imag = imag
    def __add__(self, C):
        Temp = Complex()
        Temp.real = self.real + C.real
        Temp.imag = self.imag + C.imag
        return Temp
    def display(self):
        print("(", self.real, " + ", self.imag, "i)")
C1 = Complex()
C1.setValue(1,2)
C2 = Complex()
C2.setValue(3,4)
C3 = Complex()
C3 = C1 + C2
Print("RESULT = ")
C3.display()


OUTPUT
RESULT = ( 4 + 6 i)
```

In the program, when we write C1 + C2, the __add__() function is called on C1 and C2 is passed as an argument. Remember that, user-defined classes have no + operator defined by default. The only exception is when you inherit from an existing class that already has the + operator defined.

Note The __add__() method returns the new combined object to the caller.

We can also overload the comparison operators to work with class objects. But before we write further programs, let us first have a look at Table 11.1 to know the name of the function for each operator.

Table 11.1 Operators and their corresponding function names

Operator	Function Name	Operator	Function Name
+	__add__	+=	__iadd__
-	__sub__	-=	__isub__
*	__mul__	*=	__imul__
/	__truediv__	/=	__idiv__
**	__pow__	**=	__ipow__
%	__mod__	%=	__imod__
>>	__rshift__	>>=	__irshift__
&	__and__	&=	__iand__
|	__or__	|=	__ior__
^	__xor__	^=	__ixor__
~	__invert__	~=	__iinvert__
<<	__lshift__	<<=	__ilshift__
>	__gt__	<=	__le__
<	__lt__	==	__eq__
>=	__ge__	!=	__ne__

The program given below compares two Book objects. Although the class Book has three, attributes, comparison is done based on its price. However, this is not mandatory. You can compare two objects based on any of the attributes.

Example 11.3 Program to compare two objects of user-defined class type

```
class Book:
    def __init__(self):
        title = ""
        publisher = ""
        price = 0
    def set(self, title, publisher, price):
        self.title = title
        self.publisher = publisher
        self.price = price
    def display(self):
        print("TITLE : ", self.title)
        print("PUBLISHER : ", self.publisher)
        print("PRICE : ", self.price)
    def __gt__(self, B):
        if self.price > B.price:
            return True
        else:
            return False
B1 = Book()
```

```
B1.set("OOP with C++", "Oxford University Press", 525)
B2 = Book()
B2.set("Let us C++", "BPB", 300)
if B1>B2:
    print("This book has more knowledge so I will buy")
    B1.display()
```

OUTPUT

```
This book has more knowledge so I will buy
TITLE :  OOP with C++ PUBLISHER :  Oxford University Press PRICE :   525
```

PROGRAMMING EXAMPLES

Program 11.1 Write a program that overloads the + operator on a class Student that has attributes name and marks.

```
class Student:
    def __init__(self, name, marks):
        self.name = name
        self.marks = marks
    def display(self):
        print(self.name, self.marks)
    def __add__(self, S):
        Temp = Student(S.name, [])
        for i in range(len(self.marks)):
            Temp.marks.append(self.marks[i] + S.marks[i])
        return Temp
S1 = Student("Nikhil", [87, 90, 85])
S2 = Student("Nikhil", [83, 86, 88])
S1.display()
S2.display()
S3 = Student("",[])
S3 = S1 + S2
S3.display()
```

OUTPUT

```
Nikhil [87, 90, 85]
Nikhil [83, 86, 88]
Nikhil [170, 176, 173]
```

Program 11.2 Write a program that overloads the + operator to add two objects of class Matrix.

```
class Matrix:
    def __init__(self, List):
```

```
            self.List = List
    def display(self):
        print(self.List)
    def __add__(self, M):
        Temp = Matrix([])
        for i in range(len(self.List)):
            for j in range(len(self.List[0])):
                Temp.List.append(self.List[i][j] + M.List[i][j])
        return Temp
M1 = Matrix([[1,2],[3,4]])
M2 = Matrix([[3,4],[5,1]])
M3 = Matrix([])
M3 = M1 + M2
print("RESULTANT MATRIX IS : ")
M3.display()
```

OUTPUT

```
RESULTANT MATRIX IS :  [4, 6, 8, 5]
```

Program 11.3 Write a program that overloads the + operator so that it can add two objects
of class Fraction.

```
def GCD(num, deno):
    if(deno == 0):
        return num
    else:
        return GCD(deno, num%deno)
class Fraction:
    def __init__(self):
        self.num = 0
        self.deno = 1
    def get(self):
        self.num = int(input("Enter the numerator : "))
        self.deno = int(input("Enter the denominator : "))
    def simplify(self):
        common_divisor = GCD(self.num, self.deno)
        self.num //= common_divisor
        self.deno //= common_divisor
    def __add__(self, F):
        Temp = Fraction()
        Temp.num = (self.num * F.deno) + (F.num * self.deno)
        Temp.deno = self.deno * F.deno
        return Temp
    def display(self):
        self.simplify()
        print(self.num, "/", self.deno)
F1 = Fraction()
```

```
F1.get()
F2 = Fraction()
F2.get()
F3 = Fraction()
F3 = F1 + F2
print("RESULTANT FRACTION IS : ")
F3.display()
```

OUTPUT

```
Enter the numerator : 4
Enter the denominator : 10
Enter the numerator : 2
Enter the denominator : 5
RESULTANT FRACTION IS :  4 / 5
```

Program 11.4 Write a program that overloads the + operator so that it can add a specified number of days to a given date.

```
Dict = {1:31, 3:31, 4:30, 5:31, 6:30, 7:31, 8:31, 9:30, 10:31, 11:30, 12:31}
def chk_Leap_Year(year):
    if (year%4 == 0 and year%100 != 0) or (year%400 == 0):
        return 1
    else:
        return 0
class Date:
    def __init__(self):
        d = m = y = 0
    def get(self):
        self.d = int(input("Enter the day : "))
        self.m = int(input("Enter the month : "))
        self.y = int(input("Enter the year : "))
    def __add__(self, num):
        self.d += num
        if self.m !=2:
            max_days = Dict[self.m]
        elif self.m == 2:
            isLeap = chk_Leap_Year(self.y)
            if isLeap == 1:
                max_days = 29
            else:
                max_days = 28
        while self.d > max_days:
            self.d -= max_days
            self.m += 1
        while self.m > 12:
            self.m -= 12
            self.y += 1
```

```
    def display(self):
        print(self.d, "-", self.m,"-", self.y)
D = Date()
D.get()
num = int(input("How many days to add : "))
D + num
D.display()
```

OUTPUT

```
Enter the day : 25
Enter the month : 2
Enter the year : 2016
How many days to add : 10
6 - 3 - 2016
```

Program 11.5 Write a program that has an overloads the *, /, and > operators so that it can multiply, divide, and compare two objects of class Fraction.

```
Dict = {1:31, 3:31, 4:30, 5:31, 6:30, 7:31, 8:31, 9:30, 10:31, 11:30, 12:31}
def chk_Leap_Year(year):
    if (year%4 == 0 and year%100 != 0) or (year%400 == 0):
        return 1
    else:
        return 0
class Date:
    def __init__(self):
        d = m = y = 0
    def get(self):
        self.d = int(input("Enter the day : "))
        self.m = int(input("Enter the month : "))
        self.y = int(input("Enter the year : "))
    def __add__(self, num):
        self.d += num
        if self.m !=2:
            max_days = Dict[self.m]
        elif self.m == 2:
            isLeap = chk_Leap_Year(self.y)
            if isLeap == 1:
                max_days = 29
            else:
                max_days = 28
        while self.d > max_days:
            self.d -= max_days
            self.m += 1
        while self.m > 12:
            self.m -= 12
            self.y += 1
```

```
    def display(self):
        print(self.d, "-", self.m,"-", self.y)
D = Date()
D.get()
num = int(input("How many days to add : "))
D + num
D.display()
```

OUTPUT

```
Enter the numerator : 2
Enter the denominator : 3
Enter the numerator : 4
Enter the denominator : 9
F1 > F2 True
F1 * F2 IS :  8 / 27
F1 / F2 IS :  3 / 2
```

Program 11.6 Write a program that overloads the + operator so that it can add two objects of class Binary.

```
class Binary:
    number = []
    def set(self, bnum):
        self.number = bnum
    def display(self):
        print(self. Number)
    def __add__(self, B):
        Temp = Binary()
        index = len(self.number)
        carry = []
        while len(Temp.number) != index:
            Temp.number.append(-1)
            carry.append(0)
        index -= 1
        while (index)>=0:
            if self.number[index] == 0 and B.number[index] == 0:
                Temp.number[index] = 0 + int(carry[index])
            if self.number[index] == 0 and B.number[index] == 1:
                Temp.number[index] = 1 + int(carry[index])
            if self.number[index] == 1 and B.number[index] == 0:
                Temp.number[index] = 1 + int(carry[index])
            if self.number[index] == 1 and B.number[index] == 1:
                Temp.number[index] = 0 + int(carry[index])
                carry[index-1] = 1
            if Temp.number[index] == 2:
                Temp.number[index] = 0
                if (index-1)>=0:
```

```
                        carry[index-1] = 1
                index -= 1
            return Temp
B1 = Binary()
B1.set([1,1,0,1,1])
B2 = Binary()
B2.set([0,1,1,0,1])
B3 = B1 + B2
B3.display()
```

OUTPUT

```
[0, 1, 0, 0, 0]
```

Program 11.7 Write a program to compare two Date objects.

```
class Date:
    def __init__(self):
        d = m = y = 0
    def get(self):
        self.d = int(input("Enter the day : "))
        self.m = int(input("Enter the month : "))
        self.y = int(input("Enter the year : "))
    def __eq__(self, D):
        Flag = False
        if self.d == D.d:
            if self.m == D.m:
                if self.y == D.y:
                    Flag = True
        return Flag
    def __lt__(self, D):
        Flag = False
        if self.y < D.y:
            if self.m < D.m:
                if self.d < D.d:
                    Flag = True
        return Flag
D1 = Date()
D1.get()
D2 = Date()
D2.get()
print("D1 == D2", D1 == D2)
print("D1 < D2", D1 < D2)
```

Programming Tip: The __eq__ function gives NotImplemented as result when left hand argument does not know how to test for equality with given right hand argument.

OUTPUT

```
Enter the day : 21
Enter the month : 3
```

```
Enter the year : 2017
Enter the day : 21
Enter the month : 3
Enter the year : 2017
D1 == D2 True
D1 < D2 False
```

Program 11.8 Write a program to overload the `-=` operator to subtract two `Distance` objects.

```python
class Distance:
    def __init__(self):
        self.km = 0
        self.m = 0
    def set(self, km, m):
        self.km = km
        self.m = m
    def __isub__(self, D):
        self.m = self.m - D.m
        if self.m < 0:
            self.m += 1000
            self.km -= 1
        self.km = self.km - D.km
        return self
    def convert_to_meters(self):
        return (self.km*1000 + self.m)
    def display(self):
        print(self.km, "kms", self.m, "mtrs")
D1 = Distance()
D1.set(21, 70)
D2 = Distance()
D2.set(18, 123)
D1 -= D2
print("D1 - D2 = ")
D1.display(),
print("that is", D1.convert_to_meters(), "meters")
```

OUTPUT

```
D1 - D2 =  2 kms 947 mtrs that is 2947 meters
```

11.3 REVERSE ADDING

In a program, we have added a certain number of days to our `Date` object by writing d + num. In this case, it is compulsory that the class object will invoke the __add__(). But, to provide greater flexibility, we should also be able to perform the addition in reverse order, that is, adding a non-class object to the class object. For this, Python provides the concept of reverse adding. The function to do normal addition on `Date` object is discussed in the following example.

Example 11.4   Program to illustrate adding on Date object

```
def __add__(self, num):
        self.d += num
        if self.m !=2:
            max_days = Dict[self.m]
        elif self.m == 2:
            isLeap = chk_Leap_Year(self.y)
            if isLeap == 1:
                max_days = 29
            else:
                max_days = 28
        while self.d > max_days:
            self.d -= max_days
            self.m += 1
        while self.m > 12:
            self.m -= 12
            self.y += 1
```

Programming Tip: Special methods are used for performing operator overloading.

But, had we written the same statement as num + d, then the desired task would not have been performed. The simple reason for this is that the __add__() takes self as the first argument, so the + operator has to be invoked using the Date object. But this is not the case when you work with numbers. You can either write 10 + 20 or 20 + 10, it means the same and the correct result is produced. So, we should also have the same result when we write d + num or num + d. Python has a solution to this. It has the feature of reverse adding. As you write the __add__() function, just write the __radd__() function which will do the same task.

Note   To overload the + = or – = operators, use the __iadd__() or __isub__() functions.

11.4 OVERRIDING __getitem__() AND __setitem__() METHODS

Python allows you to override __getitem__() and __setitem__() methods. We have already seen in Chapter 9 that __getitem__() is used to retrieve an item at a particular index. Similarly, __setitem__() is used to set value for a particular item at the specified index. Although they are well defined for built-in types like list, tuple, string, etc. but for user-defined classes we need to explicitly write their codes. Consider the program given below which has a list defined in a class. By default, Python does not allow you to apply indexes on class objects but if you have defined the __getitem__() and __setitem__() methods in the class, then you can simply work with indices as with any other built-in type as shown in the following example.

Example 11.5   Program that overrides __getitem__() and __setitem__() methods in a class

```
class myList:
    def __init__(self, List):
        self.List = List
    def __getitem__(self,index):
        return self.List[index]
```

```
        def __setitem__(self, index, num):
            self.List[index] = num
        def __len__(self):
            return len(self.List)
        def display(self):
            print(self.List)
L = myList([1,2,3,4,5,6,7])
print("LIST IS : ")
L.display()
index = int(input("Enter the index of List you want to access : "))
print(L[index])
index = int(input("Enter the index at which you want to modify : "))
num = int(input("Enter the correct number : "))
L[index] = num
L.display()
print("The length of my list is : ", len(L))
```

OUTPUT

```
LIST IS :  [1, 2, 3, 4, 5, 6, 7]
Enter the index of List you want to access : 3
4
Enter the index at which you want to modify : 3
Enter the correct number : 40
[1, 2, 3, 40, 5, 6, 7]
The length of my list is :  7
```

11.5 OVERRIDING THE in OPERATOR

We have seen that in is a membership operator that checks whether the specified item is in the variable of built-in type or not (like string, list, dictionary, tuple, etc.). We can overload the same operator to check whether the given value is a member of a class variable or not. To overload the in operator we have to use the function __contains__(). In the program given in the following example, we have created a dictionary that has name of the subjects as *key* and their maximum weightage as *value*. In the main module, we are asking the user to input a subject. If the subject is specified in our dictionary, then its maximum weightage is displayed.

Example 11.6 Program to override the in operator

```
class Marks:
    def __init__(self):
        self.max_marks = {"Maths":100, "Computers":50, "SST":100, "Science":75}
    def __contains__(self, sub):
        if sub in self.max_marks:
            return True
        else:
                return False
    def __getitem__(self, sub):
```

```
            return self.max_marks[sub]
        def __str__(self):
            return "The Dictionary has name of subjects and maximum marks allotted to them"
M = Marks()
print(str(M))
sub = input("Enter the subject for which you want to know extra marks : ")
if sub in M:
    print("Social Studies paper has maximum marks alloted = ", M[sub])
```

OUTPUT

```
The Dictionary has name of subjects and maximum marks allotted to them
Enter the subject for which you want to know extra marks : Computers
Social Studies paper has maximum marks alloted =  50
```

11.6 OVERLOADING MISCELLANEOUS FUNCTIONS

Python allows you to overload functions like long(), float(), abs(), and hex(). Remember that we have used these functions on built-in type variables to convert them from one type to another. We can use these functions to convert a value of one user-defined type (object) to a value of another type.

Example 11.7 Program to overload hex(), oct(), and float() functions

```
class Number:
    def __init__(self, num):
        self.num = num
    def display(self):
        return self.num
    def __abs__(self):
        return abs(self.num)
    def __float__(self):
        return float(self.num)
    def __oct__(self):
        return oct(self.num)
    def __hex__(self):
        return hex(self.num)
    def __setitem__(self, num):
        self.num = num
N = Number(-14)
print("N IS : ", N.display())
print("ABS(N) IS : ", abs(N))
N = abs(N)
print("Converting to float....., N IS : ", float(N))
print("Hexadecimal equivalent of N IS : ", hex(N))
print("Octal equivalent of N IS : ", oct(N))
```

OUTPUT

```
N IS :  -14
ABS(N) IS :  14
Converting to float....., N IS :  14.0
Hexadecimal equivalent of N IS :  0xe
Octal equivalent of N IS :  016
```

Let us take another example in which we have two classes for calculating the distance. One has distance specified in meters and the other has distance in kilometers. There are two functions–km() and mts(), which takes the argument of class Distance and then converts the distance into kilometers and meters respectively.

Example 11.8 Program to illustrate conversion of class objects

```
class Distance_m:
  def __init__(self, m):
    self.m = m
  def display(self):
    print("Distance in meters is : ", self.m)
def mts(D):
    return D.km*1000
class Distance_km:
  def __init__(self, km):
    self.km = km
  def display(self):
    print("Distance in kilometers is : ", self.km)
def km(D):
    return D.m/1000
Dm = Distance_m(12345)
Dm.display()
print("Distance in kilo metres = ", km(Dm))
Dkm = Distance_km(12.345)
Dkm.display()
print("Distance in metres = ", mts(Dkm))
```

OUTPUT

```
Distance in meters is :  12345
Distance in kilo metres =  12
Distance in kilometers is :  12.345
Distance in metres =  12345.0
```

11.7 OVERRIDING THE __call__() METHOD

The __call__() method is used to overload call expressions. The __call__() method is called automatically when an instance of the class is called. It can be passed to any positional or keyword arguments. Like other functions, the __call__() method also supports all of the argument-passing modes. The __call__() method can be declared as, def __call__(self, [args...])

Example 11.9   Program to overload the __call__() method

```
class Mult:
  def __init__(self, num):
    self.num = num
  def __call__(self, O):
    return self.num * O
x = Mult(10)
print(x(5))
```

OUTPUT

50

Summary

- The meaning of operators like +, =, *, /, >, <, etc. are pre- defined in any programming language. So, programmers can use them directly on built in data types to write their programs.
- Operator overloading allows programmers to extend the meaning of existing operators so that in addition to the basic data types, they can also be applied to user-defined data types.
- With operator overloading, a programmer is allowed to provide his own definition for an operator to a class by overloading the built-in operator.

- Operator overloading is also known as operator *ad hoc polymorphism* since different operators have different implementations depending on their arguments.
- The __add__() method returns the new combined object to the caller.
- By default, Python does not allow you to apply indexes on class objects but if you have defined the __getitem__() and __setitem__() in the class, then you can simply work with indices as with any other built-in type.

Glossary

Ad hoc polymorphism A specific case of polymorphism where different operators have different implementations depending on their arguments.
Membership operator An operator that checks whether the specified item is present in the instance of an object or not.

Operator Overloading Redefining the meaning of operators when they operate on class objects.

Exercises

Fill In The Blanks

1. _____ allows programmers to redefine the meaning of existing operators.
2. Operator overloading is also known as _____ polymorphism.
3. _____ is a specific case of polymorphism where different operators have different implementations depending on their arguments.

4. The name of the function to overload ** operator is _____.
5. The __add__() method returns _____.
6. To overload the *= operator you will use _____ function.

7. The __eq__ function gives _____ as result when left hand argument does not know how to test for equality with given right hand argument.
8. The _____ method is used to overload call expressions.
9. The __call__() method supports all of the _____ modes.
10. _____ method is written to perform longObj – Number, where Number is a user-defined class.

State True Or False

1. You can have overload only one operator per class.
2. Operator overloading allows you to create new operators.
3. With operator overloading, a programmer is allowed to provide his own definition for an operator to a class.
4. Operator overloading makes the program simple to understand.
5. To overload the <<= operator, you will write the code for __lshift__ function.
6. All the operators can be overloaded.
7. Writing intObj + classObj is same as writing classObj + intObj.
8. Special methods are used for performing operator overloading.
9. The __getitem__() and __setitem__() methods are defined for lists, tuples, and strings but not for class objects.
10. The __call__() method can be passed any positional or keyword arguments.

Multiple Choice Questions

1. Which function will be written to overload the in operator?
   (a) __call__()   (b) __contains__()
   (c) __member__()   (d) __add__()
2. Which of the following function will help you to retrieve an item at a particular index?
   (a) slice   (b) __getitem__()
   (c) __setitem__()   (d) in
3. Which of the following function is used to set value for a particular item at the specified index?
   (a) slice   (b) __getitem__()
   (c) __setitem__()   (d) in
4. Membership operator when overloaded is invoked on _____.
   (a) object   (b) class
   (c) method   (d) attribute
5. Which conversion function cannot be overloaded in a class?
   (a) long()   (b) hex()
   (c) str()   (d) None of these

6. Which function is called when the following code is executed?
   ```
   C = Complex()
   format(C)
   ```
   (a) format()   (b) __format__()
   (c) str()   (d) None of these
7. If we write the following lines of code, then which function will be invoked and what will it return?
   ```
   N1 = Number(10)
   N2 = Number(20)
   print(N1<N2)
   ```
   (a) __lt__, False   (b) __gt__, False
   (c) __lt__, True   (d) __gt__, True
8. When we add two objects of class Complex, which functions are called when we write print(C1 + C2)?
   (a) __add__(), __str__()
   (b) __str__(), __add__()
   (c) __sum__(), __str__()
   (d) __str__(), __sum__()

Review Questions

1. Define the term operator overloading.
2. Assume that you have overloaded the + operator in your program. Illustrate the cases in which the operator overloaded function will be called and the cases in which the default function will be called.
3. Define the term ad hoc polymorphism.
4. Give the advantages of operator overloading.
5. Differentiate between __add__, __radd__, and __iadd__ functions.
6. Which functions will you use to index a class object? Explain with the help of an example.
7. Which operator is used to check whether a value is present in the object or not? Can you overload this object on user-defined types? If yes, how?

8. Is it possible to convert a class object in to a floating type value? If yes, how?
9. With the help of an example explain how you can convert a value of one class type into a value of another class type.

10. When is the __call__() method invoked?

Programming Problems

1. Write a class Money with attributes Rupees and Paise. Overload operators +=, -=, and >= so that they may be used on two objects. Also write functions so that a desired amount of money can be either added or subtracted from Money.
2. Use the class defined in the previous functions to calculate the amount of money to be paid by multiplying it with a specified quantity.
3. Again, using class Money, find the price of one item given the total amount paid and number of units of item bought.
4. Write a class INR with attributes Rupees and Paise. Write another class USD with attributes dollars and cents. Write a function to convert USD into INR and vice versa.
5. Write a program that overloads the + operator to add two objects of class Time.
6. Write a menu driven program to overload +=, -=, and *= operators on the Matrix class.
7. Write a menu driven program to overload +=, -=, ==, >=, and <= operators on the Distance class.
8. Write a menu driven program to overload +=, -=, ==, >=, and <= operators on the Time class.
9. Write a menu driven program to overload +=, -=, ==, >=, and <= operators on the Height class.
10. Write a menu driven program to overload +=, -=, ==, >=, and <= operators on the Binary class.
11. Write a menu driven program to overload +=, -=, *=, /=, ==, >=, and <= operators on the Complex class.

12. Write a menu driven program to overload +=, -=, *=, /=, ==, and >=, and <= operators on the Polynomial class.
13. Write a menu driven program to overload +=, -=, *=, /=, ==, >=, and <= operators on the Fraction class.
14. Write a menu driven program to overload +=, -=, ==, >=, and <= operators on the String class.
15. Write a program to convert minutes into class Time with data members—hrs and mins.
16. Write a program to convert class Time with data members—hrs and mins into minutes.
17. Write a menu driven program that performs conversion to and from Array class.
18. Write a menu driven program that performs conversion to and from String class.
19. Write a menu driven program that performs conversion from a Square to Rectangle class.
20. Write a program to convert data of class Student having members—roll no and marks in three subjects to another class Student that stores just the roll number and the average.
21. Write a program to convert Polar co-ordinates specified in one class into Rectangular co-ordinates.
22. Write a program to convert temperature specified in Celsius in one class into Fahrenheit in another class.
23. Write a program to implement a timer using increment operator overloading.

Find the Output

1.
```
class Point:
    def __init__(self, x, y):
        self.x = x
        self.y = y
    def __abs__(self):
        return (self.x**2 + self.y**2)**0.5
    def __add__(self, P):
        return Point(self.x + P.x, self.y + P.y)
    def display(self):
        print(self.x, self.y)

P1 = Point(12, 25)
P2 = Point(21, 45)
print(abs(P2))
P1 = P1+ P2
P1.display()
```
2.
```
class A(object):
    def __init__(self, num):
        self.num = num
    def __eq__(self, other):
        return self.num == other.num
```

```
     class B(object):
         def __init__(self, num):
             self.num = num
     print(A(5) == B(5))
3.   class Circle:
         def __init__(self, radius):
           self.__radius = radius
         def getRadius(self):
           return self.__radius
         def area(self):
           return 3.14 * self.__radius ** 2
         def __add__(self, C):
           return Circle( self.__radius + C.__
     radius )
     C1 = Circle(5)
     C2 = Circle(9)
     C3 = C1 + C2
     print("RADIUS : ",C3.getRadius())
     print("AREA : ", C3.area())
4.   class Circle:
         def __init__(self, radius):
           self.__radius = radius
         def __gt__(self, another_circle):
           return self.__radius >
     another_circle.__radius
         def __lt__(self, C):
           return self.__radius < C.__radius
         def __str__(self):
           return "Circle has radius " +
     str(self.__radius)
     C1 = Circle(5)
     C2 = Circle(9)
     print(C1)
     print(C2)
     print("C1 < C2 : ", C1 < C2)
     print("C2 > C1 : ", C1 > C2)
5.   class One:
         def __init__(self):
             num = 10
         def __eq__(self, T):
             if isinstance(T, One):
                 return True
             else:
                 return NotImplemented
     class Two:
         def __init__(self):
             num = 100
     print(One() == Two())
6.   class A:
         def __bool__(self):
```

```
             return True
     X = A()
     if X:
       print('yes')
7.   class String(object):
         def __init__(self, val):
           self.val = val
         def __add__(self, other):
           return self.val + '....' + other.val
         def __sub__(self, other):
           return "Not Implemented"
     S1 = String("Hello")
     S2 = String("World")
     print(S1 + S2)
     print(S1 - S2)
8.   class String(object):
         def __init__(self, val):
           self.val = val
         def __str__(self):
           return self.val
         def __repr__(self):
           return "This is String representation
     of " + self.val
     S = String("Hi")
     print(str(S))
9.   class A:
         def __len__(self):
             return 0
     X = A()
     if not X:
       print('no')
     else:
       print('yes')
10.  class A:
         def __init__(self):
             self.str = "abcdef"
         def __getitem__(self, i):
             return self.str[i]
     x = A()
     for i in x:
       print(i,end=" ")
11.  class A:
         str = "Hi"
         def __gt__(self, str):
             return self.str > str
     X = A()
     print(X > 'hi')
```

Find the Error

```
1.  class Matrix:
        def __init__(self):
            Mat = []
        def setValue(self, number):
            self.number = number
        def display(self):
            print(self.number)
    M1 = Matrix()
    M1.setValue(([1,2],[3,4]))
    M2 = Matrix()
    M2.setValue(([5,6],[2,3]))
    M3 = Matrix()
    M3 = M1 + M2
    M3.display()
2.  class A(object):
        def __init__(self, num):
            self.num = num
        def __eq__(self, other):
            return self.num == other.num
    class B(object):
        def __init__(self, val):
            self.val = val
    print(A(5) == B(5))
3.  class Point:
        def __init__(self, x, y):
            self.x = x
```

```
            self.y = y
        def __mul__(self, num):
            return self.x * num + self.y * num
    P1 = Point(3, 4)
    print(2*P1)
4.  class String(object):
        def __init__(self, val):
            self.val = val
    S1 = String("Hello")
    print(S1[5])
5.  class Number:
        def __init__(self, num):
            self.num = num
        def __sub__(self, N):
            return Number(self.num - N)
        def __sub__(N, self):
            return Number(N - self.num)
    x = Number(4)
    y = x-4
6.  class A:
        def __init__(self):
            self.str = "abcdef"
        def __setitem__(self, i, val):
            self.str[i] = val
    x = A()
    x[2] = 'X'
```

Answers

Fill in the Blanks

1. operator overloading
2. compile time or ad hoc
3. ad hoc polymorphism
4. __pow__
5. the new combined object to the caller
6. __imul__
7. NotImplemented
8. __call__()
9. argument-passing
10. __rsub__()

State True or False

1. False   2. False   3. True   4. True   5. False   6. False   7. False   8. True   9. True   10. True

Multiple Choice Questions

1. (b)   2. (b)   3. (c)   4. (a)   5. (d)   6. (c)   7. (c)   8. (a)

12 Error and Exception Handling

> • Types of Errors and Exceptions • try - except Blocks • finally Block • Raising Exceptions • Re-raising Exceptions • Built-in and User-defined Exceptions • Handling Invoked Functions • Assertions

12.1 INTRODUCTION TO ERRORS AND EXCEPTIONS

In our programs, we had been getting some or the other errors but we had not mentioned much about them. Basically, there are (at least) two kinds of errors: *syntax errors* and *exceptions*.

The programs that we write may behave abnormally or unexpectedly because of some errors and/or exceptions (Figure 12.1). The two common types of errors that we very often encounter are *syntax errors* and *logic errors*. While logic errors occur due to poor understanding of problem and its solution,

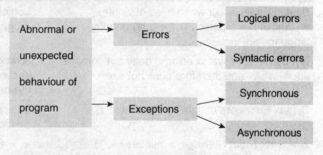

Figure 12.1 Errors and exceptions

syntax errors, on the other hand, arises due to poor understanding of the language. However, such errors can be detected by exhaustive debugging and testing of procedures.

But many a times, we come across some peculiar problems which are often categorized as *exceptions*. Exceptions are run-time anomalies or unusual conditions (such as divide by zero, accessing arrays out of its bounds, running out of memory or disk space, overflow, and underflow) that a program may encounter during execution. Like errors, exceptions can also be categorized as synchronous or asynchronous exceptions. While *synchronous* exceptions (like divide by zero, array index out of bound, etc.) can be controlled by the program, *asynchronous* exceptions (like an interrupt from the keyboard, hardware malfunction, or disk failure), on the other hand, are caused by events that are beyond the control of the program.

12.1.1 Syntax Errors

Syntax errors occurs when we violate the rules of Python and they are the most common kind of error that we get while learning a new language. For example, consider the lines of code given below.

```
>>> i=0
>>> if i == 0 print(i)
SyntaxError: invalid syntax
```

In the aforementioned code, we have missed the ':' before the keyword print. If you had run this code in a file, then the file name and line number would have also been printed to help you know where the error has occurred. Basically, in this case, the Python interpreter has found that it cannot complete the processing of the instruction because it does not conform to the rules of the language.

> **Note**   You will get syntax errors frequently as you start learning a new language.

12.1.2 Logic Error

The other type of error, known as a logic error, specifies all those type of errors in which the program executes but gives incorrect results. Logical error may occur due to wrong algorithm or logic to solve a particular program. In some cases, logic errors may lead to divide by zero or accessing an item in a list where the index of the item is outside the bounds of the list. In this case, the logic error leads to a run-time error that causes the program to terminate abruptly. These types of run-time errors are known as *exceptions*.

Many programmers may think of exception as a fatal run-time error. But programming languages provide an elegant way to deal with these errors so that the program terminates elegantly, not abruptly.

Table 12.1

Syntax Error (Compilation Error)	Logical Error (Run Time Error)
Syntax Errors occur when rules of writing instructions in a particular the programming language are violated.	Logical Errors occur due to our mistakes in programming logic.
A program with syntax error(s) does not compile successfully and therefore does not execute.	A program with logical error(s) compiles successfully and executes but does not generate the desired results.
Syntax Errors are caught by the compiler.	Logical errors are no caught by compiler. It has to be identified and corrected by the programmer.

``
x = int(input('Enter a number: '))
iff x%2 == 0:
        print(EVEN NUMBER.')
else:
        print ('ODD NUMBER')
``
	``
	x = float(input('Enter a number: '))
	y = float(input('Enter a number: '))
	z = x+y/2
	print ('The average of the two numbers = ',z)
	``

In the code, if is misspelled as iff and therefore the compiler will display an error	The results will not be as per the expectations because according to the operator precedence chart, division is evaluated before addition.

12.1.3 Exceptions

Even if a statement is syntactically correct, it may still cause an error when executed. Such errors that occur at run-time (or during execution) are known as *exceptions*. An exception is an event, which occurs during the execution of a program and disrupts the normal flow of the program's instructions. When a program encounters a situation which it cannot deal with, it raises an exception. Therefore, we can say that an exception is a Python object that represents an error.

When a program raises an exception, it must handle the exception or the program will be immediately terminated. You can handle exceptions in your programs to end it gracefully, otherwise, if exceptions are not handled by programs, then error messages are generated. Let us see some examples in which exceptions occurs.

```
• >>> 5/0
Traceback (most recent call last):
 File "<pyshell#5>", line 1, in <module>
    5/0
ZeroDivisionError: integer division or modulo by zero
  • >>> var + 10
Traceback (most recent call last):
  File "<pyshell#7>", line 1, in <module>
    var + 10
NameError: name 'var' is not defined
  • >>> 'Roll No' + 123
Traceback (most recent call last):
  File "<pyshell#8>", line 1, in <module>
    'Roll No' + 123
TypeError: cannot concatenate 'str' and 'int' objects
```

> **Programming Tip:**
> Standard exception names are built-in identifiers and not reserved keywords.

In all the three cases discussed above, we have seen three types of exceptions had occurred. Since they were not handled in the code, an appropriate error message was displayed to indicate what had happened.

The string printed as the exception type (like TypeError) is the name of the built-in exception that occurred. However, this is not true for user-defined exceptions.

12.2 HANDLING EXCEPTIONS

We can handle exceptions in our program by using try block and except block. A critical operation which can raise exception is placed inside the try block and the code that handles exception is written in except block. The syntax for try-except block can be given as,

```
try:
    statements
except ExceptionName:
    statements
```

> **Programming Tip:** Handlers do not handle exceptions that occur in statements outside the corresponding try block.

The try statement works as follows.

Step 1: First, the *try block* (statement(s) between the try and except keywords) is executed.

Step 2a: If no exception occurs, the *except block* is skipped.

Step 2b: If an exception occurs, during execution of any statement in the try block, then,

i. Rest of the statements in the try block are skipped.

ii. If the exception type matches the exception named after the except keyword, the except block is executed and then execution continues after the try statement.

iii. If an exception occurs which does not match the exception named in the except block, then it is passed on to outer try block (in case of nested try

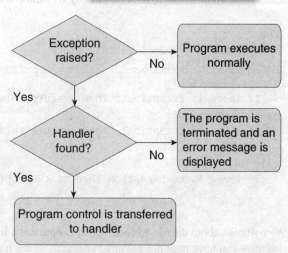

Figure 12.2 Flowchart for Case iii under Step 2b for try statements

blocks). If no exception handler is found in the program, then it is an *unhandled exception* and the program is terminated with an error message (Refer Figure 12.2).

In the aforementioned program, note that a number was divided by zero, an exception occurred so the control passed to the except block.

Example 12.1   Program to handle the divide by zero exception

```
num = int(input("Enter the numerator : "))
deno = int(input("Enter the denominator : "))
try:
  quo = num/deno
  print("QUOTIENT : ", quo)
except ZeroDivisionError:
  print("Denominator cannot be zero")
```

OUTPUT
```
Enter the numerator : 10
Enter the denominator : 0
Denominator cannot be zero
```

Note   Exceptions gives you information like what, why, and how something went wrong.

12.3 MULTIPLE EXCEPT BLOCKS

Python allows you to have multiple except blocks for a single try block. The block which matches with the exception generated will get executed. A try block can be associated with more than one except block to specify handlers for different exceptions. However, only one handler will be executed. Exception handlers only handle exceptions that occur in the corresponding try block. We can write our programs that handle selected exceptions. The syntax for specifying multiple except blocks for a single try block can be given as,

```
try:
    operations are done in this block
    .....................
except Exception1:
    If there is Exception1, then execute this block.
except Exception2:
    If there is Exception2, then execute this block.
    .....................
else:
    If there is no exception then execute this block.
    .....................
```

Programming Tip
try-except block is same as try-catch block. Exceptions are generated using raise keyword rather than throw.

We will read about the else block which is optional a little later. But for now, we have seen that a single try statement can have multiple except statements to catch different types of exceptions. For example, look at the code given below. The program prompts user to enter a number. It then squares the number and prints its result.

However, if we do not specify any number or enter a non-number, then an exception will be generated. We have two except blocks. The one matching the case will finally execute. This is very much evident from the output.

Example 12.2 Program with multiple except blocks

```
try:
    num = int(input("Enter the number : "))
    print(num**2)
except (KeyboardInterrupt):
    print("You should have enterd a number..... Program Terminating...")
except (ValueError):
    print("Please check before you enter..... Program Terminating...")
print("Bye")
```

OUTPUT

```
Enter the number : abc
Please check before you enter..... Program Terminating...
Bye
```

Note that after execution of the except block, the program control goes to the first statement after the except block for that try block.

Note The except block without an exception can also be used to print an error message and then re-raise the exception.

12.4 MULTIPLE EXCEPTIONS IN A SINGLE BLOCK

An except clause may name multiple exceptions as a parenthesized tuple, as shown in the program given below. So whatever exception is raised, out of the three exceptions specified, the same except block will be executed.

Example 12.3 Program having an except clause handling multiple exceptions simultaneously

```
    try:
    num = int(input("Enter the number : "))
    print(num**2)
except (KeyboardInterrupt, ValueError, TypeError):
    print("Please check before you enter..... Program Terminating...")
print("Bye")
```

Programming Tip: No code should be present between a list of except blocks.

OUTPUT

```
Enter the number : abc
Please check before you enter..... Program Terminating...
Bye
```

Thus, we see that if we want to give a specific exception handler for any exception raised, we can better have multiple except blocks. Otherwise, if we want the same code to be executed for all three exceptions then we can use the except(list_of_exceptions) format.

12.5 EXCEPT BLOCK WITHOUT EXCEPTION

You can even specify an except block without mentioning any exception (i.e., except:). This type of except block if present should be the last one that can serve as a wildcard (when multiple except blocks are present). But use it with extreme caution, since it may mask a real programming error.

In large software programs, may a times, it is difficult to anticipate all types of possible exceptional conditions. Therefore, the programmer may not be able to write a different handler (except block) for every individual type of exception. In such situations, a better idea is to write a handler that would catch all types of exceptions. The syntax to define a handler that would catch every possible exception from the try block is,

```
try:
    Write the operations here
    ....................
except:
    If there is any exception, then execute this block.
    ....................
else:
    If there is no exception then execute this block.
```

The except block can be used along with other exception handlers which handle some specific types of exceptions but those exceptions that are not handled by these specific handlers can be handled by the except: block. However, the default handler must be placed after all other except blocks because otherwise it would prevent any specific handler to be executed.

Example 12.4 Program to demonstrate the use of except: block

```
try:
    file = pen('File1.txt')
    str = f.readline()
    print(str)
except IOError:
    print("Error occured during Input ...... Program Terminating...")
except ValueError:
    print("Could not convert data to an integer.")
except:
    print("Unexpected error.... Program Terminating...")
```

Programming Tip: When an exception occurs, it may have an associated value, also known as the exception's *argument*.

OUTPUT
```
Unexpected error.... Program Terminating...
```

> **Note** Using except: without mentioning any specific exception is not a good programming practice because it catches all exceptions and does not make the programmer identify the root cause of the problem.

12.6 THE else CLAUSE

The try ... except block can optionally have an *else clause*, which, when present, must follow all except blocks. The statement(s) in the else block is executed only if the try clause does not raise an exception. For example, the codes given below illustrate both the cases. This will help you to visualize the relevance of the else block.

Example 12.5 Programs to demonstrate else block

```
try:
    file = open('File1.txt')
    str = file.readline()
    print(str)
except IOError:
    print("Error occurred during Input
...... Program Terminating...")
else:
    print("Program Terminating
Successfully.....")


OUTPUT
Hello
Program Terminating Successfully.....
```

```
try:
    file = open('File1.txt')
    str = f.readline()
    print(str)
except:
    print("Error occurred ...... Program
Terminating...")
else:
    print("Program Terminating
Successfully.....")


OUTPUT
Error occurred......Program
Terminating...
```

12.7 RAISING EXCEPTIONS

You can deliberately raise an exception using the raise keyword. The general syntax for the raise statement is,

```
raise [Exception [, args [, traceback]]]
```

Here, Exception is the name of exception to be raised (example, TypeError). args is optional and specifies a value for the exception argument. If args is not specified, then the exception argument is None. The final argument, traceback, is also optional and if present, is the traceback object used for the exception.

For example, the code given below simply creates a variable and prints its value. There was no error in the code but we have deliberately raised an exception.

Example 12.6 Program to deliberately raise an exception

```
try:
    num = 10
    print(num)
    raise ValueError
```

```
except:
    print("Exception occurred .... Program Terminating...")
```

OUTPUT
```
10
Exception occurred .... Program Terminating...
```

The only argument to the `raise` keyword specifies the exception to be raised. Recall that, we had earlier said that you can re-raise the exceptions in the `except:` block. This is especially important when you just want to determine whether an exception was raised but don't intend to handle it. The code given below is used to re-raise an exception from the `except:` block.

Example 12.7 Program to re-raise an exception

```
try:
    raise NameError
except:
    print("Re-raising the exception")
    raise
```

> **Programming Tip:** Avoid using except block without any exception.

OUTPUT
```
Re-raising the exception
Traceback (most recent call last):
  File "C:\Python34\Try.py", line 2, in <module>
    raise NameError
NameError
```

12.8 INSTANTIATING EXCEPTIONS

Python allows programmers to instantiate an exception first before raising it and add any attributes (or arguments) to it as desired. These attributes can be used to give additional information about the error. To instantiate the exception, the except block may specify a variable after the exception name. The variable then becomes an exception instance with the arguments stored in `instance.args`. The exception instance also has the `__str__()` method defined so that the arguments can be printed directly without using `instance.args`.

Note The contents of the argument vary based on exception type.

Example 12.8 Program to understand the process of instantiating an exception

```
try:
    raise Exception('Hello', 'World')
except Exception as errorObj:
    print(type(errorObj))        # the exception instance
```

```
    print(errorObj.args)       # arguments stored in .args
    print(errorObj)            # __str__ allows args to be printed directly
    arg1, arg2 = errorObj.args
    print('Argument1 =', arg1)
    print('Argument2 =', arg2)
```

OUTPUT

```
<type 'exceptions.Exception'>
('Hello', 'World')
('Hello', 'World')
Argument1 = Hello
Argument2 = World
```

Note   If you raise an exception with arguments but do not handle it, then the name of the exception is printed along with its arguments.

Example 12.9   Program to raise an exception with arguments

```
try:
    raise Exception('Hello', 'World')
except ValueError:
    print("Program Terminating...")
```

OUTPUT

```
Exception: ('Hello', 'World')
```

12.9 HANDLING EXCEPTIONS IN INVOKED FUNCTIONS

Till now, we have seen that exception handlers have handled exceptions if they occur in the try block. But, exceptions can also be handled inside functions that are called in the try block as shown in the program given below.

Example 12.10   Program to handle exceptions from an invoked function

```
def Divide(num, deno):
    try:
        quo = num/deno
    except ZeroDivisionError:
        print("You cannot divide a number by zero... Program Terminating...")
Divide(10,0)
```

OUTPUT

```
You cannot divide a number by zero... Program Terminating...
```

Basically, a large program is usually divided into n number of functions. The possibility that the invoked function may generate an exceptional condition cannot be ignored. Figure 12.3 shows the scenario when the function invoked by the try block throws an exception which is handled by the except block in the calling function. The syntax for such a situation can be given as,

```
function_name(arg list):
    ----------
    ----------
try
    ----------
    function_name()    // function call
    ----------

except ExceptionName:
    ----------
    // Code to handle exception
    ----------
```

Throw Point

Invoked function that generates an exception

Try Block

Invokes a function

Except Block

Catches and handles exception

| Note | Irrespective of the location of the exception, the try block is always immediately followed by the catch block. |

Figure 12.3   Function invoked by the try block throws an exception which is handled by the except block

The program given in the following example generates a divide by zero exception from a called function. The main module has a try block from which a function Divide() is invoked. In Divide(), the exception occurs which is thrown and is handled by the except block defined in the main module immediately followed by the try block.

| Example 12.11 | Program to handle exception in the calling function |

```
def Divide(num, deno):
    return num/deno
try:
    Divide(10,0)
except ZeroDivisionError:
    print("You cannot divide a number by zero... Program Terminating...")
```

OUTPUT
```
You cannot divide a number by zero... Program Terminating...
```

| Note | Python allows programmers to raise an exception in a deeply nested try block or in a deeply nested function call. |

Note that program execution creates a *stack* as one function calls another. When a function at the bottom of the stack raises an exception, it is propagated up through the call stack so that the function may handle it. If no function handles it while moving towards top of the stack, the program terminates and a `traceback` is printed on the screen. The `traceback` helps the programmer to identify what went wrong in the code.

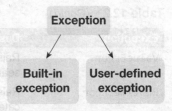

12.10 BUILT-IN AND USER-DEFINED EXCEPTIONS

Table 12.2 lists some standard exceptions that are already defined in Python. These built-in exceptions force your program to output an error when something in it goes wrong.

Table 12.2 Built-in exceptions

Exception	Description
Exception	Base class for all exceptions
StopIteration	Generated when the next() method of an iterator does not point to any object
SystemExit	Raised by sys.exit() function
StandardError	Base class for all built-in exceptions (excluding StopIteration and SystemExit)
ArithmeticError	Base class for errors that are generated due to mathematical calculations
OverflowError	Raised when the maximum limit of a numeric type is exceeded during a calculation
FloatingPointError	Raised when a floating point calculation could not be performed
ZeroDivisionError	Raised when a number is divided by zero
AssertionError	Raised when the assert statement fails
AttributeError	Raised when attribute reference or assignment fails
EOFError	Raised when end-of-file is reached or there is no input for input() function
ImportError	Raised when an import statement fails
KeyboardInterrupt	Raised when the user interrupts program execution (by pressing Ctrl+C)
LookupError	Base class for all lookup errors
IndexError	Raised when an index is not found in a sequence
KeyError	Raised when a key is not found in the dictionary
NameError	Raised when an identifier is not found in local or global namespace (referencing a non-existent variable)
UnboundLocalError, EnvironmentError	Raised when an attempt is made to access a local variable in a function or method when no value has been assigned to it.
IOError	Raised when input or output operation fails (for example, opening a file that does not exist)
SyntaxError	Raised when there is a syntax error in the program
IndentationError	Raised when there is an indentation problem in the program
SystemError	Raised when an internal system error occurs

(Contd)

Table 12.2 (*Contd*)

Exception	Description
ValueError	Raised when the arguments passed to a function are of invalid data type or searching a list for a non-existent value
RuntimeError	Raised when the generated error does not fall into any of the above category
NotImplementedError	Raised when an abstract method that needs to be implemented in an inherited class is not implemented
TypeError	Raised when two or more data types are mixed without coercion

Besides these, Python allows programmers to create their own exceptions by creating a new exception class. The new exception class is derived from the base class Exception which is pre-defined in Python. The program given below explains this concept.

Example 12.12 Program to define a user-defined exception

```
class myError(Exception):
    def __init__(self, val):
        self.val = val
    def __str__(self):
        return repr(self.val)
try:
    raise myError(10)
except myError as e:
    print('User Defined Exception Generated with value', e.val)
```

OUTPUT
```
User Defined Exception Generated with value 10
```

In the above program, the __init__() method of Exception class has been overridden by the new class. The customized exception class can be used to perform any task. However, these classes are usually kept simple and have only limited attributes to provide information about the error to be extracted by handlers for the exception. Note that creating your own exception class or defining a user defined exception is known as *custom exception*.

Note An exception can be a string, a class, or an object. Most of the exceptions raised by Python are classes, with an argument that is an instance of the class.

Moreover, when creating a module that can raise different exceptions, a better approach would be to create a base class for exceptions defined by that module, and subclasses to create specific exception classes for different error conditions.

Note 'as' is a keyword that allows programmers to name a variable within an except statement.

Example 12.13 Program to create sub-classes of Exception class to handle exceptions in a better customized way

```
class Error(Exception):
    def message(self):
        raise NotImplementedError()
class InputError(Error):
    def __init__(self, expr, msg):
        self.expr = expr
        self.msg = msg
    def message(self):
        print("Error in input in expression"),
        print(self.expr)
try:
    a = input("Enter a : ")
    raise InputError("input(\"Enter a : s\")", "Input Error")
except InputError as ie:
    ie.message()
```

OUTPUT
```
Enter a : 10
Error in input in expression input("Enter a : s")
```

Although there is no naming convention for naming a user-defined exception, it is better to define exceptions with names that end in "Error" to make it consistent with the naming of the standard exceptions.

> **Note** Many standard modules define their own exceptions to report errors that may occur in functions they define.

12.11 THE finally BLOCK

The try block has another optional block called finally which is used to define clean-up actions that must be executed under all circumstances. The finally block is always executed before leaving the try block. This means that the statements written in finally block are executed irrespective of whether an exception has occurred or not. The syntax of finally block can be given as,

```
try:
    Write your operations here
    ......................
    Due to any exception, operations written here will be skipped
finally:
    This would always be executed.
    ......................
```

Let us see with the help of a program how finally block will behave when an exception is raised in the try block and is not handled by except block.

Example 12.14 Program with finally block that leaves the exception unhandled

```
try:
    print("Raising Exception.....")
    raise ValueError
finally:
    print("Performing clean up in Finally......")

OUTPUT
Raising Exception.....
Performing clean up in Finally......
Traceback (most recent call last):
  File "C:\Python34\Try.py", line 4, in <module>
    raise ValueError
ValueError
```

From the above code, we can conclude that when an exception occurs in the try block and is not handled by an except block or if the exception occurs in the except or else block, then it is re-raised after executing the finally block. The finally block is also executed when any block of the try block is exited via a break, continue or return statement.

Now, let us see the flow of control in a program that has try, except, as well as finally block in the program given below.

Example 12.15 Program to illustrate the use of try, except and finally block all together

```
try:
    print("Raising Exception.....")
    raise ValueError
except:
    print("Exception caught.....")
finally:
    print("Performing clean up in Finally......")

OUTPUT
Raising Exception.....
Exception caught.....
Performing clean up in Finally......
```

From the output, you can see that the finally block is executed when exception occurs and also when an exception does not occur.

In real world applications, the finally clause is useful for releasing external resources like file handles, network connections, memory resources, etc. regardless of whether the use of the resource was successful.

Note You cannot have an else block with a finally block.

If you place the finally block immediately after the try block and followed by the execute block (may be in case of a nested try block), then if an exception is raised in the try block, the code in finally will be executed first. The `finally` block will perform the operations written in it and then re-raise the exception. This exception will be handled by the `except` block if present in the next higher layer of the `try-except` block. This is shown in the program given below.

Example 12.16 Program having finally block to re-raise the exception that will be handled by an outer try-except block

```
try:
    print("Dividing Strings....")
    try:
        quo = "abc" / "def"
    finally:
        print("In finally block.....")
except TypeError:
    print("In except block.. handling TypeError...")
```

> **Programming Tip:**
> finally block can never be followed by an except block.

OUTPUT

```
Dividing Strings....
In finally block.....
In except block.. handling TypeError...
```

12.12 PRE-DEFINED CLEAN–UP ACTION

In Python, some objects define standard clean-up actions that are automatically performed when the object is no longer needed. The default clean-up action is performed irrespective of whether the operation using the object succeeded or failed. We have already seen such an operation in file handling. We preferred to open the file using `with` keyword so that the file is automatically closed when not in use. So, even if we forget to close the file or the code to close it is skipped because of an exception, the file will still be closed. Consider the code given below, which opens a file to print its contents on the screen.

```
file = open('File1.txt')
str = file.readline()
print(str)
```

The code is perfectly alright except for one thing that it does not close the file after use. So the file is opened for an indeterminate amount of time after the code has finished executing. This may not be a big issue when writing small and simple programs, but can be a problem for large applications. Therefore, the `with` statement allows objects like files to be cleaned up when not in use. The better version of the code given above is therefore,

```
with open('File1.txt') as file:
    for line in file:
        print(line)
```

OUTPUT

```
Hello
# Welcome to the world of Programming
```

```
Python is a very simple and interesting language
Happy Reading
```

In the aforementioned program, after printing the contents of the file there are no more statements to execute. So just before the program completes its execution, the file is closed. The file would have closed even if any problem had occurred while executing the code.

> **Programming Tip:** Many standard modules define exceptions in a separate file known as exceptions.py or errors.py.

12.13 RE-RAISING EXCEPTION

Python allows programmers to re-raise an exception. For example, an exception thrown from the try block can be handled as well as re-raised in the except block using the keyword raise. The code given below illustrates this concept.

Example 12.17 Program to re-raise the exception

```
try:
    f = open("Abc123.txt")  # opening a non-existent file
except:
    print("File does not exist")
    raise    # re-raise the caught exception
```

OUTPUT
```
File does not exist
Traceback (most recent call last):
  File "C:\Python34\Try.py", line 2, in <module>
    f = open("Abc123.txt")  # opening a non-existent file
IOError: [Errno 2] No such file or directory: 'Abc123.txt'
```

Note To re-raise, use the raise keyword without any arguments.

12.14 ASSERTIONS IN PYTHON

An *assertion* is a basic check that can be turned on or off when the program is being tested. You can think of assert as a raise-if statement (or a raise-if-not statement). Using assert statement, an expression is tested, and if the result of the expression is False then an exception is raised. The assert statement is intended for debugging statements. It can be seen as an abbreviated notation for a conditional raise statement.

In Python, assertions are implemented using assert keyword. Assertions are usually placed at the start of a function to check for valid input, and after a function call to check for valid output.

When Python encounters an assert statement, the expression associated with it is calculated and if the expression is False, an AssertionError is raised. The syntax for assert statement is:

```
assert expression[, arguments]
```

If the expression is False (also known as assertion fails), Python uses ArgumentExpression as the argument for the AssertionError. AssertionError exceptions can be caught and handled like any other exception using the try-except block. However, if the AssertionError is not handled by the program, the program will be terminated and an error message will be displayed. In simple words, the assert statement, is semantically equivalent to writing,

```
assert <expression>, <message>
```

The above statement means if the expression evaluates to False, an exception is raised and <message> will be printed on the screen.

Consider the program given below. The program prompts a user to enter the temperature in Celsius. If the temperature is greater than 32 degree Fahrenheit, then an AssertionError is raised. Since the exception is not handled, the program is abruptly terminated with an error message.

Note   assert statement should be used for trapping user-defined constraints.

Example 12.18   Program to use the assert statement

```
c = int(input("Enter the temperature in Celsius: "))
f = (c * 9/5) + 32
assert(f<=32), "Its freezing"
print("Temperature in Fahrenheit = ", f)
```

OUTPUT

```
Enter the temperature in Celsius: 100
Traceback (most recent call last):
  File "C:\Python34\Try.py", line 3, in <module>
    assert(f<=32), "Its freezing"
AssertionError: Its freezing
```

Key points to remember

1. Do not catch exceptions that you cannot handle.
2. User defined exceptions can be very useful if some complex or specific information has to be stored in exception instances.
3. Do not create new exception classes when the built-in exceptions already have all the functionality you need.

> **Programming Tip:** When we are developing a large program, it is a good practice to place all the user-defined exceptions that the program may raise in a separate file.

PROGRAMMING EXAMPLES

Program 12.1 Write a program that prompts the user to enter a number and prints its square. If no number is entered (Ctrl + C is pressed), then a KeyboardInterrupt is generated.

```
num = int(input("Enter the numerator : "))
deno = int(input("Enter the denominator : "))
try:
  quo = num/deno
  print("QUOTIENT : ", quo)
except ZeroDivisionError:
  print("Denominator cannot be zero")
```

OUTPUT

```
Enter the numerator : 10
Enter the denominator : 0
Denominator cannot be zero
```

Program 12.2 Write a program that opens a file and writes data to it. Handle exceptions that can be generated during the I/O operations.

```
try:
    with open('myFile.txt','w') as file:
        file.write("Hello, Good Morning !!!")
except IOError:
    print("Error working with file")
else:
    print("File Writing Successful ......")
```

> **Programming Tip:** assert should not be used to catch divide by zero errors because Python traps such programming errors itself.

OUTPUT

```
File Writing Successful ......
```

Program 12.3 Write a program that deliberately raises a user-defined SocketError with any number of arguments and derived from class Runtime.

```
class SocketError(RuntimeError):
    def __init__(self, *arg):  # * because any number of arguments can be passed
        self.args = arg
try:
    raise SocketError('Socket', 'Establishment', 'Error')
except SocketError as e:
    print(e.args)
```

OUTPUT

```
('Socket', 'Establishment', 'Error')
```

Program 12.4 Write a program that prompts the user to enter a number. If the number is positive or zero print it, otherwise raise an exception.

```
try:
    num = int(input("Enter a number : "))
    if num >= 0:
        print(num)
    else:
        raise ValueError("Negative number not allowed")
except ValueError as e:
    print(e)
```

OUTPUT

```
Enter a number : -1
Negative number not allowed
```

Program 12.5 Write a number game program. Ask the user to enter a number. If the number is greater than number to be guessed, raise a ValueTooLarge exception. If the value is smaller the number to be guessed then, raise a ValueTooSmall exception and prompt the user to enter again. Quit the program only when the user enters the correct number.

```python
class ValueTooSmallError(Exception):
    def display(self):
        print("Input value is too small")
class ValueTooLargeError(Exception):
    def display(self):
        print("Input value is too large")
max = 100
while 1:
    try:
        num = int(input("Enter a number: "))
        if num == max:
            print("Great you succeeded....")
            break
        if num < max:
            raise ValueTooSmallError
        elif num > max:
            raise ValueTooLargeError
    except ValueTooSmallError as s:
        s.display()
    except ValueTooLargeError as l:
        l.display()
```

OUTPUT

```
Enter a number: 20
Input value is too small
Enter a number: 102
Input value is too large
Enter a number: 100
Great you succeeded....
```

Program 12.6 Write a program that prints the first 30 numbers. Each number should be printed after a fixed short interval of time. Make use of a timer which prints each number when the timer goes off and exception is generated.

```python
class TimeUp(Exception):
    pass
def message(c):
    start_timer = 0
    stop_timer = 10000
    count = start_timer
    try:
        while True:
```

```
            count += 1
            if count == stop_timer:
                raise TimeUp
    except TimeUp as t:
        print(c, end = " ")
for i in range(31):
    message(i)
```

OUTPUT

```
0 1 2 3 4 5 6 7 8 9 10 11 12 13 14 15 16 17 18 19 20 21 22 23 24 25 26 27 28 29 30
```

Program 12.7 Write a program which infinitely prints natural numbers. Raise the StopIteration exception after displaying first 20 numbers to exit from the program.

```
def display(n):
    while True:
        try:
            n = n+1
            if n == 21:
                raise StopIteration
        except StopIteration:
            break
        else:
            print(n, end = " ")
i = 0
display(i)
```

OUTPUT

```
1 2 3 4 5 6 7 8 9 10 11 12 13 14 15 16 17 18 19 20
```

Program 12.8 Write a program that randomly generates a number. Raise a user-defined exception if the number is below 0.1.

```
import random
class RandomError(Exception):
    pass
try:
    num = random.random()
    if num < 0.1:
        raise RandomError
except RandomError as e:
    print("Random Error Generated ....")
else:
    print("%.3f"%num)
```

> **Programming Tip:** You should only catch exceptions that you are willing to handle.

OUTPUT

```
0.696 (# Any random number will be generated)
```

Program 12.9 Write a program that validates name and age as entered by the user to determine whether the person can cast vote or not.

```
class invalidAge(Exception):
   def display(self):
      print("Sorry !!! Age cannot be below 18... You cannot vote .....")
class invalidName(Exception):
   def display(self):
      print("Please enter a valid name....")
try:
   name = input("Enter the name : ")
   if len(name) == 0:
      raise invalidName
   age = int(input("Enter the age : "))
   if age < 18:
      raise invalidAge
except invalidName as n:
   n.display()
except invalidAge as e:
   e.display()
else:
   print(name, " Congratulation !!! you can vote")
```

Programming Tip: Code in `else` block is executed if no exception was raised in the try block.

OUTPUT

```
Enter the name : Goransh
Enter the age : 10
Sorry !!! Age cannot be below 18... You cannot vote .....
```

Program 12.10 Write a program to find whether a person is eligible to vote or not.

```
try:
    age = int(input("Enter the age of the candidate : "))
    if age >= 18:
        print("You are eligible to vote")
    else:
        str1 = "You need to wait " + str(18 - age) +" more year(s) to vote"
        raise ValueError(str1)
except ValueError as e:
    print(e)
```

OUTPUT

```
Enter the age of the candidate : 12
You need to wait 6 more year(s) to vote
```

Program 12.11 Write a program to validate a user's score. Check that the marks should be in the range 0 – 100. Throw an exception, if the validation rule is violated.

```
def check(x):
    try:
        if x >= 0 and x <= 100:
            return(1)
        else:
            str1 = "Please enter valid marks in the range (0-100)"
            raise ValueError(str1)
    except ValueError as e:
            print(e)
marks = []
subjects = ['Maths','Science','Language']
flag = 0
i = 0
while i <3:
    str1 = "Enter the marks obtained in " + subjects[i] + " : "
    n = int(input(str1))
    flag = check(n)
    if flag == 1:
        marks.append(n)
        i += 1
        flag = 0

total = sum(marks)
avg = total/3.0
print("SUM = " + str(total) + "\nAVERAGE = %.2f"%avg)
```

OUTPUT

```
Enter the marks obtained in Maths : -10
Please enter valid marks in the range (0-100)
Enter the marks obtained in Maths : 98
Enter the marks obtained in Science : 102
Please enter valid marks in the range (0-100)
Enter the marks obtained in Science : 89
Enter the marks obtained in Language : 55
SUM = 242
AVERAGE = 80.67
```

Program 12.12 Student's marks' statement: Write a program that has a dictionary of names of students and a list of their marks in 4 subjects. Create another dictionary from this dictionary that has the name of the students and their total marks. Find out the topper and his/her score.

```
Marks = {'Neha' : [97,89,94, 90], 'Mitul' : [92,91,94,87], 'Shefali' : [67,99,
88,90]}
tot=0
Tot_Marks = Marks.copy()
```

```
for key, val in Marks.items():
tot = sum(val)
Tot_Marks[key] = tot
print(Tot_Marks)
max = 0
Topper = ''
for key, val in Tot_Marks.items():
if val>max:
max = val
Topper = key
print("Topper is : ", Topper, "with marks = ", max)
```

OUTPUT

```
{'Neha': 370, 'Mitul': 364, 'Shefali': 344}
Topper is : Neha with marks = 370
```

Program 12.13 Write a program for a voter's age validation.

```
try:
    age = int(input("Enter the age of the candidate : "))
    if age >= 18:
        print("You are eligible to vote")
    else:
        str1 = "You need to wait " + str(18 - age) +" more year(s) to vote"
        raise ValueError(str1)
except ValueError as e:
    print(e)
```

OUTPUT

```
Enter the age of the candidate : 12
You need to wait 6 more year(s) to vote
```

Summary

- To handle an exception means to prevent it from causing the program to crash. Exceptions are handled using try-except block.
- Exceptions can be categorized as synchronous or asynchronous exceptions.
- *Synchronous* exceptions (like divide by zero, array index out of bound, etc.) can be controlled by the program.
- *Asynchronous* exceptions (like an interrupt from the keyboard, hardware malfunction, or, disk failure), are caused by events that are beyond the control of the program.

- Logical error may occur due to wrong algorithm or logic to solve a particular program.
- Exception is a Python object that represents an error.
- When a program raises an exception, it must handle the exception or the program will be immediately terminated.
- You can handle exceptions in your programs to end it gracefully, otherwise if exceptions are not handled by programs, then error messages are generated.
- Python allows you to have multiple except blocks for a single try block. The block which matches with the exception generated will get executed.

- After execution of the except block, the program control goes to the first statement after the except block for that try block.
- The statement(s) in the else block is executed only if the try clause does not raise an exception.
- You can deliberately raise an exception by using the raise keyword.
- Python allows programmers to create their own exceptions by creating a new exception class. The new exception class is derived from the base class Exception which is pre-defined in Python.
- The finally clause is useful for releasing external resources like file handles, network connections, memory resources, etc. regardless of whether the use of the resource was successful.
- An assertion is a sanity-check that can be turned on or off when the program has been tested.

Glossary

Custom exception A user-defined exception.

Else block An optional block that is executed only when no exception is raised from the try block.

Except block Block that has statements to handle an exception raised from the try block.

Exception argument when an exception occurs Associated value.

Exception The logic error which leads to a run-time error that causes the program to terminate abruptly.

Finally block An optional block which is used to define clean-up actions that must be executed under all circumstances.

Logic error Errors that occur due to poor understanding of problem and its solution.

Raise To create a deliberate exception by making use of raise keyword.

Syntax errors Errors which occurs due to poor understanding of the language.

Try block Block that has all critical operations in the program.

Exercises

Fill in the Blanks

1. _____ errors occur due to poor understanding of a problem and its solution.
2. _____ exceptions can be controlled by the program.
3. The logic error leads to a run-time error that causes the program to terminate abruptly. These types of run-time errors are known as _____.
4. We can handle exceptions in our program by using _____ block.
5. If no exception occurs, the _____ block is skipped.
6. The default handler must be placed after all other _____ blocks.
7. The value associated with an exception is known as _____.
8. _____ and _____ are optional blocks when handling exceptions.
9. _____ block has all critical operations in the program.
10. When you raise an exception, its default argument is _____.

11. The keyword used re-raise an exception is _____.
12. _____ is the base class of all exceptions.
13. _____ exception is raised when the assert statement fails.
14. User-defined exceptions are created by inheriting the _____ class.
15. _____ keyword allows programmers to name a variable within an except statement.
16. Statements written in _____ block are executed irrespective of whether an exception has occurred or not.
17. Fill in the blanks to raise a ValueError exception, if the input is negative.
```
num = float(input("Enter the number:")
if num __ 0:
____ ValueError("Negative!")
```

State True or False

1. Syntax errors arises due to poor understanding of the language.

2. Logic errors can be detected by a Python interpreter.

3. Even if a statement is syntactically correct, it may still cause an error when executed.

4. An exception disrupts the normal flow of the program's instructions.

5. Standard exception names are reserved words in Python.

6. If an exception occurs, during execution of any statement in the try block, then, rest of the statements in the try block are skipped.

7. Exceptions gives you information like what, why, and how something went wrong.

8. Python allows you to have multiple except blocks for a single try block.

9. It is possible to execute more than one except block during the execution of the program.

10. No code should be present between the try and except block.

11. You should make extensive use of except: block to catch any type of exception that may occur.

12. else block must follow all except blocks.

13. else block has statements to handle an exception raised from the try block.

14. AttributeError exception is raised when an identifier is not found in local or global namespace.

15. An exception can be a string, a class, or an object.

Multiple Choice Questions

1. Which type of error specifies all those type of errors in which the program executes but gives incorrect results?
   (a) syntax   (b) logic
   (c) exception   (d) none of these

2. Which keyword is used to generate an exception?
   (a) throw   (b) raise
   (c) generate   (d) try

3. Which block acts as a wildcard block to handle all exceptions?
   (a) try: (b) catch:
   (c) except Exception: (d) except:

4. Which block is executed when no exception is raised from the try block?
   (a) try: (b) catch:
   (c) else: (d) except:

5. To handle an exception, try block should be immediately followed by which block?
   (a) finally: (b) catch:
   (c) else: (d) except:

6. Which exception is raised when two or more data types are mixed without coercion?
   (a) TypeError   (b) AttributeError
   (c) ValueError   (d) NameError

7. Which block can never be followed by an except block?
   (a) finally: (b) catch:
   (c) else: (d) except:

8. You cannot have which block with a finally block?
   (a) try: (b) catch:
   (c) else: (d) except:

9. Which statement raises exception if the expression is False?
   (a) Throw   (b) raise
   (c) else   (d) assert

10. '1' == 1 will result in _____
   (a) True   (b) False
   (c) TypeError   (d) ValueError

11. Which number is not printed by this code?
```
try:
    print(10)
    print(5/0)
    print(20)
except ZeroDivisionError:
    print(30)
finally:
    print(40)
```
   (a) 20   (b) 40
   (c) 30   (d) 10

Review Questions

1. Differentiate between error and exception.

2. What are logic errors? Give examples.

3. What happens when an exception is raised in a program?

4. What will happen if an exception occurs but is not handled by the program?

5. How can you handle exceptions in your program?

6. Explain the syntax of try-except block.

7. What happens if an exception occurs which does not match the exception named in the except block?

8. How can you handle multiple exceptions in a program?

9. Using except block is not recommended. Justify the statement.

10. When is the else block executed?

11. With the help of an example, explain how can you instantiate an exception?

12. Explain any three built-in exceptions with relevant examples.
13. How can you create your own exceptions in Python?
14. What will happen if an exception generated in the try block is immediately followed by a `finally` block?

Discuss both the cases (except block not present and except block present at next higher level)

15. Explain the utility of `assert` statement.

Programming Problems

1. Write a program that finds smaller of two given numbers. If the first number is smaller than the second, then generate an Assertion error.
2. Write a program to print the square root of a number. Raise an exception if the number is negative.
3. Write a program that prompts the user to enter two numbers and displays their sum. Raise an exception and handle it if a non-number value is given as input.
4. Write a program that prompts the user to enter his name. The program then greets the person with his name. But if the person's name is "Rahul" an exception is thrown and he is asked to quit the program.
5. Write a program that validates user's input.
6. Write a class `Student`. Use exception handling to read the data of a student.
7. Write a program that has multiple except blocks.
8. Write a program that re-raises an exception.
9. Write a program with `except:` handler.
10. Write a program that raises an exception of class type.
11. Write a program in which an exception raised by one function is handled by another function.
12. Write a program that raises at least two exceptions from a class.

13. Write a program that overloads the /= operator in FRACTION class. Throw an exception if a divide by zero exception occurs.
14. Write a program that overloads the -= and /= operators in COMPLEX class. The program must throw an exception if divide by zero exception occurs or if the real parts of the two objects are zero.
15. Write a program that has a class TIME. Enter the time when a user started an online test and completed the test. Subtract the two time values and display the duration in which the test was completed. Throw exceptions whenever need arises (like invalid data, or if start time is greater than completion time).
16. Write a program that accepts date of birth along with other personal details of a person. Throw an exception if an invalid date is entered.
17. Write a program that finds square root of a number. Throw an exception if a negative number is entered
18. Write a class Square that finds the square of a number. Throw an exception if instead of the number, user enters a character.

Find the Output

1.
```
>>> raise NameError('var')
```
2.
```
try:
    raise TypeError('int Expected')
except TypeError:
    raise
```
3.
```
try:
    file = open("File.txt", "r")
    file.write("Hello World")
except IOError:
    print("Error writing to file.......")
else:
    print("Write    Operation    Successful ...........")
```
4.
```
try:
    file = open("File", "r")
    try:
        file.write("This is my test file for exception handling!!")
```
```
    finally:
        print("Closing the file.....")
        file.close()
except IOError:
    print("Error: file not found .......")
```
5.
```
def convert(var):
    try:
        return int(var)
    except ValueError as e:
        print(e.args)
convert("xyz")
```
6.
```
List = ['a', 0, 2]
for i in List:
    try:
        print(i)
        r = 1/int(i)
        break
    except:
        print("Error ....")
```

```
7. >>> raise MemoryError("Problem dealing with
       memory....")
8. while 1:
       try:
          n = int(input("Enter an integer: "))
          break
       except ValueError:
          print("Enter again ...")
       else:
          print("Congratulations... number
   accepted....")
9. try:
       file = open('Integers.txt')
       num = int(file.readline())
   except (IOError, ValueError):
       print("I/O error or a ValueError occurred")
   except:
       print("An unexpected error occurred")
       raise
10. def func(i):
       List = [1,2,3]
       try:
         assert i >= 1
         return l[i]
       except TypeError,e:
         print("Dealing with TypeError")
       except IndexError, e:
         print("Dealing with IndexError")
       except:
```

```
       print("Any other error...")
    finally:
       print("Terminating the program .....")
   func(-1)
11. error = Exception("Raising my error...")
    raise error
12. def listen(name):
     raise Exception(name + " you have generated an
     error...")
    listen("Henry")
13. try:
      var = 10
      print(var)
      raise NameError("Hello")
    except NameError as e:
      print("Error occurred......")
      print(e)
14. class Error(Exception):
      def __init__(self, num):
        self.num = num
      def __str__(self):
        return repr(self.num)
    try:
      raise Error(420)
    except Error as e:
      print("Received error:", e.num)
15. str="123"
    raise NameError("String please...!")
```

Find the Error

```
1. try:
       file = open('File1.txt')
       str = f.readline()
       print(str)
   except ValueError:
         print("Error occurred ...... Program
   Terminating...")
   else:
       print("Program Terminating
   Successfully.....")
2. try:
       raise KeyboardInterrupt
   finally:
       print('Good Morning')
3. def divide(x, y):
       try:
         result = x / y
       except ZeroDivisionError:
         print("Division by zero!")
       else:
```

```
       print("result is", result)
    finally:
       print("executing finally clause")
   divide('x', 1)
4. def KelvinToFahrenheit(Temp):
    assert (Temp >= 0),"Freezing"
    return ((Temp -273)*1.8)+32
   print(KelvinToFahrenheit(-5))
5. try:
    file = open("File.txt", "r")
    file.write("Hello World")
   finally:
    print("Error writing to file.......")
6. try:
    x = float(input("Enter the number: "))
    inverse = 1.0 / x
   finally:
    print("Thank you ....")
   print("The inverse: ", inverse)
```

```
7.  try:
        x = float(input("Enter the number: "))
        inverse = 1.0 / x
    except ValueError:
        print("Number means an int or a float")
    except ZeroDivisionError:
        print("Infinity.......")
    finally:
        print("Thank you ....")
    print("The inverse: ", inverse)
8.  >>> print(var)
9.  >>> 10 + 'a'
10. Dict = {"One":1, "Two":2}
    print(Dict["Three"])
11. List = [1,2,3,4,5]
    print(List[5])
12. List = [1,2,3,4,5]
    print(List.join(100))
13. List = [1,2,3,4,5]
    print(List['one'])
```

```
14. Tup = ('abc', 'def', 'xyz', 'jkl')
    Tup[2] = 'ghi'
15. def func1(i):
        return i / 0
    def func2():
        raise Exception("Raising Exception ......")
    def func3():
        try:
            func1(5)
        except Exception as e:
            print(e)
            raise
        try:
            func2()
        except Exception as e:
            print(e)
    func3()
```

Answers

Fill in the Blanks

1. logic
2. synchronous
3. exceptions
4. try-except
5. except
6. except
7. exception's argument
8. else, finally
9. Try
10. None
11. raise
12. Exception
13. Assertion
14. Exception
15. as
16. finally
17. <, raise

State True or False

1. True 2. False 3. True 4. True 5. False 6. True 7. True 8. True 9. False 10. True
11. False 12. True 13. False 14. False 15. True

Multiple Choice Questions

1. (b) 2. (b) 3. (d) 4. (c) 5. (d) 6. (a) 7. (a) 8. (c) 9. (d) 10. (b) 11. (a)

8

Compressing String and Files

Before sending a message, storing a string in a file, it is always a good idea to compress it. Compressing means making the string smaller in terms of the number of bytes of data it contains. To be useful, compression should be lossless. That is, the compressed file when uncompressed is exactly the same as the original file. When you create a zip folder, it uses lossless compression. While all zip programs are lossless, converting uncompressed audio files to a compressed audio format such as WMA (Windows Media Audio), on the other hand, uses lossy compression. This is because data representing sound that is beyond the range of human hearing is removed from the file during the conversion process. So, the played audio with removed data will not be noticed by a listener.

Advantages of Compression

- Compressing files allows you to store more files or data in the available storage space. Lossless compression can even reduce a file to 50 percent of its original size.
- Compressed files contain fewer bits of data than uncompressed files. Therefore, they can be downloaded and transferred at a faster speed.
- Compressed files also save money. First, they use less space on hard disk. So, you need not buy additional storage space (hard disk) to save big files. They can be compressed and make efficient utilization of space on the hard disk. Second, we know that ISPs charge money used on amount of data downloaded. Compressed files means downloading fewer bits for the same file. Hence, this results in reduction in costs.

#1 Program to compress strings by the number of characters within the string

```python
def compress(msg):
    msg_list = list(msg)
    comp_str = []
    prev = msg_list[0]
    count = 1
    for i in range(1,len(msg_list)):
        if msg_list[i] == prev:
            count += 1
        else:
            comp_str.append(prev)
            comp_str.append(str(count))
            prev = msg_list[i]
            count = 1
```

```
        # add the last character
        comp_str.append(prev)
        comp_str.append(str(count))
        return ''.join(comp_str)
mes = input("Enter the message:")
print("The compressed message is:", compress(mes))
```

OUTPUT

```
Enter the message : abaabbcccdddd
The compressed message is :  a1b1a2b2c3d5
```

#2 Program to compress and decompress text stored in a file

```
import re
from ast import literal_eval
import os
def compress():
    try:
        fileName = input('Enter the name of the file to be compressed:')
        file = open(fileName)
        text = file.read()
        file.close()
        p = re.compile(r'[\w]+|[\W]')
        split = p.findall(text)
        b = []
        wordList = []
        for word in split:
            try:
                r = wordList.index(word) + 1
            except ValueError:
                wordList.append(word)
                r = len(wordList)
            b.append(r)
        file = open('compressed.txt', 'w')
        file.write(str(wordList)+'\n'+str(b))
        file.close()
    except:
        print('File does not exist')

def decompress():
    try:
        fileName = input('Enter the name of the file to be decompressed:')
        file = open(fileName)
    except:
        print('File does not exist')
    print("Contents of the compressed file is:")
    words = literal_eval(file.readline().rstrip('\n'))
```

```
    pos = literal_eval(file.readline())
    temp = []
    for index in pos:
        temp.append(words[index-1])
    sentence = ''.join(temp)
    print(sentence)
compress()
decompress()
```

OUTPUT

```
Enter the name of the file to be compressed : File.txt
Enter the name of the file to be decompressed : compressed.txt
Contents of the compressed file is :
Greetings to All !!!
Welcome to the world of programming
```

About the Author

Dr. Reema Thareja is teaching in the Department of Computer Science, Shyama Prasad Mukherji College, University of Delhi. In her 17 years of teaching experience, she has taught several courses including BA, BSc, MSc, BBA, MBA, BCA, MCA. She has authored several books in Computer Science and her books have been well accepted across the globe. She has published more than 20 researcher papers in international journals of repute. She also launched a free mobile app, Jruma, for Apple as well Android devices to promote incentive based learning through quizzing. Users can now earn while they learn.

Besides being an author, she is an eminent speaker. Dr. Thareja has conducted several Faculty Development Programs, Seminars, Webinars and Student's Workshop in India and the US. She was also invited as a speaker for the Global Virtual Summit in New York. Being a member of Computer Society of India, Editorial Board and Elite Speakers group of IMRF have added feathers in her cap. For her immense contributions in the field of education, she has received multiple awards and recognitions.

Related Titles

Fundamentals of Computers [9780199499274]

- Lab activities – Relevant chapters are followed by lab activities which provide the practical implementation of the concepts covered in the chapter
- Updated version of Windows and MS Office - numerous lab activities based on Windows 10 and MS Office 2013
- Assessment through Oxford Areal – contain numerous MCQs and True/False questions which help readers to gain immediate feedback on their understanding of the concepts

Course on Computer Concepts [9780199469390]

- The contents of the book completely conform to the latest CCC syllabus prescribed by NIELIT.
- Discusses important topics ranging from basics of computers to applications of MS Word, MS Excel, and MS PowerPoint, and recent technologies (i.e., digital financial services).
- Provides a list of shortcut keys used in MS Word, Excel, and PowerPoint for easy reference.

Introduction to C Programming [9780199452057]

- Exhaustive coverage of fundamental topics with more than 200 program code examples with outputs
- Chapter on programming languages and the generations through which these languages have evolved, which gives readers an insight into computer software
- More than 700 objective-type questions, including fill-in-the-blanks, MCQS, and true/false questions

Computer Fundamentals and Programming in C [9780199463732]

- Provides exhaustive coverage of computer fundamentals, focusing on both the hardware as well as software components
- Offers a detailed coverage of different types of number systems and computer codes
- Covers user-defined data types (arrays, strings, structures, unions) in detail, with each of the operations on these data types implemented using numerous example codes

Programming in C [9780199492282]

- Employs a very lucid style of presentation which makes the concepts easy to understand
- Provides more than 240 programming examples with outputs to illustrate the concepts
- Includes highly detailed pedagogy entailing examples, figures, algorithms, and programming tips

Object Oriented Programming with C++ [9780199485673]

- Provides plenty of programs executable on Dev C++ and g++ compilers along with their outputs to help readers enhance their programming skills
- Includes Notes and Programming tips to help readers keep in mind the critical concepts and do's and don'ts while developing a program
- Provides case-studies including programs interspersed within the text to demonstrate the implementation of the concepts learnt

Other Related Titles

9780190127275	**Sridhar & Vijayalakshmi:** Machine Learning
9780199459643	**A. Seth and B.L. Juneja:** Java: One Step Ahead
9780190124083	**Vasudevan et.al.** Data Structures Using Python
9780199456666	**H. Bhasin:** Algorithms: Design and Analysis
9780198093695	**S. Sridhar:** Design and Analysis of Algorithms